The Course of
Ideas

The Course of Ideas

SECOND EDITION

Jeanne Gunner
University of California at Los Angeles

Ed Frankel
University of California at Los Angeles

HarperCollins*Publishers*

Sponsoring Editor: Patricia Rossi
Project Editor: Ellen MacElree
Art Direction: Lucy Krikorian
Text Design: N.S.G. Design
Cover Design: Kay Cannizzaro
Cover Painting: Braque, *The Round Table*, copyright © The Phillips Collection, Washington, D.C.
Production Administrator: Paula Keller

THE COURSE OF IDEAS, Second Edition

Library of Congress Cataloging-in-Publication Data

Gunner, Jeanne, 1954-
   The course of ideas / Jeanne Gunner, Ed Frankel.—2nd ed.
      p.   cm.
   ISBN 0-06-042551-2 (teachers ed.).—ISBN 0-06-042550-4 (student ed.)
   1. College readers.   2. English language—Rhetoric.   I. Frankel, Ed.   II. Title.
PE1417.G86   1990
808'.0427—dc20   90-41489
                                                                              CIP

90 91 92 93   9 8 7 6 5 4 3 2 1

C O N T E N T S ❧

❧ CHAPTER 3 *Revolutions and Reactions in Science*   **133**

TO THE INSTRUCTOR &

The original intention of this book—to expand the type of readings typically available to instructors of freshman writing courses—remains the major goal of the second edition. *The Course of Ideas* attempts to enhance the content of freshman writing courses by incorporating reading material that is intellectually challenging and valuable in its own right. Such content seems appropriate for students who are beginning serious study of academic writing: the subjects that they discuss in their composition class and explore in their class essays should relate to the academic work they pursue in their other courses. Students are likely to encounter the classic authors and readings represented in *The Course of Ideas* in their humanities and science classes, in class lectures and texts, and in the conversations and contexts common to the academic world.

Drawing on the tradition of Western intellectual history and incorporating current critiques of it, the second edition of this text is designed to be intellectually and socially provocative. The readings provide students with an introduction to the canon of Western studies; the apparatus helps students to analyze the readings, to assess their place in Western tradition, and to consider the contemporary debate over the very notions of traditions, canons, and the Western heritage.

The second edition follows the same organizational pattern as the first. Chapter 1 covers the ancient sources of the later chapter topics of religion, science, literary art, politics, and philosophy. Each of the following chapters traces major issues and ideas, from medieval through contemporary times, in the academic field that serves as the chapter's focus. The maps and timelines at the start of the first five chapters help students to locate chapter readings in time and place.

The majority of the readings from the first edition have been retained, though additions have been made to update the text and to add perspectives on the Western tradition, both canonical and critical. The apparatus has been significantly modified to suit most instructors' actual use of the text. As in the first edition, the text includes several features to support students in reading difficult primary and secondary texts. Vocabulary words from each reading are defined in footnotes at the bottom of the page. Key concepts—ideas that students are likely to encounter in their readings in other classes—are defined before the reading passage and are highlighted where they appear in it. The reading skills covered in the first version have been condensed and reprinted in the *Instructor's Manual.*

Throughout the second edition, the number and nature of the writing topics have been expanded, both in *Questions for Discussion and Writing* that follow each reading and in *Chapter Writing Topics*. The questions that appear after each reading selection have been designed for use in class discussion and as informal writing assignments. They cover three general categories:

- Rhetorical and stylistic issues related to the reading.
- Questions related to content and key concepts defined before and in the readings.
- Interactive questions that allow for collaborative work.

The questions can be used for a prereading survey of the reading passage, homework response questions, free-writing prompts, or paragraph or essay topics.

Topics designed to elicit extended prose responses appear at the end of each chapter. These questions ask students to synthesize the ideas of several related readings in the chapter (and occasionally refer to related readings in other chapters), to use the concepts of chapter readings to analyze current social or personal issues, and to develop a critical view of some major texts that form part of the Western tradition. Topics are divided into multiple questions to allow students to generate ideas, free-write, and work through a writing process to arrive at a unified response to the question.

The readings in *The Course of Ideas* represent the intellectual history that has shaped our culture. The recent thoughtful criticism of this tradition, perhaps best articulated by Mike Rose in the excerpt from *Lives on the Boundary*, has become part of the tradition, a new stage in the story of Western intellectual history. This book attempts to provide students with an understanding of the tradition, the context of current criticism of it, and the analytical ability to decide on its worth and its future.

TO THE STUDENT &

The Course of Ideas is an overview of the Western tradition from the time of the ancient Greeks through the contemporary American social scene. Readings in religion, science, literature, politics, and philosophy provide you with an introduction to some of the writers and ideas that have historically been considered the most important, most influential, and often most challenging to the established beliefs of the Western world. These are the "Great Books" and "Great Ideas" of Western culture. You will probably recognize the names— Socrates, Plato, Homer, Dante, Muhammad, Cervantes, Voltaire, Darwin, Freud, and many others whose works form part of your college studies and who have shaped modern cultural views and scientific knowledge.

The readings in this book represent the Western intellectual tradition (the term "Western" refers generally to the countries of Europe and the Americas). The Western tradition usually cites Classical Greece as its main source, though it also recognizes the influences of the earlier Egyptian and Hebrew civilizations. The nations of the East—China, India, Japan, and other Asian countries—have traditions of equally or more ancient origin. Limited contact between East and West over the centuries has led to a division in historical study of these and other civilizations. Thus the readings in *The Course of Ideas* do not represent world civilization; they are limited to Western history, the context in which American education has traditionally taken place. As with all traditions, change takes place, authors and ideas gain and fade in the degree of attention given to them, new ideas and people become influential. The Western tradition is at such a point of revision, a reseeing of its heritage and future direction. Increasingly, the Western tradition is opening up to cultural diversity. Many of the readings in the second edition of this book address these changes, and ask you to do the same.

We hope you will find the readings challenging, informative, and entertaining. As the basis for writing, they should involve you in the issues and concerns that have absorbed some of the finest minds of Western culture over the centuries. This book is an invitation to join in the conversation that is Western history and to help shape it through examination of its traditions and your personal views.

ACKNOWLEDGMENTS &

The second edition of *The Course of Ideas* has been shaped by the informed commentary of the instructors who have used it in their classrooms. We thank the many people who have served as reviewers, formally and informally, and who have passed on along with their views their students' reactions to the text, enabling us to revise with the complete audience in mind. We hope that the additions, deletions, and unchanged parts of the book address their comments, concerns, and personal preferences.

The reviewers for the manuscript of the second edition gave very helpful advice and much appreciated encouragement. We'd like to thank Joan F. Abram, Fort Valley State College; Wendy Bishop, Florida State University; Sheryl Gowen, Georgia State University; Terri Haas, Hunter College; Raymond N. MacKenzie, College of St. Thomas; Margaret Meyer, Ithaca College; Mark Newman, Scott Community College; Anna Paveglio, Merced Junior College; Susan Popkin, University of California at Los Angeles; James Rodgers, Lawrence Technological University; William Schutzius, College of Mount St. Joseph; Marie Secor, Pennsylvania State University; and Joyce Smoot, Virginia Polytechnic Institute.

We are grateful to the many people at HarperCollins who worked on this project. Our former editor, Lucy Rosendahl, provided excellent professional guidance. We'd especially like to thank our development editor, Linda Allen; her interpretation of reviews, responses to the manuscript, and willingness to serve as a sounding board added immeasurably to the flow and effectiveness of the revision process. As project editor Ellen MacElree has been most generous with her professional attention and expertise; we are greatful to her for all her help. Patricia Rossi, Mark Paluch, and Barbara Cinquegrani also deserve thanks for the assistance they provided.

And once again, we want to recognize the help and support of our families—Ida and Mili, and Bob Muller.

Jeanne Gunner
Ed Frankel

The Course of
Ideas

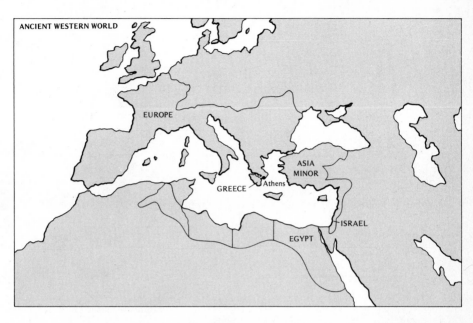

ANCIENT WESTERN WORLD

EUROPE

GREECE
Athens
ASIA MINOR

ISRAEL

EGYPT

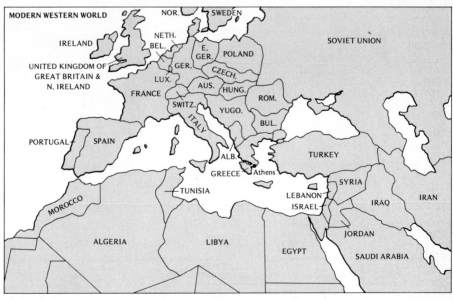

MODERN WESTERN WORLD

NOR.
SWEDEN
IRELAND
NETH.
BEL.
SOVIET UNION
E. GER.
POLAND
UNITED KINGDOM OF
GREAT BRITAIN &
N. IRELAND
GER.
CZECH.
LUX.
AUS.
HUNG.
FRANCE
SWITZ.
YUGO.
ROM.
ITALY
BUL.
PORTUGAL
SPAIN
ALB.
GREECE
Athens
TURKEY
TUNISIA
SYRIA
LEBANON
MOROCCO
ISRAEL
IRAQ
IRAN
ALGERIA
LIBYA
JORDAN
EGYPT
SAUDI ARABIA

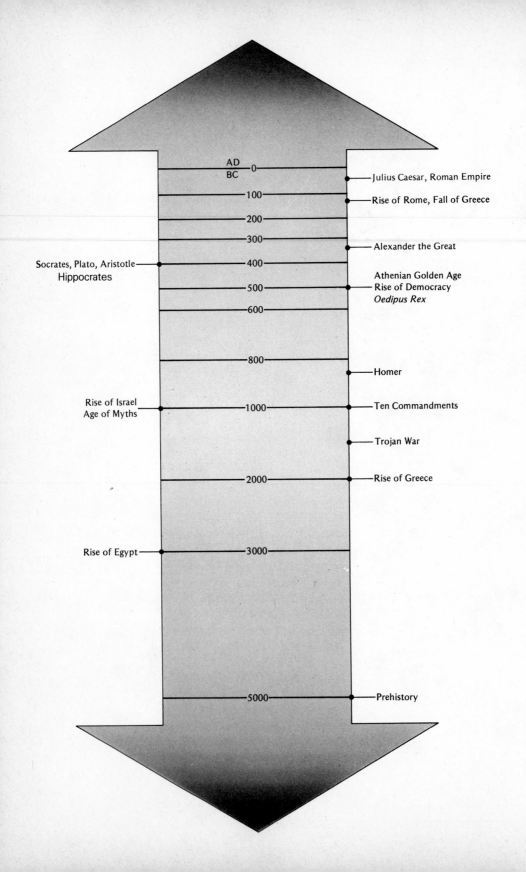

CHAPTER   *1*

The Ancient Greek Tradition

≈

Introduction

As the headings and titles that make up the framework of Chapter 1 suggest, the readings included here represent a special view of ancient Greece. "Classic" and "classical," "founders" and "origins"—these words assign cultural values to certain texts, names, and ideas. Within Western intellectual history, these texts, names, and ideas have come to be regarded as the "Great Ideas" or "Great Books" of Western culture.

The Western tradition is embodied in canonical texts—texts that scholars and educators consider part of our cultural foundation and that "educated" people are expected to know. The political theories, philosophical beliefs, and scholarly texts of ancient Greece are usually cited as the foundation of the Western tradition; Chapter 1 consists in part of readings from the "beginnings" of Western culture. That the texts have "endured" is taken as evidence of their worth and universality. But the idea of cultural tradition itself has come under scrutiny and, in some cases, attack. The Western tradition is, after all, only one cultural heritage among many.

Increasingly, other cultural traditions have gained recognition and influence in America. As we grow in diversity as a nation, and as groups whose voices were traditionally not heard gain greater social representation, social values change. These changes are clearly evident in current debates in education. Should students be schooled in the Western tradition? Should the curriculum in the schools reflect the actual social mix of the country? Of what value are the "Great Books" of Western tradition to a culturally diverse student audience? Should the curriculum be expanded to include works that specifically address the concerns of women, minorities, and a broader range of social classes?

Since the debate over the Western tradition assumes knowledge of that tradition, it seems necessary for students to be familiar with the texts, ideas, and values that make it up. This chapter introduces some of the major works of ancient Greece that form the earliest basis of the classical tradition. Classical mythology, scientific method, Platonic idealism, the theory of democracy— the topics covered in the readings—are concepts that continue to shape modern thought. The final section of Chapter 1, entitled "Rethinking the Tradition," consists of essays that detail the debate over traditional education (or, more broadly, "cultural literacy") currently taking place on campuses throughout the country.

Historically, students have played a significant role in bringing about social and educational reform; their opinions on the issue of Western tradition will no doubt have great influence on future social and educational practice. The readings, discussion questions, and writing topics in this chapter invite you to formulate your own opinions and join in the debate.

A Note on "Gendered" Language

The readings in *The Course of Ideas* have not been edited for gender-specific language. That means that traditional masculine terms ("mankind," "man," "he") are often used to designate both men and women. Because these terms are characteristic of the traditional values that these readings represent, we believe they should remain unchanged in the selections. As a critical reader, you should be aware of the historical context in which the various works were created as well as the contemporary context in which we study them today. Most academic writers avoid the use of gendered language, as the introductions, reading questions, and writing topics in this text illustrate.

RELIGIOUS AND ARTISTIC NARRATIVES: MYTH AND EPIC

Edith Hamilton, **"Introduction to Classical Mythology"** _____

    Edith Hamilton (1867–1963) in her introduction to Mythology *(1942) discusses the role of mythology in Greek life. She approaches myths as explanations of natural phenomena, a common interpretation though not the only possible one. Myths can be analyzed psychologically as well, or anthropologically, or theologically. They held religious significance for the earliest Greeks, but, by the time of the Golden Age of Athens (fifth century B.C.), myths were usually not believed literally. The Romans adapted Greek mythology, changing the names of most gods and slightly altering their nature. The Romans, too, had little actual faith in the gods. With the start of Christianity, about 400 years after the Golden Age, mythology was suppressed as pagan literature. In the Renaissance, it was resurrected as artistic material. As astronomers discovered the planets, they named them for ancient Roman gods (Mars, Jupiter, Venus, Mercury, Uranus, Saturn, Neptune, and Pluto). Much modern poetry has also incorporated mythological imagery, evident from the Renaissance through the twentieth century.*

Key Concepts

The Real and the Unreal (page 5) and the **Invisible and Visible World** (page 7) refer to philosophical concepts of two different planes of existence: "body and spirit," "material and ideal," the observable world or world of the senses versus the abstract world or the world of ideas. The **primeval forest** (page 6) is an image used to refer to the first age of humans, the earliest and most basic state of consciousness.

Anthropocentrism and **Anthropomorphism** are related anthropological concepts. The root "anthropo" means "human." In an anthropocentric view of the world, humans are "the center of the universe," (page 6) in importance and interest. Anthropomorphism is the application of human characteristics to things or natural phenomena, as when "The Greeks made their gods in their own image" (page 7).

    Greek and Roman mythology is quite generally supposed to show us the way the human race thought and felt untold ages ago. Through it, according to this view, we can retrace the path from civilized man who lives so far from nature, to man who lived in close companionship with nature; and the real interest of the myths is that they lead us back to a time when the world was young and people had a connection with the earth, with trees and seas and flowers and hills, unlike anything we ourselves can feel. When the stories were being shaped, we are given to understand, little distinction had as yet been made between **the real and**

the unreal. The imagination was vividly alive and not checked by the reason, so that anyone in the woods might see through the trees a fleeing nymph, or bending over a clear pool to drink behold in the depths a naiad's[1] face.

But a very brief consideration of the ways of uncivilized people everywhere and in all ages is enough to prick that romantic bubble. Nothing is clearer than the fact that primitive man, whether in New Guinea today or eons ago in the prehistoric wilderness, is not and never has been a creature who peoples his world with bright fancies and lovely visions. Horrors lurked in the **primeval forest,** not nymphs and naiads. Terror lived there, with its close attendant, Magic, and its most common defense, Human Sacrifice. Mankind's chief hope of escaping the wrath of whatever divinities were then abroad lay in some magical rite, senseless but powerful, or in some offering made at the cost of pain and grief.

This dark picture is worlds apart from the stories of classical mythology. The study of the way early man looked at his surroundings does not get much help from the Greeks. How briefly the anthropologists treat the Greek myths is noteworthy.

Of course the Greeks too had their roots in the primeval slime. Of course they too once lived a savage life, ugly and brutal. But what the myths show is how high they had risen above the ancient filth and fierceness by the time we have any knowledge of them. Only a few traces of that time are to be found in the stories.

We do not know when these stories were first told in their present shape; but whenever it was, primitive life had been left far behind. The myths as we have them are the creation of great poets. The first written record of Greece is the *Iliad.*[2] Greek mythology begins with Homer, generally believed to be not earlier than a thousand years before Christ. The *Iliad* is, or contains, the oldest Greek literature; and it is written in a rich and subtle and beautiful language which must have had behind it centuries when men were striving to express themselves with clarity and beauty, an indisputable proof of civilization. The tales of Greek mythology do not throw any clear light upon what early mankind was like. They do not throw an abundance of light upon what early Greeks were like—a matter, it would seem, of more importance to us, who are their descendants intellectually, artistically, and politically, too. Nothing we learn about them is alien to ourselves.

People often speak of "the Greek miracle." What the phrase tries to express is the new birth of the world with the awakening of Greece. "Old things are passed away; behold, all things are become new." Something like that happened in Greece. Why it happened, or when, we have no idea at all. We know only that in the earliest Greek poets a new point of view dawned, never dreamed of in the world before them, but never to leave the world after them. With the coming forward of Greece, **mankind became the center of the universe,** the most important thing in

[1] Female water divinity.   [2] Homer's epic poem on the Trojan War.

it. This was a revolution in thought. Human beings had counted for little heretofore. In Greece man first realized what mankind was.

The Greeks **made their gods in their own image.** That had not entered the mind of man before. Until then, gods had had no semblance of reality. They were unlike all living things. In Egypt, a towering colossus,[3] immobile, beyond the power of the imagination to endow with movement, as fixed in the stone as the tremendous temple columns, a representation of the human shape deliberately made unhuman. Or a rigid figure, a woman with a cat's head suggesting inflexible, inhuman cruelty. Or a monstrous mysterious sphinx, aloof from all that lives. In Mesopotamia,[4] bas-reliefs[5] of bestial shapes unlike any beast ever known, men with birds' heads and lions with bulls' heads and both with eagles' wings, creations of artists who were intent upon producing something never seen except in their own minds, the very consummation[6] of unreality.

These and their like were what the pre-Greek world worshiped. One need only place beside them in imagination any Greek statue of a god, so normal and natural with all its beauty, to perceive what a new idea had come into the world. With its coming, the universe became rational.

Saint Paul said **the invisible must be understood by the visible.** That was not a Hebrew idea, it was Greek. In Greece alone in the ancient world people were preoccupied with the visible; they were finding the satisfaction of their desires in what was actually in the world around them. The sculptor watched the athletes contending in the games and he felt that nothing he could imagine would be as beautiful as those strong young bodies. So he made his statue of Apollo. The storyteller found Hermes among the people he passed in the street. He saw the god "like a young man at that age when youth is loveliest," as Homer says. Greek artists and poets realized how splendid a man could be, straight and swift and strong. He was the fulfillment of their search for beauty. They had no wish to create some fantasy shaped in their own minds. All the art and all the thought of Greece centered in human beings.

Human gods naturally made heaven a pleasantly familiar place. The Greeks felt at home in it. They knew just what the divine inhabitants did there, what they ate and drank and where they banqueted and how they amused themselves. Of course they were to be feared; they were very powerful and very dangerous when angry. Still, with proper care a man could be quite fairly at ease with them. Zeus, trying to hide his love affairs from his wife and invariably shown up, was a capital figure of fun. The Greeks enjoyed him and liked him all the better for it. Hera was that stock character of comedy, the typical jealous wife, and her ingenious tricks to discomfit[7] her husband and punish her rival, far from displeasing

---

[3] Gigantic statue.
[4] Ancient Middle Eastern region.
[5] Sculpture with raised figures.

[6] Fulfillment; endpoint.
[7] Thwart; defeat.

the Greeks, entertained them as much as Hera's modern counterpart does us today. Such stories made for a friendly feeling. Laughter in the presence of an Egyptian sphinx or an Assyrian bird-beast was inconceivable; but it was perfectly natural in Olympus, and it made the gods companionable.

On earth, too, the deities were exceedingly and humanly attractive. In the form of lovely youths and maidens they peopled the woodlands, the forests, the rivers, the sea, in harmony with the fair earth and the bright waters.

That is the miracle of Greek mythology—a humanized world, men freed from the paralyzing fear of an omnipotent Unknown. The terrifying incomprehensibilities which were worshiped elsewhere, and the fearsome spirits with which earth, air and sea swarmed, were banned from Greece. It may seem odd to say that the men who made the myths disliked the irrational and had a love for facts; but it is true no matter how wildly fantastic some of the stories are. Anyone who reads them with attention discovers that even the most nonsensical take place in a world which is essentially rational and matter-of-fact. Hercules, whose life was one long combat against preposterous monsters, is always said to have had his home in the city of Thebes. The exact spot where Aphrodite was born of the foam could be visited by any ancient tourist; it was just offshore from the island of Cythera. The winged steed Pegasus, after skimming the air all day, went every night to a comfortable stable in Corinth. A familiar local habitation gave reality to all the mythical beings. If the mixture seems childish, consider how reassuring and how sensible the solid background is as compared with the Genie who comes from nowhere when Aladdin rubs the lamp and, his task accomplished, returns to nowhere.

The terrifying irrational has no place in classical mythology. Magic, so powerful in the world before and after Greece, is almost nonexistent. There are no men and only two women with dreadful, supernatural powers. The demoniac wizards and the hideous old witches who haunted Europe and America, too, up to quite recent years, play no part at all in the stories. Circe and Medea are the only witches and they are young and of surpassing beauty—delightful, not horrible. Astrology, which has flourished from the days of ancient Babylon down to today, is completely absent from classical Greece. There are many stories about the stars, but not a trace of the idea that they influence men's lives. Astronomy is what the Greek mind finally made out of the stars. Not a single story has a magical priest who is terribly to be feared because he knows ways of winning over the gods or alienating them. The priest is rarely seen and is never of importance. In the *Odyssey*[8] when a priest and a poet fall on their knees before Odysseus, praying him to spare their lives, the hero kills the priest without a thought, but saves the poet.

---

[8] Homer's epic poem on Odysseus' return from Troy.

Homer says that he felt awe to slay a man who had been taught his divine art by the gods. Not the priest, but the poet, had influence with heaven—and no one was ever afraid of a poet. Ghosts, too, which have played so large and so fearsome a part in other lands, never appear on earth in any Greek story. The Greeks were not afraid of the dead—"the piteous dead," the *Odyssey* calls them.

The world of Greek mythology was not a place of terror for the human spirit. It is true that the gods were disconcertingly incalculable. One could never tell where Zeus's thunderbolt would strike. Nevertheless, the whole divine company, with a very few and for the most part not important exceptions, were entrancingly beautiful with a human beauty, and nothing humanly beautiful is really terrifying. The early Greek mythologists transformed a world full of fear into a world full of beauty.

This bright picture has its dark spots. The change came about slowly and was never quite completed. The gods-become-human were for a long time a very slight improvement upon their worshipers. They were incomparably lovelier and more powerful, and they were of course immortal; but they often acted in a way no decent man or woman would. In the *Iliad* Hector is nobler by far than any of the heavenly beings, and Andromache infinitely to be preferred to Athena or Aphrodite. Hera from first to last is a goddess on a very low level of humanity. Almost every one of the radiant divinities could act cruelly or contemptibly. A very limited sense of right and wrong prevailed in Homer's heaven, and for a long time after.

Other dark spots too stand out. There are traces of a time when there were beast-gods. The satyrs are goat-men and the centaurs are half man, half horse. Hera is often called "cow-faced," as if the adjective had somehow stuck to her through all her changes from a divine cow to a very human queen of heaven. There are also stories which point back clearly to a time when there was human sacrifice. But what is astonishing is not that bits of savage belief were left here and there. The strange thing is that they are so few.

Greek mythology is largely made up of stories about gods and goddesses, but it must not be read as a kind of Greek Bible, an account of the Greek religion. According to the most modern idea, a real myth has nothing to do with religion. It is an explanation of something in nature; how, for instance, any and everything in the universe came into existence: men, animals, this or that tree or flower, the sun, the moon, the stars, storms, eruptions, earthquakes, and all that is and all that happens. Thunder and lightning are caused when Zeus hurls his thunderbolt. A volcano erupts because a terrible creature is imprisoned in the mountain and every now and then struggles to get free. The Dipper, the constellation called also the Great Bear, does not set below the horizon because a goddess once was angry at it and decreed that it should never sink into the sea. Myths are early science, the result of men's first trying to explain what they saw around them. But there are many so-called myths which explain nothing at all. These tales are pure entertainment, the sort of thing people would tell each other on a long winter's evening. The story of Pygmalion and Galatea is an example; it has no conceivable connection with any event in nature. Neither has the Quest of the Golden Fleece, nor Orpheus and Eurydice, nor many another. This fact is now generally accepted; and we do not have to try to find in every mythological heroine the moon or the dawn and in every hero's life a sun myth. The stories are early literature as well as early science.

But religion is there, too. In the background to be sure, but nevertheless plain to see. From Homer through the tragedians and even later, there is a deepening realization of what human beings need and what they must have in their gods.

Zeus the Thunderer was, it seems certain, once a rain-god. He was supreme even over the sun, because rocky Greece needed rain more than sunshine and the God of Gods would be the one who could give the precious water of life to his worshipers. But Homer's Zeus is not a fact of nature. He is a person living in a world where civilization has made an entry, and of course he has a standard of right and wrong. It is not very high, certainly, and seems chiefly applicable to others, not to himself; but he does punish men who lie and break their oaths; he is angered by any ill treatment of the dead; and he pities and helps old Priam when he goes as a supplicant[9] to Achilles. In the *Odyssey,* he has reached a higher level. The swineherd[10] there says that the needy and the stranger are from Zeus and he who fails to help them sins against Zeus himself. Hesiod,[11] not much later than the *Odyssey* if at all, says of a man who does evil to the supplicant and the stranger, or who wrongs orphan children, "with that man Zeus is angry."

Then Justice became Zeus's companion. That was a new idea. The buccaneering chieftains in the *Iliad* did not want justice. They wanted to be able to take whatever they chose because they were strong and they wanted a god who was on the side of the strong. But Hesiod, who was a peasant living in a poor man's world, knew that the poor must have a just god. He wrote, "Fishes and beasts and fowls of the air devour one another. But to man, Zeus has given justice. Beside Zeus on his throne Justice has her seat." These passages show that the great and bitter needs of the helpless were reaching up to heaven and changing the god of the strong into the protector of the weak.

So, back of the stories of an amorous Zeus and a cowardly Zeus and a ridiculous Zeus, we can catch sight of another Zeus coming into being, as men grew continually more conscious of what life demanded of them and what human beings needed in the god they worshiped. Gradually this Zeus displaced the others, until he occupied the whole scene. At last he became, in the words of Dio Chrysostom, who wrote during the

---

[9] Petitioner; favor-seeker.   [11] Greek poet, 8th century B.C.
[10] Hog shepherd.

second century A.D.: "our Zeus, the giver of every good gift, the common father and savior and guardian of mankind."

The *Odyssey* speaks of "the divine for which all men long," and hundreds of years later Aristotle wrote, "Excellence, much labored for by the race of mortals." The Greeks from the earliest mythologists on had a perception of the divine and the excellent. Their longing for them was great enough to make them never give up laboring to see them clearly, until at last the thunder and lightning were changed into the Universal Father.

Questions for Discussion and Writing

1. In your own essays, you probably open with an introduction, a portion of the essay designed to give readers an overview of the topic or a context for it. In what sense is Hamilton's entire essay an introduction to classical mythology, as its title claims? Analyze the elements that make it an introductory piece, such as its review of commonly held beliefs about the topic, the strong authorial thesis, the history of the topic that it gives, and so on.

2. What is Hamilton's thesis? Is she likely to agree with a view of myths as early versions of stories that we would call fantasy and science fiction today?

3. Classical myths served scientific, literary, and religious ends, Hamilton writes. What examples does she offer of each use to support her view?

4. How do Greek mythological figures differ in appearance and behavior from those developed by other cultures? Why, according to Hamilton, does "the terrifying irrational [have] no place in classical mythology?"

5. Hamilton cautions against perceiving mythology as "a kind of Greek Bible, an account of the Greek religion." Why does she find this view too restrictive? How does the changing figure of Zeus, for example, show how mythology differs from traditional religions in the depiction of God or gods?

6. What are some examples of belief systems, religious or cultural, that make no distinction between "the real and the unreal," the "invisible and visible world"? Do such systems and practices as parapsychology or voodoo exemplify the concept? Do traditional religions? Is a scientist likely to perceive the two planes of existence in a way similar to adherents of nontraditional belief systems?

7. How can the concept of anthropocentrism be used to explain the environmental problems created by the modern world?

8. What are some examples of our anthropomorphic tendencies in daily life? Consider how we perceive pets, cars, and so on.

9. According to one definition, mythic figures embody cultural ideals and reflect commonly held values. Think about contemporary mythic figures: John Wayne, Elvis Presley, Marilyn Monroe, the myth of the old west and the American cowboy, and others that come to mind. Do they reflect American cultural values? If so, what are they? How closely do they reflect your own values?

10. Choose a figure or story from classical (or contemporary) mythology that appeals to you and examine why you find it attractive. Write a brief response to help identify the mythic significance it holds for you.

"Echo and Narcissus"

The following two myths, like folktales, Bible stories, and nursery rhymes, cannot be attributed to any single author. Apart from being entertaining to read, these stories tell us a lot about Greek values and world view. They also highlight the tragedy, heroism, and comedy of the human condition.

Key Concepts

Vengeance, or the "avenging goddess" (page 13) represents a moral principle in Greek religious thought. Any offense against the gods, direct or indirect, had to be punished for the moral order to continue. A related notion of vengeance appears in the Old Testament.

Freudian theory uses **narcissism** to denote obsessive concern with the self. Narcissus in this myth "fell in love with himself" (page 13).

Echo was a beautiful nymph, fond of the woods and hills, where she devoted herself to woodland sports. She was a favorite of Diana, and attended her in the chase. But Echo had one failing; she was fond of talking, and whether in chat or argument, would have the last word. One day Juno[1] was seeking her husband, who, she had reason to fear, was amusing himself among the nymphs. Echo by her talk contrived to detain the goddess till the nymphs made their escape. When Juno discovered it, she passed sentence upon Echo in these words: "You shall forfeit the use of that tongue with which you have cheated me, except for that one purpose you are so fond of—*reply.* You shall still have the last word, but no power to speak first."

This nymph saw Narcissus, a beautiful youth, as he pursued the chase upon the mountains. She loved him and followed his footsteps. O how she longed to address him in the softest accents, and win him to conversation! But it was not in her power. She waited with impatience for him to speak first, and had her answer ready. One day the youth, being separated from his companions, shouted aloud, "Who's here?" Echo replied, "Here." Narcissus looked around, but seeing no one called out, "Come." Echo answered, "Come." As no one came, Narcissus called again, "Why do you shun me?" Echo asked the same question. "Let us join one another," said the youth. The maid answered with all her heart in the same words, and hastened to the spot, ready to throw her arms about his neck. He started back, exclaiming, "Hands off! I would rather die than you should have me!" "Have me," said she; but it was all in vain. He left her, and she went to hide her blushes in the recesses of the woods. From that time forth she lived in caves and among mountain cliffs. Her form faded with grief, till at last all her flesh shrank away. Her bones were changed into rocks and there was nothing left of her but her voice. With

---

[1] Latin for Hera, queen of the gods.

that she is still ready to reply to any one who calls her, and keeps up her old habit of having the last word.

Narcissus's cruelty in this case was not the only instance. He shunned all the rest of the nymphs, as he had done poor Echo. One day a maiden who had in vain endeavored to attract him uttered a prayer that he might some time or other feel what it was to love and meet no return of affection. The **avenging goddess** heard and granted the prayer.

There was a clear fountain, with water like silver, to which the shepherds never drove their flocks, nor the mountain goats resorted, nor any of the beasts of the forest; neither was it defaced with fallen leaves or branches; but the grass grew fresh around it, and the rocks sheltered it from the sun. Hither[2] came one day the youth, fatigued with hunting, heated and thirsty. He stooped down to drink, and saw his own image in the water; he thought it was some beautiful water-spirit living in the fountain. He stood gazing with admiration at those bright eyes, those locks curled like the locks of Bacchus or Apollo, the round cheeks, the ivory neck, the parted lips, and the glow of health and exercise over all. **He fell in love with himself.** He brought his lips near to take a kiss; he plunged his arms in to embrace the beloved object. It fled at the touch, but returned again after a moment and renewed the fascination. He could not tear himself away; he lost all thought of food or rest, while he hovered over the brink of the fountain gazing upon his own image. He talked with the supposed spirit: "Why, beautiful being, do you shun me? Surely my face is not one to repel you. The nymphs love me, and you yourself look not indifferent upon me. When I stretch forth my arms you do the same; and you smile upon me and answer my beckonings with the like." His tears fell into the water and disturbed the image. As he saw it depart, he exclaimed, "Stay, I entreat you! Let me at least gaze upon you, if I may not touch you."

With this, and much more of the same kind, he cherished the flame that consumed him, so that by degrees he lost his color, his vigor, and the beauty which formerly had so charmed the nymph Echo. She kept near him, however, and when he exclaimed "Alas! alas!" she answered him with the same words. He pined away and died; and when his shade[3] passed the Stygian river, it leaned over the boat to catch a look of itself in the waters. The nymphs mourned for him, especially the water nymphs; and when they smote[4] their breasts Echo smote hers also. They prepared a funeral pile and would have burned the body, but it was nowhere to be found; but in its place a flower, purple within, and surrounded with white leaves, which bears the name and preserves the memory of Narcissus.

Questions for Discussion and Writing

1. Myths take the form of a narrative, or story. How is this form different from the traditional essay form? Does a myth have an implied thesis? What might the implied thesis of "Echo and Narcissus" be?

---

[2] To this place.
[3] Ghost.

[4] Hit.

2. Hamilton writes that myths often explain natural phenomena. Apply this view to "Echo and Narcissus."

3. Describe the behavior of a narcissistic person as we would define the concept of narcissism today. What are the destructive effects of narcissism as they are illustrated in the myth and as they appear in real life?

4. Toward which figure, Echo or Narcissus, are you most sympathetic? Why? Can you make a case for each as a pitiable figure? As negative figures?

5. Develop your own mythical explanation for one of the following:
    (a) The man in the moon
    (b) Dressing in costumes on Halloween
    (c) Bringing an apple to the teacher
    (d) The invention of blue jeans
    (e) The custom of answering the telephone with "hello"
    (f) A superstition you believe in

"Oedipus"

Key Concepts

The **Oedipus Complex** is another Freudian term. Freud theorized that children go through a stage in which they desire the parent of opposite gender and resent the parent of the same gender, to the point of wishing him or her dead. Oedipus caused "the death of his own father and [became] the husband of his mother" (page 14).

Destiny (page 16) is the idea that every individual has a predetermined life; certain things will happen to him or her regardless of choices made or actions taken.

Vengeance and Atonement appear again in this myth. King Laius was murdered; (see page 16, **unatoned blood**) his people, the Thebans, suffer a curse until the murderer is found and punished.

Among all the descendants of Cadmus, the most famous and the most unhappy was Laius's son, doomed by an oracle[1] **to be the death of his own father and the husband of his mother.** Forewarned of such a fate, when his queen Jocasta bore a boy, Laius had him cast out on Mount Cithaeron, with his feet tightly bound to make the child more helpless against speedy death. But the goatherd charged with this cruel errand took pity on the wailing infant, and, though he told the king that his bidding was done, in truth he had given it to another herd, who took it to his master Polybus, king of Corinth. By him the boy was kindly received, and brought up under the name of Oedipus ("Swollen foot"); while Laius and Jocasta, making sure he had been torn to pieces by wild beasts, believed themselves to live childless, and thus hoped to cheat the oracle.

Polybus and his childless wife Merope adopted the outcast boy as their own son; then, as years went on, few at Corinth remembered how

---

[1] A god's message.

he was not so in truth. Oedipus grew to manhood never doubting but that these foster-parents were his father and mother, till one day, at a feast, some drunken fellow mocked at him for a base-born foundling.[2] In wrathful concern he sought to know from Merope whose son he truly was. She tried to put him off, yet could not deny that he was a stranger by birth. The dismayed youth turned to Polybus, who also gave him doubtful answers, bidding him ask no more, since it would be a woeful misfortune if ever he came to know his real parents.

But these hints only made Oedipus more eager to learn the truth, and he bethought himself of Apollo's oracle. Leaving Corinth secretly, he travelled on foot to Delphi, where the priestess vouchsafed[3] no plain answer to his question, but only this fearful warning—

"Shun thy father, ill-omened[4] youth! Shouldst thou meet with him, he will fall by thy hand; then, wedding thine own mother, thou wilt leave a race destined to fresh crimes and woe."

Oedipus turned away with a shudder. Now he believed himself to understand why Polybus and Merope had made a mystery of his birth. Fearing affliction for them, who loved him so well, he vowed never to go back to Corinth, but to seek some distant land, where, if madness came upon his mind to drive him to such wicked deeds, he might be far from the parents he took for threatened by so dire a curse.

From Delphi he was making for Boeotia, when in a narrow hollow way where three roads met, he came upon an old man in a chariot, before which ran an arrogant servant bidding all stand aside to let it pass. Oedipus, used to bid rather than to be bidden, answered the man hotly, and felled him to the ground; then his master flung a javelin at this presumptuous youth. With his staff Oedipus struck back, overturned the old man from the chariot, and left him dead by the roadside. In the pride of victory Oedipus went his way, ignorant that the proud lord he had slain in a chance quarrel was no other than his own father, Laius. A traveller who found the king's corpse buried it where it lay; and the news was brought to Thebes by the charioteer, who, having fled from the one bold assailant, to excuse his own cowardice gave out that a band of robbers had fallen upon them in the hollow pass.

Wandering from city to city, Oedipus reached Thebes, to find it all in mourning not only for the death of its king, but from the dread of a monster that haunted the rocky heights beyond the wall. This was the Sphinx, which men took to be a sister of Cerberus, that three-headed hound of Hades. To anyone coming near it, the creature put a riddle, which if he failed to answer, it devoured him on the spot. Till some man should have guessed its riddle, the Sphinx would not be gone; and so long as it brooded over the city, blight[5] and famine wasted the fields around. One or another Theban daily met death in setting his wit against this monster's, and its last victim had been a son of Creon, Jocasta's

---

[2] Abandoned baby.
[3] Gave.

[4] Having bad luck; cursed.
[5] Disease.

brother, who for a time ruled the kingless land. Seeing himself unable to get rid of the Sphinx, Creon proclaimed that whoever could answer its riddle, were he the poorest stranger, should have as reward the kingdom of Thebes, with all the dead king's treasures, and the hand of his widow, Jocasta, in marriage.

As Oedipus entered the city, a herald went through the streets to make this proclamation, that set the friendless youth pricking up his ears. Life seemed not dear to him; all he desired was to escape that **destiny** of crime threatened by the oracle. At once he presented himself before Creon, declaring that he was not afraid to answer the Sphinx.

They led him outside the walls to the stony wilderness it haunted, strewn with the bones of those who had failed to get its riddle. Here he must seek out the creature alone, for its very voice made men tremble. Soon was he aware of it perched on a rock, a most grisly monster, with the body of a lion, the wings of an eagle, and the head of a woman. But Oedipus, caring little whether he lived or died, shrank not from its appalling looks.

"Put thy riddle!" he cried; and the Sphinx croaked back—

"What creature alone changes the number of its feet? In the morning it goes on four feet, at midday on two, in the evening on three feet. And with the fewest feet, it has ever the greatest strength and swiftness."

Fixing her cruel eyes on the youth, she frowned to see him not at a loss, nay, he smiled in her stony face, answering forthwith—

"The riddle is easy. It is man that in childhood goes on all-fours, then walks firmly on two feet, and in his old age must lean upon a staff."

Furious to hear her riddle guessed for the first time, the Sphinx gave a shrill scream, flapped her gloomy wings, and vanished among the rocks, never more to be seen at Thebes. With shouts of joy the watching citizens poured out to greet that ready-witted youth that had delivered them from such a scourge.[6] They hailed him as their king; and he was married to the widowed Jocasta, the more willingly on his part, as he believed himself thus made safe against the unnatural union predicted by the oracle, for he held Merope to be his mother, for all her denial.

Years, then, he reigned at Thebes in peace and prosperity, gladly obeyed by the people, who took this young stranger for a favorite of the gods. He loved his wife Jocasta, older than himself as she was; and they had four children, the twin-sons Eteocles and Polynices, and two daughters, Antigone and Ismene. But when these were grown to full age, the fortune of the land seemed to change. For now a sore plague fell upon it, so that the people cried for help to their king, who sent to Delphi his brother-in-law, Creon, to ask of the oracle how the pestilence[7] might be stayed.

The answer was that it came as punishment for the **unatoned blood** of Laius. Now, for the first time, Oedipus set on foot enquiries as to his predecessor's death. Vowing to do justice on the criminal, whoever

---

[6] Plague.   [7] Plague.

this might prove to be, he consulted Tiresias the seer,[8] struck with blindness in his youth because he had spied upon the goddess Athena, who again, taking pity on him for the loss of his eyes, gave him marvellous sharpness of ear, so that he understood the voice of all birds, also she filled his mind with mystic knowledge of things past and of things to come. But the blind seer was loath[9] to tell what Oedipus sought to know.

"Bitter is knowing when ignorance were best. Let me go home, with a perilous secret hid in my bosom!"

In vain the people besought[10] him, in vain the king bid him speak. At last Oedipus angrily reviled[11] him as having himself had a hand in the murder he would not disclose. This rash accusation made the old man speak.

"Hear then, oh king, if thou must learn the truth. Thou thyself art the man that slew Laius in the hollow way to Delphi. For thy sake, and no other, this curse is come upon the city."

Now with a start Oedipus remembered that old lord in the chariot whom he had slain in quarrel as he came from Delphi. Anxiously he pressed Jocasta with questions about her first husband. She described his gray hair, his haughty bearing, his black steeds; she told that he had been killed by robbers in a hollow pass where three ways met; and every word made Oedipus surer of the truth. But his wife mocked at the seer's wisdom.

"Even the god's oracle may speak falsely," she said, "for Laius was warned at Delphi that he should fall by the hand of his own son, who, moreover, should marry his mother. Yet we never had but one child, and he was thrown out to die on Mount Cithaeron when not three days old, that thus our house should escape so dark a doom."

Among the bystanders chanced to be that goatherd charged long ago with the child's death; and him Jocasta called to confirm her words. But the old man fell on his knees, confessing how he had not had the heart to leave a helpless babe to be torn by wolves and eagles, but had given it alive to a servant of the king of Corinth.

Jocasta raised a cry, for she knew her husband passed for a son of that king, and she began to guess the truth, now clear to the awestruck Oedipus, that he and no other had unwittingly[12] fulfilled the oracle by slaying his own father and wedding his mother. While he stood aghast,[13] veiling his face for shame and horror, she fled to her chamber, like one out of her senses, barring herself in with her unspeakable woe. When the door was broken open, she had hanged herself with her girdle[14] rather than look again upon the husband who was no other than her son.

"Thy sorrows are ended; but for me death were too light a punishment!" he wept upon her dead body. And with the buckle of Jocasta's

---

[8] Prophet.
[9] Reluctant.
[10] Begged.
[11] Abused and accused.

[12] Unknowingly.
[13] Horrified.
[14] Sash; belt.

girdle he bored out the sight of both his eyes, so that night came upon him at noonday.

A blind old man, his hair grown suddenly gray, Oedipus groped his way out of the palace, poorly dressed as he had entered it a travel-worn youth; and leaning on the staff with which he had been the death of his father. His people turned away from him shuddering. His own sons held aloof.[15] Only his daughters, Antigone and Ismene, followed him tearfully, begging him to stay. He would not be entreated; and when they had led him out of the city, Ismene took leave of him and went back to her brothers, already quarreling over the kingdom.

But Antigone vowed that she would never desert her father, and with him she wandered away from her birthplace. Led by her, he went from city to city as a blind beggar, till they came to Athens, where Theseus was king. He gave the exiles refuge in a temple at Colonus. In this sanctuary Oedipus lived on for some years, poor and sorrowful, pitied by his neighbors as a victim of fate, and gently tended by Antigone till death came to end his strange misfortunes.

Questions for Discussion and Writing

1. We often expect that a story or film will hold us in suspense so that the ending comes as a surprise. Does reading the oracle's prediction about Oedipus at the start of the story detract from the suspense of the story's events and the drama of its ending?

2. Where does Oedipus get his name, which means "swollen foot"?

3. What do Oedipus's actions reveal about his character? Consider his reasons for leaving Corinth, his behavior when he meets Laius, his confrontation with the sphinx, his attitude in the search for the king's murderer. Why does he ultimately blind himself?

4. Jocasta kills herself when all is revealed, but Oedipus says that death is "too light a punishment" for him. How is living a greater punishment for him than dying would be?

5. If we see myth as the expression of cultural and moral ideals, what values and beliefs does "Oedipus" promote?

6. Are the events that befall Oedipus more tragic than the calamities we all face as possibilities in daily life—the death of loved ones, serious accidents, and so on? Do we have modern tragic heroes, and, if so, who are some examples? What makes them heroic?

7. The concept of "unatoned blood" has often been associated with modern criminal groups, such as the Mafia or street gangs. Is the modern criminal concept of vengeance and atonement similar to or different from the ancient belief?

Homer, from **The Odyssey** _____

> ***The earliest audiences for the Homeric texts that we see produced in book form today as*** The Iliad *and* The Odyssey *were familiar with these*

[15] Apart.

*epic poems not through reading but through oral performances. The
Homeric poet sang the stories of the legendary Greek heroes, providing entertainment for his listeners and preserving the stories and beliefs of a
rapidly evolving, preliterate culture. As the written word became an increasingly common medium, the poems were recorded, probably in the
eighth century B.C., and gradually took on the set form that we see today.
The* Iliad *tells the story of the Trojan War (begun when the Trojan prince
Paris abducted Helen, wife of the powerful Greek lord Menelaus) and of
Achilles, the greatest of the ancient Greek heroes. The* Odyssey *chronicles
the return of Odysseus to his Greek homeland after the defeat of Troy.
Friend of Achilles and winner of the great warrior's armor after Achilles
falls in battle, Odysseus represents a different kind of hero, a man whose
superiority is revealed through his intelligence and cunning. (These
qualities are shown most vividly when Odysseus devised the Trojan horse,
a huge statue offered to the Trojans as a peace token; when they brought
it into their walled city, Greek warriors emerged from it and overcame the
Trojans, putting an end to the ten-year war.) The figure of Odysseus appears in many later works, including Dante's* Inferno. *In the following
excerpt (presented here in prose form), Odysseus and his crew have been
taken prisoner by the cannibalistic, one-eyed giant, Cyclops; it is the task
of the great leader Odysseus to formulate a plan for escape.*

"Here, Cyclops: drink some wine, now you've eaten human flesh,
and see what kind of drink our ship held. I brought it as a gift for you,
hoping you would pity me and send me home. But you're an unbearable
savage—Monster! What man will ever come to visit you, now that you've
done such wrong?"

The Cyclops took the wine and drank it down. He was terribly
pleased with the sweet drink, and asked for some more.

"Please be so good as to give me still more, and tell me your name
right now, so I can give you a guest-gift, one you will like. For the fruitful
fields give even to the Cyclopes great clusters of grapes, and Zeus of the
rains makes them grow. But your wine is a bit of nectar and ambrosia."

So he spoke, and again I offered a bowl of bright wine to him. I
brought it and served him three times; three times he foolishly drank it.
And when the wine had gone to his head, I spoke to him in charming
words:

"Cyclops, you ask my well-known name? Well, then, I shall tell you.
But you must give me the guest-gift, just as you promised. My name is
Nobody. My mother and my father and all my companions call me
Nobody."

But once I told him, the Cyclops answered me cruelly: "I will eat
Nobody last of his company—the rest of them first. That will be your
gift."

Then he leaned back and fell flat. There he lay, his thick neck bent
to one side, and sleep, which masters all, overcame him. Heavy with
wine, he vomited. Wine and scraps of men poured out of his mouth. I
pushed my stake under a heap of embers to heat it, and with a speech

encouraged my companions so none would cower in fear. Just as the olive-wood stake—green as it was—was about to catch, and was glowing brightly, I snatched it from the fire, and my companions stood by me. A great god breathed courage into us. Then we took the sharp-pointed stake and plunged it into the Cyclops' eye; I, perched above, whirled it around, just as a man bores a ship-beam with a drill, and those below, taking hold on either side, keep it spinning with a strap, and it runs steadily. That is how we took hold of the fire-sharpened stake and twisted it into his eye.

Blood bubbled out and boiled around the burning stake. The fiery smoke from the burning eyeball singed off the eyelids and the eyebrows all around. The roots of the eyball hissed in the fire. As when a smith[1] dips a great axe into hissing cold water to temper it—for that is what makes it strong—so his eye sizzled around the olive stake. He bellowed[2] horribly, and the rocks resounded with it. We backed off in terror. He pulled the stake, all spattered with blood, from his eye. Then, in a frenzy, he threw it from him and called loudly to the Cyclopes who lived in the neighboring caves on the windy heights. They heard his cry and ran from every direction. They stood outside the cave and asked what his trouble was.

"What has happened to you, Polyphemus, to make you bellow through the peaceful night and ruin our sleep? Is someone stealing your sheep? Is someone trying to kill you?"

Mighty Polyphemus answered them from the cave: "Friends, Nobody is trying to kill me!"

Answering him quickly, they said, "Well, if you are alone and nobody is attacking you, you must be ill. There is no way to avoid disease, which comes from Zeus. You should pray to your father, Lord Poseidon."

They said this, and then they went away. My heart began to laugh, because my name and cleverness had deceived them. The Cyclops, groaning in agony with the pain, groped around and moved the stone from the door. He sat down in the doorway and spread out his hands, to try to catch anyone sneaking out with the sheep. He probably hoped in his heart I would be so foolish. But I was planning how to work out an escape for myself and my men. I thought of all kinds of plots and tricks to save our lives, for great danger was very near. This seemed the best plan to my heart:

There were some rams there, well-bred, heavy and fleecy, large and handsome, with dark gray wool. Silently, I tied these animals together with the flexible willows on which the monstrous Cyclops slept, brute that he was. I bound together three at a time. The one in the middle carried a man; the other two walked on either side, guarding my comrade. So three sheep carried each man. For me, I chose a ram, the best of all the flock by far. Taking hold of his back, I curled up beneath his fleecy

---

[1] Metalworker.   [2] Yelled loudly.

belly. I held on, my hands entwined firmly in the amazing fleece, waiting patiently. Thus we waited, trembling, for bright dawn.

As soon as the rosy-fingered dawn appeared, the rams rushed out to pasture, but the ewes bleated about the pen, unmilked, their udders full to the bursting point. Their master, racked[3] with terrible pain, felt all over the backs of the standing sheep. But the fool never realized how the men were fastened underneath the sheeps' fleecy breasts. Last of the flock, my ram walked to the door, weighed down by his fleece and by me, clever plotter that I am. Great Polyphemus, feeling him all over, said:

"Dear ram, why do you leave the cave last of all my flock? You never used to be left behind the other sheep, but, with your long strides, you used to be the first to graze on the tender blooms of grass; you were the first to return to the fold in the evening. But now you are the last. Maybe you miss your master's eye, which a wicked man and his wretched companions put out, after my wits were muddled with wine. That was Nobody, and I swear he hasn't escaped destruction yet. If only you could think like me, and become able to speak so you could say where he is hiding from my anger. Then, I tell you, his brains would be smashed around the cave, and splatter on the floor, and my heart would be relieved of some of the sorrows that this good-for-nothing Nobody brought upon me."

Saying this, he let the ram go outside. I came some way from the cave and the yard, then let go of the ram and released my companions. We quickly drove off the fat, long-legged sheep, looking back many times, until we came to the ships. Those of us who had escaped death were a cheerful sight to our dear friends, but they missed the others, and began to mourn loudly for them. I forbade their lamentations with a frown to each one. I told them to load the fleecy sheep quickly into the ships and sail away over the salty water. They boarded in haste and sat down at the oarlocks; sitting in order they beat the gray sea with their oars. But before we were too far away for the Cyclops to hear us, I called out these taunts:

"Cyclops, it was not your fate to eat some timid man's companions in your hollow cave. Your wicked deeds were discovered, you brute— you who dared to eat guests in your own home. That is why Zeus and the other gods have punished you."

So I spoke, and he grew still angrier in his heart. He broke off the top of a great hill, and hurled it at us. It splashed just in front of our dark-prowed ship, failing to reach the rudder's tip. The water gushed under the falling stone, and the backwash, like a wave from the deep sea, pushed us immediately back toward the land, and brought us close to shore. I took a very long pole in my hands, and pushed us off again. I encouraged my companions, and ordered them, with nods of my head, to fall to their oars again so we could get away from this danger. They leaned forward and rowed. Now when we had gone twice as far out to

---

[3] Tormented.

sea, again I was going to call to the Cyclops. But my companions all tried to restrain me, muttering in soft tones:

"Reckless fellow! Why do you want to enrage this wild savage? He just now forced the ship back to land by throwing a rock into the sea, and we thought we were lost all over again. If he had heard us speak or cry out, he would have pounded our heads and our ships' beams together, by hurling a jagged boulder at us, for he can throw very far."

So they said, but they did not dissuade my bold spirit. I taunted him again, with rage in my heart:

"Cyclops, if any mortal man asks you about the hideous blinding of your eye, say it was Odysseus who deprived you of sight—the spoiler[4] of cities, the son of Laertes, whose home is in Ithaka!"

Questions for Discussion and Writing

1. How does the adventure narrated in this excerpt support the reputation of Odysseus as a man of superior cleverness?

2. In Greek legend, the Cyclopes are a group of barbarous, cave-dwelling people. With what characteristics does the poet endow Polyphemus in order to suggest his inferiority? How does this depiction reveal the poet's own cultural values?

3. Odysseus laughs at the Cyclops' pain after blinding him. Is Odysseus as insensitive and brutal as his captor, or is he justified in rejoicing over his enemy's fall?

4. Despite pleas from his comrades to complete their escape, Odysseus continues to taunt the Cyclops and then reveals his true name to him. Why does Odysseus choose this apparently foolhardy course of action?

5. Is the graphic violence in Homer's story similar to the violence we see in horror films and stories today? Are Odysseus and Polyphemus different from the heroes and villains of modern times?

Werner Jaeger, from **Paideia** _____

In Paideia: The Ideals of Greek Culture, *the German scholar Werner Jaeger presents a three-volume study of the cultural development and values of the ancient Greeks. For Jaeger, the Greek term* paideia *sums up the educational ideals and goals of a culture, its ideal image of itself; he identifies* arete, *a Greek term that refers to the concepts of personal honor and physical bravery, as the primary cultural value of the ancient Greeks. Jaeger bases his analysis on the Homeric heroes of* The Iliad *and* The Odyssey, *and sees in figures such as Achilles and Odysseus the embodiment of the ancient Greek ideal. Although it is recognized as a work of great scholarly importance,* Paideia *has also been criticized for what some take to be an endorsement of certain values associated with Nazi Germany—fascistic control of the state and a belief in one group's innate*

---

[4] Plunderer; ruiner.

superiority. Jaeger's work was published in 1939, at the beginning of World War II. Whether Jaeger intended to draw a parallel between the ancient ideal and modern values is up to the individual reader to determine.

Key Concepts

In Greek myth, **Nemesis** (page 23) is the goddess of revenge. In common usage, *nemesis* means "downfall," a challenge too great to be overcome.

The **nobility** (page 23) are people who, by virtue of their birth, hold the highest rank or title in a society. The term refers to a class system based on hereditary privilege.

Classical **rhetoric** (page 24) is the study of persuasive speech and writing techniques. The traditional elements of rhetorical study are invention, arrangement, and style.

In Homer, the real mark of the nobleman is his sense of duty. He is judged, and is proud to be judged, by a severe standard. And the nobleman educates others by presenting to them an eternal ideal, to which they have a duty to conform. His sense of duty is *aidos.* Anyone is free to appeal to aidos; and if it is slighted the slight awakes in others the kindred[1] emotion of **nemesis.** Both aidos and nemesis are essential parts of Homer's ideal of aristocracy. The nobleman's pride in high race and ancient achievement is partnered by his knowledge that his pre-eminence[2] can be guaranteed only by the virtues which won it. The aristoi are distinguished by that name from the mass of the common people: and though there are many aristoi, they are always striving with one another for the prize of areté. The Greek nobles believed that the real test of manly virtue was victory in battle—a victory which was not merely the physical conquest of an enemy, but the proof of hard-won areté. This idea is exactly suited by the word *aristeia,* which was later used for the single-handed adventures of an epic hero The hero's whole life and effort are a race for the first prize, an unceasing strife for supremacy over his peers. (Hence the eternal delight in poetic accounts of these aristeiai.) In peace-time too, the warriors match their aretai against one another in war-games: in the *Iliad* we see them in competition even in a brief pause in the war, at the funeral games of Patroclus. It was that chivalrous rivalry which struck out the motto of knighthood throughout the centuries:

αἰὲν ἀριστεύειν χαὶ ὑπείροχον ἔμμεναι ἄλλων.[3]

(This motto, which teachers of all ages have quoted to their pupils, modern educational 'levellers' have now, for the first time, abandoned.) Into that one sentence the poet has condensed the whole educational outlook of the **nobility.** When Glaucus meets Diomedes on the battlefield, and wishes to prove himself a worthy opponent, he first (in the

---

[1] Related.
[2] Superiority.

[3] Always to be the best and to be distinguished above all others.

Homeric manner) names his illustrious ancestors, and then continues: 'Hippolochus begat me, and I claim to be his son. He sent me to Troy, and often gave me this command, to strive always for the highest areté, and to excel all others.' It is the finest possible expression of the inspiration of heroic strife: and it was familiar to the author of the eleventh book of the *Iliad*, who makes Peleus give the same counsel to his son Achilles.

There is another way in which the *Iliad* bears witness to the high educational ideals of the early Greek aristocracy. It shows that the old conception of areté as warlike prowess[4] could not satisfy the poets of a new age: their new ideal of human perfection was that character which united nobility of action with nobility of mind. And it is important to notice that the new concept is expressed by Phoenix, who is the old counsellor and teacher of Achilles, the pattern-hero of Greece. At a crisis in the action, he reminds his pupil of the ideal on which he has been moulded: 'to be both a speaker of words and a doer of deeds'. The later Greeks were right in believing this verse to be the earliest formulation of the Greek educational ideal, of its effort to express the whole of human potentialities. It was often quoted in the later ages of **rhetoric** and sophistication to set off the departed heroic world of action against the wordy and inactive present; but it can be interpreted in another way, for it shows the whole mental outlook of the aristocracy. They believed that mastery of words meant intellectual sovereignty.[5] Phoenix speaks this line to Achilles when he has just received the envoys of the Greek chiefs with sullen anger. The poet presents the eloquent Odysseus and Ajax the laconic[6] man of action as contrasts to Achilles himself. By this contrast he emphasises the highest ideal of developed humanity as personified in the greatest of the heroes—Achilles—who has been trained to it by the third envoy Phoenix. The word areté had originally meant warlike prowess; but it is clear from this passage that a later age found no difficulty in transforming the concept of nobility to suit its own higher ideals, and that the word itself was to acquire a broader meaning to suit this developing ideal.

An essential concomitant[7] of areté is honour. In a primitive community it is inseparable from merit and ability. Aristotle has well described it as a natural standard for man's half-realised efforts to attain areté. 'Men,' he says, 'seem to pursue honour in order to assure themselves of their own worth—their areté. They strive to be honoured for it, by men who know them and who are judicious.[8] It is therefore clear that they recognise areté as superior.' The philosophy of later times then bade[9] man obey an inner standard: it taught him to regard honour as the external image of his inner value, reflected in the criticism of his fellows. But the Homeric man estimated his own worth exclusively by the standards of the society to which he belonged. He was a creature of his class: he measured his own areté by the opinion which others held of

---

[4] Bravery.
[5] Power.
[6] Terse, quiet.

[7] Related quality.
[8] Wise.
[9] Ordered.

him. Yet the philosophic man of later times could dispense with such external recognition, although (as Aristotle says) he might not be entirely indifferent to it.

Homer and the aristocracy of his time believed that the denial of honour due was the greatest of human tragedies. The heroes treat one another with constant respect, since their whole social system depends on such respect. They have all an insatiable thirst for honour, a thirst which is itself a moral quality of individual heroes. It is natural for the great hero or the powerful prince to demand high and higher honour. When the Homeric man does a great deed, he never hesitates to claim the honour which is its fit reward. It is not chiefly the question of payment for services rendered which occupies him. The sources of honour and dishonour are praise and blame (ἔπαινοδ and ψόγοδ). But praise and blame were considered by the philosophic morality of later times to be the foundations of social life, the expression of objective social standards. Nowadays we must find it difficult to imagine how entirely *public* was the conscience of a Greek. (In fact, the early Greeks never conceived anything like the personal conscience of modern times.) Yet we must strive to recognise that fact, before we can comprehend what they meant by honour. Christian sentiment will regard any claim to honour, any self-advancement, as an expression of sinful vanity. The Greeks, however, believed such ambition to be the aspiration of the individual towards that ideal and supra-personal[10] sphere in which alone he can have real value. Thus it is true in some sense to say that the areté of a hero is completed only in his death. Areté exists in mortal man. Areté *is* mortal man. But it survives the mortal, and lives on in his glory, in that very ideal of his areté which accompanied and directed him throughout his life. The gods themselves claim their due honour. They jealously avenge any infringement of it, and pride themselves on the praise which their worshippers give to their deeds. Homer's gods are an immortal aristocracy. And the essence of Greek worship and piety lay in giving honour to godhead: to be pious is 'to honour the divinity'. To honour both gods and men for their areté is a primitive instinct.

Questions for Discussion and Writing

1. Define Jaeger's concept of *arete* in simple terms.
2. What is the author's attitude toward his subject? Cite lines and phrases that reveal his authorial view of the Greek heroes.
3. Jaeger sets up a relationship between *aidos,* or duty, and *nemesis,* or revenge. Apply these concepts to the excerpt from Homer's *Odyssey.* Are Odysseus's vengeful actions justified by the Cyclops' violation of *aidos*?
4. Do we have a contemporary cultural ideal equivalent to the ancient Greek concept of *arete*?
5. How can Jaeger's interpretation of the ancient hero's superiority be used to justify the existence of a master race (as Hitler envisioned the Aryan race, for

[10] Beyond the individual.

example), and how might the argument gain strength from citing the ancient Greeks as developers and practitioners of the doctrine?

6. Cite evidence for the view that Jaeger is promoting a return to the ancient ideal of the aristocratic Greeks, and then consider your own view of the issue. Use the textual evidence you've gathered to support your view, if you agree, or develop arguments that counter it, if you do not.

7. The Greeks, according to Jaeger, idealized nobility of mind as well as action. Do the heroes of later ages reflect this ideal, or does each age and culture redefine the heroic ideal? Consider some of the figures represented as heroes in other readings in this book, such as Oedipus, Socrates, Galileo, Lancelot, Don Quixote, or Candide.

8. Does Jaeger's discussion of the importance of honor help explain Odysseus's behavior at the end of the adventure with the Cyclops?

9. The term *paideia* refers to an educational ideal, a system of training that produces the finest citizen, in all senses of the word. Judging from your experience with the educational system and popular culture, can we be said to have such an ideal in contemporary America?

SYSTEMATIC THOUGHT IN PHILOSOPHY, SCIENCE, AND POLITICS

Thomas H. Greer, "The Founders of Western Philosophy" _____

Thomas H. Greer wrote "The Founders of Western Philosophy" in 1977. As Greer points out, the Golden Age Greeks originated systematic philosophical thought. They explored theories of the material world— Greek philosophies often bordered on what we consider scientific issues— as well as developing a theory of idealism. Plato was this original and greatly influential theorist. Later, Platonic theory was incorporated into Christian thought and thus survived throughout the Middle Ages and Renaissance. Nineteenth-century thought also expanded idealist theory. (Following Greer's article you'll find an excerpt from Plato's Symposium *which helps illustrate how idealism works.) Aristotle's works have had similar historical importance, especially in science and literature. As Greer explains, Aristotle defined a systematic method of inquiry.*

Key Concepts

Materialism versus **Idealism** (Plato's "Doctrine of Ideas, page 30), or a belief in "unseen essence" (page 27), is a fundamental concept in Western philosophy. Materialists claim that existence has a real foundation in the objects we perceive; idealists believe that existence is an idea, an essence, perceivable through thought, not sense.

Absolute versus **Relative Truth** is a logical concept used throughout this passage. It helps us to distinguish context: does a thing or idea depend on another thing or idea for its meaning, or does it have a constant, universal meaning?

Empirical Evidence, or "the evidence of the senses" (page 32), is information gained through observation.

Theory of Knowledge (page 29) is also called **Epistemology,** the study of the source and characteristics of knowledge.

Idea of the Soul (page 29) is another way of saying **metaphysics**—what is the nature of the spiritual world?

Sophists, Socratic Method, Dialectics, the Academy, Platonic Doctrine of Ideas, Utopia, and **The Golden Mean** are terms whose definition you will find from their context in the article. These terms will appear in your academic reading quite often because they represent some of the greatest Greek contributions to Western thought.

The earliest Greek philosophers (sixth century B.C.) began by criticizing the prevailing nature-myths. They found it hard to believe that earthquakes were caused by the stamping of Poseidon or that lightning was a bolt from Zeus. They made the crucial intellectual leap from a primitive, anthropomorphic view of nature to a rational, analytic view.

Pioneers of Rational Thought

One of the basic questions they sought to answer through rational analysis relates to the composition of the physical universe: What are the elements from which all **material things** are made? Around 600 B.C., Thales of Miletus (in Asia Minor) hypothesized that water is the basic ingredient. This was a logical inference, since water seems to be present, in various forms, throughout the world of space and matter. It fills the sea, rivers, and springs; it falls from the sky; it is found in the flesh and the organs of animal bodies. And, under varying conditions of temperature and pressure, it changes from a liquid to a solid or a vapor. Thales was no doubt aware that his hypothesis did not explain all the varied appearances of matter; but he and other Greek thinkers were convinced that nature, in its **unseen essence,** is far simpler than it appears to be.

Though later philosophers rejected Thales' belief that everything can be reduced to water, they agreed that he was on the right track. Some believed the prime substance to be air or fire; others concluded that there are four basic elements: earth, air, fire, and water. But during the fifth century B.C. Democritus of Abdera (in Thrace) developed the hypothesis that all physical things are formed by combinations of tiny particles, so small that they are both invisible and indivisible. He called them atoms. Democritus' atoms are identical in substance but differ in shape, thus making possible the great variety of perceived objects in the world. They are infinite in number, everlasting, and in constant motion. They account, said Democritus, for everything that has been or ever will be. Democritus offered no **empirical evidence** to prove the existence of atoms, but the fact that he could conceive this remarkable hypothesis demonstrates the far-reaching achievement of Greek rational thought.

By sheer logic another philosopher, Parmenides of Elea (in southern Italy), convinced himself that everything in the universe must be eternal and unchangeable. Change required motion, he reasoned, and motion required empty space. But empty space equals nonexistence, which by definition does not exist. Therefore, he concluded, motion and change are impossible. Parmenides readily admitted that some things appear to move and change; but this must be an illusion of the senses, he said, because it is contradicted by logic. And logic, the Greek philosophers thought, is the most reliable test of truth.

Logic did not always lead to the same answers, however. While Parmenides satisfied himself that matter was unchanging and permanent, another Greek reached the opposite conclusion. Heraclitus of Ephesus (in Asia Minor) insisted that the universe, instead of standing still, is in continuous motion. He declared that a person cannot step into the same river twice—in fact, the river is changing even as one steps into it. This doctrine proved most disturbing, for if everything is constantly changing (including ourselves), how can we gain true knowledge of anything? By the time our mind has been informed, the object of our attention is no longer what it was!

Discomforting suggestions such as these led many Greeks to abandon the effort to find **absolute or final truth.** As philosophic inquiry began to center in Athens during the fifth century B.C., serious thinkers there turned from baffling questions about physical matter, permanence, and change to the more immediate and engaging problems of human existence. A group of professional teachers, called **Sophists** because they claimed to make their pupils wise (sophos), played a leading part in this shift. Most prominent among them was Protagoras, who lived and taught in Athens. He declared, "Man is the measure of all things, of what is and of what is not." Completely skeptical[1] of general truths, even about the gods, he insisted that truth is different for each individual. What was true (or right) for a Spartan might be false (or wrong) for an Athenian. Furthermore, as Heraclitus had suggested, our bodies and minds are changing every moment, and our perceptions and ideas change with them.

The Sophists concluded that it is pointless to look for **absolute truth** about nature or morals. Since **truth is relative** to each individual, it is important only to know what one finds agreeable and useful, such as the arts of persuasion or how to succeed in life. As news of this teaching circulated in Athens and elsewhere in Greece, the more conservative citizens became shocked and alarmed. It smacked[2] of blasphemy[3] and threatened to subvert[4] the laws and moral codes of the state. Protagoras protested that his theories did not call for the denial of authority

---

[1] Doubting.
[2] Strongly suggested.
[3] Impiety; religious disrespect.
[4] Undercut; weaken.

(anarchy) and cautioned his pupils, "When in Athens do as the Athenians." Social order, he agreed, requires reasonable conformity to the laws of the community, whether or not they are absolutely true or right. But the conservative elders were not reassured. It was upsetting to them to think that one person's ideas are as "true" as another's. And the laws of gods and mortals, they argued, cannot be properly respected and upheld unless the citizens believe them to be true and just—in an **absolute sense.**

Socrates and Plato

The greatest teacher of the fifth century was Socrates, who met the Sophist view of how to get on in life with the full force of his intellect and will. He was not a defender of the Olympian[5] religion or of traditional morality; he was convinced, rather, of the existence of a higher truth. Socrates did not claim to know this truth but spoke of himself only as a seeker after knowledge. Because of his skeptical approach and his primary interest in human affairs, Socrates was often mistaken for one of the Sophists. He believed that knowledge must proceed from doubting, and he was forever posing questions and testing the answers people gave him. The Athenians resented having to justify their ways and ideas to Socrates, and he became increasingly unpopular. But he persisted in his arguments and discussions, for, he felt, "The unexamined life is not worth living."

Socrates believed that a technique of careful questioning can lead to the discovery and elimination of false opinions, which often pass for "truth." He cross-examined his associates on their definitions of justice, right, and beauty, moving them constantly toward answers that seemed more and more certain. This **"Socratic method,"** sometimes called the **"dialectical method,"** is simply a procedure for reaching toward truth by means of a dialogue or directed discussion. Socrates did not believe it necessary to observe and collect data in order to find **absolute knowledge;** he had a deep conviction that truth is implanted in the mind but becomes obscured by erroneous **sense impressions.** The function of the philosopher is to recover the truth that lies buried in the mind.

Socrates' **theory of knowledge** is closely related to his **idea of the soul** (the seat of the mind). Almost all we know about his idea of the soul, as well as his other views, comes to us through the writings of his brilliant pupil, Plato. In the dialogue of the *Phaedo,* Plato describes the final hours of his great teacher. Condemned to death by an Athenian jury on charges of corrupting the youth and doubting the gods, Socrates faces his fate cheerfully. He does so because he believes the soul is immortal, though during life it is hindered by the troubles and "foolishness" of the body. Death brings release for the soul and the opportunity to see the truth more clearly than before. And for Socrates the real aim of life is to

[5] Ancient Greek gods of Mt. Olympus.

know the truth, rather than to seek the satisfactions of the body. His devotion to the search for truth persisted unto death.

It is difficult to say where the ideas of Socrates end and those of Plato begin. Plato wrote masterly literary works in the form of dialogues in which Socrates usually appears as the chief speaker. It seems clear that Plato took up the main thoughts of his teacher and carried them through a full and positive development. It is even possible that Socrates would have challenged some of the conclusions reached by his pupil. Plato, after traveling widely through the Mediterranean lands, founded a philosophical school at Athens (385 B.C.). The **Academy,** as it was called, became the most influential intellectual center of the ancient world. It endured after its founder's death for over nine hundred years, and it served as a model for similar schools in other cities.

Plato continued the Socratic attack on the Sophist theory of relative truth. He refused to admit that the world consists of nothing more than imperfect nature in a constant state of flux.[6] Turning back to the conjectures[7] of the earlier Greek thinkers, who had been concerned with the "stuff" of the universe and with the question of permanence and change, Plato felt that the imperfect surface of things conceals a perfect, absolute, and eternal order. With daring imagination, he constructed a picture of the universe that satisfied the demands of his intelligence and his conservative temperament.

In his famous **"Doctrine of Ideas,"** Plato conceded that the **physical world** is just what Heraclitus and the Sophists suggested: imperfect, changeable, and different in appearance to every individual. But the physical world is superficial, possibly only an illusion of our senses; above and beyond it, Plato asserted, is the "real" **world of spirit.** This consists of perfect Ideas (Forms) authored by "God," which exist unchanged through all the ages. There are, for example, the Ideas of Man, Horse, Tree, Beauty, Justice, and the State. These exist independent of individuals and can be known to them only through the mind (soul). The physical objects that the senses report are at best imperfect reflections or copies of the master Ideas; hence, though they may offer clues to the Ideas, they have no intrinsic[8] value. Philosophers should turn away from these sensory impressions and focus upon the discovery and contemplation of the perfect, the eternal, the real. It is in the realm of Ideas (Forms) that they will discover absolute truths and standards.

Plato and thinkers of similar outlook have found this conception sublimely[9] illuminating and satisfying. It is a possible explanation of the universe, though not a convincing one for persons who place faith primarily in their senses. Many arguments can be marshaled to support it, and centuries later Plato's view was to prove adaptable to the teachings of Christianity. For the Christians, also, subordinated physical things and urged believers to think upon the world of spirit—the "other" world of divine order and perfection.

---

[6] Flow; movement.
[7] Guesses based on logic.

[8] Internal, natural.
[9] Nobly; grandly.

Affairs on earth, according to Plato, are best guided by absolute principles as interpreted by true philosophers. Partly to provide a model society and government (state), he wrote the best known of his dialogues, the *Republic.* The book is rich with suggestions on education, literature, and the arts, but its major influence has been on social and political thought. Plato believed that human institutions should aim, not at complete individual freedom and equality, but at social justice and order. Justice, to Plato, meant harmony of function within each individual and among the individual members of a state. (An aristocrat by birth and inclination, Plato admired Spartan[10] institutions and had contempt for democratic ways.) Reflecting his view of the state as an organic unity, he argued that the foot should not try to become the head—nor the head the stomach. Every part of the human body and every member of the body politic should do the job it was designed to perform. Only then can friction, envy, and inefficiency—the chief sources of human and social sickness—be eliminated.

To reach this objective, Plato felt, the state must be structured according to natural capacities. The bulk of citizens would make up the class of Workers (producers), who would be sorted into various occupations according to their aptitudes. Above them would be the Guardian class, which would be trained in the arts of war. From this disciplined class would be chosen, with the greatest care, the rulers of the state. While the Workers would be permitted to live "naturally," procreating and raising families, the Guardians would follow a most austere[11] and regulated life. Matings among them would be arranged by the state, to ensure the production of superior offspring. Any infant showing a physical defect would be left to die of exposure, and normal infants would be taken from their mothers and placed in a community nursery. Parents would not be permitted to know their own children, nor would they be allowed to possess personal property. Such extreme measures are necessary, thought Plato, if rulers are to become truly selfless and dedicated to the welfare of the whole community.

The education of the Guardians, the same for males and females, was to be closely controlled. Only the "right" kind of music, art, and poetry would be taught, so that pupils would receive the desired moral indoctrination.[12] Men and women chosen to be the rulers would have additional training in philosophy and would serve a period of political apprenticeship before taking their place as directors of the state. The Republic of Plato remains to this day an example for believers in aristocracy, planned society, equality for women, and state control over education and the arts. It was the first of a series of **utopias,** or model states, that have offered radical solutions for the problems of human society.

Aristotle

Plato's own pupil, Aristotle, combined the brilliant imagination of his master, who had made mind the sole reality, with a sense of the reality

[10] Of Sparta, ancient Greek military state.   [12] Training in a specific belief.
[11] Without excess; extremely simple.

of the physical world. Born in Stagira (in Thrace), Aristotle made his way early to Plato's Academy in Athens; years later he founded a school of his own there—the Lyceum (335 B.C.). Far more than his teacher, Aristotle was interested in the **evidence of the senses.** He was, in fact, the greatest collector and classifier in antiquity. His interests ranged from biology to poetry and from politics to ethics.

Aristotle accepted Plato's general notion of the existence of Ideas (Forms), but he held that physical matter also is a part of reality and not to be despised. Matter, he thought, constitutes the "stuff" of reality, though its shapes and purposes come from the Forms that Plato had postulated.[13] By logical thinking, men can gain knowledge of the purposes of things and of their interrelations, knowledge that will give meaning and guidance to their lives and bring them at the same time closer to God—whom Aristotle conceived as pure spirit and the source of the forms. To Aristotle, logic is the indispensable key to truth and happiness. For this reason, he worked out precise and systematic rules for logical thinking, rules that have been respected for centuries.

In his study of society and government, Aristotle began by examining existing constitutions and states. In his classic work, the *Politics,* he analyzed and evaluated the major types of political organization. He did not derive from these a model organization suitable for all cities; rather, he recognized that there are differences in local conditions and classes of inhabitants. Aristotle identified three basic types of government: rule by the one, the few, and the many. Each of these types, if dedicated to the general welfare, is legitimate, but any one of them becomes a "perversion" when the rulers pursue their own interest alone. (The worst government of all, he thought, is a perversion of rule by the many.) Under whatever constitution, Aristotle favored a strong role for the "middle class" of citizens. The more numerous poor, he stated, lack experience in directing others; the very rich are not used to obeying. The middle class knows what it is both to command and to obey and may be counted on to avoid political extremes.

The same spirit of moderation—"nothing in excess"—marks Aristotle's comments on what constitutes the "good life." In accordance with his theory that all things have a purpose, he taught that every organ and organism should function according to its design. The function of the eye is to see; the function of the ear is to hear; the function of man is to live like a man. This last calls for a harmonious balance of faculties, of both body and mind. But, since the mind is the crowning and unique part, it is clear that individuals should be governed by reason rather than by their appetites. Further, Aristotle insisted, it is not enough just to be a man; the "good life" must be nobly lived, with every act and faculty aimed at excellence.

But what makes an act excellent (virtuous)? Aristotle admitted that this is a difficult question, which cannot be answered by any exact rule.

---

[13] Assumed, hypothesized.

Excellence is more than a matter of knowledge or science; it is an art that each individual must develop through practice. He advised that, in general, excellence in a particular faculty lies somewhere between extremes. In battle, a warrior should exhibit neither a deficiency of nerve (cowardice) nor an excess (foolhardiness). Rather, he should strike a happy medium (courage). A work of sculpture or architecture should be judged by asking whether it might be improved, either by taking something away or by adding something to it. If it cannot, the work is "just right"—excellent.

Aristotle warned that his advice did not apply to things that are good or bad in themselves. Truth and beauty, for example, should be sought in the highest degree, while murder, theft, and adultery are evil in any degree. But in most affairs each person should find, through trial and self-criticism, the desired mean between extremes. This insistence on moderation has come to be known as the philosophy of **the Golden Mean.** It does not signify a pale average, or mediocre, standard; rather, it calls for the best performance of mind and body working together in harmony.

Questions for Discussion and Writing

1. In everyday speech we often use the term *philosophy* to mean "view of life" or individual opinion. But the meaning of philosophy as an academic subject differs from how we use the term generally. As you read Greer's article, did you find that the Greeks' systematic approach coincides with your impression of philosophical procedure? In other words, do the concerns of the Greek philosophers strike you as *philosophical* issues? If not, how do your impressions differ?

2. Greer describes Socrates as employing what came to be termed "the Socratic or Dialectic method" to move his students toward "answers that seemed more and more certain." He describes Socrates as "cross-examining" his associates, utilizing dialogue or "directed discussion." How does the Socratic method work? Have your teachers used it in your classes? What might be the advantages and disadvantages of the Socratic method?

3. The notions of absolute and relative truth still challenge people today in religion, personal ethics, and politics. Think about the truths you personally consider absolute. Where do your beliefs come from? Can you defend them logically? Might other people consider them relative? Can you think of some examples in history or contemporary life where issues of relative versus absolute truth have brought people into conflict?

4. Philosophers played a prominent role in the intellectual, social, and political arenas of ancient Greece. In fact, the study of philosophy may have been more popular in ancient Greece than it is in modern times. Where are our philosophers today? Who (if anyone) has replaced them? Do we still need them? What purpose could they serve?

5. Although Plato lived under Greek democracy, his political and social utopia outlined in his book *The Republic* is far from democratic. Why might Plato oppose democracy so passionately? What does he offer instead? To what extent do you agree with his ideas?

6. The Sophists, led by Protagoras, believed that truth is relative. They were opposed by Socrates and then Plato. Explain how the two positions differ.

7. Plato believed that "affairs on earth are best guided by absolute principles." Why did Christian theorists centuries after Plato find his teachings on the physical world and the world of the spirit so helpful in developing their own ideology? If you are familiar with non-Christian religions, do you find the notion of the absolute central to them as well?

8. Greer outlines the Greeks' preference for rational thought as the method of finding truth. What other methods might you argue could also lead people to truth? What methods do you use in your own life?

9. Greer points out that Greek philosophers originated systematic "Western" thought. He doesn't mention that non-Western philosophies—Taoism, Hinduism, and others—developed complex philosophical systems at the same time or even possibly earlier than the Greeks. Survey your classmates to see if anyone can explain some of the basic philosophical ideas of Taoism, Buddhism, or Hinduism, or consider researching these and other systems briefly to see how they compare to Greek philosophy.

Plato, from **Symposium** _____

Socrates was one of the greatest thinkers in Western history, but he wrote nothing. His student Plato (427–347 B.C.) recorded Socrates' philosophical thought. Plato's works are mainly dialogues or arguments between several speakers, and usually the major speaker is Socrates. Plato wrote the dialogue Symposium *around the beginning of the fourth century B.C. "Symposium" means "drinking party." Here, Socrates entertains and instructs the other guests by telling a story. He imagines a conversation between himself and Divine Wisdom, represented by the goddess Diotima who explains how physical experience in the material world can lead to comprehension of ideal beauty, goodness, and truth.*

So far, Socrates, I have dealt with love-mysteries[1] into which even you could probably be initiated, but whether you could grasp the perfect revelation to which they lead the pilgrim[2] if he does not stray from the right path, I do not know. However, you shall not fail for any lack of willingness on my part: I will tell you of it, and do you try to follow if you can.

The man who would pursue the right way to this goal must begin, when he is young, by applying himself to the contemplation of physical beauty, and, if he is properly directed by his guide, he will first fall in love with one particular beautiful person and beget noble sentiments in partnership with him. Later he will observe that physical beauty in any person is closely akin to physical beauty in any other, and that, if he is to

---

[1] Difficult concepts; secrets.   [2] Traveler to a sacred place.

make beauty of outward form the object of his quest it is great folly[3] not to acknowledge that the beauty exhibited in all bodies is one and the same; when he has reached this conclusion he will become a lover of all physical beauty, and will relax the intensity of his passion for one particular person, because he will realize that such a passion is beneath him and of small account.

The next stage is for him to reckon beauty of soul more valuable than beauty of body; the result will be that, when he encounters a virtuous soul in a body which has little of the bloom of beauty, he will be content to love and cherish it and to bring forth such notions as may serve to make young people better; in this way he will be compelled to contemplate beauty as it exists in activities and institutions, and to recognize that here too all beauty is akin,[4] so that he will be led to consider physical beauty taken as a whole a poor thing in comparison.

From morals he must be directed to the sciences and contemplate their beauty also, so that, having his eyes fixed upon beauty in the widest sense, he may no longer be the slave of a base and mean-spirited devotion to an individual example of beauty, whether the object of his love be a boy or a man or an activity, but, by gazing upon the vast ocean of beauty to which his attention is now turned, may bring forth in the abundance of his love of wisdom many beautiful and magnificent sentiments and ideas, until at last, strengthened and increased in stature by this experience, he catches sight of one unique science whose object is the beauty of which I am about to speak. And here I must ask you to pay the closest possible attention.

The man who has been guided thus far in the mysteries of love, and who has directed his thoughts towards examples of beauty in due and orderly succession, will suddenly have revealed to him as he approaches the end of initiation a beauty whose nature is marvelous indeed, the final goal, Socrates, of all his previous efforts. This beauty is first of all eternal; it neither comes into being nor passes away, neither waxes nor wanes; next, it is not beautiful in part and ugly in part, nor beautiful at one time and ugly at another, nor beautiful in this relation and ugly in that, nor beautiful here and ugly there, as varying according to its beholders, nor again will this beauty appear to him like the beauty of a face or hands or anything corporeal,[5] or like the beauty which has its seat in something other than itself, be it a living thing or the earth or the sky or anything else whatever; he will see it as **absolute,** existing alone with itself, unique, eternal, and all other beautiful things as partaking[6] of it, yet in such a manner that, while they come into being and pass away, it neither undergoes any increase or diminution[7] nor suffers any change.

When a man, starting from this sensible world and making his way upward by a right use of his feeling of love for boys, begins to catch sight

[3] Foolishness.
[4] Related.
[5] Of the flesh.

[6] Sharing; having part.
[7] Lessening; reduction.

of that beauty, he is very near his goal. This is the right way of approaching or being initiated into the mysteries of love, to begin with examples of beauty in this world, and using them as steps to ascend continually with that absolute beauty as one's aim, from one instance of physical beauty to two and from two to all, then from physical beauty to moral beauty, and from moral beauty to the beauty of knowledge, until from knowledge of various kinds one arrives at the supreme knowledge whose sole object is that absolute beauty, and knows at last what absolute beauty is.

This above all others, my dear Socrates, is the region where a man's life should be spent, in the contemplation of absolute beauty. Once you have seen that, you will not value it in terms of gold or rich clothing or of the beauty of boys or young men, the sight of whom at present throws you and many people like you into such an ecstasy that, provided that you could always enjoy the sight and company of your darlings, you would be content to go without food and drink, if that were possible, and to pass your whole time with them in the contemplation of their beauty.

What may we suppose to be the felicity[8] of the man who sees absolute beauty in its essence, pure and unalloyed,[9] who, instead of a beauty tainted[10] by human flesh and color and a mass of perishable rubbish, is able to apprehend divine beauty where it exists apart and alone? Do you think that it will be a poor life that a man leads who has his gaze fixed in that direction, who contemplates absolute beauty with the appropriate faculty and is in constant union with it? Do you not see that in that region alone where he sees beauty with the faculty capable of seeing it, will he be able to bring forth not mere reflected images of goodness but true goodness, because he will be in contact not with a reflection but with the truth? And having brought forth and nurtured[11] true goodness he will have the privilege of being beloved of God, and becoming, if a man ever can, immortal himself.

Questions for Discussion and Writing

1. Socrates, often considered the founder of Western philosophy, never wrote anything. Everything we know of his philosophy was written down by his followers, in much the same way as the teachings of Christ and Buddha have been. Why might Socrates have dispensed with the written word and declined to systematize his philosophy?

2. Socrates sets up his explanation of how to experience beauty and truth in a conversation with a Greek goddess rather than stating a step-by-step procedure himself. What are the advantages of doing this? Can you think of other forms of writing that employ this technique?

3. Outline the steps Socrates proposes to reach the experience of absolute truth and beauty.

4. Socrates suggests that people begin their quest for truth on the level of physical love and passion. Why begin an idealistic, philosophical "quest" with physical love?

[8] Happiness.
[9] Unmixed.

[10] Corrupted.
[11] Supported; nourished.

5. At the end of paragraph 2, Diotima tells Socrates that "passion is beneath him and of small account." How might you apply such an idea to a personal relationship? Is Socrates' method for seeking wisdom and experiencing beauty still possible in our modern world?

6. How do people today seek the experience of beauty and truth that Socrates describes? Does this experience concern most people? How, if at all, is it systematized in other cultures you are familiar with?

Marshall Clagett, *"Greek Science: Origins and Methods"*

Clagett wrote Greek Science in Antiquity, *from which this article is taken, in 1957. He points out that in science, as in philosophy, rationalism distinguished the Greek approach from that of earlier civilizations, like the Egyptians. The nations that would later base their scientific discoveries on Greek ideas and methods did not yet exist; Europe was inhabited by tribes that were to become the English, French, Germans, Italians, and so on. The Greeks led the intellectual world in systematic thought applied to scientific investigation. The Romans and later the Christians pursued other goals—empire and theology—at the expense of continued scientific study and experiment. In the late Middle Ages scholars took up the Greeks' knowledge, kept alive during the so-called dark ages by the Arab world. In his essay Clagett explains the stages of Greek scientific development and defines its major methods.*

Key Concepts

Natural Philosophy or Science (page 37) refers to the life sciences.

Epicurean Philosophy (page 39) states that pleasure, or the avoidance of pain, is the highest good. **Stoic Philosophy,** on the other hand, emphasizes acceptance of life's pleasures and troubles with a sense of moderation and patience. See Chapter 6, page 407.

Neo-Platonism (page 39) joins the Christian idea of spirit to Platonic idealism.

Deduction and **Induction** (page 40) are logical patterns of inquiry. Deductive reasoning tests an idea or observation against a general law; inductive reasoning works from particular observations to formulating a general law.

Aristotelian Method (page 40) involves making deductions from general principles or observations.

Much has been written concerning the seemingly sudden emergence in the Greek Ionian colonies of the sixth century B.C. of a **natural philosophy or science** rational and surprisingly secular in character. In fact, historians, in recognition of the gulf that separates the approach of this natural philosophy from that of the cosmology of the Egyptians and the Babylonians, have called this phenomenon the "Greek

Miracle." Study of the antecedents[1] in earlier Greek and Near Eastern cultures does something to lessen the miraculous element but leaves us with considerable admiration for the first two centuries of Greek science and philosophy, from about 600 B.C. to about 400 B.C.

We cannot hope to detail here the developments leading to the "Greek Miracle." But we can suggest certain crucial factors. We recognize the importance of the change from a Bronze Age[2] civilization to an Iron Age[3] civilization, a change made possible by the improvement of the techniques for reducing and working iron. These improved techniques appear toward the end of the second millennium[4] B.C. The cheap production of tools and weapons resulting from that change must have been an important factor in the ability of the smaller Greek city-states to compete successfully in trade with the more centralized monarchies of the Near East.

Of at least equal importance, no doubt, was the development of the alphabet, which tradition would have us believe originated in Phoenicia about 1200 B.C. and which spread to areas of Greek culture sometime after the turn of the millennium. Adoption of alphabetic writing did not, of course, initiate anything like popular education. But the comparative ease with which alphabetic writing can be learned certainly made possible a wider distribution of learning than had prevailed in the earlier monarchies, where writing and reading were the property of an exclusively scribal-priestly[5] class.

The independence of the commercial-minded inhabitants of Miletus, an Ionian city on the coast of Asia Minor, the possible weakness of the ties between the governing classes of Miletus and older religious orthodoxy[6] of the cities of the mainland, the immediate contact with the more cultured peoples of Asia Minor, who had drawn their culture from Mesopotamia and Egypt, and the occasional direct contacts with the culture of Mesopotamia and Egypt themselves—all these factors and no doubt others helped to produce the natural philosophy associated with the "school" of Miletus and its traditional founder, Thales (fl.[7] 575 B.C.).

But lest we ignore the intellectual past of Greece in favor of uncertain, although probable, social factors, we should not set aside the undoubted effect of the changing mythology on the evolution of natural philosophy and science among the Greeks. H. Diels, the greatest of the modern editors of the fragments remaining from the writers of the pre-Socratic period, conjectures[8] as to the very probable development of Greek thought out of earlier mythological speculations. And one of our most distinguished students of Greek culture, W. Jaeger, has led us carefully along the road from the mythological cosmogonies[9] of early Greece to the "natural" theology that is evident among the so-called "materialists" of Ionia.

[1] Predecessors.
[2] Between prehistoric Stone and Iron Ages; use of bronze for tools.
[3] Prehistoric time; use of iron for tools.
[4] 1000-year period.
[5] Clerical and religious.
[6] Official doctrine.
[7] Flourished; the high point.
[8] Guesses based on logic.
[9] Theories of the universe.

It is convenient to divide the period of Greek science into four main chronological divisions. The first and formative period is that usually called by the historians of philosophy the pre-Socratic period, from about 600 B.C. until just before 400 B.C. The second is the fourth century, the century of Plato and Aristotle and, later, of the creation of the **Epicurean** and **Stoic** philosophies. The third period is the so-called Hellenistic period, 300-100 B.C., when Greek culture behind the conquests of Alexander began to spread over the Near East and react more directly with the remains of the older cultures. This was the great period of Greek science, the period of Euclid, Archimedes, Apollonius, and many others. And the last is the Greco-Roman period, from about 100 B.C. to A.D. 600, a period in which Greek science was affected by the spiritual and nonrational currents that were in part responsible for the rise of Christianity. It was in this period that the Greek science which was to pass later to the Arabs and through them to the Latin West was epitomized,[10] reorganized, and subjected to extensive commentaries.

Initially we must insist upon the general "rational," critical, often secular and nonmythological tone that the natural philosophers of the pre-Socratic period gave to much of Greek thought and science. We hasten to add that this does not mean that Greek philosophy in general was atheistic. The briefest reading of such Pythagorean fragments as appear genuine, the references in the Ionian fragments themselves, and the subsequent **Neo-Platonic** development make any such judgment ridiculous. But the critical spirit that emerges from this period is of great moment for the subsequent growth of science.

Another distinctive feature of Greek thought that emerged during the first period was the basic concept of a "generalized" science as distinct from a set of empirical rules. It most clearly appears in the creation of a theoretical and abstract geometry. The Egyptians were accustomed in their mathematical papyri to give specific problems, such as the finding of the area of a particular field with particular dimensions. The theoretical geometry behind these empirical operations remained unexpressed and latent.[11] Now with the Greeks it was the theoretical and abstract geometry that became the object of attention. They arrived at the general solution for the area of any triangle, starting with fundamental definitions, axioms, and postulates.

Closely connected with the rise of the concept of a generalized, theoretical, and abstract science and closely connected also with the rising critical spirit among the Pre-Socratic philosophers, particularly in the so-called Eleatic school of philosophy, was the evolution among the Greeks of a strict methodology[12] of reason, or logic. Together with its kindred[13] disciplines of mathematics, logic is a fundamental instrument of science. Observed data, whether assembled by the most careful experimental means or not, would mean little if we had no rules for testing the truth and falsity of arguments. It would, of course, be impossible to

[10] Summarized.
[11] Dormant.
[12] System.
[13] Related.

say when man first used rules of logic—say, for example, the principle of noncontradiction. But it is clear that conscious and critical study of the rules of reasoning is a Greek discovery.

It is, then, among the Eleatic philosophers of the sixth and fifth centuries B.C. that we can find important beginnings in logic, particularly in **deductive logic,** which was used so skillfully by Plato, was formulated as a discipline by Aristotle, and served as the chief instrument for the extraordinary mathematics of Euclid and Archimedes—in fact, for the Hellenistic science generally (from about 300 B.C.). The Greeks, then, became masters of deduction, the drawing of <u>necessary</u> inferences from given premises.

On the other hand, less satisfactory was the Greek understanding of **induction,** the drawing of <u>probable</u> general conclusions from a multiplicity of particulars, the relative probability of the general conclusion depending on the relative completeness of the set of particulars. Also unsatisfactory was the discussion by the Greeks of the relation of argument to experience, although in practice they often exhibited an almost intuitive understanding of the proper relation of a scientific theory to observed data.

A word must be said about the very difficult question of **Aristotle's scientific method.** Although his *Posterior Analytics* is his chief discussion of this question, there is much elsewhere to throw light on it. In the first place the object of a science is to find its principles, its elements, or its causes. This is as true of physics as it is of zoology. "The natural way of doing this is to start from the things which are more knowable and observable to us and proceed toward those things which are clearer and more knowable by nature." That is, we proceed initially from complex effects to simple causes; and once we have found causes or principles we have scientific knowledge. But how do we proceed to causes? Herein lie the difficulties of Aristotelian procedure.

We have already briefly suggested above that the Greeks often had a happy faculty for following what was essentially sound use of empirical observation as a foundation of and check on theory. For example, the whole course of Greek astronomy, as one mathematical system after another attempts to account for the solar, lunar, and planetary movements, was fashioned with the avowed intention of "saving the phenomena"—i.e.,[14] accounting for appearances—and it seems that one or another of the earlier systems was rejected precisely on the grounds that the theory could not account for the phenomena, or rather that the phenomena directly contradicted some deductive conclusion of the theory. Thus the system of concentric spheres introduced by Eudoxus in the fourth century B.C. and taken up and popularized by Aristotle foundered[15] on the fact that the apparent size of the moon and planets varies. This indicates that these bodies are not always the same distance from

[14] Latin "id est": that is.   [15] Broke down.

the earth, and they would have to be as a necessary conclusion of the theory of concentric spheres.

Somewhat different was the role of observation and experience in the formation of the early systems of natural philosophy of Thales and his successors. These systems seem to have originated in the grossest analogies and patently insufficient observational data. Thus it is supposed that such gross facts as the plenitude[16] of water on the earth's surface and its ready change of form to ice or vapor led Thales to assume water as the fundamental stuff of nature and to build a system around this assumption. It may be that the insufficiency of the ties between theory and experience in the early systems is merely representative of the fact that these were the first stages of science and philosophy. It was recognized as important that there be some ties between the theoretical explanation of nature and our experience of nature; but the necessity of a multiplicity of such ties and of their surety[17] was not apparent. In a sense, the growth of modern science has been brought about on the one hand by the increasing sophistication of theoretical explanation, due largely to the use of mathematics, and on the other hand by the development of experimental ways to establish the surety and firmness of manifold[18] bonds that unite theory with experience.

It would, of course, be incorrect to state that there was no experimentation in antiquity, whether for the purpose of uncovering new facts about nature or for the purpose of confirming scientific theory. Even at the earliest stages of Greek science, in the sixth and fifth centuries B.C., there was experimentation by Pythagoras and the early Pythagoreans. Thus Pythagoras or his followers clearly established by experiment the relationship between the lengths of vibrating strings and the pitch of the notes emitted by the strings. It is true that the equally famous experiment of Empedocles (490-435 B.C.) with a water vessel to prove the corporality[19] of air was more a notation of common experience than a deliberately planned and controlled test to confirm theory. But numerous controlled experiments are recorded in the Hippocratic medical treatises, which date from the fifth and fourth centuries B.C., and when we examine the activity of the successor of Theophrastus at the famous Lyceum, Strato the Physicist, we are confronted with activity deliberately experimental for purposes of scientific investigation.

If, then, scientific investigation in antiquity involved considerable experimental activity, we may well ask why it was that Greek science falls short of modern science. It falls short in the maturity and the universality of its use of mathematical-experimental techniques. There is no question that a mathematical-experimental science existed in nascent[20] form, at least, in optics, in statics, and in applied mechanics; that a mathematical-experimental science was present in astronomy; and that an experimental science existed in zoology and physiology. But the

---

[16] Great quantity.
[17] Certainty; security.
[18] Multiple.

[19] Physical existence.
[20] Beginning.

techniques of these sciences were not yet commonly considered as the necessary methods in all fields of natural investigation. Before mathematical and experimental techniques had become the common property of Greek science, that science began to level off. The leveling off (note that reference is made to "leveling off" rather than to "dying out") of Greek science in late antiquity took place for a number of important political and social reasons: Rome's rise to political power and domination of the Mediterranean area, the rise of Christianity and the consequent funneling off of many scholars who might have been scientists into dogmatic activities, and the general effect of noncritical spiritual forces that beset[21] the Mediterranean world from at least late Hellenistic times.

Questions for Discussion and Writing

1. Clagett lists several factors that led to the sudden emergence of Greek natural philosophy and science. Consider each of these factors. How did they play a role in the development of science?

2. Think about other cultures you may have read about that did not experience the technological developments of the Greeks: the Mayans, Aztecs, Incas, Egyptians, and so on. We know that these civilizations could measure the distance from the earth to the moon and construct wonders of engineering. According to Clagett, how did their "science" differ from that of the Greeks?

3. Explain the difference between induction and deduction and construct an example of each.

4. Think about how your teachers in high school and college presented new ideas to you. Did they use inductive and deductive methods? In teaching, what might be the benefits of each approach? Which approach did/do you like the most?

5. Why did Greek science "[fall] short of modern science?" Why did science not continue to develop when Rome rose to power?

6. Clagett points out that Greek science was not atheistic. In other words, the Greeks maintained a critical scientific spirit as well as a belief in God(s). How were the Greeks able to reconcile science and religion? Do you find any contradictions in practicing both religion and science?

Hippocrates, **"The Sacred Disease"** _____

Hippocrates lived c.[1] 460–c. 377 B.C. You've probably heard that he is the "Father of Medicine" and that doctors take "the Hippocratic oath." His approach to medical science and his method for studying disease mark the beginnings of applied empirical method. The following excerpt from his scientific writings illustrates some of Clagett's major points. Hippocrates here argues against the usual perception of epilepsy as a "sacred disease."

---

[21] Came upon; plagued.   [1] Latin circa; about, approximately, around.

I am about to discuss the disease called "sacred." It is not, in my opinion, any more divine or more sacred than other diseases, but has a natural cause, and its supposed divine origin is due to men's inexperience, and to their wonder at its peculiar character. Now while men continue to believe in its divine origin because they are at a loss to understand it, they really disprove its divinity by the facile[2] method of healing which they adopt, consisting as it does of purifications and incantations.[3] But if it is to be considered divine just because it is wonderful, there will be not one sacred disease but many, for I will show that other diseases are no less wonderful and portentous,[4] and yet nobody considers them sacred. For instance, one can see men who are mad and delirious from no obvious cause, and committing many strange acts; while in their sleep, to my knowledge, many groan and shriek, others choke, others dart up and rush out of doors, being delirious until they wake, when they become as healthy and rational as they were before, though pale and weak; and this happens not once but many times.

My own view is that those who first attributed a sacred character to this malady were like the magicians, purifiers, charlatans and quacks of our own day, men who claim great piety and superior knowledge. Being at a loss, and having no treatment which would help, they concealed and sheltered themselves behind superstition, and called this illness sacred, in order that their utter ignorance might not be manifest. They added a plausible story, and established a method of treatment that secured their own position. They used purifications and incantations; they forbade the use of baths, and many foods that are unsuitable for sick folk. These observances they impose because of the divine origin of the disease, claiming superior knowledge and alleging other causes, so that, should the patient recover, the reputation for cleverness may be theirs; but should he die, they may have sure fund of excuses, with the defense that they are not at all to blame, but the gods. Having given nothing to eat or drink, and not having steeped their patients in baths, no blame can be laid, they say, upon them. So I suppose that no Libyans dwelling in the interior can enjoy good health, since they lie on goat-skins and eat goats' flesh, possessing neither coverlet nor cloak nor footgear that is not from the goat; in fact they possess no cattle save goats. But if to eat or apply these things engenders and increases the disease, while to refrain works a cure, then neither is godhead to blame nor are the purifications beneficial; it is the foods that cure or hurt, and the power of godhead disappears.

This disease styled sacred comes from the same causes as others, from the things that come to and go from the body, from cold, sun, and from the changing restlessness of winds. These things are divine. So that there is no need to put the disease in a special class and to consider it more divine than the others; they are all divine and all human. Each has a

---

[2] Overly simple.
[3] Magical chants.
[4] Significant, meaningful.

nature and power of its own; none is hopeless or incapable of treatment. Most are cured by the same things as caused them. One thing is food for one thing, and another for another, though occasionally each actually does harm. So the physician must know how, by distinguishing the seasons for individual things, he may assign to one thing nutriment and growth, and to another diminution and harm. For in this disease as in all others it is necessary, not to increase the illness, but to wear it down by applying to each what is most hostile to it, not that to which it is conformable. For what is conformity gives vigor and increase; what is hostile causes weakness and decay. Whoever knows how to cause in men by regimen moist or dry, hot or cold, he can cure this disease also, if he distinguish the seasons for useful treatment, without having recourse to purifications and magic.

Questions for Discussion and Writing

1. How does Hippocrates' method differ from nonrational approaches to medical diagnosis and treatment? How does it illustrate Clagett's description of the development of the Greek rational method?
2. How did claiming that the cause of illness was divine insure the reputations of "charlatans, quacks, and magicians," whether or not the patient was cured?
3. In paragraph 2, Hippocrates cites Libyans and their consumption and use of goat and goat products as evidence for his argument. How does this example work?
4. Throughout history, epilepsy has been considered a "sacred" disease or a form of spiritual possession. What characteristics of the disease might have suggested this misconception?
5. Some of Hippocrates' medical beliefs and practices conform to modern ones; some are clearly wrong or outdated. Isolate the "modern" and outdated parts of his work.

Moses I. Finley, "Politics"

As Moses I. Finley, the noted historian of the ancient world, argues in the following essay (written in 1981), politics as a social activity was developed in ancient Greece. Unlike the more ancient and rudimentary concept of government, which is a system of providing for and enforcing social order, politics as Finley defines it is the public discussion of and voting on policy, on how things should be done. When the citizens of a state have authority over policy, citizenship becomes a crucial status to attain. A key to power, citizenship in ancient Athens was limited to a small group of men from a particular class and background. This practice may violate our contemporary notion of democratic society; however, the collective power that these privileged citizens held was total, subject to no superior authority (such as our Supreme Court). In this sense the power of democracy in ancient Athens exceeded the power held by ordinary citizens in democratic societies today.

Key Concepts

The **Code of Hammurabi** (page 46) is the first known written legal system. Hammurabi was a Babylonian king; his code declared that all crimes should be met with punishment of equal seriousness (" an eye for an eye"), regardless of the criminal's social status.

Revelation (page 47) is a religious concept naming a direct experience of God or his "divine plan."

A **Tyrant** (page 48) is a head of state who rules absolutely without the necessary consent of the people.

In a **democracy** (page 48), people have a direct say in their government or elect their own representatives.

In Athens, explained the Sophist Protagoras, "when the subject of their deliberation involves political wisdom . . . they listen to every man, for they think that everyone must share in this virtue; otherwise there could be no poleis."[1] Euripides made the same point in his *Suppliant Women,* produced in the 420s: quoting the words of the herald at a meeting of the assembly, "What man has good advice to give the city (polis) and wishes to make it known?," Theseus comments, "This is freedom. He who wishes is illustrious; who is unwilling remains silent. For the city, what is more fair than that?"

The judgments of Protagoras and Euripides were possible only because of a fundamental Greek innovation—politics. Government is another matter: every society of any complexity requires a machinery for laying down rules and administering them, for performing community services, military and civil, and for settling disputes. Every society also requires a sanction for both the rules and the machinery, and a notion of justice. But the Greeks took a radical step, a double one: they located the source of authority in the polis, in the community itself, and they decided on policy in open discussion, eventually by voting, by counting heads. That is politics, and fifth-century Greek drama and historiography[2] reveal how far politics had come to dominate Greek culture.

Of course there was discussion about policy in neighboring and earlier societies, in the court circles of the kings of Egypt, Assyria, and Persia, or, on lower levels, in the courts of the Persian satraps[3] and the circles of the Homeric "heroes." Such discussions did not constitute politics, however, for they were neither open nor binding. The king or satrap received advice, but he was not obligated to heed it or even to request it. Those with access to him planned, maneuvered, and sometimes conspired to direct his decisions, in a procedure that has been called government by antechamber (rather than government by "chamber"). The same was true of Greek **tyrants,** whose existence was there-

---

[1] Cities.
[2] Body of historical writings.
[3] Governors.

fore a denial of the polis-idea, and in whose regimes politics ceased to exist.

It must be acknowledged that there were also some early non-Greek political communities, among the Phoenicians and the Etruscans at any rate. Nevertheless, it remains correct to say that, effectively, the Greeks "invented" politics. In the western tradition, the history of politics has always started from the Greeks; that is symbolized by the word "politics" itself, with its root in polis. In no Near Eastern society, furthermore, was the culture politicized as it was among the Greeks.

Nor did any previous society secularize[4] government in all its aspects, the ideological[5] as well as the practical, as did the Greeks. Nothing could be further removed from, for example, **Hammurabi's code.** The lengthy preamble[6] says in its opening paragraph: "Anum and Illil for the prosperity of the people called me by name Hammurabi, the reverend God-fearing prince, to make justice to appear in the land, to destroy the evil and the wicked that the strong might not oppress the weak." Solon of Athens, in contrast, was assigned the task of codification[7] by mutual agreement among the contending factions; he claimed neither divine guidance nor revelation nor "royal blood."

This insistence on the secular quality of public life appears to overlook the ubiquitous[8] piety of the Greeks. Altars were everywhere; no public actions (and not many serious private ones) were taken without a preliminary sacrifice; the oath was the standard sanction[9] in public agreements; the gods were consulted through oracles and other media; successes were shared with the gods; the management of major religious festivals was the state's responsibility, as was the punishment of impiety[10] and blasphemy.[11] Yet in neither the classical nor the Hellenistic period did this vast amount of ritual activity normally or seriously impinge[12] on, or divert, political decisions. A battle might be delayed for a few days, a conviction for impiety might damage an individual's career, but there is no known case when the Delphic oracle, for example, determined a state's course of action (as distinct from providing a retrospective[13] explanation of a failure). In the Hellenistic east after Alexander, perhaps even more significantly, kings of Egypt and Syria became gods, stressed their divinity in cult, on their coins, occasionally in their epithets[14] (Epiphanes = God Manifest), but their laws and edicts[15] were invariably issued in the name of men, not gods, and violation was never treated as a sacrilege.[16]

Likewise in the courts: witnesses continued to testify under oath, but the oath had become a ceremony, not a formal proof as it had once been. It was now necessary to persuade the judges and jurymen; the

[4] Remove from religious control.
[5] Theoretical.
[6] Introduction.
[7] Written law.
[8] Ever-present.
[9] Legal approval.
[10] Religious disrespect.

[11] Irreverence; religious treason.
[12] Interfere with.
[13] Hindsight; backward-looking.
[14] Descriptive phrases or names.
[15] Commands.
[16] Religious crime.

threat that perjury would bring down the wrath of the gods was no longer of itself persuasive. How, then, were justice and injustice to be defined and determined? That is, of course, the problem that runs through both archaic and classical Greek literature, more sharply among the philosophers beginning with the Sophists. But it was equally a problem at the level of practical affairs, not in abstract or general terms but in the day-to-day decisions of assemblies, magistrates, and courts. Since Greek religion as far back as we can trace it lacked the component of **revelation**—oracles and other forms of communication from the supernatural powers referred to specific actions, not to principles—or even of what may be called the "quasi-revelation" of a Hammurabi, man had to fall back on himself and his ancestors (tradition or custom) for the answers. At critical moments, the Greeks may have turned to a "lawgiver" to codify the right answers, but that step was no departure from the rule of human self-reliance.

For such a society to function, not to tear itself apart, a broad consensus was essential, a sense of community and a genuine willingness on the part of its members to live according to certain traditional rules, to accept the decisions of legitimate authorities, to make changes only by open debate and further consensus; in a word, to accept the "rule of law" so frequently proclaimed by Greek writers. The process thus produced both new rules and their sanction simultaneously, and, as has already been said, that is politics. In a world, furthermore, in which inequalities were sharp even among the members of the community (quite apart from those, such as slaves, who were wholly excluded), and in which communities were small in both territory and population, issues were relatively clear and obvious, and conflict was often acute. The Greek word for political conflict was stasis,[17] a very awkward term with a gamut[18] of connotations[19] ranging from day-to-day "party conflict" (to use an anachronistic[20] modern phrase) to open civil war, which marks the final breakdown of consensus and the abandonment of politics. Civil wars, with their attendant bloodshed, exiles, and property dislocations, were frequent in the classical city-states, with such notable exceptions as Athens and Sparta. They were the subject of much concern among the great surviving political writers—Thucydides, Plato, and Aristotle—and we therefore tend to misjudge the situation. Only in *Utopia* can there be a society without dissent over important issues; in a political society, "party conflict" is essential for its continued existence and well-being, and it is as wrong to regard all instances in the Greek poleis pejoratively[21] as it would be to denigrate[22] contemporary party politics in the same way.

Today the right to vote is widely believed to be the most essential privilege (and duty) of a citizen, and that was also the case, within limits, in the Roman Republic. In the Greek polis, however, though it was an

[17] Unchanged state.
[18] Wide range.
[19] Suggestions; unspoken meanings.
[20] Out of date or time period.
[21] Negatively.
[22] Downgrade.

important right, it was only one of several equally exclusive rights—the right to own real property, the right to contract a legal marriage with another citizen, the right to participate in various major cult activities— and it was available to all citizens only in the **democracies,** whereas the other rights were universal, normally even under **tyrannies.** Hence membership in the body of "active citizens" and membership in the "community of all citizens" were often not coterminous;[23] hence, too, the frequency with which stasis for access to political rights erupted into civil war.

The political rights over which they contended included but transcended[24] the right to select officials and legislative bodies. At issue was the direct share, by voice and vote, in the decision-making process and in the judicial process (understood broadly enough to include evaluation of the performance, and if necessary punishment, of civil and military officials). The right to vote, in other words, meant above all the right to vote in a legislative or judicial body, not merely at an election. That is why classical Greek governments, whether oligarchic[25] or democratic, are classified as "direct," in contrast to "representative." When, as in Athens and other democracies, every citizen became a member, barring a few excluded for specified personal offences, "rule by the people" eventually acquired a literal connotation never approached before or since in western history.

No one, however, not even the most "radical" democrat, wished to break the traditional "community" of male citizens, a closed body of families whose members succeeded each other in the orderly progress of the generations. In Greek usage, the Athenians (never "Athens") declared war on the Spartans (not "Sparta"). If one were not an indigenous[26] Athenian, only a formal act of the sovereign[27] body could admit one to the community. Not only were women, children, and slaves excluded, which is no surprise, but so were freed slaves (unlike the Roman practice), or free men who migrated from other Greek states or from the "barbarian" world, or even their children, born and raised in the cities that labelled them aliens. In the classical period, grants of citizenship to outsiders were rare and were always the consequence of exceptional actions or circumstances. Aristotle, writing at the end of the classical era, observed that more open-handed policy was a temporary measure in times of severe manpower shortage, abandoned as soon as the crisis was over. Democracies, it is worth adding, appear to have been particularly jealous of citizenship.

In political terms, the power possessed by the community was total. That is to say, within the limits imposed by "rule of law," however that was understood, and by certain taboos in the fields of cult and sexual relations, the sovereign body was unrestrictedly free in its decision-making. There were areas or facets of human behavior in which it

[23] Happening at the same time.
[24] Went beyond.
[25] Led by a group of people.

[26] Native.
[27] Ruling.

normally did not interfere, but that was only because it chose not to, or did not think to do so. There were no natural rights of the individual to inhibit action by the state, no inalienable rights granted or sanctioned by a higher authority. There was no higher authority.

Questions for Discussion and Writing

1. Clarify the distinction between politics and government by placing the terms in a familiar context, such as the family, the classroom, or the workplace. What examples of politics, as Finley defines the concept, exist in your family? In your classroom? At your job?

2. Finley makes a distinction between the terms *Athenians* and *Athens, Spartans* and *Sparta.* In what way does the first term name a different concept than the second? Why does Finley emphasize the distinction?

3. The distinction between church and state, so crucial in American political thought, was not a serious issue for the Greeks, according to Finley. What cultural differences may help explain why a major tenet of American political philosophy seemed unimportant in ancient Athens?

4. Why is conflict necessary in any state that wishes to maintain its political life, as Finley argues? Is the concept of necessary civil conflict accepted in American society?

5. Does a direct democracy seem to offer benefits which a representative democracy cannot provide to the citizen? Would you be likely to gain any benefit if the American system were direct rather than representative? Discuss specific examples.

6. Why should democracies be "particularly jealous of citizenship?" Consider who was excluded from or included in Athenian citizenship.

7. In modern usage, the term *tyrant* has deeply negative connotations. For the ancient Greeks, however, tyranny was an acceptable form of government, and tyrants were not perceived as necessarily evil figures. (The title of Sophocles' play *Oedipus Rex* can also be translated as *Oedipus Tyrannus.*) What in our modern notion of a tyrant makes the figure evil, and why might this change in the concept have come about? How might the concept of democracy have affected perceptions of tyranny?

8. How does the average citizen today perceive the right to vote? How might the average Athenian have perceived it? Is your view closer to the ancient or modern attitude?

Plato, from *"The Apology of Socrates" and "Phaedo"* _____

In two of Plato's most famous dialogues, he recreates Socrates' speech to his Athenian judges, who had charged him with promoting impiety—failure to show proper respect for the gods—and with "corrupting the youth of Athens" through his philosophical teachings. In his speech, Socrates applies his ideas of the good and the just to his own case, and points out that it is the community that will suffer if one of its best citizens is put to death. Unmoved, his judges condemn him. "Phaedo" recounts Socrates' final hours and the philosophical attitude that helped him accept his fate. As Socrates' friend and pupil, Plato uses the dialogues to depict Socrates as a hero, in life and death.

Order, please, gentlemen! Remember my request to give me a hearing without interruption; besides, I believe that it will be to your advantage to listen. I am going to tell you something else, which may provoke a storm of protest; but please restrain yourselves. I assure you that if I am what I claim to be, and you put me to death, you will harm yourselves more than me. Neither Meletus nor Anytus can do me any harm at all; they would not have the power, because I do not believe that the law of God permits a better man to be harmed by a worse. No doubt my accuser might put me to death or have me banished or deprived of civic rights; but even if he thinks, as he probably does (and others too, I dare say), that these are great calamities, I do not think so; I believe that it is far worse to do what he is doing now, trying to put an innocent man to death. For this reason, gentlemen, so far from pleading on my own behalf, as might be supposed, I am really pleading on yours, to save you from misusing the gift of God by condemning me. If you put me to death, you will not easily find anyone to take my place. It is literally true (even if it sounds rather comical) that God has specially appointed me to this city, as though it were a large thoroughbred horse which because of its great size is inclined to be lazy and needs the stimulation of some stinging fly. It seems to me that God has attached me to this city to perform the office of such a fly; and all day long I never cease to settle here, there, and everywhere, rousing, persuading, reproving[1] every one of you. You will not easily find another like me, gentlemen, and if you take my advice you will spare my life.

[The jury decides for the death penalty and Socrates is imprisoned until he can be executed. The following passage from "Phaedo" recounts Socrates' final hours.]

It was now nearly sunset. Socrates came and sat down, fresh from the bath; and he had only been talking for a few minutes when the prison officer came in, and walked up to him. "Socrates," he said, "at any rate I shall not have to find fault with you, as I do with others, for getting angry with me and cursing when I tell them to drink the poison—carrying out Government orders. I have come to know during this time that you are the noblest and the gentlest and the bravest of all the men that have ever come here, and now especially I am sure that you are not angry with me, but with them; because you know who are responsible. So now—you know what I have come to say—goodbye, and try to bear what must be as easily as you can." As he spoke he burst into tears, and turning round, went away.

Socrates looked up at him and said, "Goodbye to you, too; we will do as you say." Then addressing us he went on, "What a charming person! All the time I have been here he has visited me, and shown me the greatest kindness; and how generous of him now to shed tears for me at

[1] Correcting, reprimanding.

parting! But come, Crito, let us do as he says. Someone had better bring in the poison, if it is ready prepared; if not, tell the man to prepare it."

"But surely, Socrates," said Crito, "the sun is still upon the mountains; it has not gone down yet. Besides, I know that in other cases people have dinner and enjoy their wine, and sometimes the company of those whom they love, long after they receive the warning; and only drink the poison quite late at night. No need to hurry; there is still plenty of time."

"It is natural that these people whom you speak of should act in that way, Crito," said Socrates, "because they think that they gain by it. And it is also natural that I should not; because I believe that I should gain nothing by drinking the poison a little later—I should only make myself ridiculous in my own eyes if I clung to life and hugged it when it has no more to offer. Come, do as I say and don't make difficulties."

At this Crito made a sign to his servant, who was standing nearby. The servant went out and after a considerable time returned with the man who was to administer the poison; he was carrying it ready prepared in a cup. When Socrates saw him he said, "Well, my good fellow, you understand these things; what ought I to do?"

"Just drink it," he said, "and then walk about until you feel a weight in your legs, and then lie down. Then it will act of its own accord."

As he spoke he handed the cup to Socrates, who received it quite cheerfully, without a tremor,[2] without any change of color or expression, and said, looking up under his brows with his usual steady gaze, "What do you say about pouring a libation[3] from this drink? Is it permitted, or not?"

"We only prepare what we regard as the normal dose, Socrates," he replied.

"I see," said Socrates. "But I suppose I am allowed, or rather bound, to pray the gods that my removal from this world to the other may be prosperous. This is my prayer, then; and I hope that it may be granted." With these words, quite calmly and with no sign of distaste, he drained the cup in one breath.

Up till this time most of us had been fairly successful in keeping back our tears; but when we saw that he was drinking, that he had actually drunk it, we could do so no longer; in spite of myself the tears came pouring out, so that I covered my face and wept broken-heartedly—not for him, but for my own calamity in losing such a friend. Crito had given up even before me, and had gone out when he could not restrain his tears. But Apollodorus, who had never stopped crying even before, now broke out into such a storm of passionate weeping that he made everyone in the room break down, except Socrates himself, who said:

"Really, my friends, what a way to behave! Why, that was my main reason for sending away the women, to prevent this sort of disturbance; because I am told that one should make one's end in a tranquil frame of mind. Calm yourselves and try to be brave."

This made us feel ashamed, and we controlled our tears. Socrates

---

[2] Shaking.   [3] Liquid sacrifice.

walked about, and presently, saying that his legs were heavy, lay down on his back—that was what the man recommended. The man (he was the same one who had administered the poison) kept his hand upon Socrates, and after a little while examined his feet and legs; then pinched his foot hard and asked if he felt it. Socrates said no. Then he did the same to his legs; and moving gradually upwards in this way let us see that he was getting cold and numb. Presently he felt him again and said that when it reached the heart, Socrates would be gone.

The coldness was spreading about as far as his waist when Socrates uncovered his face—for he had covered it up—and said (they were his last words): "Crito, we ought to offer a cock to Asclepius. See to it, and don't forget."

"No, it shall be done," said Crito. "Are you sure that there is nothing else?"

Socrates made no reply to this question, but after a little while he stirred; and when the man uncovered him, his eyes were fixed. When Crito saw this, he closed the mouth and eyes.

Such was the end of our comrade, who was, we may fairly say, of all those whom we knew in our time, the bravest and also the wisest and most upright man.

Questions for Discussion and Writing

1. Does the defense that Socrates presents in "Apology" appear to be self-interested—is he seeking to save himself through clever argument? Consider how Socrates' behavior at the time of his execution, described in "Phaedo," fits in with such a reading.

2. Is Socrates' death scene depicted in a heroic manner, using Jaeger's definition of heroic behavior?

3. Can the Athenian citizens be faulted for their decision to execute Socrates, given what you know of Athenian politics from Moses Finley's article?

4. Explain how Platonic philosophy, which derives from the teachings of Socrates, may have helped Socrates to face his own death without fear or anger.

5. How does the trial, judgment, and execution of Socrates differ from the legal process leading to capital punishment in our society? Does the modern system seem more or less just than the ancient? Would a figure such as Socrates be likely to face legal prosecution today, and if so, would the death penalty be a possible sentence?

RETHINKING THE TRADITION

Carolyn J. Mooney, **"[Stanford's] Western Culture Program"** _____

This 1988 article from the Chronicle of Higher Education *outlines how Stanford minority students and faculty, critical of the traditional curriculum that presented the* **Euro-centric canon,** *initiated what was to* *become known as the Stanford Debate. Citing increased minority demographics, and voicing an insistent argument for cultural diversity at the university, they succeeded in convincing Stanford to change its Western Civilization curriculum to one that was more sensitive to the needs and issues of women and minorities.*

Key Concepts

The term **Euro-centric** (page 52) implies a bias or a favoring of European culture, values, and ideas.

Tokenism (page 58) is the symbolic, superficial recognition of accomplishment, often of a minority group.

In the months following Stanford University's controversial decision to replace its Western culture program and drop its required reading list, a monumental curricular change has been under way on this campus of golden buildings and quiet courtyards.

Some of it has been subtle, such as a professor's decision to refer in class to "cultures" in the plural rather than the singular form.

Some of it has been obvious, such as the addition of the Koran[1] to one course syllabus and the deletion of the *Odyssey* from another to make room for a new book.

All of it, however, is being watched closely, both by faculty members and administrators at Stanford and by their counterparts and critics across the country.

In March, after two years of vigorous debate that followed complaints by minority students, Stanford's Faculty Senate voted to replace the university's year-long Western culture requirement with a new requirement called "Cultures, Ideas and Values." The year-long program, which is being phased in this year and will be fully in place next fall, requires courses to give "substantial attention" to the issues of race, gender, and class, and to include the study of works by women and minority-group members.

Non-European Works

Students will continue to study ideas derived largely from European, ancient, and medieval cultures, but will also be required to study works from at least one non-European culture. Instead of selections from a common list of 15 great works, as they are frequently called, they will read a smaller number of common books to be chosen annually by those who teach in the program, giving faculty members more flexibility to choose lesser-known works.

During this transition year, the term "Western" is slowly being phased out. The program office recently printed new stationery, and an endowed chair in Western culture held by the program's director, Paul Robinson, will become an endowed chair in Cultures, Ideas and Values.

---

[1] Islamic holy book.

Many faculty members who teach in the program's eight different "tracks" have already adjusted their courses. For some professors, the changes will be minimal; for others, more substantial.

In the meantime, the transition has raised a number of questions. Among them:

■ Will most professors make a sincere effort to go along with the spirit of the new program, or will some take only token steps to comply?

■ Will there be enough professors who are knowledgeable enough about other cultures to teach in the new program? Some professors and administrators have expressed concern that Stanford doesn't have enough minority faculty members to meet the goals of the program.

■ Can the program continue to provide students with a significant common learning experience?

■ Will faculty members in the program be able to connect the readings and common themes in a coherent way? Can Vergil, the Roman poet, coexist with Frantz Fanon, the French West Indian author of anti-colonial works?

■ Will students be cheated by reading fewer well-known works, or will they gain by reading a richer variety of lesser-known works?

■ Where will the debate lead? Will a single redesigned course satisfy those who feel disenfranchised,[2] or will the changes spill over to other courses and virtually all other parts of university life?

Debate at Berkeley

Since the new program was adopted, minority student groups have continued to rally for more multicultural education. Only recently, they presented Stanford administrators with a list of demands that, among other things, called for more minority faculty members, a required ethnic-studies course, and the strengthening of several ethnic-studies programs.

"The question," says Clayborne Carson, an associate professor of history and a specialist on the Rev. Martin Luther King, Jr., "is whether we should expect changes that reflect the spirit of the reform to be taught by those who have taught in the past."

The debate over Western culture at Stanford is one that is taking place at other institutions, as well. Most recently, faculty members at the University of California at Berkeley have been debating a plan that would require all undergraduates to take a course that examines the role of minority-group members in American society. Pressure from minority students has been a big factor at Berkeley, where minority-group members make up 62 per cent of this year's freshman class and about half of the undergraduate student body.

At Stanford, the debate has been evolving since the Western culture program was adopted in 1980 as a way to give students a common learning experience. Even then, it was hardly considered perfect.

[2] Without power or rights.

Among most students, however, the Western culture program has been enormously popular. In annual surveys, most graduating seniors have consistently rated it as one of their most valuable academic experiences at Stanford.

What Does 'Western' Mean?

But in recent years, the program came under mounting criticism from minority students and some young professors, who argued that its focus was so narrow that it ignored the contributions and heritage of women and minority-group members. What, these critics asked, did the term "Western" mean? Whose culture were they studying? And how could any culture of which they were a part be represented by a core reading list with no works by women or minority-group members?

"Western culture did not try to understand the diversity of experiences of different people," says Alejandro Sweet-Cordero, a senior who, as a member of a Chicano student organization, was among those pushing for the changes. "We're not saying we need to study Tibetan philosophy; we're arguing that we need to understand what made our society what it is."

On the other side were professors who, while acknowledging that non-traditional voices were valuable, argued that students would lose an important part of their heritage without a substantial core of literature that traced the development of Western thought and institutions. "You don't fix what isn't broken," says George Dekker, an English professor who opposed the change.

200 Phone Calls

The opponents were later joined by scholars and observers around the country, including former Education Secretary William J. Bennett, who accused Stanford of trashing the classics and caving in to student demands.

Much of the hoopla that followed actually served to pique[3] public interest in reading traditional classics. Mary Rosenstock, coordinator of both the old and new programs, estimates that she got at least 200 phone calls from members of the public seeking copies of the reading list when Stanford decided to eliminate it.

John Agresto, deputy chairman of the National Endowment for the Humanities and a scholar of political philosophy, went one step further: He recently finished teaching a course at the New School for Social Research called "The Old Stanford Western Culture Course," in which students studied works from Stanford's core list. He says his students were enthusiastic.

Tracks Linked by a Core List

Until now, students could satisfy Stanford's Western culture requirement by taking a year-long, three-course sequence in one of eight

[3] Excite, stimulate.

CHANGING THE CORE AT STANFORD

The Old Reading List

While technically "required," not all the works were consistently read in all Western Culture courses.

Ancient World

Old Testament (Hebrew Bible), Genesis
New Testament, including a Gospel
Plato, *Republic*
Homer, selections from the *Iliad* and/or the *Odyssey*
One Greek tragedy

Medieval and Renaissance

Augustine, *Confessions*
Dante, *Inferno*
More, *Utopia*
Machiavelli, *The Prince*
Luther, *Christian Liberty*
Galileo, *The Starry Messenger, The Assayer*

Modern

Voltaire, *Candide*
Marx and Engels, *The Communist Manifesto*
Freud, *Outline of Psychoanalysis, Civilization and Its Discontents*
Darwin, selections

Recommended Supplements to the Old List

Ancient World
Thucydides
Aristotle, *Nicomachean Ethics, Politics*
Cicero
Vergil, *Aeneid*
Tacitus

Medieval and Renaissance
Boethius, *Consolation of Philosophy*
Aquinas
A Shakespearean tragedy
Cervantes, *Don Quixote*
Descartes, *Discourse on Method, Meditations*
Hobbes, *Leviathan*
Locke, *Second Treatise of Civil Government*

Modern

Rousseau, *Social Contract, Confessions, Emile*
Hume, *Enquiries, Dialogues on Natural Religion*
Goethe, *Faust, Sorrows of Young Werther*
A 19th-century novel
Mill, *Essay on Liberty, The Subjection of Women*
Nietzsche, *Genealogy of Morals, Beyond Good and Evil*

New Program's Common Readings

The Old and New Testaments
Selections from:
   Augustine
   Machiavelli
   Marx
   Plato
   Rousseau

tracks that focused on academic themes such as great works, history, and philosophy. They also had the option each year of taking part in an experimental track like this year's "Europe and the Americas" sequence, which focuses on the relationship and common heritage of North America and Latin America. Different tracks were linked by the core list, which in theory represented about half of the works read in each track each year.

Stanford administrators are quick to point out that Western culture has not been trashed, just broadened. Indeed, they say, the program has always had a great deal of flexibility, and many faculty members who teach in it have always discussed issues of gender, race, and class.

"The program has been inching itself along in these directions since it was created," says Marsh McCall, a classics professor who supported the new program only after provisions were made for students to read common works. "The popular notion that we've done away with a core is simply untrue—what we have done is reduce it."

Some observers have suggested that students may actually study *more* common works than before, since one recent survey showed that only two of the 14 "required" core works—Machiavelli's *The Prince* and parts of the Bible—were actually taught in all tracks. Under the new system, which requires faculty members to agree each year on an unspecified number of common elements to be taught in all tracks, six books were chosen for this year: both the Old and New Testaments of the Bible, and works by Plato, Augustine, Machiavelli, Rousseau, and Karl Marx.

That, says one faculty member, was what made the new requirement so politically ingenious: Those who believed in the integrity of the old core list could still teach many of its works, while those who chose to introduce new books would have more chance to do so.

"What we had was a classic compromise," says Renato Rosaldo, an anthropology professor who favored the changes. "What we got was some space to allow people to do new things."

Vergil, Yes; 'Odyssey,' No

Over in the School of Education's Cubberly auditorium, a visitor to the Western culture humanities course finds Vergil—or the *Aeneid,* anyway—alive and well during this transition year. Mark W. Edwards, a classics professor who teaches the course and is a supporter of the new program, has no plans to drop Vergil. He did, however, have to drop the *Odyssey* (students still read the *Iliad*) so that he could introduce his students instead to *The Epic of Gilgamesh* a story about a Babylonian king. He added *The Homeric Hymn to Demeter,* a hymn about a Greek goddess, and the Book of Esther from the Old Testament.

Incorporating other voices into a course about the ancient world is difficult, Mr. Edwards says. There are few surviving works by women, although he has been teaching the poems of Sappho for the last few years. Mr. Edwards is also devoting more time to the lives of women in the ancient world.

As for the Vergil lecture, he says: "There's a slight shift in emphasis, but it doesn't need to change that much." At one point during the class, he compares a passage from the *Aeneid* ("There all stood begging to be first across/And reached out longing hands to the far shore") to Robert Frost's poem "Stopping by Woods on a Snowy Evening." He asks those who have read the Frost poem to raise their hands, and is pleased when most do.

Mr. Edwards thinks there are some books everybody should read. But, he adds, "I wouldn't want a core list as rigid as the old one."

Augustine and a Navajo History

In the experimental "Europe and the Americas" class, students are discussing, *I, Rigoberta Menchù,* a life history told by a Guatemalan Indian woman, with Mr. Rosaldo, the professor. Throughout the quarter, students will read books about the Navajo and Mayan Indians as well as works by Herman Melville, Marx, Augustine, Sigmund Freud, Zora Neale Hurston, and Sandra Cisneros.

An exciting thing happened when Mr. Rosaldo taught Augustine's *Confessions* with *Sun of Old Man Hat,* the life history of a Navajo man. "Both books got better," he says.

Mr. Rosaldo says the new program will better serve an incoming freshman class that is nearly 40 per cent minority. How, he asks, could a Chicano student be expected to find her identity in Plato and Aristotle? Would a science student be expected to take a course that hadn't changed since 1930? "My agenda for the course is, students are coming into a multicultural, interdependent world," he says. "I tried to pick books that, within their own traditions, are classics."

Mr. Rosaldo fears some professors will resort to **tokenism** to satisfy the new requirements. "There's a big difference between tossing an extra book in and connecting the courses in a way that will reflect the spirit of the new course," he says.

Lea Wolf, a freshman in the course, says she has been surprised by how coherently the diverse subject matter has been presented. "If you only looked at the syllabus, you'd think we were out to have a revolution," she says. "But the way we read the books is much broader." Yet, she is by no means opposed to reading traditional classics. "I'm not sure I'd be so comfortable in this track if I hadn't read the *Odyssey* and Plato in high school," she says.

Professors Discuss the Koran

In a history-department conference room, a group of professors has gathered to discuss teaching the Koran, the sacred text of Islam, with Jessica A. Coope, a lecturer who specializes in Spain and Islam. The Koran is being taught in several of the Western culture tracks, but not all the faculty members know as much about it as they would like.

Ms. Coope passes around a list of suggested readings, noting several that are especially helpful "if you find yourselves in an emergency."

One professor who has taught the Koran before wants to know more about its treatment of women. For example, she says, in the book's discussion of afterlife, men are promised "chaste virgins" for companions as a reward. Are women, she wonders, also rewarded with virgins? Or is the Koran really written for men?

Among those at this morning's meeting is Ronald Rebholz, a professor of English who was opposed to the new program because it dropped the core reading list. He says he would have agreed to a list that included works by women and minority writers, but that idea was scrapped because of fears it would encourage tokenism.

The Risk of Tokenism

Indeed, some observers say tokenism is an inherent risk in the new program—and in other parts of university life—as long as a particular action can be perceived by some as having been taken to appease a particular group. Already a backlash has occurred among some scholars across the country, many of whom denounced Stanford's decision to do away with its core reading list at a recent meeting in New York (*The Chronicle,* November 23).

Most of those who have watched the debate over multicultural awareness unfold at Stanford agree that it will not end with the new requirement. But no one knows where it will lead, or what the boundaries are for those who feel disenfranchised. Will women and minority-group members, for example, insist on having their own sculptures displayed on the campus lawn alongside Rodin's "The Thinker," which has just been acquired by the university? (In fact, university officials note that Stanford's art collection includes a loaned sculpture called "Gay Liberation," which depicts two gay couples.) Will they want additional names engraved alongside those of Plato, Locke, Rousseau, and other thinkers and educators whose names now adorn the facade of the School of Education?

The best answer to where the debate ends, say those who have been closely involved in it here, is that it doesn't.

Stanford faculty members are already engaged in a new discussion about whether the university's non-Western requirement—which can now be satisfied by a number of quarter-long courses—should be replaced by an ethnic-studies course and strengthened. Minority student groups are continuing to press for a platform of changes, some of which they have demanded in response to several recent racial incidents on the campus. A long-awaited report on minority life at Stanford, prepared by a committee that was formed in response to student pressure, is to be released early next year.

"We're at an early stage in the process," says Mr. Carson, the history professor. "But you already see people putting together a new view of America, a much richer narrative."

Says Mr. Edwards, the classics professor: "Whatever we do, we'll change again in 10 years. No university curriculum can last that long."

Questions for Discussion and Writing

1. You've probably encountered some of the works of the traditional Western canon in high school or college. What were your initial impressions before studying them? Did any of your preconceptions change after reading them? What value did any of these works have for you personally? Did they speak to you in any way? Would you encourage others to study them in more depth? Why might you not want to read them if they were not required? What would you replace them with?

2. Survey your classmates or discuss in groups what students think they should be learning about the Western canon. How many are actually planning to take these classes? What do they hope to gain from them?

3. Explain the debate over curriculum that took place at Stanford and the compromise that was finally reached. Do you agree with the change?

4. Faculty members at Berkeley, where half the undergraduates are minorities and 62 percent of the freshmen are minorities, have been debating a proposal that would require all undergraduates to take a course on the role of minorities in America. What are the pros and cons of such a required course?

5. One professor at Stanford taught a work by St. Augustine along with a life history of a Navajo man claiming "both books got better." How could a traditional work and a contemporary minority book enhance each other? More broadly, how might the traditional canon and a culturally diverse canon enrich each other?

6. Should a country like the United States, whose basis is a mixture of cultures, have a single canon of knowledge and cultural values taught through the school system? What would it provide us with? How close are we to it now? Consider defending the following position, developed by a student writer: For a society to remain strong and flourish, it needs a central body of knowledge and cultural traditions to teach all its young people; otherwise things will fall apart. In fact, things are beginning to fall apart. Young people today don't know very much about American democratic ideals or about the Western civilization that is the very source of our ideals and traditions. Of course, if people want to maintain their own cultures as the Irish Americans, Jewish Americans, and Italian Americans have done for years, that's fine as long as they embrace first and foremost a mainstream American tradition based on the ideals and values of Western Civilization as taught in our schools. That's the way it has been, and that's the way it should be.

7. Will students be "cheated" by reading fewer well-known works, or should the notion of what is a well-known work and why it has been canonized be examined and reconsidered?

8. In this article, a minority student pointed out that "Western culture did not try to understand the diversity of experiences of different people." How is this a problem? Do you agree with her position?

Mike Rose, **"Crossing Boundaries"** _____

Mike Rose is a nationally known author of a number of books and articles on education, literacy, and composition. Growing up in a Los An-

geles ghetto, Rose himself experienced "life on the boundary" of mainstream America. In this excerpt from his book Lives on the Boundary *(1989), he examines how the traditional canon can present problems to underprepared minority students.*

Key Concepts

The traditional definition of **literacy** (page 61)—the ability to read and write—has evolved to include a broader concept of cultural literacy, or the ability to function and succeed in various social contexts.

The **underclass** (page 64) are those members of society who are oppressed and powerless; they have little or no access to the traditional means of social mobility, such as higher education and professional training.

A **pluralistic democracy** (page 65) is one that recognizes and accepts the differences between cultural groups and treats them equally. Unlike the "melting pot" version of democracy, in pluralistic democracies, cultural groups retain their diversity.

One who holds **egalitarian ideals** (page 65) believes in the fundamental equality of all people and promotes equal treatment in social institutions (government, schools, etc.).

There is a strong impulse in American education—curious in a country with such an ornery streak of antitraditionalism—to define achievement and excellence in terms of the acquisition of a historically validated body of knowledge, an authoritative list of books and allusions, a canon. We seek a certification of our national intelligence, indeed, our national virtue, in how diligently our children can display this central corpus[1] of information. This need for certification tends to emerge most dramatically in our educational policy debates during times of real or imagined threat: economic hard times, political crises, sudden increases in immigration. Now is such a time, and it is reflected in a number of influential books and commission reports. E. D. Hirsch argues that a core national vocabulary, one oriented toward the English literate tradition—Alice in Wonderland to zeitgeist[2]—will build a knowledge base that will foster the **literacy** of all Americans. Diane Ravitch and Chester Finn call for a return to a traditional historical and literary curriculum: the valorous historical figures and the classical literature of the once-elite course of study. Allan Bloom, Secretary of Education William Bennett, Mortimer Adler and the Paideia Group, and a number of others have affirmed, each in their very different ways, the necessity of the Great Books: Plato and Aristotle and Sophocles, Dante and Shakespeare and Locke, Dickens and Mann and Faulkner. We can call this orientation to educational achievement the canonical orientation.

At times in our past, the call for a shoring[3] up of or return to a canonical curriculum was explicitly elitist, was driven by a fear that the

---

[1] Body.
[2] Spirit of an age.

[3] Supporting, bracing.

education of the select was being compromised. Today, though, the majority of the calls are provocatively framed in the language of democracy. They assail[4] the mediocre and grinding curriculum frequently found in remedial and vocational education. They are disdainful of the patronizing perceptions of student ability that further restrict the already restricted academic life of disadvantaged youngsters. They point out that the canon—its language, conventions, and allusions—is central to the discourse of power, and to keep it from poor kids is to assure their disenfranchisement[5] all the more. The books of the canon, claim the proposals, the Great Books, are a window onto a common core of experience and civic ideals. There is, then, a spiritual, civic, and cognitive[6] heritage here, and *all* our children should receive it. If we are sincere in our desire to bring [all children] into our society—then we should provide them with this stable and common core. This is a forceful call. It promises a still center in a turning world.

I see great value in being challenged to think of the curriculum of the many in the terms we have traditionally reserved for the few; it is refreshing to have common assumptions about the capacities of under-prepared students so boldly challenged. Many . . . have displayed the ability to engage books and ideas thought to be beyond their grasp. . . . Too many people are kept from the books of the canon, the Great Books, because of misjudgments about their potential. Those books eventually proved important to me, and, as best I know how, I invite my students to engage them. But once we grant the desirability of equal curricular treatment and begin to consider what this equally distributed curriculum would contain, problems arise: If the canon itself is the answer to our educational inequities,[7] why has it historically invited few and denied many? Would the canonical orientation provide adequate guidance as to how a democratic curriculum should be constructed and how it should be taught? . . . .

Those who study the way literature becomes canonized, how linguistic creations are included or excluded from a tradition, claim that the canonical curriculum students would most likely receive would not as is claimed, offer a common core of American experience . . . . The canon has tended to push to the margin much of the literature of our nation: from American Indian songs and chants to immigrant fiction to working-class narratives. The institutional messages that students receive in the books they're issued and the classes they take are powerful and, as I've witnessed since my Voc. Ed. days, quickly internalized. And to revise these messages and redress[8] past wrongs would involve more than adding some new books to the existing canon—the very reasons for linguistic and cultural exclusion would have to become a focus of study in order to make the canon act as a democratizing force. Unless this

---

[4] Attack.
[5] Exclusion from rights, privileges.
[6] Way of thinking or knowing.

[7] Unfairness.
[8] Set right.

happens, the democratic intent of the reformers will be undercut by the content of the curriculum they propose.

And if we move beyond content to consider basic assumptions about teaching and learning, a further problem arises, one that involves the very nature of the canonical orientation itself. The canonical orientation encourages a narrowing of focus from learning to that which must be learned: It simplifies the dynamic tension between student and text and reduces the psychological and social dimensions of instruction. The student's personal history recedes as the what of the classroom is valorized[9] over the how. Thus it is that the encounter of student and text is often portrayed by canonists as a transmission. Information, wisdom, virtue will pass from the book to the student if the student gives the book the time it merits, carefully traces its argument or narrative or lyrical progression. Intellectual, even spiritual, growth will *necessarily* result from an encounter with Roman mythology, *Othello,* and "I heard a Fly buzz—when I died—," with biographies and historical sagas and patriotic lore. Learning is stripped of confusion and discord. It is stripped, as well, of strong human connection. My own initiators to the canon— Jack MacFarland, Dr. Carothers, and the rest—knew there was more to their work than their mastery of a tradition. What mattered most, I see now, were the relationships they established with me, the guidance they provided when I felt inadequate or threatened. This mentoring was part of my entry into that solemn library of Western thought—and even with such support, there were still times of confusion, anger, and fear. It is telling, I think, that once that rich social network slid away, once I was in graduate school in intense, solitary encounter with that tradition, I abandoned it for other sources of nurturance and knowledge.

The model of learning implicit in the canonical orientation seems, at times, more religious than cognitive or social: Truth resides in the printed texts, and if they are presented by someone who knows them well and respects them, that truth will be revealed. . . . But . . . there is little acknowledgment that the material in the canon can be not only difficult but foreign, alienating, overwhelming.

We need an orientation to instruction that provides guidance on how to determine and honor the beliefs and stories, enthusiasms, and apprehensions that students reveal. How to build on them, and when they clash with our curriculum—as I saw so often in the Tutorial Center at UCLA—when they clash, how to encourage a discussion that will lead to reflection on what students bring and what they're currently confronting. Canonical lists imply canonical answers, but the manifestos[10] offer little discussion of what to do when students fail. If students have been exposed to at least some elements of the canon before—as many have— why didn't it take? If they're enountering it for the first time and they're lost, how can we determine where they're located—and what do we do then?

---

[9] Given value.   [10] Public declarations.

Each member of a teacher's class, poor *or* advantaged, gives rise to endless decisions, day-to-day determinations about a child's reading and writing: decisions on how to tap strength, plumb confusion, foster growth. The richer your conception of learning and your understanding of its social and psychological dimensions, the more insightful and effective your judgments will be. Consider the sources of literacy we saw among the children in El Monte: shopkeepers' signs, song lyrics, auto manuals, the conventions of the Western, family stories and tales, and more. . . . How would these myriad sources and manifestations be perceived and evaluated if viewed within the framework of a canonical tradition, and what guidance would the tradition provide on how to understand and develop them? The great books and central texts of the canon could quickly become a benchmark[11] against which the expressions of student literacy would be negatively measured, a limiting band of excellence that, ironically, could have a dispiriting[12] effect on the very thing the current proposals intend: the fostering of mass literacy.

To understand the nature and development of literacy we need to consider the social context in which it occurs—the political, economic, and cultural forces that encourage or inhibit it. The canonical orientation discourages deep analysis of the way these forces may be affecting performance. The canonists ask that schools transmit a coherent traditional knowledge to an ever-changing, frequently uprooted community. This discordance[13] between message and audience is seldom examined. Although a ghetto child can rise on the lilt of a Homeric line—books *can* spark dreams—appeals to elevated texts can also divert attention from the conditions that keep a population from realizing its dreams. The literacy curriculum is being asked to do what our politics and our economics have failed to do: diminish differences in achievement, narrow our gaps, bring us together. Instead of analysis of the complex web of causes of poor performance, we are offered a faith in the unifying power of a body of knowledge, whose infusion will bring the rich and the poor, the longtime disaffected[14] and the uprooted newcomers into cultural unanimity. If this vision is democratic, it is simplistically so, reductive, not an invitation for people truly to engage each other at the point where cultures and classes intersect.

I worry about the effects a canonical approach to education could have on cultural dialogue and transaction—on the involvement of an abandoned **underclass** and on the movement of immigrants . . . into our nation. A canonical uniformity promotes rigor and quality control; it can also squelch new thinking, diffuse[15] the generative tension between the old and the new. It is significant that the canonical orientation is voiced with most force during times of challenge and uncertainty, for it promises the authority of tradition, the seeming stability of the past. But

---

[11] Standard of measurement.
[12] Discouraging.
[13] Conflict, difference.

[14] Alienated.
[15] Scatter, weaken.

the authority is fictive, gained from a misreading of American cultural history. No period of that history was harmoniously stable; the invocation[16] of a golden age is a mythologizing act. Democratic culture is, by definition, vibrant and dynamic, discomforting and unpredictable. It gives rise to apprehension; freedom is not always calming. And, yes, it can yield fragmentation, though often as not the source of fragmentation is intolerant misunderstanding of diverse traditions rather than the desire of members of those traditions to remain hermetically[17] separate. A truly democratic vision of knowledge and social structure would honor this complexity. The vision might not be soothing, but it would provide guidance as to how to live and teach in a country made up of many cultural traditions.

We are in the middle of an extraordinary social experiment: the attempt to provide education for all members of a vast **pluralistic democracy.** To have any prayer of success, we'll need many conceptual blessings: A philosophy of language and literacy that affirms the diverse sources of linguistic competence and deepens our understanding of the ways class and culture blind us to the richness of those sources. A perspective on failure that lays open the logic of error. An orientation toward the interaction of poverty and ability that undercuts simple polarities[18] that enables us to see simultaneously the constraints[19] poverty places on the play of mind and the actual mind at play within those constraints. We'll need a pedagogy[20] that encourages us to step back and consider the threat of the standard classroom and that shows us, having stepped back, how to step forward to invite a student across the boundaries of that powerful room. Finally, we'll need a revised store of images of educational excellence, ones closer to **egalitarian ideals**—ones that embody the reward and turmoil of education in a democracy, that celebrate the plural, messy human reality of it. At heart, we'll need a guiding set of principles that do not encourage us to retreat from, but move us closer to, an understanding of the rich mix of speech and ritual and story that is America.

Questions for Discussion and Writing

1. Explain Rose's concept of the canonical orientation in education. Has your education been influenced by this philosophy? In what way(s)?

2. In the past, Rose says, canonical education had an elitist purpose of providing a select education for an exclusive group. Today, defenders of the canon argue that such an approach enhances democracy. Explain their side of the argument—that teaching the canon can give access to power.

3. Rose mentions American Indian and working-class texts as examples of works that are marginalized in canonical education. What does "marginalization" mean as a political concept, and what might its practical effects be, particularly on members of marginalized groups?

---

[16] Appeal to.
[17] Sealed airtightly.
[18] Opposite points.

[19] Limitations.
[20] Teaching method.

4. Examine an incident in your experience which made you feel marginalized. What were the personal and social effects of the experience?

5. Rose argues that "the democratic intent of the [canonists] will be undercut by the content of the curriculum they propose." How does he reach this conclusion, and do you accept it?

6. The focus of canonical education, Rose writes, is not on learning but on "that which must be learned." In what way does education then become a simple "transmission" of information, rather than real learning?

7. What "boundaries" must the nontraditional student attempt to overcome, in the educational system and in society as a whole?

Chapter Writing Topics

1. Review the readings that deal with the current debate over the traditional Western civilization canon (see the Mooney and Rose essays). Also consider your own educational experience: your exposure to the canon, your sense of how well your home culture is represented by it, your feelings toward canonical readings such as those contained in *The Course of Ideas*. Where do you stand on the issue, and what contributions to the discussion can you make? Consider the following issues as you begin to address the topic. You may want to respond informally in writing to each issue as a way of beginning your writing process.

    (a) How do proponents of canonical education defend it? Summarize the arguments discussed in the Mooney and Rose pieces.

    (b) What are the major criticisms?

    (c) Are you the product of a canonical education? Do you feel that your education has been restricted to one cultural view, or have your course materials been culturally diverse?

    (d) Do you sympathize with the Stanford student protesters?

2. How common is familiarity with Greek mythology in contemporary American society? Survey a representative group of people (include people of different ages, backgrounds, and educational levels) to determine whether classical mythology continues to be a shared base of knowledge for us. Consider asking the following questions, and work with classmates to develop others.

    (a) Can you retell the myth of Oedipus?

    (b) Who was Narcissus? (Add other mythological figures you know and might expect others to be familiar with.)

    (c) What myth explains the natural phenomenon we call an echo?

    (d) Can you name any books, films, or products that use mythological figures?

    (e) What is the story of the Trojan War? (Ask for as many details as the person can give.)

    (f) What is the purpose of myths?

3. Several of the readings in Chapter 1 discuss the concept of heroic behavior or present the exploits or ideas of a heroic figure. From your reading, develop a description of the heroic ideals of the ancient world that have become an accepted part of the Western tradition. Heroic figures to consider include Oedipus, Odysseus, and Socrates, in addition to heroic figures whom you may know from previous reading. In your essay, discuss whether contemporary heroic figures fit into the traditional ideal and whether you endorse or disapprove of it.

   (a) Do Oedipus, Odysseus, and Socrates have specific traits in common? Analyze what these are and why they have traditionally been considered admirable.

   (b) Who are some modern counterparts of these ancient heroes? Consider historical as well as fictional heroes.

   (c) Are these modern heroes without flaws, or are they open to criticism, as the ancient heroes are?

   (d) Do you advocate the values that our modern heroes represent? Can you think of some alternative heroic figures who represent traits you respect more?

4. The Sophists and the Platonists disagreed strongly on the issue of absolute versus relative truth. Review and summarize their respective positions (see the Greer essay and review the discussion questions that follow it). Develop an essay discussing how the same intellectual debate continues into contemporary times.

   (a) How does it still bring people into conflict?

   (b) Can we attribute positive results to this debate?

   (c) Consider the relativist and absolutist positions on ethical, moral, and political issues such as abortion, affirmative action, creation versus evolution, prayer in schools, and other topical concerns you can name.

5. Define the different logical methods of induction and deduction and assess which logical method works most often and most effectively for you in your approach to learning.

   (a) Explain how the Greeks used each type of reasoning,

   (b) Consider modern uses of each in sciences such as physics and biology.

   (c) Examine a typical learning situation drawn from your experience as a student.

6. To what extent is a truly democratic classroom (as Finley describes a political democracy) possible and desirable? Explain how such a classroom would function, and consider some of the following issues:

   (a) Who would determine the curriculum? How?

   (b) How would writing assignments be performed?

   (c) How would discussions be run?

   (d) What would the role of the instructor be?

   (e) How would disciplinary issues such as incomplete work or plagiarism be handled?

(f) What benefits might such a system offer? What drawbacks might surface?

7.   The chapter readings present a selective historical view of the Classical Greek era. Our view of the era suggests the values we hold, rather than a mirror of the actual historical time period. What beliefs and qualities have we found valuable in the ancient Greek tradition? Examine the heroes, the philosophical and political ideals, and the scientific work that we continue to cite as important contributions to Western civilization. How do we use the Greeks as a mirror of our ideal selves? What sort of image do we create of the ancient world and thus of idealized modern society?

   (a) Name the heroic, philosophical, political, and scientific values represented in the chapter readings.

   (b) What view of human nature do the readings create?

   (c) How should people behave in society, according to the readings?

   (d) What value is attached to rational thought?

   (e) Describe the ideal person, as we have used the ancient Greek tradition to define this ideal.

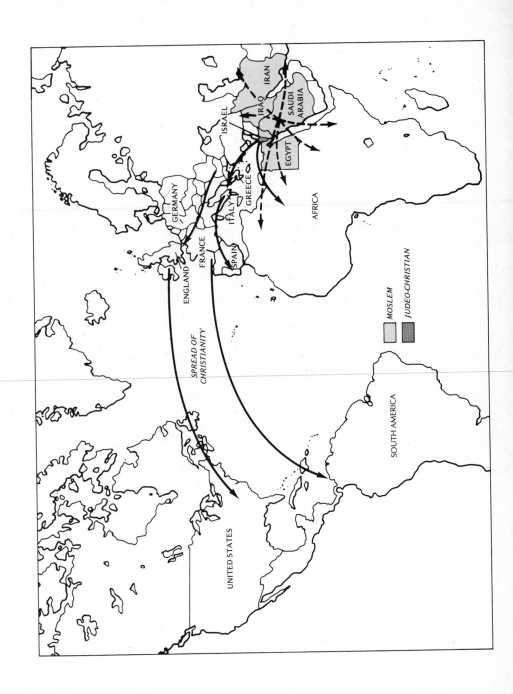

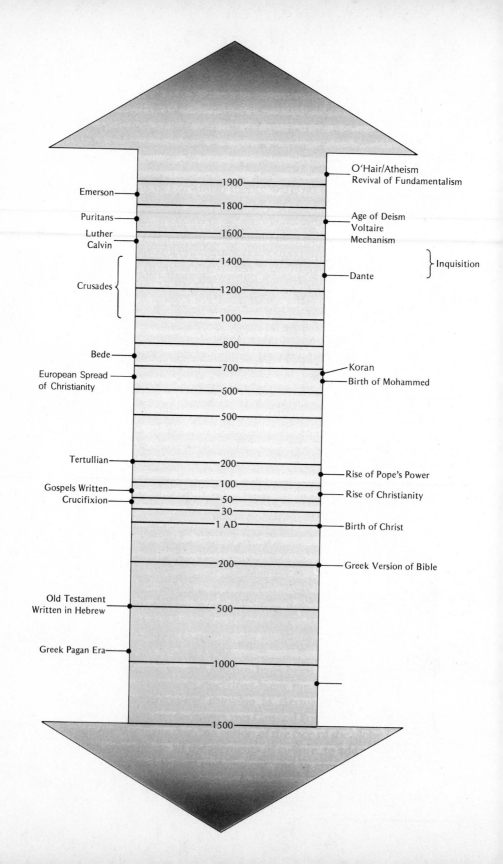

O'Hair/Atheism
Revival of Fundamentalism
1900
Emerson
1800
Puritans
Age of Deism
Voltaire
1600
Mechanism
Luther
Calvin
1400
Inquisition
Dante
1200
Crusades
1000
800
Bede
700
Koran
European Spread
Birth of Mohammed
of Christianity
600
500
Tertullian
200
Rise of Pope's Power
Gospels Written
100
Crucifixion
50
Rise of Christianity
30
1 AD
Birth of Christ
200
Greek Version of Bible
Old Testament
Written in Hebrew
500
Greek Pagan Era
1000
1500

CHAPTER 2

Religion: Changing Beliefs and Attitudes

———— ❧ ————

Introduction

For many people religion is simply a matter of expressing personal faith in God every Sunday. Throughout history, however, religion has functioned as a powerful force, intimately connected with the development of cultural and political institutions, as well as with philosophy, science, and art. To a large extent, the history of Western religion is also a history of Western art, politics, and world view.

Two stories from the Old Testament open this chapter. They portray an all-powerful Hebrew Jehovah: a lawgiver, at times merciful, comforting and sustaining, but often exacting and vengeful. Juxtaposed to Jehovah in the parable from the New Testament is the Christian concept of God the Father whose son Jesus Christ offers God's love and compassion for all. This concept changed with the authoritative attitudes of the early Church Fathers, like St. Augustine, who solidified the structure of the early Christian Church and began consolidating its political, social, and religious power. Patristic theorists like Augustine ultimately shaped Christian precepts and teachings into an organized doctrine and moral code.

Less than 200 years after St. Augustine, the prophet Muhammad recorded the Koran and the religion of Islam was born. Since then, Islam and Christianity have clashed, often violently, leading to cultural animosity, religious prejudice, and mutual distrust. Ironically, Judaism, Christianity, and Islam share a good deal in common. Parts of the Koran, as the selections in this chapter demonstrate, read much like the Bible, but the clash of Islam and Christianity can be vividly seen in the selection from Dante's *Divine Comedy*. Dante's graphic imagery of fire and infernal suffering reflects the very real medieval conception of Hell and its tortures. The rise of Lutheranism and the Reformation marked a split in the organized Catholic Church and the beginning of the Protestant era, continued by Calvin, whose doctrine was less tolerant and hopeful than Luther's. The Puritans continued the Calvinist tradition, bringing it with them to the new world of America.

In the late sixteenth and seventeenth centuries, the Age of Reason, scientists increased our understanding of the physical universe and hence changed the image and role of God. God became less of an active force in everyday affairs than a "Divine Clockmaker" who designed the universe as a well-oiled and-running machine, but who did not interfere in daily life. Voltaire's "Of Universal Tolerance" embodies the Age of Reason's deistic view of God as benevolent, rational, and independent of any organized church. The later Romantics, reacting in part against the mechanistic world view of the Age of Reason, emphasized individual spirituality rather than organized religion or rational faith. The famous American poet and transcendentalist Ralph Waldo Emerson conceived of the universe as a great and holy spirit, a living "oversoul" of which all people are a part. The extreme end of the spiritual continuum, the historical progression of religion away from an organized social institution to a less public, individual practice, is found in atheistic doctrine, represented here by Madalyn Murray O'Hair, a contemporary American atheist.

The final article in this chapter offers a radical feminist argument against traditional religions, which historically have been patriarchal, established and still controlled by men. Although a minority position, this article reflects the continued impetus for change in Western religious practice and values.

As you read this chapter, keep in mind that Western society in general and American society in particular has been continually enriched by many non-Western religions. Many of these religions may be traced back as far as, or further than, Western religions and can claim achievements of equal magnitude. Because the Judeo-Christian religion has been the historical center in Western culture, the chapter readings are drawn largely from this tradition.

THE ANCIENT WORLD

The Old Testament is a collection of the writings of ancient Hebrew scholars and the teachings of the Hebrew prophets. We can trace the origins of some Bible stories, such as the great flood, back through the Egyptians, Babylonians, and Assyrians. The Judeo-Christian tradition considers the Bible the "word of God," but others view it as moral philosophy written by several different hands, probably from the eighth through second centuries B.C. In either case, Old Testament teachings and imagery continue to have a strong influence on Western thought. The New Testament, deriving from the teachings of Jesus Christ and passed on orally until the second century A.D., has also greatly influenced all aspects of Western culture. Both parts of the Bible survive today as the definitive beliefs of the Jewish and Christian religions. Like Greek myths, Bible stories embody moral beliefs and teachings. In these stories, the moral and religious message is strongly implied in the characters and the events.

"The Golden Calf"

Key Concepts

Idolatry consists of object-worship; instead of a spiritual notion of God, idolators worship a representation of God, usually some sort of statue. Here, the people say, ". . . make us a god" (page 73).

The Old Testament notion of **atonement** means an individual must pay for his or her sins with an equivalent sacrifice (page 75).

When the people became aware of Moses' delay in coming down from the mountain, they gathered around Aaron and said to him, "Come, **make us a god** who will be our leader; as for the man Moses who brought us out of the land of Egypt, we do not know what has happened to him." Aaron replied, "Have your wives and sons and daughters take off the golden earrings they are wearing, and bring them to me." So all the people took off their earrings and brought them to Aaron, who accepted their offering, and fashioning this gold with a graving tool, made a molten[1] calf. Then they cried out, "This is your God, O Israel, who brought you out of the land of Egypt." On seeing this, Aaron built an altar before the calf and proclaimed, "Tomorrow is a feast of the Lord." Early the next day the people offered holocausts[2] and brought peace offerings. Then they sat down to eat and drink, and rose up to revel.[3]

---

[1] Made from melted metal.
[2] Burnt sacrifices.

[3] Celebrate.

With that, the Lord said to Moses, "Go down at once to your people, whom you brought out of the land of Egypt, for they have become depraved. They have soon turned aside from the way I pointed out to them, making for themselves a molten calf and worshiping it, sacrificing to it and crying out, 'This is your God, O Israel, who brought you out of the land of Egypt!' I see how stiff-necked[4] this people is," continued the Lord to Moses. "Let me alone, then, that my wrath may blaze up against them to consume them. Then I will make of you a great nation."

But Moses implored the Lord, his God, saying, "Why, O Lord, should your wrath blaze up against your own people, whom you brought out of the land of Egypt with such great power and with so strong a hand? Why should the Egyptians say, 'With evil intent he brought them out, that he might kill them in the mountains and exterminate them from the face of the earth'? Let your blazing wrath die down; relent[5] in punishing your people. Remember your servants Abraham, Isaac and Israel, and how you swore to them by your own self, saying, 'I will make your descendants as numerous as the stars in the sky; and all this land that I promised, I will give your descendants as their perpetual heritage.'" So the Lord relented in the punishment he had threatened to inflict on his people.

Moses then turned and came down the mountain with the two tablets of the Commandments in his hands, tablets that were written on both sides, front and back; tablets that were made by God, having inscriptions on them that were engraved by God himself. Now, when Joshua heard the noise of the people shouting, he said to Moses, "That sounds like a battle in the camp." But Moses answered, "It does not sound like cries of victory, nor does it sound like cries of defeat; the sounds that I hear are sounds of revelry." As he drew near the camp, he saw the calf and the dancing. With that, Moses' wrath flared up, so that he threw the tablets down and broke them on the base of the mountain. Taking the calf they had made, he fused it in the fire and then ground it down to powder, which he scattered on the water and made the Israelites drink.

Moses asked Aaron, "What did this people ever do to you that you should lead them into so grave a sin?" Aaron replied, "Let not my lord be angry. You know well enough how prone the people are to evil. They said to me, 'Make us a god to be our leader; as for the man Moses who brought us out of the land of Egypt, we do not know what has happened to him.' So I told them, 'Let anyone who has gold jewelry take it off.' they gave it to me, and I threw it into the fire, and this calf came out."

When Moses realized that, to the scornful joys of their foes, Aaron had let the people run wild, he stood at the gate of the camp and cried, "Whoever is for the Lord, let him come to me!" All the Levites[6] then

---

[4] Stubborn.
[5] Be less stubborn or stern.

[6] Members of one of the twelve tribes.

rallied to him, and he told them, "Thus says the Lord, the God of Israel: Put your sword on your hip, every one of you! Now go up and down this camp, from gate to gate, and slay your own kinsmen, your friends and neighbors!" The Levites carried out the command of Moses and that day there fell about three thousand of the people. Then Moses said, "Today you have been dedicated to the Lord, for you were against your own sons and kinsmen, to bring a blessing upon yourselves this day."

On the next day Moses said to the people, "You have committed a grave sin. I will go up to the Lord, then; perhaps I may be able to make **atonement** for your sin." So Moses went back to the Lord and said, "Ah, this people has indeed committed a grave sin in making a god of gold for themselves! If you would only forgive their sin! If you will not, then strike me out of the book that you have written." The Lord answered, "Him only who has sinned against me will I strike out of my book. Now, go and lead the people whither I have told you. My angel will go before you. When it is time for me to punish, I will punish them for their sin."

Thus the Lord smote[7] the people for having had Aaron make the calf for them.

Questions for Discussion and Writing

1. Most stories contain a conflict and a resolution as well as an implied message. In the case of the "Golden Calf," the message is a religious one. Why is Jehovah angered at the creation of the Golden Calf? Why are the sinners punished? What is the religious message(s) and purpose behind this story?

2. The early Hebrew tribes of the Old Testament were tough, nomadic desert people, often surviving in a harsh, unforgiving environment. Examine this and other stories from the Old Testament and build a picture of what daily life may have been like for the first Hebrew people. What did they eat and drink? Where did they sleep? How did they travel? What was the land like that they inhabited? How does this depiction of God in the "Golden Calf" story reflect the Hebrew people's culture and environment?

3. Twice Moses attempts to intervene directly with God on behalf of his people. How does he convince God not to let [His] "wrath blaze up against" them and "consume" them, when God first finds out that they have constructed an idol? What does he offer God when he pleads for atonement at the end of the story?

4. Other major world religions utilize statues and images of God in their religious practice. What function do religious symbols serve in the religions you are familiar with?

---

[7] Struck; afflicted.

The Book of Jonah

Like the story of "The Golden Calf," the Bible story of Jonah, the reluctant prophet who was swallowed by a whale, functions as a parable with important theological messages. It was written later than "The Golden Calf," possibly in the fifth century B.C.

THE FIRST MISSION

[1] This is the word of the Lord that came to Jonah, son of Amittai: [2] "Set out for the great city of Nineveh, and preach against it; their wickedness has come up before me." [3] But Jonah made ready to flee to Tarshish away from the Lord. He went down to Joppa, found a ship going to Tarshish, paid the fare, and went aboard to journey with them to Tarshish, away from the Lord.

[4] The Lord, however, hurled a violent wind upon the sea, and in the furious tempest that arose the ship was on the point of breaking up. [5] Then the mariners became frightened and each one cried to his god. To lighten the ship for themselves, they threw its cargo into the sea. Meanwhile, Jonah had gone down into the hold of the ship, and lay there fast asleep. [6] The captain came to him and said, "What are you doing asleep? Rise up, call upon your God! Perhaps God will be mindful of us so that we may not perish."

[7] Then they said to one another, "Come, let us cast lots to find out on whose account we have met with this misfortune." So they cast lots, and thus singled out Jonah. [8] "Tell us," they said, "what is your business? Where do you come from? What is your country, and to what people do you belong?" [9] "I am a Hebrew," Jonah answered them; "I worship the Lord, the God of heaven, who made the sea and the dry land."

[10] Now the men were seized with great fear and said to him, "How could you do such a thing!"—They knew that he was fleeing from the Lord, because he had told them—[11] "What shall we do with you," they asked, "that the sea may quiet down for us?" For the sea was growing more and more turbulent. [12] Jonah said to them, "Pick me up and throw me into the sea, that it may quiet down for you; since I know it is because of me that this violent storm has come upon you."

[13] "Still the men rowed hard to regain the land, but they could not, for the sea grew ever more turbulent. [14] Then they cried to the Lord: "We beseech[1] you, O Lord, let us not perish for taking this man's life; do not charge us with shedding innocent blood, for you, Lord, have done as you saw fit." [15] Then they took Jonah and threw him into the sea, and the sea's raging abated. [16] Struck with great fear of the Lord, the men offered sacrifice and made vows to him.

---

[1] Beg.

¹ But the LORD sent a large fish, that swallowed Jonah; and he remained in the belly of the fish three days and three nights. ² From the belly of the fish Jonah said this prayer to the LORD, his God:

Psalm of Thanksgiving

³ Out of my distress I called to the LORD,
  and he answered me;
From the midst of the nether² world I cried for help,
  and you heard my voice.
⁴ For you cast me into the deep, into the heart of the sea,
  and the flood enveloped me;
All your breakers and your billows passed over me.
⁵ Then I said, "I am banished from your sight!
  yet would I again look upon your holy temple."
⁶ The waters swirled about me, threatening my life;
  the abyss enveloped me; seaweed clung about my head.
⁷ Down I went to the roots of the mountains;
  the bars of the nether world were closing behind me forever,
But you brought up my life from the pit,
  O LORD, my God.
⁸ When my soul fainted within me,
  I remembered the LORD;
My prayer reached you
  in your holy temple.
⁹ Those who worship vain idols
  forsake their source of mercy.
¹⁰ But I, with resounding praise,
  will sacrifice to you;
What I have vowed I will pay:
  deliverance is from the LORD.
¹¹ Then the LORD commanded the fish to spew³
  Jonah upon the shore.

CONVERSION OF NINEVEH

¹ The word of the LORD came to Jonah a second time: ² "Set out for the great city of Nineveh, and announce to it the message that I will tell you." ³ So Jonah made ready and went to Nineveh, according to the LORD's bidding. Now Nineveh was an enormously large city; it took three days to go through it. ⁴ Jonah began his journey through the city, and had gone but a single day's walk announcing, "Forty days more and Nineveh shall be destroyed," ⁵ when the people of Nineveh believed God; they proclaimed a fast and all of them, great and small, put on sackcloth.

---

² Lower, under.   ³ Vomit.

⁶ When the news reached the king of Nineveh, he rose from his throne, laid aside his robe, covered himself with sackcloth, and sat in the ashes. ⁷ Then he had this proclaimed throughout Nineveh, by decree of the king and his nobles: "Neither man nor beast, neither cattle nor sheep, shall taste anything; they shall not eat, nor shall they drink water. ⁸ Man and beast shall be covered with sackcloth and call loudly to God; every man shall turn from his evil way and from the violence he has in hand. ⁹ Who knows, God may relent and forgive, and withhold his blazing wrath, so that we shall not perish." ¹⁰ When God saw by their actions how they turned from their evil way, he repented of the evil that he had threatened to do to them; he did not carry it out.

JONAH'S ANGER: GOD'S REPROOF [4]

¹ But this was greatly displeasing to Jonah, and he became angry. ² "I beseech you, LORD," he prayed, "is not this what I said while I was still in my own country? This is why I fled at first to Tarshish. I knew that you are a gracious and merciful God, slow to anger, rich in clemency, loathe to punish. ³ And now, LORD, please take my life from me; for it is better for me to die than to live." ⁴ But the LORD asked, "Have you reason to be angry?"

⁵ Jonah then left the city for a place to the east of it, where he built himself a hut and waited under it in the shade, to see what would happen to the city. ⁶ And when the LORD God provided a gourd plant, that grew up over Jonah's head, giving shade that relieved him of any discomfort, Jonah was very happy over the plant. ⁷ But the next morning at dawn God sent a worm which attacked the plant, so that it withered. ⁸ And when the sun arose, God sent a burning east wind; and the sun beat upon Jonah's head till he became faint. Then he asked for death, saying, "I would be better off dead than alive."

⁹ But God said to Jonah, "Have you reason to be angry over the plant?" "I have reason to be angry," Jonah answered, "angry enough to die." ¹⁰ Then the LORD said, "You are concerned over the plant which cost you no labor and which you did not raise; it came up in one night and in one night it perished. ¹¹ And should I not be concerned over Nineveh, the great city, in which there are more than a hundred and twenty thousand persons who cannot distinguish their right hand from their left, not to mention the many cattle?"

Questions for Discussion and Writing

1. Identify the points of conflict in the story of Jonah and how they are resolved. What issues does the story raise? What does the story teach?

2. From the belly of the whale Jonah prays to the Lord for deliverance, and the Lord has the whale vomit Jonah onto the shore. What does Jonah say in the prayer? What lesson has Jonah learned?

---

[4] Reprimand, scolding.

3. Examine Jehovah's actions throughout the story. How different is the image of God in the story of Jonah from that in "The Golden Calf"?

4. What do the preceding two stories reveal about the cultural and religious values of the society at that time? Do some aspects of the stories seem relevant today? If so, what are they?

5. How would you respond to the perception that the Old Testament God often appears cruel, vengeful, and harsh?

Psalms 23 and 24

The Psalms, like the rest of the Old Testament, were originally written in Aramaic (ancient Hebrew) and then translated into Greek, Latin, and finally into English in the King James version which, for over 300 years, has been the most commonly used and most popular version of the Bible. Attributed to David (the same David who killed the giant Goliath with his slingshot), the Psalms are "songs to God."

PSALM 23

The LORD is my shepherd; I shall not want.
2 He maketh me to lie down in green pastures: he leadeth me beside the still waters.
3 He restoreth my soul: he leadeth me in the paths of righteousness for his name's sake.
4 Yea, though I walk through the valley of the shadow of death, I will fear no evil: for thou art with me; thy rod and thy staff they comfort me.
5 Thou preparest a table before me in the presence of mine enemies: thou anointest[1] my head with oil; my cup runneth over.
6 Surely goodness and mercy shall follow me all the days of my life: and I will dwell in the house of the LORD for ever.

PSALM 24

The earth is the LORD's, and the fulness thereof; the world, and they that dwell therein.
2 For he hath founded it upon the seas, and established it upon the floods.
3 Who shall ascend into the hill of the LORD? or who shall stand in his holy place?
4 He that hath clean hands, and a pure heart; who hath not lifted up his soul unto vanity, nor sworn deceitfully.
5 He shall receive the blessing from the LORD, and righteousness from the God of his salvation.

[1] Rub oil on as part of a religious ceremony.

⁶ This *is* the generation of them that seek him, that seek thy face, O
   Jā′cob.
⁷ Lift up your heads, O ye gates; and be ye lift up, ye everlasting
   doors; and the King of glory shall come in.
⁸ Who *is* this King of glory? The LORD strong and mighty, the LORD
   mighty in battle.
⁹ Lift up your heads, O ye gates; even lift *them* up, ye everlasting
   doors; and the King of glory shall come in.
¹⁰ Who is this King of glory? The LORD of hosts, he *is* the King of
   glory.

Questions for Discussion and Writing

1. As "songs to God," the Psalms praise God and describe who can receive
   His Blessing. For what is God praised? What does the Twenty-Fourth Psalm
   say about those who want God's blessing?

2. Read these psalms out loud as well as to yourself. Pay attention to the
   images they evoke. What feeling(s) do they call up as you read them?

3. Look for the words that describe God or names that refer to Him. Is He
   depicted in the same way in "The Golden Calf" and "The Story of Jonah?"

4. Why do you think these psalms have remained popular over the centuries?

"The Prodigal¹ Son"

*"The Prodigal Son" is a parable, a story that illustrates a moral or
religious message. In the New Testament, Jesus uses this parable as a
method of teaching a model of Christian love and forgiveness.*

A certain man had two sons. And the younger of them said to his
father, "Father, give me the share of the property that falls to me." And he
divided his means between them.

And not many days later, the younger son gathered up all his
wealth, and took his journey into a far country; and there he squandered
his fortune in loose living. And after he had spent all, there came a
grievous famine over that country, and he began himself to suffer want.
And he went and joined one of the citizens of that country, who sent him
to his farm to feed swine.² And he longed to fill himself with the pods that
the swine were eating, but no one offered to give them to him.

But when he came to himself, he said, "How many hired men in my
father's house have bread in abundance, while I am perishing here with
hunger! I will get up and go to my father, and will say to him, Father, I
have sinned against heaven and before thee. I am no longer worthy to be
called thy son; make one of thy hired men." And he arose and went to his
father.

¹ Extremely wasteful.

But while he was yet a long way off, his father saw him and was moved with compassion, and ran and fell upon his neck and kissed him. And the son said to him, "Father, I have sinned against heaven and before thee. I am no longer worthy to be called thy son." But the father said to his servants, "Fetch quickly the best robe and put it on him, and give him a ring for his finger and sandals for his feet; and bring out the fattened calf and kill it, and let us eat and make merry; because this my son was dead, and has come to life again; he was lost, and is found." And they began to make merry.

Now his elder son was in the field; and as he came and drew near to the house, he heard music and dancing. And calling one of the servants he inquired what this meant. And he said to him "Thy brother has come, and thy father has killed the fattened calf, because he has got him back safe." But he was angered and would not go in.

His father, therefore, came out and began to entreat[3] him. But he answered and said to his father, "Behold these many years I have been serving thee, and have never transgressed[4] one of thy commands; and yet thou hast never given me a kid that I might make merry with my friends. But when this thy son comes, who has devoured his means with harlots, thou hast killed for him the fattened calf."

But he said to him, "Son, thou art always with me, and all that is mine is thine; but we were bound to make merry and rejoice, for this thy brother was dead, and has come to life; he was lost, and is found."

Questions for Discussion and Writing

1. Paraphrase the events in the parable and analyze the religious and moral lessons in the story, focusing on the conflicts and problems. How are they resolved?

2. This parable teaches the major Christian precept of forgiveness. What are the implications of the father's forgiveness? How does the parable's significance extend beyond the story of father and son?

3. Parables usually function allegorically, often on different levels. If the father in this parable represents God the Father, who does the prodigal son represent? What then does the parable teach?

4. Consider the types of people whom Jesus was usually addressing. Why might he have chosen to teach through parables? We find parables used as forms of teaching in many religions; why have they remained a popular means of religious instruction and transmission?

5. Consult with your classmates to develop a list of some non-Christian parables. How are they similar to "The Prodigal Son"? How do they differ?

---

[3] Beg. [4] Sinned against.

THE MIDDLE AGES

St. Augustine, from **Confessions**

St. Augustine (A.D. 354–430) was an early Church Father who preached and wrote extensively. His theories of sin and grace helped con-solidate Church doctrine and an ascetic tradition that continued up to the medieval period, when a more humanistic scholarly approach emerged with the rise of the great universities. In Book II, Augustine describes his experiences with love and sexuality as well as his initial relationship with God.

BOOK II

1   I want to call back to mind my past impurities and the carnal[1] corruptions of my soul, not because I love them, but so that I may love you, my God. It is for the love of your love that I do it, going back over those most wicked ways of mine in the bitterness of my recollection so that the bitterness may be replaced by the sweetness of you, O unfailing sweetness, happy sweetness and secure! And gathering myself together from the scattered fragments into which I was broken and dissipated during all that time when, being turned away from you, the One, I lost myself in the distractions of the Many.

For in that youth of mine I was on fire to take my fill of hell. Outrageously in all my shady loves I began to revert to a state of savagery: *my beauty consumed away* and I stank in your sight; pleasing myself and being anxious to please in the eyes of men. . . .

2   And what was it that delighted me? Only this—to love and be loved. But I could not keep that true measure of love, from one mind to another mind, which marks the bright and glad area of friendship. Instead I was among the foggy exhalations which proceed from the muddy cravings of the flesh and the bubblings of first manhood. These so clouded over my heart and darkened it that I was unable to distinguish between the clear calm of love and the swirling mists of lust. I was storm-tossed by a confused mixture of the two and, in my weak unstable age, swept over the precipices of desire and thrust into the whirlpools of vice. Your wrath had gathered above me, and I was not aware of it. I had grown deaf through the clanking of the chain of my mortality. This was your punish-ment for my soul's pride. I was going further and further from you, and you let me be. I was tossed here and there, spilled on the ground, scattered abroad; I boiled over in my fornications. And still you were

[1] Physical.

silent, O my joy so slow in coming! Then you were silent, and I went on going further from you and further, making my way into more and more of these sterile plantations of sorrow, arrogant in my dejection and still restless in my weariness.

How I wish that there had been someone at that time to put a measure on my disorder and to turn to good use the fleeting beauties of these new temptations and to put limits to their delights. Then the waves of my youth might at last have spent themselves on the shore of marriage, if tranquility could not be found simply in the purposeful begetting[2] of children, as your law, Lord, prescribes; for you shape even the offspring of our mortality and are able with a gentle hand to blunt the thorns which were excluded from your paradise. And not far from us is your omnipotence even when we are far from you. Or certainly I ought to have listened with greater heed to the voice from those clouds of yours: *Nevertheless such shall have trouble in the flesh, but I spare you.* And, *it is good for a man not to touch a woman.* And, *he that is without a wife thinketh of the things of God, how he may please God; but he that is married thinketh of the things of the world, how he may please his wife.* I should have listened more carefully to words such as these and should have become a *eunuch for the kingdom of heaven's sake,* so in greater happiness awaiting your embraces.

But I, poor wretch, boiled up and ran troubled along the course of my own stream, forsaking you. I broke through all the boundaries of your law but did not escape your chastisement.[3] What mortal can? For you were always with me, angered against me in your mercy, scattering the most bitter discontent over all my illicit[4] pleasures, so that thus I might seek for pleasure in which there was no discontent and be unable to find such a thing except in you, Lord, except in you, who shape sorrow to be an instructor, who give wounds in order to heal, who kill us lest we should die away from you. Where was I, and how far was I banished from the delights of your house in that sixteenth year of my flesh when the madness of lust (forbidden by your laws but too much countenanced[5] by human shamelessness) held complete sway over me and to this madness I surrendered myself entirely! And those about me took no care to save me from falling by getting me married; their one aim was that I should learn how to make a good speech and become an orator capable of swaying his audience. . . .

BOOK III

1   I came to Carthage, and all around me in my ears were the sizzling and frying of unholy loves. I was not yet in love, but I loved the idea of love, and from a hidden want I hated myself for not wanting more. Being in love with love I looked for something to love; I hated security and a

---

[2] Producing.
[3] Criticism.
[4] Illegal, improper.
[5] Supported.

path without snares. I was starved inside me for inner food (for you yourself, my God), yet this starvation did not make me hungry. I had no desire for the food that is incorruptible, and this was not because I was filled with it; no, the emptier I was, the more my stomach turned against it. And for this reason my soul was in poor health; it burst out into feverish spots which brought the wretched longing to be scratched by contact with the objects of sense. Yet if these had no soul, they could certainly not be loved. It was a sweet thing to me both to love and to be loved, and more sweet still when I was able to enjoy the body of my lover.

And so I muddied the clear spring of friendship with the dirt of physical desire and clouded over its brightness with the dark hell of lust. And still, foul and low as I was, I would, in the exorbitance of my vanity, give myself the airs of a fine man of fashion. Desiring to be captivated in this way, I fell headlong into love. My God and my mercy, how good you were to me in sprinkling so much bitterness over that sweetness! For I was loved myself, and I reached the point where we met together to enjoy our love, and there I was fettered happily in bonds of misery.

Questions for Discussion and Writing

1. Just as Jesus had a religious and moral purpose for telling his parables, St. Augustine writes of his youth in his *Confessions* to teach a religious and moral lesson. Outline St. Augustine's beliefs on physical love versus love of God. Does he imply that we can enjoy both?

2. To describe physical love and desire, St. Augustine uses strong imagery. Read through the text and identify these descriptions. What do they reveal about Augustine's bias toward physical love?

3. What is St. Augustine's attitude toward marriage? Explain your reasoning for the stand you believe he would take.

4. St. Augustine describes God as "sprinkling bitterness over that sweet-ness . . . of falling headlong into love." What does the bitterness symbolize? Why does he thank God for it?

5. Why does early Christianity take such a harsh stand on physical love and desire, a position very different from that of the Greeks? Do you know of other religions critical of physical pleasure in the same way? What reasons might exist for a suspicious attitude toward earthly pleasures?

Bede, from **Life of Cuthbert** _____

The Venerable Bede (c. 672–735) wrote histories of England in the early Middle Ages, the most famous of which is Ecclesiastical History of the English People. *The title of the work reveals his interest; he was a chronicler of the Church, a Christian historian of the Anglo-Saxon people's conversion from paganism to Christianity. It was Bede who began dating events according to their relation to Christ's birth; he was the first to use* "A.D." *as a measure of time. The following passage comes from Bede's chronicle of St. Cuthbert, a seventh-century religious figure.*

From having shown what power the venerable Cuthbert had against the deceits and frauds of the devil, we can now go on to reveal his strength in combating the fiend's undisguised fury. There was a sheriff of Kind Ecgfrith, called Hildmer, a man dedicated to good works along with all his household and therefore specially loved by Cuthbert. He visited Hildmer whenever he happened to be in the neighborhood. His wife, though zealous in almsgiving[1] and all the other fruits of virtue, was suddenly possessed of a devil. She was so sorely vexed[2] that she would gnash[3] her teeth, let out frightful howls, and fling her arms and legs about. It was terrifying to see or hear her. The convulsions gradually exhausted her, and she was already at death's door, or so it seemed, when her husband galloped off to fetch Cuthbert.

"My wife is ill," he pleaded. "She is very near her end. Send a priest before she goes, to give her the Body and Blood of the Lord and to bury her in holy ground."

He was ashamed to admit that she whom Cuthbert was used to seeing well was now out of her mind. Cuthbert went off to see whom he could send when it suddenly came to him that she was in the grip of no ordinary illness; she was possessed. He returned.

"I will not send anyone else. I ought to go back with you and see her myself."

As they were going along the sheriff began to weep. The bitterness of his anguish was apparent from the floods of his tears. He was afraid that when Cuthbert found that she was mad he might think she had served God up to now only in feigned[4] faith. But the man of God gently soothed his fears.

"Do not weep. Your wife's condition will not astonish me. I know, even though you are ashamed to admit it, that she is afflicted by a demon. I know too that before I arrive the demon will have left her and that she herself will come running out to meet us as sound as ever. She will take the reins, bid us come in quickly, and treat us with all her usual attention. It is not only the wicked who are stricken down in this way. God, in his inscrutable designs, sometimes lets the innocent in this world be blighted[5] by the devil, in mind as well as body.

Cuthbert continued to console and instruct his friend in this vein,[6] and as they approached the house the evil spirit, unable to bear the coming of the Holy Spirit with whom Cuthbert was filled, suddenly departed. The woman, loosed from the chains of the devil, jumped up as though woken from a deep sleep, rushed out in gratitude to the saint, and caught hold of his bridle. Her bodily and mental strength soon completely returned. She asked him to dismount and come in to bless the house and waited on him with her most devoted attention. She admitted quite openly that at the first touch of his bridle all trace of her affliction had vanished.

---

[1] Giving money or food to the poor.
[2] Troubled and disturbed.
[3] Grind.

[4] Pretended, false.
[5] Destroyed.
[6] Manner.

Questions for Discussion and Writing

1. Consider Bede's audience, the actual people who might have read or listened to this account. What can you infer about their beliefs and world view?

2. How does St. Cuthbert explain the Sheriff's wife's illness? Compare the wife's physical condition and subsequent treatment with Hippocrates' description of "the divine illness" in Chapter 1.

3. What is Bede's implied message in the story?

4. Bede uses Cuthbert to illustrate the qualities of a saint. What are Cuthbert's saintly characteristics?

5. Do religions you have studied accept or conflict with the belief in demonic possession that Bede describes? If so, how?

Barbara W. Tuchman, from **A Distant Mirror** _____

Barbara Tuchman wrote A Distant Mirror *in 1978. She is an historian, not a theologian like St. Augustine, and her account of medieval religion focuses on its role in the everyday lives of people. This was the era of the great heresies, expounded by sects that split from the main Church over doctrinal differences. They met with aggressive repression at the hands of the Inquisition. None of the contemporary Protestant religions—which successfully challenged Catholic, or papist, hegemony[1]— yet existed.*

Key Concepts

Penitence/absolution (page 90) and **repentance/salvation** both refer to the process of atoning for sin and being rewarded with forgiveness for doing so (page 88).

The **chosen,** like the Israelites in the Old Testament, are those selected by God for protection or salvation (page 88).

The term **inherent conditions** makes the same distinction as the term **innate vs. acquired** (page 88).

Asceticism involves leading a life of renunciation, in which a person gives up wealth, physical comforts, and sexual relations to devote himself or herself to spiritual contemplation (page 90).

Mystical experience involves direct, intuitive knowledge of God (page 90).

In the sin of **heresy,** considered by the Church to be one of the most serious sins, a person challenges God's law or the Church's interpretation of it (page 90).

The **inquisition** was the Church's organized campaign against heresy, which threatened its authority. Inquisitors often used torture to extract confessions and in some cases put heretics to death (page 90).

_____

[1] Dominance.

A believer in the **supremacy of the state** recognizes national law over ecclesiastical, or Church, law (page 90).

Nominalism, unlike idealism, recognizes no essential ideas or objects; all things are distinct in their existence (page 90).

In daily life the Church was comforter, protector, physician. The Virgin and patron saints gave succor in trouble and protection against the evils and enemies that lurked along every man's path. Craft guilds,[1] towns, and functions had patron saints, as did individuals. Archers and crossbowmen had St. Sebastian, martyr of the arrows; bakers had St. Honore, whose banner bore an oven shovel argent and three loaves gules; sailors had St. Nicholas with the three children he saved from the sea; travelers had St. Christopher carrying the infant Jesus on his shoulder; charitable brotherhoods usually chose St. Martin, who gave half his cloak to the poor man; unmarried girls had St. Catherine, supposed to have been very beautiful. The patron saint was an extra companion through life who healed hurts, soothed distress, and in extremity could make miracles. His image was carried on banners in processions, sculpted over the entrance to town halls and chapels, and worn as a medallion on an individual's hat.

Above all, the Virgin was the ever-merciful, ever-dependable source of comfort, full of compassion for human frailty, caring nothing for laws and judges, ready to respond to anyone in trouble; amid all the inequities,[2] injuries, and senseless harms, the one never-failing figure. She frees the prisoner from his dungeon, revives the starving with milk from her own breasts. When a peasant mother takes her son, blinded by a thorn in his eye, to the Church of St. Denis, kneels before Our Lady, recites an Ave Maria, and makes the sign of the cross over the child with a sacred relic, the nail of the Saviour, "at once," reports the chronicler, "the thorn falls out, the inflammation disappears, and the mother in joy returns home with her son no longer blind."

A hardened murderer has no less access. No matter what crime a person has committed, though every man's hand be against him, he is still not cut off from the Virgin. In the *Miracles of Notre Dame,* a cycle of popular plays performed in the towns, the Virgin redeems every kind of malefactor[3] who reaches out to her through the act of **repentance.** A woman accused of incest with her son-in-law has procured his assassination by two hired men and is about to be burned at the stake. She prays to Notre Dame, who promptly appears and orders the fire not to burn. Convinced of a miracle, the magistrates free the condemned woman, who, after distributing her goods and money to the poor, enters a convent. The act of faith through prayer was what counted. It was not justice one received from the Church but forgiveness.

---

[1] Associations.
[2] Injustices.

[3] Doer of bad deeds.

More than comfort, the Church gave answers. For nearly a thousand years it had been the central institution that gave meaning and purpose to life in a capricious world. It affirmed that man's life on earth was but a passage in exile on the way to God and the New Jerusalem, "our other home." Life was nothing, wrote Petrarch to his brother, but "a hard and weary journey toward the eternal home for which we look; or, if we neglect our salvation, an equally pleasureless way to eternal death." What the Church offered was salvation, which could be reached only through the rituals of the established Church and by the permission and aid of its ordained priests. *"Extra ecclesium nulla salus"* (No **salvation** outside the Church) was the rule.

Salvation's alternative was Hell and eternal torture, very realistically pictured in the art of the time. In Hell the damned hung by their tongues from trees of fire, the impenitent burned in furnaces, unbelievers smothered in foul smelling smoke. The wicked fell into the black waters of an abyss[4] and sank to a depth proportionate to their sins; fornicators[5] up to the nostrils, persecutors of their fellow man up to the eyebrows. Some were swallowed by monstrous fish, some gnawed by demons, tormented by serpents, by fire or ice or fruits hanging forever out of the reach of the starving. In Hell men were naked, nameless, and forgotten. No wonder salvation was important and the Day of Judgment present in every mind. Over the doorway in every cathedral it was carved in vivid reminder, showing the numerous sinners roped and led off by devils toward a flaming cauldron[6] while angels led the fewer elect to bliss in the opposite direction.

No one doubted in the Middle Ages that the vast majority would be eternally damned. *Salvandorum paucitas, damnandorum multitudo* (Few saved, many damned) was the stern principle maintained from Augustine to Aquinas. Noah and his family were taken to indicate the proportion of the saved, usually estimated at one in a thousand or even one in ten thousand. No matter how few were to be **chosen,** the Church offered hope to all. Salvation was permanently closed to non-believers in Christ, but not to sinners, for sin was an **inherent condition** of life which could be canceled as often as necessary by **penitence and absolution.** "Turn thee again, turn thee again, thou sinful soul," spoke a Lollard preacher, "for God knoweth thy misgovernance[7] and will not forsake thee. Turn thou to me saith the Lord and I shall receive thee and take thee to grace."

The Church gave ceremony and dignity to lives that had little of either. It was the source of beauty and art to which all had some access and which many helped to create. To carve the stone folds of an apostle's gown, to paste with infinite patience the bright mosaic[8] chips into a

---

[4] Bottomless pit.
[5] People engaging in illicit sexual intercourse.
[6] A large pot.

[7] Poor management.
[8] Pieces of colored stones.

picture of winged angels in a heavenly chorus, to stand in the towering space of a cathedral nave[9] amid pillars rising and rising to an almost invisible vault and know this to be man's work in honor of God, gave pride to the lowest and could make the least man an artist.

The Church, not the government, sponsored the care of society's helpless—the indigent[10] and sick, orphan and cripple, the leper, the blind, the idiot—by indoctrinating the laity in the belief that alms bought them merit and a foothold in Heaven. Based on this principle, the impulse of Christian charity was self-serving but effective. Nobles gave alms daily at the castle gate to all comers, in coin and in leftover food from the hall. Donations from all sources poured into the hospitals, favorite recipients of Christian charity. Merchants bought themselves peace of mind for the non-Christian business of making profit by allocating a regular percentage to charity. This was entered in the ledger under the name of God as the poor's representative. A Christian duty of particular merit was the donation of dowries to enable poor girls to marry, as in the case of a Gascon seigneur[11] of the 14th century who left 100 livres to "Those whom I deflowered, if they can be found."

Corporate bodies accepted the obligation to help the poor as a religious duty. The statutes of craft guilds set aside a penny for charity, called "God's penny," from each contract of sale or purchase. Parish councils of laymen superintended maintenance of the "table of the Poor" and of a bank for alms. On feast days it was a common practice to invite twelve poor to the banquet table, and on Holy Thursday, in memory of Christ, the mayor of a town or other notable would wash the feet of a beggar. When St. Louis conducted the ceremony, his companion and biographer, the Sire de Joinville, refused to participate, saying it would make him sick to touch the feet of such villains. It was not always easy to love the poor.

The clergy on the whole were probably no more lecherous or greedy or untrustworthy than other men, but because they were supposed to be better or nearer to God than other men, their failings attracted more attention. If Clement VI was luxury-loving, he was also generous and warm-hearted. The Parson among the Canterbury pilgrims is as benign and admirable as the Pardoner is repulsive, always ready to visit on foot the farthest and poorest house of his parish, undeterred by thunder or rain.

Nevertheless, a wind of discontent was rising. Papal tax-collectors were attacked and beaten, and even bishops were not safe. In 1326, in a burst of anti-clericalism, a London mob beheaded the Bishop and left his body naked in the street. In 1338 two "rectors of churches" joined two knights and a "great crowd of country folk" in attacking the Bishop of Constance, severely wounding several of his retinue,[12] and holding him

---

[9] Main part of a church from altar to
   entrance.
[10] Impoverished.

[11] Nobleman.
[12] People serving someone important.

in prison. Among the religious themselves, the discontent took serious form. In Italy arose the Fraticelli, a sect of the Franciscan order, in another of the poverty-embracing movements that periodically tormented the Church by wanting to disendow it. The Fraticelli or spiritual Franciscans insisted that Christ had lived without possessions, and they preached a return to that condition as the only true "imitation of Christ."

The poverty movements grew out of the essence of Christian doctrine: renunciation of the material world—the idea that made the great break with the classical age. It maintained that God was positive and life on earth negative, that the world was incurably bad and holiness achieved only through renunciation of earthly pleasures, goods, and honors. To gain victory over the flesh was the purpose of fasting and celibacy, which denied the pleasures of this world for the sake of reward in the next. Money was evil, beauty vain, and both were transitory.[13] Ambition was pride, desire for gain was avarice,[14] desire of the flesh was lust, desire for honor, even for knowledge and beauty, was vainglory. Insofar as these diverted man from seeking the life of the spirit, they were sinful. The Christian ideal was **ascetic:** the denial of sensual man. The result was that, under the sway of the Church, life became a continual struggle against the senses and a continual engagement in sin, accounting for the persistent need for **absolution.**

Repeatedly, **mystical** sects arose in an effort to sweep away the whole detritus[15] of the material world, to become nearer to God by cutting the earth-binding chains of property. Embedded in its hands and buildings, the Church could only react by renouncing the sects as **heretical.** The Fraticelli's stubborn insistence on the absolute poverty of Christ and his twelve Apostles was acutely inconvenient for the Avignon papacy,[16] which condemned their doctrine as "false and pernicious"[17] heresy in 1315 and, when they refused to desist, excommunicated them and other associated sects at various times during the next decade. Twenty-seven members of a particularly stubborn group of Spiritual Franciscans of Provence were tortured by the **Inquisition** and four of them burned at the stake at Marseille in 1318.

The wind of temporal[18] challenge to papal supremacy was rising too, focusing on the Pope's right to crown the Emperor, and setting the claims of the state against those of the Church. The Pope tried to excommunicate this temporal spirit in the person of its boldest exponent, Marsilius of Padua, whose *Defensor Pacis* in 1324 was a forthright assertion of the **supremacy of the state.** Two years later the logic of the struggle led John XXII to excommunicate William of Ockham, the English Franciscan, known for his forceful reasoning as "the invincible doctor." In expounding a philosophy called **"nominalism,"** Ockham opened a dangerous door to direct intuitive knowledge of the physical

---

[13] Temporary.
[14] Greed.
[15] Trash.

[16] Rule by a Pope.
[17] Harmful.
[18] Worldly.

world. He was in a sense a spokesman for intellectual freedom, and the Pope recognized the implications by his ban. In reply to the excommunication, Ockham promptly charged John XXII with seventy errors and seven heresies.

Questions for Discussion and Writing

1. What does the image of a "distant mirror" suggest, and what might be seen in the mirror? How does the title reflect the author's thesis?

2. Tuchman writes that a "wind of discontent was rising." What problem does this discontent point to?

3. What was the major criticism voiced by the Fraticelli? What defense might the Church offer against the criticisms of poverty movements like the Fraticelli?

4. Compare the medieval Church's doctrine of "no salvation outside the Church" with the Old Testament notion of the chosen people as portrayed in "The Golden Calf." Consider why such a doctrine might be beneficial to both believer and organized religion alike. How did the requirements for attaining salvation differ for Christian and Israelite?

5. In some ways, Oedipus served a similar function in his society as the Church served in medieval society. Compare their roles: What did they give to their people? How did their roles differ?

6. How has the role of religion in daily life changed from ancient and medieval times to the present day? Consider purpose, practice, and participants.

7. William of Occam (also Ockham) was excommunicated for expounding nominalism, direct intuitive knowledge of the physical world. Why did the Church consider such a philosophy a threat?

8. The accumulation of money by religious institutions and religious leaders has become a prominent issue recently, as in the case of Jim Bakker, the evangelist who was convicted of accumulating wealth illegally. How does this case reflect current attitudes toward the finances of religions and religious leaders? Explain possible justifications for donating money to religious groups.

Harvey Cox, "Understanding Islam: No More Holy Wars" _____

During the "dark ages" from the fall of Rome in 476 to approximately 900 and into the Middle Ages, the Islamic culture preserved, assimilated, and added to the advances made by ancient Greek scientists and mathematicians. The Christian Crusades, beginning in the eleventh century, marked the rise of religious and political hostility between Christian and Moslem that has kept cultural exchange to a minimum. Hostility continues to this day. Harvey Cox, the author of the following article, is a well-known contemporary scholar of theology currently teaching at Harvard. "Understanding Islam" first appeared in The Atlantic *in 1981. Its focus is just as urgent today in its call for Islam and Christianity to recognize their many similarities and resolve their differences.*

Key Concepts

According to the psychological theory of Carl Jung, a pioneer of modern psychology early in this century and one of Freud's original pupils, we all have **primal** experiences (page 93), that is, experiences that remind us of some basic human event: birth, for example. The word "primal" derives from the Latin word for "first."

Jung also theorized that our minds recognize certain **archetypes** (page 94), prime, essential models of objects or experiences, such as an archetypal mother.

Freud developed the theory of **psychoanalysis** (page 94), a method of exploring dreams, memories, and feelings to explain how the individual mind is formed.

Freudian psychology also discusses **sibling rivalry** (page 94), the competition between brothers and sisters for their parents' affection.

The terms **particular** and **universal** refer to the relativity or specificity of a thing versus its general truth (page 94).

Church versus **civil polity** names the rivalry of church versus state over legal and political power (page 95).

Odious Western images of Muhammad and of Islam have a long and embarrassingly honorable lineage. Dante places the prophet in that circle of hell reserved for those stained by the sin he calls *seminator di scandalo e di scisma* [sewing of scandal and schism]. As a schismatic[1] Muhammad's fitting punishment is to be eternally chopped in half from his chin to his anus, spilling entrails and excrement at the door of Satan's stronghold. His loyal disciple Ali, whose sins of division were presumably on a lesser scale, is sliced only "from forelock to chin." There is scandal, too. A few lines later, Dante has Muhammad send a warning to a contemporary priest whose sect was said to advocate the community of goods and who was also suspected of having a mistress. The admonition[2] cautions the errant[3] padre that the same fate awaits him if he does not quickly mend his ways. Already in Dante's classic portrait, we find the image of the Moslem linked with revolting violence, distorted doctrine, a dangerous economic idea, and the tantalizing hint of illicit sensuality.

Nothing much has changed in the 600 years since. Even the current wave of interest in Eastern spirituality among many American Christians has not done much to improve the popular estimate of Islam. It is fashionable now in the West to find something of value in Buddhism or Hinduism, to peruse the *Sutras*[4] or the *Bhagavad Gita,*[5] to attend a lecture by Swami Muktamanda or the Dalai Lama, even to try a little yoga or meditation. But Americans in general and Christians in particular seem

---

[1] A person who causes a split or division in a religion.
[2] Warning.

[3] Someone going off the proper course.
[4] Hindu and Buddhist religious writings.
[5] A Hindu religious text.

unable to find much to admire in Islam. As G. H. Hansen observes, with only a modicum[6] of hyperbole,[7] in his book *Militant Islam,* the mental picture most Westerners hold of this faith of 750 million people is one of ". . . strange bearded men with burning eyes, hieratic[8] figures in robes and turbans, blood dripping from the amputated hands and from the striped backs of malefactors,[9] and piles of stones barely concealing the battered bodies of adulterous couples." Lecherous, truculent,[10] irrational, cruel, conniving, excitable, dreaming about lascivious[11] heavens while hypocritically enforcing oppressive legal codes: the stereotype of the Moslem is only partially softened by a Kahlil Gibran who puts it into sentimental doggerel[12] or a Rudolph Valentino who does it with zest and good humor.

There is, of course, one important exception to the West's rejection of the religious value of Islam. This exception's most visible representatives have been Muhammad Ali and the late Malcolm X. Most Americans who seem genuinely drawn to the call of the minaret[13] are blacks. But given racial myopia[14] that continues to affect almost all American cultural perceptions, this exception has probably deepened the distrust most white Americans feel toward Islam. The dominant image was summed up brilliantly in a Boston newspaper's cartoon showing a Moslem seated in prayer. Over his head the balloon contained one word: "Hate!"

This captious[15] caricaturing of Moslems and Arabs is not confined to the popular mentality. In his *Orientalism,* Edward Said describes a study published in 1975 of Arabs in American textbooks that demonstrates how prejudices continue to be spread through respectable sources. One textbook, for example, sums up Islam in the following manner:

The Moslem religion, called Islam, began in the seventh century. It was started by a wealthy businessman of Arabia, called Muhammad. He claimed that he was a prophet. He found followers among the other Arabs. He told them they were picked to rule the world.

This passage is, unfortunately, not atypical. Although phrased with some degree of restraint, it coheres all too well with the popular medieval picture of Muhammad as a sly trickster or the current comic-book depictions of the sated,[16] power-mad Arab. Moreover, Dante's unflattering portrait of the prophet was rooted in traditions that existed long before his time. These **primal** shadowgraphs[17] have notoriously long half-lives, and they continue to darken our capacity to understand Islam to this day.

[6] A small amount.
[7] Exaggeration.
[8] Priestlike.
[9] Evil doers.
[10] Argumentative.
[11] Lustful.
[12] Poorly written poetry.

[13] Tower of Moslem mosque.
[14] Nearsightedness.
[15] Finding fault easily.
[16] Completely satisfied or full.
[17] Images made by projecting a shadow on a screen.

Allah works in mysterious ways. Through the stubborn geopolitics of oil, Westerners are being forced, like it or not, to learn more about Islam than they ever thought they would. Inevitably this reappraisal has begun to include a rethinking of the relationship between Islam and Christianity. In the fall of 1979, the World Council of Churches sponsored a conference on the subject of Kenya, and Christian scholars with direct experience of Islam were invited from all over the world. The results were mixed since, ironically, theologians from countries where Islam is a small minority seemed much more eager to enter into dialogue with their Moslem counterparts than did those from countries where Christians form a small minority in an Islamic world. Still, the recent upsurge of Islamic visibility will surely increase enrollment in courses on Islam whereever they are offered, and sales of books on the subject are up.

All such activities are welcome. But what about the shadowgraphs? Conferences and courses will help only if their participants become aware of the deep-lying, nearly **archetypal** images that subvert[18] the whole enterprise from the outset. Along with study and analysis, a kind of cultural archaeology or even a collective **psychoanalysis** may be necessary if we are to leave Dante's *Inferno* behind and live in peace with our Moslem neighbors on the planet Earth. The question is, How can Westerners, and Christians in particular, begin to cut through the maze of distorting mirrors and prepare the ground for some genuine encounter with Moslems?

The first thing we probably need to recognize is that the principal source of the acrimony[19] underlying the Christian-Moslem relationship is a historical equivalent of **sibling rivalry.** Christians somehow hate to admit that in many ways their faith stands closer to Islam than to any other world religion. Indeed, that may be the reason Muhammad was viewed for centuries in the West as a charlatan and an impostor. The truth is, theologically speaking at least, both faiths are the offspring of an earlier revelation through the Law and the Prophets to the people of Israel. Both honor the Virgin Mary and Jesus of Nazareth. Both received an enormous early impetus from an apostle—Paul for Christianity and Muhammad for Islam—who translated a **particularistic** vision into a **universal** faith. The word "Allah" (used in the core formula of Islam: "There is no God but Allah and Muhammad is his prophet") is not an exclusively Moslem term at all. It is merely the Arabic word for God, and is used by Arabic Christians when they refer to the God of Christian faith.

There is nothing terribly surprising about these similarities since Muhammad, whose preaching mission did not begin until he reached forty, was subjected to considerable influence from Christianity during his formative years and may have come close—according to some scholars—to becoming an Abyssinian Christian. As Artend van Leeuwen points

---

[18] Overthrow or destroy.
[19] Bitter hatred.

out in his thoughtful treatment of Islam in *Christianity in World History,* "The truth is that when Islam was still in the initial stages of its development, there was nothing likely to prevent the new movement from being accepted as a peculiar version of Arabian Christianity." Maybe the traditional Christian uneasiness with Islam is that it seems just a little <u>too</u> similar. We sense the same aversion we might feel toward a twin brother who looks more like us than we want him to and whose habits remind us of some of the things we like least in ourselves.

The actual elements of the Koran's message—faith, fasting, alms, prayer, and pilgrimage—all have Christian analogues.[20] Despite its firm refusal to recognize any divine being except God (which is the basis for its rejection of Christ's divinity), Islam appears sometimes to be a pastiche[21] of elements from disparate[22] forms of Christianity molded into a potent unity. Take the Calvinist emphasis on faith in an omnipotent deity, the pietistic[23] cultivation of daily personal prayer, the medieval teaching on charity, the folk-Catholic fascination with pilgrimage, and the monastic[24] practice of fasting, and you have all the essential ingredients of Islam. All that is, except the confluence[25] of forces which, through the personality of Muhammad and the movement he set off, joined these elements in the white heat of history and fused them into a coherent faith of compelling attractiveness.

No one should minimize the fact that in any genuine conversation between Christians and Moslems certain real differences in theology and practice will have to be faced, what scholars so often call "rival truth claims." But such conflicting assertions can be properly understood only against the flesh-and-blood history that has somehow made them rivals. Religious teachings do not inhabit a realm apart. They mean what they do to people because of the coloration given to them by long historical experience. Therefore a previous question has to be asked. It is this: If Christianity and Islam share such common roots and, despite real differences, some striking similarities, why have they grown so bitter toward each other over the centuries? Why did the average white American feel less sympathetic to Islam than to any other world religion even <u>before</u> our current flap with the ayatollahs[26]?

Curiously, after being warned for years that our greatest enemies in the world were godless and atheistic, Americans are now faced with a challenge that emanates from profoundly religious sources. Although Islam has never accepted the dichotomy between religion and the **civil polity** that has arisen in the West, there can be little doubt that the present Islamic renaissance is not a deviation but an authentic expression of the elements that were there at its origin. So we are now told that, instead of atheists, we are dealing with "fanatics," or "Moslem fundamentalists." This language is not very helpful either.

---

[20] Similarities, counterparts.
[21] Mixture.
[22] Different.
[23] Religiously devoted.

[24] Pertaining to monks or nuns.
[25] Flowing together.
[26] Islamic religious leaders.

Sometime soon a real conversation must begin. Perhaps the moment has come to set aside Dante, Urban II, and the rest; to remember instead the two children of Father Abraham, from both of whom God promised to make great nations; to recall that Jesus also cast his lot with the wounded and wronged of his time; to stop caricaturing the faith of Arabia's apostle; and to try to help both Christians and Moslems to recover what is common to them in a world that is just too small for any more wars, especially holy ones.

Questions for Discussion and Writing

1. What similarities between Islam and Christianity does Cox identify? How does he explain these similarities? What are the major differences between the two religions?

2. How does Cox use the notion of sibling rivalry to explain why religions that are more alike than different oppose each other so fervently?

3. Which Islamic beliefs might St. Augustine condone? Why so?

4. What does Cox mean when he writes that "Islam has never accepted the dichotomy between religion and the civil polity that has arisen in the West"? How is this similar to the relationship of church and state in Western Europe during the Middle Ages?

5. What solution does Cox propose to end the "acrimony underlying the Christian–Moslem relationship"? How feasible is his proposal?

6. Many black Americans such as Malcolm X, Muhammad Ali, and Kareem Abdul Jabar have converted to the Islamic faith. Why in your opinion has Islam attracted so many black converts in the United States?

7. What is the Western stereotype of Moslems, according to Cox?

8. Do the media perpetuate a negative stereotype of Moslems today? Consider how Moslems are portrayed in movies, on news programs, and in other media.

The Koran

In the previous reading, Harvey Cox pointed out the many similarities between Christianity and Islam. The following hymn comes from the Koran (A.D. 651–652), the holy book of Islam, which Moslems believe was given as revelation to Muhammad. The Koran shares many common themes, images, and stories with both the New and Old Testament of the Bible. The following readings are similar to the psalms that appear earlier in this chapter.

Whatever is in Heaven and Earth
celebrates God. He is
the Powerful, the Wise!

He holds control
over Heaven and Earth.
He grants life and brings death;
He is Capable of everything!

He is the First and the Last,
the Outward and the Innermost.
He is Aware of everything!

He is the One Who created
Heaven and Earth in six days;
then He mounted on the Throne.
He knows what penetrates the earth
and what issues from it,
and what comes down from the sky
and what soars up into it.
He is with you (all) wherever you may be!
God is Observant of anything you do.

He holds control
over Heaven and Earth;
unto God do matters return.

He wraps night up in daytime;
and wraps daytime up in night.
He is Aware of whatever is on our minds.

Such is God, my Lord;
on Him have I relied
and to Him do I refer.

Originator of Heaven and Earth,
He has granted you spouses
from among yourselves,
as well as pairs of livestock
by means of which He multiplies you.

There is nothing like Him!
He is the Alert, the Observant.

He holds the controls over Heaven and Earth;
He extends sustenance and measures it out
to anyone He wishes.
He is Aware of everything!

Questions for Discussion and Writing

1. What similarities do you find between this portion of the Koran and the Old Testament, particularly the Twenty-third and Twenty-fourth Psalms? How is God depicted? What does the scripture praise God for?

2. As a text, in what ways does the Koran excerpt structurally resemble the Psalms or other parts of the Old Testament with which you are familiar?

3. In what ways do the passages differ from biblical scripture?

Dante, **Inferno,** *Canto XXVIII* _____

One of the greatest names in Western literature is Dante Alighieri, an Italian poet. Dante wrote his epic poem, The Divine Comedy, *in 1320. The work has three parts:* Inferno, Purgatorio, *and* Paradiso. *In each part, Dante depicts his imaginary voyage through the regions of the afterlife, with the Roman poet Virgil as his guide. He intended his poem to be a theological tract as well as a criticism of his contemporaries, especially those holding political power. His work illustrates Tuchman's thesis that religious concerns were central to medieval life and that people then had a literal notion of Hell and damnation. It also illustrates Cox's thesis that the Islamic prophet Muhammad was feared and hated by Christian society of the time.*

In the Inferno, *the source of the following passage, Dante divides Hell into nine circles, each of which has several subdivisions. The more serious the sin, the graver the punishment and the lower the placement in the descending circles. The following passage depicts part of the ninth circle, reserved for "schismatics." A schismatic is one who intentionally causes division or strife between the individual and the Church, the king, or the family. Heresy was the major and most serious form of schismatic sin in the eyes of the Church. Dante's characters represent the prevailing views of his era; the poem contains some of the religious and racial biases common at the time.*

Even if someone tried, over and over again, who could ever really tell of all the blood and gore that I now saw before me?

Surely no human language has the words, the meanings, that could convey such awful tales.

Imagine an assembly of all the people who already mourned their dead through the long Trojan war, which the infallible Livy wrote about, and all those who suffered such painful wounds when they fought against Robert Guiscard, and the others whose heaps of bones still lie at Ceperano, where Apulians turned traitors, and at Tagliacozzo, where old Alardo, without weapons, was victorious; imagine one man showing his pierced limb, another holding up his stump for all to see. Even so, none of this would equal the hideous ninth chasm.

I saw a man who looked like a barrel that had lost its staves: he was split open from his chin to his anus, and his intestines hung down between his legs. All his guts showed, even the pathetic sack that makes filth out of what we swallow. He looked at me, displaying all his innards to my startled stare, and with his hands he ripped apart his chest, saying:

"Now see how torn up I am! See how mutilated Mohammed is! Before me goes my apostle Ali, crying, with his face split open from chin to scalp. And all the others that you see here, sewers of scandal and schism while they lived, are laid open like this as punishment. Behind us a devil cruelly cuts us in two. As we pass by him on our painful path, he makes new sword-slashes in each of us, because our wounds close up before we pass by again.

But who are you, looking at us, loitering on that bank, perhaps to avoid recognizing the torment that your own conscience sentences you to?"

My guide answered him: "Death hasn't brought him here, nor have sins led him to this place of punishment. I, who am dead, must lead him through every level of hell, to give him full experience here below; and that's as true as my speaking to you."

More than a hundred, when they heard his words, stopped in their tracks, forgetting their torture. They looked at me in wonder.

Another, who had his throat pierced through and his nose cut away from right below his eyebrows, and who had only one ear, stopped with the pack to stare in awe. In front of all the others, he tore open his windpipe, which was soaked with blood through and through, and said:

"You, not damned by sin, I have seen you in your Italian land, if appearances don't deceive me. Think of Pier da Medicina if ever again you see the pretty slope between Vercelli and Marcabo. And let the two best men of Fano, Guido and Angiolello, know that, if our foreknowledge here isn't worthless, they will be thrown from their boat and drowned, near la Cattolica, through the treason of a wicked tyrant. Neptune never saw such an evil deed done by pirates or Argives between the Isle of Capri and Majorca. That traitor who has only one eye, and holds the land that one here with me wishes he had never seen, will call them to a conference with him. Then he'll arrange it so they'll need to make no oath or prayer on the agreement."

I said to him: "If you want me to carry your news, show me, tell me who he is that has such bitter sight." Then he put his hand on the jaw of one of his companions and opened his mouth, crying, "Here's the man himself, but no speech comes from him. This man, an exile, calmed Caesar's doubts, telling him that trouble awaits those who delay."

Oh how shocking Curio appeared, with his tongue carved from his throat—he used to speak so boldly!

And one who had only stumps at the end of each arm, lifting up his mutilated limbs so that blood dripped down and stained his face, cried: "Remember Mosca, too, who said—alas!—what's done is done, which was the start of trouble for the Tuscan people." I added: "And the death of your own." He went on his way, like a mournful madman, grief piled on grief.

But I remained to watch the group, and I saw something that I would be afraid to describe without having a witness other than myself, if my conscience, that good companion that gives a man courage, didn't reassure me; its purity is like armor. I'm sure I saw, and still see in my mind, a trunk without a head go by, just like all the others of this sad crowd passed; and this body held its head by the hair, swinging it like a lantern in its hand. And the head looked at us and said, "Oh me!" For

itself, it made of itself a light—it was two in one, and one in two: how that
was possible, God only knows. When it was right at the foot of the bridge,
it raised its arm up high, with its head in hand—to bring its words near
us—and it said:

"Now see this awful punishment, you who, still breathing, walk
among the dead: see if any pain is as great as mine. And so that you can
bring news of me, know that I am Bertran de Born, who gave the young
King such wicked guidance. I made father and son turn against each
other; Achitophel created no greater malice between Absalom and David.
Because I divided once-united people, I carry my brain, alas! divided
from my body, its former home. Divine revenge shows itself in me."

Questions for Discussion and Writing

1. Barbara Tuchman claims that the medieval vision of Hell was literal. How
   does this passage from Dante support her view?

2. Dante writes that people condemned to Hell as "sewers of scandal and
   schisms" are "laid open" as punishment. Why would creating schisms in the
   Church be so severely punished? Why might the Church be fearful of
   schismatics?

3. Explain how the punishment of sinners in Dante's ninth circle of Hell corresponds to their specific crime of causing religious, political, or family dissent.

4. Would St. Augustine approve of Dante's depiction of Hell? Does Augustine
   envision divine punishment in the same way?

5. Many religious systems include the concept of Hell or an underworld of some
   sort. Discuss with your classmates their religious heritage to discover how
   different religions depict Hell and what purpose it serves in their religious
   system.

REFORM MOVEMENTS

Harold J. Grimm, **"The Growth of Lutheranism"** _____

   *Harold J. Grimm in "The Growth of Lutheranism" (1963) traces the
rise of Lutheranism during the Reformation. This period—the early sixteenth century—marks a major change in Western Christianity. The
Church of Rome lost much of its authority and power to Protestant factions. Political repercussions included animosity between Catholic and
Protestant countries or opposing factions within nations; England, France,
and Spain saw continuing religious/political conflict over the next few
centuries. Even today, the Protestant/Catholic split causes political turmoil; Northern Ireland is a violent example.*

Key Concepts

The **reformation,** which challenged the authority of the Catholic Church, took place in the sixteenth century under the leadership of Martin Luther (page 101).

Conservatism refers to a political attitude, specifically one that involves resistance to change or a desire to maintain the status quo (page 101).

A **dualistic** doctrine proposes that two forces exist in the universe, a positive/good one and a negative/evil one (page 101).

The fear of popular unrest, expressed by religious and secular[1] authorities during the first years of the **Reformation,** had been well founded. It seemed as though every German with grievances looked to Luther for redress,[2] especially after the publication of his revolutionary pamphlets of 1520. Luther's own religious program, which he expressed in a forcible idiomatic[3] German as well as in Latin, became the program of the masses, and such words as gospel and liberty became the watchwords[4] of a movement that tended to become much broader than the purely religious reforms envisioned by Luther.

Luther at the Wartburg and the Radicals at Wittenberg

At the Wartburg Luther had an opportunity to consider those events that had driven him inexorably[5] from the position of a monk, professor, and preacher demanding reforms in conformity with his new theology to the position of a leader of a widespread national movement against Rome. Frequently he was troubled by doubts whether he, one person among many thousands, was able to oppose the entire medieval Church supported by the Empire. But he eventually dispelled such doubts by doing hard work of a constructive nature. By gradually building an evangelical[6] church separated from Rome, he carried into practice, as far as circumstances would permit, his new theology and demonstrated his innate **conservatism.**

Luther's inner conflict during his stay of almost ten months at the Wartburg was accentuated by his physical inactivity, by lack of contact with his friends, and by disturbing news from the outside. This conflict found characteristic expression in his many references to the devil. He was quick to see in every opponent and obstacle the work of Satan. This tendency is an indication of the religious **dualism** that became so pronounced in his theology. Although God's grace was for him a dynamic force for good, struggling for the soul of man and his regeneration, he picturesquely conceived of evil, engineered by the devil, as a dynamic force working for the destruction of the soul. By faith in God the individual permitted the forces of good to operate successfully against

---

[1] Nonreligious, worldy.
[2] Correction, satisfaction.
[3] Common regional speech.
[4] Slogans.

[5] Relentlessly.
[6] Protestant, pertaining to the New Testament.

the forces of evil; but because evil was not vanquished in this life, the struggle continued until the soul was released from the body. One's own ability and the use of force were of no avail, for only the preaching of the gospel would provide victory.

This certainty that God would combat the forces of evil without man's efforts was reflected in all Luther's letters and sermons sent to his friends from Wartburg. The many rumors and the popular excitement that followed his disappearance after the Diet of Worms were soon allayed[7] when he established contact with his friends, without divulging the exact location of his "island of Patmos," or "region of the birds." By his voluminous correspondence he attempted to keep the Reformation in line with his own doctrines and to prevent the uncertainty and violence that, he felt, would destroy all that had thus far been achieved. He urged Melanchthon and others to preach the evangelical message in the vernacular,[8] made suggestions for reorganizing the University of Wittenberg, gave encouragement to those who feared the future, and answered the polemical[9] tracts of his enemies.

Meanwhile Luther applied still further his new doctrines to Christian life and practice. In a pamphlet, *Concerning Confession, Whether the Pope Has Power to Order It,* he adduced[10] Bible passages to show that the Christian had the right to confess his sins to God alone; that priestly confession and absolution, though not denied by the Bible, were inventions designed to enslave Christians; and that the power of forgiving sins was given by Christ to the entire Church, not only to the clergy. Even more significant was his opposition to what he considered the distorted views concerning the role of the clergy in the Church. Arguing that the Bible and the early Church sanctioned the marriage of priests and that the Western Church had imposed celibacy as a further means for suppressing freedom, Luther came to the defense of one of his students, a priest, who had taken a wife and whom his ecclesiastical[11] superior had accused of an infraction[12] of the canon[13] law.

Luther's attack upon the unique position of the clergy was extended to the monks in his work *On Monastic Vows,* also written at the Wartburg. He maintained that because virtually all monks took the monastic vows in the hope of earning merits on a higher plane than ordinary Christians—contrary to the "New Testament reign of liberty and faith"— these vows were not binding, despite ecclesiastical authority to the contrary. Moreover, the chastity that they vowed was contrary to human nature and reason. The vow of poverty, he insisted, was in most instances a sham, for the monks did not seek out those monasteries that rigidly practiced that virtue but used monasticism[14] to obtain false religious security and live lives of ease. Obedience was generally looked upon as

---

[7] Calmed.

[8] Common native language of a country or area.

[9] Argumentative.

[10] Gave as evidence.

[11] Of the church.

[12] Breaking of a law.

[13] Church laws.

[14] Life as a monk or nun.

mere obedience to a prior,[15] whereas the true Christian was obedient to God above all; and God demanded an active life of service to others, not withdrawal from the community. Although he stated his case against monastic vows with dogmatic[16] certainty, he cautioned his friends at Wittenberg to permit monks and nuns to exercise complete freedom in determining whether or not they should revoke their vows. Yet when he returned to Wittenberg, only the prior had remained in the Augustinian monastery.

Luther was also compelled to give his attention to the practical question of the celebration of the Mass and Communion in both kinds when Carlstadt, his colleague at the university, and Gabriel Zwilling, a forceful preacher of the Augustinian order, attempted to enforce changes in Wittenberg. In order to clarify still further the doctrines that he had expressed in *The Babylonian Captivity,* he wrote his pamphlet *On the Abrogation of Private Mass.* Like the priestly hierarchy of the Middle Ages, he maintained, the Mass as a sacrifice had no sanction in the New Testament, which refers only to a memorial of Christ's sacrifice.

The news that Luther received concerning the overzealous[17] activities of some of his followers in carrying out his reforms filled him with forebodings[18] of serious social as well as religious disturbances. Although he wrote Spalatine and Elector Frederick, criticizing them for withholding from publication some of his polemical writings, and demanded of the archbishop of Mainz that he cease encouraging superstitious practices by permitting the sale of indulgences, he consistently refrained from inciting revolt and urged his followers to carry on reforms through duly constituted political authorities.

In defiance of the Edict of Worms and contrary to the wishes of his elector, Luther traveled incognito[19] to Wittenberg to learn firsthand how serious the disturbances had become. Upon his return to the Wartburg he once more made clear his views with respect to the importance of obeying the political authorities in his *Faithful Exhortation to All Christians to Guard Against Revolt and Tumult.* Although he can be justly criticized for not realizing that a revolt against ecclesiastical authority might lead to a revolt against the political and social order, he cannot be accused of inconsistency. His entire concern centered in a religious problem and excluded political, economic and social considerations, except insofar as these could be improved by praying, hearing the Gospel, and requesting reforms of the established authorities.

In further preparation for the preaching of the gospel of Christ, which he considered his chief mission, Luther continued his study of Hebrew and Greek. As an aid to those preachers who could not write their own sermons, he prepared his first collection of short sermons, called *Postils* or *Homilies,* in which he expounded his evangelical doctrines in simple, homely language, free of all scholastic subtleties.[20] As

[15] Head of a monastery.
[16] Strictly held.
[17] Overenthusiastic.

[18] Fears; premonitions.
[19] Disguised.
[20] Very fine points.

the father of the modern evangelical sermon, he demonstrated how the Bible could be made a lively, dynamic force. For him, the entire Bible was primarily a testimony of Christ that he, like Paul, felt compelled to bring to all people.

Undoubtedly, the greatest product of the Wartburg days was Luther's translation into German of the New Testament, achieved in the unbelievably short period of eleven weeks. Numerous translations of the New Testament and the Bible as a whole had previously been made; but this was the first one not based on the Vulgate translation of Jerome. Luther used the second edition of Erasmus' New Testament, published in 1519. By using the official German of the Saxon Chancery, not his own colloquial Saxon dialect, he helped create a standard German for all Germay.

Organization and Spread of Lutheranism

As soon as order had been established at Wittenberg, Luther and his friends took up the task of constructing an evangelical church along conservative lines. Although urging leaders to follow moderation and tolerance toward those who had not yet comprehended the significance of the Gospel, Luther insisted that those who had should be firm in their opposition to the forces of evil.

Contrary to Luther's expectations, the simple preaching of the Gospel did not solve all difficulties and differences of opinion. Consequently he resorted upon occasion to vigorous practical measures for the maintenance of order. He went on numerous missions to those centers where serious controversies had developed and wrote many letters and pamphlets urging vigorous action in abolishing the Mass, relic worship, and other nonevangelical usages. He also persisted in his demands that his elector put an end to the old practices in All Saints Church in Wittenberg until the latter finally agreed to do so in 1524. Like Carlstadt during the Wittenberg disturbances, Luther now argued that in matters of the conscience a Christian should obey God rather than man.

Meanwhile, Luther also reformed the order of service in the parish church at Wittenberg, substituting for the defunct[21] daily Masses a short daily worship, in which the chief emphasis was placed upon reading and expounding the Bible. In the Sunday service, in which the Lord's Supper was celebrated, the preaching of the Gospel in the vernacular likewise received chief emphasis, although Luther retained most of the medieval liturgy,[22] including the Gloria, the Hallelujah, the Nicene Creed, the Sanctus, and the Agnus Dei. With the assistance of two able musicians he adapted the Gregorian music to the German translation with happy artistic results. Communion in both kinds followed the sermon. But Luther did not insist that congregations elsewhere follow the service at Wittenberg in every detail, for he maintained that freedom should be practiced in all externals, such as the use of vestments,[23] candles, and

[21] No longer existing.   [23] Clergyman's robes.
[22] Religious services.

music. Although the private Mass was abolished, individual confession before Communion was permitted. The great concern in making changes in the service was to make it intelligible to the participants; therefore the vernacular was used both in the liturgy and in the singing of the hymns.

The Baptismal service was also translated into German, for Luther wished to make the parents of those baptized aware of the importance of this sacrament, by means of which the infant became regenerated, was "delivered from the devil, sin and death," and was made a member of the Christian communion of saints. Although he wished to simplify the rite, he retained it in its traditional form, for he did not want to offend weak Christians.

Luther's emphasis upon the preaching of the Gospel and the participation of the members of the congregation in the religious services was reflected also in his plans for the administration of the Church. In his significant work *On Secular Government,* he distinguished between the spiritual realm, which consisted of preaching the Gospel and in which no force should be used, and the secular realm, which was divinely ordained to maintain order and which the Christians must obey in secular matters. The ideal society, according to Luther, would be the one in which the Christian government would protect all divinely created classes in their respective callings and maintain order in the preaching of the Gospel. Thus preaching and governing were, according to him, complementary[24] callings, the former operating the the sphere of religion and ethics, the latter in matters pertaining to order.

In his attempts to approximate the conditions of the primitive Christian Church, Luther replaced the ecclesiastical hierarchy of the medieval Church with the spiritual democracy of the New Testament. He insisted that the congregation had the right not only to decide doctrinal matters and call pastors and teachers but to appropriate and administer ecclesiastical revenues[25] for the good of the whole community. Accordingly, a common treasury received money from the entire community, and from it the congregations paid their teachers and preachers, maintained schools, and cared for the poor. The wishes of the congregation were usually executed by both the city council as the chief administrative body and the chief pastor as a superintendent, or bishop.

Questions for Discussion and Writing

1. Review the "winds of discontent" that Barbara Tuchman writes of that describe deep problems in the Catholic Church. List the reasons for the emergence and survival of the Reformation.

2. Why didn't/couldn't the Reformation have happened in the Middle Ages? Consider the political and social climate as well as the central role of the Catholic Church.

3. Why did Luther insist on individual prayer and reading the Gospel in the vernacular? What effect did this have on churchgoers?

[24] Completing or perfecting something.   [25] Income from taxes.

4. Despite its radical break from the Catholic Church, why is Lutheranism described by Grimm as a conservative "evangelical church?" Why was Luther personally described as a conservative?

5. In the last paragraph, Grimm writes that Luther attempted to "approximate the conditions of the primitive Christian Church," the first organization of early Christians that banded together directly after the death of Christ before the Church became highly structured under the teachings of Augustine and other ideologists. What purposes did Luther hope a return to this earlier concept of a church would serve?

6. Explain Luther's position on the relationship of church and state.

Thomas J. Wertenbaker *"The Rule of Conduct"* _____

Thomas Wertenbaker's discussion of the Puritan code of behavior appeared in his book The First Americans *(1927). Puritans practiced a form of Calvinism, a Protestant religion that was similar to Lutheranism but emphasized human sinfulness and the uncertainty of redemption. The American Puritan ethic defined the earliest non-Indian American culture. Its restrictive, disciplined influence is still evident in American society today.*

Key Concepts

The elect, a Calvinist term, refers to those people whom God has chosen for salvation (page 107).

A **theocracy** is a form of government in which religious leaders administer the state and determine its laws (page 107).

To the Puritan, this world seemed a place of temptation and danger. On trial before an exacting God, he was constantly subjected to the wiles of Satan and his minions.[1] In what form the spirits of evil would assail him he knew not, so that safety lay only in unceasing vigilance. "Was ever man more tempted . . . ," wrote Cotton Mather in his *Diary*. "Should I tell, in how many Forms the Divel[2] has assaulted me, and with what Subtilty and Energy, his assaults have been carried on, it would strike my Friends with Horrour." Again and again this eminent divine implored "the Help of Heaven" against "the Buffetings[3] of Satan." With eternal happiness or eternal punishment hanging in the balance, the Puritan had for earthly pleasures a mingled feeling of contempt and fear. They were but baubles[4] placed before him in seductive forms by the Evil One to divert him from the great goal of salvation.

This state of mind brought about constant self-searchings and a rigid code of personal conduct. The Puritan had few diversions, and these few he took with some qualms of conscience. To go into the country in

---

[1] Followers.
[2] Devil.
[3] Blows.
[4] Cheap jewelry.

quest of chestnuts, to smoke a pipe, to read a beautiful poem, to play shuffleboard, amusements innocent in themselves, might afford some opening to Satan to lure the godly man from the path of duty. Safety could be assured only by constant meditation on religious matters, regular attendance at divine service, copious reading of the Bible, much prayer, and sobriety[5] in the tasks of everyday life.

Nor was the Puritan content with maintaining this rigid standard for himself—he insisted that his neighbor should conform to it also. Sin and worldliness, dread diseases of the soul, are no less contagious than diseases of the body, and like them must be stamped out in order to insure the safety of the community, save **the elect** from annoyance, and protect God from mockery. The New England leaders set up for their Zion[6] the most severe moral code; that their system interfered seriously with individual liberty did not in the least give them pause.

Laws for the observance of the Sabbath were everywhere rigidly enforced. In Massachusetts a law was passed in 1653 which made it a misdemeanor to waste time by taking walks on the streets or by visiting ships in the port on Sunday. It was forbidden to travel, cook, sweep or make up beds on that day. In New London, John Lewis and Sara Chapman were brought before the court in 1670, "for sitting together on the Lord's day, under an apple tree, in Goodman Chapman's orchard." From time to time laws were passed in various New England colonies against observing Christmas, indulging in mixed dances, playing cards, or performing on certain musical instruments. God's time must not be frittered away, as anyone who read the book of Proverbs well understood.

This ascetiscism[7] entailed no great hardships upon the moving spirits of the **theocracy** themselves. For them there were many compensations—the interest that comes from creative leadership, the inspiration derived from reading and study, the anticipated joy of a heaven easily within the grasp of their imaginations. Beyond doubt the virile, rosy-cheeked John Cotton delighted in his religion quite as today the great surgeon and the captain of industry feel the thrill of accomplishment. But for those in the humbler walks of life—the farmer, the fisherman, the ship carpenter or the blacksmith—the system of repression must have been irksome. The reverence which they entertained for their leaders, their fear of damnation, their respect for the law might keep them within the narrow limits of Puritan life, but the effort was hard. Even in the days of the exodus,[8] when men's minds were fired with zeal for the new state which they were building in the forests of America, there must have been in many a humble breast the fierce beating of suppressed desire.

Questions for Discussion and Writing

1. Define the term *Puritan.*
2. According to Puritanism, in what ways can dancing, cardplaying, or even taking walks be construed as sinful activities?

---

[5] Seriousness.
[6] Holyland.

[7] Religious self-denial.
[8] Puritans' flight to America.

3. How does the Puritan differ from the Lutheran? What major theological beliefs separate the two religious doctrines?

4. Wertenbaker refers to the Puritans' asceticism. The early Church Fathers were also ascetics. What are the shared goals of such believers?

5. Asceticism is common in non-European religious practices. Consider Native Americans, Asians, Africans, Arabs, or other groups you may have studied. What ascetic practices come to mind? What purposes do they serve? How are they similar to or different from the practices and goals of the Puritans?

Ian G. Barbour, *"God as Divine Clockmaker"*

The following article depicts the age of rationalism (the late sixteenth and seventeenth centuries), which saw the rise of modern scientific method and major scientific discoveries, like Newton's theory of gravity and his development of calculus. The search for knowledge through rational thought altered theological views, as Ian Barbour explains here. It also lead to the Age of Reason, or the Enlightenment, in the eighteenth century.

Key Concepts

In a **mechanistic** view of the universe (page 108), all forces and objects run according to a prearranged plan, like parts in a machine, one thing infallibly causing another thing to happen.

Revelation (page 109) involves direct experience of God's existence and of His divine plan.

Providence (page 109) refers to God's ordained plan for the universe, or a kind of Christian fate.

The **first cause** (page 110) is God, who built the universe and set the mechanism in motion.

Divine immanence (page 110) is the belief that we can know God by observing the order of the universe, that is, God's existence in the actual parts of the universal machine.

Status quo (page 110) is the middle-of-the-road or generally accepted position; it usually implies a desire to maintain conditions unchanged.

Deism (page 110) is a form of Christian faith outside the organized Church, emphasizing God's benevolence and rationality.

The **primacy of spirit over matter** (page 110) is another way of naming **platonic idealism.**

Pantheistic absolute (page 111) is similar to **divine immanence** but emphasizes God's existence in all natural things.

Nowhere was the impact of scientific on religious thought greater than in the modification of views of the function of God in relation to nature. God became primarily the divine Architect, though various attempts were made to find a place for God's continuing activity within **a mechanical natural order.** Boyle's favorite analogy for the world was the famous clock at Strasbourg. The analogy served him well in arguing for the divine Clockmaker, for a clock is obviously not the work of chance but of skillful artifice[1] by its original creator. But the analogy also makes clear the difficulties in finding any room for present divine activity, for a clock once started runs its own independent mechanical course.

Most of the virtuosi,[2] at least until the end of the century, were willing to make an exception to the rule of law in the case of biblical miracles, which they felt to be part of their Christian heritage. God may intervene on rare occasions for special reasons since he is not bound by his creation. Some authors felt that miracles and the fulfillment of prophecies were evidence for the validity of **revelation;** they claimed that miracles were public events observable by the senses and attested by reliable witnesses. Other interpreters showed more ambivalent attitudes; having used the regularity of the world as their main argument for God, they did not want to make too much of the irregularities. Thus Boyle started by affirming God's freedom to rule his creatures, but ended by asserting that God's wisdom was displayed primarily in planning things so he would not have to intervene. God demonstrated his care for the welfare of his creatures in the perfection of the original creative act, which was itself the greatest miracle. Laws are the instruments through which he governs, and he violates them "very rarely." The unfailing rule of law, not miraculous intervention, is the chief evidence of God's wisdom.

There were various attempts to preserve the doctrine of **providence.** Some writers simply affirmed a mechanical universe and a God who cares about each detail, without attempting to reconcile the two assertions. Others equated providence with God's prevision; foreseeing the chain of causes, he could adjust his agents in advance to secure his providential ends without violating the ensuing[3] order. More commonly, providence received a very general interpretation. Not the particular events but the total design represented God's benevolence. He set things in motion in a harmonious way, planning the overall structure and order of the world for the welfare of his creatures. Once started, the operation of nature would follow fixed laws, with material causes acting from their own necessity.

God's function in the present was thus reduced to the preservation of the cosmic order. God's concurrence[4] had traditionally been conceived as an active participation, and some of the virtuosi so interpreted it. Boyle, like Descartes, stated that if the Almighty were to discontinue his support of the universe it would collapse. Continuing divine involvement is necessary, he said, since a law is not a real power but only a

---

[1] Craftsmanship.
[2] Accomplished scholars or practitioners.

[3] Coming after.
[4] Power; jurisdictional role.

pattern of regularity. But it was the clock analogy that provided the basic interpretive image of the world as a perfect machine, autonomous and self-sufficient, with natural causes acting in independence of God. "Divine preservation" started as an active sustenance,[5] became passive acquiescence,[6] and was then forgotten.

Perhaps partly because he did not want to see God's role limited to that of **First Cause,** and partly because his scientific data were inaccurate, Newton asserted that God has a continuing function in adjusting the solar system. He believed that there is no scientific explanation for the pattern of the planets, holding that coplanar orbits with velocities in the same direction cannot be accounted for by natural causes. There are also continuing irregularities in motion, he said, which would build up if God did not occasionally step in to correct them. In addition, God somehow prevents the stars from collapsing together under gravitational attraction. Newton also identified absolute space and time with God's omnipresence[7] and eternity, but this was a purely passive role. God was represented primarily as the Maker external to what he has made; like the clockmaker, he could act only by intervening from outside. The traditional idea of **divine immanence** in nature was virtually lost until its recovery by eighteenth-century Romanticism[8] and, in a different form, by Protestant liberalism in the light of evolution in the nineteenth century.

The scientific inadequacy of Newton's references to divine intervention became obvious in the next century; Laplace's nebular[9] hypothesis was able to account for the coplanar character of the solar system, and the "irregularities" were shown to be due either to inaccurate observations or to perturbations[10] that would eventually cancel each other out. Laplace was correct in saying of God's role in planetary motion, "I had no need of that hypothesis." The theological inadequacy of Newton's assertions was pointed out by Leibniz: a perfect God would not have created an imperfect mechanism requiring periodic correction. We might object further that God the Cosmic Plumber, mending the leaks in his system, would be the Ultimate Conservative, concerned only to maintain the **status quo.** This was "the God of the gaps," introduced to explain areas of scientific ignorance, and destined to retreat in the light of new knowledge to become the Retired Architect, the inactive God of **deism.**

Most of the virtuosi thus ended by reducing God's role to that of First Cause; the divine benevolence was expressed in his original act of creation and not in continuing fatherly care. But they defended this limited fatherly role with vigor, for they wanted to assert the **primacy of spirit over matter** without compromising the orderliness of the uni-

---

[5] That which supports life.
[6] Peaceful agreement.
[7] Being everywhere.
[8] Literary movement sanctifying nature.

[9] Cloudlike clusters of gases or far-distant stars.
[10] Disturbances.

verse. Against Hobbes, they maintained that the universe is the product of intelligent purpose, not of blind chance. Against Leibniz, they maintained that creation was an act of God's will and freedom, not of rational necessity. Against Spinoza, they maintained that God is separate from the world and external to it, not identical with the nexus[11] of inexorable[12] law. Though the function of God was drastically reduced, the conception of God was still the traditional one of personal intelligence and will, not the **pantheistic absolute.**

Questions for Discussion and Writing

1. Why did the image of God change so radically during the Enlightenment? How did the emerging rationalism and growth of science reduce God's role to that of "first cause"?

2. Explain the analogy of God as "divine architect." What are its implications for the nature of God and the universe?

3. How does the term *retired architect* change the original analogy of God as an architect?

4. Explain God as the "cosmic plumber." What particular attitude toward God does such an analogy suggest?

5. Is a mechanistic view of the universe, in which "all forces and objects run . . . like parts of a machine," still possible today?

6. If you have studied physics or are familiar with other religious world views, what other analogies can be or have been used to explain the way the universe works?

7. To what extent do we continue to use "mechanistic" metaphors to describe ourselves and the world around us? Consider, for example, the common image of the brain as a comuter. What other metaphors have been used in previous readings that are not mechanistic?

Voltaire, *"Of Universal Tolerance"* _____

The French philosopher and writer Voltaire (1694–1778) embodied the beliefs of the typical Enlightenment thinker: reason as the prime value, tolerance for religious and intellectual differences, and freedom to pursue and express one's beliefs. Voltaire was one of the Encyclopedists, the group of French thinkers who put together the first encyclopedia. He is also the author of Candide, *a portion of which is included in Chapter 4. The theorists behind the American Revolution were Enlightenment thinkers: Locke, Paine, Jefferson. Deism, the belief that God created the world but that humans are responsible for their own actions and are not under divine guidance, flourished in the eighteenth century. Here, Voltaire, a deist, writes satirically on Christian intolerance.*

[11] Central point.
[12] Unstoppable.

* Translated by Jeanne Gunner.

Key Concept

Infallibility, a major Roman Catholic doctrine, states that the Pope's doctrinal decisions come directly from God and therefore cannot be wrong (page 112).

It doesn't take great art or refined eloquence to prove that Christians ought to have tolerance for each other. I will go even further: I say that we should consider all men as brothers. What! A Turk my brother? A Chinese my brother? A Jew? A Siamese? Yes, certainly; aren't we all children of the same father, and creatures of the same God?

But these people scorn us; but they treat us as idolaters! Oh well—I will tell them that they're wrong. It seems to me that I would be able at least to astonish the conceited obstinacy of an imam[1] or Buddhist priest, if I said something like this to them:

"This little globe, which is just a speck, revolves in space, just like so many other globes; we're lost in the universe. Mankind, in the neighborhood of above five feet tall, surely isn't much in all of creation. One of these imperceptible beings says to some of his neighbors, in Arabia or Africa: Listen to me, because the God of all these worlds enlightened me: there are 900,000,000 ants like us on earth, but only my ant-hill is dear to God; all the others, for all eternity, are loathsome to him; mine alone will prosper, and all the others will be eternally unlucky."

They would stop me then, and they would ask me who the madman was who said this nonsense. I would be obliged to tell them: "You yourselves." Then I would try to soothe them, but that would be very difficult.

I would speak now to the Christians, and I would dare to say to, for example, a fervent Dominican Inquisitor: "My brother, you know that each province in Italy has its slang, and that people don't speak alike from Venice to Bergamo to Florence. The Crusca Academy has set the language; one must not deviate from the rule of its dictionary, and Buonmattei's *Grammar* is an **infallible** guide that one has to follow; but do you believe that the Academy's consul, and Buonmattei, in his absence, would have been able to cut out the tongue of all the Venetians and all the Bergamese who persisted in their dialect?"

The Inquisitor answers me: "Differences always exist; what matters here is the salvation of your soul: it's for your own good that the Grand Inquisitor orders your arrest on the testimony of a single individual, even if he be a hardened criminal; that you have no lawyer to defend you; that you never know the name of your accuser; that the Inquisitor first promise you grace, and then condemn you; that he put you through five different tortures, and then that you be either whipped, or sentenced to hard labor, or burned at the stake. This pious practice doesn't suffer contradiction." I would take the liberty of answering him: "My brother,

---

[1] Persian priest.

you may perhaps be right; I'm sure you want to do me good; but can't I be saved without all that?"

It's true that these absurd horrors don't daily stain the face of the earth; but they have been frequent, and one would easily be able to compose from them a volume much heavier than the Gospels that damn them. Not only is it terribly cruel in this short life to persecute those who don't think as we do, I don't know that it isn't risky to pronounce their eternal damnation. It seems to me that it's not for little specks of time like us to anticipate the Creator's decrees. I'm far from opposing this sentence: "No salvation outside the Church"; I respect it, and all that it teaches, but, really, do we know all the ways of God and the full extent of his mercy? Isn't it allowed to hope in him as much as to fear him? Isn't it enough to support the Church? Must each individual person usurp[2] the rights of Divinity and decide before him the eternal fate of all men?

When we wear mourning for the king of Sweden, or Denmark, or England, or Prussia, do we say that we're mourning for one of the damned who burns eternally in hell? In Europe there are 40,000,000 inhabitants who don't belong to the Church of Rome; will we say to each of these: "Sir, considering that you are infallibly damned, I don't want to eat, do business, or converse with you?"

What French ambassador, having been presented to some great lord, would say from deep down inside his heart, Your Majesty will infallibly burn for all eternity, because you submitted to circumcision? If he really believed that the great lord is God's mortal enemy and the object of his vengeance, would he be able to talk to him? Should he have been sent to him? With what man would one be able to do business, what duty of civil life would one be able to fulfill, if in effect one was convinced of this idea that he was dealing with the damned?

O sectarians[3] of a merciful God! if you have had a cruel heart; if, while adoring him whose whole law consists of these words: "Love God and your neighbor," you have overworked this pure and holy law with sophisms[4] and incomprehensible arguments; if you have kindled discord, now for a single word, now for a single letter of the alphabet; if you have assigned eternal punishment to the omission of a few words, a few rites that people elsewhere cannot possibly know, I would say to you, shedding tears on all humankind, "Come with me to the day of final judgment, where God will treat each one according to his deeds.

I see all the dead from centuries past and present brought before his presence. Are you very sure that our Creator and our Father will say to the wise and virtuous Confucius, to the lawmaker Solon, to Pythagoras, to Zaleucus, to Socrates, to Plato, to the divine Antoninus, to good Trajan, to Titus, the delights of the human race, to Epictetus, and so many others, models of humanity: Go, monsters, go suffer punishment infinite in

---

[2] Take over.
[3] Narrowminded people.
[4] Clever but incorrect arguments.

intensity and duration; so that your torment will be as eternal as I am! And you, my beloved, Jean Chatel, Ravaillac, Damiens, Cartouche, etc., who died with the prescribed ceremonies, sit forever at my right hand and share my empire and my bliss."

. You recoil in horror from these words; and, after they have escaped me, I have nothing more to say to you.

Questions for Discussion and Writing

1. Is Voltaire's essay satirical, or does he write in a serious voice?
2. Summarize Voltaire's views. In what ways do they embody the beliefs of a typical Enlightenment thinker?
3. Explain how the following people or institutions would react to Voltaire's position: the Puritan church, St. Augustine, Martin Luther, Plato, or other figures whose religious views you have studied.
4. Voltaire examines the issue of "no salvation outside the Church," a concept you first read about in Tuchman's essay. Why is he unable to accept it?
5. Which of the attitudes toward tolerance or salvation in the readings on religion do you find the least acceptable? Summarize the view and then respond with your own argument.
6. Deism is the belief that people are responsible for their own actions and are not under divine guidance. To what extent do we find this attitude present in American society today?
7. Deism and Puritanism both constitute the roots of American spiritual beliefs. How have they come into conflict historically? How are they still in conflict?

Brooks Atkinson, **"Emerson"** _____

Ralph Waldo Emerson was a major American writer and philosopher of the nineteenth century. He's known for his poems and essays, which are considered Romantic works. Romanticism is an attitude rather than one systematic philosophy: Most Romantic thinkers emphasized the freedom of the individual and the oppressive nature of organized society and religion. Emerson was a major spokesperson for the American brand of Romanticism. In his life, he moved slowly away from the Unitarian Church to what was then considered a radical doctrine of spirituality. He believed that spiritual nature came from an all-encompassing higher force, the Oversoul. To get in touch with the spiritual world, one had to transcend the material world, to move beyond physical reality into the realm of the spirit. Romantics in general believed that the world of nature helped people to connect with the spiritual realm. Emerson helped define the American version of Romanticism by emphasizing civic life in addition to the natural world. Like Walt Whitman, the American poet who shared some of Emerson's beliefs, he taught that the real American spirit involved action as well as thought. Romantic thought can be seen as a reaction to the Age of Reason (which Voltaire was part of and Barbour wrote about); Emerson and the American Romantics can be seen as the antithesis or reaction to the previous centuries' Puritan culture. In the following essay, Brooks Atkinson, a contemporary scholar of American literature, explains Emerson's transcendentalism.

Key Concepts

A **transcendentalist** (page 115) seeks truth in the realm of ideas or spirits, rejecting the material world and believing instead in his or her own mind, experience, and energy.

Idealism is the philosophical basis of transcendentalism. As Plato first formulated it, idealism states that reality resides in ideas, not things. The **materialist,** on the other hand, believes that sense perceptions tell us about the real nature of the world (page 115).

Intuition (page 115) is usually considered an irrational mental process, the opposite of reason, related to emotion, not logic.

Pantheism (page 115) is a form of religious belief. A pantheist adores nature, taking it to be the physical presence of God.

Emerson was a **transcendentalist.** He believed in the "over-soul" —the universal soul of which everything living was a part. Even in Emerson's own day the word "transcendentalism" was considered confusing, and the popular meaning of the word is still "vague, obscure, visionary." Scholars accustomed to exact knowledge could not make head or tail of Emerson's school of thought. That was not surprising. Transcendentalism had no system; it was more poetry than thought. "What is popularly called transcendentalism among us is **idealism,**" Emerson once said. In contrast with the **materialist,** who reasoned from facts, history, and the animal wants of man, the idealist believed in "the power of thought and of will, in inspiration, in miracle, in individual culture."

To a young country just beginning to enjoy its independence and lustily expanding in all directions, this style of thinking was natural and satisfying. It believed that anything could be accomplished. Systems of thought and methods of reasoning seemed stifling to people of exultant temperament who were looking on all the fruits of the earth and finding them good. It was easy for them to give their **intuitions** authority over experience. Not what had been done but what might be done seemed to them the greater truth. Life flowed into the transcendentalist from the flowers, the clouds, the birds, the sun, the chill and warmth of the weather, the beauty of the evening, and from the farms, the shops and the railroads where life was stirring and good things seemed to be happening.

Although Emerson's philosophy was not a system, it had something of a plan in the way he developed it. His attitude toward life was based on his love of nature and is stated in his first book, *Nature.* A short book, published anonymously, it was generally dismissed by the reviewers as **pantheistic** rapture, charmingly written but without much significance.

Yet it represented several years of deliberate thought when Emerson was trying to put his ideas in order. He began in the introduction with a definition of terms: "Nature, in the common sense, refers to essences unchanged by man: space, the air, the river, the leaf. Art is applied to the mixture of his will with the same things, as in a house, a canal, a statue, a picture." He rejoiced that man is part of nature and that nature is his home. The most significant statement he made is that man becomes a part of God when he surrenders himself to association with nature: "I become a transparent eyeball; I am nothing; I see all; the currents of the Universal Being circulate through me; I am part or parcel of God."

Five years later Emerson published his first book of *Essays,* made from lectures he had been reading chiefly in Boston. The new book contained the essay on "The Over-Soul" which may be regarded as the cornerstone of his faith. In the notes to the complete works, Emerson's son has pointed out that the first series of essays derive from a plan set down in the journals:

There is one soul.
It is related to the world.
Art is its action thereon.
Science finds its methods.
Literature is its record.
Religion is the emotion of reverènce that it inspires.
Ethics is the soul illustrated in human life.
Society is the finding of this soul by individuals in each other.
Trades are the learning of the soul in nature by labor.
Politics is the activity of the soul illustrated in power.
Manners are silent and mediate expressions of soul.

Not everybody was willing to follow Emerson so far from the material world into the world of intuition. Identifying man with God seemed like heresy to some of the clergy. Others thought it was mere rhapsody[1] or wishful thinking. And, of course, many hardheaded men did not know what he was talking about. But the effect of this belief on Emerson was transcendent. To believe himself part of universal wisdom gave him a wonderful sense of freedom. It was the ultimate liberation. It was creative. Life seemed good fundamentally; nature and man could be trusted. Life was something not to be learned but to be lived. Now was the appointed hour for making a fresh start. The doctrine was a receptive one. Better an imperfect theory, with glimpses of the truth, then digested systems that were dead.

Emerson's faith was dynamic. And that was why he seemed to the young people of his time to be the great cultural liberator. He was always on the side of imaginative exploration. In "The American Scholar," he said the sole use of books is to inspire: "One must be a creator to read

---

[1] Ecstatic expression.

well." The scholar's preoccupation with bookish learning seemed mori-
bund[2] to him. He urged the scholar to become a man of action and learn
directly from life: "Life is our dictionary. Years are well spent in country
labors; in town; in the insight into trades and manufactures; in frank
intercourse with many men and women; in science; in art; to the end of
mastering in all facts a language by which to illustrate and embody our
perceptions." He enkindled[3] the hearts of the young divinity students
with the same criticisms of institutions and the same invitation to life.
Religion should have a common accent away from the cloister[4]: "The
time is coming when all men will see that the gift of God to the soul is not
a vaunting,[5] overpowering, excluding sanctity, but a sweet, natural goodness, a goodness like thine[6] and mine, and that so invites thine and mine
to be and to grow." He complained that religion was treated in the pulpit
"as if God were dead."

Questions for Discussion and Writing

1. The social attitudes of a given age are usually reactions to previous social
   attitudes or beliefs. As a Romantic, what attitudes of the Age of Reason was
   Emerson reacting against?

2. Summarize the definition of transcendentalism.

3. Atkinson describes Emerson's first work, *Nature,* as being "dismissed by
   reviewers as pantheistic rapture." What were the reviewers criticizing? Did
   you have a similar reaction as you read?

4. Think about the hippies of the 1960s and their lifestyle. In what ways would
   Emerson's ideas find acceptance in this counterculture?

5. What areas of contemporary life and culture still show the influence of
   Romanticism and Emerson's thoughts?

Madalyn Murray O'Hair, *"Arguments for God, Historical and Contemporary, with Refutation"* _____

*Madalyn Murray O'Hair is a contemporary advocate of atheism and
atheists' rights. Atheism, or disbelief in God and religion, is largely a
twentieth-century phenomenon, perhaps because in the twentieth century
people with nontraditional views on religion have met with more tolerance than they would have in earlier times. Atheism has emerged as a
contemporary issue particularly in the school prayer controversy, which
involves the constitutional issue of separation of church and state.
O'Hair's essay (transcribed from a radio broadcast in 1972) attempts to
refute major arguments for the existence of God.*

---

[2] Deathlike.
[3] Inspired; fired up.
[4] Monastery.

[5] Boastful.
[6] Yours.

Key Concepts

Aristotelian syllogistics (page 119) refers to Aristotle's method of deductive reasoning.

An **empirical argument** (page 119) depends on observable evidence to prove its point.

An **a priori** (page 120) statement is an assumption, a given.

A **cosmological** view (page 120) addresses the whole universe as a single entity.

A **teleological** view (page 120) claims that life has some detectable design, some purpose.

An **ontological** view (page 120) is a metaphysical view: God must exist because we can imagine something called "God."

Good evening. This is Madalyn Murray O'Hair, American Atheist, back to talk to you again.

The Society of Separationists, my sponsors, sell booklets, and some of these are authored by me. One of them is titled, "Why I Am an Atheist." This booklet is a capsule description of what an atheist is, what an atheist believes and what an atheist thinks about religion.

A part of it deals with the so called "Arguments for god" and "his existence." I would like to read some of this to you tonight, for it is imperative that you know that religious people of all the time of recorded history have admitted that there is no god.

You are not hearing things at all. They have admitted this.

When? When? Who?

Just listen.

We all agree, you and I and all of the religious people, everybody, on one rule of logic when we discuss things logically. The rule is that when anyone postulates[1] a theory, that person has the burden of proof. He must show the proof of his theory. The classic example is Newton. When he postulated a theory of gravity, which later became a law, it was necessary for him to prove that his theory was correct before it was accepted by the world community of scholars, and by people in general.

It is not a surprise then, to you, to discover here with me tonight that the religious community, its scholars, teachers and theologians, churchmen of every kind, have admitted that god is only a theory. They have admitted this by their constant attempts to offer proof of their proposition and theory. They put forth more and different proofs in a constant stream in order to do this. Now, If a god really <u>was</u>, it would not be necessary for them to do this. From the way they define him, it is obvious that <u>he</u> would be able to offer this proof and not leave it to their puny efforts. He could just appear, just once, or give incontrovertible[2] proof in some set of laboratory conditions and that would end the

---

[1] Takes as true.   [2] Unable to be disproved.

argument for all time. He does not, of course, because there is no god. He can't be called forth because he doesn't exist.

The theories, however, are interesting. The religionists have been putting them forth for thousands of years. Knowing that the burden of proof is on them, the religionists have assumed that burden.

We Atheists merely evaluate and categorize their arguments, and decide if we want to accept them or reject them. For us, it is as simple as that. So, any good Atheist simply acquaints himself with every argument that has been set forth in support of the god theory since human history began.

This is impossible, you say? Not at all. The arguments are not too good and there are not too many of the basic arguments. There are elaborations on certain theme arguments, but the basics are simple. It will surprise you to hear that in thousands of years of arguments, there have only been a half a dozen basic arguments. That's right—six of them.

But, think of this a moment. Why would even six arguments be needed? If there were a god, his existence would be argument enough. There would be no need to prove it a half a dozen times, would there? It is only when you lose an argument that you need so much proof. Isn't it curious that with all of this, every religious person says, "I believe in god"? He does not say, "There is a god." It only indicates that the proposition is indeed very tenuous,[3] even with the help of **Aristotelian syllogistics.**

I am sure you are impatient. What are the possible arguments for a belief in god? First, I must give you those arguments which have been abandoned.

The first group of arguments cluster around the idea of direct sensory experience. This is the **empirical argument.** Someone says he has actually talked to god, or heard him, or seen him, or smelled him, or touched him. Today when people say this, the psychiatrists say they are having hallucinations, and classify the hallucinations as auditory, visual, tactile, or olfactory, but an hallucination, no less. Have you seen god? Have you personally talked to him? Well, you can trust your own senses if you are a normal human being. If you have not seen him, felt him, talked with him, smelled him, you know no one else has. Included in this category of arguments are the ideas of "mystical insights," which "tell" you there is a god, and "intuition," which does the same. The group of ideas concerned with direct sensory experience (real or imagined) and insight or intuition (real or imagined) has been abandoned now for many years and is not any longer considered as valid argument.

The second group of arguments has to do with "Faith." This is your accepting someone else having experienced the first group of ideas, your blind acceptance of someone else's talking with god, or seeing him, or having "insight," or "intuition" which tells him there is a god. When two people share a delusion like this, the psychiatrist calls it "folie à deux"[4]

---

[3] Shaky; flimsy.

[4] Shared delusion.

and when a large group shares this delusion, it is popularly called "religion." For the most part the modern theologians have abandoned this argument too.

The third group of older arguments has to do with authority, and depends on your acceptance of that authority. There are different kinds of authority here involved. The authority of an institution, a book, an individual person. If you accept the authority of an institution, this is the authority of a particular church: the Moslem church, the Hindu church, the pagan church, the Roman Catholic Church, your particular protestant church.

You choose what you want to choose, unless you live in an era when choice is not approved, and then you have a certain religion rammed down your throat, whether you like it or not, by a powerful institution. If you accept the authority of a book, again you have a lot of choices: the Koran, the Veda, the Old Testament, the New Testament, the Apocrypha, the Upanishads, the Torah.

Again, what would have happened to you in old Mexico had you said that you did not accept their holy book? The old Aztecs would have torn your heart out of your body on one of their altars. If you accept the authority of a person, again you have a lot of choices: Mohammed, Confucius, Buddha, Moses, Fatima, Christ, Quoxichochtle. Authority, whoever is in power, rules. That is why this argument has been abandoned.

The fourth group of arguments has to do with rational and/or logical proofs. The Roman Catholic Church was the longest holdout before turning to this group. But even now that church expects arguments to be logical. The kicker in the woodpile is that these so-called rational or logical proofs are based simply on **a priori** grounds. This is a so-called high fallutin' way of saying that the religionists start out with so-called "self-evident truths." One of these is "In the beginning was the word." One then gets into nonsense for that sentence has absolutely no meaning at all. Understanding this we can proceed tongue in cheek. Rational arguments can be reduced to three main categories also: the **cosmological,** the **teleological,** and the **ontological.** Let's just look at these jawbreakers for a moment.

The cosmological argument is the most popular. This is the oldest argument and was advanced by Thomas Aquinas. It is based on the principle of cause and is called the principle of "causality." It holds that everything requires a cause to account for its existence. John Stuart Mill is the person who is credited with having put the K.O. to this argument. He tells the story that it was his little child who revealed the truth to him.

He was holding forth on his argument one day about everything needing to be caused, and his pre-school age child was listening. He said that since everything had to be caused, god caused everything. His child interrupted and said, "Daddy, if everything is caused, who caused god?"

At first sight, of course, this argument does sound convincing, but a very brief consideration reveals that it offers no real proof at all. That is, the theorist cannot solve his dilemma by postulating an uncaused first cause, when by his first premise everything must have a cause. That is to say, who gave god the wherewithal to begin everything? Who caused god? Who is god's mother? The cosmological argument is worthless.

The old Indian myths were that the world rested on an elephant, and the elephant rested on a tortoise (a huge turtle) and then a little Indian boy who tended elephants said, "Well, what does the turtle rest on?" and the great religious philosophers there said, "Let's change the subject."

The Atheist is very practical about this. We say simply, we do not know how the universe came into being, or what caused life at all. Let us all admit our ignorance and attempt to find out the answer through science and research.

Be man enough to say with us, "We don't know, either."

The second argument, the teleological argument, is also known as the natural law argument. This was the favorite of the eighteenth century, especially under the influence of Sir Isaac Newton and the cosmographists. Generally it goes this way: as we look at the world around us, we observe an order and design which makes the assumption of a planning intelligence unavoidable. Look at the stars, the moon, the plants, the seasons, day and night, with rhythm. Actually, though, the teleological argument lies open to such easy attack that the modern theologians avoid it. What very little evidence there is of a purpose in this world, is overwhelmed by the conspicuous lack of benevolent purpose. The most unprejudiced mind can only allow that the universe appears indifferent to the life that swarms over it. Surely only a very evil deity, a very evil god, would create and smile upon the diseases of man, on war, earthquakes, defective children, floods, drought, hurricanes, polio. The teleological argument is worthless.

The ontological argument is the chief hope of the theologians. This holds that god's existence is implied by his nature, which the theologians define. This is an argument by definition. If we can define perfection, then it must exist. Oh, come now! It is impossible to prove existence merely by the process of definition. If I try to describe an elf to you, or a leprecaun, no matter how much detail can be given, this does not make that elf exist. Dickens could describe his characters like no other author. Yet this did not make David Copperfield become a real-live person. The ontological argument is worthless.

Immanuel Kant tried to introduce the "moral" argument for god. This was that goodness, justice, truth, love and wisdom flow from god and therefore he exists. However, it left unsolved the problem of badness, injustice, untruth, hate and folly, and this argument fails also. After all, if god is omnipotent, omnipresent, omniscient, omnibenevolent, i.e. all powerful, always present, all knowing and always good, how could he permit evil? This argument fails.

The latest argument, coming from America, is the pragmatic[5] argument and this asks us, "Does it work?" Is mankind advanced or retarded

---

[5] Practical.

by faith in a god? Well, you have history to answer that. Religion has caused more misery to all men in every single stage of history than any other single idea. I need only recount human sacrifices, the use of humans to build pyramids, the religious wars, the crusades, the crime of the Inquisition, the burning of witches, even here in America, the inter-necine[6] warfare between religious groups. If that does not answer the question, then we propose that the question be asked, "has not the idea of Santa Claus alone brought more happiness?" Of course it has. The pragmatic argument fails.

We Atheists might be pleased to accept the idea of god if a god was invented who loved people—a kind and good and honorable god. Until he is invented someday by man, we merely look at your arguments and your beliefs and your conduct and say, "This is not for us. We want something better for people."

Questions for Discussion and Writing

1. O'Hair's purpose is to refute, to argue against, the existence of God. How does she structure her argument? What arguments for God does she refute?

2. Briefly summarize each of the refutations O'Hair offers.

3. If you believe in God, which, if any, of the arguments for God's existence best reflect your position?

4. If you disagree with O'Hair's position, how would you argue against her?

5. O'Hair asserts that atheists want "something better for people." Can a society flourish without religion, in your opinion? Some societies, such as the Soviet Union, have been officially without religion. What, if anything, re-placed religion in such a society?

6. Are religious beliefs an inherent part of human nature? Why or why not?

7. The United States government is based partially on the separation of church and state. Are there ways in which religious groups circumvent this separa-tion? If so, how and to what purpose(s)?

Carol P. Christ, **"Why Women Need the Goddess"** _____

Before Western religion began, people worshiped female deities, and many societies were matriarchal. Some non-Western peoples still worship female deities, and even in the West, we still refer to the giver and sus-tainer of life, "Mother Nature," as a female. However, the major Western religions today, Christianity and Judaism, are patriarchal religions. The God of the Bible, in both the Old and New Testaments, is a male God and a father figure, and men have historically controlled all forms of power in Western religion, with women playing secondary, subservient roles in religious activities. In this reading, written in 1979, feminist Carol Christ examines the problems women encounter in patriarchal religions and ex-

---

[6] Internally divisive and destructive.

plains some of the social and psychological benefits women would enjoy if they followed a Goddess-based religion.

Key Concepts

The Goddess (page 123) in this reading refers to both the symbol of a female divinity that replaces the Judeo-Christian God and the acknowledgment of female power and will.

A **patriarchal religion** (page 124) is a religion that worships a male god or gods and that is controlled by men. The Judeo-Christian tradition represents patriarchal religious attitudes, for example.

At the close of Ntosake Shange's stupendously successful Broadway play *For Colored Girls Who Have Considered Suicide When the Rainbow Is Enuf,* a tall beautiful black woman rises from despair to cry out, "I found God in myself and I loved her fiercely." Her discovery is echoed by women around the country who meet spontaneously in small groups on full moons, solstices, and equinoxes to celebrate **the Goddess** as symbol of life and death powers and waxing and waning energies in the universe and in themselves.

What are the political and psychological effects of this fierce new love of the divine in themselves for women whose spiritual experience has been focused by the male God of Judaism and Christianity? Is the spiritual dimension of feminism a passing diversion, an escape from difficult but necessary political work? Or does the emergence of the symbol of Goddess among women have significant political and psychological ramifications for the feminist movement?

To answer this question, we must first understand the importance of religious symbols and rituals in human life and consider the effect of male symbolism of God on women. According to anthropologist Clifford Geertz, religious symbols shape a cultural ethos[1] defining the deepest values of a society and the persons in it. "Religion," Geertz writes, "is a system of symbols which act to produce powerful, pervasive, and long-lasting moods and motivations" in the people of a given culture. A "mood" for Geertz is a psychological attitude such as awe, trust, and respect, while a "motivation" is the *social* and *political* trajectory created by a mood that transforms mythos into ethos, symbol system into social and political reality. Symbols have both psychological and political effects, because they create the inner conditions (deep-seated attitudes and feelings) that lead people to feel comfortable with or to accept social and political arrangements that correspond to the symbol system.

Because religion has such a compelling hold on the deep psyches of so many people, feminists cannot afford to leave it in the hands of the fathers. Even people who no longer "believe in God" or participate in the

---

[1] Attitudes and beliefs.

institutional structure of **patriarchal religion** still may not be free of the power of the symbolism of God the Father. A symbol's effect does not depend on rational assent, for a symbol also functions on levels of the psyche other than the rational. Religion fulfills deep psychic needs by providing symbols and rituals that enable people to cope with limit situations in human life (death, evil, suffering) and to pass through life's important transitions (birth, sexuality, death).

Religions centered on the worship of a male God create "moods" and "motivations" that keep women in a state of psychological depen- dence on men and male authority, while at the same time legitimating the *political* and *social* authority of fathers and sons in the institutions of society.

Religious symbol systems focused around exclusively male images of divinity create the impression that female power can never be fully legitimate or wholly beneficent. This message need never be explicitly stated (as, for example, it is in the story of Eve) for its effect to be felt. A woman completely ignorant of the myths of female evil in biblical religion nonetheless acknowledges the anomaly[2] of female power when she prays exclusively to a male God. She may see herself as like God (created in the image of God) only by denying her own sexual identity and affirming God's transcendence[3] of sexual identity. But she can never have the experience that is freely available to every man and boy in her culture, of having her full sexual identity affirmed as being in the image and likeness of God. In Geertz' terms, her "mood" is one of trust in male power as salvific[4] and distrust of female power in herself and other women as inferior or dangerous. Such a powerful, pervasive, and long- lasting "mood" cannot fail to become a "motivation" that translates into social and political reality.

Philosopher Simone de Beauvoir was well aware of the function of patriarchal religion as legitimater of male power. As she wrote, "Man enjoys the great advantage of having a god endorse the code he writes; and since man exercises a sovereign authority over women it is es- pecially fortunate that this authority has been vested in him by the Supreme Being. For the Jews, Mohammedans, and Christians, among others, man is Master by divine right; the fear of God will therefore repress any impulse to revolt in the downtrodden female."

The simplest and most basic meaning of the symbol of Goddess is the acknowledgement of the legitimacy of female power as a beneficent and independent power. A woman who echoes Ntosake Shange's dra- matic statement, "I found God in myself and I loved her fiercely," is saying "Female power is strong and creative." She is saying that the divine principle, the saving and sustaining power, is in herself, that she will no longer look to men or male figures as saviors. The strength and independence of female power can be intuited by contemplating ancient

---

[2] Abnormality.   [4] Redemptive.
[3] Being above or beyond.

and modern images of the Goddess. This meaning of the symbol of Goddess is simple and obvious, and yet it is difficult for many to comprehend. It stands in sharp contrast to the paradigms[5] of female dependence on males that have been predominant in Western religion and culture.

The affirmation of female power contained in the Goddess symbol has both psychological and political consequences. Psychologically, it means the defeat of the view engendered[6] by patriarchy that women's power is inferior and dangerous. This new "mood" of affirmation of female power also leads to new "motivations"; it supports and undergirds women's trust in their own power and the power of other women in family and society.

If the simplest meaning of the Goddess symbol is an affirmation of the legitimacy and beneficence of female power, then a question immediately arises, "Is the Goddess simply female power writ large, and if so, why bother with the symbol of Goddess at all? Or does the symbol refer to a Goddess 'out there' who is not reducible to a human potential?" The many women who have rediscovered the power of Goddess would give three answers to this question: (1) The Goddess is divine female, a personification who can be invoked in prayer and ritual; (2) the Goddess is symbol of the life, death, and rebirth energy in nature and culture, in personal and communal life; and (3) the Goddess is symbol of the affirmation of the legitimacy and beauty of female power (made possible by the new becoming of women in the women's liberation movement). If one were to ask these women which answer is the "correct" one, different responses would be given. Some would assert that the Goddess definitely is *not* "out there," that the symbol of a divinity "out there" is part of the legacy of patriarchal oppression, which brings with it the authoritarianism, hierarchicalism, and dogmatic rigidity associated with biblical monotheistic religions. They might assert that the Goddess symbol reflects the sacred power within women and nature, suggesting the connectedness between women's cycles of menstruation, birth, and menopause and the life and death cycles of the universe. Others seem quite comfortable with the notion of Goddess as a divine female protector and creator and would find their experience of Goddess limited by the assertion that she is not *also* out there as well as within themselves and in all natural processes. When asked what the symbol of Goddess means, feminist priestess Starhawk replied, "It all depends on how I feel. When I feel weak, she is someone who can help and protect me. When I feel strong, she is the symbol of my own power. At other times I feel her as the natural energy in my body and the world." How are we to evaluate such a statement? Theologians might call these the words of a sloppy thinker. But my deepest intuition tells me they contain a wisdom that Western theological thought has lost.

---

[5] Patterns or models. [6] Produced.

The "mood" created by the symbol of the Goddess in triple aspect is one of positive, joyful affirmation of the female body and its cycles and acceptance of aging and death as well as life. The "motivations" are to overcome menstrual taboos, to return the birth process to the hands of women, and to change cultural attitudes about age and death. Changing cultural attitudes toward the female body could go a long way toward overcoming the spirit-flesh, mind-body dualisms of Western culture, since, as Ruether has pointed out, the denigration of the female body is at the heart of these dualisms. The Goddess as symbol of the revaluation of the body and nature thus also undergirds the human potential and ecology movements. The "mood" is one of affirmation, awe, and respect for the body and nature, and the "motivation" is to respect the teachings of the body and the rights of all living beings. Patriarchal religion has enforced the view that female initiative and will are evil through the juxtaposition of Eve and Mary. Eve caused the fall by asserting her will against the command of God, while Mary began the new age with her response to God's initiative, "Let it be done to me according to thy word" (Luke 1:38). Even for men, patriarchal religion values the passive will subordinate to divine initiative. The classical doctrines of sin and grace view sin as the prideful assertion of will and grace as the obedient subordination of the human will to the divine initiative or order. While this view of will might be questioned from a human perspective, Valerie Saiving has argued that it has particularly deleterious[7] consequences for women in Western culture. According to Saiving, Western culture en-courages males in the assertion of will, and thus it may make some sense to view the male form of sin as an excess of will. But since culture discourages females in the assertion of will, the traditional doctrines of sin and grace encourage women to remain in their form of sin, which is self-negation or insufficient assertion of will. One possible reason the will is denigrated[8] in a patriarchal religious framework is that both human and divine will are often pictured as arbitrary, self-initiated, and exer-cised without regard for other wills.

In a Goddess-centered context, in contrast, the will is valued. *A woman is encouraged to know her will, to believe that her will is valid, and to believe that her will can be achieved in the world,* three powers traditionally denied to her in patriarchy. In a Goddess-centered frame-work, a woman's will is not subordinated to the Lord God as king and ruler, nor to men as his representatives. Thus a woman is not reduced to waiting and acquiescing[9] in the wills of others as she is in patriarchy. But neither does she adopt the egocentric form of will that pursues self-interest without regard for the interest of others.

The Goddess-centered context provides a different understanding of the will than that available in the traditional patriarchal religious framework. In the Goddess framework, will can be achieved only when it

---

[7] Harmful.   [9] Yielding or giving in without complaint.
[8] Harshly criticized.

is exercised in harmony with the energies and wills of other beings. Wise women, for example, raise a cone of healing energy at the full moon or solstice when the lunar or solar energies are at their high points with respect to the earth. This discipline encourages them to recognize that not all times are propitious[10] for the achieving of every will. Similarly, they know that spring is a time for new beginnings in work and love, summer a time for producing external manifestations of inner potentialities, and fall or winter times for stripping down to the inner core and extending roots. Such awareness of waxing and waning processes in the universe discourages arbitrary ego-centered assertion of will, while at the same time encouraging the assertion of individual will in cooperation with natural energies and the energies created by the wills of others. Wise women also have a tradition that whatever is sent out will be returned and this reminds them to assert their wills in cooperative and healing rather than egocentric and destructive ways. This view of will allows women to begin to recognize, claim, and assert their wills without adopting the worst characteristics of the patriarchal understanding and use of will. In the Goddess-centered framework, the "mood" is one of positive affirmation of personal will in the context of the energies of other wills or beings. The "motivation" is for women to know and assert their wills in cooperation with other wills and energies. This of course does not mean that women always assert their wills in positive and life-affirming ways. Women's capacity for evil is, of course, as great as men's. My purpose is simply to contrast the differing attitudes toward the exercise of will *per se,*[11] and the female will in particular, in Goddess-centered religion and in the Christian God-centered religion.

The final aspect of Goddess symbolism that I will discuss here is the significance of the Goddess for a revaluation of woman's bonds and heritage. As Virginia Woolf has said, "Chloe liked Olivia," a statement about a woman's relation to another woman, is a sentence that rarely occurs in fiction. Men have written the stories, and they have written about women almost exclusively in their relations to men. The celebrations of women's bonds to each other, as mothers and daughters, as colleagues and coworkers, as sisters, friends, and lovers, is beginning to occur in the new literature and culture created by women in the women's movement. While I believe that the revaluing of each of these bonds is important, I will focus on the mother-daughter bond, in part because I believe it may be the key to the others.

Adrienne Rich has pointed out that the mother-daughter bond, perhaps the most important of woman's bonds, "resonant with charges . . . the flow of energy between two biologically alike bodies, one of which has lain in amniotic[12] bliss inside the other, one of which has labored to give birth to the other," is rarely celebrated in patriarchal religion and culture. Christianity celebrates the father's relation to the

---

[10] Favorable.
[11] In itself.

[12] Fluid that surrounds the embryo.

son and the mother's relation to the son, but the story of mother and daughter is missing. So, too, in patriarchal literature and psychology the mothers and the daughters rarely exist. Volumes have been written about the oedipal complex, but little has been written about the girl's relation to her mother. Moreover, as de Beauvoir has noted, the mother-daughter relation is distorted in patriarchy because the mother must give her daughter over to men in a male-defined culture in which women are viewed as inferior. The mother must socialize her daughter to become subordinate to men, and if her daughter challenges patriarchal norms, the mother is likely to defend the patriarchal structures against her own daughter. . . .

Almost the only story of mothers and daughters that has been transmitted in Western culture is the myth of Demeter and Persephone that was the basis of religious rites celebrated by women only, the Thesmophoria, and later formed the basis of the Eleusian mysteries, which were open to all who spoke Greek. In this story, the daughter, Persephone, is raped away from her mother, Demeter, by the God of the underworld. Unwilling to accept this state of affairs, Demeter rages and withholds fertility from the earth until her daughter is returned to her. What is important for women in this story is that a mother fights for her daughter and for her relation to her daughter. This is completely different from the mother's relation to her daughter in patriarchy. The "mood" created from the story of Demeter and Persephone is one of celebration of the mother-daughter bond, and the "motivation" is for mothers and daughters to affirm the heritage passed on from mother to daughter and to reject the patriarchal pattern where the primary loyalties of mother and daughter must be to men.

The symbol of Goddess has much to offer women who are struggling to be rid of the "powerful, pervasive, and long-lasting moods and motivations" of devaluation of female power, denigration of the female body, distrust of female will, and denial of the women's bonds and heritage that have been engendered by patriarchal religion. As women struggle to create a new culture in which women's power, bodies, will, and bonds are celebrated, it seems natural that the Goddess would reemerge as symbol of the newfound beauty, strength, and power of women.

Questions for Discussion and Writing

1. How does religion as a system of symbols affect our moods and motivation?

2. How do traditional religions "keep women in a state of psychological dependency through religious symbols and fail to legitimize female power," as Christ argues?

3. Explain how contemplating ancient and modern images of the Goddess affirms a woman's sense of empowerment.

4. How does Christ deal with the question of whether the Goddess exists "out there" or within women? How do other religions, including your own, answer this question?

5. One woman describes the Goddess as "someone who can help and protect me. . . the symbol of my own power. . . I feel her as the natural energy in my body and the world." How does this description differ from the way God is often conceived? How is it similar to Emerson's conception of God?

6. Do you agree with the author's statement that "patriarchal religion has enforced the view that female initiative and will are evil"? How does Christ argue this point?

7. What is the importance of Goddess symbolism to women who are establishing bonds between themselves and their perception of their historical heritage?

8. Reread the next to last paragraph and Simone de Beauvoir's description of mother–daughter relationships in a male-defined culture. Do you agree with her position?

9. How feasible is the establishment of a Goddess-centered religion today? What counterarguments would traditional religions respond with? What are your personal reactions to a "Goddess" instead of a God?

Chapter Writing Topics

1. American society and culture have been shaped by two diametrically opposed religious forces: the God-fearing ascetic Puritan influence and the expansive liberal tradition of Deists like Voltaire or the American transcendentalist Emerson. Write an essay showing where both of these influences appear in daily American life and then analyze and evaluate their impact. The following questions can help you structure your response.

   (a) What are the characteristics and values of Puritanism and the liberal/deist tradition?

   (b) How have these values been conveyed? How and why have they become part of our culture?

   (c) In what areas of American life do these values appear? Consider the censoring of books and rock and roll music, the abortion issue, prayer in schools, the Moral Majority, and other social movements and controversies. What have been the positive and negative effects of each of these traditions?

   (d) Can you imagine America without either of these two traditions? What differences might we expect to see?

   (e) Are these traditions reconciled or are they still in conflict? Could they and should they ever be completely reconciled?

2. You have read how the image of God and His role in people's daily lives have changed from biblical times through the present. Write an essay that explains how and why God's image and role have changed over the centuries. Consider the following topics in your writing process.

   (a) Note God's actual behavior in the Bible stories, what you can infer about perceptions of God from other readings such as the

Tuchman piece, or what is actually said about the role of God, as in the essays by Voltaire and Barbour.

(b) Consider how the changes in culture and world view influenced the depiction of God, as Barbour does in "The Divine Clockmaker," for example.

(c) How can you account for the fact that many people still picture God as He is depicted in the Old Testament?

3. Write an essay speculating on how our society would be affected if we followed a religion based on a Goddess instead of a God. To develop a response, address some of the following issues:

(a) Summarize Carol Christ's argument on the negative effects of patriarchal religion on woman in "Why Women Need the Goddess."

(b) Consider whether men might encounter negative effects in a matriarchal religion.

(c) What other changes might take place psychologically, politically, and institutionally?

(d) Would your hypothetical society be different and improved or just different and equally problematic?

(e) Can you propose a religious system that would offer a better alternative?

4. The three Bible stories in this chapter served to teach a religious or moral lesson. In Chapter 1 the myths of Oedipus and Echo and Narcissus also contained religious and moral themes. Using the parables or myths as a model, write a story with a moral for our time.

(a) Review the myths and parables you read. Examine how the symbolism and analogies work in each story.

(b) Consider basing your story on a moral or religious lesson you have learned in your own life or a situation in which an individual you know has confronted a conflict of values.

(c) Be certain to convey the moral or religious lesson clearly: the value of forgiveness, the need to have faith or hope, the virtue of honesty, and so on.

5. From ancient times through the Middle Ages, religion has played a major role in daily life. According to Barbara Tuchman, the church of the Middle Ages was "comforter, protector and physician." Today, it continues to play a central role in many people's lives. How has the role of religion in daily life changed from ancient times to the present day? Consider religion's purpose, practice, and participants.

(a) List the different purposes of religion over the centuries. Review the myths in Chapters 1 and 2.

(b) Does religion still function as healer and physician, as described by Bede and Tuchman?

(c) How did science take over much of religion's responsibility?

(d) How and why have religious practices changed? Think about the major changes that took place during the Reformation and how the role of religion was transformed at that time. How is religion changing now? Consider the Catholic mass recited in English instead of Latin; the use of electric guitars in some services; and the radical political involvement of some clergy.

(e) Are women undertaking more responsible roles in major religions today? Why might such changes have come about?

(f) Can you speculate on the future role of the major Western religions in our society?

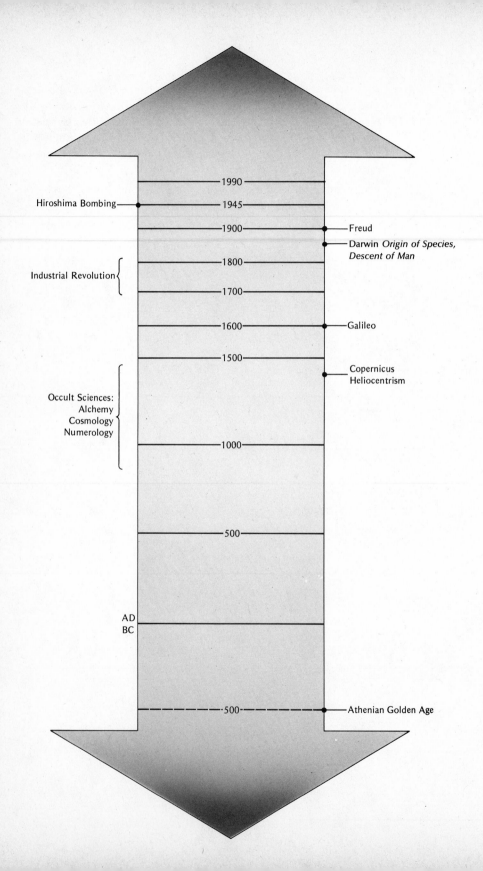

Revolutions and
Reactions in Science
～

Introduction

The word "science" comes from the Latin verb *scire,* which means "to know."
The ancient Greeks are credited with the development of systematic thought,
which gave rise to scientific inquiry and the scientific method of observation
and generalization. Scientific inquiry, the desire to know the nature of the
world and to understand its workings, did not follow a completely smooth
and continuous path from the time of the Greeks.

Ancient science, or natural philosophy, as it was called, saw no conflict between scientific knowledge and religious faith. However, conflict between
scientists and religious leaders arose in the medieval age, the age of theological inquiry. The relationship between Christianity and science became
increasingly adversarial as scientific researchers developed new ways of
seeing the natural world—ways that contradicted Christian theology. Such beliefs as creation and geocentrism (the theory that the earth is the center of
the universe) were increasingly open to rational doubt, which in turn threatened to undermine the authority and power of Church leaders. Galileo, the
Italian scientist who advanced the notion of a heliocentric (sun-centered) universe, stands as the traditional symbol of the conflict of this age. The excerpt
from Friedrich Heer's *The Medieval World* and Bertrand Russell's "The
Copernican Revolution" depict the origins of the conflict (and the Church's
response in the form of the Inquisition).

The events and effects of the industrial revolution are clear evidence of
which side emerged victorious in the battle. Scientists needed the skills of
craftsmen, who in turn sought the practical benefits that science produced in
the form of technological inventions. As never before, science (or at least the
products of science) became part of daily life. Christe McMenomy analyzes
this phenomenon in "The Scientific Background to the Industrial Revolution."

Along with welcome innovations, however, came theories that were much
less appealing to the modern mind. Charles Darwin and Sigmnd Freud ad-

vanced theories of human origin and human nature that still trouble people today; their ideas rocked the traditional faith in natural human goodness and superiority. The theories (and some social reactions to them) are chronicled in Russell's "Evolution" and in excerpts from Darwin's *Descent of Man,* Kagan and Havemann's "Psychoanalytic Theory," and Freud's *Interpretation of Dreams.*

The political implications of Darwinian theory were no less unsettling, and sometimes horrific, as scientific theory was put to ideological ends in the form of Social Darwinism, the subject of two essays in this chapter: George Simpson's "Early Social Darwinism" and Adolf Hitler's "Man Must Kill." The development and use of the atomic bomb, described in Sidney Shalett's news report and by surviving Japanese eyewitnesses (in *Unforgettable Fire*), and the continuing destruction of the environment have fueled modern inquiry into the proper role of science, the ethical issues it has raised, and the nature of scientific knowledge itself.

Today the scientist's ability to be objective and to stand as an outside observer of the world has come under intense scrutiny. Many contemporary theorists deny the possibility of scientific objectivity. Claims to absolute knowledge, discovery of "truth," and belief in scientific neutrality have all come into serious question. Stephen Jay Gould, in "On Heroes and Fools in Science," and Stephen Toulmin, in "Modern and Postmodern Science," argue that scientific "knowledge" reflects the context out of which it comes—the biases and assumptions that mark its historical age. What we "know" is how we see; science interprets the world, and its interpretations can never be objective, for they are shaped by the values of the observer. How such bias affects the scientific "truths" we have historically accepted is one of the issues that Ruth Bleier takes up in her Introduction to *Feminist Approaches to Science.* She discusses the role of power in constructing scientific "knowledge" and the way the scientific method serves those in power. Like the theories of Galileo, Darwin, and Freud, the contemporary critiques of science may be the start of another revolution in scientific thinking.

THE HISTORICAL CONTEXT: MEDIEVAL, RENAISSANCE, MODERN

Friedrich Heer, from **The Medieval World** _____

"Medieval science" is often said to be a self-contradictory term. The Middle Ages, as the medieval era is also called (or, in the negative view of the later Age of Reason, the "dark ages," from the fifth to the fourteenth century A.D.), was dominated by concerns other than the scientific. With many of the texts of ancient scientists destroyed or unavailable, medieval scientists pursued private, usually unsystematic investigations, making little distinction between the supernatural and the natural worlds. Today's occult arts, such as astrology and numerology, were largely the sciences of the medieval world. Yet as Friedrich Heer points out in the following article, a culture whose primary values were defined by religious authority may have had very good reasons to consider the "seeking out of the secrets of nature" to be a questionable, if not actually heretical, pursuit.

Key Concepts

The eighteenth century is commonly referred to as the Age of Reason or the **enlightenment** (page 136). Rational thought came to be the guiding philosophical value in science, religion, art, and politics.

An **empirical** view states that we can gain knowledge through observation, or the use of our senses (page 137).

The **macrocosm and the microcosm** (page 137) represent two views of the universe. "Macrocosm" refers to the universe as a whole, a single entity, and "microcosm" refers to a single part of the universe as an analogy for the whole—in the part one finds a model of the whole system.

About the middle of the fourteenth century John of Rupescissa, a Franciscan, complained that there were so few genuine and pious natural philosophers;[1] most of those who pretended to pursue the sciences were magicians, sorcerers, swindlers and false coiners. "It is of no avail to strive for perfection in this art if a man has not first purified his mind by a devout life and profound contemplation, so that he not only recognizes nature for what it is but also understands how to change what can be changed; but this is given to all too few."

John's own scientific knowledge came to him "through divine enlightenment," during a stay of seven years in prison. His subjects were medicine, chemistry and alchemy,[2] and he attracted much attention in his own day by his prophecies of changes in Church and State. He foretold that the Papacy, then captive at Avignon, would lose its power

[1] Early organic scientists.   [2] Study of turning metals into gold.

and worldly possessions and return to apostolic poverty. His years of imprisonment were passed first at Toulouse, as the prisoner of the Franciscan Provincial of Aquitaine, and afterwards in a papal jail at Avignon. Primarily "a seeker out of the secrets of nature," he falls, with other Franciscans, alchemists, soothsayers[3] and astrologers, into that line of European natural philosophers which leads through Dr. Faustus, Boyle and Erasmus Darwin down into the nineteenth century and indeed into the present.

This "seeking out of the secrets of nature" should not be regarded as something set apart from the religious and political preoccupations of the moment; it was intimately bound up with the prevailing outlook on the world. Those most active and most activating in this field were attempting nothing less than the transformation of the "elements of nature" and of society, the metamorphosis which should alter the age itself and all human relations. A high value has often been set on natural science as the coadjutor[4] of religious and political advancement. Erasmus Darwin, for example, the grandfather of Charles Darwin, was at once a doctor of medicine, a religious reformer, a man of the **enlightenment** and a revolutionary. It can be shown that the reforming ideal of using science to "make the world a better place," which in the twentieth century is bound up with the two great questions of the relationship of science and religion and the social and political uses of atomic energy, has a long ancestry. In Europe the pedigree reaches back at least into the twelfth century, though it was mainly in the thirteenth and early fourteenth centuries that the natural sciences began to emerge in their own right, and even then in a peculiarly ambiguous role. Anyone who concerned himself with the "secrets of nature" and was bold enough to seek them out by experiment was committed to a perilous association with magicians, sorcerers and alchemists, that is to say with underground conspirators dedicated to uncovering the secrets God had veiled in mystery, impelled by motives of ambition and vanity or in consequence of a sworn compact with the devil. Gerbert of Aurillac, the tenth century scholar with mathematical and scientific interests who on his election to the Papacy took the name Sylvester II, was famous in the Middle Ages not for his pontificate[5] but as a magician and a sorcerer. As late as the seventeenth century the same German word still served both for "spirit" and for "gas" and the distinction between the two was arrived at only very slowly. Boyle, friend of Newton and the "father of modern chemistry," was a practicing alchemist, and Newton himself derived some of the basic elements of his color theory from the natural philosophers of the thirteenth and fourteenth centuries.

During the Middle Ages those who pursued the natural sciences had no legitimate niche in society, nor were they recognized by the

---

[3] Fortune tellers, prophets.   [5] Term as Pope.
[4] Assistant.

Church. The universities eschewed[6] technical activities (the necessary basis of experiment and of empirical research) as "illiberal arts," banishing them to the backrooms and workshops of small craftsmen and persons of dubious reputation. Theology frowned on any attempt at reaching into the secrets of nature, an unlawful invasion of the sacred womb of the Great Mother. Even in the nineteenth century the Spanish Academy of Sciences could reject on these grounds a proposal for controlling the river Manzanares. Anyone who persisted in flying in the face of public opinion by meddling with science was forced to consort with outcasts of all kinds: with Provencal Jews, because they could translate Arabic texts dealing with alchemy, chemistry, medicine and astrology, and with eccentrics who lived out their lives in dark secluded basements, dedicated to their quest for the "philosopher's stone," the transmutation[7] of quicksilver into gold. Anyone who like Roger Bacon was bold enough to convert his monastic cell into a cell of early scientific endeavor had to be prepared to exchange it for a prison.

The pattern of development in medieval ideas about the natural sciences provides as conspicuous an example of that broad co-existence of opposites as any we have yet met with: it can never be sufficiently stressed that medieval society, medieval piety and medieval learning were all compounded of numerous contradictory and diverse elements. Scholars who engaged in scientific pursuits did so from a mixture of motives, rational and irrational, scholarly and superstitious; their methods were a combination of **empiricism** and bold speculation. The stresses of contemporary political and religious pressures were such that although these activities may have made a satisfying life's work for an individual, what emerged from them was certainly not science. The different subjects went together in pairs, some of them so closely linked as to become hybrids. Chemistry went with alchemy, astronomy with astrology, mathematics with cosmology[8] (numbers were regarded as sacred cyphers in which were hidden all the secrets of **the macrocosm and the microcosm**), technology with magic, medicine with philosophy, and optics with mystical ideas about light.

Questions for Discussion and Writing

1. What is the author's view of medieval science? Does he believe that it was a period of scientific stagnation unrelated to later scientific efforts?

2. According to Heer, "Theology frowned on any attempt at reaching into the secrets of nature, an unlawful invasion of the sacred womb of the Great Mother." Analyze the medieval theologians' use of female imagery for nature: what does it suggest about their view of the world, of science, and of women in their society?

3. What beliefs made medieval scientists consider empirical method—objec-

---

[6] Avoided.
[7] Change in form.

[8] Study of the universe's structure.

tive observation and generalization—an insufficient base for scientific inquiry?

4. During the medieval age, religion and science became competing pursuits, and scientists were often imprisoned by Church officials. Why might theologians and scientists have become caught up in a power struggle? Over what aspects of life might each seek to have power?

5. John of Rupescissa argues that a scientist should be pure, devout, and respectful of nature. Does his view have any place in scientific fields today? Consider current examples of scientific work that reflect his view and work that violates it, in your opinion. (The readings on the first atomic bomb, at the end of this chapter, may be useful material for this topic.)

6. Has science (and the technology that derives from it) lived up to early expectations—that it would help "make the world a better place"?

7. Many people continue to place faith in astrology, numerology, and other "occult" sciences. To what extent is this belief still considered uninformed, unscientific, unacceptable? Why did the public react so negatively when former First Lady Nancy Reagan admitted that she and the former president regularly met with an astrologer?

8. On what issues do scientists today continue to face social or religious opposition? Is the basis of such opposition related to medieval fears and beliefs?

Bertrand Russell, "*The Copernican Revolution*" _____

In the following essay, Bertrand Russell (1872–1970), a prolific scholar of philosophy and mathematics, chronicles the increasingly negative and finally oppressive reaction of the established Church to the theories of Copernicus (1473–1543). The Italian astronomer Galileo Galilei (1564–1642) took up the Copernican theory—that the sun, not the earth, is the center of the universe—and made advances in its defense. The theory offended not only religious dogma but popular sensibilities as well. The idea that humans were not the center of the divinely designed universe had psychological ramifications of an upsetting and anxiety-producing nature.

Key Concepts

Impiety (page 139) is the sin of disrespectfulness toward God or Church teachings.

Stoic philosophy (page 139) advocates avoiding extremes as a way of assuring a good and happy life.

In theological terms, **infidelity** means unfaithfulness to one's God or to Church doctrine, and is one of the most serious charges possible (page 140).

The **Inquisition** was the Catholic Church's organized campaign against heresy (page 141).

The first pitched battle between theology and science, and in some ways the most notable, was the astronomical dispute as to whether the earth or the sun was the center of what we now call the solar system. The orthodox theory was the Ptolemaic, according to which the earth is at rest in the center of the universe, while the sun, moon, planets, and system of fixed stars revolve round it, each in its own sphere. According to the new theory, the Copernican, the earth, so far from being at rest, has a twofold motion: it rotates on its axis once a day, and it revolves round the sun once a year.

The theory which we call Copernican, although it appeared with all the force of novelty in the sixteenth century, had in fact been invented by the Greeks, whose competence in astronomy was very great. It was advocated by the Pythagorean school, who attribute it, probably without historical truth, to their founder Pythagoras. The first astronomer who is known definitely to have taught that the earth moves was Aristarchus of Samos, who lived in the third century B.C. He was in many ways a remarkable man. He invented a theoretically valid method of discovering the relative distances of the sun and moon, though through errors of observation his result was far from correct. Like Galileo, he incurred the imputation[1] of **impiety,** and he was denounced by the **Stoic** Cleanthes. But he lived in an age when bigots had little influence on governments, and the denunciation apparently did him no harm.

The Greeks had great skill in geometry, which enabled them to arrive at scientific demonstration in certain matters. They knew the cause of eclipses, and from the shape of the earth's shadow on the moon they inferred that the earth is a sphere. Eratosthenes, who was slightly later than Aristarchus, discovered how to estimate the size of the earth. But the Greeks did not possess even the rudiments of dynamics, and therefore those who adhered to the Pythagorean doctrine of the earth's motion were unable to advance any very strong arguments in favor of their view. Ptolemy, about the year A.D. 130, rejected the view of Aristarchus, and restored the earth to its privileged position at the center of the universe. Throughout later antiquity and the Middle Ages, his view remained unquestioned.

The theory of Copernicus, though important as a fruitful effort of imagination which made further progress possible, was itself still very imperfect. The planets, as we now know, revolve about the sun, not in circles, but in ellipses, of which the sun occupies, not the center, but one of the foci. Copernicus adhered to the view that their orbits must be circular, and accounted for irregularities by supposing that the sun was not quite in the center of any one of the orbits. This partially deprived his system of the simplicity which was its greatest advantage over that of Ptolemy, and would have made Newton's generalization impossible if it had not been corrected by Kepler. Copernicus was aware that his central

---

[1] Accusation, charge.

doctrine had already been taught by Aristarchus—a piece of knowledge which he owed to the revival of classical learning in Italy, and without which, in those days of unbounded admiration for antiquity, he might not have had the courage to publish his theory. As it was, he long delayed publication because he feared ecclesiastical censure. Himself an ecclesiastic, he dedicated his book to the Pope, and his publisher, Osiander, added a preface (which may perhaps have not been sanctioned by Copernicus) saying that the theory of the earth's motion was put forward solely as a hypothesis, and was not asserted as positive truth. For a time, these tactics sufficed, and it was only Galileo's bolder defiance that brought retrospective official condemnation upon Copernicus.

At first, the Protestants were almost more bitter against him than the Catholics. Luther said that "People give ear to an upstart astrologer who strove to show that the earth revolves, not the heavens or the firmament,[2] the sun and the moon. Whoever wishes to appear clever must devise some new system, which of all systems is of course the very best. This fool wishes to reverse the entire science of astronomy; but sacred Scripture tells us that Joshua commanded the sun to stand still, and not the earth." Melanchthon was equally emphatic; so was Calvin, who after quoting the text: "The world also is stablished, that it cannot be moved," triumphantly concluded: "Who will venture to place the authority of Copernicus above that of the Holy Spirit?" Even Wesley, so late as the eighteenth century, while not daring to be quite so emphatic, nevertheless stated that the new doctrines in astronomy "tend toward **infidelity.**"

In this, I think, Wesley was, in a certain sense, in the right. The importance of Man is an essential part of the teaching of both the Old and New Testaments; indeed God's purposes in creating the universe appear to be mainly concerned with human beings. The doctrines of the Incarnation and the Atonement could not appear probable if Man were not the most important of created beings. Now there is nothing in the Copernican astronomy to prove that we are less important than we naturally suppose ourselves to be, but the dethronement of our planet from its central position suggests to the imagination a similar dethronement of its inhabitants. While it was thought that the sun and moon, the planets and the fixed stars, revolved once a day about the earth, it was easy to suppose that they existed for our benefit, and that we were of special interest to the Creator. But when Copernicus and his successors persuaded the world that it is we who rotate while the stars take no notice of our earth; when it appeared further that our earth is small compared to several of the planets, and that they are small compared to the sun; when calculation and the telescope revealed the vastness of the solar system, of our galaxy and finally of the universe of innumerable galaxies—it became increasingly difficult to believe that such a remote and parochial[3]

[2] Sky.   [3] Narrow.

retreat could have the importance to be expected of the home of Man, if Man had the cosmic significance assigned to him in traditional theology. Mere considerations of scale suggested that perhaps we were not the purpose of the universe: lingering self-esteem whispered that, if we were not the purpose of the universe, it probably had no purpose at all. I do not mean to say that such reflections have any logical cogency, still less that they were widely aroused at once by the Copernican system. I mean only that they were such as the system was likely to stimulate in those to whose minds it was vividly present. It is therefore not surprising that the Christian Churches, Protestant and Catholic alike, felt hostility to the new astronomy, and sought out grounds for branding it as heretical.

Galileo Galilei (1564-1642) was the most notable scientific figure of his time, both on account of his discoveries and through his conflict with **the Inquisition.** It was the telescope that led Galileo on to more dangerous ground. Hearing that a Dutchman had invented such an instrument, Galileo reinvented it, and almost immediately discovered many new astronomical facts, the most important of which, for him, was the existence of Jupiter's satellites.

Besides Jupiter's moons, the telescope revealed other things horrifying to theologians. It showed that Venus has phases like the moon; Copernicus had recognized that his theory demanded this, and Galileo's instrument transformed an argument against him into an argument in his favor. The moon was found to have mountains, which for some reason was thought shocking. More dreadful still, the sun had spots! This was considered as tending to show that the Creator's work had blemishes; teachers in Catholic universities were therefore forbidden to mention sun-spots, and in some of them this prohibition endured for centuries. A Dominican was promoted for a sermon on the punning text: "Ye men of Galilee, why stand ye gazing up into the heaven?" in the course of which he maintained that geometry is of the devil, and that mathematicians should be banished as the authors of all **heresies.** Theologians were not slow to point out that the new doctrine would make the Incarnation difficult to believe. Moreover, since God does nothing in vain, we must suppose the other planets inhabited; but can their inhabitants be descended from Noah or have been redeemed by the Savior? Such were only a few of the dreadful doubts which, according to Cardinals and Archbishops, were liable to be raised by the impious inquisitiveness of Galileo.

The result of all this was that the Inquisition took up astronomy, and arrived, by deduction from certain texts of Scripture, at two important truths:

The first proposition, that the sun is the center and does not revolve about the earth, is foolish, absurd, false in theology, and heretical, because expressly contrary to Holy Scripture . . . The second proposition, that the earth is not the center, but revolves about the sun, is absurd, false in philosophy, and, from a theological point of view at least, opposed to the true faith.

Galileo, hereupon, was ordered by the Pope to appear before the Inquisition, which commanded him to abjure[4] his errors, which he did on February 26, 1616. He solemnly promised that he would no longer hold the Copernican opinion, or teach it whether in writing or by word of mouth. It must be remembered that it was only sixteen years since the burning of Bruno.[5]

At the instance of the Pope, all books teaching that the earth moves were thereupon placed upon the Index;[6] and now for the first time the work of Copernicus himself was condemned. Galileo retired to Florence, where, for a while, he lived quietly and avoided giving offense to his victorious enemies.

During the time of Galileo's enforced silence, his enemies had taken the opportunity to increase prejudice by arguments to which it would have been imprudent to reply. It was urged that his teaching was inconsistent with the doctrine of the Real Presence. The Jesuit Father Melchior Inchofer maintained that "the opinion of the earth's motion is of all heresies the most abominable, the most pernicious, the most scandalous; the immovability of the earth is thrice sacred; argument against the immortality of the soul, the existence of God, and the incarnation, should be tolerated sooner than an argument to prove that the earth moves." By such cries of "tally-ho" the theologians had stirred each other's blood, and they were now all ready for the hunt after one old man, enfeebled by illness and in process of going blind.

Galileo was once more summoned to Rome to appear before the Inquisition, which, feeling itself flouted,[7] was in a sterner mood than in 1616.

When he reached Rome he was thrown into the prisons of the Inquisition, and threatened with torture if he did not recant. The Inquisition, "invoking the most holy name of our Lord Jesus Christ and of His most glorious Virgin Mother Mary," decreed that Galileo should not incur the penalties provided for heresy, "provided that with a sincere heart and unfeigned faith, in Our presence, you abjure, curse, and detest the said errors and heresies." Nevertheless, in spite of recantation and penitence, "We condemn you to the formal prison of this Holy Office for a period determinable at Our pleasure; and by way of salutary penance, we order you during the next three years to recite, once a week, the seven penitential psalms."

The comparative mildness of this sentence was conditional upon recantation. Galileo, accordingly, publicly and on his knees, recited a long formula drawn up by the Inquisition, in the course of which he stated: "I abjure, curse, and detest the said errors and heresies . . . and I swear that I will never more in future say or assert anything, verbally or in writing, which may give rise to a similar suspicion of me." He went on to promise that he would denounce to the Inquisition any heretics whom

---

[4] Renounce.
[5] 16th-century Italian philosopher.

[6] List of forbidden works.
[7] Treated with contempt.

he might hereafter find still maintaining that the earth moved, and to swear, with his hands on the Gospels, that he himself had abjured this doctrine. Satisfied that the interests of religion and morals had been served by causing the greatest man of the age to commit perjury, the Inquisition allowed him to spend the rest of his days in retirement and silence, not in prison, it is true, but controlled in all his movements, and forbidden to see his family or his friends. He became blind in 1637, and died in 1642—the year in which Newton was born.

Questions for Discussion and Writing

1. Analyze the ways in which Russell's writing style creates a sympathetic view of science and scientists and a harsh view of theology and Church figures. Examine his word choice closely.

2. Reread the final sentence in the passage. What connection to later scientific inquiry does Russell seek to make? Is his sentence an effective way of ending his essay?

3. Why should the Copernican theory have raised fears of the purposelessness of human life?

4. Were early theologians justified in their fears that science would undermine Church authority and diminish religious faith?

5. According to Russell, one reason for the initial rejection of Copernican theory was its "dethronement of our planet from its central position [and] a similar dethronement of its inhabitants." Has this anthropocentric urge—the urge to identify humans as the center of importance—affected the role that science and technology have had on our planet, in ecological terms?

6. Russell casts Galileo in the role of martyr and theologians in the role of persecutors. How justified are his characterizations? Do they serve to promote modern scientific views, and if so, how? Is it significant that the probe recently sent to Jupiter has been named "Galileo"?

7. Do you believe that students should know about the story of Galileo's life as well as his scientific contributions? What purpose(s) could such study serve?

8. Are there modern methods of suppressing scientific theories that challenge traditional doctrine? Consider recent controversies over nontraditional medical practices and medicines (laetrile for cancer treatment, faith healing, etc.), the existence of parapsychological phenomena such as ESP, and other issues you have read about that have caused public controversy. How are these theories treated in the media? What stand do scientists in industry, government agencies, and universities tend to take?

Christe McMenomy, "The Scientific Background to the Industrial Revolution"

In the following article Christe McMenomy, an historian of science, outlines the causes and effects of the industrial revolution, which began in the seventeenth century and, some would argue, continues in the form of the technological revolution today. With the invention of steam en-

gines, the rise of factories, and the construction of canals, traditional
ways of life and commerce were disrupted, sometimes with disastrous re-
sults but, overall, McMenomy argues, with beneficial social effects for a
population in need of food, sanitation, and health care.

Key Concepts

Dialectic (page 144) is a form of logical argumentation, beginning with a
material base, or observation, and following through the implications
that arise from it. It is dynamic logic in that one proposition leads to
others, creating new knowledge.

In **humanism,** (page 144) the center of interest and basis of values is human
life and human concerns (versus theological concerns, for example).

The period between Galileo and Darwin was one of great change in
the definition of science, its methodology and subject matter, and in the
status and education of the scientist. At the end of the middle ages,
natural philosophers were trained in the universities of Europe in logic
and **dialectic,** and their texts were primarily commentaries on Aristotle.
Scientific method was defined by logical demonstration of known conclusions, as exemplified by Aristotle's discussions of physics and cosmology. The relationship between physics, astronomy, and mathematics
was defined in hierarchical terms, and conclusions in one discipline
could not be used in demonstrations of conclusions in another discipline.

By the time of Galileo's death in 1642, both the method of training
scientists and the methods scientists used were changing. Renaissance
humanism fostered the development of an educational system emphasizing useful knowledge, not merely theoretical demonstration. Francis
Bacon described a national program of scientific investigation, a fact-
gathering method of science, with the ultimate goal being the control of
nature for the benefit of mankind. While his programs were never
adopted as he envisioned them, Bacon's view of nature as knowable
and controllable, and science as an enterprise devoted to discovering
new facts, rather than proving old observations, reveals a conception
of science drastically different from that of the medieval natural
philosophers.

Galileo used mathematics to describe the behavior of bodies in
motion, and developed a method of experimental mechanics based on
measurement of isolatable phenomena. Kepler defined five parts for
astronomy, including observations, hypotheses to explain planetary motion, cosmology or metaphysics, prediction, and instruments. For Kepler,
development of the cosmology was least important: if hypotheses explaining the observations could be fitted to a cosmological or metaphysical system, that was an advantage, but if not, it was the cosmological
system which had to be discarded, not the hypotheses which accounted
for the observations. Gilbert, who pioneered work on magnetism, also
favored an observational approach which was not bound to outdated

theories, and dedicated his work to those men who sought answers not in old books, but in things themselves.

The emphasis on measurement and experimentation, and the new goal of finding useful knowledge, brought theoretical science closer ties with technology. Scientific measurement requires precise instruments. Experimenters were forced to become craftsmen to make instruments to carry out their tests, or at least to explain their needs to craftsmen who could make the instruments for them. The need for certain kinds of knowledge also defined those areas where science could most usefully benefit society. In the two centuries before Galileo, the requirements of navigators sailing out of sight of land for long periods on voyages to the New World had stimulated the spread of knowledge of astronomical calculation and geometric mapping techniques by the end of the sixteenth century. In the seventeenth and eighteenth centuries, the need for better agricultural techniques to support growing populations, the need for more fuel for production and heating, and the need for better timing devices, as well as the needs of warfare, all promoted theoretical investigation in biology, mechanics, mining technology, ballistics[1] and engineering which resulted in new technology, and ultimately, in the industrial revolution of the late eighteenth century.

The new view of man as an active intellectual with wide interests and abilities broke down some of the old barriers between the theoretical and practical sciences. The printing press made publication of books by many different authors possible. Craftsmen who produced works on mining, ballistics and architecture were largely self-taught, not scholars of the great universities, and their knowledge came from experience with the coal mines of Germany, and the cannon and fortifications used in Italy. Practical sciences became part of the university curriculum. In London, Gresham College was founded in 1600 to provide free education in mechanical and navigational arts in addition to traditional studies.

The seventeenth century is also the period in which the great scientific societies were founded. The Lincei of Rome, which counted Galileo among its members, was shortlived, but the Royal Society of London and the Académie des Sciences of Paris were permanent foundations, whose goals were the advancement of knowledge for human use. Newton, Boyle, and Hooke were Fellows of the Royal Society; in France, Huygens, and later Lavoisier and Coulomb, belonged either to the Académie or to the Ecole Polytechnique. The societies stimulated the dissemination of theories, experimental methods and results, the development of instruments, and at times, unhealthy rivalry. The status of the scientist had become one of both personal and national prestige, and there was competition between the scientists of England and France, who debated for decades over whether Newton or Leibniz had invented calculus first.

---

[1] Study of firearms.

In contrast to the seventeenth century, the early eighteenth century was a period of relatively few important major scientific advances. Instead, there were major technological implementations of the seventeenth century theories, leading to the industrial revolution, which were made possible by the changes in both science and society which had taken place since the middle ages. Besides the new experimental methods of science, and the cooperation of the scientific societies, the dissemination[2] of scientific ideas was increased by popularizations of new theories. Newton's *Principles of Mathematical Physics* appeared in a new version in the 1730s, written especially for the edification of ladies. Such popularizations interested the general public in the advances and possibilities of scientific theories.

There were other major developments in society which aided the industrial revolution. Economic institutions such as banks, insurance companies and trading companies were willing and able to advance the capital necessary to build new factories and means of transportation, in return for a share of the profits. Religious reformation provided new ways of evaluating success and challenging the authority of old institutions and ideas, and encouraged reception of new ideas. There was a general shift towards practical application of new knowledge in all areas of public and private life, which fed on the closer relationship between theoretical science and technology.

The industrial revolution was really a group of several revolutions. These were changes in transportation, architecture, energy use, and manufacturing. The transportation and architecture revolutions have their origins in the Renaissance, when the new astronomy made possible navigation beyond sight of land, and the ideas from perspective aided the Italian painters to design new buildings. As long distance voyages became safer, the demand for better shipping increased, to allow manufacturers in Europe to take advantage of cheap raw materials available in the New World. Ships increased in size and sail power, and changed shape to allow for greater maneuverability.

The new relationship between science and technology fostered the science of engineering. Systematic studies of how weight could be supported by beams led to stronger and safer building, road and bridge design, and the development of stronger materials allowed construction of larger factories.

The availability of steam power, iron and steel, and the machines to produce precision tools provided the materials and energy sources necessary for the invention of the railway engine. The earliest engines were used in England for mining, but by the mid-nineteenth century, the railroad had become the major source of goods transportation in England and in America, and was opening the American West to immigration and settlement.

---

[2] Spread.

The industrial revolution of the eighteenth and nineteenth centuries emphasized the interdependence of science and technology. Not only in the fields mentioned here, but also in the study of ballistics and chemistry, theoretical science provided the information necessary for improvements in cannon and dyes. Society came to expect that new scientific theories would result in new products, new sources of energy, and a better standard of living. By the nineteenth century, the scientist was a professional, supported by industrial or government institutions as well as academic ones, and his discoveries and inventions brought him prestige among his colleagues, and often financial reward from ownership of patents. The technical craftsman was educated in theoretical science and capable of applying new theories to improve production, make new tools, or invent new machines.

The social impact of the industrial revolution and the scientific discoveries of the seventeenth and eighteenth centuries was tremendous. In medicine, agriculture and factory production, new knowledge and techniques both improved the lives of many people and created new problems for others.

The study of medicine was freed from the authority of Galen and Hippocrates, and Harvey and others determined finally the circulation of the blood. The use of the microscope in medical research led to the discovery of germs and the invention of preventative innoculations for such diseases as small pox. Doctors were able to cure or prevent more diseases, with the result that more people lived longer and more had productive lives.

In agriculture, the enclosure laws permitted the landed gentry[3] to consolidate their lands, and take over untenanted areas for cultivation. The new attitude toward experimentation and technology led to the introduction of more effective draining techniques, better crop rotation, and the use of new food crops from plants discovered in the New World. Agricultural output increased significantly in England and the United States, with the result that fewer people were needed as farm laborers to produce the food necessary to support the population.

The displacement of poor farmers from the land caused an urban growth crisis. People flooded into the new industrial centers seeking jobs in the factories. Because the machines performed the work, they needed only to be overseen and refitted with supplies of thread or raw cotton. Factory owners set wages for women and children lower than those for men, as was true with farm labor. But factory work required less strength than outdoor labor; women and children were often hired to supervise the machines or work in the mines, leaving many men out of work. The work involved little mental effort but long hours. Children working thoughout the day had no time for education, and adults were frustrated by a type of work which emphasized the worth of machines over people.

---

[3] Upper middle class.

For those who could afford the new goods of the factories, living standards improved significantly. Cheap cloth from the textile revolution made it possible for all but the very poor to afford a change of clothes. Dishes, pot and pans, and soap improved home food preparation and sanitation, resulting in better general health. Cheaper transportation made a wide variety of other goods available for the first time to many people who would otherwise never have been able to afford them.

The changes brought by the industrial revolution raised new fears and expectations among the people it affected. Traditional jobs and social positions were threatened as women took more wage-earning posts, and populations shifted from the farms to the cities. The landed gentry and aristocracy lost some prestige as enterprising inventors produced new goods and became wealthy enough to influence political decisions. On the other hand, the availability of new products and cheaper goods made possible better standards of living for people who were not wealthy. And the new interdependence between science and technology had already solved energy and health problems and promised to answer more.

Questions for Discussion and Writing

1. McMenomy ends her essay with a discussion of the social effects of industrialism. How do the ideas in this final section affect our view of the essay's central topic, the industrial revolution itself?

2. Is the image of Galileo created by Bertrand Russell in "The Copernican Revolution" reinforced or weakened by the way in which McMenomy makes reference to him in her essay?

3. McMenomy writes that Francis Bacon's view of science differs radically from that of the medieval scientists. Explain the differences, and assess how closely Bacon's view is reflected in the role science plays in contemporary society.

4. In the fourth paragraph of her essay, McMenomy suggests that scientific research and technology were fueled by social needs. Does this picture of science serving society hold true in the twentieth century? Consider, in particular, recent technological inventions.

5. Humanism, according to McMenomy, encouraged education to provide not just theory but useful knowledge. Is the humanist bias still at work in education today? Draw on your own experience as a student to justify your conclusion(s).

6. How can you account for the prestige accorded scientists, historically and in our culture today? McMenomy suggests possible origins; consider her ideas as well as your own perceptions. What organizations and awards exist today to honor scientists?

7. The industrial revolution had a tremendous social impact, as McMenomy describes. Consider the many developing countries today that are becoming industrialized. What similar problems should they expect to encounter? Can they avoid the problems that Western societies experienced—a rise in unemployment, the exploitation of workers, rapid urban growth? Will the social benefits outweigh the costs of industrialization?

8. How has modern technology affected you, as a student and as a worker? Have the effects been largely positive? What negative effects, if any, have you noted, and are they likely to be resolved by "new and improved" technological developments?

Bertrand Russell, "Evolution"

Still furiously debated today in religious circles, the theory of evolution encountered intense hostility when its formulator, Charles Darwin (1809-1882), published his famous scientific works. But Darwin had gathered enough evidence in his field research (recounted in The Voyage of the Beagle, *1845) to convince him that the ideas he advanced in* Origin of Species *(1859) and* The Descent of Man *(1871) provided a more accurate account of the beginnings of the human race than did the Old Testament's Book of Genesis. In the following article Bertrand Russell explains the basic content of Darwin's theory as well as possible reasons for the reactions it continues to evoke.*

Key Concepts

When little government regulation of commerce exists, the system is called **laissez-faire economics** (page 149).

Providence (page 151) refers to the idea of Christian fate.

The doctrine of the gradual evolution of plants and animals by descent and variation, which came into biology largely through geology, may be divided into three parts. There is first the fact, as certain as a fact about remote ages can hope to be, that the simpler forms of life are the older, and that those with a more complicated structure make their first appearance at a later state of the record. Second, there is the theory that the later and more highly organized forms did not arise spontaneously, but grew out of the earlier forms through a series of modifications; this is what is specially meant by "evolution" in biology. Third, there is the study, as yet far from complete, of the mechanism of evolution, i.e., of the causes of variation and of the survival of certain types at the expense of others. The general doctrine of evolution is now universally accepted among biologists, though there are still doubts as to its mechanism. The chief historical importance of Darwin lies in his having suggested a mechanism—natural selection—which made evolution seem more probable; but his suggestion, while still accepted as valid, is less completely satisfying to modern men of science than it was to his immediate successors.

Darwin's theory was essentially an extension to the animal and vegetable world of **laissez-faire economics,** and was suggested by Malthus's theory of population. All living things reproduce themselves so fast that the greater part of each generation must die without having reached the age to leave descendants. A female cod-fish lays about 9,000,000 eggs a year. If all came to maturity and produced other cod-fish, the sea would, in a few years, give place to solid cod, while the land would be covered by a new deluge.[1] Even human populations, though their rate of natural increase is slower than that of any other animals except elephants, have been known to double in twenty-five years. If this rate continued thoughout the world for the next two centuries, the resulting population would amount to five hundred thousand millions. But we find, in fact, that animal and plant populations are, as a rule, roughly stationary; and the same has been true of human populations at most periods. There is therefore, both within each species and as be-tween different species, a constant competition, in which the penalty of defeat is death. It follows that, if some members of a species differ from others in any way which gives them an advantage, they are more likely to survive. If the difference has been acquired, it will not be transmitted to their descendants, but if it is congenital[2] it is likely to reappear in at least a fair proportion of their posterity.[3] Lamarck thought that the giraffe's neck grew long as a result of stretching up to reach high branches, and that the results of this stretching were hereditary; the Darwinian view, at least as modified by Weismann, is that giraffes which, from birth, had a tendency to long necks, were less likely to starve than others, and therefore left more descendants, which, in turn, were likely to have long necks—some of them, probably, even longer necks than their already long-necked parents. In this way the giraffe would gradually develop its peculiarities until there was nothing to be gained by developing them further.

Darwin's theory depended upon the occurrence of chance varia-tions, the causes of which, as he confessed, were unknown. It is an observed fact that the posterity of a given pair are not all alike. Domestic animals have been greatly changed by artificial selection: through the agency of man cows have come to yield more milk, race-horses to run faster, and sheep to yield more wool. Such facts afforded the most direct evidence available to Darwin of what selection could accomplish. It is true that breeders cannot turn a fish into a marsupial,[4] or a marsupial into a monkey; but changes as great as these might be expected to occur during the countless ages required by the geologists. There was, more-over, in many cases, evidence of common ancestry. Fossils showed that animals intermediate between widely separated species of the present had existed in the past; the pterodactyl, for example, was half bird, half reptile. Embryologists discovered that, in the course of development, immature animals repeat earlier forms; a mammalian fetus, at a certain stage, has the rudiments[5] of a fish's gills, which are totally useless, and hardly to be explained except as a recapitulation[6] of ancestral history.

---

[1] Flood.
[2] From birth.
[3] Descendants.

[4] Mammals having pouches.
[5] Basic elements.
[6] Summary.

Many different lines of argument combined to persuade biologists both of the fact of evolution, and of natural selection as the chief agent by which it was brought about.

Darwinism was as severe a blow to theology as Copernicanism. Not only was it necessary to abandon the fixity of species and the many separate acts of creation which Genesis seemed to assert; not only was it necessary to assume a lapse of time, since the origin of life, which was shocking to the orthodox; not only was it necessary to abandon a host of arguments for the beneficence of **Providence,** derived from the exquisite adaptation of animals to their environment, which was now explained as the operation of natural selection—but, worse than any or all of these, the evolutionists ventured to affirm that man was descended from the lower animals. Theologians and uneducated people, indeed, fastened upon this one aspect of the theory. "Darwin says that men are descended from monkeys!" the world exclaimed in horror. It was popularly said that he believed this because he himself looked like a monkey (which he did not). When I was a boy, I had a tutor who said to me, with the utmost solemnity: "If you are a Darwinist, I pity you, for it is impossible to be a Darwinist and a Christian at the same time." To this day in Tennessee [1935], it is illegal to teach the doctrine of evolution, because it is considered to be contrary to the Word of God.

As often happens, the theologians were quicker to perceive the consequences of the new doctrine than were its advocates, most of whom, though convinced by the evidence, were religious men, and wished to retain as much as possible of their former beliefs. Progress, especially during the nineteenth century, was much facilitated by lack of logic in its advocates, which enabled them to get used to one change before having to accept another. When all the logical consequences of an innovation are presented simultaneously, the shock to habits is so great that men tend to reject the whole, whereas, if they had been invited to take one step every ten or twenty years, they could have been coaxed along the path of progress without much resistance. The great men of the nineteenth century were not revolutionaries, either intellectually or politically, though they were willing to champion a reform when the need for it became overwhelmingly evident. This cautious temper in innovators helped to make the nineteenth century notable for the extreme rapidity of its progress.

The theologians, however, saw what was involved more clearly than did the general public. They pointed out that men have immortal souls, which monkeys have not; that Christ died to save men, not monkeys; that men have a divinely implanted sense of right and wrong, whereas monkeys are guided solely by instinct. If men developed by imperceptible steps out of monkeys, at what moment did they suddenly acquire these theologically important characteristics? At the British Association in 1860 (the year after *The Origin of Species* appeared), Bishop Wilberforce thundered against Darwinism, exclaiming: "The principle of natural selection is absolutely incompatible with the word of God."

Questions for Discussion and Writing

1. Is Russell more sympathetic in his depiction of the outrage provoked by evolutionary theory than he is in his depiction of reactions to Galileo and Copernican theory? Compare his treatment of the critics of Darwin in this essay and those of Galileo in "The Copernican Revolution."

2. Russell uses two direct quotations in his essay, one from his tutor ("If you are a Darwinist, I pity you, for it is impossible to be a Darwinist and a Christian at the same time") and one from a bishop ("The principle of natural selection is absolutely incompatible with the word of God"). Are these quotations well chosen as support for his thesis in the essay?

3. Explain how Darwin's theory extends the concept of laissez-faire economics to the natural world, as Russell states in the second paragraph.

4. We often use the evolution image to describe developments in technology or to trace social change (the evolution of computers, the evolution of the feminist movement). Russell defines evolution in one sense as "the causes of variation and of the survival of certain types at the expense of others." Does the evolution image help to explain *why* change happens, technologically and/or socially? Explore the implications of the evolution image, using Russell's definition of the term.

5. Why have many people found the (oversimplified) Darwinian idea that "men are descended from monkeys" so upsetting?

6. Russell points out that "Darwinism was as severe a blow to theology as Copernicanism." How do these two theories conflict with traditional religious beliefs? Is the conflict primarily one of faith or is it the product of a power struggle—or both?

7. Would the theory of evolution have found acceptance in the ancient Greek world? Consider Greek scientific practice (see Clagett, "Greek Science," in Chapter 1) and the uses of mythology in formulating your response.

8. Do you believe that both creation theory and evolutionary theory should be taught in the schools? What defense can you offer for your position?

Charles Darwin, from **The Descent of Man** _____

In The Descent of Man, *(1871) Darwin detailed his theory of human evolution. Well aware that his ideas would be met with enormous resistance, especially from religious leaders, Darwin sought to ground his work in a convincing mass of evidence that would place his conclusions in the context of the authority of science. Still his work reflects the values of his time despite its heretical implications; in his evolutionary scheme, evolution means progress, improvement, true civilization. Thus he provided his society with a complimentary view of its culture which, for many, balanced out what was considered a degrading picture of human origins.*

A brief summary will be sufficient to recall to the reader's mind the more salient[1] points in this work. Many of the views which have been advanced are highly speculative, and some no doubt will prove erroneous; but I have in every case given the reasons which have led me to one view rather than to another. It seemed worth while to try how far the principle of evolution would throw light on some of the more complex problems in the natural history of man. False facts are highly injurious to the progress of science, for they often endure long; but false views, if supported by some evidence, do little harm, for every one takes a salutary pleasure in proving their falseness and when this is done, one path towards error is closed and the road to truth is often at the same time opened.

The main conclusion here arrived at, and now held by many naturalists who are well competent to form a sound judgment, is that man is descended from some less highly organised form. The grounds upon which this conclusion rests will never be shaken, for the close similarity between man and the lower animals in embryonic development, as well as in innumerable points of structure and constitution, both of high and of the most trifling importance,—the rudiments which he retains, and the abnormal reversions to which he is occasionally liable,—are facts which cannot be disputed. They have long been known, but until recently they told us nothing with respect to the origin of man. Now when viewed by the light of our knowledge of the whole organic world, their meaning is unmistakable. The great principle of evolution stands up clear and firm, when these groups or facts are considered in connection with others, such as the mutual affinities of the members of the same group, their geographical distribution in past and present times, and their geological succession. It is incredible that all these facts should speak falsely. He who is not content to look, like a savage, at the phenomena of nature as disconnected, cannot any longer believe that man is the work of a separate act of creation. He will be forced to admit that the close resemblance of the embryo of man to that, for instance, of a dog—the construction of his skull, limbs and whole frame on the same plan with that of other mammals, independently of the uses to which the parts may be put—the occasional re-appearance of various structures, for instance of several muscles, which man does not normally possess, but which are common to the Quadrumana—and a crowd of analogous facts—all point in the plainest manner to the conclusion that man is the co-descendant with other mammals of a common progenitor.

We have seen that man incessantly presents individual differences in all parts of his body and in his mental faculties. These differences or variations seem to be induced by the same general causes, and to obey the same laws as with the lower animals. In both cases similar laws of

---

[1] Prominent.

inheritance prevail. Man tends to increase at a greater rate than his means of subsistence; consequently he is occasionally subjected to a severe struggle for existence, and natural selection will have effected whatever lies within its scope. A succession of strongly marked variations of a similar nature is by no means requisite;[2] slight fluctuating differences in the individual suffice for the work of natural selection; not that we have any reason to suppose that in the same species, all parts of the organisation tend to vary to the same degree. We may feel assured that the inherited effects of the long-continued use or disuse of parts will have done much in the same direction with natural selection. Modifications formerly of importance, though no longer of any special use, are long-inherited. When one part is modified, other parts change through the principle of correlation, of which we have instances in many curious cases of correlated monstrosities. Something may be attributed to the direct and definite action of the surrounding conditions of life, such as abundant food, heat or moisture; and lastly, many characters of slight physiological importance, some indeed of considerable importance, have been gained through sexual selection. . . .

Through the means just specified, aided perhaps by others as yet undiscovered, man has been raised to his present state. But since he attained to the rank of manhood, he has diverged into distinct races, or as they may be more fitly called, sub-species. Some of these, such as the Negro and European, are so distinct that, if specimens had been brought to a naturalist without any further information, they would undoubtedly have been considered by him as good and true species. Nevertheless all the races agree in so many unimportant details of structure and in so many mental peculiarities that these can be accounted for only by inheritance from a common progenitor; and a progenitor thus characterised would probably deserve to rank as man.

It must not be supposed that the divergence of each race from the other races, and of all from a common stock, can be traced back to any one pair of progenitors. On the contrary, at every stage in the process of modification, all the individuals which were in any way better fitted for their conditions of life, though in different degrees, would have survived in greater numbers than the less well-fitted. The process would have been like that followed by man, when he does not intentionally select particular individuals, but breeds from all the superior individuals, and neglects the inferior. He thus slowly but surely modifies his stock, and unconciously forms a new strain. So with respect to modifications acquired independently of selection, and due to variations arising from the nature of the organism and the action of the surrounding conditions, or from changed habits of life, no single pair will have been modified much more than the other pairs inhabiting the same country, for all will have been continually blended through free intercrossing. . . .

[2] Necessary.

The belief in God has often been advanced as not only the greatest, but the most complete of all the distinctions between man and the lower animals. It is however impossible, as we have seen, to maintain that this belief is innate or instinctive in man. On the other hand a belief in all-pervading spiritual agencies seems to be universal; and apparently follows from a considerable advance in man's reason, and from a still greater advance in his faculties of imagination, curiosity and wonder. I am aware that the assumed instinctive belief in God has been used by many persons as an argument for His existence. But this is a rash argument, as we should thus be compelled to believe in the existence of many cruel and malignant spirits, only a little more powerful than man; for the belief in them is far more general than in a beneficent[3] Deity. The idea of a universal and beneficent Creator does not seem to arise in the mind of man, until he has been elevated by long-continued culture.

He who believes in the advancement of man from some low organised form, will naturally ask how does this bear on the belief in the immortality of the soul. The barbarous races of man, as Sir J. Lubbock has shewn, possess no clear belief of this kind; but arguments derived from the primeval beliefs of savages are, as we have just seen, of little or no avail. Few persons, feel any anxiety from the impossibility of determining at what precise period in the development of the individual, from the first trace of a minute germinal[4] vesicle, man becomes an important being; and there is no greater cause for anxiety because the period cannot possibly be determined in the gradually ascending organic scale.

I am aware that the conclusions arrived at in this work will be denounced by some as highly irreligious; but he who denounces them is bound to shew why it is more irreligious to explain the origin of man as a distinct species by descent from some lower form, through the laws of variation and natural selection, than to explain the birth of the individual through the laws of ordinary reproduction. The birth both of the species and of the individual are equally parts of that grand sequence of events, which our minds refuse to accept as the result of blind chance. The understanding revolts at such a conclusion, whether or not we are able to believe that every slight variation of structure,—the union of each pair in marriage,—the dissemination of each seed,—and other such events, have all been ordained for some special purpose. . . .

The main conclusion arrived at in this work, namely, that man is descended from some lowly organised form, will, I regret to think, be highly distasteful to many. But there can hardly be a doubt that we are descended from barbarians. The astonishment which I felt on first seeing a party of Fuegians on a wild and broken shore will never be forgotten by me, for the reflection at once rushed into my mind—such were our ancestors. These men were absolutely naked and bedaubed with paint, their long hair was tangled, their mouths, frothed with excitement, and

---

[3] Producing good.   [4] Membrane.

their expression was wild, startled, and distrustful. They possessed hardly any arts, and like wild animals lived on what they could catch; they had no government, and were merciless to every one not of their own small tribe. He who has seen a savage in his native land will not feel much shame, if forced to acknowledge that the blood of some more humble creature flows in his veins. For my own part I would as soon be descended from that heroic little monkey, who braved his dreaded enemy in order to save the life of his keeper, or from that old baboon, who descending from the mountains, carried away in triumph his young comrade from a crowd of astonished dogs—as from a savage who delights to torture his enemies, offers up bloody sacrifices, practises infanticide without remorse, treats his wives like slaves, knows no decency, and is haunted by the grossest superstitions.

Man may be excused for feeling some pride at having risen, though not through his own exertions, to the very summit of the organic scale; and the fact of his having thus risen, instead of having been aboriginally placed there, may give him hope for a still higher destiny in the distant future. But we are not here concerned with hopes or fears, only with the truth as far as our reason permits us to discover it; and I have given the evidence to the best of my ability. We must, however, acknowledge, as it seems to me, that man with all his noble qualities, with sympathy which feels for the most debased, with benevolence which extends not only to other men but to the humblest living creature, with his god-like intellect which has penetrated into the movements and constitution of the solar system—with all these exalted powers—Man still bears in his bodily frame the indelible stamp of his lowly origin.

Questions for Discussion and Writing

1. Can you detect any effort on Darwin's part to present his ideas in a way that might help curtail negative responses from readers? Does he write defensively, or does he seem unconcerned about his readers' reactions?

2. How does Darwin's writing style differ from the writing you've seen in your science textbooks or in other scientific works you've read? Would you use a similar style in preparing a lab report, for example? What differences would you expect to see?

3. Darwin developed his theory of human evolution in the context of "the whole organic world." Is his view different from the traditional belief that the world was created with humans as the highest form of life and the natural rulers of the lower orders? If so, how?

4. Darwin refers to our progenitors as "barbarians." Does evolution necessarily lead to progress and improvement, or is it more a matter of simple adaptation for survival purposes? How might the notion of progress be self-serving?

5. Analyze Darwin's descriptions of the Fuegians. What cultural values does he reveal in the features he chooses to comment on—the nakedness, body painting, long hair, and so on? He condemns specific Fuegian social practices; again, how do his remarks reveal his own cultural values?

6. Should Darwin's works continue to be read as part of the "Great Books" tradition? Why or why not?

Jerome Kagan and Ernest Havemann, "Psychoanalytic Theory" _____

*The authors of the following textbook excerpt provide an overview
of the basic model of human psychology developed by Sigmund Freud
(1856-1939). Freud's influence on modern thought has been extensive; as
Kagan and Havemann show, his work consists of "key concepts." The authors note that Freud himself "made the comparison of psychoanalysis
with Copernican and Darwinian theory in terms of the three historical
blows which human narcissism has had to undergo: the cosmological
blow administered by Copernicus, the biological blow administered by
Darwin and his group, and the psychological blow administered by psychoanalysis." Among his theories, the importance Freud assigns to
sexuality created (and continues to create) the greatest dissent. Many contemporary theorists, feminist and otherwise, have condemned his views of
women and female sexuality. Again, the values of a particular historical
age are apparent in the "objective" scientific work that came out of it.*

The most influential personality theory during the past half century
has been "psychoanalytic theory," originally formulated by Sigmund
Freud. Freud began his career in Vienna in the 1880s as a physician and
neurologist. He became interested in psychological processes as the
result of his experiences with patients who were suffering from hysteria—that is, from paralysis of the legs or arms that seemed to have no
physical cause. His final theories represent a lifetime of treating and
observing many kinds of neurotic patients and also of attempting to
analyze the unconscious aspects of his own personality.

When Freud introduced his ideas around the turn of the century,
they were bitterly attacked. Many people were repelled by his notion
that man, far from being a rational animal, is largely at the mercy of his
irrational unconscious thoughts. Many were shocked by Freud's emphasis on the role of sexual impulses and particularly by his insistence that
young children have intense sexual motives. Over the years, however,
the furor has died down. There is considerable controversy over the
value of psychoanalytic methods in treating neurotic[1] patients, but even
those who criticize psychoanalysis as a form of therapy accept some of
Freud's basic notions about personality and its formation.

Freud's most influential ideas concerned concepts central to the
study of psychology. One of them was the role of anxiety. Freud was a
pioneer in emphasizing the importance of anxiety, which he believed to
be the central problem in mental disturbance. Another was repression
and the other defense mechanisms. Freud believed that these mechanisms, and especially the process of repression,[2] are frequently used to
eliminate from conscious awareness any motive or thought that threatens to cause anxiety. Another influential idea was his concept of the
unconscious mind, composed in part of repressed motives and thoughts.

---

[1] Showing slight maladjustment.   [2] Blocking out upsetting thoughts.

Freud was the first to suggest the now widely held theory that the human mind and personality are like an iceberg, with only a small part visible and the great bulk submerged and concealed. All of us, he maintained, have many unconscious motives of which we are never aware but which nonetheless influence our behavior. An example is the case of a man who sincerely believes that he has no hostile motives, yet who in subtle ways performs many acts of aggression against his wife, his children, and his business associates.

The core of the unconscious mind, according to Freud, is the "id," composed of raw, primitive, inborn forces that constantly struggle for gratification. Even the baby in his crib, Freud said, is swayed by two powerful drives. One is what he called the "libido," embracing sexual urges and such related desires as to be kept warm, well-fed, and comfortable. The other is aggression—the urge to fight, dominate, and where necessary destroy.

The id operates on what Freud called the "pleasure principle," insisting on immediate and total gratification of all its demands. Freud felt, for example, that the baby—though unable to think as yet like a human being and thus more like a little animal—wants to satisfy his libido by possessing completely everything he desires and loves and to satisfy his aggressive urges by destroying everything that gets in his way. As the child grows up, he learns to control the demands of the id, at least in part. But the id remains active and powerful throughout life; it is indeed the sole source of all the psychic energy put to use in behaving and thinking. It is unconscious and we are not aware of its workings, but it continues to struggle for the relief of all its tensions.

The conscious, logical part of the mind that develops as the child grows up was called by Freud the ego—the "real" us, as we like to think of ourselves. In contrast to the id, the ego operates on the "reality principle"; it tries to mediate between the demands of the id and the realities of the environment. Deriving its energies from the id, the ego perceives what is going on in the environment and develops the operational responses (such as finding food) necessary to satisfy the demands of the id. The ego does our logical thinking; it does the best it can to help us lead sane and satisfactory lives. To the extent that the primitive drives of the id can be satisfied without getting us into danger or harm, the ego permits them satisfaction. But when the drives threaten to get us jailed as a thief or rejected by society as a brawler and a rake, the ego represses them or attempts to satisfy them with substitutes that are socially acceptable.

In the ego's constant struggle to satisfy the demands of the id without permitting the demands to destroy us, it has a strong but troublesome ally in the third part of the mind as conceived by Freud—the "superego." In a sense the superego is our conscience, our sense of right and wrong. It is partly acquired by adopting the notions of right and wrong that we are taught by society from the earliest years. However,

Freud's concept of the superego represents a much stronger and more dynamic notion than the word "conscience" implies. Much like the id, the superego is mostly unconscious, maintaining a far greater influence over our behavior than we realize. It is largely acquired as a result of that famous process that Freud called the "Oedipus complex," which can be summarized as follows.

According to Freud, every child between the ages of about two and a half through six is embroiled in a conflict of mingled affection and resentment for his parents. The child has learned that the outer world exists and that there are other people in it, and the id's demands for love and affection reach out insatiably toward the person he has been closest to—the mother. Although the child has only the haziest notion of sexual feelings, he wants to possess his mother totally and to take the place of his father with her. But his anger against his father, the rival with whom he must share her, makes him fearful that his father will somehow retaliate against his mother—so that he becomes overwhelmed with strong feelings of mingled love, anger, and fear toward both parents at once.

The Oedipus conflict must somehow be resolved; the way this is done, according to Freud, is through identification with the parents. The child ends his mingled love and hate for his parents by becoming like them, by convincing himself that he shares their strength and authority and the affection they have for each other. The parents' moral judgments, or what the child conceives to be their moral judgments, become his superego. This helps him hold down the drives of the id, which have caused him such intense discomfort during the Oedipal period. But, forever after, the superego tends to oppose the ego. As his parents once did, the superego punishes him or threatens to punish him for his transgressions. And, since its standards were rigidly set in childhood, its notions of crime and guilt are likely to be completely illogical and unduly harsh.

In their own way the demands of the superego are just as insatiable as the id's blind drives. Its standards of right and wrong and its rules for punishment are far more rigid, relentless, and vengeful than anything in our conscious minds. Formed at a time when the child was unable to distinguish between a "bad" wish and a "bad" deed, the superego may sternly disapprove of the merest thought of some transgression—the explanation, according to Freud, of the fact that some people who have never actually committed a "bad" deed nonetheless feel guilty all their lives.

The three parts of the human personality are in frequent conflict. One of the important results of the conflict is anxiety, which is produced in the ego whenever the demands of the id threaten danger or when the superego threatens disapproval or punishment. Anxiety, though unpleasant, is a tool that the ego uses to fight the impulses or thoughts that have aroused it. In one way or another—by using repression and the other defense mechanisms, by turning the mind's attention elsewhere, by gratifying some other impulse of the id—the ego defends itself against the threat from the id or superego and gets rid of the anxiety.

In a sense the conscious ego is engaged in a constant struggle to satisfy the insatiable demands of the unconscious id without incurring the wrath and vengeance of the largely unconscious superego. To the extent that a person's behavior is controlled by the ego, it is sensible and generally satisfying. To the extent that it is governed by the childish passions of the id and the unrelenting demands of the superego, it tends to be foolish, unrewarding, painful, and neurotic.

If the ego is not strong enough to check the id's drives, a person is likely to be a selfish and hot-headed menace to society. But if the id is checked too severely, other problems may arise. Too much repression of the libido can make a person unable to enjoy a normal sex life or to give and take competition. Too strong a superego may result in vague and unwarranted feelings of guilt and unworthiness, and sometimes in an unconscious need for self-punishment.

There can be little question that Freud was an important innovator who had a number of most useful insights into the human personality. He was the first to recognize the role of the unconscious and the importance of anxiety and defenses as a factor in personality. He also dispelled the myth, widely accepted before his time, that children do not have the sexual urges and hostile impulses that characterize adults.

One criticism of Freud is that he may have overemphasized the role of sexual motivation in personality. In Freud's nineteenth and early twentieth century Vienna, with its strict sexual standards, it is perhaps only natural that many of his neurotic patients should have had conflicts and guilt feelings centering around their sexual desires. In today's Western world, with its more permissive attitudes toward sexual behavior, this kind of conflict and guilt seems to be less frequent. Yet people continue to have personality problems and the incidence of serious mental disturbance seems to remain about the same as ever. This would indicate that conflicts over sexuality cannot be the sole or perhaps even the most important cause of personality disturbances. Another frequent criticism of Freud is that many of his ideas about the dynamics of human behavior can be explained more economically without using his concepts of the id, ego, and superego.

Questions for Discussion and Writing

1. Explain how the image of an iceberg helps to describe Freud's notion of personality. Would the image of a house with a subterranean foundation be equally effective? Why or why not?

2. How does the term *egotistic* as we use it in everyday speech relate to Freud's notion of the ego and how it operates on the reality principle? Do we mean that an egotist has a distorted view of reality? What might it mean when we say that someone's "ego was wounded?"

3. Explain in your own words the role of the superego, its origins in the Oedipal stage, and our capacity to feel guilt as a result of simple thoughts. Is the formation of a superego a beneficial human capability, or is it the source primarily of neurosis and resulting unhappiness?

4. Why might conventional adult feelings toward infants have made (or make) Freud's concept of the id so difficult to believe?

5. When we can't satisfy the "primitive drives of the id," according to Freud, we seek socially acceptable substitutes. The primary drives of the id are sexual desire and aggression. What are some socially acceptable substitutes for indirect expression of these drives?

6. How does Freudian theory threaten the ideal of human innocence and natural goodness?

7. Freud theorized that we often express hostility indirectly and unconsciously, especially if we are angry at people whom we love or fear (or both). Think of examples from your own experience, both as the aggressor and as the recipient of another person's indirectly expressed anger. Is this behavior mainly positive in that it allows expression without confrontation, or is it mainly negative, for the same reason?

8. Many people reading about Freudian theory for the first time feel an immediate reaction against Freud's ideas. As you read this essay, did you find that you strongly disagreed with some of his propositions? Which ones? Why, according to Freud, might a reader have this reaction?

9. List the terms that make up the Freudian vocabulary (psychoanalysis, hysteria, neurosis, the unconscious, etc.). How common are these terms in conversation and general reading material, such as magazine and newspaper stories? To what extent has Freudian thought become part of the way we perceive our lives?

Sigmund Freud, *"The Embarrassment-Dream of Nakedness"* from *The Interpretation of Dreams*

That dreams might have symbolic meaning for the dreamer was not a new concept with Freud; dream interpretation has a history that is probably as long as conscious thought about dreams is. But Freud articulated a method for analyzing dreams that provided insight into the life of the unconscious mind, rather than the mystical or occult worlds that were the traditional contexts of dream interpreters. Thousands of hours spent analyzing the dreams of his patients led Freud to the conclusions he presents in his famous work, The Interpretation of Dreams *(published in 1900). In the following excerpt, he theorizes about a commonly experienced type of dream and shows how it functions as wish fulfillment.*

In a dream in which one is naked or scantily clad in the presence of strangers, it sometimes happens that one is not in the least ashamed of one's condition. But the dream of nakedness demands our attention only when shame and embarrassment are felt in it, when one wishes to escape or to hide, and when one feels the strange inhibition of being unable to stir from the spot, and of being utterly powerless to alter the painful situation. It is only in this connection that the dream is typical; otherwise the nucleus of its content may be involved in all sorts of other connections, or may be replaced by individual amplifications. The essential point is that one has a painful feeling of shame, and is anxious to hide one's nakedness, usually by means of locomotion, but is absolutely unable to do so. I believe that the great majority of my readers will at some time have found themselves in this situation in a dream. . . .

The persons before whom one is ashamed are almost always strangers, whose faces remain indeterminate. It never happens, in the typical dream, that one is reproved[1] or even noticed on account of the lack of clothing which causes one such embarrassment. On the contrary, the people in the dream appear to be quite indifferent; or, as I was able to note in one particularly vivid dream, they have stiff and solemn expressions. This gives us food for thought.

The dreamer's embarrassment and the spectator's indifference constitute a contradiction such as often occurs in dreams. It would be more in keeping with the dreamer's feelings if the strangers were to look at him in astonishment, or were to laugh at him, or be outraged. I think, however, that this obnoxious feature has been displaced by wish-fulfilment, while the embarrassment is for some reason retained, so that the two components are not in agreement. We have an interesting proof that the dream which is partially distorted by wish-fulfilment has not been properly understood; for it has been made the basis of a fairy-tale familiar to us all in Andersen's version of *The Emperor's New Clothes,* and it has more recently received poetical treatment by Fulda in *The Talisman.* In Andersen's fairy-tale we are told of two impostors who weave a costly garment for the Emperor, which shall, however, be visible only to the good and true. The Emperor goes forth clad in this invisible garment, and since the imaginary fabric serves as a sort of touchstone,[2] the people are frightened into behaving as though they did not notice the Emperor's nakedness.

But this is really the situation in our dream. It is not very venturesome to assume that the unintelligible dream-content has provided an incentive to invent a state of undress which gives meaning to the situation present in the memory. This situation is thereby robbed of its original meaning, and made to serve alien ends. . . . The impostor is the dream, the Emperor is the dreamer himself, and the moralizing tendency betrays a hazy knowledge of the fact that there is a question, in the latent[3] dream-content, of forbidden wishes, victims of repression. The connection in which such dreams appear during my analyses of neurotics proves beyond a doubt that a memory of the dreamer's earliest child-

[1] Scolded.   [3] Hidden.
[2] Test of worth.

hood lies at the foundation of the dream. Only in our childhood was there a time when we were seen by our relatives, as well as by strange nurses, servants and visitors, in a state of insufficient clothing, and at that time we were not ashamed of our nakedness. In the case of many rather older children it may be observed that being undressed has an exciting effect upon them, instead of making them feel ashamed. They laugh, leap about, slap or thump their own bodies; the mother, or whoever is present scolds them, saying: "Fie, that is shameful—you mustn't do that!" Children often show a desire to display themselves; it is hardly possible to pass through a village in country districts without meeting a two- or three-year-old child who lifts up his or her blouse or frock before the traveller, possibly in his honour. One of my patients has retained in his conscious memory a scene from his eighth year, in which, after undressing for bed, he wanted to dance into his little sister's room in his shirt, but was prevented by the servant. In the history of the childhood of neurotics exposure before children of the opposite sex plays a prominent part; in paranoia the delusion of being observed while dressing and undressing may be directly traced to these experiences; and among those who have remained perverse there is a class in whom the childish impulse is accentuated into a symptom: the class of *exhibitionists.*

This age of childhood, in which the sense of shame is unknown, seems a paradise when we look back upon it later, and paradise itself is nothing but the mass-phantasy of the childhood of the individual. This is why in paradise men are naked and unashamed, until the moment arrives when shame and fear awaken; expulsion follows, and sexual life and cultural development begin. Into this paradise dreams can take us back every night; we have already ventured the conjecture that the impressions of our earliest childhood (from the prehistoric period until about the end of the third year) crave reproduction for their own sake, perhaps without further reference to their content, so that their repetition is a wish-fulfilment. Dreams of nakedness, then, are *exhibition-dreams.*

The relation of our typical dreams to fairy-tales and other fiction and poetry is neither sporadic nor accidental. Sometimes the penetrating insight of the poet has analytically recognized the process of transformation of which the poet is otherwise the instrument, and has followed it up in the reverse direction; that is to say, has traced a poem to a dream. A friend has called my attention to the following passage in G. Keller's *Der Grüne Heinrich:* "I do not wish, dear Lee, that you should ever come to realize from experience the exquisite and piquant[4] truth in the situation of Odysseus, when he appears, naked and covered with mud, before Nausicaä and her playmates! Would you like to know what it means? Let us for a moment consider the incident closely. If you are ever parted from your home, and from all that is dear to you, and wander about in a strange country; if you have seen much and experienced much; if you

---

[4] Stimulating.

have cares and sorrows, and are, perhaps, utterly wretched and forlorn, you will some night inevitably dream that you are approaching your home; you will see it shining and glittering in the loveliest colours; lovely and gracious figures will come to meet you; and then you will suddenly discover that you are ragged, naked, and covered with dust. An indescribable feeling of shame and fear overcomes you; you try to cover yourself, to hide, and you wake up bathed in sweat. As long as humanity exists, this will be the dream of the care-laden, tempest-tossed man, and thus Homer has drawn the situation from the profoundest depths of the eternal nature of humanity."

What are the profoundest depths of the eternal nature of humanity, which the poet commonly hopes to awaken in his listeners, but these stirrings of the psychic life which are rooted in that age of childhood, which subsequently becomes prehistoric? Childish wishes, now suppressed and forbidden, break into the dream behind the unobjectionable and permissibly conscious wishes of the homeless man, and it is for this reason that the dream which is objectified in the legend of Nausicaä regularly develops into an anxiety-dream.

Questions for Discussion and Writing

1. Freud and later psychologists have often commented on the psychological content of fairy tales. Relate a fairy tale or nursery rhyme that you recall hearing as a child. Work with class members to create a Freudian reading of its content, using Kagan and Havemann's article as well as this excerpt from Freud.

2. Does Freud view this common type of dream as a positive expression of natural feelings or as evidence of possible neurosis? Cite lines from his essay to support your view.

3. Freud writes that "childhood . . . seems a paradise when we look back upon it later." How is the child's experience similar to the biblical story of life in Paradise or the Garden of Eden?

4. Explain how the experience depicted in the legend from Homer's *Odyssey* reveals a conflict between childhood desires and adult reality.

5. Name other common dream experiences, both typically negative ones (dreams related to test-taking, for example, or dreams about death) and more positive ones (dreams of flying or meeting an ideal mate). How might Freud explain these common dream experiences? Would you accept his probable reading of them?

SOME SOCIAL CONSEQUENCES OF SCIENTIFIC PROGRESS

*George E. Simpson, **"Early Social Darwinism"*** _____

Darwinian theory, particularly the concept of "survival of the fittest," has, over time, been taken up as scientific justification for certain social and political views. Social Darwinists, the term applied to one such school of thought popular in Europe and America during the late nineteenth and early twentieth centuries, believed that, by nature, the "best" humans rise to positions of power and so to wealth, social status, and political control. Social Darwinist theory was used to justify aggressive capitalism, colonialism, and imperialism. Rudyard Kipling, a British poet of the period, expressed a Social Darwinist sentiment when he wrote "That they should take who have the power/And they should keep who can." Darwin himself intended no such application of his theory. The following article explains the motives for and effects of applying the scientific model to social life.

Key Concepts

Colonial expansion (page 165) means that one nation increases its political or economic dominance over a subject nation. **Imperialism** (page 166) is a related concept; in this case, the stronger nation acquires dominance over the actual land of the subject nation.

A **naturalistic** world view involves belief in observable physical laws that determine biology and behavior (page 166).

Eugenics is the study of human breeding, emphasizing continued physical and mental improvement through genetic manipulation (page 166).

The application of Darwin's principle of natural selection to human society, with special emphasis on competition and struggle, became known as "Social Darwinism." This doctrine, congenial to the intellectual climate of the end of the nineteenth century, was endorsed by the advocates of unrestricted competition in private enterprise, the **colonial expansionists,** and the opponents of voluntary social change. Among others, Ernest Haeckel provided scientific sanction for this point of view:

The theory of selection teaches that in human life, as in animal and plant life, everywhere and at all times, only a small and chosen minority can exist and flourish, while the enormous majority starve and perish miserably and more or less prematurely. . . . The cruel and merciless struggle for existence which rages through living nature, and in the course of nature must rage, this unceasing and inexorable[1] competition of all living creatures is an incontestable fact; only the picked minority of the qualified fittest is in a position to resist it successfully, while the great majority of the competitors must necessarily perish miserably. We may profoundly lament this tragical state of things, but we can neither controvert[2] nor alter it. "Many are called, but few are chosen." This principle of selection is as far as possible from democratic, on the contrary it is aristocratic in the strictest sense of the word.

Herbert Spencer and William Graham Sumner were prominent in advancing the doctrine of the social Darwinists. Despite differences in their philosophies, both saw the poor as the "unfit." Because they are the result of the operations of the laws of evolution, they cannot be assisted

---

[1] Unstoppable. [2] Disprove.

and efforts to help them through legislation, public charity, and social reconstruction are evil. According to Spencer, "The whole effort of nature is to get rid of them, and make room for better . . . If they are sufficiently complete to live, they do live, and it is well they should live. If they are not sufficiently complete to live, they die, and it is best they should die."

Although Darwin pointed out that militarism and war occasion reverse selection by exposing the biologically soundest young men to early death or preventing them from marrying during the prime of their life and, at the same time, by providing those with poorer constitutions with greater opportunity to marry and propagate[3] their kind, many of the social Darwinists praised war as a means of furthering social progress. An English scientist, Karl Pearson, wrote: "History shows me one way and one way only, in which a high state of civilization has been produced, namely the struggle of race with race, and the survival of the physically and mentally fitter race. If men want to know whether the lower races of man can evolve a higher type, I fear the only course is to leave them to fight it out among themselves."

Nineteenth century **imperialists,** calling upon Darwinism in defense of the subjugation[4] of "backward" races, could point to *The Origin of Species* which had referred in its sub-title to *The Preservation of Favored Races in the Struggle for Life.* Darwin had been talking about pigeons but they saw no reason why his theories should not apply to men, and the whole spirit of the **naturalistic** world view seemed to call for a vigorous and unrelenting thoroughness in the application of biological concepts. Darwinian theory was utilized to justify the conflicts of rival empires, the ententes[5] and the alliances of the "balance of power." Bismarck in Germany, Chamberlain in England, and Theodore Roosevelt in the United States found in social Darwinism a sanction for their theories of force and expansion.

Another aspect of social Darwinism at the turn of the century was the **eugenics** movement. Like other early social Darwinists, the eugenicists equated the "fit" with the upper classes and the "unfit" with the poor. Believing that disease, poverty, and crime are due largely to heredity, they warned against the high reproductive rates of the lower classes.

Social Darwinism in Recent Years

Adolf Hitler's racism and Nazism have been called perversions of Darwinism. Hitler's virulent[6] doctrines were the culmination of a half-century of social Darwinistic thinking in Germany. One of his most influential immediate predecessors was General Freidrich von Bernhardi, who said of the Germans that "no nation of the face of the globe is so able to grasp and appropriate all the elements of culture, to add to them from the stores of its own spiritual endowment, and to give back to mankind

---

[3] Breed.
[4] Enslavement.

[5] Agreements.
[6] Bitter, poisonous.

richer gifts than it received." Bernhardi glorified war as a biological necessity, as the greatest factor in the furtherance of culture and power, and claimed that the Germans could fulfill their great and urgent duty toward civilization only by the sword.

Hitler's doctrines are so well-known that extended reference to them here is unnecessary. According to *Mein Kampf,* the "Aryan" alone "furnishes the great building-stones and plans for all human progress." The Aryan had subjugated "lower races" and made them do his will, the Jew's "intellect is never constructive," "the mingling of blood . . . is the sole reason for the dying-out of old cultures," and hyperindividualism had cheated Germany of world domination and a peace "founded on the victorious sword of a lordly people . . ." Hitlerism represents the most extreme variety of social Darwinism and the one which has had the most powerful effects on the destinies of modern peoples.

Conclusion

One hundred years after the publication of *The Origin of Species,* and eighty-eight years after the appearance of *The Descent of Man,* natural selection remains an important concept in biology, anthropology, sociology, even in international relations. Modern man is subject to selection, natural and artificial. If this were not so, all human genotypes would produce surviving children in the same ratio as the occurrence of these genotypes in existing populations. Today the adaptive value of co-operation is more widely acknowledged and the role of ruthless aggression as a factor in the evolution of man, society, and culture is given smaller significance. Social Darwinistic thinking has not disappeared, but increasingly the "nature, red in tooth and claw" version of natural selection is regarded as an outdated brand of Darwinism.

Questions for Discussion and Writing

1. Welfare programs today are sometimes cited as the cause of a family's continued poverty; families get caught in a welfare "cycle," the argument goes. How is this view different from the Social Darwinist view of the poor? Is it important which view members of our society adopt? Why or why not?

2. Explain the logic behind a Social Darwinist view of war as a beneficial social force.

3. How can Darwinian theory be used to support imperialism? Why might imperialist nations have desired scientific support for their policies and actions?

4. Scientists have developed various ways of manipulating conception and genetic programming: artificial insemination, in vitro fertilization, and sperm donors selected by IQ, among other techniques. Do any of these practices suggest the rise of a modern system of eugenics? If so, do the practices threaten certain social groups and favor others?

5. Simpson writes that "Today the adaptive value of co-operation is more widely acknowledged and the role of ruthless aggression . . . is given smaller significance." Surveying world events, American social practices,

and your own experiences as a student, do you find that cooperation is indeed the common and preferred model for social interaction, rather than aggression?

Adolf Hitler, **"Man Must Kill"** _____

The leader of the German National Socialist (Nazi) Party, Adolf Hitler (1889-1945) promoted his version of Social Darwinism in speeches that deeply appealed to many Germans of his day. The Holocaust, in which Hitler's forces rounded up and murdered six million Jews and other "unfit" types such as homosexuals, was a radical extension of Social Darwinist theory. In the following excerpt from one of these popular speeches, Hitler explains why he believes his policies are right and necessary—and how Germany intends to see them through.

Key Concepts

Darwin theorized that **self-preservation** (page 168) is the primary natural law; all species seek to maintain their individual existence at any cost.

The **struggle for survival** (page 168) is the process by which an animal (the human included) preserves itself, a process that often involves violence against other animals.

If men wish to live, then they are forced to kill others. The entire struggle for survival is a conquest of the means of existence which in turn results in the elimination of others from these same sources of subsistence.[1] As long as there are peoples on this earth, there will be nations against nations and they will be forced to protect their vital rights in the same way as the individual is forced to protect his rights.

There is in reality no distinction between peace and war. Life, no matter in what form, is a process which always leads to the same result. **Self-preservation** will always be the goal of every individual. Struggle is ever present and will remain. This signifies a constant willingness on the part of man to sacrifice to the utmost. Weapons, methods, instruments, formations, these may change, but in the end the **struggle for survival** remains.

One is either the hammer or the anvil. We confess that it is our purpose to prepare the German people again for the role of the hammer. For ten years we have preached, and our deepest concern is: How can we again achieve power? We admit freely and openly that, if our Movement is victorious, we will be concerned day and night with the question of how to produce the armed forces which are forbidden us by the peace treaty. We solemnly confess that we consider everyone a scoundrel who

[1] Basic survival.

does not try day and night to figure out a way to violate this treaty, for we have never recognized this treaty.

We admit, therefore, that as far as we are concerned the German army in its present form is not permanent. For us it will serve only as a great cadre[2] army, that is, as a source of sergeants and officers. And in the meantime we will be continuously at work filling in the ranks. We will take every step which strengthens our arms, which augments the number of our forces, and which increases the strength of our people.

We confess further that we will dash anyone to pieces who should dare to hinder us in this undertaking. . . . Our rights will never be represented by others. Our rights will be protected only when the German Reich[3] is again supported by the point of the German dagger.

Questions for Discussion and Writing

1. Connect Hitler's image of the hammer and the anvil to Social Darwinist principles. What does it mean for a country or race to play the part of the anvil? The part of the hammer?

2. Hitler's speech opens with a major logical assumption. To what extent do you agree with his opening assertion?

3. Is Hitler's view of Germany's right to world domination an outmoded one, or is it conceivable for nations today to adopt a similar view of their own right to world power?

4. Why might the people of Germany have found Hitler's doctrine appealing? Consider the appeal of the doctrine in contemporary America: which group(s) might support it, and which group(s) might most energetically oppose it?

Sidney Shalett, **"First Atomic Bomb Dropped on Japan; Missile Is Equal to 20,000 Tons of TNT; Truman Warns Foe of a 'Rain of Ruin'"** _____

At the time of this article, World War II (1939–1945) was nearing its end. The Allies (the United States, Great Britain, and Russia, along with other countries fighting against Germany, Italy, and Japan) had already defeated the Nazis, and Japan was on the verge of defeat. With the stated goal of ending the war quickly, U.S. military and scientific leaders tested their new "super weapon," the atomic bomb, by exploding it over two Japanese cities, Hiroshima and Nagasaki. The people and their cities were devastated, physically wrecked by the blast and its deadly radiation, and psychologically suffering shock and horror at the new weapon's power. Throughout history, advances in weaponry have changed the nature of warfare, but crossbows and rifles were minor innovations compared to the radical implications of "the bomb."

---

[2] Special corps.   [3] State.

Washington, Aug. 6—The White House and War Department announced today that an atomic bomb, possessing more power than 20,000 tons of TNT, a destructive force equal to the load of 2,000 B-29s and more than 2,000 times the blast power of what previously was the world's most devastating bomb, had been dropped on Japan.

The announcement, first given to the world in utmost solemnity by President Truman, made it plain that one of the scientific landmarks of the century had been passed, and that the "age of atomic energy," which can be a tremendous force for the advancement of civilization as well as for destruction, was at hand.

At 10:45 o'clock this morning, a statement by the President was issued at the White House that sixteen hours earlier—about the time that citizens on the Eastern seaboard were sitting down to their Sunday suppers—an American plane dropped the single atomic bomb on the Japanese city of Hiroshima, an important army center.

What happened at Hiroshima is not yet known. The War Department said it "as yet was unable to make an accurate report" because "an impenetrable cloud of dust and smoke" masked the target area from reconnaissance[1] planes. The Secretary of War will release the story "as soon as accurate details of the results of the bombing become available."

But in a statement vividly describing the results of the first test of the atomic bomb in New Mexico, the War Department told how an immense steel tower had been "vaporized" by the tremendous explosion, how a 40,000-foot cloud rushed into the sky, and two observers were knocked down at a point 10,000 yards away. And President Truman solemnly warned:

It was to spare the Japanese people from utter destruction that the ultimatum of July 26 was issued at Potsdam. Their leaders promptly rejected that ultimatum. If they do not now accept our terms, they may expect a rain of ruin from the air the like of which has never been seen on this earth.

The President referred to the joint statement issued by the heads of the American, British and Chinese governments, in which terms of surrender were outlined to the Japanese and warning given that rejection would mean complete destruction of Japan's power to make war.

[The atomic bomb weighs about 400 pounds and is capable of utterly destroying a town, a representative of the British Ministry of Aircraft Production said in London, the United Press reported.]

What is this terrible new weapon, which the War Department also calls the "Cosmic Bomb"? It is the harnessing of the energy of the atom, which is the basic power of the universe. As President Truman said, "the force from which the sun draws its power has been loosed against those who brought war to the Far East."

The imagination-sweeping experiment in harnessing the power of the atom had been the most closely guarded secret of the war. America

[1] Spying, information-gathering.

to date has spent nearly $2,000,000,000 in advancing its research. Since 1939, American, British and Canadian scientists have worked on it. The experiments have been conducted in the United States, both for reasons of achieving concentrated efficiency and for security; the consequences of having the material fall into the hands of the enemy, in case Great Britain should have been successfully invaded, were too awful for the Allies to risk.

All along, it has been a race with the enemy. Ironically enough, Germany started the experiments, but we finished them. Germany made the mistake of expelling, because she was a "non-Aryan," a woman scientist who held one of the keys to the mystery, and she made her knowledge available to those who brought it to the United States. Germany never quite mastered the riddle, and the United States, Secretary Stimson declared, is "convinced that Japan will not be in a position to use an atomic bomb in this war."

Not the slightest spirit of braggadocio[2] is discernible either in the wording of the official announcements or in the mien[3] of the officials who gave out the news. There was an element of elation in the realization that we had perfected this devastating weapon for employment against an enemy who started the war and has told us she would rather be destroyed than surrender, but it was grim elation. There was sobering awareness of the tremendous responsibility involved.

Secretary Stimson said that this new weapon "should prove a tremendous aid in the shortening of the war against Japan," and there were other responsible officials who privately thought that this was an extreme understatement and that Japan might find herself unable to stay in the war under the coming rain of atom bombs.

It was obvious that officials at the highest levels made the important decision to release news of the atomic bomb because of the psychological effect it may have in forcing Japan to surrender. However, there are some officials who feel privately it might have been well to keep this completely secret. Their opinion can be summed up in the comment by one spokesman: "Why bother with psychological warfare against an enemy that already is beaten and hasn't sense enough to quit and save herself from utter doom?"

No details were given on the plane that carried the bomb. Nor was it stated whether the bomb was large or small. The President, however, said the explosive charge was "exceedingly small." It is known that tremendous force is packed into tiny quantities of the element that constitutes these bombs. Scientists, looking to the peacetime uses of atomic power, envisage submarines, ocean liners and planes traveling around the world on a few pounds of the element. Yet, for various reasons, the bomb used against Japan could have been extremely large.

Hiroshima, first city on earth to be the target of the "Cosmic Bomb," is a city of 318,000 which is—or was—a major quartermaster

[2] Italian: bragging.   [3] Appearance.

depot and port of embarkation for the Japanese. In addition to large military supply depots, it manufactured ordnance,[4] mainly large guns and tanks, and machine tools and aircraft-ordnance parts.

President Truman grimly told the Japanese that "the end is not yet. In their present form these bombs are now in production," he said, "and even more powerful forms are in development."

He sketched the story of how the late President Roosevelt and Prime Minister Churchill agreed that it was wise to concentrate research in America, and how great secret cities sprang up in this country, where, at one time, 125,000 men and women labored to harness the atom. Even today more than 65,000 workers are employed.

"What has been done," he said, "is the greatest achievement of organized science in history. We are now prepared to obliterate more rapidly and completely every productive enterprise the Japanese have above ground in any city. We shall destroy their docks, their factories and their communications. Let there be no mistake; we shall completely destroy Japan's power to make war."

The President emphasized that the atomic discoveries were so important, both for the war and for the peace, that he would recommend to Congress that it consider promptly establishing "an appropriate commission to control the production and use of atomic power within the United States."

"I shall give further consideration and make further recommendations to the Congress as to how atomic power can become a powerful and forceful influence toward the maintenance of world peace," he said.

Secretary Stimson called the atomic bomb "the culmination of years of herculean[5] effort on the part of science and industry, working in cooperation with the military authorities." He promised that "improvements will be forthcoming shortly which will increase by several fold the present effectiveness."

"But more important for the long-range implications of this new weapon," he said, "is the possibility that another scale of magnitude will be developed after considerable research and development." The scientists are confident that over a period of many years atomic bombs may well be developed which will be very much more powerful than the atomic bombs now at hand.

[The plants which manufactured the atom bombs] were amazing phenomena in themselves. They grew into large, self-sustaining cities, employing thousands upon thousands of workers. Yet, so close was the secrecy that not only were the citizens of the area kept in darkness about the nature of the project, but the workers themselves had only the sketchiest ideas—if any—as to what they were doing. This was accomplished, Mr. Stimson said, by "compartmentalizing" the work so "that no one had been given more information than was absolutely necessary to his particular job."

---

[4] Weapons and ammunition.   [5] Heroic, great.

A special laboratory also has been set up near Santa Fe, N.M., under direction of Dr. J. Robert Oppenheimer of the University of California. Dr. Oppenheimer also supervised the first test of the atomic bomb on July 16, 1945. This took place in a remote section of the New Mexico desert lands, with a group of eminent scientists gathered, frankly fearful to witness the results of the invention which might turn out to be either the salvation or the Frankenstein's monster of the world.

"Atomic fission holds great promise for sweeping developments by which our civilization may be enriched when peace comes, but the overriding necessities of war have precluded the full exploration of peacetime applications of this new knowledge," Mr. Stimson said. "However, it appears inevitable that many useful contributions to the well-being of mankind will ultimately flow from these discoveries when the world situation makes it possible for science and industry to concentrate on these aspects."

Although warning that many economic factors will have to be considered "before we can say to what extent atomic energy will supplement coal, oil and water as fundamental sources of power," Mr. Stimson acknowledged that "we are at the threshold of a new industrial art which will take many years and much expenditure of money to develop."

The War Department gave this supplementary background on the development of the atomic bomb:

The series of discoveries which led to the development of the atomic bomb started at the turn of the century when radioactivity became known to science. Prior to 1939, the scientific work in this field was world-wide, but more particularly so in the United States, the United Kingdom, Germany, France, Italy, and Denmark. One of Denmark's great scientists, Dr. Neils Bohr, a Nobel prize winner, was whisked from the grasp of the Nazis in his occupied homeland and later assisted in developing the atomic bomb.

It is known that Germany worked desperately to solve the problem of controlling atomic energy.

Questions for Discussion and Writing

1. What image of Japan and Germany does the writer try to create in the report?

2. Why might the War Department have used the term *cosmic bomb* for its new weapon? Does it carry a political message?

3. Is the view of atomic energy as "a tremendous force for the advancement of civilization" still a common one? Would people today describe the value of atomic energy in these terms? If not, what terms might they use?

4. With other class members, clarify the writer's image of the atom bomb as potentially "the Frankenstein's monster of the world." In your opinion, is atomic energy closer to being a monstrous invention or a source of salvation?

5. How important a development is the atomic bomb? Is it equivalent in its social and psychological effects to earlier developments such as Darwinian and Freudian theory? Cite examples of how it has affected modern life and thought.

The Japanese Broadcasting Corporation, from **Unforgettable Fire** _____

Unforgettable Fire *is a collection of drawings by survivors of the atomic bomb attacks on Hiroshima and Nagasaki. The book's introduction, reprinted below, describes the heavily populated Hiroshima as it existed before the blast, and then takes us through a detailed account of the first moments, hours, and days following the explosion. Part of the horror lies in the fact that this single attack continues to claim victims even today: many people who lived through the actual event suffer the effects of radiation exposure, with cancer still taking many lives. The article also describes the psychological scars of this "unforgettable fire" which marks all of us in the atomic age.*

That morning . . .

On August 6, 1945, the morning started with a cloudless blue sky characteristic of the Inland Sea's summer. In March the big Tokyo air raid had killed 120,000 citizens. Many other cities in Japan were also violently bombed and burned by the American air attacks so that many non-combatants continued to be cruelly killed. In April American armed forces landed in Okinawa and the whole island became a battlefield. 90,000 Japanese soldiers were killed and 100,000 civilians died. Japanese people cried loudly that they would fight a decisive battle on the mainland.

Hiroshima remained unharmed. A wild rumor spread that the Americans were not bombing in Hiroshima because it was a religious city with many Buddhist believers. Though not known at the time, in fact, the American military had ordered that Hiroshima be spared from bombing raids in order to later calculate accurately the full effects of the A-Bomb.

Hiroshima developed on the delta at the mouth of the Ota River that ran from the Chugoku mountains into the Seto Inland Sea. In line with the Meiji government's policy to make the country rich and the army strong, Hiroshima became a strategic center for the Japanese military. From Hiroshima's Ujina Port soldiers recruited from all over Japan were sent to battle on the Asian continent. As World War II continued, Hiroshima developed into a major military city.

Before daybreak of August 6 an air raid alarm was given in Hiroshima. At 7:00 A.M. another air raid alarm was sounded. But at 7:31 A.M. the all clear was given. Soldiers at the anti-aircraft machine guns on the roofs of the miltary installations and munitions[1] factories were released by an air defense order.

Just before the fateful moment the seven rivers which ran through the city looked stagnant because of the high tide and reflected the deep-blue of the summer sky. Wearing work clothes and gaiters,[2] with air defense hoods thrown back, people were running on the big and small

---

[1] War supplies.   [2] Overshoes.

bridges throughout the city. One of these was the Aioi Bridge, an unusual T-type bridge. It was the target of the A-Bomb. The mobilized students, even school girls, were hurrying to the munitions factories by streetcar. A horsedrawn farmer's cart, taking nightsoil[3] from the city to outlying farms, passed by at a leisurely pace with a clop-clop noise. Small clouds of dust rose here and there among the crowded, tile-roofed houses. These showed that work had begun on pulling down evacuated buildings to make compulsory firelanes. Members of the Women's Society of Labor Service, National Volunteers from the suburban districts, and junior high school students put their lunches in the shade of nearby trees before beginning a long day of sweaty, dusty work.

In public offices and businesses workers had begun their jobs after their section chiefs had given their morning instructions. In public schools morning assemblies had begun because even during summer vacation, students who had not been evacuated had lessons there. Little children were busy playing in the streets. There were even foreigners in Hiroshima. Several thousand Koreans who had been taken from their country were working as forced laborers in an armament factory. There were some foreign students from Southeast Asian countries. And there were even Americans, POW Army pilots who had been shot down. Suddenly a bell rang in the broadcasting department of NHK. It was a warning given from the Army Headquarters of Chugoku District Army Information. The radio announcer began to read the bulletin, "Chugoku District Army Information. Three enemy airplanes have been spotted over the Saijo area. . . ." Just then there was a dreadful shaking and loud crash of iron and concrete. The announcer was thrown into the air.

The flash: 8:15

The A-Bomb, which was nicknamed "Little Boy," was dropped from the B-29, Enola Gay. It exploded 570 meters above the ground with a light blue flash. The diameter of the fireball was 100 meters and the temperature at its center was 300,000 C. Soon after the explosion black and white smoke covered the whole city and rose thousands of meters high. The pressure of the blast directly under the center of the explosion was from 4.5 to 6.7 tons per square meter. Wooden houses within a radius of two kilometers of the hypocenter[4] collapsed and completely burned from the wind and heat. The fires continued for two days. Some people who were near the center of the explosion literally evaporated and only their shadows remained; others were turned to charred corpses. Those who survived were badly burned. Usually their clothes were scorched and burned so they were practically naked. Their skin peeled off and hung down. They rushed to nearby fire prevention water boxes and river banks seeking water. Friends and relatives trapped under collapsed houses were crying for help. But flames surrounded them so closely that they were about to burn.

---

[3] Human waste used as fertilizer.   [4] Area directly beneath the bomb blast.

Later large black drops of rain poured down. It was a deadly rain which contained mud, ash, and other radioactive fallout. Through burning flames and pouring black rain there was an endless line of injured people heading for the outskirts of the city. The burns on their hands made the skin hang down. Their hands looked like those of ghosts.

"Give me water."

The security functions of the army, police, prefecture,[5] and city agencies practically ceased. Under such circumstances medical treatment was started by doctors and nurses who were injured themselves. Damage to nearby army posts was rather slight and so soldiers from them first began the relief job. Hospitals soon became full, so public schools around the city were used as first-aid stations. They were also crowded by the rush of wounded persons. Countless dead bodies and seriously wounded people, who barely breathed, were left on the road or the riverbanks of the city. Medical supplies were used up immediately because of the unimaginable number of wounded persons. The untreated people took their last breath moaning, "Give me water." What is now called radiation sickness soon appeared. People began suffering from diarrhea as if they had dysentery, losing clumps of their hair, and developing purple colored spots on their skin which made them look like a map. Such people soon died, their bodies full of big maggots they were too weak to remove.

Those who were looking for their relatives walked around in the still smoldering city with the rescue parties. What they saw were dead bodies piled up on the ground and filling up the rivers. Figures of mothers who died protecting their own children were especially heartbreaking. People were deeply scarred by the indiscriminate cruelty of the new styled bomb and the dreadfulness of war itself.

Among those who entered the city later, there were a large number of people who were affected by lingering radioactivity, and died. Cremation of dead bodies continued for many days throughout the city. On top of some wood dead bodies were piled up, oil poured on them, and a fire was lit. The smell of dead bodies and the wail of sutra-chanting spread over the vast scorched desolation.

And on August 9, the second A-Bomb was dropped on Nagasaki.

Questions for Discussion and Writing

1. Contrast the details of the Hiroshima bombing selected by the authors of this piece to the details Shalett emphasizes in his newspaper account of it. What makes the Japanese Broadcasting Corporation (JBC) story a more personal account?

2. What made the casualties caused by this "new styled bomb" more horrible than those caused by conventional warfare?

---

[5] Local government.

3. The authors open the selection by detailing the typical events of the morning of August 6, 1945. How does this approach affect the reader's response to the section entitled "The flash"?

4. Hiroshima was selected as the first bomb site in part because it was undamaged by previous bombing, and so scientists would be able to calculate the atom bomb's effect. If the United States were the victim of an atomic attack, what area(s) might be targeted as bomb sites, and for what possible reasons?

5. Is the typical attitude toward "the bomb" today one of horror at its effects, or have we become hardened to the idea of nuclear warfare?

David Attenborough, from **The Living Planet** _____

David Attenborough might best be described as an environmental educator. The Living Planet (1984) is his explanation of how the earth's systems—ecological and technological—interact, compete, and clash, to the detriment of the natural world and, as a necessary result, to human life as well. In the following essay, he details one example of natural imbalance caused by poor planning and seemingly willful destruction of natural resources. Acknowledging that as a technological society we will use the planet in ways that must affect nature, he urges not a return to nontechnological ways but an increase in environmental responsibility.

Some of the most fertile waters in the world lie just off the coast of Peru, around two groups of islands, the Chinchas and the Sangallans. Here an ocean current brings up nutrients from the deep sea floor to the surface in much the same way as happens on the Grand Banks of Newfoundland and with much the same result. Plankton blooms and supports great shoals of fish. The major direct consumers of the plankton are small shoaling fish, the anchovetas. These, in turn, are eaten by bigger fish such as sea bass and tunny and by vast numbers of birds which roost and nest on the bare rocks of the islands. Terns, gulls, pelicans and boobies swarm in huge flocks. Most numerous of all, fifty years ago, was a kind of cormorant called the guanay. Five and a half million of these birds alone nested there. Unlike the gannets and the pelicans, the guanay does not range far for its food, nor does it dive deep for it. It gets all it requires from the shoals of anchovetas, swimming close by and near the surface.

The guanay's digestion is odd, and it seems, not very efficient, for it absorbs only a relatively small proportion of the nutriment in the anchovetas it catches and excretes the remainder. The greater part of its droppings fall into the sea, where they fertilise the water and promote still further the growth of the plankton. But about a fifth of the guanay's droppings fall on to the rocks of the islands. Rain rarely falls in this part of Peru. In consequence, the droppings do not wash away but accumulate, forming deposits that were once over 50 metres deep. The Indians on the

mainland, in pre-Columbian times, knew very well that this was a magnificent fertiliser and used it on their plantations. It was not until the
nineteenth century that other peoples made the same discovery. Guano,
as it was called, proved to be thirty times richer, in terms of nitrogen,
than ordinary farmyard manure and contained many other important
elements besides. It was exported all over the world. Distant countries
based whole agricultural industries on it. Its price rose and rose. Sales of
guano abroad contributed more than half of Peru's national income. And
fleets of fishing boats working around the islands harvested the sea bass
and the tunny to provide food for the people all over Peru. It would have
been difficult to find a richer, more productive natural treasury
anywhere.

Then, some thirty years ago, chemical fetilisers were developed and
marketed. Though not as good as guano, nonetheless the price of guano
began to fall and some people on the coast decided it would be mar-
ginally more profitable to harvest the anchovetas instead. They were not
suitable for human consumption, but they could be turned into meal
which would be eaten by chicken, cattle and pet animals. Netting the
gigantic shoals was only too easy. The fishing was uncontrolled. In a
single year, 14 million tons of anchovetas were hauled out of the waters.
Within a few years, the shoals had all but disappeared. The guanays, in
consequence, starved. Millions of the birds were washed up dead along
the Peruvian coast. The survivors were so few in number that they no
longer produced enough guano to make its collection worthwhile and
the guano market collapsed completely. Neither were there enough
guanay birds to fertilise the sea and sustain the plankton at its previous
levels, so even though the anchovy fleet has stopped fishing, the recovery
of the shoals is by no means assured. Certainly it will not be swift.
Mankind, by not accepting his responsibility to manage, has succeeded in
damaging not only the guanay, the anchoveta and the tuna, but himself.

The other great natural resource of the world, second only to the
oceans, is the tropical rain forest. That too is being plundered in a
similarly reckless way. We know that it plays a key role in the worldwide
balance of life, absorbing the heavy equatorial rains and releasing them in
a steady flow down the rivers to irrigate the lower fertile valleys. It has
given us immense riches. Some 40 per cent of all the drugs we use
contain natural ingredients, many of them deriving from the forest.
Timber from the trunks of its trees is the most valued of all wood. For
centuries, foresters have collected it, seeking particular kinds of trees,
pulling them out and leaving the rest of the forest community little
damaged. They planned their activities carefully so that they did not
return to the same area for several years and gave the forest time to
recover.

But now pressures on the rain forest have intensified. The increase
of human beings in the surrounding countryside has led, understandably,
to more and more of the jungle being cut down so that the land can be
used to grow food. As we now know, the fertility of the jungle lies more

in substance of its plants than in its leached-out soil and the cleared land becomes exhausted and infertile after a few years. So the people fell more forest. Adding to this encroachment, modern machinery makes it easier than ever before to turn timber into cash. A tree that took two centuries to grow can now be knocked down in an hour. Powerful tractors can drag the fallen trunks out through dense forest with comparative ease, even if, in the process, they destroy many other trees that have no immediate cash value. So the jungle is disappearing at a swifter rate than ever before. Every year an area the size of Switzerland is being cut down. Once it has gone, the roots of the trees no longer hold the soil together. The lashing rains wash it away. So the rivers turn to brown roaring torrents, the land becomes a soil-less waste and the richest treasury of plants and animals in the world has vanished.

The roll call of such ecological disasters could be extended almost endlessly. It is only too easy to demonstrate the damage we have now inflicted on the wildernesses of the world. It is more important to consider what should be done about it.

We have to recognise that the old vision of a world in which human beings played a relatively minor part is done and finished. The notion that an ever-bountiful nature, lying beyond man's habitations and influence, will always supply his wants, no matter how much he takes from it or how he maltreats it, is false. We can no longer rely on providence to maintain the delicate interconnected communities of animals and plants on which we depend. Our success in controlling our environment, that we first achieved 10,000 years ago in the Middle East, has now reached its culmination. We now, whether we want to or not, materially influence every part of the globe.

The natural world is not static, nor has it ever been. Forests have turned into grassland, savannahs have become deserts, estuaries[1] have silted up and become marshes, ice caps have advanced and retreated. Rapid though these changes have been, seen in the perspective of geological history, animals and plants have been able to respond to them and so maintain a continuity of fertility almost everywhere. But man is now imposing such swift changes that organisms seldom have time to adapt to them. And the scale of our changes is now gigantic. We are so skilled in our engineering, so inventive with chemicals, that we can, in a few months, transform not merely a stretch of a stream or a corner of a wood, but a whole river system, an entire forest.

If we are to manage the world sensibly and effectively we have to decide what our management objectives are. Three international organisations, the International Union for the Conservation of Nature, the United Nations Environmental Programme, and the World Wildlife Fund, have cooperated to do so. They have stated three basic principles that should guide us.

---

[1] River's mouth.

First, we must not exploit natural stocks of animals and plants so intensively that they are unable to renew themselves, and ultimately disappear. This seems such obvious sense that it is hardly worth stating. Yet the anchoveta shoals were fished out in Peru, the herring has been driven away from its old breeding grounds in European waters, and many kinds of whales are still being hunted and are still in real danger of extermination.

Second, we must not so grossly change the face of the earth that we interfere with the basic processes that sustain life—the oxygen content of the atmosphere, the fertility of the seas—and that could happen if we continue destroying the earth's green cover of forests and if we continue using the oceans as a dumping ground for our poisons.

And third, we must do our utmost to maintain the diversity of the earth's animals and plants. It is not just that we depend on many of them for our food—though that is the case. It is not just that we still know so little about them or the practical value they might have for us in the future—though that, too, is so. It is, surely, that we have no moral right to exterminate for ever the creatures with which we share this earth.

As far as we can tell, our planet is the only place in all the black immensities of the universe where life exists. We are alone in space. And the continued existence of life now rests in our hands.

Questions for Discussion and Writing

1. Why, in Attenborough's estimation, is the interdependent system of sea–bird–humans, described in the opening of his essay, more natural and balanced than the system introduced by the development of chemical fertilizers?

2. Is Attenborough's purpose to urge us to reject technology and industrialization?

3. Describe the environmental changes you have witnessed in your home town throughout the years of your childhood and adolescence. Has the government controlled the changes, or have they been unintentional byproducts of the town's expansion or industrial base?

4. Examine the three earth management principles listed at the end of the essay. Do our environmental laws and current practices actively support these principles?

5. What steps can the average citizen take to enact the principles of environmental responsibility that Attenborough lays out?

RETHINKING SCIENTIFIC OBJECTIVITY

Stephen Jay Gould, **"On Heroes and Fools in Science"** _____

The author of, among other works, Ever Since Darwin *(1977), from which the following essay was taken,* The Panda's Thumb *(1980), and The*

Mismeasure of Man *(1981), Stephen Jay Gould has been an enormously successful popularizer of science, as well as being himself an eminent research scientist in the field of biology. Gould is credited with correcting Darwin's original formulation of the evolutionary process (though the idea of "correcting" earlier scientific views is one which his essay finds is itself in need of correction). The views Gould expresses in this excerpt illustrate the shift in scientific values which Stephen Toulmin analyzes in "Modern and Postmodern Science." Just as Darwin's notion of evolutionary progress has been questioned, Gould questions our belief in scientific progress as a matter of increased knowledge.*

Key Concepts

A priori (page 182) reasoning proceeds from cause to effect, from general law to particular instance. The term also refers to inherent, given knowledge or traits considered to exist independently of experience.

The Latin term **reductio ad absurdum** (page 183) names the logical technique of refuting a point or theory by taking it to a logical extreme, thus suggesting its falseness by showing that it ultimately leads to absurdity.

As a romantic teen-ager, I believed that my future life as a scientist would be justified if I could discover a single new fact and add a brick to the bright temple of human knowledge. The conviction was noble enough; the metaphor was simply silly. Yet that metaphor still governs the attitude of many scientists toward their subject.

In the conventional model of scientific "progress," we begin in superstitious ignorance and move toward final truth by the successive accumulation of facts. In this smug perspective, the history of science contains little more than anecdotal interest—for it can only chronicle past errors and credit the bricklayers for discerning glimpses of final truth. It is as transparent as an old-fashioned melodrama: truth (as we perceive it today) is the only arbiter and the world of past scientists is divided into good guys who were right and bad guys who were wrong.

Historians of science have utterly discredited this model during the past decade. Science is not a heartless pursuit of objective information. It is a creative human activity, its geniuses acting more as artists than as information processors. Changes in theory are not simply the derivative results of new discoveries but the work of creative imagination influenced by contemporary social and political forces. We should not judge the past through anachronistic spectacles of our own convictions— designating as heroes the scientists whom we judge to be right by criteria that had nothing to do with their own concerns. We are simply foolish if we call Anaximander (sixth century B.C.) an evolutionist because, in advocating a primary role for water among the four elements, he held that life first inhabited the sea; yet most textbooks so credit him.

In this essay, I will take the most notorious of textbook baddies and try to display their theory as both reasonable in its time and enlightening in our own. Our villains are the eighteenth century "preformationists," adherents to an outmoded embryology.[1] According to the textbooks, preformationists believed that a perfect miniature homunculus[2] inhabited the human egg (or sperm), and that embryological development involved nothing more than its increase in size. The absurdity of this claim, the texts continue, is enhanced by its necessary corollary of *emboîtement* or encasement—for if Eve's ovum contained a homunculus, then the ovum of that homunculus contained a tinier homunculus, and so on into the inconceivable—a fully formed human smaller than an electron. The preformationists must have been blind, antiempirical dogmatists supporting an **a priori** doctrine of immutability against clear evidence of the senses—for one only has to open a chicken's egg in order to watch an embryo develop from simplicity to complexity. Indeed, their leading spokesman, Charles Bonnet, had proclaimed that "preformationism is the greatest triumph of reason over the senses." The heroes of our textbooks, on the other hand, were the "epigeneticists"; they spent their time looking at eggs rather than inventing fantasies. They proved by observation that the complexity of adult form developed gradually in the embryo. By the mid-nineteenth century, they had triumphed. One more victory for unsullied observation over prejudice and dogma.

In reality, the story is not so simple. The preformationists were as careful and accurate in their empirical observations as the epigeneticist. Moreover, if heroes we must have, that honor might as well fall to the preformationists who upheld, against the epigeneticists, a view of science quite congenial with our own.

The imagination of a few peripheral figures must not be taken as the belief of an entire school. The great preformationists—Malpighi, Bonnet, and von Haller—all knew perfectly well that the chick embryo seemed to begin as a simple tube and become more and more complex as organs differentiated within the egg. They had studied and drawn the embryology of the chick in a series of astute observations that matched anything achieved by contemporary epigeneticists.

Preformationists and epigeneticists did not disagree about their observations; but, whereas epigeneticists were prepared to take those observations literally, the preformationists insisted on probing "behind appearance." They claimed that the visual manifestations of development were deceptive. The early embryo is so tiny, so gelatinous, and so transparent that the preformed structures could not be discerned by the crude microscopes then available. Bonnet wrote in 1762: "Do not mark the time when organized beings begin to exist by the time when they begin to become visible; and do not constrain nature by the strict limits of our senses and instruments." Moreover, the preformationists never believed that preformed structures were organized into a perfect miniature homunculus in the egg itself. The rudiments existed in the egg to be sure, but in relative positions and proportions bearing little relationship to adult morphology. Again, Bonnet in 1762: "While the chick is

---

[1] Study of embryos and their development.   [2] Little person.

still a germ, all its parts have forms, proportions and positions which differ greatly from those that they will attain during development. If we were able to see the germ enlarged, as it is when small, it would be impossible for us to recognize it as a chick. All the parts of the germ do not develop at the same time and uniformly."

But how did the preformationists explain the **reductio ad absurdum** of encasement—the encapsulation of our entire history in the ovaries of Eve? Very simply—this concept was not absurd in an eighteenth-century context.

First of all, scientists believed that the world had existed—and would endure—for only a few thousand years. One had, therefore, to encapsulate only a limited number of generations, not the potential products of several million years on a twentieth-century geological time chart.

Secondly, the eighteenth century had no cell theory to set a lower boundary to organic size. It now seems absurd to postulate a fully formed homunculus smaller than the minimum size of a single cell. But an eighteenth-century scientist had no reason to postulate a lower limit to size. In fact, it was widely believed that Leeuwenhoek's animalcules, the single-celled microscopic creatures that had so aroused the imagination of Europe, had complete sets of miniature organs. Thus Bonnet, supporting the corpuscular theory (that light is made of discrete particles), rhapsodized[3] about the inconceivable tininess of the several million globules of light that penetrate all at once into the supposed eyes of animalcules. "Nature works as small as it wishes. We know not at all the lower boundary of the division of matter, but we see that it has been prodigiously[4] divided. From the elephant to the mite, from the whale to the animalcule 27 million times smaller than the mite, from the globe of the sun to the globule of light, what an inconceivable multitude of intermediate degrees!"

Why did the preformationists feel such a need to penetrate behind appearances? Why would they not accept the direct evidence of their senses? Consider the alternatives. Either the parts are present from the first or the fertilized egg is utterly formless. If the egg is formless, then some external force must unerringly impose a design upon matter only potentially capable of producing it. But what kind of a force could this be? And must there be a different force for each species of animal? How can we learn about it, test it, perceive it, touch it, or understand it? How could it represent any more than an insubstantial appeal to a mysterious and mystical vitalism?

Preformationism represented the best of Newtonian science. It was designed to save a general attitude, which we would recognize today as "scientific," from a vitalism that the evidence of raw sensation implied. If the egg were truly unorganized, homogeneous material without preformed parts, then how could it yield such wondrous complexity with-

---

[3] Gushed.   [4] To an amazing degree.

out a mysterious directing force? It does so, and can do so, only because the structure (not merely the raw material) needed to build this complexity already resides in the egg. In this light, Bonnet's statement about the triumph of reason over the senses seems itself more reasonable.

Finally, who can say that our current understanding of embryology marks the triumph of epigenesis? Most great debates are resolved at Aristotle's golden mean, and this is no exception. From our perspective today, the epigeneticists were right; organs differentiate sequentially from simpler rudiments during embryological development; there are no preformed parts. But the preformationists were also right in insisting that complexity cannot arise from formless raw material—that there must be something within the egg to regulate its development. All we can say (as if it mattered) is that they incorrectly identified this "something" as preformed parts, where we now understand it as encoded instructions built of DNA. But what else could we expect from eighteenth-century scientists, who knew nothing of the player piano, not to mention the computer program? The idea of a coded program was not part of their intellectual equipment.

And, come to think of it, what could be more fantastic than the claim that an egg contains thousands of instructions, written on molecules that tell the cell to turn on and off the production of certain substances that regulate the speed of chemical processes? The notion of preformed parts sounds far less contrived to me. The only thing going for coded instructions is that they seem to be there.

Questions for Discussion and Writing

1. Explain how the theory of encasement, which seems absurd in modern terms, might seem acceptable to an eighteenth-century scientific mind. What point about scientific knowledge and belief is Gould making?

2. Why might historians of science have oversimplified the theories of the preformationists in order to make heroes of the epigeneticists? Why might it be useful to science and scientists to have heroes and fools?

3. Gould and other writers such as Carl Sagan and Lewis Thomas are known as "popularizers" of science. What aspects of Gould's style in this essay make it accessible to readers outside Gould's specialized scientific field? How would you define the term *popularizer*?

4. Why should what Gould calls "mystical vitalism"—the belief in a force or forces outside of material nature—be considered detrimental to the development of a "scientific attitude"?

5. How does Gould defend the preformationists' theory by drawing a parallel to DNA?

6. What view would you expect Gould to have of medieval science and scientists? Explain your reasoning.

7. Instead of considering former scientific theories outdated and foolish, Gould argues, we should understand scientific "progress" as a different way of seeing or representing the world. Does his view call for an alteration in our traditional notion of scientific discovery? Can his view be applied to other

fields in which we commonly assume we have "progressed"? Think about other areas of life in which the progress model is popular—in educaton or history, for example, or the development of maturity. Do you accept or reject it in these and other areas you can identify?

8. In what way(s) is Gould's view of science as an art rather than as the pursuit of information a postmodern view, as Stephen Toulmin defines it in the following essay?

Stephen Toulmin, "Modern and Postmodern Science" _____

The term postmodern *is generally used to indicate a critical perspective characterized by the rejection of absolutes and a recognition of relative, subjective values. More simply, postmodernist critics examine an idea or text in order to reveal the hidden values it promotes. A central postmodern premise is that all ideas and texts are the products of their age and are thus inevitably imbued with the values of their authors, who are themselves the products of the larger social context in which they live. Clearly, the traditional belief in scientific objectivity clashes with postmodern thought. In the following essay, written in 1982, Stephen Toulmin, a contemporary critic-philosopher, analyzes whether there is a logical contradiction inherent in the notion that subjective researchers can produce objective results.*

Key Concepts

Empiricist knowledge is derived from observation rather than from theorizing (page 185).

A **positivist** (page 185) believes that facts can be determined through sense perception and then general laws can be articulated through inductive reasoning.

According to **Newtonian mechanics** (page 186), physical laws can be absolutely calculated; Newtonian theory was later supplanted by Einsteinian relativity.

1. The doctrines of the natural sciences are critical interpretations of their subject matter, no less than those of the humanities.

Among the spokesmen for the new "mathematical and experimental philosophy" of the seventeenth century, there were some who claimed to rest their scientific conclusions on simple deductions and/or generalizations from the "facts" of observation. This claim, from time to time, has been revived by enthusiastic scientists interested in affirming a unique kind of rationality or objectivity for their results as well as by **empiricist** philosophers interested in using science to support a **positivist** theory of knowledge. This positivist view of scientific argument is, however, deceptive: scientists always approach their investigations with specific problems in mind and view the phenomena or processes that they study with the hope of shedding light on those problems. As a result, scientific discoveries are typically arrived at not by generalizing from preexisting *facts* but by providing answers to preexisting *questions.*

2. Significant changes have occurred in the current styles of interpretation as the natural sciences have moved from one stage of historical development to another.

The interpretive standpoint characteristic of the physical sciences in the "classical" period, which lasted from the mid-seventeenth century until around 1920, required scientists to approach the world as pure *spectators.* In theory, at least, the ideal viewpoint for observing the processes of nature was one that permitted scientists to look on at them and describe them without significantly influencing them. Whereas the alchemists had been continually open to the worry that their own states of mind might be altering the very phenomena they were hoping to control, the "new philosophers" thought they had hit on a method for obtaining truly objective knowledge of nature which was in no way affected by their own motives and prejudices. Thus the intellectual program and strategy of modern science was established, and this dominated the thinking of physical scientists until well into the twentieth century. It was nicely captured in Pierre Simon Laplace's image of the Omniscient Calculator, who looked on at the universe *from outside* and predicted its entire future course as a straightforward exercise in **Newtonian mechanics.**

During the heyday of the modern scientific program, the inherent limits to the scope of this method were not, however, borne in mind as carefully as they might have been. It was too often assumed that the particular ideal of objective, scientific knowledge on which it was based could, in principle, be extended without limit to embrace natural systems and phenomena of all kinds. This method could be applied without difficulty—not surprisingly—to inert physical or material *objects* and also to other natural happenings that follow the same course, regardless of whether they were observed or not. But once the scope of investigation was extended to include systems and subjects whose behavior may be changed by the very fact that they are being investigated, it could no longer play the same exclusive part.

At first this meant only that modern science provided an unsuitable method and an irrelevant ideal of objectivity for the *human* sciences. (Human beings—qua[1] research subjects—are normally aware when their behavior is being studied and are capable of reacting countersuggestibly.) That is to say, at first this limitation served merely to reinforce the contrast between the passivity and objectivity of material nature, on the one hand, and the activity and subjectivity of human beings, on the other. During the first thirty years of the twentieth century, however, these difficulties began to cut deeper. All along, it now appeared, the

---

[1] As.

standpoint of the detached onlooker, from which—in theory at least—classical scientists had observed and speculated about the world, was no more than an abstraction.

It was convenient to *assume* that such detachment was possible, for the purposes of interpretation, but that assumption misrepresented the actual situation. As we now realize, the interaction between scientists and their objects of study is always a *two-way* affair. There is no way in which scientists can continue to reduce the effects of their observations on those objects without limit. Even in fundamental physics, for instance, the fact that subatomic particles are under observation will make the influence of the physicists' instruments a significant element in the phenomena themselves. As a result, during the twentieth century scientists have had to change their interpretive standpoint not merely in the human sciences but elsewhere. In quantum mechanics as much as in psychiatry, in ecology as much as in anthropology, the scientific observer is now—willy-nilly—also a *participant.* The scientists of the mid-twentieth century, then, have entered the period of postmodern science. For natural scientists today, the classical posture of pure spectator is no longer available even on the level of pure theory; and the objectivity of scientific knowledge can no longer rely on the passivity of the scientists' objects of knowledge alone. In the physical sciences, objectivity can now be achieved only in the way it is in the human sciences: the scientist must acknowledge and discount his own reactions to and influence on that which he seeks to understand. . . .

This shift within the physical sciences—from the detached point of view of the uninfluencing spectator to the interactive point of view of the participant-observer—is only one (though perhaps the most radical) illustration of the multiplicity of interpretive standpoints that twentieth-century scientists have occasion to adopt.

So, we may say, in postmodern science *nature is no longer held at arm's length.* The objectivity of the sciences today is no different from the objectivity aimed at in other fields of judgment—the objectivity, for example, at which a judge must aim in trying a case or to which a parent should aspire when mediating a quarrel between children. In all these cases, to be objective does not require us to be *un*interested, that is, devoid of interests or feelings; it requires us only to acknowledge those interests and feelings, to discount any resulting biases and prejudices, and to do our best to act in a *dis*interested way.

The postmodern scientist may, thus, still be something of a spectator, but he need no longer be a purely *detached* spectator. The human ecologist, for instance, has the task of studying the modes of interaction between human agents or communities and the natural environment and explaining the effects of, for example, land use or agriculture on the lives of other species. But, in doing so, he is not required to pretend that he has no interests of his own in water supply and food production. At most, he is required to discount his own needs and hopes in this work and to analyze the manner in which the activities of human beings and other species influence each other in terms that "do equal justice" to all of the species involved. At times, the resulting accounts may surprise the lay public as much as the older-style explanations of the modern scientists did: many Americans found it hard to view snail darters with the required degree of piety and equity. But it is important to recognize how, through the shift from the modern to the postmodern standpoint, questions of justice have taken a place in the forum of scientific judgment alongside the questions of truth.

In the course of this shift, the very concept of "scientific truth" has itself been clarified. The truth of theories turns out to resemble the truth of plain, factual statements, which aim at being straightforward, veracious, and undistorted reports, less than it does the truth of portraits, which aim at being faithful, just, or "unmisleading" likenesses. What puzzles a scientist about any phenomenon is less the queston What is *true* about this? than the question What can we *make* of this?; and there the interpretive element is quite explicit.

Accordingly, in both today's postmodern natural and human sciences and the critical disciplines of the humanities, we are concerned with a mix, or blend, of explanation and interpretation. All of our scientific explanations and critical readings start from, embody, and imply some interpretive standpoint, conceptual framework, or theoretical perspective. The relevance and adequacy of our explanations can never be demonstrated with Platonic rigor or geometrical necessity. . . . Instead, the operative question is, Which of our positions are rationally warranted, reasonable, or defensible—that is, well-founded rather than groundless opinions, sound *doxal*[2] rather than shaky ones?

Questions for Discussion and Writing

1. Restate Toulmin's phrase "the multiplicity of interpretive standpoints" in simpler terms. Work with other class members to reformulate the phrasing.

2. Toulmin concludes by suggesting that "scientific truth" is more like a portrait, which is someone's attempt at a fair likeness of some thing or person, than it is a clear-cut, factual, undistorted report. How well does his formulation of scientific knowledge fit with Stephen Jay Gould's in "On Heroes and Fools in Science"?

3. Explain the contemporary view that the traditional scientific method, which is based on the principle of objective observation, is limited and naive.

4. How can the presence of an observer affect the behavior of the person or thing being studied? Think of examples to illustrate how observers affect and are affected by their objects of study.

5. Why should the fact that scientists are trying to answer specific questions through their research affect the "discoveries" they make? Try drawing a parallel to some activity of your own that might have different goals at different times. Does your reading of a novel, for example, change according to whether you're studying it for an exam or reading it for personal interest?

[2] Doctrines.

Ruth Bleier, Introduction to **Feminist Approaches to Science** _____

The belief in scientific objectivity has served not only to promote the authority of science, but also to conserve that authority as the domain of male researchers, according to the arguments put forth by feminists and many postmodern critics. The traditional stereotype of women as intuitive, emotional types has helped to keep them from advancing in scientific fields; "feminine" ways of thinking have traditionally been considered inferior to "masculine" ways. The world of science has thus been shaped by a certain ideology that Bleier and other feminist critics are challenging today. In the following essay, written in 1988, she outlines the historical exclusion of women from science and the promotion of "masculine" scientific values.

Key Concepts

Determinist (page 193) thinking states that all actions are the product of preceding causes, hereditary or environmental in nature; behavior is the product of predestining factors.

Dualism is the belief that two forces are always in operation in the world, that all knowledge can be broken down into two, usually opposing elements (page 193).

In **patriarchal** structuring, laws and customs are determined by a ruling male, either in society as a whole or within the family (page 193).

What is it about science—or about women—or about feminists—that explains the virtual absence of a feminist voice in the natural sciences, as an integral part *of* the sciences, with the single exception of primatology?[1] And what would such a voice sound like? How would science be different? How would our perceptions of the natural world, of women and men, be transformed? While, over the past 10-12 years, feminists within science and without have been dissenting from and criticizing the many damaging and self-defeating features of science (the absolutism, authoritarianism, **determinist** thinking, cause-effect simplifications, androcentrism,[2] ethnocentrism, pretensions to objectivity and neutrality), the elephant has not even flicked its trunk or noticeably glanced in our direction, let alone rolled over and given up.

Yet, we may ask, is that what is most important? Is our only goal to change science itself? I would say it is, indeed, a goal, but one among many. Not the least important aim, as in the rest of feminist scholarship and practices, is to win the struggle for the minds of those women, perhaps the majority, who are constrained or oppressed by internalized scientific judgments about our presumed biological limitations. For then, together we can change science, like the rest of society. The reading public, including feminists, who have been dazzled by the real and life-

[1] The study of primates.   [2] Centering on males.

saving and life-improving accomplishments of science but also intimidated by its life-threatening and life-killing technological "achievements" and mystified by its esoteric[3] language and techniques, need to gain access to its practices and familiarity with its language, methods and theories. One route to such knowledge, short of becoming scientists, is through the writings of feminist scientists and historians and philosophers of science and other radical social critics. Their articles and books . . . not simply conceived *within* a particular social and political context, are themselves *part* of the large international social struggle about the political-symbolic structure, history, and future of Woman and women. . . . Feminists criticize the authoritarianism, detachment from nature and its "objects" of study, and the denial of responsibility for the life-threatening and nature-destroying applications of scientific knowledge and technology as stereotypically masculine. . . . Feminist analyses of important areas of research in the natural sciences (both contemporary and historical) have revealed many levels of distortion and bias in assumptions, methods, and interpretations. Yet, on further analysis, this discovery need not be surprising. Science is a socially produced body of knowledge and a cultural institution. Our culture is deeply and fundamentally structured socially, politically, ideologically, and conceptually by gender as well as by race, class, and sexuality. It then follows that the dominant categories of cultural experience (white, male, middle/upper class, and heterosexual) will be reflected within the cultural institution of science itself: in its structure, theories, concepts, values, ideologies, and practices . . . science is done by means of human relationships, and these relationships are unequal in terms of power across several different boundaries—of class and race as well as of gender. . . . Each scientist has a particular history of experiences and social relationships and, therefore, a particular worldview and set of values, beliefs, hopes, and needs that are reflected—as they are for everyone else—in what scientists do, how they (we) perceive the world, how they view and experience social relationships and questions of power, and how they practice their science.

There is an oral tradition and set of idealized practices known as the scientific method, which includes making observations, forming hypotheses or tentative explanations for the observations, and then testing the validity of the hypotheses by further observations or experiments. This method is generally viewed as the protector against rampant subjectivities and the guarantor of the objectivity and validity of scientific knowledge. Yet each step in the scientific method is profoundly affected by the values, opinions, biases, beliefs, and interests of the scientist. These values and beliefs affect what observations scientists make and, therefore, what they believe needs explaining in the world, what questions they ask: for example, what are the origins of gender differences in status and roles or the origins of IQ differences between blacks and

[3] Restricted, uncommon.

whites? They affect the assumptions scientists make: what language they use to pose questions; what they see and fail to see; how they interpret their data; what they hope, want, need, and believe to be true.

While we all have the experience of not seeing things that are before our eyes, it still may be difficult for most nonscientists (or scientists) to believe that scientists' values, beliefs, and expectations can influence what they are actually able to *see* or *hear* with their perfectly functioning senses. For example, leading microscopists of the 17th and 18th centuries, including the great van Leeuwenhoek, claimed they had seen "exceedingly minute forms of men with arms, heads and legs complete inside sperm" under the microscope. Their observations were constrained not by the limited resolving power of the microscopes of the time, but rather by the 2,000-year-old concept, dating from the time of Aristotle, that women, as totally passive beings, contribute nothing to conception but the womb as incubator. Except for Japanese field workers, primatologists in the 1950s and 1960s could not *see* what female primates were doing; and even if they could see something, their hypotheses, observations, and interpretations were clearly constrained by the cultural concepts available. Attempts to explain female leadership, or dominance, or sexual aggressivity and initiative had to be accommodated within male-centered explanatory systems.

As human beings we *all* have deep-seated beliefs on most important issues and those beliefs derive from sources that are other than scientific. In turn, when such issues, like gender or race differences, become the subject of scientific investigation, scientists are not magically capable of suspending belief and judgment in their approach to the problem. And this is true for scientists on all sides of any controversy. Suspensions of belief, emotion, and judgment are no more possible in the pursuit of answers about gender than they were in the race to reveal the structure of DNA (or, more accurately, the race to win the Nobel Prize) by Watson, Crick, and Wilkins. There is hardly a significant area of science, however remote from gender or race or other social issues, that does not engender wildly differing opinions, intense passions, irrational responses, and personal antagonisms. And, furthermore, I would maintain that most scientists would not be happy in their work nor would science have accomplished so much as it has in understanding natural phenomena and applying the knowledge to social uses were these passions and drives absent from the laboratory.

The problem is that, more often than not, these passions and commitments have more to do with drives for personal power than with the pursuit of the truths of nature. And when the questions being investigated have important social implications about the "nature" of women, the commitment is to the social status quo rather than to a disinterested and unemotional consideration of the range of possible interpretations of a body of observations. That is, scientists, like the majority of men in our society, have a personal stake in a system and ideology that reinforce belief in the biological inferiority of women and, thus, justify women's subordinate position within the home *and* the laboratory. (The phe-nomenon of the eminent scientist could hardly exist without a veritable army of unpaid and underpaid women who have facilitated his career—as wife, technician, secretary, and underacknowledged scientific col-league contributing essentially to his research.) Yet scientists would still maintain that what they do in their laboratory is neutral, objective, and value-free; and that their differences of opinion, emotions, and drives are objective—based on rational differences in techniques or interpreta-tions—all quite separate from who they are as people. . . .

The field of the sociology of scientific knowledge attempts to relate the production of scientific knowledge by scientists to scientists' social, political, and personal contexts. Sociologists of scientific knowledge (Karin Knorr-Cetina, Michael Mulkay, G. Nigel Gilbert, Bruno Latour, and others), through their participatory observations of daily life in particular science laboratories, record and analyze the patterns of daily scientific laboratory work and conversations, written communications with other scientists, lectures, and publications. They have documented the com-monplace fact that scientists—in their drives, motives, and operations—are influenced by many of the same considerations that affect others trying to get ahead and keep ahead in the world—competitiveness, envy, and dependence on recognition and rewards. . . .

Yet, in the face of all of this, we know that the objectivity and social neutrality of science and scientists are supposed to be what distinguishes the pursuit of knowledge by scientific means from that pursuit by other means. Neutrality is believed to be an inherent and defining feature of science. It is an interesting paradox, however, that even the idea itself of objectivity and social neutrality as a characteristic or even requirement of science is not an inherently logical internal achievement of modern science, but rather the product of social and political forces in the 17th century, in the view of van den Daele (1977). A part of the reform and New Learning movements of Puritan England prior to 1660, Baconian science represented one aspect of the battle against the philosophical authority of the ancients, against received wisdom. Its antielitism and antiauthoritarianism were expressed in its emphasis on empiricism, on experimentalism (manual labor integrated with intellectual labor) as essential features of natural philosophy. Furthermore, Baconian science was associated with the goals of social, political, and educational reform and emancipation. But the end of the Puritan Revolution, with the Restoration in 1660, terminated this association of science with social and political concerns. This separation "is a historical compromise that follows not only from scientific purposes but also from the exploitation of opportunities for institutionalization offered within the context of Absolutism." The separation of science from social reform was essential for retaining royal protection and support for the important processes of the institutionalization of science, begun with the establishment of the Royal Society in London in 1662.

Retained from Baconian science was the emphasis on experimen-talism which could be defended as culturally neutral because of its universalistic character, and its association with utilitarian concerns, which were important to Absolutist rulers. Thus, in van den Daele's view, "The normative (social, political, religious) neutralization of the knowledge of nature, which for us is an essential element of the 'positive,' objective, and concrete character of scientific knowledge, was a condition for the institutionalization of science in the seventeenth century." His thesis suggests "that there is a connection between the rise of science as a cognitive program and the rise of science as a social structure." Thus, even though there exists for us a categorical distinction between social reform and knowledge of nature, 17th century science, in fact, *made a choice* for the institutionalization of a positivist science, objective and neutral, to the exclusion of alternative cognitive programs of knowledge of nature as well as alternative social structures of science, such as those that "would at least institutionally and normatively be associated with the requirements of human progress, enlightenment and emancipation."

It is striking and ironic that while the enlightened and emancipatory goals of 17th century Baconian science were aborted, Bacon's influence on molding science in the image of men and masculinity was considerable and long-lived—with us, in fact, to this day. Though Bacon rejected all *other* kinds of recognizable established authority, he accepted and *established* male authority as integral to the practice and philosophy of science. Continuing a process begun at least in the 16th century, Bacon elaborated the metaphors of science in sexual and gendered terms, with science as male and nature as female, a mystery to be unveiled and penetrated. Woman as a reproductive being embodied the natural, the disordered, the emotional, the irrational; man as a thinker empitomized objectivity, rationality, culture, and control. The subject of these **dualisms** and metaphors has been explored by feminist philosophers and historians of science . . . because of their importance in the molding of gender-differentiated stereotypes and in the structuring of science as male, both conceptually and organizationally. Since ideas are not generated in cultural vacuums, the exclusion of women from the practice of science and the consequent male, **patriarchal** structuring of science is reflected in the concerns, concepts, metaphors, assumptions, and language of science.

Questions for Discusson and Writing

1. Compare Bleier's analysis of the preformationists (seventeenth- and eighteenth-century scientists who believed that sperm contained completely formed, tiny humans) with Stephen Jay Gould's view of them. Do their analyses reflect gender biases?

2. According to Bleier, many feminist scholars believe that traditional scientific methods and values are male-dominated, expressed through "absolutism, authoritarianism, determinist thinking, cause-effect simplifications, androcentrism, ethnocentrism, [and] pretensions to objectivity and neutrality." How can these ways of thinking be used to increase and maintain male power in society?

3. Does the image of science as a "masculine" field persist? Develop a list of other academic and professional fields that are traditionally identified by gender. Why should feminists object to such identification? Examine the list to see if economic reward, social prestige, possibility for advancement, or other measures of professional benefits vary according to the gender assigned to the field or profession.

4. Do you accept Bleier's argument that science is a cultural institution and therefore it reflects cultural biases? Consider a scientific field that you have studied, such as biology or psychology. What (perhaps biased) beliefs about and attitudes toward females are accepted and taught in these fields?

5. Bleier states that one of the greatest motivators in scientific work is the drive for personal power. Does her view conflict with our cultural ideal of the scientist? Do you accept her observation?

Chapter Writing Topics

1. Discuss the many stereotypes that have been applied to scientists in our culture over the centuries. Draw on Heer's depiction of medieval scientists, on the revolutionaries Galileo, Darwin, and Freud, and on twentieth-century views questioning scientific attitudes and motives (Gould, Toulmin, Bleier). Why does the image of the scientist change over time?

   (a) Begin your writing process by describing scientists from different periods, perhaps freewriting on specific historical figures such as Galileo or Darwin.

   (b) Identify changes in the image according to historical ages. For example, did certain ages hold a more positive view than others? Why did this change come about?

   (c) What role does religion play in the changing status of the scientist? What other social factors might have an influence?

   (d) How have twentieth-century critics reacted to the preceding centuries' view of "men of science"? What changes can you predict will take place in coming generations, and why?

2. From the time of the industrial revolution, critics have protested the destructive environmental effects of industry and technology and have questioned the ethics of various scientific practices. What are the primary environmental concerns and ethical questions about scientific practices that concern people today? Interview a representative group of people from your campus, workplace, and neighborhood, and present your survey findings in report form. If you prefer, focus your survey on one specific issue instead—contemporary views on evolution, energy sources, or the role of women in science, for example.

3. Contemporary critics argue that scientific "knowledge" is inevitably shaped by specific cultural values. Explain how religious beliefs have historically affected the reception of scientific theories. Consider the cases of Galileo, Darwin, and Freud in particular, in addition to other

scientists and scientific theories that you may have studied. Consider the following subtopics.

(a) What were the primary religious criticisms of Copernican, Darwinian, and Freudian theory?

(b) Did such criticism limit scientific inquiry to a significant extent? Why or why not?

(c) What issues are a source of scientific/religious conflict today?

4. Develop a Freudian reading of a familiar fairy tale or nursery rhyme. Explain how it might be used to teach children about the need to control basic drives and to enhance development of the superego. Summarize the tale or rhyme for your audience. The following Freudian concepts may be of value for your analytic reading.

(a) The tale may teach children to *repress* feelings of anger or sexual desire.

(b) The tale may show the dangers of acting on the basic drives of the id.

(c) The tale may teach children that they must give up the *pleasure principle* and accept the *reality principle.*

(d) The *Oedipus complex* may serve as the tale's structuring principle.

5. Construct your own version of how daily life would be transformed in the wake of a nuclear attack, as the bombing of Hiroshima was chronicled in *Unforgettable Fire.* Consider using the following writing strategies and techniques.

(a) Use the first-person voice ("I") to personalize and dramatize the account.

(b) Set your account in an identifiable geographic and physical location—the center of town, the classroom, or a shopping mall, for example. Use actual place names.

(c) Use details from the Shalett and JBC essays for realistic descriptions of the atomic bomb's power.

(d) Consider various ways of ending the essay: an argument about nuclear war; a personal statement on the issue; a possible solution to any future perceived need for nuclear attack.

6. Explain why women and minorities have historically been marginal forces in science. Use the Bleier essay in this chapter and the Rose essay in Chapter 1 to help trace the social factors that have hindered members of either group from being represented in the Western scientific tradition. Observations drawn from personal experience may also be helpful. Analyze the importance of the following factors: economic standing; access to education; traditional assumptions about interests and ability; exposure to science and related professional fields; traditional scientific attitudes (consider the Bleier and Toulmin essays).

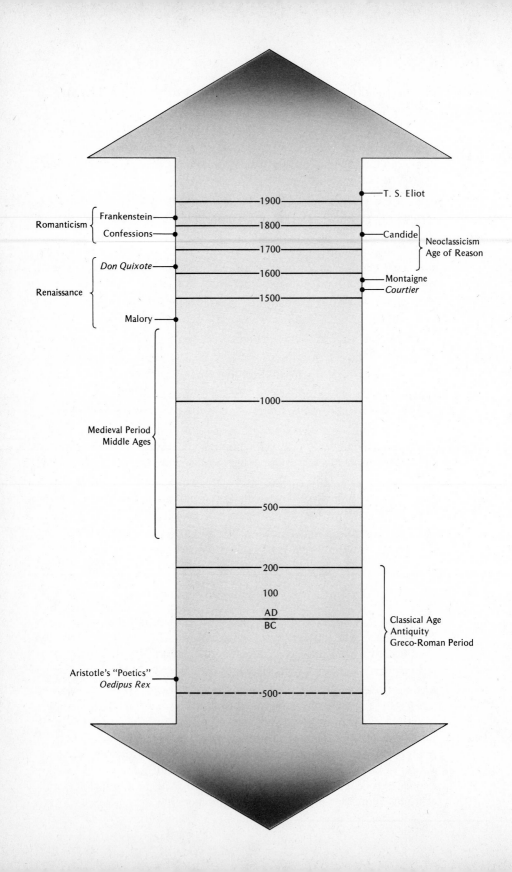

1900 — T. S. Eliot

Romanticism { Frankenstein
Confessions

1800

Candide } Neoclassicism
Age of Reason

1700

Renaissance { Don Quixote

1600 — Montaigne
— Courtier

1500

Malory

Medieval Period
Middle Ages

1000

500

200

100

AD
BC

Classical Age
Antiquity
Greco-Roman Period

Aristotle's "Poetics"
Oedipus Rex

500

CHAPTER   *4*

The Literary Tradition
≥å

Introduction

The readings in Chapter 4 are organized chronologically and include diverse genres, periods, and themes; the traditional categories of fiction and nonfiction, literature and criticism, are represented. Most of the selections are taken from the "Great Books" of Western culture. For the past two decades, however, literary critics have been absorbed in some fundamental questions relating to the nature of literary art and literary tradition. Does the term "literature" refer to any text that employs written language? Do traditional definitions of literature promote specific values and suppress the writings of certain social groups? What role should traditionally defined literary texts play in education, especially in the multicultural classrooms found in American society today?

Questions such as these have opened up the discussion of what "real" literature is and what value we should attach to the traditional Great Books. Critic Adalaide Morris, in "Dick, Jane, and American Literature: Fighting with Canons" (the final selection in this chapter), leads her readers to question whether the Western literary canon tells a story beyond the plot lines of the individual texts themselves. As a reader, you may want to consider the tradition represented here from more than the traditional perspective. The "meaning" of the texts, and of the tradition they are part of, is open to *your* interpretation. That means that the knowledge you bring to each text alters the sense you can make of it. Your familiarity with the historical period of each work, and your sensitivity to the values of your own historical age, affect the meaning you assign to each text. As you read the ancient text *Oedipus Rex,* for example, your interpretation will differ from that of a member of the original audience; you "know" a different text, one whose meaning has been altered by intervening ages and ideas—by the works of Aristotle and Sigmund Freud, for example, whose critical commentaries on the play are included.

The values of each age—the medieval ideals of chivalry, illustrated by Malory's *Le Morte D'Arthur,* for example—are present in reformulated ways in the works of later ages—in Cervantes' *Don Quixote* or in the Italian Renaissance writer Castiglione's redefinition of the courtier. The very notion of "hero" undergoes continual redefinition, with the Romantic heroes of Rousseau and Mary Shelley showing how, within the same historical period, conventions and ideals shift and change in reaction to social, historical, and subjective events.

The readings in this section call for your active critical involvement and a willingness to question received wisdom. They are representative of the ideas and writing styles that have been highly prized over the centuries. Audiences have found these works entertaining and thought-provoking, and have used them as sources of intellectual and moral instruction. As you read them, your voice will add to the continuing critical exchange that determines their place in our culture.

CLASSICAL TEXTS

Sophocles, **Oedipus Rex**

> *From the time of its composition (429 B.C.), Sophocles' Oedipus Rex has served as the classical standard against which critics have measured the success of later tragic plays. Aristotle, the ancient Greek critic, rhetorician, and philosopher, used Oedipus Rex in his Poetics to describe the elements of the perfectly conceived and produced tragedy. In its concentrated action and in the hero's rise to power, recognition of guilt, and reversal of fortune, Oedipus Rex embodies the essence of tragedy, according to Aristotle. For Sigmund Freud, the play also embodies the primal struggle children face as they establish an identity separate from that of their parent: the Oedipus complex names the psychological process of conquering the desire to overpower the father and possess the mother, which young boys experience, or the desire of young girls to compete with the mother for the father's affection. Oedipus Rex has maintained its appeal into modern times. It is still a classic play in the most fundamental sense of the term—a text deemed especially valuable for class study.*

Key Concepts

Revelation means direct communication from a god (page 202).

An **oracle** (page 202) names either the place devoted to devine revelation, a god's mouthpiece, usually a priest or priestess, or an actual revelation.

An **exile** (page 203) is a criminal or "persona non grata"—an unwanted person—who has been punished by ejection from his or her community or country.

Vengeance, or **to take revenge,** means claiming retribution for some wrong suffered (page 203).

Divination is the art of telling the future from signs in natural phenomena or dreams (page 208).

According to ancient Greek belief, one who commits an offense against a god, nature, or the moral code is in a state of **pollution** (page 209).

Statesmanship refers to the handling of political affairs; a statesman is a leader or diplomat (page 210).

Regicide means murdering a king (page 212).

The word **policy** (page 215) is sometimes used to name behavior that is shrewd, manipulative, or has some ulterior purpose, usually a political one.

Anarchy is a state of political chaos (page 215).

A **tyrant** maintains absolute power (page 222).

Someone who shows irreverence for the gods is guilty of the sin of **blas-phemy** (page 222).

The Greek notion of **fate** (page 225) means that the gods have predestined the course of a person's life.

The word **primal** (page 234) refers to an origin or archetypal experience.

Sexual relations between close blood relatives is called **incest** (page 235).

A **parricide** (page 236) is a person who has killed his father, mother, or other close relative.

To **purge** (page 237) oneself is to cleanse oneself of sin or disease.

PERSONS REPRESENTED:

OEDIPUS	MESSENGER
A PRIEST	SHEPHERD OF LAIOS
CREON	SECOND MESSENGER
TEIRESIAS	CHORUS OF THEBAN ELDERS
IOCASTE	

THE SCENE: Before the palace of Oedipus, King of Thebes. A central door and two lateral doors open onto a platform which runs the length of the facade. On the platform, right and left, are altars; and three steps lead down into the "orchestra," or chorus-ground. At the beginning of the action these steps are crowded by suppliants[1] who have brought branches and chaplets[2] of olive leaves and who lie in various attitudes of despair. OEDIPUS enters.

Prologue

OEDIPUS: My children, generations of the living
    In the line of Kadmos, nursed at his ancient hearth:
    Why have you strewn yourselves before these altars
    In supplication,[3] with your boughs and garlands?
    The breath of incense rises from the city
    With a sound of prayer and lamentation.

                        Children,
    I would not have you speak through messengers,
    And therefore I have come myself to hear you—
    I, Oedipus, who bear the famous name.

                     [To a PRIEST:
    You, there, since you are the eldest in the company,
    Speak for them all, tell me what preys upon you,
    Whether you come in dread, or crave some blessing:
    Tell me, and never doubt that I will help you
    In every way I can; I should be heartless
    Were I not moved to find you suppliant here.

---

[1] People seeking favors.   [3] Favor-seeking.
[2] Garlands; wreaths.

PRIEST: Great Oedipus, O powerful King of Thebes!
　　　You see how all the ages of our people
　　　Cling to your altar steps: here are boys
　　　Who can barely stand alone, and here are priests
　　　By weight of age, as I am a priest of God,
　　　And young men chosen from those yet unmarried;
　　　As for the others, all that multitude,
　　　They wait with olive chaplets in the squares
　　　At the two shrines of Pallas, and where Apollo
　　　Speaks in the glowing embers.
　　　　　　　　　　　　　　　Your own eyes
　　　Must tell you: Thebes is tossed on a murdering sea
　　　And can not lift her head from the death surge.
　　　A rust consumes the buds and fruits of the earth;
　　　The herds are sick; children die unborn,
　　　And labor is vain. The god of plague and pyre[4]
　　　Raids like detestable lightning through the city,
　　　And all the house of Kadmos is laid waste,
　　　All emptied, and all darkened: Death alone
　　　Battens[5] upon the misery of Thebes.

　　　You are not one of the immortal gods, we know;
　　　Yet we have come to you to make our prayer
　　　As to the man surest in mortal ways
　　　And wisest in the ways of God. You saved us
　　　From the Sphinx, that flinty singer, and the tribute
　　　We paid to her so long; yet you were never
　　　Better informed than we, nor could we teach you:
　　　It was some god breathed in you to set us free.

　　　Therefore, O mighty King, we turn to you:
　　　Find us our safety, find us a remedy,
　　　Whether by counsel of the gods or men.
　　　A king of wisdom tested in the past
　　　Can act in a time of troubles, and act well.
　　　Noblest of men, restore
　　　Life to your city! Think how all men call you
　　　Liberator for your triumph long ago;
　　　Ah, when your years of kingship are remembered,
　　　Let them not say *We rose, but later fell*—
　　　Keep the State from going down in the storm!
　　　Once, years ago, with happy augury,[6]
　　　You brought us fortune; be the same again!
　　　No man questions your power to rule the land:

---

[4] Cremation site.　　　　　　　　　　　　[6] Predicting the future.
[5] Clings to.

But rule over men, not over a dead city!
Ships are only hulls,[7] citadels[8] are nothing,
When no life moves in the empty passageways.
OEDIPUS: Poor children! You may be sure I know
All that you longed for in your coming here.
I know that you are deathly sick; and yet,
Sick as you are, not one is as sick as I.
Each of you suffers in himself alone
His anguish, not another's; but my spirit
Groans for the city, for myself, for you.

I was not sleeping, you are not waking me.
No, I have been in tears for a long while
And in my restless thought walked many ways.
In all my search, I found one helpful course,
And that I have taken: I have sent Creon,
Son of Menoikeus, brother of the Queen,
To Delphi, Apollo's place of **revelation,**
To learn there, if he can,
What act or pledge of mine may save the city.
I have counted the days, and now, this very day,
I am troubled, for he has overstayed his time.
What is he doing? He has been gone too long.
Yet whenever he comes back, I should do ill
To scant[9] whatever duty God reveals.
PRIEST: It is a timely promise. At this instant
They tell me Creon is here.
OEDIPUS: O Lord Apollo!
May his news be fair as his face is radiant!
PRIEST: It could not be otherwise: he is crowned with bay,
The chaplet is thick with berries.
OEDIPUS: We shall soon know;
He is near enough to hear us now.

                                             [*Enter* CREON

                         O Prince:
Brother: son of Menoikeus:
What answer do you bring us from the god?
CREON: A strong one. I can tell you, great afflictions
Will turn out well, if they are taken well.
OEDIPUS: What was the **oracle?** These vague words
Leave me still hanging between hope and fear.
CREON: Is it your pleasure to hear me with all these
Gathered around us? I am prepared to speak,
But should we not go in?

---

[7] Frames.   [9] Minimize.
[8] Fortresses.

OEDIPUS: Let them all hear it.
    It is for them I suffer, more than for myself.
CREON: Then I will tell you what I heard at Delphi.

    In plain words
    The god commands us to expel from the land of Thebes
    An old defilement[10] we are sheltering.
    It is a deathly thing, beyond cure;
    We must not let it feed upon us longer.
OEDIPUS: What defilement? How shall we rid ourselves of it?
CREON: By **exile** or death, blood for blood. It was
    Murder that brought the plague-wind on the city.
OEDIPUS: Murder of whom? Surely the god has named him?
CREON: My lord: long ago Laïos was our king,
    Before you came to govern us.
OEDIPUS: I know;
    I learned of him from others; I never saw him.
CREON: He was murdered; and Apollo commands us now
    To take revenge upon whoever killed him.
OEDIPUS: Upon whom? Where are they? Where shall we find a clue
    To solve that crime, after so many years?
CREON: Here in this land, he said.
                            If we make enquiry,
    We may touch things that otherwise escape us.
OEDIPUS: Tell me: Was Laïos murdered in his house,
    Or in the fields, or in some foreign country?
CREON: He said he planned to make a pilgrimage.
    He did not come home again.
OEDIPUS: And was there no one,
    No witness, no companion, to tell what happened?
CREON: They were all killed but one, and he got away
    So frightened that he could remember one thing only.
OEDIPUS: What was that one thing? One may be the key
    To everything, if we resolve to use it.
CREON: He said that a band of highwaymen attacked them,
    Outnumbered them, and overwhelmed the King.
OEDIPUS: Strange, that a highwayman should be so daring—
    Unless some faction here bribed him to do it.
CREON: We thought of that. But after Laïos' death
    New troubles arose and we had no avenger.
OEDIPUS: What troubles could prevent your hunting down the killers?
CREON: The riddling Sphinx's song
    Made us deaf to all mysteries but her own.
OEDIPUS: Then once more I must bring what is dark to light.
    It is most fitting that Apollo shows,

---

[10] Shameful corruption.

As you do, this compunction[11] for the dead.
You shall see how I stand by you, as I should,
To avenge the city and the city's god,
And not as though it were for some distant friend,
But for my own sake, to be rid of evil.
Whoever killed King Laïos might—who knows?—
Decide at any moment to kill me as well.
By avenging the murdered king I protect myself.
Come then, my children: leave the altar steps,
Lift up your olive boughs!

                             One of you go
And summon the people of Kadmos to gather here.
I will do all that I can; you may tell them that.

                                      [Exit a PAGE

So, with the help of God,
We shall be saved—or else indeed we are lost.

PRIEST: Let us rise, children. It was for this we came,
And now the King has promised it himself.
Phoibos has sent us an oracle; may he descend
Himself to save us and drive out the plague.

        [Exeunt[12] OEDIPUS *and* CREON *into the palace by the central
        door. The* PRIEST *and the* SUPPLIANTS *disperse R and L[13]. After a
        short pause the* CHORUS[14] *enters the orchestra.*

CHORUS: What is God singing in his profound
     Delphi of gold and shadow?
     What oracle for Thebes, the sunwhipped city?

Fear unjoints[15] me, the roots of my heart tremble.

Now I remember, O Healer, your power, and wonder:
Will you send doom like a sudden cloud, or weave it
Like nightfall of the past?

Speak, speak to us, issue of holy sound:
Dearest to our expectancy: be tender!

Let me pray to Athenê, the immortal daughter of Zeus,
And to Artemis her sister
Who keeps her famous throne in the market ring,
And to Apollo, bowman at the far butts of heaven—

O gods, descend! Like three streams leap against
The fires of our grief, the fires of darkness;
Be swift to bring us rest!

---

[11] Concern.
[12] Exit.
[13] Stage right and stage left.

[14] Representative group of citizens.
[15] Disturbs.

As in the old time from the brilliant house
Of air you stepped to save us, come again!

Now our afflictions have no end,
Now all our stricken host[16] lies down
And no man fights off death with his mind;

The noble plowland bears no grain,
And groaning mothers can not bear—

See, how our lives like birds take wing,
Life sparks that fly when a fire soars,
To the shore of the god of evening.

The plague burns on, it is pitiless,
Though pallid[17] children laden[18] with death
Lie unwept in the stony ways,

And old gray women by every path
Flock to the strand about the altars

There to strike their breasts and cry
Worship of Phoibos in wailing prayers:
Be kind, God's golden child!

There are no swords in this attack by fire,
No shields, but we are ringed with cries.
Send the besieger plunging from our homes
Into the vast sea-room of the Atlantic
Or into the waves that foam eastward of Thrace—

For the day ravages what the night spares—

Destroy our enemy, lord of the thunder!
Let him be riven[19] by lightning from heaven!

Phoibos Apollo, stretch the sun's bowstring,
That golden cord, until it sing for us,
Flashing arrows in heaven!
                              Artemis Huntress,
Race with flaring lights upon our mountains!

O scarlet god, O golden-banded brow,
O Theban Bacchos in a storm of Maenads,
                              [*Enter* OEDIPUS, *C.*

---

[16] Large gathering of people.   [18] Afflicted; weighed down.
[17] Pale; ashen.   [19] Split in two.

Whirl upon Death, that all the Undying hate!
Come with blinding torches, come in joy!

Scene I

OEDIPUS: Is this your prayer? It may be answered. Come,
Listen to me, act as the crisis demands,
And you shall have relief from all these evils.

Until now I was a stranger to this tale,
As I had been a stranger to the crime.
Could I track down the murderer without a clue?
But now, friends,
As one who became a citizen after the murder,
I make this proclamation to all Thebans:
If any man knows by whose hand Laïos, son of Labdakos,
Met his death, I direct that man to tell me everything,
No matter what he fears for having so long withheld it.
Let it stand as promised that no further trouble
Will come to him, but he may leave the land in safety.

Moreover: If anyone knows the murderer to be foreign,
Let him not keep silent: he shall have his reward from me.
However, if he does conceal it; if any man
Fearing for his friend or for himself disobeys this edict,
Hear what I propose to do:

I solemnly forbid the people of this country,
Where power and throne are mine, ever to receive that man
Or speak to him, no matter who he is, or let him
Join in sacrifice, lustration,[20] or in prayer.
I decree that he be driven from every house,
Being, as he is, corruption itself to us: the Delphic
Voice of Zeus has pronounced this revelation.
Thus I associate myself with the oracle
And take the side of the murdered king.

As for the criminal, I pray to God—
Whether it be a lurking thief, or one of a number—
I pray that that man's life be consumed in evil and wretchedness.
And as for me, this curse applies no less
If it should turn out that the culprit is my guest here,
Sharing my hearth.
                              You have heard the penalty.
I lay it on you now to attend to this

---

[20] Ceremonial offering.

For my sake, for Apollo's, for the sick
Sterile city that heaven has abandoned.
Suppose the oracle had given you no command:
Should the defilement go uncleansed forever?
You should have found the murderer: your king,
A noble king, had been destroyed!

Now I,

Having the power that he held before me,
Having his bed, begetting children there
Upon his wife, as he would have, had he lived—
Their son would have been my children's brother,
If Laïos had had luck in fatherhood!
(But surely ill luck rushed upon his reign)—
I say I take the son's part, just as though
I were his son, to press the fight for him
And see it won! I'll find the hand that brought
Death to Labdakos' and Polydoros' child,
Heir of Kadmos' and Agenor's line.
And as for those who fail me,
May the gods deny them the fruit of the earth,
Fruit of the womb, and may they rot utterly!
Let them be wretched as we are wretched, and worse!

For you, for loyal Thebans, and for all
Who find my actions right, I pray the favor
Of justice, and of all the immortal gods.
CHORAGOS:[21] Since I am under oath, my lord, I swear
    I did not do the murder, I can not name
    The murderer. Might not the oracle
    That has ordained the search tell where to find him?
OEDIPUS: An honest question. But no man in the world
    Can make the gods do more than the gods will.
CHORAGOS: There is one last expedient[22]—
OEDIPUS: Tell me what it is.
    Though it seem slight, you must not hold it back.
CHORAGOS: A lord clairvoyant to the lord Apollo,
    As we all know, is the skilled Teiresias.
    One might learn much about this from him, Oedipus.
OEDIPUS: I am not wasting time:
    Creon spoke of this, and I have sent for him—
    Twice, in fact; it is strange that he is not here.
CHORAGOS: The other matter—that old report—seems useless.
OEDIPUS: Tell me. I am interested in all reports.
CHORAGOS: The King was said to have been killed by highwaymen.
OEDIPUS: I know. But we have no witnesses to that.

---

[21] Chorus member.   [22] Way, method.

Choragos: If the killer can feel a particle of dread,
   Your curse will bring him out of hiding!
Oedipus: No.
   The man who dared that act will fear no curse.

> [*Enter the blind seer*
> teiresias, *led by a*
> page

Choragos: But there is one man who may detect the criminal.
   This is Teiresias, this is the holy prophet
   In whom, alone of all men, truth was born.
Oedipus: Teiresias: seer: student of mysteries,
   Of all that's taught and all that no man tells,
   Secrets of Heaven and secrets of the earth:
   Blind though you are, you know the city lies
   Sick with plague; and from this plague, my lord,
   We find that you alone can guard or save us.
   Possibly you did not hear the messengers?
   Apollo, when we sent to him,
   Sent us back word that this great pestilence
   Would lift, but only if we established clearly
   The identity of those who murdered Laïos.
   They must be killed or exiled.
                       Can you use
   Birdflight or any art of **divination**
   To purify yourself, and Thebes, and me
   From this contagion? We are in your hands.
   There is no fairer duty
   Than that of helping others in distress.
Teiresias: How dreadful knowledge of the truth can be
   When there's no help in truth! I knew this well,
   But made myself forget. I should not have come.
Oedipus: What is troubling you? Why are your eyes so cold?
Teiresias: Let me go home. Bear your own fate, and I'll
   Bear mine. It is better so: trust what I say.
Oedipus: What you say is ungracious and unhelpful
   To your native country. Do not refuse to speak.
Teiresias: When it comes to speech, your own is neither temperate
   Nor opportune. I wish to be more prudent.
Oedipus: In God's name, we all beg you—
Teiresias: You are all ignorant.
   No; I will never tell you what I know.
   Now it is my misery; then, it would be yours.
Oedipus: What! You do know something, and will not tell us?
   You would betray us all and wreck the State?
Teiresias: I do not intend to torture myself, or you.
   Why persist in asking? You will not persuade me.

OEDIPUS: What a wicked old man you are! You'd try a stone's
      Patience! Out with it! Have you no feeling at all?
TEIRESIAS: You call me unfeeling. If you could only see
      The nature of your own feelings . . .
OEDIPUS: Why,
      Who would not feel as I do? Who could endure
      Your arrogance toward the city?
TEIRESIAS: What does it matter!
      Whether I speak or not, it is bound to come.
OEDIPUS: Then, if "it" is bound to come, you are bound to tell me.
TEIRESIAS: No, I will not go on. Rage as you please.
OEDIPUS: Rage? Why not!
                      And I'll tell you what I think:
      You planned it, you had it done, you all but
      Killed him with your own hands: if you had eyes,
      I'd say the crime was yours, and yours alone.
TEIRESIAS: So? I charge you, then,
      Abide by the proclamation you have made:
      From this day forth
      Never speak again to these men or to me;
      You yourself are the **pollution** of this country.
OEDIPUS: You dare say that! Can you possibly think you have
      Some way of going free, after such insolence?
TEIRESIAS: I have gone free. It is the truth sustains me.
OEDIPUS: Who taught you shamelessness? It was not your craft.
TEIRESIAS: You did. You made me speak. I did not want to.
OEDIPUS: Speak what? Let me hear it again more clearly.
TEIRESIAS: Was it not clear before? Are you tempting me?
OEDIPUS: I did not understand it. Say it again.
TEIRESIAS: I say that you are the murderer whom you seek.
OEDIPUS: Now twice you have spat out infamy. You'll pay for it!
TEIRESIAS: Would you care for more? Do you wish to be really angry?
OEDIPUS: Say what you will. Whatever you say is worthless.
TEIRESIAS: I say you live in hideous shame with those
      Most dear to you. You can not see the evil.
OEDIPUS: It seems you can go on mouthing like this for ever.
TEIRESIAS: I can, if there is power in truth.
OEDIPUS: There is:
      But not for you, not for you,
      You sightless, witless, senseless, mad old man!
TEIRESIAS: You are the madman. There is no one here
      Who will not curse you soon, as you curse me.
OEDIPUS: You child of endless night! You can not hurt me
      Or any other man who sees the sun.
TEIRESIAS: True: it is not from me your fate will come.
      That lies within Apollo's competence,

    As it is his concern.

OEDIPUS: Tell me:

    Are you speaking for Creon, or for yourself?

TEIRESIAS: Creon is no threat. You weave your own doom.

OEDIPUS: Wealth, power, craft of **statesmanship!**

    Kingly position, everywhere admired!

    What savage envy is stored up against these,

    If Creon, whom I trusted, Creon my friend,

    For this great office which the city once

    Put in my hands unsought—if for this power

    Creon desires in secret to destroy me!

    He has brought this decrepit fortune-teller, this

    Collector of dirty pennies, this prophet fraud—

    Why, he is no more clairvoyant than I am!

                          Tell us:

    Has your mystic mummery[23] ever approached the truth?

    When that hellcat the Sphinx was performing here,

    What help were you to these people?

    Her magic was not for the first man who came along:

    It demanded a real exorcist. Your birds—

    What good were they? or the gods, for the matter of that?

    But I came by,

    Oedipus, the simple man, who knows nothing—

    I thought it out for myself, no birds helped me!

    And this is the man you think you can destroy,

    That you may be close to Creon when he's king!

    Well, you and your friend Creon, it seems to me,

    Will suffer most. If you were not an old man,

    You would have paid already for your plot.

CHORAGOS: We can not see that his words or yours

    Have been spoken except in anger, Oedipus,

    And of anger we have no need. How can God's will

    Be accomplished best? That is what most concerns us.

TEIRESIAS: You are a king. But where argument's concerned

    I am your man, as much a king as you.

    I am not your servant, but Apollo's.

    I have no need of Creon to speak for me.

    Listen to me. You mock my blindness, do you?

    But I say that you, with both your eyes, are blind:

    You can not see the wretchedness of your life,

    Nor in whose house you live, no, nor with whom.

    Who are your father and mother? Can you tell me?

    You do not even know the blind wrongs

---

[23] Hypocritical acting.

That you have done them, on earth and in the world below.
But the double lash of your parents' curse will whip you
Out of this land some day, with only night
Upon your precious eyes.
Your cries then—where will they not be heard?
What fastness[24] of Kithairon will not echo them?
And that bridal-descant[25] of yours—you'll know it then,
The song they sang when you came here to Thebes
And found your misguided berthing.[26]
And this, and more, that you can not guess at now,
Will bring you to yourself among your children.

Be angry, then. Curse Creon. Curse my words.
I tell you, no man that walks upon the earth
Shall be rooted out more horribly than you.

OEDIPUS: Am I to bear this from him?—Damnation
    Take you! Out of this place! Out of my sight!

TEIRESIAS: I would not have come at all if you had not asked me.

OEDIPUS: Could I have told that you'd talk nonsense, that
    You'd come here to make a fool of yourself, and of me?

TEIRESIAS: A fool? Your parents thought me sane enough.

OEDIPUS: My parents again!—Wait: who were my parents?

TEIRESIAS: This day will give you a father, and break your heart.

OEDIPUS: Your infantile riddles! Your damned abracadabra!

TEIRESIAS: You were a great man once at solving riddles.

OEDIPUS: Mock me with that if you like; you will find it true.

TEIRESIAS: It was true enough. It brought about your ruin.

OEDIPUS: But if it saved this town?

TEIRESIAS:
    [To the PAGE:
                        Boy, give me your hand.

OEDIPUS: Yes, boy; lead him away.
                        —While you are here
    We can do nothing. Go; leave us in peace.

TEIRESIAS: I will go when I have said what I have to say.
    How can you hurt me? And I tell you again:
    The man you have been looking for all this time,
    The damned man, the murderer of Laïos,
    That man is in Thebes. To your mind he is foreign-born,
    But it will soon be shown that he is a Theban,
    A revelation that will fail to please.
                        A blind man,
    Who has his eyes now; a penniless man, who is rich now;
    And he will go tapping the strange earth with his staff
    To the children with whom he lives now he will be

---

[24] Remote area.   [26] Home.
[25] Marriage song.

Brother and father—the very same; to her
Who bore him, son and husband—the very same
Who came to his father's bed, wet with his father's blood.

Enough. Go think that over.
If later you find error in what I have said,
You may say that I have no skill in prophecy.

> [*Exit* TEIRESIAS, *led by his*
> PAGE. OEDIPUS *goes into the*
> *palace.*

CHORUS: The Delphic stone of prophecies
Remembers ancient **regicide**
And a still bloody hand.
That killer's hour of flight has come.
He must be stronger than riderless
Coursers[27] of untiring wind,
For the son of Zeus armed with his father's thunder
Leaps in lightning after him;
And the Furies[28] follow him, the sad Furies.
Holy Parnassos' peak of snow
Flashes and blinds that secret man,
That all shall hunt him down:
Though he may roam the forest shade
Like a bull gone wild from pasture
To rage through glooms of stone.
Doom comes down on him; flight will not avail him;
For the world's heart calls him desolate,
And the immortal Furies follow, for ever follow.

But now a wilder thing is heard
From the old man skilled at hearing Fate in the wingbeat of a bird.
Bewildered as a blown bird, my soul hovers and can not find
Foothold in this debate, or any reason or rest of mind,
But no man ever brought—none can bring
Proof of strife between Thebes' royal house,
Labdakos' line, and the son of Polybos;
And never until now has any man brought word
Of Laïos' dark death staining Oedipus the King.

Divine Zeus and Apollo hold
Perfect intelligence alone of all tales every told;
And well though this diviner works, he works in his own night;
No man can judge that rough unknown or trust in second sight,
For wisdom changes hands among the wise.

---

[27] Fast horses.   [28] Avenging goddesses.

Shall I believe my great lord criminal
At a raging word that a blind old man let fall?
I saw him, when the carrion woman faced him of old,
Prove his heroic mind! These evil words are lies.

Scene II

CREON: Men of Thebes:
   I am told that heavy accusations
   Have been brought against me by King Oedipus.

   I am not the kind of man to bear this tamely.

   If in these present difficulties
   He holds me accountable for any harm to him
   Through anything I have said or done—why, then,
   I do not value life in this dishonor.
   It is not as though this rumor touched upon
   Some private indiscretion. The matter is grave.
   The fact is that I am being called disloyal
   To the State, to my fellow citizens, to my friends.
CHORAGOS: He may have spoken in anger, not from his mind.
CREON: But did you not hear him say I was the one
   Who seduced the old prophet into lying?
CHORAGOS: The thing was said; I do not know how seriously.
CREON: But you were watching him! Were his eyes steady?
   Did he look like a man in his right mind?
CHORAGOS: I do not know.
   I can not judge the behavior of great men.
   But here is the King himself.
                                          [*Enter* OEDIPUS
OEDIPUS: So you dared come back.
   Why? How brazen of you to come to my house,
   You murderer!
                          Do you think I do not know
   That you plotted to kill me, plotted to steal my throne?
   Tell me in God's name: am I coward, a fool,
   That you should dream you could accomplish this?
   A fool who could not see your slippery game?
   A coward, not to fight back when I saw it?
   You are the fool, Creon, are you not? hoping
   Without support or friends to get a throne?
   Thrones may be won or bought: you could do neither.
CREON: Now listen to me. You have talked; let me talk, too.
   You can not judge unless you know the facts.
OEDIPUS: You speak well: there is one fact; but I find it hard
   To learn from the deadliest enemy I have.

CREON: That above all I must dispute with you.

OEDIPUS: That above all I will not hear you deny.

CREON: If you think there is anything good in being stubborn
    Against all reason, then I say you are wrong.

OEDIPUS: If you think a man can sin against his own kind
    And not be punished for it, I say you are mad.

CREON: I agree. But tell me: what have I done to you?

OEDIPUS: You advised me to send for that wizard, did you not?

CREON: I did. I should do it again.

OEDIPUS: Very well. Now tell me:
    How long has it been since Laïos—

CREON: What of Laïos?

OEDIPUS: Since he vanished in that onset by the road?

CREON: It was long ago, a long time.

OEDIPUS: And this prophet,
    Was he practicing here then?

CREON: He was; and with honor, as now.

OEDIPUS: Did he speak of me at that time?

CREON: He never did;
    At least, not when I was present.

OEDIPUS: But . . . the enquiry?
    I suppose you held one?

CREON: We did, but we learned nothing.

OEDIPUS: Why did the prophet not speak against me then?

CREON: I do not know; and I am the kind of man
    Who holds his tongue when he has no facts to go on.

OEDIPUS: There's one fact that you know, and you could tell it.

CREON: What fact is that? If I know it, you shall have it.

OEDIPUS: If he were not involved with you, he could not say
    That it was I who murdered Laïos.

CREON: If he says that, you are the one that knows it!—
    But now it is my turn to question you.

OEDIPUS: Put your questions. I am no murderer.

CREON: First, then: You married my sister?

OEDIPUS: I married your sister.

CREON: And you rule the kingdom equally with her?

OEDIPUS: Everything that she wants she has from me.

CREON: And I am the third, equal to both of you?

OEDIPUS: That is why I call you a bad friend.

CREON: No. Reason it out, as I have done.
    Think of this first: Would any sane man prefer
    Power, with all a king's anxieties,
    To that same power and the grace of sleep?
    Certainly not I.
    I have never longed for the king's power—only his rights.
    Would any wise man differ from me in this?
    As matters stand, I have my way in everything

With your consent, and no responsibilities.
If I were king, I should be a slave to **policy.**

How could I desire a scepter[29] more
Than what is now mine—untroubled influence?
No, I have not gone mad; I need no honors,
Except those with the perquisites[30] I have now.
I am welcome everywhere; every man salutes me,
And those who want your favor seek my ear,
Since I know how to manage what they ask.
Should I exchange this ease for that anxiety?
Besides, no sober mind is treasonable.
I hate **anarchy**
And never would deal with any man who likes it.

Test what I have said. Go to the priestess
At Delphi, ask if I quoted her correctly.
And as for this other thing: if I am found
Guilty of treason with Teiresias,
Then sentence me to death! You have my word
It is a sentence I should cast my vote for—
But not without evidence!
                    You do wrong
When you take good men for bad, bad men for good.
A true friend thrown aside—why, life itself
Is not more precious!
                    In time you will know this well:
For time, and time alone, will show the just man,
Though scoundrels are discovered in a day.
CHORAGOS: This is well said, and a prudent man would ponder it.
     Judgments too quickly formed are dangerous.
OEDIPUS: But is he not quick in his duplicity?
     And shall I not be quick to parry[31] him?
     Would you have me stand still, hold my peace, and let
     This man win everything, through my inaction?
CREON: And you want—what is it, then? To banish me?
OEDIPUS: No, not exile. It is your death I want,
     So that all the world may see what treason means.
CREON: You will persist, then? You will not believe me?
OEDIPUS: How can I believe you?
CREON: Then you are a fool.
OEDIPUS: To save myself?
CREON: In justice, think of me.
OEDIPUS: You are evil incarnate.[32]

---

[29] Symbol of authority.
[30] Benefits.

[31] Fight off.
[32] In the flesh.

CREON: But suppose that you are wrong?
OEDIPUS: Still I must rule.
CREON: But not if you rule badly.
OEDIPUS: O city, city!
CREON: It is my city, too!
CHORAGOS: Now, my lords, be still. I see the Queen,
      Iocastê, coming from her palace chambers;
      And it is time she came, for the sake of you both.
      This dreadful quarrel can be resolved through her.

                                        [*Enter* IOCASTE

IOCASTE: Poor foolish men, what wicked din is this?
      With Thebes sick to death, is it not shameful
      That you should rake some private quarrel up?

                              [*To* OEDIPUS:
      Come into the house.

                  —And you, Creon, go now:
      Let us have no more of this tumult over nothing.
CREON: Nothing? No, sister: what your husband plans for me
      Is one of two great evils: exile or death.
OEDIPUS: He is right.

            Why, woman I have caught him squarely
      Plotting against my life.
CREON: No! Let me die
      Accurst[33] if ever I have wished you harm!
IOCASTE: Ah, believe it, Oedipus!
      In the name of the gods, respect this oath of his
      For my sake, for the sake of these people here!
CHORAGOS: Open your mind to her, my lord. Be ruled by her, I beg you!
OEDIPUS: What would you have me do?
CHORAGOS: Respect Creon's word. He has never spoken like a fool,
      And now he has sworn an oath.
OEDIPUS: You know what you ask?
CHORAGOS: I do.
OEDIPUS: Speak on, then.
CHORAGOS: A friend so sworn should not be baited so,
      In blind malice; and without final proof.
OEDIPUS: You are aware, I hope, that what you say
      Means death for me, or exile at the least.
CHORAGOS: No, I swear by Helios, first in Heaven!
      May I die friendless and accurst,
      The worst of deaths, if ever I meant that!
      It is the withering fields
      That hurt my sick heart:
      Must we bear all these ills,
      And now your bad blood as well?

[33] Cursed.

OEDIPUS: Then let him go. And let me die, if I must,
　　　Or be driven by him in shame from the land of Thebes.
　　　It is your unhappiness, and not his talk,
　　　That touches me.
　　　　　　　　　　As for him—
　　　Wherever he goes, hatred will follow him.
CREON: Ugly in yielding, as you were ugly in rage!
　　　Natures like yours chiefly torment themselves.
OEDIPUS: Can you not go? Can you not leave me?
CREON:　　　　　　　　　　　　　　　　I can.
　　　You do not know me; but the city knows me,
　　　And in its eyes I am just, if not in yours.

　　　　　　　　　　　　　　　　　　[*Exit* CREON

CHORAGOS: Lady Iocastê, did you not ask the King to go to his chambers?
IOCASTE: First tell me what has happened.
CHORAGOS: There was suspicion without evidence; yet it rankled[34]
　　　As even false charges will.
IOCASTE:　　　　　　　　　　On both sides?
CHORAGOS:　　　　　　　　　　　　　On both.
IOCASTE:　　　　　　　　　　　　　　　But what was said?
CHORAGOS: Oh let it rest, let it be done with!
　　　Have we not suffered enough?
OEDIPUS: You see to what your decency has brought you:
　　　You have made difficulties where my heart saw none.
CHORAGOS: Oedipus, it is not once only I have told you—
　　　You must know I should count myself unwise
　　　To the point of madness, should I now forsake you—
　　　　　You, under whose hand,
　　　　　　In the storm of another time,
　　　　　Our dear land sailed out free.
　　　　　　But now stand fast at the helm!
IOCASTE: In God's name, Oedipus, inform your wife as well:
　　　Why are you so set in this hard anger?
OEDIPUS: I will tell you, for none of these men deserves
　　　My confidence as you do. It is Creon's work,
　　　His treachery, his plotting against me.
IOCASTE: Go on, if you can make this clear to me.
OEDIPUS: He charges me with the murder of Laïos.
IOCASTE: Has he some knowledge? Or does he speak from hearsay?
OEDIPUS: He would not commit himself to such a charge,
　　　But he has brought in that damnable soothsayer[35]
　　　To tell his story.
IOCASTE:　　　　　Set your mind at rest.
　　　If it is a question of soothsayers, I tell you

---

[34] Irritated.　　　　　　　　　　[35] Fortuneteller.

That you will find no man whose craft gives knowledge
Of the unknowable.
                        Here is my proof:

An oracle was reported to Laïos once
(I will not say from Phoibos himself, but from
His appointed ministers, at any rate)
That his doom would be death at the hands of his own son—
His son, born of his flesh and of mine!

Now, you remember the story: Laïos was killed
By marauding[36] strangers where three highways meet;
But his child had not been three days in this world
Before the King had pierced the baby's ankles
And left him to die on a lonely mountainside.

Thus, Apollo never caused that child
To kill his father, and it was not Laïos' fate
To die at the hands of his son, as he had feared.
This is what prophets and prophecies are worth!
Have no dread of them.
                        It is God himself
Who can show us what he wills, in his own way.

OEDIPUS: How strange a shadowy memory crossed my mind,
    Just now while you were speaking; it chilled my heart.

IOCASTE: What do you mean? What memory do you speak of?

OEDIPUS: If I understand you, Laïos was killed
    At a place where three roads meet.

IOCASTE: So it was said;
    We have no later story.

OEDIPUS: Where did it happen?

IOCASTE: Phokis, it is called: at a place where the Theban Way
    Divides into the roads toward Delphi and Daulia.

OEDIPUS: When?

IOCASTE: We had the news not long before you came
    And proved the right to your succession here.

OEDIPUS: Ah, what net has God been weaving for me?

IOCASTE: Oedipus! Why does this trouble you?

OEDIPUS: Do not ask me yet.
    First, tell me how Laïos looked, and tell me
    How old he was.

IOCASTE: He was tall, his hair just touched
    With white; his form was not unlike your own.

OEDIPUS: I think that I myself may be accurst
    By my own ignorant edict.

---

[36] Raiding.

Iocaste: You speak strangely.
It makes me tremble to look at you, my King.

Oedipus: I am not sure that the blind man can not see.
But I should know better if you were to tell me—

Iocaste: Anything—though I dread to hear you ask it.

Oedipus: Was the King lightly escorted, or did he ride
With a large company, as a ruler should?

Iocaste: There were five men with him in all: one was a herald,
And a single chariot, which he was driving.

Oedipus: Alas, that makes it plain enough!
                    But who—
Who told you how it happened?

Iocaste: A household servant,
The only one to escape.

Oedipus: And is he still
A servant of ours?

Iocaste: No; for when he came back at last
And found you enthroned in the place of the dead king,
He came to me, touched my hand with his, and begged
That I would send him away to the frontier district
Where only the shepherds go—
As far away from the city as I could send him.
I granted his prayer; for although the man was a slave,
He had earned more than this favor at my hands.

Oedipus: Can he be called back quickly?

Iocaste: Easily.
But why?

Oedipus: I have taken too much upon myself
Without enquiry; therefore I wish to consult him.

Iocaste: Then he shall come.
                    But am I not one also
To whom you might confide these fears of yours?

Oedipus: That is your right; it will not be denied you,
Now least of all; for I have reached a pitch
Of wild foreboding.[37] Is there anyone
To whom I should sooner speak?

Polybos of Corinth is my father.
My mother is a Dorian: Meropê.
I grew up chief among the men of Corinth
Until a strange thing happened—
Not worth my passion, it may be, but strange.

At a feast, a drunken man maundering in his cups[38]
Cries out that I am not my father's son!

---

[37] Sense of coming evil.   [38] Self-pitying.

I contained myself that night, though I felt anger
And a sinking heart. The next day I visited
My father and mother, and questioned them. They stormed,
Calling it all the slanderous rant[39] of a fool;
And this relieved me. Yet the suspicion
Remained always aching in my mind;
I knew there was talk; I could not rest;
And finally, saying nothing to my parents,
I went to the shrine at Delphi.
The god dismissed my question without reply;
He spoke of other things.
                              Some were clear,
Full of wretchedness, dreadful, unbearable:
As, that I should lie with my own mother, breed
Children from whom all men would turn their eyes;
And that I should be my father's murderer.

I heard all this, and fled. And from that day
Corinth to me was only in the stars
Descending in that quarter of the sky,
As I wandered farther and farther on my way
To a land where I should never see the evil
Sung by the oracle. And I came to this country
Where, so you say, King Laïos was killed.

I will tell you all that happened there, my lady.
There were three highways
Coming together at a place I passed;
And there a herald came towards me, and a chariot
Drawn by horses, with a man such as you describe
Seated in it. The groom leading the horses
Forced me off the road at his lord's command;
But as this charioteer lurched over towards me
I struck him in my rage. The old man saw me
And brought his double goad[40] down upon my head
As I came abreast.
                        He was paid back, and more!
Swinging my club in this right hand I knocked him
Out of his car, and he rolled on the ground.
                                                  I killed him.

I killed them all.
Now if that stranger and Laïos were—kin,
Where is a man more miserable than I?
More hated by the gods? Citizen and alien alike

---

[39] Raving.   [40] Whip.

Must never shelter me or speak to me—
I must be shunned by all.

                    And I myself
Pronounced this malediction[41] upon myself!

Think of it: I have touched you with these hands,
These hands that killed your husband. What defilement!

Am I all evil, then? It must be so,
Since I must flee from Thebes, yet never again
See my own countrymen, my own country,
For fear of joining my mother in marriage
And killing Polybos, my father.

                         Ah,
If I was created so, born to this fate,
Who could deny the savagery of God?

O holy majesty of heavenly powers!
May I never see that day! Never!
Rather let me vanish from the race of men
Then know the abomination[42] destined me!

CHORAGOS: We too, my lord, have felt dismay at this.
    But there is hope: you have yet to hear the shepherd.

OEDIPUS: Indeed, I fear no other hope is left me.

IOCASTE: What do you hope from him when he comes?

OEDIPUS: This much:
If his account of the murder tallies with yours,
Then I am cleared.

IOCASTE: What was it that I said
Of such importance?

OEDIPUS: Why, "marauders," you said,
Killed the King, according to this man's story.
If he maintains that still, if there were several,
Clearly the guilt is not mine: I was alone.
But if he says one man, singlehanded, did it,
Then the evidence all points to me.

IOCASTE: You may be sure that he said there were several;
And can he call back that story now? He can not.
The whole city heard it as plainly as I.
But suppose he alters some detail of it:
He can not ever show that Laïos' death
Fulfilled the oracle: for Apollo said
My child was doomed to kill him; and my child—
Poor baby!—it was my child that died first.

---

[41] Curse.   [42] Loathsome act.

No. From now on, where oracles are concerned,
I would not waste a second thought on any.
OEDIPUS: You may be right.

                                  But come: let someone go
For the shepherd at once. This matter must be settled.
IOCASTE: I will send for him.

        I would not wish to cross you in anything,
And surely not in this.—Let us go in.

                              [Exeunt into the palace

CHORUS: Let me be reverent in the ways of right,
    Lowly the paths I journey on;
    Let all my words and actions keep
    The laws of the pure universe
    From highest Heaven handed down.
    For Heaven is their bright nurse,
    Those generations of the realms of light;
    Ah, never of mortal kind were they begot,
    Nor are they slaves of memory, lost in sleep:
    Their Father is greater than Time, and ages not.

    The **tyrant** is a child of Pride
    Who drinks from his great sickening cup
    Recklessness and vanity,
    Until from his high crest[43] headlong
    He plummets to the dust of hope.
    That strong man is not strong.
    But let no fair ambition be denied;
    May God protect the wrestler for the State
    In government, in comely policy,
    Who will fear God, and on His ordinance[44] wait.

    Haughtiness and the high hand of disdain
    Tempt and outrage God's holy law;
    And any mortal who dares hold
    No immortal Power in awe
    Will be caught up in a net of pain:
    The price for which his levity[45] is sold.
    Let each man take due earnings, then,
    And keep his hands from holy things,
    And from **blasphemy** stand apart—
    Else the crackling blast of heaven
    Blows on his head, and on his desperate heart;
    Though fools will honor impious[46] men,
    In their cities no tragic poet sings.

---

[43] High point.
[44] Command, law.

[45] Disrespect; joking.
[46] Blasphemous.

Shall we lose faith in Delphi's obscurities,[47]
We who have heard the world's core
Discredited, and the sacred wood
Of Zeus at Elis praised no more?
The deeds and the strange prophecies
Must make a pattern yet to be understood.
Zeus, if indeed you are lord of all,
Throned in light over night and day,
Mirror this in your endless mind:
Our masters call the oracle
Words on the wind, and the Delphic vision blind!
Their hearts no longer know Apollo,
And reverence for the gods has died away.

Scene III

[*Enter* IOCASTE

IOCASTE: Princes of Thebes, it has occurred to me
    To visit the altars of the gods, bearing
    These branches as a suppliant, and this incense.
    Our King is not himself: his noble soul
    Is overwrought with fantasies of dread,
    Else he would consider
    The new prophecies in the light of the old.
    He will listen to any voice that speaks disaster,
    And my advice goes for nothing.

                        [*She approaches the altar, R.*
                        To you, then, Apollo,
    Lycean lord, since you are nearest, I turn in prayer.
    Receive these offerings, and grant us deliverance
    From defilement. Our hearts are heavy with fear
    When we see our leader distracted, as helpless sailors
    Are terrified by the confusion of their helmsman.

                                    [*Enter* MESSENGER

MESSENGER: Friends, no doubt you can direct me:
    Where shall I find the house of Oedipus,
    Or, better still, where is the King himself?
CHORAGOS: It is this very place, stranger; he is inside.
    This is his wife and mother of his children.
MESSENGER: I wish her happiness in a happy house,
    Blest in all the fulfillment of her marriage.
IOCASTE: I wish as much for you: your courtesy
    Deserves a like good fortune. But now, tell me:
    Why have you come? What have you to say to us?
MESSENGER: Good news, my lady, for your house and your husband.

---

[47] Mysteries.

IOCASTE: What news? Who sent you here?

MESSENGER: I am from Corinth.
   The news I bring ought to mean joy for you,
   Though it may be you will find some grief in it.

IOCASTE: What is it? How can it touch us in both ways?

MESSENGER: The word is that the people of the Isthmus
   Intend to call Oedipus to be their king.

IOCASTE: But old King Polybos—is he not reigning still?

MESSENGER: No. Death holds him in his sepulchre.[48]

IOCASTE: What are you saying? Polybos is dead?

MESSENGER: If I am not telling the truth, may I die myself.

IOCASTE:

                                    [To a MAIDSERVANT:

   Go in, go quickly; tell this to your master.

   O riddlers of God's will, where are you now!
   This was the man whom Oedipus, long ago,
   Feared so, fled so, in dread of destroying him—
   But it was another fate by which he died.

                              [Enter OEDIPUS, C.

OEDIPUS: Dearest Iocastê, why have you sent for me?

IOCASTE: Listen to what this man says, and then tell me
   What has become of the solemn prophecies.

OEDIPUS: Who is this man? What is his news for me?

IOCASTE: He has come from Corinth to announce your father's death!

OEDIPUS: Is it true, stranger? Tell me in your own words.

MESSENGER: I can not say it more clearly: the King is dead.

OEDIPUS: Was it by treason? Or by an attack of illness?

MESSENGER: A little thing brings old men to their rest.

OEDIPUS: It was sickness, then?

MESSENGER: Yes, and his many years.

OEDIPUS: Ah!
   Why should a man respect the Pythian hearth, or
   Give heed to the birds that jangle above his head?
   They prophesied that I should kill Polybos,
   Kill my own father; but he is dead and buried,
   And I am here—I never touched him, never,
   Unless he died of grief for my departure,
   And thus, in a sense, through me. No. Polybos
   Has packed the oracles off with him underground.
   They are empty words.

IOCASTE: Had I not told you so?

OEDIPUS: You had; it was my faint heart that betrayed me.

IOCASTE: From now on never think of those things again.

OEDIPUS: And yet—must I not fear my mother's bed?

---

[48] Tomb.

IOCASTE: Why should anyone in this world be afraid,
   Since **Fate** rules us and nothing can be foreseen?
   A man should live only for the present day.
   Have no more fear of sleeping with your mother:
   How many men, in dreams, have lain with their mothers!
   No reasonable man is troubled by such things.

OEDIPUS: That is true; only—
   If only my mother were not still alive!
   But she is alive. I can not help my dread.

IOCASTE: Yet this news of your father's death is wonderful.

OEDIPUS: Wonderful. But I fear the living woman.

MESSENGER: Tell me, who is this woman that you fear?

OEDIPUS: It is Meropê, man; the wife of King Polybos.

MESSENGER: Meropê? Why should you be afraid of her?

OEDIPUS: An oracle of the gods, a dreadful saying.

MESSENGER: Can you tell me about it or are you sworn to silence?

OEDIPUS: I can tell you, and I will.
   Apollo said through his prophet that I was the man
   Who should marry his own mother, shed his father's blood
   With his own hands. And so, for all these years
   I have kept clear of Corinth, and no harm has come—
   Though it would have been sweet to see my parents again.

MESSENGER: And is this the fear that drove you out of Corinth?

OEDIPUS: Would you have me kill my father?

MESSENGER: As for that
   You must be reassured by the news I gave you.

OEDIPUS: If you could reassure me, I would reward you.

MESSENGER: I had that in mind, I will confess: I thought
   I could count on you when you returned to Corinth.

OEDIPUS: No: I will never go near my parents again.

MESSENGER: Ah, son, you still do not know what you are doing—

OEDIPUS: What do you mean? In the name of God tell me!

MESSENGER: —If these are your reasons for not going home.

OEDIPUS: I tell you, I fear the oracle may come true.

MESSENGER: And guilt may come upon you through your parents?

OEDIPUS: That is the dread that is always in my heart.

MESSENGER: Can you not see that all your fears are groundless?

OEDIPUS: How can you say that? They are my parents, surely?

MESSENGER: Polybos was not your father.

OEDIPUS: Not my father?

MESSENGER: No more your father that the man speaking to you.

OEDIPUS: But you are nothing to me!

MESSENGER: Neither was he.

OEDIPUS: Then why did he call me son?

MESSENGER: I will tell you:
   Long ago he had you from my hands, as a gift.

OEDIPUS: Then how could he love me so, if I was not his?

MESSENGER: He had no children, and his heart turned to you.

OEDIPUS: What of you? Did you buy me? Did you find me by chance?

MESSENGER: I came upon you in the crooked pass of Kithairon.

OEDIPUS: And what were you doing there?

MESSENGER: Tending my flocks.

OEDIPUS: A wandering shepherd?

MESSENGER: But your savior, son, that day.

OEDIPUS: From what did you save me?

MESSENGER: Your ankles should tell you that.

OEDIPUS: Ah, stranger, why do you speak of that childhood pain?

MESSENGER: I cut the bonds that tied your ankles together.

OEDIPUS: I have had the mark as long as I can remember.

MESSENGER: That was why you were given the name you bear.

OEDIPUS: God! Was it my father or my mother who did it?
     Tell me!

MESSENGER: I do not know. The man who gave you to me
     Can tell you better than I.

OEDIPUS: It was not you that found me, but another?

MESSENGER: It was another shepherd gave you to me.

OEDIPUS: Who was he? Can you tell me who he was?

MESSENGER: I think he was said to be one of Laïos' people.

OEDIPUS: You mean the Laïos who was king here years ago?

MESSENGER: Yes; King Laios; and the man was one of his herdsmen.

OEDIPUS: Is he still alive? Can I see him?

MESSENGER: These men here
     Know best about such things.

OEDIPUS: Does anyone here
     Know this shepherd that he is talking about?
     Have you seen him in the fields, or in the town?
     If you have, tell me. It is time things were made plain.

CHORAGOS: I think the man he means is that same shepherd
     You have already asked to see. Iocastê perhaps
     Could tell you something.

OEDIPUS: Do you know anything
     About him, Lady? Is he the man we have summoned?
     Is that the man this shepherd means?

IOCASTE: Why think of him?
     Forget this herdsman. Forget it all.
     This talk is a waste of time.

OEDIPUS: How can you say that,
     When the clues to my true birth are in my hands?

IOCASTE: For God's love, let us have no more questioning!
     Is your life nothing to you?
     My own is pain enough for me to bear.

OEDIPUS: You need not worry. Suppose my mother a slave,
     And born of slaves: no baseness can touch you.

IOCASTE: Listen to me, I beg you: do not do this thing!

OEDIPUS: I will not listen; the truth must be made known.

IOCASTE: Everything that I say is for your own good!

OEDIPUS: My own good

Snaps my patience, then; I want none of it.

IOCASTE: You are fatally wrong! May you never learn who you are!

OEDIPUS: Go, one of you, and bring the shepherd here.

Let us leave this woman to brag of her royal name.

IOCASTE: Ah, miserable!

That is the only word I have for you now.

That is the only word I can ever have.

[*Exit into the palace*

CHORAGOS: Why has she left us, Oedipus? Why has she gone

In such a passion of sorrow? I fear this silence:

Something dreadful may come of it.

OEDIPUS: Let it come!

However base my birth, I must know about it.

The Queen, like a woman, is perhaps ashamed

To think of my low origin. But I

Am a child of Luck; I can not be dishonored.

Luck is my mother; the passing months, my brothers,

Have seen me rich and poor.

If this is so,

How could I wish that I were someone else?

How could I not be glad to know my birth?

CHORUS: If ever the coming time were known

To my heart's pondering,

Kithairon, now by Heaven I see the torches

At the festival of the next full moon,

And see the dance, and hear the choir sing

A grace to your gentle shade:

Mountain where Oedipus was found,

O mountain guard of a noble race!

May the god who heals us lend his aid,

And let that glory come to pass

For our king's cradling-ground.[49]

Of the nymphs that flower beyond the years,

Who bore you, royal child,

To Pan of the hills or the timberline Apollo,

Cold in delight where the upland clears,

Or Hermês for whom Kyllenê's heights are piled?

Or flushed as evening cloud,

Great Dionysos, roamer of mountains,

He—was it he who found you there,

And caught you up in his own proud

---

[49] Birthplace.

Arms from the sweet god-ravisher
Who laughed by the Muses' fountains?

Scene IV

OEDIPUS: Sirs: though I do not know the man,
I think I see him coming, this shepherd we want:
He is old, like our friend here, and the men
Bringing him seem to be servants of my house.
But you can tell, if you have ever seen him.

[Enter SHEPHERD *escorted by servants*

CHORAGOS: I know him, he was Laïos' man. You can trust him.
OEDIPUS: Tell me first, you from Corinth: is this the shepherd
We were discussing?
MESSENGER: This is the very man.
OEDIPUS: *[To* SHEPHERD

Come here. No, look at me. You must answer
Everything I ask.—You belonged to Laïos?
SHEPHERD: Yes: born his slave, brought up in his house.
OEDIPUS: Tell me: what kind of work did you do for him?
SHEPHERD: I was a shepherd of his, most of my life.
OEDIPUS: Where mainly did you go for pasturage?
SHEPHERD: Sometimes Kithairon, sometimes the hills near-by.
OEDIPUS: Do you remember ever seeing this man out there?
SHEPHERD: What would he be doing there? This man?
OEDIPUS: This man standing here. Have you ever seen him before?
SHEPHERD: No. At least, not to my recollection.
MESSENGER: And that is not strange, my lord. But I'll refresh
His memory: he must remember when we two
Spent three whole seasons together, March to September,
On Kithairon or thereabouts. He had two flocks;
I had one. Each autumn I'd drive mine home
And he would go back with his to Laïos sheepfold.—
Is this not true, just as I have described it?
SHEPHERD: True, yes; but it was all so long ago.
MESSENGER: Well, then: do you remember, back in those days,
That you gave me a baby boy to bring up as my own?
SHEPHERD: What if I did? What are you trying to say?
MESSENGER: King Oedipus was once that little child.
SHEPHERD: Damn you, hold your tongue!
OEDIPUS: No more of that!
It is your tongue needs watching, not this man's.
SHEPHERD: My King, my Master, what is it I have done wrong?
OEDIPUS: You have not answered his question about the boy.
SHEPHERD: He does not know . . . He is only making trouble . . .
OEDIPUS: Come, speak plainly, or it will go hard with you.
SHEPHERD: In God's name, do not torture an old man!

OEDIPUS: Come here, one of you; bind his arms behind him.
SHEPHERD: Unhappy king! What more do you wish to learn?
OEDIPUS: Did you give this man the child he speaks of?
SHEPHERD: I did.
    And I would to God I had died that very day.
OEDIPUS: You will die now unless you speak the truth.
SHEPHERD: Yet if I speak the truth, I am worse than dead.
OEDIPUS: Very well; since you insist upon delaying—
SHEPHERD: No! I have told you already that I gave him the boy.
OEDIPUS: Where did you get him? From your house? From somewhere
      else?
SHEPHERD: Not from mine, no. A man gave him to me.
OEDIPUS: Is that man here? Do you know whose slave he was?
SHEPHERD: For God's love, my King, do not ask me any more!
OEDIPUS: You are a dead man if I have to ask you again.
SHEPHERD: Then . . . Then the child was from the palace of Laïos.
OEDIPUS: A slave child? or a child of his own line?
SHEPHERD: Ah, I am on the brink of dreadful speech!
OEDIPUS: And I of dreadful hearing. Yet I must hear.
SHEPHERD: If you must be told, then . . .
                        They said it was Laïos' child;
    But it is your wife who can tell you about that.
OEDIPUS: My wife!—Did she give it to you?
SHEPHERD: My lord, she did.
OEDIPUS: Do you know why?
SHEPHERD: I was told to get rid of it.
OEDIPUS: An unspeakable mother!
SHEPHERD: There had been prophecies . . .
OEDIPUS: Tell me.
SHEPHERD: It was said that the boy would kill his own father.
OEDIPUS: Then why did you give him over to this old man?
SHEPHERD: I pitied the baby, my King,
    And I thought that this man would take him far away
    To his own country.
                  He saved him—but for what a fate!
    For if you are what this man says you are,
    No man living is more wretched than Oedipus.
OEDIPUS: Ah God!
    It was true!
           All the prophecies!
                 —Now,
    O Light, may I look on you for the last time!
    I, Oedipus,
    Oedipus, damned in his birth, in his marriage damned,
    Damned in the blood he shed with his own hand!
                      [*He rushes into the palace*

CHORUS: Alas for the seed of men.

What measure shall I give these generations
That breathe on the void and are void
And exist and do not exist?

Who bears more weight of joy
Than mass of sunlight shifting in images,
Or who shall make his thought stay on
That down time drifts away?

Your splendor is all fallen.

O naked brow of wrath and tears,
O change of Oedipus!
I who saw your days call no man blest—
Your great days like ghósts góne.

That mind was a strong bow.

Deep, how deep you drew it then, hard archer,
At a dim fearful range,
And brought dear glory down!

You overcame the stranger—
The virgin with her hooking lion claws—
And though death sang, stood like a tower
To make pale Thebes take heart.

Fortress against our sorrow!

True king, giver of laws,
Majestic Oedipus!
No prince in Thebes had ever such renown,
No prince won such grace of power.

And now of all men ever known
Most pitiful is this man's story:
His fortunes are most changed, his state
Fallen to a low slave's
Ground under bitter fate.

O Oedipus, most royal one!
The great door that expelled you to the light
Gave at night—ah, gave night to your glory:
As to the father, to the fathering son.

All understood too late.

How could that queen whom Laios won,
The garden that he harrowed[50] at his height,
Be silent when that act was done?

But all eyes fail before time's eye,
All actions come to justice there.
Though never willed, though far down the deep past,
Your bed, your dread sirings,[51]
Are brought to book at last.
Child by Laïos doomed to die,
Then doomed to lose that fortunate little death,
Would God you never took breath in this air
That with my wailing lips I take to cry:

For I weep the world's outcast.

I was blind, and now I can tell why:
Asleep, for you had given ease of breath
To Thebes, while the false years went by.

[*Enter, from the palace,* SECOND MESSENGER

SECOND MESSENGER: Elders of Thebes, most honored in this land,
What horrors are yours to see and hear, what weight
Of sorrow to be endured, if, true to your birth,
You venerate the line of Labdakos!
I think neither Istros nor Phasis, those great rivers,
Could purify this place of the corruption
It shelters now, or soon must bring to light—
Evil not done unconsciously, but willed.
The greatest griefs are those we cause ourselves.
CHORAGOS: Surely, friend, we have grief enough already;
What new sorrow do you mean?
SECOND MESSENGER: The Queen is dead.
CHORAGOS: Iocastê? Dead? But at whose hand?
SECOND MESSENGER: Her own.
The full horror of what happened you can not know,
For you did not see it; but I, who did, will tell you
As clearly as I can how she met her death.

When she had left us,
In passionate silence, passing through the court,
She ran to her apartment in the house,
Her hair clutched by the fingers of both hands.

[50] Ploughed.   [51] Offspring.

She closed the doors behind her; then, by that bed
Where long ago the fatal son was conceived—
That son who should bring about his father's death—
We heard her call upon Laïos, dead so many years,
And heard her wail for the double fruit of her marriage,
A husband by her husband, children by her child.

Exactly how she died I do not know:
For Oedipus burst in moaning and would not let us
Keep vigil to the end: it was by him
As he stormed about the room that our eyes were caught.
From one to another of us he went, begging a sword,
Cursing the wife who was not his wife, the mother
Whose womb had carried his own children and himself.
I do not know: it was none of us aided him,
But surely one of the gods was in control!
For with a dreadful cry
He hurled his weight, as though wrenched out of himself,
At the twin doors: the bolts gave, and he rushed in.
And there we saw her hanging, her body swaying
From the cruel cord she had noosed about her neck.
A great sob broke from him, heartbreaking to hear,
As he loosed the rope and lowered her to the ground.

I would blot out from my mind what happened next!
For the King ripped from her gown the golden brooches
That were her ornament, and raised them, and plunged them down
Straight into his own eyeballs, crying, "No more,
No more shall you look on the misery about me,
The horrors of my own doing! Too long you have known
The faces of those whom I should never have seen,
Too long been blind to those for whom I was searching!
From this hour, go in darkness!" And as he spoke,
He struck at his eyes—not once, but many times;
And the blood spattered his beard,
Bursting from his ruined sockets like red hail.

So from the unhappiness of two this evil has sprung,
A curse on the man and woman alike. The old
Happiness of the house of Labdakos
Was happiness enough: where is it today?
It is all wailing and ruin, disgrace, death—all
The misery of mankind that has a name—
And it is wholly and for ever theirs.
CHORAGOS: Is he in agony still? Is there no rest for him?
SECOND MESSENGER: He is calling for someone to lead him to the gates
    So that all the children of Kadmos may look upon

His father's murderer, his mother's—no,
I can not say it!
                    And then he will leave Thebes,
Self-exiled, in order that the curse
Which he himself pronounced may depart from the house.
He is weak, and there is none to lead him,
So terrible is his suffering.
                    But you will see:
Look, the doors are opening; in a moment
You will see a thing that would crush a heart of stone.
                    [*The central door is opened;* OEDIPUS, *blinded, is led in*

CHORAGOS: Dreadful indeed for men to see.
Never have my own eyes
Looked on a sight so full of fear.
Oedipus!
What madness came upon you, what daemon[52]
Leaped on your life with heavier
Punishment than a mortal man can bear?
No: I can not even
Look at you, poor ruined one.
And I would speak, question, ponder,
If I were able. No.
You make me shudder.

OEDIPUS: God. God.
Is there a sorrow greater?
Where shall I find harbor in this world?
My voice is hurled far on a dark wind.
What has God done to me?

CHORAGOS: Too terrible to think of, or to see.

OEDIPUS: O cloud of night,
Never to be turned away: night coming on,
I can not tell how: night like a shroud![53]
My fair winds brought me here.
                    O God. Again
The pain of the spikes where I had sight,
The flooding pain
Of memory, never to be gouged out.

CHORAGOS: This is not strange.
You suffer it all twice over, remorse in pain,
Pain in remorse.

OEDIPUS: Ah dear friend
Are you faithful even yet, you alone?
Are you still standing near me, will you stay here,
Patient, to care for the blind?
                    The blind man!

---

[52] Demon; evil spirit.   [53] Burial gown.

Yet even blind I know who it is attends me,
By the voice's tone—
Though my new darkness hide the comforter.
CHORAGOS: Oh fearful act!
What god was it drove you to rake black
Night across your eyes?
OEDIPUS: Apollo. Apollo. Dear
Children, the god was Apollo.
He brought my sick, sick fate upon me.
But the blinding hand was my own!
How could I bear to see
When all my sight was horror everywhere?
CHORAGOS: Everywhere; that is true.
OEDIPUS: And now what is left?
Images? Love? A greeting even,
Sweet to the senses? Is there anything?
Ah, no, friends: lead me away.
Lead me away from Thebes.

                       Lead the great wreck
And hell of Oedipus, whom the gods hate.
CHORAGOS: Your fate is clear, you are not blind to that.
Would God you had never found it out!
OEDIPUS: Death take the man who unbound
My feet on that hillside
And delivered me from death to life! What life?
If only I had died,
This weight of monstrous doom
Could not have dragged me and my darlings down.
CHORAGOS: I would have wished the same.
OEDIPUS: Oh never to have come here
  . With my father's blood upon me! Never
To have been the man they call his mother's husband!
Oh accurst! Oh child of evil,
To have entered that wretched bed—

                         the selfsame one!
More **primal** than sin itself, this fell to me.
CHORAGOS: I do not know how I can answer you.
You were better dead than alive and blind.
OEDIPUS: Do not counsel me any more. This punishment
That I have laid upon myself is just.
If I had eyes,
I do not know how I could bear the sight
Of my father, when I came to the house of Death,
Or my mother: for I have sinned against them both
So vilely that I could not make my peace
By strangling my own life.

Or do you think my children,
Born as they were born, would be sweet to my eyes?
Ah never, never! Nor this town with its high walls,
Nor the holy images of the gods.

For I,

Thrice miserable!—Oedipus, noblest of all the line
Of Kadmos, have condemned myself to enjoy
These things no more, by my own malediction
Expelling that man whom the gods declared
To be a defilement in the house of Laïos.
After exposing the rankness[54] of my own guilt,
How could I look men frankly in the eyes?
No, I swear it,
If I could have stifled my hearing at its source,
I would have done it and made all this body
A tight cell of misery, blank to light and sound:
So I should have been safe in a dark agony
Beyond all recollection.

Ah Kithairon!

Why did you shelter me? When I was cast upon you,
Why did I not die? Then I should never
Have shown the world my execrable[55] birth.

Ah Polybos! Corinth, city that I believed
The ancient seat of my ancestors: how fair
I seemed, your child! And all the while this evil
Was cancerous within me!

For I am sick

In my daily life, sick in my origin.

O three roads, dark ravine, woodland and way
Where three roads met: you, drinking my father's blood,
My own blood, spilled by my own hand: can you remember
The unspeakable things I did there, and the things
I went on from there to do?

O marriage, marriage!

The act that engendered me, and again the act
Performed by the son in the same bed—

Ah, the net

Of **incest,** mingling fathers, brothers, sons,
With brides, wives, mothers: the last evil
That can be known by men: no tongue can say
How evil!

---

[54] Corruption; rottenness.   [55] Detestable; hateful.

No. For the love of God, conceal me
Somewhere far from Thebes; or kill me; or hurl me
Into the sea, away from men's eyes for ever.

Come, lead me. You need not fear to touch me.
Of all men, I alone can bear this guilt.

[*Enter* CREON

CHORAGOS: We are not the ones to decide; but Creon here
        May fitly judge of what you ask. He only
        Is left to protect the city in your place.
OEDIPUS: Alas, how can I speak to him? What right have I
        To beg his courtesy whom I have deeply wronged?
CREON: I have not come to mock you, Oedipus,
        Or to reproach you, either.

[*To* ATTENDANTS:
        —You, standing there:
        If you have lost all respect for man's dignity,
        At least respect the flame of Lord Helios:
        Do not allow this pollution to show itself
        Openly here, an affront[56] to the earth
        And Heaven's rain and the light of day. No, take him
        Into the house as quickly as you can.
        For it is proper
        That only the close kindred[57] see his grief.
OEDIPUS: I pray you in God's name, since your courtesy
        Ignores my dark expectation, visiting
        With mercy this man of all men most execrable:
        Give me what I ask—for your good, not for mine.
CREON: And what is it that you would have me do?
OEDIPUS: Drive me out of this country as quickly as may be
        To a place where no human voice can ever greet me.
CREON: I should have done that before now—only,
        God's will had not been wholly revealed to me.
OEDIPUS: But his command is plain: the **parricide**
        Must be destroyed. I am that evil man.
CREON: That is the sense of it, yes; but as things are,
        We had best discover clearly what is to be done.
OEDIPUS: You would learn more about a man like me?
CREON: You are ready now to listen to the god.
OEDIPUS: I will listen. But it is to you
        That I must turn for help. I beg you, hear me.

The woman in there—
Give her whatever funeral you think proper:
She is your sister.

---

[56] Insult.   [57] Relatives.

—But let me go, Creon!
Let me **purge** my father's Thebes of the pollution
Of my living here, and go out to the wild hills,
To Kithairon, that was won such fame with me,
The tomb my mother and father appointed for me,
And let me die there, as they willed I should.
And yet I know
Death will not ever come to me through sickness
Or in any natural way: I have been preserved
For some unthinkable fate. But let that be.

As for my sons, you need not care for them.
They are men, they will find some way to live.
But my poor daughters, who have shared my table,
Who never before have been parted from their father—
Take care of them, Creon; do this for me.
And will you let me touch them with my hands
A last time, and let us weep together?
Be kind, my lord,
Great prince, be kind!
                    Could I but touch them,
They would be mine again, as when I had eyes.
                    [*Enter* ANTIGONE *and* ISMENE, *attended*

Ah, God!
Is it my dearest children I hear weeping?
Has Creon pitied me and sent my daughters?
CREON: Yes, Oedipus: I knew that they were dear to you
In the old days, and know you must love them still.
OEDIPUS: May God bless you for this—and be a friendlier
Guardian to you than he has been to me!
Children, where are you?
Come quickly to my hands: they are your brother's—
Hands that have brought your father's once clear eyes
To this way of seeing—
                    Ah dearest ones,
I had neither sight nor knowledge then, your father
By the woman who was the source of his own life!
And I weep for you—having no strength to see you—
I weep for you when I think of the bitterness.
That men will visit upon you all your lives.
What homes, what festivals can you attend
Without being forced to depart again in tears?
And when you come to marriageable age,
Where is the man, my daughters, who would dare
Risk the bane[58] that lies on all my children?

---

[58] Disease.

Is there any evil wanting? Your father killed
His father; sowed the womb of her who bore him;
Engendered[59] you at the fount[60] of his own existence!
That is what they will say of you.

                                        Then, whom
Can you ever marry? There are no bridegrooms for you,
And your lives must wither away in sterile dreaming.

O Creon, son of Menoikeus!
You are the only father my daughters have,
Since we, their parents, are both of us gone for ever.
They are your own blood: you will not let them
Fall into beggary and loneliness;
You will keep them from the miseries that are mine!
Take pity on them; see, they are only children,
Friendless except for you. Promise me this,
Great Prince, and give me your hand in token of it.

                          [CREON *clasps his right hand*
Children, I could say much, if you could understand me,
But as it is, I have only this prayer for you:
Live where you can, be as happy as you can—
Happier, please God, than God has made your father!

CREON: Enough. You have wept enough. Now go within.
OEDIPUS: I must; but it is hard.
CREON: Time eases all things.
CREON: But you must promise—
CREON: Say what you desire.
OEDIPUS: Send me from Thebes!
CREON: God grant that I may!
OEDIPUS: But since God hates me . . .
CREON: No, he will grant your wish
OEDIPUS: You promise?
CREON: I can not speak beyond my knowledge.
OEDIPUS: Then lead me in.
CREON: Come now, and leave your children.
OEDIPUS: No! Do not take them from me!
CREON: Think no longer
That you are in command here, but rather think
How, when you were, you served your own destruction.

                          [*Exeunt into the house all but the* CHORUS; *the*
                          CHORAGOS *chants directly to the audience:*
CHORAGOS: Men of Thebes: look upon Oedipus.

This is the king who solved the famous riddle
And towered up, most powerful of men.

[59] Fathered.   [60] Origin.

No mortal eyes but looked upon him with envy,
Yet in the end ruin swept over him.

Let every man in mankind's frailty
Consider his last day; and let none
Presume on his good fortune until he find
Life, at his death, a memory without pain.

Questions for Discussion and Writing

1. The term *tragedy* in everyday speech refers to some terrible occurrence usually involving death or extreme loss. Compare our contemporary sense of tragedy with the classical notion (described in the questions below) in the following ways. Use contemporary examples to illustrate and support your responses.

    - To what extent does our sense of tragedy depend on the stature of the person(s) involved, a reversal of fortune, and a personal flaw that leads to the tragic event?
    - In what way(s) are the story and character of Oedipus different from our contemporary notion of tragedy? Consider the rule of "hubris" (as the ancient Greeks called ruinous pride) in his fall, the idea of fate, and the notion of divine retribution (tragedy as a kind of punishment sent by the gods).

2. In one modern formulation of tragedy, the quality that makes a hero great is also the one that ironically brings about the hero's tragic fate. Apply this theory to the play: what quality elevates Oedipus, and is that quality responsible for his later tragic fall? Test the theory on contemporary tragic situations (political assassinations, terrorist attacks, the sudden death of a young person) to see if it helps explain our sense of what "tragic" means.

3. Examine the opening exchange between Oedipus and the priest of the city. What sort of a ruler is Oedipus?

4. Oedipus sets off the tragic chain of events by announcing his intention to find and punish the murderer of Laios. Reread his speech in Scene I: how does knowing the outcome of the story affect your understanding of his words?

5. When Tiresias refuses to answer his questions, Oedipus turns on Tiresias and treats him in an increasingly brutal way. What role do power and authority play in creating the conflict between them? Is Tiresias a threat to the king?

6. Why does Oedipus blind himself after discovering the truth? Why does Jocasta commit suicide? How do their different fates reflect their different characters?

7. How are women and lower class people depicted in the play? Does the author depend on stereotypes, or are these figures realistically drawn?

8. Are modern audiences likely to accept the ancient Greek view that Oedipus was fated to commit his crimes? Would they consider his crimes unpardonable?

9. Freud believed that the story of Oedipus teaches a powerful lesson to all

people to overcome the oedipal urges of childhood. In what way(s) does the play convey the message that oedipal impulses must be repressed?

10. In your view, does the play illustrate the ancient Greeks' mythological way of thinking or the rational method they are also known for developing? Does it illustrate both types of thinking? Refer to the Chapter 1 readings (Hamilton, Greer, and Clagett) to help formulate your response.

11. How might the ending of the play be altered in a Christian version of it? Consider Chapter 2 readings such as "The Prodigal Son."

Aristotle, from **Poetics** _____

The text of Aristotle's Poetics *not one that the author carefully designed and revised; it is a compilation of class notes and lecture fragments jotted down by Aristotle's students at some point during the fourth century* B.C. *Traditionally viewed as one of the earliest works of literary criticism, the* Poetics *takes a descriptive approach to literary works, asking such questions as: What are the work's major elements? How does the action come about? What is the source of its effects on an audience? In later ages, the Aristotelian principles outlined in the* Poetics *became prescriptive "rules" that playwrights had to follow if their works were to be accepted as having "classical" value. (This was particularly true in the Neoclassical age of the seventeenth century.) Aristotle's theory of catharsis, described in the following excerpt, can also be seen as an early version of a concept later articulated by Sigmund Freud: tragedy, and* Oedipus Rex *in particular, helps us work through deeply felt conflicts in order to find release from the tensions they produce.*

Key Concepts

The theory of **imitation** (page 240) is fundamental to Western art; Aristotle defines it in the following passage. Basically, the theory states that art duplicates life, that it re-creates experience and observation.

Aristotle's theory of **purgation** (page 241) states that viewing art, especially tragedy, rids the audience of harmful or dangerous emotions.

An Aristotelian **whole** (page 241) is another artistic concept fundamental to Western literature. All works should have a distinct beginning, a developed middle section, and a definite end.

Poetry in general seems to have sprung from two causes, each of them lying deep in our nature. First, the instinct of **imitation** is implanted in man from childhood, one difference between him and other animals being that he is the most imitative of living creatures, and through imitation learns his earliest lessons; and no less universal is the pleasure felt in things imitated. We have evidence of this in the facts of experience. Objects which in themselves we view with pain, we delight to contemplate when reproduced with minute fidelity, such as the forms of the most ignoble[1] animals and of dead bodies.

Tragedy—as also Comedy—was at first mere improvisation. The one originated with the authors of the Dithyramb,[2] the other with those of the phallic songs,[3] which are still in use in many of our cities. Tragedy advanced by slow degrees; each new element that showed itself was in turn developed. Having passed through many changes, it found its natural form, and there it stopped.

Epic poetry agrees with Tragedy in so far as it is an imitation in verse of characters of a higher type. They differ in that Epic poetry admits but one kind of meter,[4] and is narrative in form. They differ, again, in their length: for Tragedy endeavors, as far as is possible, to confine itself to a single revolution of the sun, or but slightly to exceed this limit; whereas the Epic action has no limits of time. This, then, is a second point of difference, though at first the same freedom was admitted in Tragedy as in Epic poetry.

Tragedy is an imitation of an action that is serious, complete, and of a certain magnitude; in language embellished with each kind of artistic ornament, the several kinds being found in separate parts of the play; in the form of action, not of narrative; through pity and fear effecting the proper **purgation** of these emotions.

Now, according to our definition, tragedy is an imitation of an action that is complete, and whole, and of a certain magnitude; for there may be a **whole** that is wanting in magnitude. A whole is that which has a beginning, a middle, and an end. A beginning is that which does not follow anything by causal necessity, but after which something naturally is or comes to be. An end, on the contrary, is that which itself naturally follows some other thing, either by necessity, or as a rule, but has nothing following it. A middle is that which follows something as some other thing follows it. A well-constructed plot, therefore, must neither begin nor end at haphazard, but conform to these principles.

It is evident from what has been said that it is not the function of the poet to relate what has happened, but what may happen—what is possible according to the law of probability or necessity. The poet and the historian differ not by writing in verse or in prose. The work of Herodotus might be put into verse, and it would still be a species of history, with meter no less than without it. The true difference is that one relates what has happened, the other what may happen. Poetry, therefore, is a more philosophical and a higher thing than history, for poetry tends to express the universal, history the particular.

Plots are either simple or complex, for the actions in real life, of which the plots are an imitation, obviously show a similar distinction. An action which is one and continuous in the sense above defined, I call

---

[1] Lowly, base.
[2] Irregular short poem.
[3] Cult songs.
[4] Beat of a poem by syllables.

simple, when the change of fortune takes place without reversal of the situation and without recognition.

A complex action is one in which the change is accompanied by such reversal, or by recognition, or by both. These last should arise from the internal structure of the plot, so that what follows should be the necessary or probable result of the preceding action. It makes all the difference whether any given event is a case of propter hoc or post hoc.[5] Reversal of the situation is a change by which the action veers round to its opposite, subject always to our rule of probability or necessity.

Recognition, as the name indicates, is a change from ignorance to knowledge, producing love or hate between the persons destined by the poet for good or bad fortune. The best form of recognition is coincident with a reversal of the situation, as in the *Oedipus*. This recognition, combined with reversal, will produce either pity or fear; and actions producing these effects are those which, by our definition, Tragedy represents.

A perfect tragedy should, as we have seen, be arranged not on the simple but on the complex plan. It should, moreover, imitate actions which excite pity and fear, this being the distinctive mark of tragic imitation. It follows plainly, in the first place, that the change of fortune presented must not be the spectacle of a virtuous man brought from prosperity to adversity, for this moves neither pity nor fear; it merely shocks us. Nor, again, that of a bad man passing from adversity to prosperity, for nothing can be more alien to the spirit of Tragedy: it possesses no single tragic quality; it neither satisfies the moral sense nor calls forth pity or fear. Nor, again, should the downfall of the utter villain be exhibited. A plot of this kind would, doubtless, satisfy the moral sense, but it would inspire neither pity nor fear; for pity is aroused by un-merited misfortune, fear by the misfortune of a man like ourselves. Such an event, therefore, will be neither pitiful nor terrible. There remains, then, the character between these two extremes—that of a man who is not eminently good and just, yet whose misfortune is brought about not by vice or depravity,[6] but by some error or frailty. He must be one who is highly renowned and prosperous—a personage like Oedipus, Thyestes, or other illustrious men of such families.

Fear and pity may be aroused by spectacular means; but they may also result from the inner structure of the piece, which is the better way, and indicates a superior poet. For the plot ought to be so constructed that, even without the aid of the eye, he who hears the tale told will thrill with horror and melt to pity at what takes place. This is the impression we should receive from hearing the story of the *Oedipus*. But to produce this effect by the mere spectacle is a less artistic method, and dependent on extraneous[7] aids. Those who employ spectacular means to create a

---

[5] Result of some cause.   [7] External, uninvolved.
[6] Corruption, evil.

sense not of the terrible but only the monstrous, are strangers to the purpose of Tragedy; for we must not demand of Tragedy any and every kind of pleasure, but only that which is proper to it. And since the pleasure which the poet should afford is that which comes from pity and fear through imitation, it is evident that this quality must be impressed upon the incidents. Let us then determine what are the circumstances which strike us as terrible or pitiful.

Actions capable of this effect must happen between persons who are either friends or enemies or indifferent to one another. If an enemy kills an enemy, there is nothing to excite pity either in the act or the intention—except so far as the suffering in itself is pitiful. So again with indifferent persons. But when the tragic incident occurs between those who are near or dear to one another—if, for example, a brother kills, or intends to kill, a brother, a son his father, a mother her son, a son his mother, or any other deed of the kind is done—these are the situations to be looked for by the poet.

Questions for Discussion and Writing

1. Why is imitation of life in artistic form so appealing to an audience, according to Aristotle?

2. Explain Aristotle's theory of how art works as purgation. Why does he cite pity and fear as the two emotions that most need purging and that produce the greatest sense of release?

3. Does Aristotle's theory of catharsis explain the popularity of certain films and television programs today? Apply the theory to disaster films, horror films, and television dramas to see how well the Aristotelian notion of catharsis explains our popular culture. Which films most closely match Aristotle's descriptive guidelines?

4. Aristotle writes that a successful work has three elements: a beginning, a middle, and an end. What would the effect be if one of these elements were omitted from the following texts? How would the clarity of the text be affected? How would audience reaction be changed?
   (a) An academic essay without a beginning (an introduction).
   (b) A sitcom without the middle section (the complicating part of the plot that creates some threat of disaster, embarrassment, etc.).
   (c) A biography without a conclusion about the subject.
   (d) Other common types of texts that you can name.

5. Using Aristotle's definition of plot, outline the plot of Sophocles' *Oedipus Rex*.

6. Using the same definition, outline the plot of a well-known contemporary work (a film, a popular book, or a children's story).

7. Think of a situation (either real or hypothetical) which you consider to be tragic. What elements of the situation make it tragic in the ancient Greek sense of a complex action?

Sigmund Freud, **"Oedipus Rex"** _____

*In the following essay, Sigmund Freud uses the myth of Oedipus to
illustrate his theory of children's sexual development. (See the Kagan and
Havemann article, "Psychoanalytic Theory," in Chapter 3 for an outline of
Freud's basic theories.) He cites the continual appeal of Sophocles' play—
an appeal he claims is "universal"—as support for his theory. We would
not respond so deeply and so uniformly to the tragedy, Freud believes, if it
did not stir some deeply hidden, deeply felt conflict in us. As you read,
consider whether Freud's argument lends support to Aristotle's theory of
catharsis.*

In my experience, which is already extensive, the chief part in the
mental lives of all children who later become psycho-neurotics[1] is played
by their parents. Being in love with one parent and hating the other are
among the essential constituents of the stock of psychical impulses
which is formed at that time and which is of such importance in determining the symptoms of the later neurosis. It is not my belief, however,
that psycho-neurotics differ sharply in this respect from other human
beings who remain normal—that they are able, that is, to create something absolutely new and peculiar to themselves. It is far more probable—and this is confirmed by occasional observations on normal
children—that they are only distinguished by exhibiting on a magnified
scale feelings of love and hatred to their parents which occur less
obviously and less intensely in the minds of most children.

This discovery is confirmed by a legend that has come down to us
from classical antiquity: a legend whose profound and universal power to
move can only be understood if the hypothesis I have put forward in
regard to the psychology of children has an equally universal validity.
What I have in mind is the legend of King Oedipus and Sophocles' drama
which bears his name.

The action of the play consists of nothing other than the process of
revealing, with cunning delays and ever-mounting excitement—a process than can be likened to the work of a psychoanalysis—that Oedipus
himself is the murderer of Laius, but further that he is the son of the
murdered man and of Jocasta. Appalled at the abomination[2] which he has
unwittingly perpetrated, Oedipus blinds himself and forsakes his home.
The oracle has been fulfilled.

Oedipus Rex is what is known as a tragedy of destiny. Its tragic
effect is said to lie in the contrast between the supreme will of the gods
and the vain attempts of mankind to escape the evil that threatens them.
The lesson which, it is said, the deeply moved spectator should learn
from the tragedy is submission to the divine will and realization of his
own impotence. Modern dramatists have accordingly tried to achieve a
similar tragic effect by weaving the same contrast into a plot invented by

---

[1] Anxious, disturbed people.   [2] Unnatural crime.

themselves. But the spectators have looked on unmoved while a curse or an oracle was fulfilled in spite of all the efforts of some innocent man: later tragedies of destiny have failed in their effect.

If *Oedipus Rex* moves a modern audience no less than it did the contemporary Greek one, the explanation can only be that its effect does not lie in the contrast between destiny and human will, but is to be looked for in the particular nature of the material on which that contrast is exemplified. There must be something which makes a voice within us ready to recognize the compelling force of destiny in the *Oedipus,* while we can dismiss as merely arbitrary[3] such dispositions[4] as are laid down in modern tragedies of destiny. And a factor of this kind is in fact involved in the story of King Oedipus. His destiny moves us only because it might have been ours—because the oracle laid the same curse upon us before our birth as upon him. It is the fate of all of us, perhaps, to direct our first sexual impulse towards our mother and our first hatred and our first murderous wish against our father. Our dreams convince us that that is so. King Oedipus, who slew his father Laius and married his mother Jocasta, merely shows us the fulfillment of our own childhood wishes. But, more fortunate than he, we have meanwhile succeeded insofar as we have not become psycho-neurotics, in detaching our sexual impulses from our mothers and in forgetting our jealousy of our fathers. Here is one in whom these primeval wishes of our childhood have been fulfilled, and we shrink back from him with the whole force of the repression by which those wishes have since that time been held down within us. While the poet, as he unravels the past, brings to light the guilt of Oedipus, he is at the same time compelling us to recognize our own inner minds, in which those same impulses, though suppressed, are still to be found. The contrast with which the closing Chorus leaves us confronted—

> . . . Fix on Oedipus your eyes,
> Who resolved the dark enigma, noblest champion and most wise.
> Like a star of his envied fortune mounted beaming far and wide:
> Now he sinks in seas of anguish, whelmed[5] beneath a raging
> tide . . .

—strikes as a warning at ourselves and our pride, at us who since our childhood have grown so wise and so mighty in our own eyes. Like Oedipus, we live in ignorance of these wishes, repugnant to morality, which have been forced upon us by Nature, and after their revelation we may all of us well seek to close our eyes to the scenes of our childhood.

There is an unmistakable indication in the text of Sophocles' tragedy itself that the legend of Oedipus sprang from some primeval dream-material which had as its content the distressing disturbance of a child's relation to his parents owing to the first stirrings of sexuality. At a point

---

[3] Not following any law.
[4] Explanations, opinions.

[5] Overtaken.

when Oedipus, though he is not yet enlightened, has begun to feel troubled by his recollection of the oracle, Jocasta consoles him by referring to a dream which many people dream, though, as she thinks, it has no meaning:

> Many a man ere now in dreams hath lain
> With her who bare him. He hath least annoy
> Who with such omens troubleth not his mind.

Today, just as then, many men dream of having sexual relations with their mothers, and speak of the fact with indignation and astonishment. It is clearly the key to the tragedy and the complement to the dream of the dreamer's father being dead. The story of Oedipus is the reaction of the imagination to these two typical dreams. And just as these dreams, when dreamt by adults, are accompanied by feelings of repulsion, so too the legend must include horror and self-punishment.

Questions for Discussion and Writing

1. Freud's theories on infant and child sexuality created intense hostility even within the medical profession of his time. Do you see evidence that as a writer he was aware of the potential for audience hostility? Cite examples from the text that suggest his sensitivity to his potentially critical audience.

2. Illustrate Freud's concept of the Oedipus conflict by giving concrete examples of how a child might express it through his or her actual behavior. Consider examples first of how a child might show special attachment to a parent and then of how a child might express hostility.

3. What, according to Freud, is the tragedy of Oedipus?

4. In what sense is *Oedipus Rex* a play about psychological destiny, to use Freud's term?

5. Freud sees the emotional power of the play as being in part a "warning at ourselves and our pride, at us . . . who have grown so wise and mighty in our own eyes." Explain how Oedipus embodies this kind of ruinous pride.

6. Do the literary and popular works we read or view today have the same kind of educational impact that Freud sees in the story of Oedipus? Do you believe that plays such as *Oedipus Rex* are more valuable than contemporary works as educational tools?

MEDIEVAL TALES AND RENAISSANCE PROSE

Sir Thomas Malory, from **Le Morte D'Arthur** _____

The medieval romances consist of tales of brave knights, beautiful ladies, beloved kings, and powerful sorcerers. The best known tales of this tradition are the Arthurian legends, the stories of King Arthur, his teacher the magician Merlin, Excalibur, the "sword in the stone," and the rise of Camelot, home to the Knights of the Round Table. Arthur may have been based on an historical figure, perhaps of Roman lineage. (The Romans had once conquered Great Britain.) In the legend, Arthur's most devoted knight is Sir Lancelot. This devotion does not prevent Lancelot from loving Queen Guenivere, Arthur's wife, and, as seen in the following tale, from performing chivalrous acts in her name. The code of chivalry—the ideals that governed the behavior of the fictional medieval knights—is embodied in Lancelot's deeds. The tales were printed in 1485, fourteen years after Malory's death.

Sir Lancelot departed, and when he came to the Chapel Perilous he alighted and tied his horse to a little gate. As soon as he was within the churchyard he saw on the front of the Chapel many fair rich shields turned upside-down, and many of these shields Sir Lancelot had seen knights bear beforehand. With that, he saw standing by him there thirty huge knights, taller by a yard than any man he had ever seen; they all grimaced and gnashed[1] at Lancelot. When he saw their countenances[2] he was sorely[3] afraid; so he put his shield before him and took his sword in his hand, ready for battle. The knights were all armed in black armor, ready with their shields and their drawn swords. As Sir Lancelot would have gone through them, they scattered on every side of him and gave him the way. He waxed[4] all bold and entered into the Chapel, and there he saw no light except a dim lamp burning. Then he was aware of a corpse covered with a cloth of silk, and he stooped down and cut away a piece of that cloth. At that, he felt as if beneath him the earth had quaked a little, and he was frightened. Then he saw a fair sword lying by the dead knight, and he got it in his hand and hurried out of the Chapel.

As soon as he was in the Chapel-yard, all the knights spoke to him with a grim voice and said, "Knight, Sir Lancelot, put that sword from thee or else thou shalt die!"

"Whether I live or die," said Sir Lancelot, "with no such words shall ye get it again. Therefore fight for it, if ye list.[5]

But then he past through them, and beyond the Chapel yard a fair damosel[6] met him and said, "Sir Lancelot, leave that sword behind thee or thou will die for it."

"I will not leave it," said Sir Lancelot, "for any threats."

"No," she said, "if thou did leave that sword, thou would never see Queen Guenivere."

"Then I would be a fool if I should leave this sword," said Lancelot.

"Now gentle knight," said the damosel, "I require thee to kiss me but once."

"Nay," said Sir Lancelot, "That God forbid."

"Well, sir," said she, "if thou had kissed me thy life-days had been done. But now, alas, I have lost all my labor, for I ordained this chapel for

---

[1] Grinded their teeth.
[2] Face, looks.
[3] Exceedingly.

[4] Grew.
[5] Want.
[6] Lady.

thy sake and for Sir Gawain. I once had Sir Gawain with me, and at that time he fought with that knight who lieth[7] there dead in yonder chapel, Sir Gylbert the Bastard; and at that time he smote[8] off the left hand of Sir Gylbert. Sir Lancelot, now I tell thee that I have loved thee for seven years, but no woman may have thy love except Queen Guenivere. Since I may not rejoice thee and have thy body alive, I had thought of no greater joy in this world than to have thy body dead. Then I would have embalmed it and wrapped it and so kept it for all my life-days, and daily I would have embraced thee and kissed thee as spite to Queen Guenivere."

"Ye say well!" said Sir Lancelot. "Jesus preserve me from your subtle crafts."

He took his horse and departed from her, and as the book sayeth, when Sir Lancelot had departed she made such sorrow that she died within a fortnight.[9] Her name was Hellawes the Sorceress, Lady of the Castle Nygramous.

Soon Sir Lancelot met the damosel, Sir Melyot's sister, and when she saw him she clapped her hands and wept for joy. Then they rode unto a castle nearby, where Sir Melyot lay, and as soon as Sir Lancelot saw him he knew him; but he was pale as the earth from bleeding. When Sir Melyot saw Sir Lancelot he kneeled upon his knees and cried on high, "Oh lord, Sir Lancelot, help me!"

At once Sir Lancelot leapt unto him and touched his wounds with Sir Gylbert's sword; then he wiped his wounds with a part of the bloody cloth that Sir Gylbert was wrapped in. At once he was as well as he ever was. Then there was great joy among them, and they made Sir Lancelot all the cheer that they might. So on the morn Sir Lancelot took his leave and bade Sir Melyot to hurry "to the court of my lord Arthur, for it draweth nigh[10] to the feast of the Pentecost; and there by the grace of God ye shall find me." And they parted.

Then Sir Lancelot rode through many strange countries, over moors and valleys, till by fortune he came to a fair castle. As he passed beyond the castle he thought he heard two bells ring, and then he was aware of a falcon which came flying over his head toward a high elm, with long leashes about her feet. As she flew unto the elm to take her perch, the leashes wrapped about a bough; when she would have taken flight she hung there, held fast by the legs. Sir Lancelot saw how she hung and beheld the fair falcon dangling, and he was sorry for her.

Meanwhile a lady came out of the castle and cried on high, "Oh Lancelot, Lancelot, as thou art the flower of all knights, help me to get my hawk. For if my hawk is lost, my lord will destroy me; I guarded the hawk but she slipped away from me. And if my lord husband knows it, he is so hasty that he will slay me."

---

[7] Is stretched out.   [9] Two weeks.
[8] Cut, hit.   [10] Near.

"What is your lord's name?" said Sir Lancelot.

"Sir," she said, "his name is Sir Phelot, a knight who belongs to the king of North Wales."

"Well fair lady, since you know my name and require me of knighthood to help you, I will do what I may to get your hawk; yet God knoweth I am a poor climber and the tree is passing high, with few boughs to help me."

Sir Lancelot alighted, tied his horse to the same tree, and prayed the lady to unarm him. When he was unarmed he put off all his clothes except his shirt and breeches. Then with might and force he climbed up to the falcon and tied the leashes to a large rotten bough and threw the hawk down with the bough. At once the lady got the hawk in her hand.

Sir Phelot came out of the thicket suddenly, he who was her husband, all armed and with his naked sword in his hand. He said "Oh knight Lancelot, now I have found thee as I wished!"—and stood at the bole[11] of the tree to slay him.

"Ah, lady," said Sir Lancelot, "why have ye betrayed me?"

"She hath done," said Sir Phelot, "only as I commanded her. Therefore there is no other help, for the hour has come when thou must die."

"That would be a shame to thee," said Sir Lancelot: "thou, an armed knight, to slay a naked man by treason."

"Thou gettest no other grace," said Sir Phelot, "and therefore help thyself if thy canst."

"Truly," said Sir Lancelot, "that shall be thy shame. But since thou wilt not do otherwise, take my armor with thee and hang my sword upon a bough where I may get it, then do thy best to slay me if thou canst."

"Nay, nay," said Sir Phelot, "for I know thee better than thou thinkest. Therefore thou gettest no weapon if I may keep you therefrom."

"Alas," said Sir Lancelot, "that ever a knight should die weaponless!"

Then he looked above him and below him, and over his head he saw a rough limb, a big leafless bough. He broke it off from the trunk; then he came lower and saw where his own horse stood, and suddenly he leapt on the farther side of his horse, away from the knight. Then Sir Phelot lashed at him eagerly, thinking to have slain him, but Sir Lancelot put the stroke away with the rough bough; with it he smote Sir Phelot on one side of the head, so that he fell down in a swoon on the ground. Then Sir Lancelot took Sir Phelot's sword out of his hand and struck his neck from the body.

The lady cried, "Alas, why have you slain my husband?"

"I am not the cause," said Sir Lancelot. "With falsehood you would have me slain by treason, and now it has fallen on you both."

Then she swooned as though she would die. Sir Lancelot got all his armor as quickly as he might and put it upon him for fear of further

---

[11] Trunk.

attack, since the knight's castle was so near him. Then as soon as he could he took his horse and departed, thanking God that he had escaped from that hard adventure.

So Sir Lancelot rode in many wild ways throughout moors and marshes, and as he rode in a valley he saw a knight chasing a lady with a naked sword in order to slay her. But just as the knight would have slain this lady, she cried to Sir Lancelot and prayed him to rescue her. When he saw that mischief, he took his horse and rode between them saying, "Knight, fie,[12] for shame! Why wilt thou slay this lady? Thou dost shame unto thee and all knights."

"What hast thou to do between me and my wife?" said the knight. "I will slay her despite thy head."

"That shall ye not," said Sir Lancelot, "for instead we two will have ado[13] together."

"Sir Lancelot," said the knight, "thou dost not thy part, for this lady hath betrayed me."

"It is not so," said the lady. "Truly he sayeth wrong about me. Because I love and cherish my cousin-germane,[14] he is jealous; but as I shall answer to God, there was never sin between us. But sir, as thou art called the most worshipful[15] knight of the world I require thee of true knighthood to help me and save me. For what so ever he says, he will slay me; he is without mercy."

"Have ye no fear," said Lancelot. "It shall not lie in his power."

"Sir," said the knight, "In your sight I will be ruled as ye will have me."

So Sir Lancelot rode with the knight on one side and the lady on the other. They had ridden only a short while when the knight bade Sir Lancelot turn and look behind him, and said, "Sir, yonder come men of arms riding after us."

So Sir Lancelot turned and suspected no treason. But the knight went to his lady's side and suddenly cut off her head. When Sir Lancelot had spied what he had done, he said, "Traitor, thou hast shamed me forever!" And suddenly he alighted from his horse and pulled out his sword to slay the knight. But he fell flat to the earth and gripped Sir Lancelot by the thighs and cried mercy.

"Fie on thee!" said Sir Lancelot. "Thou shameful knight, thou maist[16] have no mercy; therefore arise and fight with me."

"Nay," said the knight, "I will never arise till ye grant me mercy."

"Now I will offer thee fairly," said Lancelot. "I will unarm myself to my shirt, and I will have nothing upon me but my shirt and my sword in my hand. Then if thou canst slay me, thou art quit[17] forever."

"Nay, Sir, that I will never do."

---

[12] Oh!
[13] Fight.
[14] Blood relative.

[15] Honorable.
[16] May.
[17] Pardoned, released.

"Well," said Sir Lancelot, "take this lady and her head and bear them with thee. And here thou shalt swear upon my sword to bear them always upon thy back and never to rest till thou come to Queen Guenivere."

"Sir," said he, "that I will do, by the faith of my body."

"Now," said Lancelot, "tell me, what is your name?"

"Sir, my name is Pedyvere."

"In a shameful hour thou were born," said Lancelot.

So Pedyvere departed with the dead lady and the head and found the queen with King Arthur at Winchester. There he told all the truth.

"Sir Knight," said the queen, "This is a horrible and shameful deed, and a great rebuke for Sir Lancelot; but, not withstanding, his worship is known in many diverse countries. I shall give you this as a penance. Make ye as good shift[18] as ye can: ye shall bear this lady with you on horseback unto the Pope of Rome, and from him receive your penance for your foul deeds. And ye shall never rest one night where ye rest another; if ye go to any bed, the dead body shall lie with you."

He made his oath and so departed. And it telleth the French book, when he came to Rome the Pope bade him go back to Queen Guenivere; and in Rome his lady was buried by the Pope's commandment. Later this knight, Sir Pedyvere, fell into great goodness and was a holy man and a hermit.

Questions for Discussion and Writing

1. Describe the way the characters sound in this tale. How does their speech affect the reader's perceptions of them?

2. Is the story structured according to Aristotle's definition of a plot? If not, how is it different?

3. In the story, Lancelot is clearly a hero, one of the "good guys." Using his motives and acts as illustrations of the chivalric code, name the values the code promotes.

4. How and why is Lancelot protected from the spells of Hellawes the Sorceress?

5. What in Sir Phelot's behavior marks him as a "bad guy," an evil knight?

6. What aspect of Sir Pedyvere's murder of his wife makes it a "horrible and shameful deed"—the murder itself, or the insult it represents to Lancelot?

7. Explain the rationale behind the penance that Queen Guenivere imposes on Sir Pedyvere.

8. Does Lancelot bear any resemblance to typical comic-book heroes? How are they alike, and how are they different? Might the Arthurian stories have served the same purpose(s) for fifteenth-century audiences as comic books do for audiences today?

9. Generate in class a list of some of the popular films, television programs, and games that draw on medieval romances. What is the appeal of the tradition for modern audiences?

---

[18] Arrangements.

10. In what way(s) does the story contribute to and depart from traditional stereotypes about women and feminine behavior?

Cervantes, from **Don Quixote**

The Spanish writer Miguel de Cervantes (1547–1616) wrote what is considered to be the first novel in European literature. Before Cervantes' work, most long narratives had no unifying plot; they usually consisted of a series of adventures. Don Quixote also is organized by adventures, but it has progressive character development (meaning that we can understand a character's psychological motivation and can see him or her change throughout the story) and an overall theme. The following selection presents two episodes from Cervantes' work, completed in 1614. Cervantes treats some of the same themes as Malory did in Le Morte d'Arthur, but Cervantes' work satirizes chivalry. Still, the work has serious elements in addition to its humor; it philosophizes as well as entertains.

Chapter VIII. Of the valorous Don Quixote's success in the dreadful and never before imagined Adventure of the Windmills.

At that moment they caught sight of some thirty or forty windmills, which stand on that plain, and as soon as Don Quixote saw them he said to his squire: "Fortune is guiding our affairs better than we could have wished. Look over here, friend Sancho Panza, where more than thirty monstrous giants appear. I intend to do battle with them and take all their lives. With their spoils we will begin to get rich, for this is a fair war, and it is a great service to God to wipe such a wicked brood from the face of the earth."

"What giants?" asked Sancho Panza.

"Those you see there," replied his master, "with their long arms. Some giants have them about six miles long."

"Take care, your worship," said Sancho; "those things over there are not giants but windmills, and what seem to be their arms are the sails, which are whirled round in the wind and make the millstone turn."

"It is quite clear," replied Don Quixote, "that you are not experienced in this matter of adventures. They are giants, and if you are afraid, go away and say your prayers, whilst I advance and engage them in fierce and unequal battle."

As he spoke, he dug his spurs into his steed Rocinante, paying no attention to his squire's shouted warning that beyond all doubt they were windmills and not giants he was advancing to attack. But he went on, so positive that they were giants that he neither listened to Sancho's cries nor noticed what they were, even when he got near them. Instead he went on shouting in a loud voice: "Do not fly, cowards, vile creatures, for it is one knight alone who assails you."

At that moment a slight wind arose, and the great sails began to move. At the sight of which Don Quixote shouted: "Though you wield more arms than the giant Briareus, you shall pay for it!" Saying this, he commended himself with all his soul to his Lady Dulcinea, beseeching her aid in his great peril. Then, covering himself with his shield and putting his lance in the rest, he urged Rocinante forward at a full gallop and attacked the nearest windmill, thrusting his lance into the sail. But the wind turned it with such violence that it shivered his weapon in pieces, dragging the horse and his rider with it, and sent the knight rolling badly injured across the plain. Sancho Panza rushed to his assistance as fast as his ass could trot, but when he came up he found that the knight could not stir. Such a shock had Rocinante given him in their fall.

"O my goodness!" cried Sancho. "Didn't I tell your worship to look what you were doing, for they were only windmills? Nobody could mistake them, unless he had windmills on the brain."

"Silence, friend Sancho," replied Don Quixote. "Matters of war are more subject than most to continual change. What is more, I think—and that is the truth—that the same sage Friston who robbed me of my room and my books has turned those giants into windmills, to cheat me of the glory of conquering them. Such is the enmity he bears me; but in the very end his black arts shall avail[1] him little against the goodness of my sword."

"God send it as He will," replied Sancho Panza, helping the knight to get up and remount Rocinante, whose shoulders were half dislocated.

As they discussed this last adventure they followed the road to the pass of Lapice where, Don Quixote said, they could not fail to find many adventures, as many travellers passed that way. He was much concerned, however, at the loss of his lance, and, speaking of it to his squire, remarked: "I remember reading that a certain Spanish knight called Diego Perez de Vargas, having broken his sword in battle, tore a great bough or limb from an oak, and performed such deeds with it that day, and pounded so many Moors, that he earned the surname of the Pounder, and thus he and his descendants from that day onwards have been called Vargas y Machuca. I mention this because I propose to tear down just such a limb from the first oak we meet, as big and as good as his; and I intend to do such deeds with it that you may consider yourself most fortunate to have won the right to see them. For you will witness things which will scarcely be credited."

"With God's help," replied Sancho, "and I believe it all as your worship says. But sit a bit more upright, sir, for you seem to be riding lop-sided. It must be from the bruises you got when you fell."

"That is the truth," replied Don Quixote. "And if I do not complain of the pain, it is because a knight errant[2] is not allowed to complain of any wounds, even though his entrails[3] may be dropping out through them."

[1] Help.
[2] Wandering knight.

[3] Guts, intestines.

"If that's so, I have nothing more to say," said Sancho, "but God knows I should be glad if your worship would complain if anything hurt you. I must say, for my part, that I have to cry out at the slightest twinge, unless this business of not complaining extends to knight errants' squires as well."

Don Quixote could not help smiling at his squire's simplicity, and told him that he could certainly complain how and when he pleased, whether he had any cause or not, for up to that time he had never read anything to the contrary in the law of chivalry.

Chapter X. In which is related the device Sancho adopted to enchant the Lady Dulcinea, and other incidents as comical as they are true.

As soon as Don Quixote had hidden himself in the thicket, or oak wood, or forest, beside great El Toboso, he ordered Sancho to go back to the city, and not return to his presence without first speaking to his lady on his behalf, and begging her to be so good as to allow herself to be seen by her captive knight, and to deign[4] to bestow her blessing on him, so that he might hope thereby to meet with the highest success in all his encounters and arduous enterprises. Sancho understood to do as he was commanded, and to bring his master as favorable reply as he had brought him the last time.

This colloquy[5] Sancho held with himself: "I have seen from countless signs that this master of mine is a raving lunatic who ought to be tied up—and me, I can't be much better, for since I follow him and serve him, I'm more of a fool than he—if the proverb is true that says: tell me what company you keep and I will tell you what you are; and that other one too: not with whom you are born but with whom you feed. Well, he's mad—that he is—and it's the kind of madness that generally mistakes one thing for another, and thinks white black and black white, as was clear when he said that the windmills were giants and the friars' mules dromedaries,[6] and the flocks of sheep hostile armies, and many other things to this tune. So it won't be very difficult to make him believe that the first peasant girl I run across about here is the Lady Dulcinea. If he doesn't believe it I'll swear, and if he swears I'll outswear him, and if he sticks to it I shall stick to it harder, so that, come what may, my word shall always stand up to his. Perhaps if I hold out I shall put an end to his sending me on any more of these errands, seeing what poor answers I bring back. Or perhaps he'll think, as I fancy he will, that one of those wicked enchanters who, he says, have a grudge against him, had changed her shape to vex and spite him."

With these thoughts Sancho quieted his conscience, reckoning the business as good as settled. And there he waited till afternoon, to convince Don Quixote that he had time to go to El Toboso and back. And so well did everything turn out that when he got up to mount Dapple he

---

[4] Condescend.
[5] Conversation.

[6] Camels.

saw three peasant girls coming in his direction, riding on three young asses or fillies[7]—our author does not tell us which—though it is more credible that they were she-asses, as these are the ordinary mounts of village women; but as nothing much hangs on it, there is no reason to stop and clear up the point. To continue—as soon as Sancho saw the girls, he went back at a canter[8] to look for his master and found him, sighing and uttering countless amorous lamentations. But as soon as Don Quixote saw him, he cried: "What luck Sancho? Shall I mark this day with a white stone or a black?"

"It'll be better," replied Sancho, "for your worship to mark it in red chalk, like the college lists, to be plainly seen by all who look."

"At that rate," said Don Quixote, "you bring good news."

"So good," answered Sancho, "that your worship has nothing more to do than to spur Rocinante and go out into the open to see Lady Dulcinea del Toboso, who is coming to meet your worship with two of her damsels."

"Holy Father! What is that you say, Sancho my friend," cried Don Quixote. "See that you do not deceive me, or seek to cheer my real sadness with false joys."

"What could I gain by deceiving your worship?" replied Sancho. "Especially as you are so near to discovering the truth of my report. Spur on, sir, come, and you'll see the princess, our mistress, coming dressed and adorned—to be brief, as befits her. Her maidens and she are one blaze of gold, all ropes of pearls, all diamonds, all rubies, all brocade[9] of more than ten gold strands; their hair loose on their shoulders, like so many sunrays sporting in the wind and, what's more, they are riding on three piebald[10] nackneys, the finest to be seen."

"Hackneys[11] you mean, Sancho."

"There is very little difference," replied Sancho, "between nackneys and hackneys. But let them come on whatever they may, they are the bravest ladies you could wish for, especially the Princess Dulcinea, my lady, who dazzles the senses."

"Let us go, Sancho my son," replied Don Quixote, "and as a reward for this news, as unexpected as it is welcome, I grant you the best spoil I shall gain in the first adventure that befalls me; and, if that does not content you, I grant you the fillies that my three mares will bear this year, for you know that I left them foal on our village common."

"The fillies for me," cried Sancho, "for it is not too certain that the spoils of the first adventure will be good ones."

At this point they came out of the wood and discovered the three village girls close at hand. Don Quixote cast his eye along the El Toboso road, and seeing nothing but the three peasant girls, asked Sancho in great perplexity whether he had left the ladies outside the city.

---

[7] Female ponies.
[8] Slow run.
[9] Woven fabric.

[10] Spotted.
[11] Horses.

"How outside the city?" he answered. "Can it be that your worship's eyes are in the back of your head that you don't see that these are they, coming along shining like the very sun at noon?"

"I can see nothing, Sancho," said Don Quixote, "but three village girls on three donkeys."

"Now God deliver me from the Devil," replied Sancho. "Is it possible that three hackneys, or whatever they're called, as white as driven snow, look to your worship like asses? Good Lord, if that's the truth, may my beard be plucked out."

"But I tell you, Sancho my friend," said Don Quixote, "that it is as true that they are asses, or she-asses, as that I am Don Quixote and you Sancho Panza. At least they look so to me."

"Hush sir!" said Sancho. "Don't say such a thing, but wipe those eyes of yours, and come and do homage[12] to the mistress of your thoughts who is drawing near."

As he spoke he rode forward to receive the three village girls, and dismounting from Dapple, took one of the girl's asses by the bridle and sank on both knees to the ground, saying: "Queen and Princess and Duchess of beauty, may your Highness and Mightiness deign to receive into your grace and good liking your captive knight, who stands here, turned to marble stone, all troubled and unnerved[13] at finding himself in your magnificent presence. I am Sancho Panza, his squire, and he is the travel-weary knight, Don Quixote de la Mancha, called also by the name of the Knight of the Sad Countenance."

By this time Don Quixote had fallen on his knees beside Sancho, and was staring, with his eyes starting out of his head, and a puzzled look on his face, to the person whom Sancho called Queen and lady. And as he could see nothing in her but a country girl, and not a very handsome one at that, she being round-faced and flat-nosed, he was bewildered and amazed, and did not dare to open his lips. The village girls were equally astonished at seeing these two men, so different in appearance, down on their knees and preventing their companion from going forward. But the girl they had stopped broke the silence by crying roughly and angrily: "Get out of the way, confound[14] you, and let us pass. We're in a hurry."

To which Sancho replied: "O Princess and world famous Lady of El Toboso! How is it that your magnanimous heart is not softened when you see the column and prop[15] of knight errantry kneeling before your sublimated[16] presence?"

On hearing this, one of the two others exclaimed: "Wait till I get my hands on you, you great ass! See how these petty gentry come and make fun of us village girls, as if we couldn't give them as good as they bring! Get on your way, and let us go on ours. You had better!"

---

[12] Honor.
[13] Nervous.
[14] Damn.

[15] Foundation.
[16] (Here misused; intended: beyond description).

"Rise Sancho," said Don Quixote at this, "For I see that Fortune unsatisfied with the ill already done me, has closed all roads by which any comfort may come to this wretched soul I bear in my body. And you, O perfection of all desire! Pinnacle[17] of human gentleness! Sole remedy of this afflicted heart, that adores you! Now that the malignant enchanter persecutes me, and has put clouds and cataracts into my eyes, and for them alone, and for no others, has changed and transformed the peerless[18] beauty of your countenance into the semblance[19] of a poor peasant girl, if he has not at the same time turned mine into the appearance of some spectre[20] to make it abominable to your sight, do not refuse to look at me softly and amorously, perceiving in this submission and prostration,[21] which I make before your deformed beauty, the humility with which my soul adores you."

"Tell that to my grandmother!" replied the girl. "Do you think I want to listen to that nonsense? Get out of the way and let us go on, and we'll thank you."

Sancho moved off and let her pass, delighted at having got well out of his fix. And no sooner did the girl who had played the part of Dulcinea find herself free than she prodded her nackney with the point of a stick that she carried, and set off at a trot across the field. But when the she-ass felt the point of the stick, which pained her more than usual, she began to plunge so wildly that my lady Dulcinea came off upon the ground. When Don Quixote saw this accident, he rushed to pick her up, and Sancho to adjust the strap on the saddle which had slipped under the ass's belly. But when the saddle was adjusted and Don Quixote was about to lift his enchanted mistress in his arms and place her on her ass, the lady picked herself up from the ground and spared him the trouble. For, stepping back a little, she took a short run, and resting both her hands on the ass's rump, swung her body into the saddle, lighter than a hawk, and sat astride like a man.

At which Sancho exclaimed: "By St. Roque, the lady, our mistress, is lighter than a falcon, and she could train the nimblest Cordovan or Mexican to mount like a jockey. She was over the cropper[22] of the saddle in one jump, and now without spurs she's making that hackney gallop like a zebra. And her maidens are not much behind her. They're all going like the wind."

And so they were, for once Dulcinea was mounted, they all spurred after her and dashed away at full speed, without once looking behind them till they had gone almost two miles. Don Quixote followed them with his eyes, and, when he saw that they had disappeared, turned to Sancho and said:

"Do you see now what a spite the enchanters have against me,

---

[17] High point.
[18] Without Equal.
[19] Shape, order.

[20] Ghost.
[21] Groveling.
[22] Back.

Sancho? See to what extremes the malice and hatred they bear me
extend, for they have sought to deprive me of the happiness I should
have enjoyed in seeing my mistress in her true person. In truth, I was
born a very pattern for the unfortunate, and to be a target and mark for
the arrows of adversity. You must observe also, Sancho, that these traitors
were not satisfied with changing and transforming Dulcinea, but transformed her and changed her into a figure as low and ugly as that peasant
girl's. And they have deprived her too of something most proper to great
ladies, which is the sweet smell they have from always moving among
ambergris[23] and flowers. For I must tell you, Sancho, that when I went to
help my Dulcinea on to her hackney, as you say it was, though it seemed
a she-ass to me, I got such a whiff of raw garlic as stank me out and
poisoned me to the heart."

"Oh the curs!"[24] cried Sancho at this. "Oh wretched and spiteful
enchanters! I should like to see you strung up by the gills like pilchards[25]
on a reed. Wise you are and powerful—and much evil you do! It should
be enough for you, ruffians, to have changed the pearl of my lady's eyes
into corktree galls, and her hair of purest gold into red ox tail bristles,
and all her features, in fact, from good to bad, without meddling with her
smell. For from that at least we have gathered what lay concealed
beneath that ugly crust. Though, to tell you the truth, I never saw her
ugliness, but only her beauty, which was enhanced and perfected by a
mole she had on her right lip, like a moustache, with seven or eight red
hairs like threads of gold more than nine inches long."

"To judge from that mole," said Don Quixote, "by the correspondence there is between those on the face and those on the body,
Dulcinea must have another on the fleshy part of her thigh, on the same
side as the one on her face. But hairs of the length you indicate are very
long for moles."

"But I can assure your worship," replied Sancho, "that there they
were, as if they had been born with her."

"I believe it friend," said Don Quixote, "for nature has put nothing
on Dulcinea which is not perfect and well-finished. And so, if she had a
hundred moles like the one you speak of on her, they would not be
moles, but moons and shining stars. But tell me, Sancho, that which
appears to me to be a pack-saddle and which you set straight—was it a
plain saddle or a side-saddle?"

"It was just a lady's saddle," replied Sancho, "with an outdoor
covering so rich that it was worth half a kingdom."

"And to think that I did not see all this Sancho!" cried Don Quixote.
"Now I say once more—and I will repeat it a thousand times—I am the
most unfortunate of men."

And that rascal Sancho had all he could do to hide his amusement

---

[23] Perfume base.   [25] Sardines.
[24] Dogs.

on hearing this crazy talk from his master, whom he had so beautifully deceived.

Questions for Discussion and Writing

1. The passage consists of two episodes: the windmill adventure and Dulcinea's "transformation." Which elements of chivalry does Cervantes satirize in each instance?

2. To which social class does Sancho Panza belong? Consider how Don Quixote treats him and speaks to him. Why could a character such as Sancho not have appeared in Arthurian legends or Greek myths and tragedies?

3. How realistic is the story of Don Quixote compared to the story of Sir Lancelot? Examine the details of the setting, the psychological depictions of each character, and the plausibility of their actions. What changes in society and world view in Cervantes' time might account for this increased realism? Consider the readings on the Middle Ages and the Renaissance in Chapters 2–3.

4. Sancho Panza is one of literature's first "sidekicks." Define his role: What literary purpose does he serve alongside Don Quixote? Consider other sidekicks and their partners in literature, film, and television—Tonto and the Lone Ranger, Batman and Robin, Chewbaca and Han Solo in *Star Wars,* the Tin man, the Lion, the Scarecrow, and Dorothy from the *Wizard of Oz.* Do modern sidekicks serve different purposes than did their predecessors?

5. Three elements of humor are incongruity (not being consistent with what is correct or logical), exaggeration, and embarrassment. Apply these elements to those scenes in the story which you found humorous. How well do they account for the humorous effect?

6. What role does Lady Dulcinea play in the adventures? How does she compare to Guenivere or the other women in the stories of Lancelot?

7. What popular contemporary books or movies satirize a previous time in our history and its values? Consider Monty Python's movies, "Saturday Night Live," and movies such as *Blazing Saddles* which satirize the "old West." Why do we find them humorous? Do they contain serious messages or are they strictly entertainment?

Castiglione, from **The Book of the Courtier**

Baldassare Castiglione (1478-1529), one of the most influential men of letters in Europe during the Renaissance, was an Italian diplomat, writer, and courtier. His Book of the Courtier *typifies Renaissance literature in its emphasis on stylistic accomplishment in art, conversation, and behavior. The conversation that makes up the following reading takes place in the Renaissance court of an Italian duke. The court members are entertaining themselves by playing "parlor games" of a sort. In this particular game, they describe the ideal courtier. In doing so, they show off their ability to speak eloquently and wittily at a moment's notice. They admire a certain style of behavior called* sprezzatura, *a kind of cool, sophisticated manner that understates their accomplishments, while still clearly demonstrating them for the admiring world to see.*

At a sign from the Duchess, Cesare Gonzaga began:

"If I well remember, Count, it seems to me you have repeated several times this evening that the Courtier[1] must accompany his actions, his gestures, his habits, in short, his every movement, with grace. And it strikes me that you require this in everything as that seasoning without which all the other properties and good qualities would be of little worth. And truly I believe that everyone would easily let himself be persuaded of this, because, by the very meaning of the word, it can be said that he who has grace finds grace. But since you have said that this is often a gift of nature and the heavens, and that, even if it is not quite perfect, it can be much increased by care and industry, those men who are born as fortunate and as rich in such treasure as some we know have little need, it seems to me, of any teacher in this, because such benign favor from heaven lifts them, almost in spite of themselves, higher than they themselves had desired, and makes them not only pleasing but admirable to everyone. Therefore I do not discuss this, it not being in our power to acquire it of ourselves. But as for those who are less endowed by nature and are capable of acquiring grace only if they put forth labor, industry, and care, I would wish to know by what art, by what discipline, by what method, they can gain this grace, both in bodily exercises, in which you deem it to be so necessary, and in every other thing they do or say. Therefore, since by praising this quality so highly you have, as I believe, aroused in all of us an ardent desire, according to the task given you by signora Emilia, you are still bound to satisfy it."

"I am not bound," said the Count, "to teach you how to acquire grace or anything else, but only to show you what a perfect Courtier ought to be. Nor would I undertake to teach you such a perfection; especially when I have just now said that the Courtier must know how to wrestle, vault,[2] and so many other things which, since I never learned them myself, you all know well enough how I should be able to teach them. Let it suffice that just as a good soldier knows how to tell the smith[3] what shape, style, and quality his armor must have, and yet is not able to teach him to make it, nor how to hammer or temper[4] it; just so I, perhaps, shall be able to tell you what a perfect Courtier should be, but not to teach you what you must do to become one. Still, in order to answer your question in so far as I can (although it is almost proverbial that grace is not learned), I say that if anyone is to acquire grace in bodily exercises (granting first of all that he is not by nature incapable), he must begin early and learn the principles from the best of teachers. And how important this seemed to King Philip of Macedon can be seen by the fact

---

[1] Member of a royal court.
[2] Jump.

[3] Metalworker.
[4] Make strong.

that he wished Aristotle, the famous philosopher and perhaps the greatest the world has ever known, to be the one who should teach his son Alexander the first elements of letters. And among men whom we know today, consider how well and gracefully signor Galeazzo Sanseverino, Grand Equerry of France, performs all bodily exercises; and this because, besides the natural aptitude of person that he possesses, he has taken the greatest care to study with good masters and to have about him men who excel, taking from each the best of what they know. For just as in wrestling, vaulting, and in the handling of many kinds of weapons, he took our messer Pietro Monte as his guide, who is (as you know) the only true master of every kind of acquired strength and agility—so in riding, jousting,[5] and the rest he has ever had before his eyes those men who are known to be most perfect in these matters.

"Therefore, whoever would be a good pupil must not only do things well, but must always make every effort to resemble and, if that be possible, to transform himself into his master. And when he feels that he has made some progress, it is very profitable to observe different men of that profession; and, conducting himself with that good judgment which must always be his guide, go about choosing now this thing from one and that from another. And even as in green meadows the bee flits[6] about among the grasses robbing the flowers, so our Courtier must steal this grace from those who seem to him to have it, taking from each the part that seems most worthy of praise; not doing as a friend of ours whom you all know, who thought he greatly resembled King Ferdinand the Younger of Aragon, but had not tried to imitate him in anything save in the way he had of raising his head and twisting one side of his mouth, which manner the King had contracted through some malady. And there are many such, who think they are doing a great thing if only they can resemble some great man in something; and often they seize upon that which is his only bad point.

"But, having thought many times already about how this grace is acquired (leaving aside those who have it from the stars), I have found quite a universal rule which in this matter seems to me valid above all others, and in all human affairs whether in word or deed: and that is to avoid affectation in every way possible as though it were some very rough and dangerous reef; and (to pronounce a new word perhaps) to practice in all things a certain *sprezzatura* [nonchalance], so as to conceal all art and make whatever is done or said appear to be without effort and almost without any thought about it. And I believe much grace comes of this: because everyone knows the difficulty of things that are rare and well done; wherefore facility[7] in such things causes the greatest wonder; whereas, on the other hand, to labor and, as we say, drag forth by the hair of the head, shows an extreme want of grace, and causes everything, no matter how great it may be, to be held in little account.

---

[5] Fighting with lances.
[6] Flies about.

[7] Ease, ability.

"Therefore we may call that art true art which does not seem to be art; nor must one be more careful of anything than of concealing it, because if it is discovered, this robs a man of all credit and causes him to be held in slight esteem. And I remember having read of certain most excellent orators in ancient times who, among the other things they did, tried to make everyone believe that they had no knowledge whatever of letters; and, dissembling[8] their knowledge, they made their orations appear to be composed in the simplest manner and according to the dictates[9] of nature and truth rather than of effort and art; which fact, had it been known, would have inspired in the minds of the people the fear that they could be duped by it.

"So you see how art, or any intent effort, if it is disclosed, deprives everything of grace. Who among you fails to laugh when our messer Pierpaolo dances after his own fashion, with those capers[10] of his, his legs stiff on tiptoe, never moving his head, as if he were a stick of wood, and all this so studied that he really seems to be counting his steps? What eye is so blind as not to see in this the ungainliness[11] of affectation; and not to see the grace of that cool *disinvoltura* [ease] (for when it is a matter of bodily movements many call it that) in many of the men and women here present, who seem in words, in laughter, in posture not to care; or seem to be thinking more of everything than of that, so as to cause all who are watching them to believe that they are almost incapable of making a mistake?"

Questions for Discussion and Writing

1. Define the perfect courtier as Castiglione depicts him. What physical characteristics and abilities should he have? What intellectual skill should he cultivate?

2. The Count advises that an aspiring courtier must imitate the actions and style of those around him, to "steal this grace from those who seem to him to have it." What problems can imitating the style of others present, as in the example of King Ferdinand?

3. Name the qualities and behavior a perfect courtier does *not* display and why.

4. The Count advises that people should avoid affectation and not put on false airs. Does this advice conflict with his advice to imitate others? Is there necessarily a contradiction?

5. Define *sprezzatura*. Why is it important in a courtier's life-style? What does it reveal about him?

6. Why should the courtier's style appear effortless? What does the Count mean when he says that "we may call that art true art which does not seem to be art"?

7. Being spontaneous is a personal trait that is still admired today. Consider

---

8 Hiding.   10 Fancy steps.
9 Laws.   11 Awkwardness.

examples such as improvisation in jazz or rapping. What do we value about spontaneity? What characteristics does it reflect?

8. Do other cultures that you are familiar with value spontaneity? If so, name some examples. In what situations is it not valued, and why?

9. How do people acquire their models of individual style and social presentation of self?

10. Is style often "a gift of nature and the heavens," as the Count suggests, or can it be acquired? If so, how? If not, why not?

Michel de Montaigne, "Of Not Communicating One's Glory" _____

Michel de Montaigne (1533–1592) was a mixture of the Renaissance man (exemplified in his skill and knowledge in many areas) and a forerunner of the Age of Reason (shown by his famous skepticism and discursive mind). His motto, "What do I know?," symbolizes his ironic view of human ideals and shortcomings. Montaigne lived in a time of political turmoil caused by religious factions in France and other European countries—this was the era of the Reformation. In this essay, Montaigne explores an aspect of personal style and behavior, much the way Castiglione does in the previous reading, though in this case the question is, why pursue fame and reputation?

Of all the illusions in the world, the most universally received is the concern for reputation and glory, which we espouse[1] even to the point of giving up riches, rest, life, and health, which are effectual[2] and substantial goods, to follow that vain phantom and mere sound that has neither body nor substance:

> The fame that charms proud mortals with sweet sound,
> And seems so fair, is but an echo, a dream,
> The shadow of a dream, beyond repair
> Dispersed and scattered by a puff of air.

And of the irrational humors[3] of men, it seems that even the philosophers get rid of this one later and more reluctantly than any other.

It is the most contrary and stubborn of all, "because it does not cease to tempt even souls that are making good progress" [Saint Augustine]. There is hardly any other illusion whose vanity reason condemns so clearly; but it has such live roots in us that I do not know whether anyone yet has ever been able to get clean rid of it. After you have said everything and believed everything to disown it, it produces such an ingrained inclination against your arguments that you have little power to withstand it. For as Cicero says, even those who combat it still

---

[1] Adopt, defend.
[2] Useful.

[3] Moods.

want the books that they write about it to bear their name on the title page, and want to become glorious for having despised glory.

All other things can be traded; we lend our goods and our lives to the need of our friends; but to communicate one's honor and endow another with one's glory, that is hardly ever seen.

Catalus Luctatius, in the war against the Cimbrians, after making every effort to stop his soldiers from fleeing before the enemy, himself joined the fugitives and played the coward, so that they should seem rather to be following their captain than fleeing from the enemy. That was abandoning his reputation to cover the shame of others.

When the Emperor Charles V came into Provence in the year 1537, they say that Antonio de Leyva, seeing his master resolved on this expedition and believing that it would add wonderfully to his glory, nevertheless expressed a contrary opinion and advised him against it; to this end, that all the glory and honor of this plan should be attributed to his master, and that it might be said that his good judgment and foresight had been such that, against the opinion of everyone, he had carried out such a splendid enterprise: which for de Leyva, was to honor his master at his own expense.

When the Thracian ambassadors, in consoling Argileonis, the mother of Brasidas, for the death of her son, praised him so highly as to say that he had not left his like behind him, she refused this private and particular praise and gave it back to the public: "Don't tell me that," she said; "I know that the city of Sparta has many citizens greater and more valiant than he was."

In the battle of Crecy the prince of Wales, still a very young man, was in charge of the vanguard.[4] The principal stress of the encounter was at that point. The lords who were with him, finding themselves in a tough fight, sent word to King Edward to come up and help them. He inquired about the condition of his son, and being answered that he was alive and on his horse, he said: "I should be doing him wrong to go now and rob him of the honor of victory in this combat that he has sustained so long; whatever risk there may be, this shall be all his own." And he would not go or send to him, knowing that if he went, it would be said that all would have been lost without his help, and that the credit for this exploit would be attributed to him: "for it is always what is thrown in last that seems to have accomplished the whole thing" [Livy].

Many in Rome thought, and it was commonly said, that the principal great deeds of Scipio were due in part to Laelius, who was always promoting and seconding Scipio's greatness and glory without any care for his own. And Theopompus, king of Sparta, to the man who told him that the republic remained on its feet because he knew how to command well, said: "It is rather because the people know how to obey well."

---

[4] Front lines.

As women who succeeded to peerages,[5] in spite of their sex, had the right to attend and deliberate in cases pertaining to the jurisdiction of peers, so the ecclesiastical peers, in spite of their profession, were obliged to assist our kings in their wars, not only with their friends and retainers,[6] but also in person. The bishop of Beauvais, finding himself with Philip Augustus at the battle of Bouvines, participated very courageously in the action; but it seemed to him he should not touch the fruit and glory of this bloody and violent activity. With his own hand he got the better of several of the enemy that day; and he would give them to the first gentleman he found, to cut their throats or take them as prisoners, letting him handle them as he chose; and he so delivered William, earl of Salisbury, to Jean de Nesle. With a like subtlety of conscience he was willing to club a man to death but not to wound him, and therefore fought only with a mace.[7]

Someone in my day, being reproached by the king for having laid hands on a priest, strongly and stoutly denied it: the fact was that he had cudgeled[8] and kicked him.

Questions for Discussion and Writing

1. Explain how each of Montaigne's examples supports his view of "glory" and his concern for personal reputation.

2. Although Montaigne provides several examples to make his point and says that "even the philosophers get rid of this [concern for reputation] later and more reluctantly than any other," he does not say *why* people should not seek fame. What is the philosophical reason for his position? What does Montaigne say is wrong with being concerned about fame and reputation?

3. Both Montaigne and Castiglione recommend that people be modest about their accomplishments. How do the two authors' *motives* for praising modesty differ? How would Montaigne view Castiglione's ideal courtier and vice versa?

4. Do many Americans embrace Montaigne's views? If so, what examples can you cite? If not, why not?

5. Young people of the 1970s–1980s have been described as the "me" generation, people who are concerned only with advancing themselves. How might they argue against Montaigne's views?

6. Do other cultures that you are familiar with consider seeking fame and reputation to be an undesirable trait? How do they discourage this behavior through their philosophy or education?

---

[5] Ranks of nobility.
[6] Attendants, servants.

[7] Spiked club.
[8] Clubbed.

ENLIGHTENMENT SATIRE AND ROMANTIC HEROES

François-Marie Arouet de Voltaire, from **Candide**

Philosopher, tragedian, poet, encyclopedist: François-Marie Arouet de Voltaire (1694–1778) was all these things, and more. One of the leading thinkers of the Age of Reason in France, the early Voltaire championed a doctrine of Optimism—a view he later rejected and satirized in his tale Candide *(published in 1759), which bears "Optimism" as its subtitle. Having read widely in the history of human injustice (the Inquisition was a particularly hateful example of evil, in Voltaire's eyes, as he writes in "Of Universal Tolerance," Chapter 2), and contemplating the cruelties of nature (the 1755 Lisbon earthquake in particular, in which close to 40,000 people died), Voltaire found it increasingly difficult to believe that "all is for the best in the best of all possible worlds." He advocated the use of reason as the best route to happiness, although he also recognized the limited degree of human control over life and nature. "To cultivate one's garden" strikes the balance between the ideal and the possible, as the tale of* Candide *suggests.*

CHAPTER I

HOW CANDIDE WAS BROUGHT UP IN A NOBLE CASTLE AND HOW HE WAS EXPELLED FROM THE SAME

In the castle of Baron Thunder-ten-tronckh in Westphalia there lived a youth, endowed by Nature with the most gentle character. His face was the expression of his soul. His judgment was quite honest and he was extremely simple-minded; and this was the reason, I think, that he was named Candide. Old servants in the house suspected that he was the son of the Baron's sister and a decent honest gentleman of the neighborhood, whom this young lady would never marry because he could only prove seventy-one quarterings, and the rest of his genealogical tree was lost, owing to the injuries of time. The Baron was one of the most powerful lords in Westphalia, for his castle possessed a door and windows. His Great Hall was even decorated with a piece of tapestry. The dogs in his stableyards formed a pack of hounds when necessary; his grooms were his huntsmen; the village curate was his Grand Almoner. They all called him "My Lord," and laughed heartily at his stories. The Baroness weighed about three hundred and fifty pounds, was therefore greatly respected, and did the honors of the house with a dignity which rendered her still more respectable. Her daughter Cunegonde, aged seventeen, was rosy-cheeked, fresh, plump and tempting. The Baron's son appeared in every respect worthy of his father. The tutor Pangloss was the oracle of the house, and little Candide followed his lessons with all the candor of his age and character. Pangloss taught metaphysicotheologo-cosmolonigology. He proved admirably that there is no effect without a cause and that in this best of all possible worlds, My Lord the Baron's castle was the best of castles and his wife the best of all possible Baronesses. " 'Tis demonstrated," said he, "that things cannot be otherwise; for, since everything is made for an end, everything is necessarily for the best end. Observe that noses were made to wear spectacles; and so we have spectacles. Legs were visibly instituted to be breeched, and we have breeches. Stones were formed to be quarried and to build castles; and My Lord has a very noble castle; the greatest Baron in the province should have the best house; and as pigs were made to be eaten, we eat pork all the year round; consequently, those who have asserted that all is well talk nonsense; they ought to have said that all is for the best." Candide listened attentively and believed innocently; for he thought Mademoiselle Cunegonde extremely beautiful, although he was never bold enough to tell her so. He decided that after the happiness of being born Baron of Thunder-ten-tronckh, the second degree of happiness was to be Mademoiselle Cunegonde; the third, to see her every day; and the fourth to listen to Doctor Pangloss, the greatest philosopher of the province and therefore of the whole world. One day when Cunegonde was walking near the castle, in a little wood which was called The Park, she observed Doctor Pangloss in the bushes, giving a lesson in experimental physics to her mother's waiting-maid, a very pretty and docile brunette. Mademoiselle Cunegonde had a great inclination for science and watched breathlessly the reiterated experiments she witnessed; she observed clearly the Doctor's sufficient reason, the effects and the causes, and returned home very much excited, pensive, filled with the desire of learning, reflecting that she might be the sufficient reason of young Candide and that he might be hers. On her way back to the castle she met Candide and blushed; Candide also blushed. She bade him good morning in a hesitating voice; Candide replied without knowing what he was saying. Next day, when they left the table after dinner, Cunegonde and Candide found themselves behind a screen; Cunegonde dropped her handkerchief, Candide picked it up; she innocently held his hand; the young man innocently kissed the young lady's hand with remarkable vivacity, tenderness and grace; their lips met, their eyes sparkled, their knees trembled, their hands wandered. Baron Thunder-ten-tronckh passed near the screen, and, observing this cause and effect, expelled Candide from the castle by kicking him in the backside frequently and hard. Cunegonde swooned; when she recovered her senses, the Baroness slapped her in the face; and all was in consternation in the noblest and most agreeable of all possible castles.

CHAPTER II

WHAT HAPPENED TO CANDIDE AMONG THE BULGARIANS

Candide, expelled from the earthly paradise, wandered for a long time without knowing where he was going, turning up his eyes to

Heaven, gazing back frequently at the noblest of castles which held the most beautiful of young Baronesses; he lay down to sleep supperless between two furrows in the open fields; it snowed heavily in large flakes. The next morning the shivering Candide, penniless, dying of cold and exhaustion, dragged himself toward the neighboring town, which was called Waldberghoff-trarbk-dikdorff. He halted sadly at the door of an inn. Two men dressed in blue noticed him. "Comrade," said one, "there's a well-built young man of the right height." They went up to Candide and very civilly invited him to dinner. "Gentlemen," said Candide with charming modesty, "you do me a great honor, but I have no money to pay my share." "Ah, sir," said one of the men in blue, "persons of your figure and merit never pay anything; are you not five feet five tall?" "Yes, gentlemen," said he, bowing, "that is my height." "Ah, sir, come to table; we will not only pay your expenses, we will never allow a man like you to be short of money; men were only made to help each other." "You are in the right," said Candide, "that is what Doctor Pangloss was always telling me, and I see that everything is for the best." They begged him to accept a few crowns, he took them and wished to give them an I O U; they refused to take it and all sat down to table. "Do you not love tenderly . . ." "Oh, yes," said he. "I love Mademoiselle Cunegonde tenderly." "No," said one of the gentlemen. "We were asking if you do not tenderly love the King of the Bulgarians." "Not a bit," said he, "for I have never seen him." "What! He is the most charming of Kings, and you must drink his health." "Oh, gladly, gentlemen." And he drank. "That is sufficient," he was told. "You are now the support, the aid, the defender, the hero of the Bulgarians; your fortune is made and your glory assured." They immediately put irons on his legs and took him to a regiment. He was made to turn to the right and left, to raise the ramrod and return the ramrod, to take aim, to fire, to double up, and he was given thirty strokes with a stick; the next day he drilled not quite so badly, and received only twenty strokes; the day after, he only had ten and was looked on as a prodigy by his comrades. Candide was completely mystified and could not make out how he was a hero. One fine spring day he thought he would take a walk, going straight ahead, in the belief that to use his legs as he pleased was a privilege of the human species as well as of animals. He had not gone two leagues when four other heroes, each six feet tall, fell upon him, bound him and dragged him back to a cell. He was asked by his judges whether he would rather be thrashed thirty-six times by the whole regiment or receive a dozen lead bullets at once in his brain. Although he protested that men's wills are free and that he wanted neither one nor the other, he had to make a choice; by virtue of that gift of God which is called *liberty,* he determined to run the gauntlet thirty-six times and actually did so twice. There were two thousand men in the regiment. That made four thousand strokes which laid bare the muscles and nerves from his neck to his backside. As they were about to proceed to a third turn, Candide, utterly exhausted, begged as a favor that they would be so kind as to smash his head; he obtained this favor; they bound his eyes and he was made to kneel down. At that moment the King of the Bulgarians came by and inquired the victim's crime; and as this King was possessed of a vast genius, he perceived from what he learned about Candide that he was a young metaphysician very ignorant in worldly matters, and therefore pardoned him with a clemency which will be praised in all newspapers and all ages. An honest surgeon healed Candide in three weeks with the ointments recommended by Dioscorides. He had already regained a little skin and could walk when the King of the Bulgarians went to war with the King of the Abares.

CHAPTER III

HOW CANDIDE ESCAPED FROM THE BULGARIANS
AND WHAT BECAME OF HIM

Nothing could be smarter, more splendid, more brilliant, better drawn up than the two armies. Trumpets, fifes, hautboys, drums, cannons, formed a harmony such as has never been heard even in hell. The cannons first of all laid flat about six thousand men on each side; then the musketry removed from the best of worlds some nine or ten thousand blackguards who infested its surface. The bayonet also was the sufficient reason for the death of some thousands of men. The whole might amount to thirty thousand souls. Candide, who trembled like a philosopher, hid himself as well as he could during this heroic butchery. At last, while the two Kings each commanded a Te Deum in his camp, Candide decided to go elsewhere to reason about effects and causes. He clambered over heaps of dead and dying men and reached a neighboring village, which was in ashes; it was an Abare village which the Bulgarians had burned in accordance with international law. Here, old men dazed with blows watched the dying agonies of their murdered wives who clutched their children to their bleeding breasts; there, disemboweled girls who had been made to satisfy the natural appetites of heroes gasped their last sighs; others, half-burned, begged to be put to death. Brains were scattered on the ground among dismembered arms and legs. Candide fled to another village as fast as he could; it belonged to the Bulgarians, and Abarian heroes had treated it in the same way. Candide, stumbling over quivering limbs or across ruins, at last escaped from the theater of war, carrying a little food in his knapsack, and never forgetting Mademoiselle Cunegonde. His provisions were all gone when he reached Holland; but, having heard that everyone in that country was rich and a Christian, he had no doubt at all but that he would be as well treated as he had been in the Baron's castle before he had been expelled on account of Mademoiselle Cunegonde's pretty eyes. He asked an alms of several grave persons, who all replied that if he continued in that way he would be shut up in a house of correction to teach him how to live. He then addressed himself to a man who had been discoursing on charity in a large assembly for an hour on end. This orator, glancing at him askance, said: "What are you doing here? Are you for a good cause?" "There is no effect without a cause," said Candide modestly. "Everything is necessarily linked up and arranged for the best. It was necessary that I should be expelled from the company of Mademoiselle Cunegonde, that I ran the gauntlet, and that I beg my bread until I can earn it; all this could not have happened differently." "My friend," said the orator, "do you believe that the Pope is Anti-Christ?" "I had never heard so before," said Candide, "but whether he is or isn't, I am starving." "You don't deserve to eat," said the other. "Hence, rascal; hence, you wretch; and never come near me again." The orator's wife thrust her head out of the window and seeing a man who did not believe that the Pope was Anti-Christ, she poured on his head a full . . . O Heavens! To what excess religious zeal is carried by ladies? A man who had not been baptized, an honest Anabaptist named Jacques, saw the cruel and ignominious treatment of one of his brothers, a featherless two-legged creature with a soul; he took him home, cleaned him up, gave him bread and beer, and presented him with two florins, and even offered to teach him to work at the manufacture of Persian stuffs which are made in Holland. Candide threw himself at the man's feet, exclaiming: "Doctor Pangloss was right in telling me that all is for the best in this world, for I am vastly more touched by your extreme generosity than by the harshness of the gentleman in the black cloak and his good lady." The next day when he walked out he met a beggar covered with sores, dull-eyed, with the end of his nose fallen away, his mouth awry, his teeth black, who talked huskily, was tormented with a violent cough and spat out a tooth at every cough.

CHAPTER IV

HOW CANDIDE MET HIS OLD MASTER IN PHILOSOPHY, DOCTOR PANGLOSS, AND WHAT HAPPENED

Candide, moved even more by compassion than by horror, gave this horrible beggar the two florins he had received from the honest Anabaptist, Jacques. The phantom gazed fixedly at him, shed tears and threw its arms round his neck. Candide recoiled in terror. "Alas!" said the wretch to the other wretch, "don't you recognize your dear Pangloss?" "What do I hear? You, my dear master! You, in this horrible state! What misfortune has happened to you? Why are you no longer in the noblest of castles? What has become of Mademoiselle Cunegonde, the pearl of young ladies, the masterpiece of Nature?" "I am exhausted," said Pangloss. Candide immediately took him to the Anabaptist's stable where he gave him a little bread to eat; and when Pangloss had recovered: "Well!" said he, "Cunegonde?" "Dead," replied the other. At this word Candide swooned; his friend restored him to his senses with a little bad vinegar which happened to be in the stable. Candide opened his eyes. "Cunegonde dead! Ah! best of worlds, where are you? But what illness did she die of? Was it because she saw me kicked out of her father's noble castle?" "No," said Pangloss. "She was disemboweled by Bulgarian soldiers, after having been raped to the limit of possibility; they broke the

Baron's head when he tried to defend her; the Baroness was cut to pieces; my poor pupil was treated exactly like his sister; and as to the castle, there is not one stone standing on another, not a barn, not a sheep, not a duck, not a tree; but we were well avenged, for the Abares did exactly the same to a neighboring barony which belonged to a Bulgarian Lord." At this, Candide swooned again; but, having recovered and having said all that he ought to say, he inquired the cause and effect, the sufficient reason which had reduced Pangloss to so piteous a state. "Alas!" said Pangloss, " 'tis love; love, the consoler of the human race, the preserver of the universe, the soul of all tender creatures, gentle love." "Alas!" said Candide, "I am acquainted with this love, this sovereign of hearts, this soul of our soul; it has never brought me anything but one kiss and twenty kicks in the backside. How could this beautiful cause produce in you so abominable an effect?" Pangloss replied as follows: "My dear Candide! You remember Paquette, the maid-servant of our august Baroness; in her arms I enjoyed the delights of Paradise which have produced the tortures of Hell by which you see I am devoured; she was infected and perhaps is dead. Paquette received this present from a most learned monk, who had it from the source; for he received it from an old countess, who had it from a cavalry captain, who owed it to a marchioness, who derived it from a page, who had received it from a Jesuit, who, when a novice, had it in a direct line from one of the companions of Christopher Columbus. For my part, I shall not give it to anyone, for I am dying." "O Pangloss!" exclaimed Candide, "this is a strange genealogy! Wasn't the devil at the root of it?" "Not at all," replied that great man. "It was something indispensable in this best of worlds, a necessary ingredient; for, if Columbus in an island of America had not caught this disease, which poisons the source of generation, and often indeed prevents generation, we should not have chocolate and cochineal; it must also be noticed that hitherto in our continent this disease is peculiar to us, like theological disputes. The Turks, the Indians, the Persians, the Chinese, the Siamese and the Japanese are not yet familiar with it; but there is a sufficient reason why they in their turn should become familiar with it in a few centuries. Meanwhile, it has made marvelous progress among us, and especially in those large armies composed of honest, well-bred stipendiaries who decide the destiny of States; it may be asserted that when thirty thousand men fight a pitched battle against an equal number of troops, there are about twenty thousand with the pox on either side." "Admirable!" said Candide. "But you must get cured." "How can I?" said Pangloss. "I haven't a sou, my friend, and in the whole extent of this globe, you cannot be bled or receive an enema without paying or without someone paying for you." This last speech determined Candide; he went and threw himself at the feet of his charitable Anabaptist, Jacques, and drew so touching a picture of the state to which his friend was reduced that the good easy man did not hesitate to succor Pangloss; he had him cured at his own expense. In this cure Pangloss only lost one eye and one ear. He could write well and knew arithmetic perfectly. The Anabaptist made him his bookkeeper. At the end of two months he was compelled to go to Lisbon on business and took his two philosophers on the boat with him. Pangloss explained to him how everything was for the best. Jacques was not of this opinion. "Men," said he, "must have corrupted nature a little, for they were not born wolves, and they have become wolves. God did not give them twenty-four-pounder cannons or bayonets, and they have made bayonets and cannons to destroy each other. I might bring bankruptcies into the account and Justice which seizes the goods of bankrupts in order to deprive the creditors of them." "It was all indispensable," replied the one-eyed doctor, "and private misfortunes make the public good, so that the more private misfortunes there are, the more everything is well." While he was reasoning, the air grew dark, the winds blew from the four quarters of the globe and the ship was attacked by the most horrible tempest in sight of the port of Lisbon.

In the intervening chapters, Candide, Pangloss, and Jacques barely survive the Lisbon earthquake and are tortured in the Inquisition; Candide finds Cunegonde alive but, under threat of death, must leave her behind as he flees to Paraguay; with this valet Cacambo he visits Eldorado and finds great riches; he travels back to Europe with the philosopher Martin, finding that bribery is the necessary path home. Pangloss meanwhile has been "hanged, dissected, beaten to a pulp, and sentenced to the galleys," though he lives and persists in his optimistic beliefs. Once home, Candide rejoins Cunegonde and her companion, an old woman.

CHAPTER XXIX

HOW CANDIDE FOUND CUNEGONDE AND THE OLD WOMAN AGAIN

While Candide, the Baron, Pangloss, Martin and Cacambo were relating their adventures, reasoning upon contingent or noncontingent events of the universe, arguing about effects and causes, moral and physical evil, free will and necessity, and the consolations to be found in the Turkish galleys, they came to the house of the Transylvanian prince on the shores of Propontis. The first objects which met their sight were Cunegonde and the old woman hanging out towels to dry on the line. At this sight the Baron grew pale. Candide, that tender lover, seeing his fair Cunegonde sunburned, blear-eyed, flat-breasted, with wrinkles round her eyes and red, chapped arms, recoiled three paces in horror, and then advanced from mere politeness. She embraced Candide and her brother. They embraced the old woman; Candide bought them both. In the neighborhood was a little farm; the old woman suggested that Candide should buy it, until some better fate befell the group. Cunegonde did not know that she had become ugly, for nobody had told her so; she reminded Candide of his promises in so peremptory a tone that the good Candide dared not refuse her. He therefore informed the Baron that he was about to marry his sister. "Never," said the Baron, "will I endure such baseness on her part and such insolence on yours; nobody shall ever reproach me with this infamy; my sister's children could never enter the chapters of Germany. No, my sister shall never marry anyone but a Baron of the Empire." Cunegonde threw herself at his feet and bathed them in tears; but he was inflexible. "Madman," said Candide, "I rescued you from the galleys, I paid your ransom and your sister's; she was washing dishes here, she is ugly, I am so kind as to make her my wife, and you pretend to oppose me! I should kill you again if I listened to my anger." "You may kill me again," said the Baron, "but you shall never marry my sister while I am alive."

CHAPTER XXX

CONCLUSION

At the bottom of his heart Candide had not the least wish to marry Cunegonde. But the Baron's extreme impertinence determined him to complete the marriage, and Cunegonde urged it so warmly that he could not retract. He consulted Pangloss, Martin and the faithful Cacambo. Pangloss wrote an excellent memorandum by which he proved that the Baron had no rights over his sister and that by all the laws of the empire she could make a left-handed marriage with Candide. Martin advised that the Baron should be thrown into the sea; Cacambo decided that he should be returned to the Levantine captain and sent back to the galleys, after which he would be returned by the first ship to the Vicar-General at Rome. This was thought to be very good advice; the old woman approved it; they said nothing to the sister; the plan was carried out with the aid of a little money and they had the pleasure of duping a Jesuit and punishing the pride of a German Baron. It would be natural to suppose that when, after so many disasters, Candide was married to his mistress, and living with the philosopher Pangloss, the philosopher Martin, the prudent Cacambo and the old woman, having brought back so many diamonds from the country of the ancient Incas, he would lead the most pleasant life imaginable. But he was so cheated by the Jews that he had nothing left but his little farm; his wife, growing uglier every day, became shrewish and unendurable; the old woman was ailing and even more bad-tempered than Cunegonde. Cacambo, who worked in the garden and then went to Constantinople to sell vegetables, was overworked and cursed his fate. Pangloss was in despair because he did not shine in some German university. As for Martin, he was firmly convinced that people are equally uncomfortable everywhere; he accepted things patiently. Candide, Martin, and Pangloss sometimes argued about metaphysics and morals. From the windows of the farm they often watched the ships going by, filled with effendis, pashas, and cadis, who were being exiled to Lemnos, to Mitylene and Erzerum. They saw other cadis, other pashas, and other effendis coming back to take the place of the exiles and to be exiled in their turn. They saw the neatly impaled heads which were taken to the Sublime Porte. These sights redoubled their discussions; and when they were not arguing, the boredom was so excessive that one day the old woman dared to say to them: "I should like to know which is worse, to be raped a hundred times by Negro pirates, to have a buttock cut off, to run the gauntlet among the Bulgarians, to be whipped and flogged in an *auto-da-fé,* to be dissected, to row in a galley, in short, to endure all the miseries through which we have passed, or to remain here doing nothing?" " 'Tis a great question," said Candide. These remarks led to new reflections, and Martin especially concluded that man was born to live in the convulsions of distress or in the lethargy of boredom. Candide did not agree, but he asserted nothing. Pangloss confessed that he had always suffered horribly; but, having once maintained that everything was for the best, he had continued to maintain it without believing it. One thing confirmed Martin in his detestable principles, made Candide hesitate more than ever, and embarrassed Pangloss. And it was this. One day there came to their farm Paquette and Friar Giroflée, who were in the most extreme misery; they had soon wasted their three thousand piastres, had left each other, made it up, quarreled again, been put in prison, escaped, and finally Friar Giroflée had turned Turk. Paquette continued her occupation everywhere and now earned nothing by it. "I foresaw," said Martin to Candide, "that your gifts would soon be wasted and would only make them the more miserable. You and Cacambo were once bloated with millions of piastres and you are no happier than Friar Giroflée and Paquette." "Ah! Ha!" said Pangloss to Paquette, "so Heaven brings you back to us, my dear child? Do you know that you cost me the end of my nose, an eye, and an ear! What a plight you are in! Ah! What a world this is!" This new occurrence caused them to philosophize more than ever. In the neighborhood there lived a very famous Dervish, who was supposed to be the best philosopher in Turkey; they went to consult him; Pangloss was the spokesman and said: "Master, we have come to beg you to tell us why so strange an animal as man was ever created." "What has it to do with you?" said the Dervish. "Is it your business?" "But, reverend father," said Candide, "there is a horrible amount of evil in the world." "What does it matter," said the Dervish, "whether there is evil or good? When his highness sends a ship to Egypt, does he worry about the comfort or discomfort of the rats in the ship?" "Then what should we do?" said Pangloss. "Hold your tongue," said the Dervish. "I flattered myself," said Pangloss, "that I should discuss with you effects and causes, this best of all possible worlds, the origin of evil, the nature of the soul and pre-established harmony." At these words the Dervish slammed the door in their faces. During this conversation the news went round that at Constantinople two viziers and the mufti had been strangled and several of their friends impaled. This catastrophe made a prodigious noise everywhere for several hours. As Pangloss, Candide, and Martin were returning to their little farm, they came upon an old man who was taking the air under a bower of orange-trees at his door. Pangloss, who was as curious as he was argumentative, asked him what was the name of the mufti who had just been strangled. "I do not know," replied the old man. "I have never known the name of any mufti or of any vizier. I am entirely ignorant of the occurrence you mention; I presume that in general those who meddle with public affairs sometimes perish miserably and that they deserve it; but I never inquire what is going on in Constantinople, I content myself with sending there for sale the produce of the garden I cultivate." Having spoken thus, he took the strangers into his house. His two daughters and his two sons presented them with several kinds of sherbet which they made themselves, caymac flavored with candied citron peel, oranges, lemons, limes, pineapples, dates, pistachios, and Mocha coffee which had not been mixed with the bad coffee of Batavia and the Isles. After which this good Mussulman's two daughters perfumed the beards of Candide, Pangloss, and Martin. "You must have a vast and magnificent estate?" said Candide to the Turk. "I have only twenty acres," replied the Turk. "I cultivate them with my children; and work keeps at bay three great evils: boredom, vice and need." As Candide returned to his farm he reflected deeply on the Turk's remarks. He said to Pangloss and Martin: "That good old man seems to me to have chosen an existence preferable by far to that of the six kings with whom we had the honor to sup." "Exalted rank," said Pangloss, "is very dangerous, according to the testimony of all philosophers; for Eglon, King of the Moabites, was murdered by Ehud; Absalom was hanged by the hair and pierced by three darts; King Nadab, son of Jeroboam, was killed by Baasha; King Elah by Zimri; Ahaziah by Jehu; Athaliah by Jehoiada; the Kings Jehoiakim, Jeconiah, and Zedekiah were made slaves. You know in what manner died Croesus, Astyages, Darius, Denys of Syracuse, Pyrrhus, Perseus, Hannibal, Jugurtha, Ariovistus, Caesar, Pompey, Nero, Otho, Vitellius, Domitian, Richard II of England, Edward II, Henry VI, Richard III, Mary Stuart, Charles I, the three Henrys of France, the Emperor Henry IV. You know . . ." "I also know," said Candide, "that we should cultivate our gardens." "You are right," said Pangloss, "for, when man was placed in the Garden of Eden, he was placed there *ut operaretur eum,* to dress it and to keep it; which proves that man was not born for idleness." "Let us work without theorizing," said Martin; "'tis the only way to make life endurable." The whole small fraternity entered into this praiseworthy plan, and each started to make use of his talents. The little farm yielded well. Cunegonde was indeed very ugly, but she became an excellent pastrycook; Paquette embroidered; the old woman took care of the linen. Even Friar Giroflée performed some service; he was a very good carpenter and even became a man of honor; and Pangloss sometimes said to Candide: "All events are linked up in this best of all possible worlds; for, if you had not been expelled from the noble castle by hard kicks in your backside for love of Mademoiselle Cunegonde, if you had not been clapped into the Inquisition, if you had not wandered about America on foot, if you had not stuck your sword in the Baron, if you had not lost all your sheep from the land of Eldorado, you would not be eating candied citrons and pistachios here." "'Tis well said," replied Candide, "but we must cultivate our gardens."

Questions for Discussion and Writing

1. *Candide* parodies the philosophy of optimism, among other things, and as a parody it employs humorous, sometimes ridiculous images and ideas. Name some techniques that Voltaire uses to create these comic effects and cite examples of them. Exaggeration is one such technique. Voltaire creates humorous images of the Baroness by exaggerating her weight, of Pangloss by exaggerating his quotation of philosophical propositions, and so on.

2. What makes the tale biting social commentary, despite the humorous effects created through exaggeration and other comic techniques? Are all the events of the story fictional?

3. In what ways is Candide, whose name means "honest," "simple," and "pure," different from the people around him?

4. What is Voltaire's attitude toward the doctrine of optimism? In what way(s) is optimism a problematic philosophical stand, especially as Pangloss represents it?

5. Restate Candide's concluding line ("we must cultivate our garden") in your own words to explain the value system he promotes.

6. To what extent do you endorse the final statement in the story as a useful philosophical stand in life? How would adopting it affect your behavior as a student? As a worker? In personal relationships?

7. According to the tale, the three chief evils in life are boredom, vice, and poverty. Does Voltaire believe that people themselves are responsible for the existence of evil in life? Are these conditions the source of personal and social problems today?

8. How receptive would you expect middle-class Americans to be to the message of *Candide*? Explain the reasoning behind your response. Would members of other social classes be more or less likely to accept Voltaire's views? Why?

9. Do you see support for the eighteenth-century belief in human equality in Voltaire's story, or does he think that people are born with different levels of ability and worth?

10. Given what you know of Voltaire's beliefs from reading this excerpt and his essay "Of Universal Tolerance" (Chapter 2), where would you expect Voltaire to stand on the issue of the canon, as it is discussed in the Mooney and Rose essays (Chapter 1)?

Rousseau, from The Confessions of Jean Jacques Rousseau _____

Jean-Jacques Rousseau (1712–1778), a later contemporary of Voltaire, represented an age in revolt against the philosophical views of the Enlightenment. With Rousseau, the Age of Romanticism began in Europe, an age whose influence continued to spread through the end of the nineteenth century. The Romantic writers replaced the values of reason with feeling, mechanism with wild nature, and equality with individual genius. Attention shifted from the social world to the inner experience of the sensitive soul. In his Confessions *(1766–1770), Rousseau claims to lay bare such a soul, to provide an honest portrait of the natural man made unique by his extraordinary capacity to feel.*

Key Concepts

The concept of **Nature** (page 277), especially in its Romantic usage, refers to the entire divine plan of existence, to human nature in relation to the rest of the world.

The term **Romantic** (page 279) has come to name an attitude toward nature and human life, one that emphasizes feelings and perception over reason and logic.

BOOK ONE

1712–1719 I have resolved on an enterprise which has no precedent, and which, once complete, will have no imitator. My purpose is to display to my kind a portrait in every way true to nature, and the man I shall portray will be myself.

Simply myself. I know my own heart and understand my fellow man. But I am made unlike any one I have ever met; I will even venture to say that I am like no one in the whole world. I may be no better, but at least I am different. Whether **Nature** did well or ill in breaking the mould in which she formed me, is a question which can only be resolved after the reading of my book.

Let the last trump[1] sound when it will, I shall come forward with this work in my hand, to present myself before my Sovereign Judge, and proclaim aloud: 'Here is what I have done, and if by chance I have used some immaterial embellishment it has been only to fill a void due to a defect of memory. I may have taken for fact what was no more than probability, but I have never put down as true what I knew to be false. I have displayed myself as I was, as vile and despicable when my behaviour was such, as good, generous, and noble when I was so. I have bared my secret soul as Thou thyself hast seen it, Eternal Being! So let the numberless legion of my fellow men gather round me, and hear my confessions. Let them groan at my depravities, and blush for my misdeeds. But let each one of them reveal his heart at the foot of Thy throne with equal sincerity, and may any man who dares, say "I was a better man than he."

I was born at Geneva in 1712, the son of Isaac Rousseau, a citizen of that town, and Susanne Bernard, his wife. My father's inheritance, being a fifteenth part only of a very small property which had been divided among as many children, was almost nothing, and he relied for his living entirely on his trade of watchmaker, at which he was very highly skilled. My mother was the daughter of a minister of religion and rather better-off. She had besides both intelligence and beauty, and my father had not found it easy to win her. Their love had begun almost with their birth; at

[1] Trumpet.

eight or nine they would walk together every evening along La Treille, and at ten they were inseparable. Sympathy and mental affinity strengthened in them a feeling first formed by habit. Both, being affectionate and sensitive by nature, were only waiting for the moment when they would find similar qualities in another; or rather the moment was waiting for them, and both threw their affections at the first heart that opened to receive them. Fate, by appearing to oppose their passion, only strengthened it. Unable to obtain his mistress, the young lover ate out his heart with grief, and she counselled him to travel and forget her. He travelled in vain, and returned more in love than ever, to find her he loved still faithful and fond. After such a proof, it was inevitable that they should love one another for all their lives. They swore to do so, and Heaven smiled on their vows.

Gabriel Bernard, one of my mother's brothers, fell in love with one of my father's sisters, and she refused to marry him unless her brother could marry my mother at the same time. Love overcame all obstacles, and the two pairs were wedded on the same day. So it was that my uncle married my aunt, and their children became my double first cousins. Within a year both couples had a child, but at the end of that time each of them was forced to separate.

My uncle Bernard, who was an engineer, went to serve in the Empire and Hungary under Prince Eugène, and distinguished himself at the siege and battle of Belgrade. My father, after the birth of my only brother, left for Constantinople, where he had been called to become watchmaker to the Sultan's Seraglio.[2] While he was away my mother's beauty, wit, and talents brought her admirers, one of the most pressing of whom was M. de la Closure, the French Resident in the city. His feelings must have been very strong, for thirty years later I have seen him moved when merely speaking to me about her. But my mother had more than her virtue with which to defend herself; she deeply loved my father, and urged him to come back. He threw up everything to do so, and I was the unhappy fruit of his return. For ten months later I was born, a poor and sickly child, and cost my mother her life. So my birth was the first of my misfortunes.

I never knew how my father stood up to his loss, but I know that he never got over it. He seemed to see her again in me, but could never forget that I had robbed him of her; he never kissed me that I did not know by his sighs and his convulsive embrace that there was a bitter grief mingled with his affection, a grief which nevertheless intensified his feeling for me. When he said to me, 'Jean-Jacques, let us talk of your mother,' I would reply: 'Very well, father, but we are sure to cry.' 'Ah,' he would say with a groan; 'Give her back to me, console me for her, fill the void she has left in my heart! Should I love you so if you were not more to me than a son?' Forty years after he lost her he died in the arms of a

[2] Harem.

second wife, but with his first wife's name on his lips, and her picture imprinted upon his heart.

Such were my parents. And of all the gifts with which Heaven endowed them, they left me but one, a sensitive heart. It had been the making of their happiness, but for me it has been the cause of all the misfortunes in my life.

I was almost born dead, and they had little hope of saving me. I brought with me the seed of a disorder which has grown stronger with the years, and now gives me only occasional intervals of relief in which to suffer more painfully in some other way. But one of my father's sisters, a nice sensible woman, bestowed such care on me that I survived; and now, as I write this, she is still alive at the age of eighty, nursing a husband rather younger than herself but ruined by drink. My dear aunt, I pardon you for causing me to live, and I deeply regret that I cannot repay you in the evening of your days all the care and affection you lavished on me at the dawn of mine. My nurse Jacqueline is still alive too, and healthy and strong. Indeed the fingers that opened my eyes at birth may well close them at my death.

I felt before I thought: which is the common lot of man, though more pronounced in my case than in another's. I know nothing of myself till I was five or six. I do not know how I learnt to read. I only remember my first books and their effect upon me; it is from my earliest reading that I date the unbroken consciousness of my own existence. My mother had possessed some novels, and my father and I began to read them after our supper. At first it was only to give me some practice in reading. But soon my interest in this entertaining literature became so strong that we read by turns continuously, and spent whole nights so engaged. For we could never leave off till the end of the book. Sometimes my father would say with shame as we heard the morning larks: 'Come, let us go to bed. I am more of a child than you are.'

In a short time I acquired by this dangerous method, not only an extreme facility in reading and expressing myself, but a singular insight for my age into the passions. I had no idea of the facts, but I was already familiar with every feeling. I had grasped nothing; I had sensed everything. The confused emotions which I experienced one after another, did not warp my reasoning powers in any way, for as yet I had none. But they shaped them after a special pattern, giving me the strangest and most **romantic** notions about human life, which neither experience nor reflection has ever succeeded in curing me of.

Questions for Discussion and Writing

1. Throughout the passage, Rousseau uses the first person, or "I" voice. In many paragraphs, "I" appears in almost every line. Connect Rousseau's use of "I" with the point(s) he wishes to make in this excerpt.

2. Why might Rousseau have chosen the title "Confessions" over "Autobiography" or "The Story of My Life?" In what sense is his work confessional?

3. What value does Rousseau attach to Romantic love? Why does he detail the story of his parents' courtship?

4. Often, Romantic heroes bear some physical or emotional "mark," a sign of their special nature. How does the death of his mother "mark" Rousseau?

5. Given the Romantic preference for feeling over reason, why do novels appeal to the young Rousseau, rather than science or history books?

6. What view of human nature does Rousseau seem to hold? Does he believe people are born equal? Does he believe people are naturally good?

7. Rousseau exults in being "different." Why do some people take pleasure in nonconformity? Are there nonconformist groups today, and if so, what motive(s) and goal(s) do they have? Are they reenacting Romantic values?

8. Rousseau witnessed the effects of the industrial revolution on the cities of Europe. In what way(s) is his philosophy a reaction to the social and environmental changes that were taking place?

Mary Shelley, from **Frankenstein**

The "creature" created by Mary Wollstonecraft Shelley (1797–1851) in her novel Frankenstein *(1818) has become part of our cultural context. The many film versions of Shelley's book have transformed the creature into a nonverbal and usually violent monster. Shelley's original, however, is far more the suffering poet than the stiff-legged subhuman we have come to associate with the novel's name. In fact, "Frankenstein" is the name not of the creature but of the central character, Victor Frankenstein, the "modern Prometheus" of the book's subtitle. Victor, the creator and re-animator of the creature, represents another version of the Romantic hero, an "over-reacher" whose unique attainment has tragic consequences. The following excerpt depicts the creature's "birth" scene and Victor's tortured reaction to his superhuman achievement. He is joined by his boyhood friend, Henry Clerval, who bears greetings from Victor's family and from Elizabeth, his fiancee.*

It was on a dreary night of November that I beheld the accomplishment of my toils. With an anxiety that almost amounted to agony, I collected the instruments of life around me, that I might infuse a spark of being into the lifeless thing that lay at my feet. It was already one in the morning; the rain pattered dismally against the panes, and my candle was nearly burnt out, when, by the glimmer of the half-extinguished light, I saw the dull yellow eye of the creature open; it breathed hard, and a convulsive motion agitated its limbs.

How can I describe my emotions at this catastrophe, or how delineate the wretch whom with such infinite pains and care I had endeavoured to form? His limbs were in proportion, and I had selected his features as beautiful. Beautiful! Great God! His yellow skin scarcely covered the work of muscles and arteries beneath; his hair was of a lustrous black, and flowing; his teeth of a pearly whiteness; but these luxuriances only formed a more horrid contrast with his watery eyes, that seemed almost of the same colour as the dun-white sockets in which they were set, his shrivelled complexion and straight black lips.

The different accidents of life are not as changeable as the feelings of human nature. I had worked hard for nearly two years, for the sole purpose of infusing life into an inanimate body. For this I had deprived myself of rest and health. I had desired it with an ardour that far exceeded moderation; but now that I had finished, the beauty of the dream vanished, and breathless horror and disgust filled my heart. Unable to endure the aspect of the being I had created, I rushed out of the room and continued a long time traversing my bed-chamber unable to compose my mind to sleep. At length lassitude[1] succeeded to the tumult I had before endured, and I threw myself on the bed in my clothes, endeavouring to seek a few moments of forgetfulness. But it was in vain; I slept, indeed, but I was disturbed by the wildest dreams. I thought I saw Elizabeth, in the bloom of health, walking in the streets of Ingolstadt. Delighted and surprised, I embraced her, but as I imprinted the first kiss on her lips, they became livid with the hue of death; her features appeared to change, and I thought that I held the corpse of my dead mother in my arms; a shroud enveloped her form, and I saw the grave-worms crawling in the folds of the flannel. I started from my sleep with horror; a cold dew covered my forehead, my teeth chattered, and every limb became convulsed; when, by the dim and yellow light of the moon, as it forced its way through the window shutters, I beheld the wretch— the miserable monster whom I had created. He held up the curtain of the bed; and his eyes, if eyes they may be called, were fixed on me. His jaws opened, and he muttered some inarticulate sounds, while a grin wrinkled his cheeks. He might have spoken, but I did not hear; one hand was stretched out, seemingly to detain me, but I escaped and rushed downstairs. I took refuge in the courtyard belonging to the house which I inhabited, where I remained during the rest of the night, walking up and down in the greatest agitation, listening attentively, catching and fearing each sound as if it were to announce the approach of the demoniacal corpse to which I had so miserably given life.

Oh! No mortal could support the horror of that countenance. A mummy again endued[2] with animation could not be so hideous as that wretch. I had gazed on him while unfinished; he was ugly then, but when those muscles and joints were rendered capable of motion, it became a thing such as even Dante could not have conceived.

I passed the night wretchedly. Sometimes my pulse beat so quickly and hard that I felt the palpitation of every artery; at others, I nearly sank to the ground through languor and extreme weakness. Mingled with this horror, I felt the bitterness of disappointment; dreams that had been my

---

[1] Weariness.   [2] Endowed.

food and pleasant rest for so long a space were now become a hell to me; and the change was so rapid, the overthrow so complete!

Morning, dismal and wet, at length dawned and discovered to my sleepless and aching eyes the church of Ingolstadt, its white steeple and clock, which indicated the sixth hour. The porter opened the gates of the court, which had that night been my asylum, and I issued into the streets, pacing them with quick steps, as if I sought to avoid the wretch whom I feared every turning of the street would present to my view. I did not dare return to the apartment which I inhabited, but felt impelled to hurry on, although drenched by the rain which poured from a black and comfortless sky.

I continued walking in this manner for some time, endeavouring by bodily exercise to ease the load that weighed upon my mind. I traversed the streets without any clear conception of where I was or what I was doing. My heart palpitated in the sickness of fear, and I hurried on with irregular steps, not daring to look about me:

> Like one who, on a lonely road,
>   Doth walk in fear and dread,
> And, having once turned round, walks on,
>   And turns no more his head;
> Because he knows a frightful fiend
>   Doth close behind him tread.

> Coleridge's "Ancient Mariner"

Continuing thus, I came at length opposite to the inn at which the various diligences[3] and carriages usually stopped. Here I paused, I knew not why; but I remained some minutes with my eyes fixed on a coach that was coming towards me from the other end of the street. As it drew nearer I observed that it was the Swiss diligence; it stopped just where I was standing, and on the door being opened, I perceived Henry Clerval, who, on seeing me, instantly sprung out. "My dear Frankenstein," exclaimed he, "how glad I am to see you! How fortunate that you should be here at the very moment of my alighting!"

Nothing could equal my delight on seeing Clerval; his presence brought back to my thoughts my father, Elizabeth, and all those scenes of home so dear to my recollection. I grasped his hand, and in a moment forgot my horror and misfortune; I felt suddenly, and for the first time during many months, calm and serene joy. I welcomed my friend, therefore, in the most cordial manner, and we walked towards my college. Clerval continued talking for some time about our mutual friends and his own good fortune in being permitted to come to Ingolstadt. "You may easily believe," said he, "how great was the difficulty to persuade my father that all necessary knowledge was not comprised in the noble art of bookkeeping; and, indeed, I believe I left him incredulous to the last, for his constant answer to my unwearied entreaties was the same as that of

---

[3] Stagecoach.

the Dutch schoolmaster in *The Vicar of Wakefield:* 'I have ten thousand florins[4] a year without Greek, I eat heartily without Greek.' But his affection for me at length overcame his dislike of learning, and he has permitted me to undertake a voyage of discovery to the land of knowledge."

"It gives me the greatest delight to see you; but tell me how you left my father, brothers, and Elizabeth."

"Very well, and very happy, only a little uneasy that they hear from you so seldom. By the by, I mean to lecture you a little upon their account myself. But, my dear Frankenstein," continued he, stopping short and gazing full in my face, "I did not before remark how very ill you appear; so thin and pale; you look as if you had been watching for several nights."

"You have guessed right; I have lately been so deeply engaged in one occupation that I have not allowed myself sufficient rest, as you see; but I hope, I sincerely hope, that all these employments are now at an end and that I am at length free."

I trembled excessively; I could not endure to think of, and far less to allude to, the occurrences of the preceding night. I walked with a quick pace, and we soon arrived at my college. I then reflected, and the thought made me shiver, that the creature whom I had left in my apartment might still be there, alive and walking about. I dreaded to behold this monster, but I feared still more that Henry should see him. Entreating him, therefore, to remain a few minutes at the bottom of the stairs, I darted up towards my own room. My hand was already on the lock of the door before I recollected myself. I then paused, and a cold shivering came over me. I threw the door forcibly open, as children are accustomed to do when they expect a spectre to stand in waiting for them on the other side; but nothing appeared. I stepped fearfully in: the apartment was empty, and my bedroom was also freed from its hideous guest. I could hardly believe that so great a good fortune could have befallen me, but when I became assured that my enemy had indeed fled, I clapped my hands for joy and ran down to Clerval.

We ascended into my room, and the servant presently brought breakfast; but I was unable to contain myself. It was not joy only that possessed me; I felt my flesh tingle with excess of sensitiveness, and my pulse beat rapidly. I was unable to remain for a single instant in the same place; I jumped over the chairs, clapped my hands, and laughed aloud. Clerval at first attributed my unusual spirits to joy on his arrival, but when he observed me more attentively, he saw a wildness in my eyes for which he could not acccount, and my loud, unrestrained, heartless laughter frightened and astonished him.

"My dear Victor," he cried, "what for God's sake, is the matter? Do not laugh in that manner. How ill you are! What is the cause of all this?"

"Do not ask me," cried I, putting my hands before my eyes, for I

---

[4] Dutch coins

thought I saw the dreaded spectre glide into the room; "*he* can tell. Oh, save me! Save me!" I imagined that the monster seized me; I struggled furiously and fell down in a fit.

Poor Clerval! What must have been his feelings? A meeting, which he anticipated with such joy, so strangely turned to bitterness. But I was not the witness of his grief, for I was lifeless and did not recover my sense for a long, long time.

This was the commencement of a nervous fever which confined me for several months. During all that time Henry was my only nurse. I afterwards learned that, knowing my father's advanced age and unfitness for so long a journey, and how wretched my sickness would make Elizabeth, he spared them this grief by concealing the extent of my disorder. He knew that I could not have a more kind and attentive nurse than himself; and, firm in the hope he felt of my recovery, he did not doubt that, instead of doing harm, he performed the kindest action that he could towards them.

But I was in reality very ill, and surely nothing but the unbounded and unremitting[5] attentions of my friend could have restored me to life. The form of the monster on whom I had bestowed existence was forever before my eyes, and I raved incessantly concerning him. Doubtless my words surprised Henry; he at first believed them to be the wanderings of my disturbed imagination, but the pertinacity[6] with which I continually recurred to the same subject persuaded him that my disorder indeed owed its origin to some uncommon and terrible event.

By very slow degrees, and with frequent relapses that alarmed and grieved my friend, I recovered. I remember the first time I became capable of observing outward objects with any kind of pleasure, I perceived that the fallen leaves had disappeared and that the young buds were shooting forth from the trees that shaded my window. It was a divine spring, and the season contributed greatly to my convalescence. I felt also sentiments of joy and affection revive in my bosom; my gloom disappeared, and in a short time I became as cheerful as before I was attacked by the fatal passion.

"Dearest Clerval," exclaimed I, "how kind, how very good you are to me. This whole winter, instead of being spent in study, as you promised yourself, has been consumed in my sick room. How shall I ever repay you? I feel the greatest remorse for the disappointment of which I have been the occasion, but you will forgive me."

"You will repay me entirely if you do not discompose[7] yourself, but get well as fast as you can; and since you appear in such good spirits, I may speak to you on one subject, may I not?"

I trembled. One subject! What could it be? Could he allude to an object on whom I dared not even think?

"Compose yourself," said Clerval, who observed my change of colour, "I will not mention it if it agitates you; but your father and cousin

---

[5] Ceaseless.
[6] Persistence.

[7] Upset.

would be very happy if they received a letter from you in your own handwriting. They hardly know how ill you have been and are uneasy at your long silence."

"Is that all, my dear Henry? How could you suppose that my first thought would not fly towards those dear, dear friends whom I love and who are so deserving of my love?"

"If this is your present temper, my friend, you will perhaps be glad to see a letter that has been lying here some days for you; it is from your cousin, I believe. . . ."

Questions for Discussion and Writing

1. Describing the creature, Victor says it is "a thing such as even Dante could not have conceived." Explain why Shelley uses this allusion to Dante: how does the allusion help evoke a sense of the creature's appearance? (An excerpt from Dante's *Inferno* appears in Chapter 2.)

2. Compare the actual text of *Frankenstein* with the film versions you have seen: how do the actions in the film alter Shelley's original? What might the cause(s) and purpose(s) of the alterations be?

3. Using the Romantic values you can infer from your reading of Rousseau, analyze Victor Frankenstein as a Romantic hero. Is he a tragic hero as well, in the classical sense?

4. Victor dreams that as he embraces his fiancée, Elizabeth, she dies in his arms and is transformed into the corpse of his dead mother. What interpretation might a Freudian reading of this episode produce?

5. Analyze the passage as a symbolic treatment of pregnancy and birth. What attitudes and feelings does Shelley attach to giving birth? What fears are associated with it?

6. Does Victor embody the traditional notion of the scientist? Consider critiques of the scientist stereotype (see the Gould, Toulmin, and Bleier essays in Chapter 3): to what extent is Victor an example of the stereotype, and in what way(s) does he differ from it?

7. Do you see parallels between Victor's research and various scientific developments today? Does the Frankenstein image—the popular one of the monster as well as the original one of the tortured seeker of knowledge—apply as a caution against exceeding the bounds of nature?

TRADITION IN THE TWENTIETH CENTURY

T. S. Eliot, from **"Tradition and the Individual Talent"** _____

Born in St. Louis, T. S. Eliot (1888–1965) moved to England as a young man and spent the rest of his life there, in the early years as a bank clerk and later as one of the most acclaimed poets and critics of Western literature. A philosophy major at Harvard, Eliot pored over the "Great Books," studying the classics of the ancient world and the Euro-

*pean tradition. These years of study led him to adopt a definite critical
stance in his later essays, the most famous of which is excerpted below.
Eliot opposed the cult of the individual that he perceived to be increasingly in favor, both in literature and in life. His essay is a reasoned
argument that favors recognition of values beyond the individual and the
particular age. The essay was published in 1920.*

In English writing we seldom speak of tradition, though we occasionally apply its name in deploring its absence. We cannot refer to "the
tradition" or to "a tradition"; at most, we employ the adjective in saying
that the poetry of So-and-so is "traditional" or even "too traditional."
Seldom, perhaps, does the word appear except in a phrase of censure. If
otherwise, it is vaguely approbative,[1] with the implication, as to the work
approved, of some pleasing archaeological reconstruction. You can
hardly make the word agreeable to English ears without this comfortable
reference to the reassuring science of archaeology.

Certainly the word is not likely to appear in our appreciations of
living or dead writers. Every nation, every race, has not only its own
creative, but its own critical turn of mind; and is even more oblivious of
the shortcomings and limitations of its critical habits than of those of its
creative genius. We know, or think we know, from the enormous mass of
critical writing that has appeared in the French language the critical
method or habit of the French; we only conclude (we are such unconscious people) that the French are "more critical" than we, and sometimes even plume[2] ourselves a little with the fact, as if the French were
the less spontaneous. Perhaps they are; but we might remind ourselves
that criticism is as inevitable as breathing, and that we should be none
the worse for articulating what passes in our minds when we read a book
and feel an emotion about it, for criticizing our own minds in their work
of criticism. One of the facts that might come to light in this process is
our tendency to insist, when we praise a poet, upon those aspects of his
work in which he least resembles anyone else. In these aspects or parts of
his work we pretend to find what is individual, what is the peculiar
essence of the man. We dwell with satisfaction upon the poet's difference
from his predecessors, especially his immediate predecessors; we en-
deavour to find something that can be isolated in order to be enjoyed.
Whereas if we approach a poet without this prejudice we shall often find
that not only the best, but the most individual parts of his work may be
those in which the dead poets, his ancestors, assert their immortality
most vigorously. And I do not mean the impressionable period of adolescence, but the period of full maturity.

Yet if the only form of tradition, of handing down, consisted in
following the ways of the immediate generation before us in a blind or
timid adherence to its successes, "tradition" should positively be dis-

[1] Approving.   [2] Flatter.

couraged. We have seen many such simple currents soon lost in the sand; and novelty is better than repetition. Tradition is a matter of much wider significance. It cannot be inherited, and if you want it you must obtain it by great labour. It involves, in the first place, the historical sense, which we may call nearly indispensable to anyone who would continue to be a poet beyond his twenty-fifth year; and the historical sense involves a perception, not only of the pastness of the past, but of its presence; the historical sense compels a man to write not merely with his own generation in his bones, but with a feeling that the whole of the literature of Europe from Homer and within it the whole of the literature of his own country has a simultaneous existence and composes a simultaneous order. This historical sense, which is a sense of the timeless as well as of the temporal and of the timeless and of the temporal together, is what makes a writer most acutely conscious of his place in time, of his contemporaneity.

No poet, no artist of any art, has his complete meaning alone. His significance, his appreciation is the appreciation of his relation to the dead poets and artists. You cannot value him alone; you must set him, for contrast and comparison, among the dead. I mean this as a principle of aesthetic, not merely historical, criticism. The necessity that he shall conform, that he shall cohere, is not one-sided; what happens when a new work of art is created is something that happens simultaneously to all the works of art which preceded it. The existing monuments form an ideal order among themselves, which is modified by the introduction of the new (the really new) work of art among them. The existing order is complete before the new work arrives; for order to persist after the supervention of novelty, the *whole* existing order must be, if ever so slightly, altered; and so the relations, proportions, values of each work of art toward the whole are readjusted; and this is conformity between the old and the new. Whoever has approved this idea of order, of the form of European, of English literature, will not find it preposterous that the past should be altered by the present as much as the present is directed by the past. And the poet who is aware of this will be aware of the great difficulties and responsibilities.

In a peculiar sense, he will be aware also that he must inevitably be judged by the standards of the past. I say judged, not amputated, by them; not judged to be as good as, or worse or better than, the dead; and certainly not judged by the canons of dead critics. It is a judgment, a comparison, in which two things are measured by each other. To conform merely would be for the new work not really to conform at all; it would not be new, and would therefore not be a work of art. And we do not quite say that the new is more valuable because it fits in; but its fitting in is a test of its value—a test, it is true, which can only be slowly and cautiously applied, for we are none of us infallible judges of conformity. We say: it appears to conform, and is perhaps individual, and may conform; but we are hardly likely to find that it is one and not the other.

To proceed to a more intelligible exposition of the relation of the poet to the past: he can neither take the past as a lump, an indiscriminate bolus,[3] nor can he form himself wholly on one or two private admirations, nor can he form himself wholy upon one preferred period. The first course is inadmissible, the second is an important experience of youth, and the third is a pleasant and highly desirable supplement. The poet must be very conscious of the main current, which does not at all flow invariably through the most distinguished reputations. He must be quite aware of the obvious fact that art never improves, but that the material of art is never quite the same. He must be aware that the mind of Europe— the mind of his own country—a mind which he learns in time to be much more important than his own private mind—is a mind which changes, and that this change is a development which abandons nothing *en route,* which does not superannuate[4] either Shakespeare, or Homer, or the rock drawing of the Magdalenian draughtsmen. That this development, refinement perhaps, complication certainly, is not, from the point of view of the artist, any improvement. Perhaps not even an improvement from the point of view of the psychologist or not to the extent which we imagine; perhaps only in the end based upon a complication in economics and machinery. But the difference between the present and the past is that the conscious present is an awareness of the past in a way and to an extent which the past's awareness of itself cannot show.

Some one said: "The dead writers are remote from us because we *know* so much more than they did." Precisely, and they are that which we know.

I am alive to a usual objection to what is clearly part of my programme for the *métier*[5] of poetry. The objection is that the doctrine requires a ridiculous amount of erudition (pedantry), a claim which can be rejected by appeal to the lives of poets in any pantheon.[6] It will even be affirmed that much learning deadens or perverts poetic sensibility. While, however, we persist in believing that a poet ought to know as much as will not encroach upon his necessary receptivity and necessary laziness, it is not desirable to confine knowledge to whatever can be put into a useful shape for examinations, drawing-rooms, or the still more pretentious modes of publicity. Some can absorb knowledge, the more tardy must sweat for it. Shakespeare acquired more essential history from Plutarch than most men could from the whole British Museum. What is to be insisted upon is that the poet must develop or procure the consciousness of the past and that he should continue to develop this consciousness throughout his career.

What happens is a continual surrender of himself as he is at the moment to something which is more valuable. The progress of an artist is a continual self-sacrifice, a continual extinction of personality . . . .

---

[3] Mass.
[4] Make outdated.

[5] Field, profession.
[6] Groups of gods or idols.

Questions for Discussion and Writing

1. One of Eliot's major purposes in writing this essay is to define the concept of tradition. How has he developed the opening two paragraphs to make defining the term seem like a necessary task?

2. Eliot writes in a formal, elaborate prose style. Why would a colloquial style (one that resembles the common speaking style) be inappropriate, given his thesis on the individual voice?

3. What, finally, is Eliot's definition of tradition?

4. In Eliot's view, how should a critic determine the worth of a new work of art?

5. Eliot rejects equating the term *individual* with the term *different*. Explain how an artist's "voice" can be individual and traditional at the same time by incorporating what Eliot calls "the historical sense."

6. Explain Eliot's notion of how works of art form an "ideal order," a conformity of the new with the old.

7. Why must the artist undergo an "extinction of personality"?

8. Would artistic works by members of minority groups in Western culture be admitted to the tradition as Eliot conceives it? Why or why not? What difficulties might such an artist encounter?

9. In Eliot's conception of the ideal order of art, can certain works in the tradition lose their status as great works of art? Can works from earlier historical periods become part of the ideal order even if they were not perceived as valuable at the time of their creation?

10. Apply Eliot's critical method to a traditional work of art and to a contemporary work you know. What makes the former a part of the tradition? Would the contemporary work meet the same criteria?

Adalaide Morris, **"Dick, Jane, and American Literature: Fighting with Canons"** _____

In the followng essay, published in 1985, Adalaide Morris, a professor of English literature, examines the controversial issue of canonicity. The "canon" of American literature consists of the texts that are accepted as classics, as important, as representative of the "best." The canon thus comes to have a symbolic value and power beyond the individual texts that make it up. Critics of the canon have called attention to its exclusionary nature: few works by women, minorities, or working-class people are included. Other critics have attacked the very notion of a canon, seeing it as a misguided attempt to institutionalize a certain set of values, or ideology. As a student, your views become part of this debate over the canon, for it is an issue that affects everyone associated wth American educational practice and policy.

Key Concepts

A **world view** (page 292) is our perception of reality (how the world operates, how the individual relates to society) and the values we endorse in it.

Mainstream society refers to the majority group, to the people whose opinions and behavior determine what the norms of society are (page 293).

The very first book I remember reading had bold pictures and clean, brisk words. "See Spot run," I read, sliding a stubby finger along the line. "See Puff play." It was the story of Dick and Jane, the boy and girl who lived with their dog and cat, Mother and Father, and baby sister Sally in a little house with a red door, a curving walk, and a bright green lawn with bushy trees. Father was tall and wore a suit, Mother was shorter and wore an apron, and baby Sally crawled and cried, making us feel proud to be grown-up first-graders reading books. This was my world, and I recognized its every striped ball, spotless pinafore,[1] and smiling postman.

At about the same time I was seeing Spot run, another American girl was also reading *Dick and Jane.* The Native American writer Leslie Silko grew up on the Laguna Pueblo in the Southwest. To her the father with his briefcase, the mother with her cookie pans, the children cavorting on the lawn must have seemed strange creatures. What worried her, however, was the robins. Dick and Jane (and children in the Chicago suburbs) know when winter comes robins fly south. What, then, was the matter with the Pueblo robins? Why didn't they leave?

Toni Morrison's first novel, *The Bluest Eye,* starts with *Dick and Jane:* "Here is the house. It is green and white. It has a red door. It is very pretty. Here is the family. Mother, Father, Dick, and Jane live in the green-and-white house. They are very happy." Her second paragraph runs the sentences together without breaks ("Here is the house it is green and white it has a red door"), and the third drops the spaces between the words ("Hereisthehouseitisgreenandwhite"). The stately, reassuring rhythms of *Dick and Jane* undergo nightmare acceleration, and the words fuse into a monolithic chunk of type, a block as heavy as a tablet of commandments. Chips from this block introduce Morrison's chapters about a poor black family: Cholly Breedlove, Mrs. Breedlove, Sammy, and Pecola, who live in an abandoned store underneath the headquarters of three whores named China, Poland, and the Maginot Line. Cholly drinks and beats his wife, Sammy runs away, and each night Pecola prays for blue eyes. She, like her mother, like the girls at school, like all of us first graders, knew that if she resembled Jane she would be all right. Like Silko's robins, however, by any standard we recognized, she was not all right. Out of his own tenderness and agony, her father rapes her, goes to jail, and dies; she bears a dead baby and goes mad. The ironic interplay between the chapterheads ("fatherwillyouplaywithjanesmilefathersmile") and the chapter contents indicts a whitewashed world so sure of itself it has no space between its words for little black girls in abandoned stores.

No one told us, perhaps no one in my early fifties school system *could* have told us, that Dick and Jane were a special case, a small

---

[1] Child's apron.

minority of suburban, white, middle-class children of Anglo-Saxon parentage and Protestant heritage. We thought, and our parents thought, and Native American, Black, Jewish, and Asian-American children were urged to think that when the robins left for us, they should leave for all.

When many of us reached college in the early sixties and studied what was now called "American literature," Jane and baby Sally fell away, but we continued to read about Dick. Now Dick becomes Franklin's Poor Richard who knows that *God helps them that help themselves* or Horatio Alger's Ragged Dick the Match Boy who rises from rags to riches to become, in Fitzgerald's mythic rewriting, The Great Gatsby. Or he becomes Nick, Hemingway's Nick Adams making his separate peace in the Michigan woods, or Ike, Isaac McCaslin in Faulkner's "The Bear" who earns his manhood in the Mississippi wilderness. These two great paradigms of American literature—the success story and the story of rugged individualism—are our primers. Like *Dick and Jane,* they are training tales, stories that tell us how to live, what to do. They are the stories that we have institutionalized as the "American literary canon."

Like the schools in which it is taught, like the church, like the legal system, what we call "American literature" is an institution: an authoritative organization of principles and precepts. The canon is its charter: an official designation of membership and a certification of rights and privileges. As all first graders once read *Dick and Jane,* college students now read Emerson, Thoreau, Melville, Whitman, and Twain. We like to think of literature as a representation of experience, but the question Silko and Morrison ask is blunt: *whose* experience? How have Ahab, Walt, Huck, Nick, and Ike come to stand for *the* "American" experience? Who made Injun Joe and Nigger Jim? And where in the world is Jane?

I'd like to approach these questions by rethinking a word central to the problem: the word *canon.* This is a mighty word, a word that decrees, regulates, codifies, and constitutes. With others of its family, however, it starts from a slim and supple source: the Greek word *kanna,* meaning a hollow tube or reed. If we use this reed to measure things, it becomes a *canon:* a general rule, formula, or table. Mounted on the parapets of a fort, it becomes the *cannon* we shoot at those who are unlucky enough to live outside or disobey our rules. If long enough and strong enough, this reed becomes a *cane* which can support us or flog others. Unlike a reed, which may be swayed or woven or even whistled through, the canon, cannons, and canes have fixed functions. They don't invite rethinking. It seems to be no accident that *canon* sounds so much like *cannot.*

In our profession, the literary canon not only regulates, defends, and supports us: it seems to sanctify us. In the precise sense we appropriate from ecclesiastical parlance,[2] the canon is an authoritative list of books accepted as holy scripture. Our canon is the "great books," the

---

[2] Church terminology.

Modern Library list of classics, or, most pertinently here, the Library of America volumes now emerging in a uniform format, each printed on Oxford style onion paper and bound, like a bible, with a grosgrain ribbon placemarker. These books are the basis for the lists academics live by (course lists, M.A. Exam lists, Ph.D. Comprehensive Examination lists, the list of "books I want to read" or "books I'll never admit I haven't read" or "books I swear I'll read next summer"). Lined down the page, these texts become the table of contents for anthologies, the schedule of sessions at conventions, and the subjects of scrutiny in our favorite professional journals. When we as students and teachers try to understand what we're doing in this world, the canon seems to offer a center for all our peripheries. It is, in another ecclesiastical borrowing, our mission or missal: a catalogue of saints, a liturgical sequence, an annual or customary payment or tribute.

And it should be. The canon is for us what the epic was for the Greeks: an encyclopedia of culture, a compendium[3] of what we know, a background against which forms the figure of what we read and what we write. "Masterpieces are never single and solitary births. They are," as Virginia Woolf has reminded us, "the outcome of many years of thinking in common, of thinking by the body of the people, so that the experience of the mass is behind the single voice." Reading any text is necessarily listening to a voice in conversation with other voices. No writer, no artist of any art, has his or her complete meaning alone. To understand the soliloquist,[4] we need also to listen to the chorus.

The problem arises when the canon becomes a cane by which we yank the soliloquist off the stage or a piece of artillery we use to hurl her or him into the outer darkness. The problem arises when, to alter the metaphor slightly, the chorus rises and says to the soliloquist something like "you're not the best that has been thought and said," a formula inevitably followed by adjectives like "propagandist," "second-rate," "narrow," "partial," "distorted," or "subjective." At this moment it is hard not to notice that the chorus consists almost entirely of white gentlemen of the middle or upper classes and that they're toting signs emblazoned with the words "universal," "timeless," "natural," and "self-evident."

The fact of canonization puts any work beyond questions of establishing its merit and, instead, invites us to offer only increasingly more ingenious readings and interpretations, the purpose of which is to validate labels like "great" or "universal." The general effect of canonization, as it became evident in the sixties, is threefold:

1. to propagandize the **world view** of canonized works, which tends to be almost entirely the world view of relatively privileged social classes in societies actively engaged in conquering and ruling other peoples

---

[3] Summary.   [4] Single speaker.

2. to reinforce our own authority and position as students and professors of literature who possess valuable knowledge, social usefulness, and, above all, superior taste, and

3. to substitute a tiny part for the whole, demeaning as subliterary almost the entire body of literature, especially popular literature, folk literature, oral literature, literature based on the experience of work, and almost all literature by nonwhite, nonmale peoples.

Much has happened since the sixties: we have grown suspicious of words like "timeless" and "self-evident"; we have understood the canon as, among other things, a political document; and we have begun to admit some women, a few Blacks, and here and there a Native American. . . .

It may be that we do not need a larger canon. Instead we need to do the legwork to find and the reference work to value the multiple and conflicting canons that we have always had.

This is a rigorous ideal. What it means is that when we read Leslie Silko's novel *Ceremony,* we make ourselves responsible for knowing not only the white **mainstream** canon of the American novel but also something about the oral traditions of the Pueblo people and something about the rich interconnections among contemporary Native American women writers. It means that when we read Morrison's *The Bluest Eye* we recognize not only our own Dick and Jane but also the traditions of Afro-American storytelling from the folktales, spirituals, blues, and slave narratives to the work of Richard Wright, Zora Neale Hurston, and Alice Walker. It means, finally, that we commit money to Black Studies, Native American Studies, and Women's Studies Programs, that we work to keep the writings from these traditions in cheap paperback editions and thick American anthologies, and that we require ourselves and our students to become literate in a number of the many traditions of American writing.

Defenders of the expanded canon argue that if we are to be a community we must discover or create a common intellectual heritage, a heritage that would bind us into an understanding of our enterprise as Americans. The problem with this, of course, is that it results in one of two formulations: either what a colleague of mine calls the "pale male" canon, the familiar story of Walt, Huck, Nick, Ike, and Old Ez, or its bland liberal replacement, a canon so diversified and disorganized we cannot locate a narrative to unify it.

Traditionally a canon is defined as that which is shared. For Americans, however, it is the battle that is shared, not the canons that fight it. Our common heritage is struggle. We are not and never have been a mono-cultural people; we haven't even been a mono-linguistic people. American literature is a clash of contending canons, a vital argument about how to live, what to do. There is no center, except as we enter and momentarily inhabit a writer's consciousness. We don't need to remain entrenched, but we do need to perceive and protect our differences. Fighting with canons can open a way to see not only Dick but also Jane and baby Sally, Pecola Breedlove, and Leslie Silko's stubbornly persisting robins.

Questions for Discussion and Writing

1. Outline Morris's support for and critique on the canon. In her view, are changes in the content of the canon necessary? Does she finally reject the concept of a canon?

2. In paragraph 9, Morris paraphrases a line from Eliot's "Tradition and the Individual Talent": "No writer, no artist of any art, has his or her complete meaning alone." To what extent does she agree with Eliot's concept of tradition?

3. What does Morris consider our common heritage as Americans to be?

4. How does the traditional canon promote the importance of one social group over another, or, as Morris puts it, "propagandize the world view"?

5. Choose a canonical work from the readings you've completed in *The Course of Ideas*. Apply the three effects of canonization that Morris describes to determine how the work may function as a text promoting propagandistic, elitist, and/or exclusionary values.

6. How might someone outside the mainstream group feel if he or she only encounters canonical works in school and in other institutionalized contexts? Consider Morris's reference to Leslie Silko's childhood experience.

7. Explain the idea that Morris cites in her analysis of Toni Morrison's *The Bluest Eye* that "[Pecola], like her mother, like the girls at school, like all of us first graders, knew that if she resembled Jane she would be all right." How does this view make Pecola feel responsible for her family and social situation?

8. Describe the earliest stories and books that you can recall hearing or reading as a child. Do you see the same cultural limitations reflected in them as Morris detects in the "Dick and Jane" reader? How closely do the stories reflect the actual social context of your personal background and experience?

9. What values institutionalized in the American literary canon are also reflected in the rest of your educational experience? Consider the goals that schools encourage, the type of behavior that is rewarded, and the ideas and texts promoted in class work. Analyze this textbook as one concrete example of educational ideology.

Maxine Hong Kingston, from **The Woman Warrior** _____

As a Chinese-American, and as a woman, Maxine Hong Kingston writes with a voice whose context is a mixture of different traditions. In the following passage from The Woman Warrior (published in 1975), she describes the state of silence that cultural tradition, gender, and language itself imposed on her as a child. Only at Chinese school, surrounded by people who shared her family's language and customs, did she feel free to speak without self-conciousness. But even within this familiar environment, the restrictions of gender are clear to her.

My silence was thickest—total—during the three years that I covered my school paintings with black paint. I painted layers of black over houses and flowers and suns, and when I drew on the blackboard, I put a layer of chalk on top. I was making a stage curtain, and it was the moment before the curtain parted or rose. The teachers called my parents to school, and I saw they had been saving my pictures, curling and cracking, all alike and black. The teachers pointed to the pictures and looked serious, talked seriously too, but my parents did not understand English. ("The parents and teachers of criminals were executed," said my father.) My parents took the pictures home. I spread them out (so black and full of possibilities) and pretended the curtains were swinging open, flying up, one after another, sunlight underneath, mighty operas.

During the first silent year I spoke to no one at school, did not ask before going to the lavatory, and flunked kindergarten. My sister also said nothing for three years, silent in the playground and silent at lunch. There were other quiet Chinese girls not of our family, but most of them got over it sooner than we did. I enjoyed the silence. At first it did not occur to me I was supposed to talk or to pass kindergarten. I talked at home and to one or two of the Chinese kids in class. I made motions and even made some jokes. I drank out of a toy saucer when the water spilled out of the cup, and everybody laughed, pointing at me, so I did it some more. I didn't know that Americans don't drink out of saucers.

I liked the Negro students (Black Ghosts) best because they laughed the loudest and talked to me as if I were a daring talker too. One of the Negro girls had her mother coil braids over her ears Shanghai-style like mine; we were Shanghai twins except that she was covered with black like my paintings. Two Negro kids enrolled in Chinese school, and the teachers gave them Chinese names. Some Negro kids walked me to school and home, protecting me from the Japanese kids, who hit me and chased me and stuck gum in my ears. The Japanese kids were noisy and tough. They appeared one day in kindergarten, released from concentration camp, which was a tic-tac-toe mark, like barbed wire, on the map.

It was when I found out I had to talk that school became a misery, that the silence became a misery. I did not speak and felt bad each time that I did not speak. I read aloud in first grade, though, and heard the barest whisper with little squeaks come out of my throat. "Louder," said the teacher, who scared the voice away again. The other Chinese girls did not talk either, so I knew the silence had to do with being a Chinese girl.

Reading out loud was easier than speaking because we did not have to make up what to say, but I stopped often, and the teacher would think I'd gone quiet again. I could not understand "I." The Chinese "I" has seven strokes, intricacies. How could the American "I," assuredly wearing a hat like the Chinese, have only three strokes, the middle so straight? Was it out of politeness that this writer left off strokes the way a Chinese has to write her own name small and crooked? No, it was not politeness; "I" is a capital and "you" is lower-case. I stared at the middle line and waited so long for its black center to resolve into tight strokes and dots that I forgot to pronounce it. The other troublesome word was "here," no strong consonant to hang on to, and so flat, when "here" is two mountainous ideographs.[1] The teacher, who had already told me every day how to read "I" and "here," put me in the low corner under the stairs again, where the noisy boys usually sat.

When my second grade class did a play, the whole class went to the auditorium except the Chinese girls. The teacher, lovely and Hawaiian, should have understood about us, but instead left us behind in the classroom. Our voices were too soft or nonexistent, and our parents never signed the permission slips anyway. They never signed anything unnecessary. We opened the door a crack and peeked out, but closed it again quickly. One of us (not me) won every spelling bee, though.

I remember telling the Hawaiian teacher, "We Chinese can't sing 'land where our fathers died.'" She argued with me about politics, while I meant because of curses. But how can I have that memory when I couldn't talk? My mother says that we, like the ghosts, have no memories.

After American school, we picked up our cigar boxes, in which we had arranged books, brushes, and an inkbox neatly, and went to Chinese school, from 5:00 to 7:30 P.M. There we chanted together, voices rising and falling, loud and soft, some boys shouting, everybody reading together, reciting together and not alone with one voice. When we had a memorization test, the teacher let each of us come to his desk and say the lesson to him privately, while the rest of the class practiced copying or tracing. Most of the teachers were men. The boys who were so well behaved in the American school played tricks on them and talked back to them. The girls were not mute. They screamed and yelled during recess, when there were no rules; they had fistfights. Nobody was afraid of children hurting themselves or of children hurting school property. The glass doors to the red and green balconies with the gold job symbols were left wide open so that we could run out and climb the fire escapes. We played capture-the-flag in the auditorium, where Sun Yat-sen and Chiang Kai-shek's[2] pictures hung at the back of the stage, the Chinese flag on their left and the American flag on their right. We climbed the teak ceremonial chairs and made flying leaps off the stage. One flag headquarters was behind the glass door and the other on stage right. Our feet drummed on the hollow stage. During recess the teachers locked themselves up in their office with the shelves of books, copybooks, inks from China. They drank tea and warmed their hands at a stove. There was no play supervision. At recess we had the school to ourselves, and also we could roam as far as we could go—downtown, Chinatown stores, home—as long as we returned before the bell rang.

At exactly 7:30 the teacher again picked up the brass bell that sat on his desk and swung it over our heads, while we charged down the stairs, our cheering magnified in the stairwell. Nobody had to line up.

---

[1] Written symbol of an idea.   [2] Chinese revolutionary leaders.

Not all of the children who were silent at American school found voice at Chinese school. One new teacher said each of us had to get up and recite in front of the class, who was to listen. My sister and I had memorized the lesson perfectly. We said it to each other at home, one chanting, one listening. The teacher called on my sister to recite first. It was the first time a teacher had called on the second-born to go first. My sister was scared. She glanced at me and looked away; I looked down at my desk. I hoped that she could do it because if she could, then I would have to. She opened her mouth and a voice came out that wasn't a whisper, but it wasn't a proper voice either. I hoped that she would not cry, fear breaking up her voice like twigs underfoot. She sounded as if she were trying to sing though weeping and strangling. She did not pause or stop to end the embarrassment. She kept going until she said the last word, and then she sat down. When it was my turn, the same voice came out, a crippled animal running on broken legs. You could hear splinters in my voice, bones rubbing jagged against one another. I was loud, though. I was glad I didn't whisper. There was one little girl who whispered.

Questions for Discussion and Writing

1. Why are the author and the other Chinese girls silent?

2. How does her parents' lack of English fluency affect Kingston's school experiences? Does she seem to feel shame about her family's linguistic difference?

3. Why does Kingston as a young child respond most positively to her black schoolmates? Do these children face similar cultural alienation, or is their ability to be what Kingston perceives as "daring talkers" evidence of their mainstream membership?

4. Kingston reports that she "could not understand 'I.'" How is the Western concept of "I" different from the Chinese concept? How significant is the difference?

5. How and why do the students behave differently in Chinese school than they do in the public school?

6. Compare the experiences of Kingston and Richard Rodriguez (Chapter 6, from *Hunger of Memory*) as children of immigrants, growing up with English as a second language and being acutely aware of their difference from the cultural mainstream.

7. In "Crossing Boundaries" (Chapter 1), Mike Rose discusses the effects of cultural difference and exclusion, especially in education. Does Kingston's account of her early school experience support Rose's thesis?

8. Does Kingston experience her ethnic and gender difference in the same way that Dick Gregory experiences his ethnic and class difference, as he depicts in his autobiographical essay "Shame" (Chapter 6)?

9. Many schoolchildren fear speaking in the unfamiliar public setting of the classroom. How does being different from the mainstream add to a child's fear and self-consciousness? Use your own experience or personal observations to explore the possible educational effects of cultural difference.

Chapter Writing Topics

1. King Oedipus, as he is depicted in myth, in the tragedy by Sophocles, and
    in the writings of Sigmund Freud, plays a dual role: On the one hand, he is
    a tragic hero, a symbol of the human condition, and on the other, he is
    very realistic, very much the loving, proud, flawed person. Discuss this
    split in his nature and explain its importance. As a figure in myth,
    literature, and psychological theory, why must his character be at once
    human and superhuman? How is his symbolic power related to his
    human qualities? Use the following questions to help break the essay into
    focused units of discussion, and refer to all the sources (myth, Sophocles,
    and Freud) for your analysis.

    (a) What reactions and events in the story of Oedipus emphasize his
         common human qualities?

    (b) How does the reader react to these qualities and events? Consider
         referring to Aristotle's analysis of the effects of tragedy to address
         this issue.

    (c) How does Oedipus's recognition of his guilt make the audience
         feel? Do we empathize with him or feel alienated from him? Refer to
         Freud and to the reactions of other characters in Sophocles' play.

    (d) What makes Oedipus a tragic hero? How does his tragedy separate
         him from average human experience? What does he come to
         symbolize?

    (e) Come to some conclusion about the final issue in the assignment:
         How is Oedipus's symbolic power related to his human qualities?

2. Both Oedipus Rex and Sir Lancelot embody traditional heroic charac-
    teristics. Outline the heroic traits of one or both of these heroes and then
    compare them to a contemporary hero of your choice. Has our concep-
    tion of the heroic figure changed over the centuries? To what extent is it
    still the same? Use the following organizational plan or develop your own
    structural approach to the topic.

    (a) Define the characteristics of the two types of heroes, the tragic
         (Oedipus) and the chivalric (Lancelot).

    (b) Introduce the contemporary hero. Discuss the points he or she has
         in common with the earlier heroic types.

    (c) Come to a conclusion about the nature of the contemporary hero:
         is he or she part of the heroic tradition? If so, in what way(s)? If not,
         what are the major characteristics of this new type, and what other
         examples of the type exist?

3. Construct the ideal female hero that would be most appropriate as a role
    model for young readers today. Develop your concept of the hero in
    either essay or story form. Use the assignment to promote your vision of
    the ideal female hero, and include (or create) examples. Consider the

following topics along with other issues that arise in your writing process.

(a) Clarify the most important characteristics of the hero and why you consider them to be important.

(b) How does the female heroic figure differ from traditional literary depictions of females (if you see differences)?

(c) How does this heroic figure interact with males and other females?

(d) What effect on the reading audience, especially children, will these female heroes have? What values will their stories promote?

4. Compare and contrast Malory's Arthurian tales and Cervantes' *Don Quixote* and analyze their similarities and differences. Consider how realistic or idealized the stories are. Examine the characters, settings and plots, the depiction of chivalry, the effect of the stories on readers, and the implied world views. Think about the following questions as you write.

(a) Why is Malory's story less realistic than that of Cervantes? How do the characters speak? Does Malory give any insight into their psychology and emotions? What makes Cervantes' characters more believable? How plausible are the characters' actions?

(b) How are women depicted? What is the role of Dulcinea, and how does she compare to Guenivere and the other women in the Lancelot tales?

(c) How is chivalry presented? How is it idealized and satirized?

(d) Examine the social classes of the characters. How are they idealized in Malory? How does Cervantes depict the upper and lower classes? Could characters from one story appear in the other?

(e) Review the readings on the Middle Ages and the Renaissance in Chapters 2-3. What changes in society and world view in Cervantes and Malory's time might account for the differences between the stories?

5. Review the personal styles depicted in Castiglione's description of the ideal courtier and the notion of *sprezzatura,* and in Montaigne's personal aesthetic of "not communicating one's glory." Both writers describe a way of presenting oneself to society as well as a way of judging beauty, grace, and goodness. Write an essay defining and analyzing your own personal style or the style of another person, perhaps a media figure (a rock or film star, for example). Consider some of the following questions as you write.

(a) Examine the tangible and intangible elements of the style: hairstyle, clothing, cosmetics, jewelry, behavior, body language, speech. What messages do they convey? How are they perceived?

(b) How would you classify the style—radical, conservative, innovative, conventional, humorous, creative, hip, chic, punk, heavy metal? Do people have more than one style? Under what circumstances do they change styles?

(c) How was the style acquired? Is it informed by religious or philosophical beliefs? Is it a reaction to a previous style? Do people initially imitate the styles of others, "steal this grace from those who have it," as Castiglione writes? What are the sources for style—television, movies, magazines, friends?

(d) Analyze the criteria people use to evaluate style.

(e) Consider some of the broader issues: Who sets the trends most people follow? Is conforming to a style almost contradictory to having style? What cultural values underlie the style? Are they always positive and beneficial to people and society? To what degree are modern styles formalized and structured?

6. Read one of the texts that precedes the Romantic age from the perspective of the Romantic figure Jean-Jacques Rousseau or Victor Frankenstein. Examine "Echo and Narcissus," the excerpt from *The Odyssey,* Darwin's theory of evoluton, or excerpts from *Don Quixote* or *Candide.* Present your interpretation of the text as you believe each of these figures would read it. Address some of the following questions.

(a) Would the Romantic figure's view of the text and its ideas be mainly positive or mainly negative? Why?

(b) How important is emotional response in the earlier text? Would emotional effect be a criterion of judgment for the Romantic figure?

(c) Would the Romantic figure find the view of human nature present in the text acceptable? Why or why not? What is the nature of the hero (if one exists) in the text?

(d) Does the earlier text emphasize the value of love and the idea of "soul-mates"? How would the Romantic figure react to the presence or absence of this element?

7. Summarize the arguments concerning canonicity and traditional education set forth by two or more of the following authors: T. S. Eliot, in "Tradition and the Individual Talent," Adalaide Morris, in "Dick, Jane, and American Literature," Mike Rose in "Crossing Boundaries" (Chapter 1), and Carolyn J. Mooney, in "[Stanford's] Western Culture Program" (Chapter 1). Clarify for the reader your own stand on the issues, speaking from your status as a student and a representative of a particular social group.

8. Select a reading from Chapter 4 (or a reading from another chapter you've read) and rewrite it so that it reflects your personal view of what apppropriate literary content is. You can alter the story in various ways:

(a) Change the gender or class status of a hero.

(b) Change the plot or the resolution of the action.

(c)   Make a serious tone humorous, or vice versa.

(d)   Alter the hero's world view, making him or her tragic, chivalric, rationalistic, Romantic.

(e)   Alter the genre from drama to biography, from heroic tale to confessional essay.

(f)   Change the time period, cultural setting, or other fundamental aspect of the text.

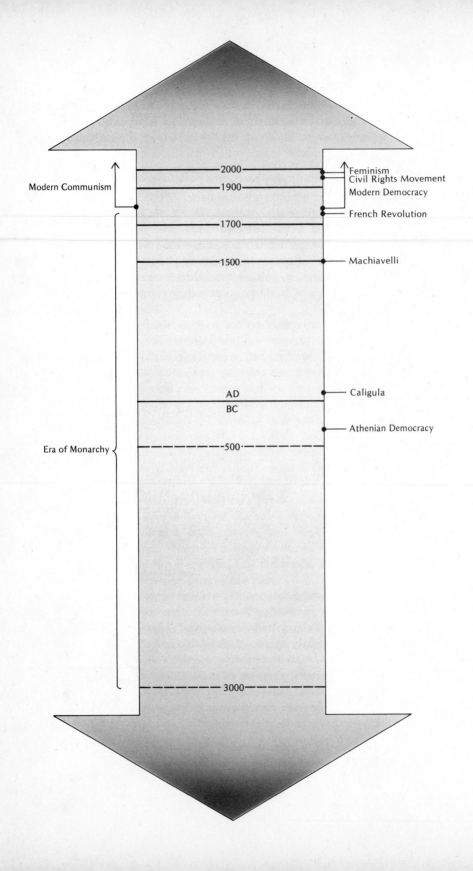

C H A P T E R   5

Political Theory and
Practice

—————— ❧ ——————

Introduction

The readings in this chapter present political theory and reflect actual practice. The beginning of each section provides a theoretical definition of a
particular political system or ideology, including democracy, monarchy, communism, imperialism, and terrorism. Each definition is followed by several
passages depicting the historical problems that have surfaced when theory
was put into practice. The passages focus on the costs and shortcomings inherent in any political system. The readings highlight discrepancies, contradictions, and dissatisfactions that inevitably arise in any society's system of
government, for no political system has shown itself to be perfect. There are
many other political systems and ideologies not covered by this chapter, and
those included here are treated generally and over large time periods. Therefore, be careful of making political judgments based on these readings alone.

In the first section, Democracy and Oppression, the readings illustrate that inequality and oppression can still exist in ostensibly egalitarian democracies,
and that democratic revolutions can lead to anarchy and terror on the way to
freedom. The section covers the place of women in ancient Athenian democracy, the French Revolution's Reign of Terror, and the struggle of women and
minorities in American democratic society.

Although they have almost disappeared from the contemporary political picture, monarchies were the predominant form of government in Western
Europe beginning with the ancient world and continuing to modern times.
The theoretical basis of monarchy is surveyed in Edenstein's "Monarchy." In
Suetonius's "Gaius [Caligula]," Caligula demonstrates the political truism that
absolute power corrupts absolutely. Of the Roman people Caligula said, "Let
them hate me as long as they fear me." This political philosophy is related to

303

Machiavelli's pronouncement in *The Prince:* "to be feared is much safer than to be loved."

Lewis L. Lorwin distinguishes Marxist and socialist thought in the first reading in the next section, The Costs of Communism. The two following essays show the past and future costs of communism. Alexander Weissberg, in an excerpt from *The Accused,* gives a victim's account of Stalin's Great Purge during the 1930s. The second reading, Dianne Feeley's "The Family," proposes that, according to Marxist theory, women's full emancipation can be achieved only by abolishing the family as a social unit.

All forms of government—democracies, monarchies, and communist states— have practiced imperialism, which is the subject of the next section, The Imperialist Heritage. Robin Winks defines imperialism in the first essay of this section. W.E.B. Dubois' essay, "The White Masters of the World" and George Orwell's essay, "Marrakech" each point out the human costs of imperialism to both oppressed and oppressor.

Terrorism, an instrument of political change which concerns everyone in the contemporary world, is examined in the next section, Contemporary Terror. Baljit Singh explains its effectiveness in "An Overview of Terrorism," and Martin Oppenheimer argues for its justification in situations of extreme oppression in "Is Terrorism Sometimes Justified?" Melanie McFadyean's interview with opposing Protestant and Catholic fighters in Northern Ireland reveals the human faces behind the terrorist masks.

The final essay of Chapter 5, co-authored by Russian Anatolii Gromyko and American Martin Hellerman, steps back and questions whether traditional political and military solutions are still feasible in a world that is rapidly becoming a "global village."

DEMOCRACY AND OPPRESSION

Sidney Hook, **"Democracy"** _____

*In the following article, Sidney Hook develops an extended defini-
tion of democracy, explaining the distinctions between direct and indirect
democracy, democracy versus republic, and democracy versus totalitarianism. He also explains the relationship between majority rule and minority
rights, the conditions for democracy, and even powerful arguments
against democracy, arguments that have been voiced from antiquity
through modern times.*

Key Concepts

The Declaration of Independence formulated an ethical principle of **inalienable rights** (page 306), which states that every individual has the right
to "life, liberty, and the pursuit of happiness." These rights are "inalienable": they cannot be taken away.

Delegation of authority in a democracy means that the people have elected
representatives to speak for them (page 307).

A **dictator** or **absolute monarch** (page 307) has total control of a nation's
government and armed forces; the people hold no power over their
leader and cannot elect any representatives.

The principle of **majority rule** (page 307) means that whatever most of the
people want will become law despite the possibly opposing wishes of the
minority.

The modern meaning of a **tyranny** is a dictatorship, a form of government by a
single leader without the necessity of popular consent (page 308).

Anarchy is the lack of any organized governing system (page 308).

The notion of **the herd** (page 308) derives from the notion of the **elite;** the
first term, an animal image, refers to the masses and carries with it the
connotation "stupid"; the second term refers to some group that expects
special privileges or recognition based on some quality, like education,
that separates them from "the herd."

Big Brother's government in Orwell's *Nineteen Eighty-Four* is an example of a
totalitarian regime. It is characterized by authoritarian control of the
people (page 309).

A **benevolent despot** (page 310) holds absolute power over a nation in an
attempt to improve or maintain the nation's economic or political
condition.

The word "democracy" has many meanings, but in the modern
world its use signifies that the ultimate authority in political affairs
rightfully belongs to the people. The term characteristically evokes
positive emotional responses among those who utter it as well as those

who hear it. There was a time when "democrat" was a term of abuse. Today its connotations are honorable.

Democracy is a form of government in which the major decisions of government—or the direction of policy behind these decisions—rest directly or indirectly on the freely given consent of a majority of the adults governed. This makes democracy essentially a political concept even when it is used—and sometimes misused—to characterize non-political institutions.

Democracy as a political process is obviously a matter of degree—depending on the area of life within the bounds of political experience and the number and qualifications of those considered adults. Because no ideal democracies exist and because there are always some areas in which the voice or wishes of the multitude[1] can be heard or can make itself felt, the difference between non-democratic and democratic states are sometimes characterized as being "merely" one of degree. This is incontestable, but usually the argument of difference "merely in degree" is employed to minimize, and often confuse, the difference between democratic and non-democratic states.

Freely Given Consent

It becomes necessary, therefore, to supplement the above definition with a working conception that will enable us to distinguish democratic regimes from others. One such working conception is the view that a democratic government is one in which the minority or its representatives may peacefully become the majority or the representatives of the majority. The presupposition[2] is, of course, that this transition is made possible by, and expresses, the freely given consent of the majority of the adults governed. The implications of the presence of freely given consent call attention to the difference between ancient democracies, which stressed only majority rule as a validating principle, and modern democracies, which since the birth of the American republic have stressed the operating presence of **inalienable rights.**

Direct and Indirect Democracy

Before developing the implications of this distinction, it is necessary to dissolve certain misconceptions that have often plagued discussions of democracy. The first is the view that the only genuine democracy is "direct" democracy in which all citizens of the community are present and collectively pass on all legislation, as was practiced in ancient Athens or as is the case in a New England town meeting. From this point of view an indirect or representative democracy is not a democracy but a constitutional republic or commonwealth. This distinction breaks down because, literally construed,[3] there can be no direct democracy if laws are defined not only in terms of their adoption but also

---

[1] The masses, common people.   [3] Translated, interpreted.
[2] That which is supposed or assumed
beforehand.

in terms of their execution. For **delegation of authority** is inescapable in any political assemblage[4] unless all citizens are in continuous service at all times, not only legislating but executing the laws together. The basic question is whether the delegation of authority is reversible—controlled by those who delegated it.

Democracy vs. Republic

The second misconception is the identification of, or confusion between, the terms "democracy" and "republic." Strictly speaking, a republican form of government is one in which the chief titular[5] head of government is not hereditary. A republic can have an undemocratic form of government (for example, Nazi Germany or the Soviet Union) whereas a monarchy can be a democracy (for example, Britain and the Scandinavian countries). There is no organic or logical connection between the two terms.

Majority Rule and Minority Rights

From one point of view, any community in which a majority of the adult population were slaves cannot be considered democratic. Nonetheless, there is a valid distinction between the kinds of government that existed in antiquity in which the freemen—however limited in numbers—were the source of ultimate political authority and governments in which the authority of government was vested in a **dictator** or **absolute monarch.** The former were ancient democracies even though the free citizenry or its representatives recognized no limitation on the nature and exercise of their rule and others enjoyed no political rights. The result of elections in the ancient democracies often was the civil equivalent of a military victory, and "vae victis" ("woe to the vanquished") often described the fate of the defeated. Under such circumstances "democratic" rule was bloody, disorderly, and often a preface to the emergence of a strong man or dictator. Even where power was in the hands of the majority, there was no democracy in the modern sense for minority rights were not considered.

With the emergence of a theory of human rights beginning in the 17th century and its explicit development in the writings of Thomas Hobbes and, above all, John Locke, the way was prepared for a conception of democracy in which the principle of **majority rule** was a necessary but not a sufficient condition. The will of the majority was to enjoy democratic legitimacy only if it was an expression of freely given consent. The specific provisions of the American Bill of Rights, and the unwritten, but not unspoken, assumptions of the British Constitution after the Cromwellian Revolution expressed, in the idiom[6] of the time, the limits set by human rights on the power of ruling majorities, minorities, or kings.

---

[4] Group.
[5] Only in name.

[6] Common language.

Majorities could do everything except deprive minorities of the freedoms—of speech, press, assembly, rights to a fair trial, and so on—the exercise of which might enable the minority peacefully to win over the electorate and come to power. Minorities might do everything within the context of these human rights to present their case. But so long as they accepted the principles of democratic organization, they were bound by the outcome of the give and take of free discussion and debate until another opportunity for persuasion might present itself. Since unanimity among human beings about matters of great and topical concern is impossible, the majority principle, insofar as it truly respects the existence of human rights, is the only one that makes democracy a viable alternative to tyranny. The other alternative to **tyranny** is **anarchy,** which is the rule of a thousand tyrants.

Conditions for Democratic Rule

What are the signs of "freely given consent" or under what conditions is it present? Briefly, when there is no physical coercion or threat of coercion employed against expression of opinion; when there is no arbitrary restriction placed on freedom of speech, press, and assembly; where there is no monopoly of propaganda by the ruling party; and where there is no institutional control over the instruments or facilities of communication. These are minimal conditions for the existence of freely given consent. In their absence a plebiscite,[7] even if unanimous, is not democratically valid.

From one point of view these may be considered negative conditions for the presence of democratic rule. But it may be necessary for a government to take positive measures to ensure that different groups in the population have access to the means by which public opinion is swayed. If, for example, an individual or a group had an economic monopoly of newsprint or television channels and barred those with contrary views from using them, both the spirit and letter of democracy would be violated.

Informed Citizenry

Philosophers of democracy, especially Thomas Jefferson, John Stuart Mill, and John Dewey, have called attention to certain positive conditions whose presence quickens and strengthens the democratic process. Foremost of these is the spread of education, allowing for an informed and critical awareness of the issues and problems of the times. If the avenues of communication are open, an educated electorate[8] can become aware of the consequences and costs of past policies and the present alternatives of action.

If, as Spinoza declared, men may become enslaved by their ignorance, uninformed freedom of choice may take the road of disaster. It is this fear of mass ignorance or the stupidity of **the herd** that is one root of

---

[7] Direct vote on an issue.   [8] People who vote.

opposition to democracy. H. L. Mencken referred to democracy as "the dictatorship of the booboisie." The more informed and better educated the electorate, the healthier is the democracy.

Citizen Participation

A second positive condition for the existence of an effective democracy is the active participation of the citizens in the processes of government. Participation is all the more essential as government grows in size and complexity and a mood develops that the individual citizen is ineffective and ineffectual in the face of anonymous forces controlling his destiny. The result of such a mood may be widescale apathy and the decay in democratic vitality even when democratic forms are preserved. "The food of feeling," observed Mill, "is action. Let a person have nothing to do for his country, and he will not care for it."

Inviolable Rights for Minorities

The acceptance of the inviolable rights of minorities reduces the danger of dictatorship by the majority in a democracy. The rights of minorities, however, cannot be construed literally as absolute, independent of the consequences of the actions of such rights on the rights of majorities or on the welfare of society as a whole. In addition, rights may conflict. Freedom of speech may interfere with a man's right to a fair trial and sometimes, as when an orator is inciting a lynching mob, with the victim's right to life. In such circumstances the rights of a minority may have to be abridged. What, then, is the difference between democratic and **totalitarian** governments? Do not the latter also abridge the rights of citizens in the alleged interests of the common good?

Democracy vs. Totalitarianism

The differences are profound. The first distinction is that democratic government recognizes the intrinsic as well as the instrumental value of civil rights, and when it moves to restrict or abridge them, it does so slowly and reluctantly, prepared to put up with considerable disorder as a price for their preservation. Second, if and when the exercise of a civil right creates a clear and present danger of a social evil that threatens other human rights, it is abridged for a limited period and restored as soon as normalcy returns. Third, the restrictions of government agencies on every level in a democracy are subject to appeal, review, and check by an independent judiciary.[9]

Arguments against Democracy

The most powerful arguments against democratic government have been formulated by its honest opponents from Plato to George Santayana, not by modern totalitarians professing to be democrats. The nub[10] of these arguments is that most human beings are either too stupid or too vicious, or both, to be entrusted with self-government, that the

---

[9] Court system.   [10] Main point.

upshot of majority rule therefore is **tyranny** and terror, and that the nature of the public good—which is the end of government—is so complex, so largely a matter of administrative wisdom and skill, that only an elite of the intellectually gifted and spiritually elect can discover and implement it. "Knowledge, and knowledge alone," writes Santayana, "gives divine right to rule."

The weakness in these arguments was exposed by Plato himself. If most human beings are vicious, who is to control the guardians? Who can guarantee the benevolence of the **benevolent despot?** In his account of the inevitable decline from the ideal aristocracy of his Republic to the depths of the irresponsible tyrant, Plato admits that rule of the philosophers is also flawed. And although he uses the analogy of the ship to argue that just as it makes no sense to elect the pilot of a ship, who must be specifically trained for the task, so it makes no sense to elect the pilot of the ship of state, he overlooks the fact that the destination of the ship is not within the competence of the pilot. Indeed, his other analogies reinforce the argument for democracy. For example, he eloquently points out that it is not the cobbler[11] who knows best what a good pair of shoes is, but the wearer. The whole philosophy of democracy may be expressed in the implications of the homely maxim that he who wears the shoes knows best where they pinch. Despite all the drawbacks and limitations of democracy, there is considerable point to Winston Churchill's declaration: "Democracy is the worst possible form of government—except all the others that have been tried."

Faith in Democracy

The faith in democracy ultimately rests not in the belief in the natural goodness of man but in the belief that most human beings can learn by experience. In a world in which science can command unlimited natural power, it can be said that its basic values, shared knowledge, mutual discussion, and the institutionalization of consent can solve more problems with less friction than is possible by entrusting decisive power to minorities who claim to be better judges of the true interests of citizens than the citizens themselves. It is true that democracies have made foolish decisions. But where such errors have not been rectified by better and more informed democratic action, salvation has been sought in a dictator or charismatic[12] leader, and the result has more often than not ended in disaster.

Democracy, as we have seen, is not indivisible—all or nothing—in the sense that its political form necessitates the extension of the democratic principle to other areas of experience. It only makes an extension possible to those who have the vision, courage, and intelligence to struggle for it. Nor is democracy indivisible on the international scene in the sense that the world must soon become one democratic community.

---

[11] Shoemaker.   [12] Inspiring; attractive.

Even under a world government, plural political systems may be feasible if each is prepared to sacrifice some national sovereignty[13] for the sake of peace.

What can be expected is that the ideals of freedom in flourishing democratic cultures, which are on their way to solving the problems of poverty and unemployment, will always function as an inspiration to the subjects of totalitarian societies. In time, if peace is preserved, and democratic cultures do not yield to the military threats of totalitarian Communist regimes, the masses in those countries may bring about democratic changes by their own efforts. Freedom is infectious. The appetite for freedom grows on what it feeds. And once the process of liberalization begins, there is no telling where it will end.

Questions for Discussion and Writing

1. Explain the differences between a direct and an indirect democracy. Why is proper delegation of authority crucial for an indirect democracy to succeed?

2. What are the benefits of direct and indirect democracies? Why is a direct democracy impractical in the United States?

3. Explain the differences between a democracy and a republic and give examples of each.

4. Explain the concept of freely given consent. What political conditions are required for it to function? How is the notion of freely given consent critical to the modern implementation of majority rule?

5. How have some modern governments that claim to be democratic failed to provide for "freely given consent"? Consider communist and totalitarian states as well as supposed democracies.

6. Democracy has been criticized as well as praised. What does Mencken mean when he refers to democracy as the "dictatorship of the booboisie"? What are Plato and Santayana's arguments against democracy? What is the weakness in their arguments, if any?

7. Under what kind of social and cultural conditions could you imagine a democracy *not* working? Review what Mill and Jefferson say about the positive conditions for democracy.

8. If you or people whom you know have lived in other countries under nondemocratic political systems, what was your or their reaction to American democracy? What did they like/not like about it? What are some of the everyday problems with the political systems in nondemocratic countries?

9. Given the many benefits and privileges Hook attributes to democracy, elections in the United States, particularly those on the state and local level, are often poorly supported. How can you explain voter apathy? What is your own attitude toward voting, and do you vote regularly?

10. Could some people in the United States be politically disenfranchised under American democracy?

11. Consider the vast amounts of money it takes to run for political office in the

---

[13] Political authority.

United States, the growing role of the media, and the importance of "political imagemakers." To what extent do such factors compromise American democracy? In what way(s)?

Amaury de Riencourt, "Women in Athens"

The Athenian democracy is often held up for admiration and even adulation in the Western world. Athens did institute the first democracy, but it contained what to modern eyes are two glaring flaws: slavery and female oppression. We point these flaws out not to condemn or minimize the achievements of Athenian society, but to illustrate the dangers of assuming that a theory *of democracy precludes inequities in practice. The ancient world did not share the modern view that "all men are created equal." This statement asserts a belief in American democracy, but its wording conceivably excludes women from sharing in democratic rights.*

Key Concepts

A culture that practices **infanticide** (page 314) controls its population by killing unwanted newborn infants at birth.

Freud theorized that humans, on both an individual level and a group level, may indulge in a **death-wish** (page 314), a desire for their own extinction.

With the development of Greek culture came a steady regression of woman's status; from Herodotus to Thucydides, she gradually faded into the home, and Plutarch takes pleasure in quoting Thucydides to the effect that "the name of a decent woman, like her person, should be shut up in the house." Greek literature was suddenly full of disparaging remarks about woman and her innumerable faults—witness the writings of Hesiod, Lucian, Aristophanes, and Simonides of Amorgos. Her legal status deteriorated: inheritance through the mother disappeared; she could not make contracts or incur large debts or bring actions at law. Solon even went so far as to legislate that anything done under the influence of woman could not be legally binding. Furthermore, she did not even inherit her husband's property after his death. She retreated to a virtual purdah.[1] locked in her home and advised not to be seen near a window; she spent most of her life in the women's quarters and never appeared when male friends visited her husband.

Such downgrading at the height of Greek cultural achievements is striking, especially in Periclean Athens.[2] But Pericles himself approved; in his famous Funeral Speech, he summed up his views: "If I must also speak a word to those who are in widowhood on the powers and duties of women, I will cast all my advice in one brief sentence. Great will be

---

[1] Hindu custom of keeping women in the house.

[2] Golden Age of Athens.

your glory if you do not lower the nature which is within you—hers most of all whose praise or blame is least bruited[3] on the lips of men."

The strongly masculine character of Greek culture may in part account for this, but it is also weird reversal of the basic concepts of sexual creativity. In the old days men were suitably ignorant about their creative role in life. Athenian lore claimed that before Cecrops, the legendary founder of Athens, "children did not know their own fathers." The discovery of their role as sexual inseminators gave them a new pride and stimulated the patriarchal revolution. Now the Greeks went a step further. They fancied that men alone were endowed with generative power, women being merely empty vessels or, at best, sort of incubators designed to carry their child and nurse it in life's early stages. Like the Persians' divine Ohrmazd, more than one Greek sighed and uttered the famous "If only we could have children without having recourse to women!" This recurring theme of extreme misogynists[4] was echoed again, some two thousand years later, by Thomas Browne: "I could be content that we might procreate like trees, without conjunction, or that there were any way to perpetuate the World without this trivial and vulgar way of union."

Athenian women were hardly educated, in accord with Euripides' view that women were harmed by an overly developed intellect. In the sixth century B.C., women still contributed somewhat to Greek literature; by the fifth century B.C., they were culturally barren. Having turned their respectable women into bores, men then searched elsewhere for entertainment and inspiration—in the extraordinary development of homosexuality and in the company of the only free women in Athens, the hetairai,[5] the "companions," the most accomplished courtesans[6] of the times. Demosthenes summed up the Athenian view of woman's uses in the following statement: "We have courtesans for the sake of pleasure, concubines[7] for the daily health of our bodies, and wives to bear us lawful offspring and be the faithful guardians of our homes."

The only attractive—and therefore influential—women were the hetairai, women of some social standing, endowed with a veneer[8] of culture, and capable of witty and learned conversation. They were denied civil rights but were entitled to the protection of their special goddess, Aphrodite Pandemos. Many of them left some mark on Greek history and literature—Aspasia, one of the precursors, who seduced Pericles and opened a school of rhetoric and philosophy; the famous Clepsydra, who timed her lovers' visits with an hourglass; Thargelia, the great spy for the account of the Persians; Danae, who influenced Epicurus in his philosophic views; Archenassa and Theoris, who amused respectively Plato and Sophocles; and countless others. Some whose plastic[9]

---

[3] Repeated.
[4] Women-haters.
[5] Highly cultured females.
[6] "High-class" prostitutes kept by nobles.

[7] Unmarried in-house female companions.
[8] Superficial appearance.
[9] Well-formed.

beauty was breathtaking inspired artists and served as models—Phryne, who appeared stark naked at the Eleusinian festival and posed for Praxiteles' "Aphrodite"; and also Lais of Corinth, one of the great beauties of all time, whose eccentric adventures stunned her contemporaries. In fact, nothing symbolizes more aptly the Greek view of the female sex's social role and value as Praxiteles' two antipodal[10] statues, "The Weeping Wife" and "The Laughing Hetairai."

Greek men held a contemptuous view of the opposite sex; even the best-endowed hetairai had a difficult time competing with their clients' male lovers. Even in Sparta, where women enjoyed more prestige and influence than in the rest of Greece, Alcman could pay no greater compliment to his women companions than to call them his "female boy-friends!" The poet-politician Critias stated that girls were charming only to the extent that they were slightly boyish—and vice versa. Homosexuality was both a cause and consequence of this steady downgrading of the female of the species; and rave against it as they might, the hetairai proved unable to curb it. At any rate, the Greek example makes it plain that the prevalence of male homosexuality in any given society is tightly linked with increasing misogyny and the social repression of woman; a kind of horror feminae[11] pervades the social atmosphere, springing from the fact that the typical feminine attributes—maternal procreativity and sexual-libidinal[12] endowments—are no longer appreciated. Havelock Ellis quite rightly pointed out the close connection between **infanticide** (birth control) and homosexuality, a connection that is stamped by an incipient[13] **death-wish** on the part of any society where they prevail. When the point is reached that woman is rejected, even as a sex object, this society is, psychologically, committing suicide—as the Greek example made plain a few generations after Pericles.

If we dig further, it becomes clear that one main reason for this degradation of the female sex is that, whereas we put the emphasis of love on its object and think of it in terms of the worthiness of the object, the ancient Greeks put it on the urge itself, honoring the feeling even if it happened to focus on an unworthy recipient. This made it easier for the Greeks to restrict their eroticism largely to homosexual relations. Its prevalence was such that it became part of public education in Sparta and Crete; it became the essential element in Greek military formations where pairs of lovers and male beloved ones formed the basic tactical unit, fighting side by side—the Sacred Band at Thebes, presumed to be the finest fighting force in the Hellenic world, was made up entirely of homosexuals.

Most Greeks had only pity for those few men who could fall in love with women with the same passion as with members of their own sex. Even the famous Platonic love is, in fact, sublimated love of an exclusively homosexual nature. In the Symposium, Pausanias states:

---

[10] Directly opposing.
[11] Fear of woman.

[12] Pertaining to pleasure.
[13] Just starting.

There are two goddesses of love, and therefore, also two forms of Eros. The Eros of the earthly Aphrodite is earthly, universal, common and casual. And everything common worships her. Both sexes, man and woman, had part in the creation and birth of the earthly Aphrodite. The higher love comes from the heavenly Aphrodite and she is the creation of man. Therefore all youths and men who are seized with this love strive after their own sex, full of longing for the manly; they love the stronger nature and the higher mind.

Such an outlook was devastating to feminine status, dignity, and influence.

Questions for Discussion and Writing

1. In what ways were the status and the rights of women limited in ancient Athens?

2. How does Riencourt use the "strongly masculine character of Greek culture" and a "weird reversal of the basic concepts of sexual creativity" to account for Greek misogyny, or hatred of women?

3. What are the differences between concubines, hetairai, and traditional Greek wives? Who were the most educated? Who had the most freedom? For what were traditional wives valued?

4. What advantages might a social system that included hetairai and courtesans offer men?

5. How was widespread homosexuality in Greek society both a cause and a result of the downgrading of women?

6. Women's rights in ancient Athens were severely restricted. How are women's rights restricted in contemporary American society?

Albert Parry, *"Robespierre's Bloody Virtue"*

Robespierre's bloody career illustrates how one can be devoted to a seemingly admirable ideal while debasing its very premises. As a leader of the French Revolution, Robespierre (1758–1794) ostensibly[1] fought for "liberty, fraternity, and equality" (the Revolution's motto). But he used tactics of oppression, violence, and terror. His "Reign of Terror," which may seem like a deviation from revolutionary ideals, finds parallels in the bloodletting of the Russian Revolution, the purges of China's Cultural Revolution, Idi Amin's rule in the newly independent Uganda, and other collisions of political ideals and atrocities.

Key Concepts

The readings by Baljit Singh and Martin Oppenheimer explain the theory of **terrorism;** see pages 377–389.

Tyrannical laws (page 318) are those that oppress a people and are imposed without their consent.

---

[1] Supposedly.

As a negative term, **sophist** (page 318) means one who uses empty rhetoric
and false reasoning.

The opening article in this chapter defines **inalienable rights;** see page 306.

Disciples of Rousseau are believers in the natural goodness, or **inborn
sinlessness,** of humankind (page 318). Rousseau was an eighteenth
century French writer and philosopher; his *Social Contract* treats the
theory of representative democracy.

One common meaning of the word **idealist** (page 319) is someone who is
unrealistically optimistic. The term is loosely related here to the philosophical notion of idealism.

What is happening now is related to what has happened in the past.
And because **terrorism** so threatens our lives today, it is important for us
to know its history and tradition.

Historically, terrorism's main stages have taken place in Western
Europe and Russia; then, North America, and latterly, Asia and Latin
America, followed by Africa.

First, this was the phenomenon chosen by Karl Marx, Friedrich
Engels, and Vladimir Lenin as the subject of their intense study and the
foremost model for their own preachments and activities. Since, overwhelmingly, Marx, Engels, and Lenin are the prime sources of inspiration
for modern terrorists throughout the world, it is through them that these
terrorists owe their beginnings to Maximilien Robespierre and his Reign
of Terror.

Second, this Great Terror of 1793-94 was the first in history to
attempt the elevation of primitive passion into a high-flown political
philosophy, and to create an organization that tried to systematize
murder and other lawlessness into a set of rules.

Of course, political slayers had, for thousands of years, tried to
manipulate people through violence and fear. But Robespierre's reign
was the first terror organized nationwide by revolutionaries actually
seizing power and becoming a punitive government proclaiming murder
as the law of the land. The very terms "terror," "terrorism," and "terrorists," used in their modern sense in so many languages, have come to
us mainly from Robespierre's Reign of Terror—one more confirmation
that today's exercises of terror trace their lineage to Robespierre.

The French Revolution came with its guillotine—history's first
campaign of political terror to be legislated by a people's duly elected
representatives into a state-authorized system. And so, though terror had
been used by individuals and groups before Robespierre's rule, his Reign
of Terror systematized violence, hallowed[1] it by the state's prestige, and
created an intense fear in a way and on a scale heretofore unknown, a
way that gave rise to the concept of modern terrorism.

---

[1] Made holy.

As for the theory of terror, it was Danton who, among the first, formulated its purpose: terror was a most desirable, most urgent weapon to defend the young Republic against its foes, both foreign and domestic. To an extent he was echoed by Lazare Carnot, the revolutionist who had been trained as a military engineer, and who from 1792 on was to go into history as the organizer of the new revolutionary armies of France and the architect of her eventual military victories over the Austrians and other foreign enemies. Carnot proclaimed that the Great Terror was the explanation of these triumphs. In truth, however, the principal successes of the French armies came before, not during, the Terror's sharpest crests. The Great Terror did not inspirit[2] the citizen-soldiers; it frightened not the invaders, but the French themselves.

Danton, in his speech at the chaotic session of the Convention of August 12, 1793, urged, as one of the measures of stepping up the Terror, the arrest—as hostages—of all "suspects" in Paris and the provinces. In the Convention's session of September 5 commemorating the first anniversary of the Massacres, it was decided to expand the Revolutionary Tribunal and to form a special army of 6,000 infantrymen and 1,200 cannoneers to carry terror throughout the nation.

In addition, Danton proposed revolutionizing all worthy men, particularly in Paris, by providing every worker with a rifle. Revolutionaries everywhere were to have arbitrary[3] power to detain, judge, and execute any and all "suspects."

Bertrand Barere, an ardent Jacobin,[4] summarized: "Let us make terror the order of the day!" Terror was not to be an exception to the new life—it was to be its ambiance[5] and prime rule. People would have to accept it for their own welfare. Another Jacobin summarized: "Since neither our virtue nor our moderation nor our philosophic ideas have been of use to us, let us be brigands for the good of the people." This was the phraseology[6] that would live for generations, and with such pithy[7] excuses generations of men would be made to suffer and die. Those excuses would reappear in the slogans of Lenin and Trotsky, of Hitler and Mussolini, of Mao Tse-tung and Ho Chi Minh, of Castro and Guevara, of DeFreeze and Arafat.

Thus, in France in 1793-94, terror was justified not alone as a means of the survival of the French people threatened by its enemies, but also as a path to the people's welfare and virtue. In November 1793, Jean Nicolas Billaud-Varenne, the secretary of the Jacobin club, elucidated the principles of a complete revolutionary centralization of state power to be based on the smiting[8] ax, so that the French government could be "purified" instead of remaining "a volcano of villainy." On December 4 these postulates were formally incorporated into a law of terror.

[2] Give courage to.
[3] According to individual judgment.
[4] Radical revolutionary.
[5] Surrounding atmosphere.
[6] Slogan.
[7] Clear and direct.
[8] Striking.

Finally and authoritatively, Robespierre himself invoked the good of the people as the paramount reason for terror. In his speech of December 25, 1793, on "the Principles of the Revolutionary Government," the advocate from Arras intoned that the theory of this government was as new as the very revolution that gave it birth—it could be found in no books but only in the life and strife of that specific era. Robespierre explained the difference between two regimes as he saw them—the revolutionary and the constitutional. The former regime had as its task the creation of a republic; the latter, the safeguard of that republic. Robespierre viewed the world of politics quite narrowly: to him there were only two positive kinds of governments. He elucidated these two regimes: A revolution meant war by the legions of freedom against their adversaries. A constitution came after the triumph of the revolution—it was the regime of a victorious and peaceful freedom. This specific time in France was one of war. Therefore the nation's revolutionary government must defend good citizens with all possible force, implacably[9] dealing out death to the enemies of the people.

These concepts were enough, Robespierre declaimed, to make clear the origin and nature of revolutionary laws. But the opponents of these concepts and these laws, the captious[10] persons who called these laws **tyrannical,** were either stupid individuals or vice-ridden **sophists.** Robespierre asked: "If the revolutionary government must be more energetic in its actions and freer in its steps, does this mean that it is less just and less lawful?" He answered, "No! For it bases itself on the holiest of all laws—the good of the people; and on the most **inalienable of all rights**—necessity."

This argument served as an all-important part of almost every public statement by Robespierre, always ending in his call to improve yet further the work of the Revolutionary Tribunal and to bring to the guillotine blade yet another rollcall of persons, yet more categories of men and women.

Through all this, Robespierre claimed to be the truest of all the **disciples of Rousseau.** He reminded his listeners that Rousseau had described man as good by nature but corrupted by civilization. This idea was twisted by Robespierre into his burning conviction that man could be saved from himself, from his meanness and criminality, by the guillotine. Robespierre would help man get rid of the evil not recognized by man himself; he would restore man's pristine purity by the death penalty. By executing them en masse,[11] this provincial lawyer would be doing his victims the valiant favor of restoring virtue to them and to society. Their execution would be less of a punishment, more of a gift— the gift of the original, **inborn sinlessness** returned to them as their heads rolled off the bloody block. This Republic of Virtue via Blood,

---

[9] Mercilessly.
[10] Always finding petty faults.

[11] Together; in great numbers.

ushered in by Robespierre, would surely be blessed by the Supreme Being, by Robespierre's own version of the Supreme Being, the new revolutionary deity whose worship Robespierre decreed as a new state religion, in whose honor he arranged his peculiar pageants of worship.

Because of this singular fanaticism, he has been called by some a mistaken **idealist.** In sober reality he was mistaken, but he was not an idealist. To apply this noun to him is an insult to idealism. Robespierre was a sick, demented man who caused wholesale deaths while emitting high-sounding but vapid phrases. His was not an ideology; it was a phraseology.

And yet, at first, many Frenchmen and Frenchwomen took his oratory for an ideology as well as for a viable revolutionary religion. Many willingly, even enthusiastically, followed him. As an illness often overcomes an individual by degrees, so the Grand Terror, charged up and maintained by this extraordinary zealot,[12] grew in phases so insidious[13] that even decent persons sometimes failed to notice they were being drawn in as his followers; too late did these followers realize that soon they were to join his victims on the tragic scaffold.[14] Their hysterical applause for the tyrant was replaced by sheer fright when, alas, nothing was left for them to do but mount the steps and submit to the blade.

First tried out in 1792, the guillotine was to gain worldwide fame as the most chilling memory of the French Revolution. For generations to come it would be a dreaded symbol. But in our own 1970s a weird North American counterculture entertainer, Vincent Damon Furnier, better known as "Alice Cooper," drew a mindless laugh out of his audiences by including a guillotine in his stage show: he would stick his repugnantly untidy head into Dr. Guillotin's machine, the stage crew substituting a fake head before the blade would fall. Thus old terror thrilled the mob of our violence-filled times. Fun, not fright, was the new response.

Questions for Discussion and Writing

1. What are some typical stereotypes Americans have of the French Revolution? Where do they come from? Does Parry's article change your image of the French Revolution?

2. What was the rationale for the Reign of Terror? How was terrorism justified as a "path to the people's welfare and virtue" as well as a means of defeating the enemy?

3. What distinction does Robespierre make between the role of the revolutionary regime and the constitutional regime?

4. Review the definition of inalienable rights in the Hook essay. How does Robespierre distort its meaning? What is the problem with the argument that necessity is an inalienable right?

---

[12] Fanatic.

[13] Treacherous.

[14] Platform for executing people.

5. Rousseau wrote that man is good by nature "but corrupted by civilization." How did Robespierre use Rousseau's position to justify mass executions?

6. In Parry's view, why can violence and terror never "purify" a nation?

Hiram Wesley Evans, **"The Klan's Fight for Americanism"** _____

The Ku Klux Klan (KKK) was originally formed as a protective order to prevent Northern carpetbaggers from exploiting the post-Civil War Southerners. Although it had benevolent intentions at its start, the KKK soon became synonymous with racism and segregation. Its members perpetrated violent acts on blacks, Jews, and other minorities. The white sheet and burning cross symbolize their policies of white supremacy through terrorist tactics. Again, as with Robespierre, a terrible irony appears in the clash of the group's asserted goal—defense of American democracy—with their actual beliefs and tactics that subvert the democratic system. The following essay written by a KKK member in 1926, when the Klan was still at the height of its power, uses the language of justice and patriotism to disguise its radical WASP (White Anglo Saxon Protestant) bias.

Key Concepts

Imperialism is defined in a later essay in this chapter; see page 366.

Autocracy (page 322) means absolute rule by a single person without the people's necessary consent.

In an **aristocracy,** the nobility, or titled class, holds political, economic, and social power (page 322).

First in the Klansman's mind is patriotism—America for Americans. He believes religiously that a betrayal of Americanism or the American race is treason to the most sacred of trusts, a trust from his fathers and a trust from God. He believes, too, that Americanism can only be achieved if the pioneer stock[1] is kept pure. There is more than race pride in this. Mongrelization[2] has been proven bad. It is only between closely related stocks of the same race that interbreeding has improved men; the kind of interbreeding that went on in the early days of America between English, Dutch, German, Huguenot, Irish and Scotch.

Racial integrity[3] is a very definite thing to the Klansman. It means even more than good citizenship, for a man may be in all ways a good citizen and yet a poor American, unless he has racial understanding of Americanism, and instinctive loyalty to it. It is in no way a reflection on any man to say that he is un-American; it is merely a statement that he is not one of us. It is often not even wise to try to make an American of the best of aliens. What he is may be spoiled without his becoming American.

[1] Ancestry, lineage.
[2] Mixture of races.
[3] Wholeness.

The races and stocks of men are as distinct as breeds of animals, and every boy knows that if one tries to train a bulldog to herd sheep, he has in the end neither a good bulldog nor a good collie.

Americanism, to the Klansman, is a thing of the spirit, a purpose and a point of view, that can only come through instinctive racial understanding. It has, to be sure, certain defined principles, but he does not believe that many aliens understand those principles, even when they use our words in talking about them. Democracy is one, fairdealing, impartial justice, equal opportunity, religious liberty, independence, self-reliance, courage, endurance, acceptance of individual responsibility as well as individual rewards for effort, willingness to sacrifice for the good of his family, his nation and his race before anything else but God, dependence on enlightened conscience for guidance, the right to unhampered development—these are fundamental. But within the bounds they fix there must be the utmost freedom, tolerance, liberalism. In short, the Klansman believes in the greatest possible diversity and individualism within the limits of the American spirit. But he believes also that few aliens can understand that spirit, that fewer try to, and that there must be resistance, intolerance even, toward anything that threatens it, or the fundamental national unity based upon it.

The second word in the Klansman's trilogy is "white." The white race must be supreme, not only in America but in the world. This is equally undebatable, except on the ground that the races might live together, each with full regard for the rights and interests of others, and that those rights and interests would never conflict. Such an idea, of course, is absurd; the colored races today, such as Japan, are clamoring not for equality but for their supremacy. The whole history of the world, on its broader lines, has been one of race conflicts, wars, subjugation or extinction. This is not pretty, and certainly disagrees with the maudlin[4] theories of cosmopolitanism, but it is truth. The world has been so made that each race must fight for its life, must conquer, accept slavery or die. The Klansman believes that the whites will not become slaves, and he does not intend to die before his time.

Moreover, the future of progress and civilization depends on the continued supremacy of the white race. The forward movement of the world for centuries has come entirely from it. Other races each had its chance and either failed or stuck fast, while white civilization shows no sign of having reached its limit. Until the whites falter, or some colored civilization has a miracle of awakening, there is not a single colored stock that can claim even equality with the white, much less supremacy.

The third of the Klan principles is that Protestantism must be supreme; that Rome shall not rule America. The Klansman believes this not merely because he is a Protestant, nor even because the Colonies that are now our nation were settled for the purpose of wresting[5] America from the control of Rome and establishing a land of free conscience. He

---

[4] Sentimental.   [5] Taking away.

believes it also because Protestantism is an essential part of Americanism; without it America could never have been created and without it she cannot go forward. Roman rule would kill it.

Protestantism contains more than religion. It is the expression in religion of the same spirit of independence, self-reliance and freedom which are the highest achievements of the Nordic[6] race. It sprang into being automatically at the time of the great "upsurgence" of strength in the Nordic peoples that opened the spurt of civilization in the fifteenth century. It has been a distinctly Nordic religion, and it has been through this religion that the Nordics have found strength to take leadership of all whites and the supremacy of the earth. Its destruction is the deepest purpose of all other peoples, as that would mean the end of Nordic rule.

It is the only religion that permits the unhampered individual development and the unhampered conscience and action which were necessary in the settling of America. Our pioneers were all Protestants, except for an occasional Irishman—Protestants by nature if not by religion—for though French and Spanish dared and explored and showed great heroism, they made little of the land their own. America was Protestant from birth.

She must remain Protestant, if the Nordic stock is to finish its destiny. We of the old stock Americans could not work—and the work is mostly ours to do, if the record of the past proves anything—if we became priestridden, if we had to submit our consciences and limit our activities and suppress our thoughts at the command of any man, much less of a man sitting upon Seven Hills[7] thousands of miles away. This we will not permit. Rome shall not rule us. Protestantism must be supreme.

Let it be clear what is meant by "supremacy." It is nothing more than power of control, under just laws. It is not **imperialism,** far less is it **autocracy** or even **aristocracy** of a race or stock of men. What it does mean is that we insist on our inherited right to insure our own safety, individually and as a race, to secure the future of our children, to maintain and develop our racial heritage in our own, white, Protestant, American way, without interference. . . . We are accused of injecting old prejudices, hatred, race and religion into politics, of creating an un-American class division, of trying to profit by race and religious enmities,[8] of violating the principle of equality, and of ruining the Democratic party.

Most of these charges are not worth answering. So long as politicians cater to alien racial and religious groups, it is the merest self-defense to have also a Protestant and an American "vote" and to make it respected. The hatred and prejudice are, as has been evident to every candid person, displayed by our enemies and not by us. As to the charge that the Klan brought race and religion into politics, that simply is not true. That was done by the very people who are now accusing us,

---

[6] Northern European Caucasian.   [8] Hostility.
[7] The Seven Hills of Rome (the Pope).

because we are cutting into the profits they had been making in politics out of their races and their religions. Race and religion have for years been used by the aliens as political platforms. The Klan is in no way responsible for this condition. We merely recognized it when others dared not, and we fight it in the open. Our belief is that any man who runs for office or asks political favors, or advocates policies or carries on any other political activity, either as a member of any racial or religious group, or in the interests of or under orders from such a group or of any non-American interest whatever, should be opposed for that very reason. The Klan's ambition is to get race and religion out of politics, and that cannot be done so long as there is any profit in exploiting them. It therefore fights every attempt to use them.

One of the Klan's chief interests is in education. We believe that it is the duty of government to insure to every child opportunity to develop its natural abilities to their utmost. We wish to go to the very limit in the improvement of the public schools; so far that there will be no excuse except snobbery for the private schools.

Further, the Klan wishes to restore the Bible to the school, not only because it is part of the world's great heritage in literature and philosophy and has profoundly influenced all white civilization, but because it is the basis on which all Christian religions are built, and to which they must look for their authority. . . . Jews or Catholics are lavish with their caustic[9] criticism of anything American. Nothing is immune; our great men, our historic struggles and sacrifices, our customs and personal traits, our "Puritan consciences"—all have been scarified[10] without mercy . . . we of the Klan admit that we are intolerant and narrow in a certain sense. . . . We are intolerant of everything that strikes at the foundations of our race, our country or our freedom of worship. We are narrowly opposed to the use of anything alien—race, loyalty to any foreign power or to any religion whatever—as a means to win political power. We are prejudiced against any attempt to use the privileges and opportunities which aliens hold only through our generosity as levers to force us to change our civilization, to wrest from us control of our own country, to exploit us for the benefit of any foreign power—religious or secular—and especially to use America as a tool for the advantage of any side in the hatreds and quarrels of the Old World. This is our intolerance; based on the sound instincts which have saved us many times from the follies of the intellectuals. We admit it. More and worse, we are proud of it.

. . . The Negro, the Klan considers a special duty and problem of the white American. He is among us through no wish of his; we owe it to him and to ourselves to give him full protection and opportunity. But his limitations are evident; we will not permit him to gain sufficient power to control our civilization. Neither will we delude him with promises of social equality which we know can never be realized. The Klan looks

---

[9] Sarcastic, biting.   [10] Inflicted with small cuts.

forward to the day when the Negro problem will have been solved on some much saner basis than miscegenation,[11] and when every State will enforce laws making any sex relations between a white and a colored person a crime.

For the alien in general we have sympathy, opportunity, justice, but no permanent welcome unless he becomes truly American. It is our duty to see that he has every chance for this, and we shall be glad to accept him if he does. We hold no rancor[12] against him; his race, instincts, training, mentality and whole outlook of life are usually widely different from ours. We cannot blame him if he adheres to them and attempts to convert us to them, even by force. But we must see that he can never succeed.

The Jew is a more complex problem. His abilities are great; he contributes much to any country where he lives. This is particularly true of the Western Jew, those of the stocks we have known so long. Their separation from us is more religious than racial. When freed from persecution these Jews have shown a tendency to disintegrate and amalgamate.[13] We may hope that shortly, in the free atmosphere of America, Jews of this class will cease to be a problem. Quite different are the Eastern Jews of recent immigration, the Jews known as the Askhenasim. It is interesting to note that anthropologists now tell us that these are not true Jews, but only Judaized Mongols—Chazars. These, unlike the true Hebrew, show a divergence from the American type so great that there seems little hope of their assimilation.

The most menacing and most difficult problem facing America today is this of the permanently unassimilable alien. The only solution so far offered is that of Dr. Eliot, president emeritus of Harvard. After admitting that the melting pot has failed—thus supporting the primary position of the Klan!—he adds that there is no hope of creating here a single, homogeneous[14] race-stock of the kind necessary for national unity. He then suggests that instead, there shall be a congeries[15] of diverse peoples, living together in sweet harmony, and all working for the good of all and of the nation! This solution is on a par with the optimism which foisted the melting pot on us. Diverse races never have lived together in such harmony; race antipathies[16] are too deep and strong. If such a state were possible, the nation would be too disunited for the progress. One race always ruled, one always must, and there will be struggle and reprisals till the mastery is established—and bitterness afterwards. And, speaking for us Americans, we have come to realize that if all this could possibly be done, still within a few years we should be supplanted[17] by the "mere force of breeding" of the low standard peoples. We intend to see that the American stock remains supreme.

[11] Mixing of races.
[12] Hatred.
[13] Join into a whole.
[14] Of the same composition.

[15] Group.
[16] Dislikes.
[17] Removed and replaced.

Questions for Discussion and Writing

1. This essay uses strong patriotic language and a common-sense tone. On the surface, the rhetoric reads logically. What image of the Klan is the writer trying to portray? Why? Does the writer succeed?

2. Who would be the audience for such an essay?

3. Although it achieves a logical tone, the essay bases its argument on many assumptions, or statements accepted to be true without proof, and fallacies, or illogical statements with invalid conclusions. Read through the essay and locate the author's assumptions and fallacies—for example, "the future of progress and civilization depends on the continued supremacy of the white race."

3. Choose one of the assumptions or fallacies and see how the author supports it. Can you identify inconsistencies in the logic?

4. The Klan is particularly concerned about the steady influx of "aliens" into the United States. Which ones is it most worried about? Why?

5. The author recognizes a paternal duty to protect blacks and to give them full opportunity. How has history shown this statement to be false, and why is its paternalistic attitude offensive?

6. The Klan strongly opposes miscegenation and mixed marriages. Do some ethnic minorities discourage interracial marriages? How is this different from what the Klan advocates?

7. Describe what the United States would be like if Klan values were imposed. Which racial groups would be considered acceptable? How would religion, education, television, and so on, be different?

8. Although the piece is titled "The Klan's Fight for Americanism," the Klan's actions throughout history clash with the most basic rights of American democracy. What actions has the Klan taken, and what actual positions has it supported, that make it "un-American?"

Malcolm X, *"The Ballot or the Bullet"* _____

Malcolm X was a militant black nationalist during the early 1960s, the era of the civil rights movement. Malcolm's father was murdered by the Ku Klux Klan in Michigan when Malcolm was a child. At the height of his influence as a black leader, Malcolm was himself murdered by followers of his former associate, the black Muslim leader, Elijah Muhammad. Unlike Martin Luther King, Jr., who advocated nonviolent protest, Malcolm X preached militant, that is, radical black activism, as reflected in the rhetoric of the speech below. His formulation of "the ballot or the bullet" shows the ultimatum with which Malcolm X challenged the democratic system.

The question tonight, as I understand it, is "The Negro Revolt, and Where Do We Go From Here?" or "What Next?" In my little humble way of understanding it, it points toward either the ballot or the bullet.

Before we try and explain what is meant by the ballot or the bullet, I would like to clarify something concerning myself. I'm still a Muslim, my religion is still Islam. That's my personal belief. Just as Adam Clayton Powell is a Christian minister who heads the Abyssinian Baptist Church in New York, but at the same time takes part in the political struggles to try and bring about rights to the black people in this country; and Dr. Martin Luther King is a Christian minister down in Atlanta, Georgia, who heads another organization fighting for the civil rights of black people in this country; and Rev. Galamison, I guess you've heard of him, is another Christian minister in New York who has been deeply involved in the school boycotts to eliminate segregated education; well, I myself am a minister, not a Christian minister, but a Muslim minister; and I believe in action on all fronts by whatever means necessary.

Although I'm still a Muslim, I'm not here tonight to discuss my religion. I'm not here to try and change your religion. I'm not here to argue or discuss anything that we differ about, because it's time for us to submerge our differences and realize that it is best for us to first see that we have the same problem, a common problem—a problem that will make you catch hell whether you're a Baptist, or a Methodist, or a Muslim, or a nationalist. Whether you're educated or illiterate, whether you live on the boulevard or in the alley, you're going to catch hell just like I am. We're all in the same boat and we all are going to catch the same hell from the same man. He just happens to be a white man. All of us have suffered here, in this country, political oppression at the hands of the white man, economic exploitation at the hands of the white man, and social degradation at the hands of the white man.

Now in speaking like this, it doesn't mean that we're anti-white, but it does mean we're anti-exploitation, we're anti-degradation, we're anti-oppression. And if the white man doesn't want us to be anti-him, let him stop oppressing and exploiting and degrading us. Whether we are Christians or Muslims or nationalists or agnostics[1] or atheists, we must first learn to forget our differences. If we have differences, let us differ in the closet; when we come out in front, let us not have anything to argue about until we get finished arguing with the man. If the late President Kennedy could get together with Khrushchev and exchange some wheat, we certainly have more in common with each other than Kennedy and Khrushchev had with each other.

If we don't do something real soon, I think you'll have to agree that we're going to be forced either to use the ballot or the bullet. It's one or the other in 1964. It isn't that time is running out—time has run out! 1964 threatens to be the most explosive year America has ever witnessed. The most explosive year. Why? It's also a political year. It's the year when all of the white politicians will be back in the so-called Negro community jiving[2] you and me for some votes. The year when all of the white political crooks will be right back in your and my community with

---

[1] Religious doubters.   [2] Deceiving, talking nonsense.

their false promises, building up our hopes for a letdown, with their trickery and their treachery, with their false promises which they don't intend to keep. As they nourish these dissatisfactions, it can only lead to one thing, an explosion; and now we have the type of black man on the scene in America today—I'm sorry, Brother Lomax—who just doesn't intend to turn the other cheek any longer.

Don't let anybody tell you anything about the odds are against you. If they draft you, they send you to Korea and make you face 800 million Chinese. If you can be brave over there, you can be brave right here. These odds aren't as great as those odds. And if you fight here, you will at least know what you're fighting for.

I'm not a politician, not even a student of politics; in fact, I'm not a student of much of anything. I'm not a Democrat, I'm not a Republican, and I don't even consider myself an American. If you and I were Americans, there'd be no problem. Those Hunkies[3] that just got off the boat, they're already Americans; Polacks[4] are already Americans; the Italian refugees are already Americans. Everything that came out of Europe, every blue-eyed thing, is already an American. And as long as you and I have been over here, we aren't Americans yet.

Well, I am one who doesn't believe in deluding myself. I'm not going to sit at your table and watch you eat, with nothing on my plate, and call myself a diner. Sitting at the table doesn't make you a diner, unless you eat some of what's on that plate. Being here in America doesn't make you an American. Being born here in America doesn't make you an American. Why, if birth made you American, you wouldn't need any legislation, you wouldn't need any amendments to the Constitution, you wouldn't be faced with civil-rights filibustering[5] in Washington, D.C., right now. They don't have to pass civil-rights legislation to make a Polack an American.

No, I'm not an American. I'm one of the 22 million black people who are the victims of Americanism. One of the 22 million black people who are the victims of democracy, nothing but disguised hypocrisy. So, I'm not standing here speaking to you as an American, or a patriot, or a flag-saluter, or a flag-waver—no, not I. I'm speaking as a victim of this American system. And I see America through the eyes of the victim. I don't see any American dream; I see an American nightmare.

So it's time in 1964 to wake up. And when you see them coming up with that kind of conspiracy, let them know your eyes are open. And let them know you got something else that's wide open too. It's got to be the ballot or the bullet. The ballot or the bullet. If you're afraid to use an expression like that, you should get on out of the country, you should get back in the cotton patch, you should get back in the alley. They get all the Negro vote, and after they get it, the Negro gets nothing in return. All they did when they got to Washington was give a few big Negroes big

---

[3] Derogatory term for Hungarians.
[4] Derogatory term for Polish people.

[5] Blocking legislation by making a very long speech.

jobs. Those big Negroes didn't need big jobs, they already had jobs. That's camouflage, that's trickery, that's treachery, window-dressing. I'm not trying to knock out the Democrats for the Republicans, we'll get to them in a minute. But it is true—you put the Democrats first and the Democrats put you last.

I say again, I'm not anti-Democrat, I'm not anti-Republican, I'm not anti-anything. I'm just questioning their sincerity, and some of the strategy that they've been using on our people by promising them promises that they don't intend to keep. When you keep the Democrats in power, you're keeping the Dixiecrats[6] in power. I doubt that my good Brother Lomax will deny that. A vote for a Democrat is a vote for a Dixiecrat. That's why, in 1964 it's time now for you and me to become more politically mature and realize what the ballot is for; what we're supposed to get when we cast a ballot; and that if we don't cast a ballot, it's going to end up in a situation where we're going to have to cast a bullet. It's either a ballot or a bullet.

Questions for Discussion and Writing

1. Malcolm X's reputation and image are highly controversial. For some people he remains a hero, but for others he is a dangerous revolutionary. What image did you have of Malcolm X before reading this speech? Did the speech differ from what you expected?

2. Malcolm X chose a particularly strong, defiant title for this speech. How did he want both black and white listeners to react and respond? How does it make you react?

3. Although parts of this text read like an essay, it was composed as a speech. Rhetorically, what makes it different from an essay?

4. What argument does Malcolm X make against the Democratic party, the party that blacks have historically supported the most loyally?

5. What would a staunch supporter of the democratic system such as Sidney Hook say about Malcolm X's position? How would Malcolm X respond?

James Farmer, "A Night of Terror in Plaquemine, Louisiana, 1963"

James Farmer was another civil rights activist in the 1960s who went on to become the national leader of CORE (the Congress of Racial Equality). This group, along with Martin Luther King's Southern Christian Leadership Conference, the NAACP, and the Student Non-violent Coordinating Committee, led the nonviolent struggle for equality. This passage illustrates how blacks suffered under segregation and in many cases were denied even the right to vote. The civil rights workers used boycotts, sit-ins, and protest marches in their fight for justice. Farmer recounts one instance of the often violent treatment which civil rights workers faced.

---

[6] White Southern Democrats.

I went down to Plaquemine toward the end of August 1963 on the first day of what I innocently assumed would be a routine three-day trip. We staged a protest march into town after my speech. When the march was over, all the leaders, myself included, were arrested and taken off to jail in nearby Donaldsonville (which hospitably offered us its facilities in lieu[1] of the already overcrowded Plaquemine jail).

We stayed in jail for a week and a half. When we came out, the spirit of militancy was spreading in Plaquemine, and two days later a group of young people organized another demonstration, protesting segregation in public places as well as exclusion from the city. This time, however, the marchers did not even get into town. The chief of police stopped them halfway, arrested the leaders, and held the rest of the marchers where they were until state troopers arrived. The troopers came on horseback, riding like cowboys, and they charged into the crowd of boys and girls as if they were rounding up a herd of stampeding cattle. They were armed with billy clubs and cattle prods, which they used mercilessly. Many of the youngsters who fell under the blows were trampled by the horses. (The children of Selma, whose suffering at the hands of police appalled the nation two years later, were but a part of a spiritual community of brave Southern youngsters like these who for years have been deprived of national attention by inadequate press coverage.)

This gratuitous[2] savagery inflicted upon their children immediately aroused the adults to a pitch of militancy much more intense than anything the organizational effort had been able to achieve. The ministers, who had previously hung back, united for the first time. (Only one minister, the Rev. Jetson Davis, had been active in the movement. It was his Plymouth Rock Baptist Church to which the injured boys and girls had fled for comfort and medical assistance.) Apathy or fear or whatever had caused their reluctance dissolved in outrage. The next morning, Sunday, every minister in the Negro quarter preached a sermon extolling freedom and condemning police brutality. After church, according to agreement, they led their congregations to Reverend Davis' church and organized a massive march in protest against the rout of the previous day. As the time approached for the march to begin, some of the ministers began to waver. One of them hesitated on his way to the front of the line. "Where's my wife?" he said, looking around fearfully. "I don't see my wife. I think I'd better just go on home." His wife was standing right behind him. "Man," she said, "if you don't get up there in the front of that line, you ain't got no wife."

He marched, all right, but his presence could not alter the course of events. This time when the troopers intercepted the marchers there was nothing impromptu about the confrontation. They did not even come on horseback; they came in patrol cars and the horses arrived in vans. The troopers mounted their horses and assembled their weapons as if the crowd of unarmed men and women before them were an opposing army;

---

[1] In place of.   [2] Unnecessary.

they charged into the mass as they had done the day before, flailing with billy clubs and stabbing with cattle prods. "Get up, nigger!" one would shout, poking a man with an electric prod and beating him to the ground with a club. "Run, nigger, run!"

I was waiting at the Plymouth Rock Church. I watched the Negroes come running back, those who could run, bleeding, hysterical, faint, some of the stronger ones carrying the injured. The nurse started to bandage the wounds and the rest of us began to sing "We Shall Overcome," but the troopers rode roaring through the streets right up to the door of the church. The Freedom Rock Church, we call it now. They dismounted and broke into the church, yelling and hurling tear gas bombs in front of them—bomb after bomb, poisoning the air. The gas masks protecting the troopers' faces transformed them into monsters as they stood and watched our people growing more and more frantic, screaming with pain and terror, trampling on one another in their frenzied efforts to escape through the back door to the parsonage behind the church. When the people had finally escaped, the troopers set about destroying the empty church. They knocked out the windows, overturned the benches, laid waste everything they could reach, and flooded the gutted building with high-pressure hoses until Bibles and hymnals floated in the aisles.

Then they attacked the parsonage to which we had fled. They sent tear gas bombs smashing through the windows, until all the windows were shattered and almost everyone inside was blinded and choking. The screaming was unbearable, I caught sight of Ronnie Moore administering mouth-to-mouth resuscitation to a young woman. People writhed on the floor, seeking oxygen. A few managed to push through the rear door into the parsonage yard, but the troopers, anticipating them, had ridden around to the back with more bombs to force them in again. And then bombs thrown into the parsonage forced them back out into the yard. All these men and women, who just that morning had resolutely banded together to reach out for freedom and dignity, were reduced now to running from torment, helpless victims of a bitter game.

We tried to telephone for help, but the operators were not putting through any outgoing calls from the Negro section. Within the community, though, there was telephone service, and several calls got through to us at the parsonage. What had appeared to be random and mindless brutality proved to have had a mad purpose after all. It was a manhunt. Troopers were in the streets, kicking open doors, searching every house in the Negro community, overturning chairs and tables, looking under beds and in closets, yelling, "Come on out, Farmer, we know you're in there. Come on out, Farmer! We're going to get you." We could hear the screaming in the streets as the troopers on horseback resumed their sport with the cattle prods and billy clubs: "Get up, nigger! Run, nigger, run!" Holding their victims down with the cattle prod, they were saying, "We'll let you up nigger, if you tell us where Farmer is." Two of our girls, hiding beneath the church, overheard one trooper saying to another, "When we catch that goddam nigger Farmer, we're gonna kill him."

Spiver Gordon, CORE field secretary in Plaquemine, who, people say, looks like me, told me later that he wandered out of the church into the street at this time. Sighting him, state troopers ran up shouting, "Here he is boys. We got Farmer. We got their m — — — f — — — Jesus." A trooper beckoned to a crowd of hoodlums who were watching nearby, many holding chains, ropes, clubs. "What post we gonna hang him from?" said one. After Spiver convinced them he wasn't me, he took a good lacing[3] for looking like me. An officer said, "He ain't Farmer. You've beat him enough. Put him in the car and arrest him."

There seemed no prospect of aid from any quarter. We were all suffering intensely from the tear gas, and the troopers kept us running with the bombs. In desperation I sent two people creeping through the grass from the parsonage to a funeral hall half a block away to ask for refuge. The owners of the hall agreed to shelter us (although I doubt that they knew what they were taking on). So we crawled on our bellies through the grass, in twos, threes, fours, making use of guerrilla[4] tactics that some remembered from the war but none of us had ever learned as a technique of non-violent demonstration, until we reached our new sanctuary. Night had fallen by the time all three hundred of us were safely inside, jammed together like straws in a broom into two rooms and a hallway. The sound of screaming still echoed in the streets as the troopers beat down another Negro ("Run, nigger, run!") or invaded another house. The telephones were still useless.

Very shortly the troopers figured out where we were. One of them—a huge, raging, red-faced man—kicked open the back door of the funeral home and screamed, "Come on out, Farmer. We know you're in there. We're gonna get you." I was in the front room. I could look down the hallway, over all the heads, right into his face: it was flushed and dripping with sweat; his hair hung over his eyes, his mouth was twisted. Another trooper burst through the door to stand beside him. "Farmer! Come out!"

I had to give myself up. I felt like a modern Oedipus who, unaware, brought down a plague upon the city. In this hall, their lives endangered by my presence, were three hundred people, many of whom had never even seen me before that day. I began to make my way into the hall, thinking that I would ask to see the warrant for my arrest and demand to know the charges against me. But before I could take three steps the men around me grabbed me silently and pulled me back into the front room, whispering fiercely, "We're not going to let you go out there tonight. That's a lynch mob. You go out there tonight, you won't be alive tomorrow morning."

The trooper, meanwhile, had discovered a large Negro in the back room. He shouted triumphantly: "Here he is, we got that nigger Farmer! Come on in boys. We got him here."

"I'm not Farmer," the man said. A third trooper came in.

---

[3] Beating.　　　　　　　　[4] Irregular, behind the lines soldier.

"That ain't Farmer," he said. "I know that nigger." They went through his identification papers. He wasn't Farmer.

Suddenly, to everyone's astonishment, a woman pushed her way through the crowd to the back room and confronted the troopers. It was the owner of the funeral home, a "Nervous Nellie," as they say, who had previously held herself apart from the movement. I can never know—she herself probably does not know—what inner revolution or what mysterious force generated in that crowded room plucked her from her caul[5] of fear and thrust her forth to assert with such a dramatic and improbable gesture her new birth of freedom. A funeral hall is as good a place as any for a person to come to life, I suppose, and her action sparked a sympathetic impulse in everyone who watched as she planted herself in front of the first trooper and shook a finger in his face: "Do you have a search warrant to come into my place of business?"

The trooper stared down at her, confounded, and backed away. "No," he said.

"You're not coming into my place of business without a search warrant. I'm a taxpayer and a law-abiding citizen. I have a wake going on here."

"This ain't no wake," the trooper said, looking around at the throng of angry, frightened people crushed together before him. "These people ain't at no wake."

"Well, you're not coming into my place of business without a search warrant." The accusing finger pushed him back to the door, where he muttered for a moment to his men outside, then turned and yelled, "All right. We got all the tear gas and all the guns. You ain't got nothin'. We'll give you just five minutes to get Farmer out here. Just five minutes, that's all." He slammed the door.

The door clanged in my ears like the door of a cell in death row. "I'll go out and face them," I said, but once again I was restrained. They would stick by me, these strangers insisted, even if they all had to die, but they would not let me out to be lynched. Someone standing near me pulled out a gun. "Mr. Farmer," he said, "if a trooper comes through that door, he'll be dead."

"If a trooper comes through that door, he may be dead," I conceded. "But what about the trooper behind him and all the ones behind that one? You'll only provoke them into shooting and we won't have a chance." Very reluctantly he allowed me to take the gun from him. It is hard for people to practice non-violence when they are looking death in the face.

Questions for Discussion and Writing

1. Despite the violence and threats of death, Farmer and the other civil rights workers and supporters maintained their nonviolent philosophy. Why did nonviolence prove to be a successful tactic in the civil rights struggle?

[5] Insulating membrane.

2. What might be the criticism of nonviolence? What would Malcolm X say about nonviolent protest?

3. Some people might argue that nonviolence was *not* a successful tactic in the civil rights movement and that the racial "riots" in America's cities pressured the government to begin making real changes. How reasonable is this argument?

4. Would nonviolence have been a successful tactic in the American or French Revolution? Is it working in South Africa? How well did it work in the overthrow of President Ferdinand Marcos in the Philippines? Consider what social and political conditions are needed for nonviolence to have an effect.

5. Some people would argue that the civil rights struggle succeeded, and others would contend that a great deal more remains to be done. What were the direct and indirect results of the civil rights movement? What laws were changed? What equalities were recognized in practice as well as law? What results of the civil rights movement appear in daily life?

Hunter College Women's Studies Collective, from **Women's Realities, Women's Choices: An Introduction to Women's Studies** _____

While most blacks recognized the oppressive conditions of pre-civil rights America, the "women's liberation" movement, both at its start and to this day, has found unity among women a difficult goal to achieve. The feminist movement itself consists of several factions, such as radical feminism or socialist feminism, some of whose ideology conflicts with that of other groups despite their similar political dissatisfactions. Feminism remains a potent political force in contemporary society, but the feminist struggle transcends politics: religion, medicine, psychology, education, business, law, all have had to respond to feminist issues. This book was written by a group of women in 1986 who pooled their knowledge and resources and worked cooperatively rather than writing individually. They recognize the gains women have made in their struggle for equality, but point out the dangers of a political backlash that could wipe out these gains. They also discuss an ideological conflict among feminists, some of whom believe "equality in the present capitalist system to be impossible," and others who "do not advocate a radical transformation of the system," but believe that it is possible to get a fair share of the "political and economic pie."

Key Concepts

A political **backlash** (page 335) is an antagonistic reaction, often conservative, to political and/or social gains achieved by the opposition.

The **liberation ethic** (page 337) in this context recognizes that both men and women are oppressed by a social system that must be transformed.

The **egalitarian ethic** (page 337) holds that women must seek equality within a system that does not need to be replaced.

Taking Stock of the Present: The Early 1980s

The status of women today encourages two views—one optimistic and the other more pessimistic. Regardless of how one rates its success, in many ways it appears as though the women's movement is at its height in the early 1980s. Hardly a day passes when a women's issue is not raised in major newspapers. . . .

An Optimistic Picture?

Women and society   Women in religious organizations are rebelling against both our low status and the sexist imagery and language in religious services. Some groups are receiving support from church officials; others are not. Nonetheless, feminists are taking (we are not being "given") positions of authority in the church and are rewriting the Scriptures. Women are dissenting in Third World countries as well as in the Western world.

Areas in which women are underrepresented, such as in police forces, corporate hierarchies, and government, show a slight increase of women in high-ranking positions. But these are for the most part token gains. In business, women are pressing employers for less discriminatory hiring and promotion procedures and are frequently successful. Women are demanding training programs which will facilitate our advancement and we are increasingly performing nontraditional jobs such as telephone repair workers, plumbers, jockeys, and construction workers. "Displaced homemaker" programs have been established to counsel women who have spent years as homemakers and now seek job training or retraining.

In the creative arts, women's productions are receiving growing attention. More than in the past, our work depicts the female experience. Women's art galleries, craft centers, and bookstores are beginning to appear in the cities. Women's magazines are increasingly feminist, led by the popularity of *Ms.* magazine. And the media are paying greater attention to women's issues than in the past.

More and more women are acquiring professional training previously reserved for men. Textbook publishers, sensitized to sexist language and concepts, have established guidelines to avoid them. An increasing number of children's books are designed to avoid subliminal sexist messages. At colleges, women's studies programs have increased and, in the face of a considerable struggle for academic credibility, have gained respect. As the preceding chapters indicate, many trained in the older academic disciplines are critically reviewing old assumptions and raising new questions. Sexism is on the defensive.

Women and the family   Women's roles in the family are also changing. A growing number of women with preschool children are working at paid jobs, and dual-career families are more common. Fathers are playing an increasingly active role in child care. Whereas books on mothering have always been plentiful, the shelves of local bookstores now contain many books for fathers, about fathering, and for parents about parenting.

Child-rearing practices are still largely sexist, but nonsexist ideas are increasingly being communicated in children's entertainment. For example, in the 1970s, Marlo Thomas's record and book *Free to Be You and Me* was a popular gift. This work, written for children, addresses the acceptability of such things as boys crying or playing with dolls and nobody liking to do housework. At the Collegiate School, a private boys' school in New York City, fifth- and sixth-grade boys could choose a six-week course in infant care. . . .

The Other Side of the Picture

*Are we witnessing a **backlash**?* Political sentiments in the United States of the early 1980s may be an omen of the future. After legislation and court rulings which promoted women's status in the 1960s and 1970s, 1980 saw the election of a president whose policies threaten to reverse many of these gains. Ronald Reagan openly opposed the Equal Rights Amendment as well as access to abortions. His spending cuts in social programs represent an enormous setback for women. Many legislators sympathetic to the women's movement were defeated in 1980 and replaced by politicians supported by unusually reactionary groups with substantial followings.

The push for the Equal Rights Amendment itself has had disappointing results, as feminists have failed to obtain sufficient support in state legislatures to achieve ratification. In 1973, the Supreme Court ruled that abortion was the personal right of a woman (in consultation with her doctor). Since then, antiabortion groups have put powerful pressure on politicians to limit severely the legality of abortions. Reagan's secretary of health and human services, Richard Schweiker, suggests that doctors should not be permitted to prescribe contraceptives to poor, unmarried teenagers under Medicaid. Many legislators and citizens support a constitutional amendment that would make abortion in almost all circumstances illegal. A basic human right that feminists have been demanding for over a century—the right to control whether our bodies are to be used for reproduction—is in jeopardy.*

In the personal sphere, traditional attitudes about women are being promoted. The lectures of Marabel Morgan attract large audiences. Her book, ironically titled *The Total Woman* (1973), encourages women to return to the home and to the service of men. She advises women to adopt the image of "sex object." (It is worth noting that she herself is an ambitious, successful woman.) Neoconservative articles warn of the hazards of day care, and books claim that equality for women will cause impotence or violence in men.

What is the appeal of these messages to those women who are influenced by them? Answering this question may help feminists to understand better some of the fears, conflicts, and survival strategies of

---

* The book this excerpt first appeared in was written in 1983. Since that time, there has been a serious but unsuccessful attempt to overturn *Roe* vs. *Wade* and a consolidation of anti-abortion forces as witnessed in Project Rescue.

many of our sisters. It may also provide information about a source of resistance that the women's movement must confront.

On December 28, 1980, the *New York Times* published the results of a survey of Ivy League women college students. The greater number sampled desired to lead rather traditional lives—get married, have a family, and stay at home, for at least a while, to raise children. These traditional family goals were given priority over career goals. While studies at other colleges have not found similar results, the women in this survey represent a group of academically superior students. What phenomena are prompting such a choice? . . .

A lesson from history   "Two steps forward, one back." In the history of the women's movement, successes have been followed by reversals or lulls. Is history to repeat itself?

The women's movement has always had strong opposition. As it becomes stronger, so will the resistance. The movement threatens to change the status quo, and any kind of significant change is frightening to many people. Change is even upsetting to people who have little, for they fear they will have even less. Change threatens the power structure, and it threatens men, who fear they will lose their privileged status. It also threatens many women: those who fear losing what is thought of as security; those who believe the women's movement denies domestic values and family life; and those who see a whole pattern of life being questioned by uncomfortable, new points of view.

The women's movement needs to address such fears, not ignore them. The greatest danger facing women is that feminists will become complacent. No situation will improve without organized action. This is a lesson to be learned from the history of the women's movement and from that of the well-organized groups that would oppress us . . . .

Sisterhood and feminism   The women's movement has sometimes been accused of being a white middle-class movement, insensitive to and irrelevant for poor and minority women. There is no question that women's concerns throughout history have been articulated by those of us who had the education and social resources to gain a hearing. Moreover, revolutions are always led by those with sufficient material resources to concern themselves with more than survival. But the women's movement today represents far more than just the concerns of middle-class women. The drive for women to be able to control our own reproduction affects all women. Demands for welfare reform and assistance to the poor have been continuing goals; the vast majority of those who *are* poor are women and children. The mean earnings of fully employed white males in the United States are already three times as high as those of everyone else in the labor force. Raising income levels of women, together with those of nonwhites and the unemployed, to the levels of white males would constitute enormous progress toward social justice in the United States, even without any significant shift in the class structure as traditionally understood. But it is highly unlikely that this could happen without many very significant changes in the structure of society. The seemingly more moderate demands of "liberal" feminists and the seemingly more radical demands of "socialist" feminists are coming more and more to coincide. Women realize we will never be able to have genuinely equal opportunities for individual progress without an array of social supports . . . .

"A piece of the pie" or a new world?   Feminists fall along a continuum as to the extent of change we think is required for society and our sisters. Many feminists regard equality in the present capitalist system to be impossible. We believe the system is structured for the benefit of a few and requires the oppression of most of the world's population. Rather than "make it" in the present system, we envision new systems which would emphasize other values than the corporate interests we see as dominant in society in the United States. We want to replace the hierarchical structure of a "business civilization" with an egalitarian one. We want governing institutions that will represent the interests of all people, and in which the people affected by decisions are involved in making them. We strive for a society in which power will not be used in ways that enable some to dominate others, but in which human beings will freely treat one another with respect. We envision a society in which people will feel concern for the well-being of others, rather than a society in which the strong seek to take advantage of the weak, and usually succeed.

Jo Freeman refers to such rhetoric as the *liberation ethic*. In this view, it is not sufficient to have both women and men participate in the various social roles that now exist; the roles themselves must change. The liberation ethic holds that men as well as women have deplorable lives and are oppressed by the present structure. The system must be transformed to provide humane lives for all.

Other feminists are more concerned with getting a piece of the pie that now exists. We strive for greater equality immediately in the present system. We feel that once we obtain power in existing institutions, we can more easily implement whatever further social and political policies are needed. These feminists among us recognize that major changes have to occur, but do not advocate a radical transformation of the system.

Freeman refers to the goals at this end of the continuum as the *egalitarian ethic*—equality for the sexes and elimination of gender roles. "Our history has proven that institutional differences inevitably mean inequity, and sex-role stereotypes have long since become anachronistic. . . . This means that there will be an integration of social functions and life-styles of women and men as groups until, ideally, one cannot tell anything relevant about a person's social role by knowing that person's sex." The result will be increased choices and greater diversity for people.

Feminists who adhere to this position do so either because we think the present economic system should be limited rather than replaced or because we feel it is a more practical and realistic approach.

Carolyn Heilbrun agrees with the latter position. She feels that the goal of shattering society and building another may be possible for small groups, but it is too remote for the larger society. Such an attempt would divert attention from the here and now of women's daily lives. She supports, instead, women's struggle for selfhood but points out that even this is becoming more difficult in light of the rise of conservatism.

Freeman cautions that both the egalitarian ethic and the liberation ethic must work in tandem. "To seek for equality alone, given the current bias of the social values, is to assume that women want to be like men or that men are worth emulating. It is to demand that women be allowed to participate in society . . . without questioning whether that society is worth participating in." By definition, the "male" role necessitates a "female" role; it exists by the oppression of women. Equality, Freeman says, requires the destruction of these roles, which will lead to basic changes in the system itself.

Similarly, Freeman points out, there are dangers in adopting various existing revolutionary ideologies and programs. It should not be assumed that a social revolution will result in equality for women. She notes that "women have yet to be defined as people, even among radicals, and it is erroneous to assume their interests are identical to those of men." To work for a revolution without paying equal attention to women's roles would be a mistake. Revolutionary systems proposed by nonfeminist theorists have not eliminated sexual inequality or a gender-role structure. Stokely Carmichael, a leader of the nonviolent civil rights organization SNCC, said in 1966, "The only position for women in SNCC is prone." Nearly all radical and revolutionary groups other than feminist ones have had a gender-role structure. In addition, too much of a focus on a massive global revolution can leave one without a battle to fight.

Separated from each other, the Egalitarian Ethic and the Liberation Ethic can be crippling, but together they can be a very powerful force. . . . Separately, they afford but superficial solutions; together they recognize that sexism not only oppresses women but limits the potentiality of men. Separately, neither will be achieved because both are too narrow in scope; together they provide a vision worthy of our devotion. Separately, these two ethics liberate neither women nor men; together they can liberate both.

Women's condition and the human condition The women's movement has always been highly sensitive to the human condition. As we have seen, many women have worked to improve conditions for all people. Women are not, however, limitless sources of energy. As individuals and as a movement, we must often choose what to focus on—the larger concern of the human condition or the more narrow area of women's issues as these touch us in our daily lives. These areas are not, of course, mutually exclusive, and the two very often affect each other. However, when it comes to expending time, energy, and money and developing a shared power for the most effective outcome, a single direction at a given time must often be decided upon.

Increasingly, feminists are insisting that women's issues must become the primary concern of women. In the past, women's goals have repeatedly taken a back seat to other concerns. Labor rights took precedence over women's concerns in England in the nineteenth century. Efforts to enlarge the franchise in England and in the United States gave the vote to ever-wider groups of men before any women were given the right. Women were used and scorned in the French Revolution, in the abolitionist movement, in the Russian Revolution, and in the civil rights movement. Many feel that granting priority to "human" concerns, rather than to women's concerns, may continue to support a male culture and male values. Of course, feminists need to keep in view the concerns of all women, not just those of a privileged few in the Western World.

One problem is that the dominant culture tends to view women's concerns as trivial. We have been criticized for asking for anything for ourselves, in the face of "more important" matters. Over and over again in history, when men have been granted rights that women have helped them to fight for, and women have asked for these same rights, we have been told "it's not your turn." Women have been asked to postpone our demands for even the most elementary aspects of equality because of the supposedly "more pressing" concerns of the proletariat or the poor or the racially disadvantaged.

It is difficult for women, particularly when we lack a strong support group, to articulate the things we feel are important when our demands are continually dismissed as insignificant. Thus, men frequently express impatience when women wish to discuss such "unimportant" issues as the division of household chores. Requests by women for even minimal respect are met with ridicule. We saw the advent of women's studies considered trivial by the academic community. When women within scholarly fields do pioneering work in feminist theory, or when we investigate whole areas of economic or historical reality ignored by our male colleagues, our work is often dismissed as "not really scholarly" or as "nonserious."

If women "buy" the male view of what is important, we feel foolish and confused. We cannot dismiss the weight of our own oppression, yet we are told we are not (and should not feel) oppressed. When feminists talk with each other, when we seriously address the realities of women's lives hidden by centuries of male inattention, we are often able to restore our sense of what is truly important. Obviously, the oppression of half of humanity *should not* be dismissed as unimportant, or turned into a joke.

Strongly asserting that women's aims must be of paramount importance for women, Heilbrun states: "Women have behaved not as an oppressed class struggling to overcome their oppression, but as a caste identifying with their oppressors, internalizing their oppressors' views of them. Since men do not take women's rights seriously, most women also refuse to do so. Until women adopt a model for action that sustains the primacy of their own claims, they will not achieve full equality" . . . .

Questions for Discussion and Writing

1. This article was written in the 1980s. How positively do the authors rate the success of the women's movement at that time?

2. The article predicts a political "backlash" against the gains made by the feminist movement. Explain what this means. What evidence does the article cite? Has this backlash increased or decreased since then?

3. Poll your classmates and compare your results to those of the *New York Times* reported in the article. How many women in class would like to "lead rather traditional lives—get married, have a family, and stay at home, for at least a while, to raise children," instead of giving priority to career goals?

4. What evidence supports the view that the women's movement is a "white middle class movement, insensitive to and irrelevant for poor and minority women"? How does the article answer these charges?

5. The article describes two feminist political positions: the liberation ethic, concerned with creating new social structures; and the egalitarian ethic, devoted to seeking equality and an end to gender roles. Explain both positions. Which, if either, do you prefer? Can they work together?

6. Why do the authors argue that women's issues must become women's primary concerns above other social and humanitarian issues? What is the argument against this position? Could women do both at the same time?

7. To what extent does the dominant culture view women's issues such as household chores and the establishment of women's study groups and centers as unimportant?

8. What aspects of the essay's rhetoric suggest the authors' positions and points of view? Consider diction (choice of verbs and adjectives and tone of voice) as well as the outside sources the authors use to support their position.

Karen Kenyon, from **"A Pink-Collar Worker's Blues"** _____

Writing in 1982, journalist Karen Kenyon describes her experience as a part-time secretary and her confrontation with the "second-class" status accorded to secretaries—almost always women. Kenyon discovers that, despite the feminist movement, for most women "liberation from home [into the workplace] is no liberation at all."

More and more women every day are going out to work. A myth has grown around them: the myth of the "new woman." It celebrates the woman executive. It defines her look (a suit), and her drink (Dewar's or perhaps a fine white wine). It puts her "in charge." But it neglects to say whom she is in charge of—probably some other women.

The world still needs helpers, secretaries and waitresses, and the sad truth is that mostly women fill these serving roles. Today more women hold clerical jobs than ever before (4 million in 1950 and 20 million in 1981). Wherever we look, we see the image of the successful woman executive but, in fact, most women are going out to become secretaries. The current totals: 3 million women in management and 20 million clerical employees. So for the majority of working women—the so-called "pink-collar workers"—liberation from home is no liberation at all.

Recently I took a job as a part-time secretary in a department office of a university. I thought the financial security would be nice (writers never have this) and I needed the sense of community a job can bring. I found there is indeed a sense of community among secretaries. It is, in fact, essential to their emotional survival.

Human Beings

I felt a bit like the author of "Black Like Me," a Caucasian who had his skin darkened by dye and went into the South, where he experienced what it was like to be black. Here I was, "a person," disguised as "a secretary." This move from being a newly published author to being a secretary made it very clear to me that the same people who are regarded as creative human beings in one role will be demeaned and ignored in another.

I was asked one day to make some Xerox invitations to a party, then told I could keep one (not exactly a cordial invitation, I thought.) The next day I was asked, "Are you coming to the party?" I brightened and said, "Well, maybe I will." I was then told, "Well, then, would you pick up the pizza and we'll reimburse you."

A friend of mine who is an "administrative assistant" told me about a campus party she attended. She was engaged in a lively, interesting conversation with a faculty wife. The wife then asked my friend, "Are you teaching here?" When my friend replied, "Well, no, actually I'm a secretary," the other woman's jaw dropped. She then said, "Don't worry. Nobody will ever guess."

I heard secretaries making "grateful" remarks like, "They really treat us like human beings here." To be grateful for bottom-line treatment was, I felt, a sorry comment.

We think we have freed our slaves, but we have not. We just call them by a different name. Every time people reach a certain status in life they seem to take pride in the fact that they now have a secretary.

It is a fact that it has to be written very carefully into a job description just what a secretary's duties are, or she will be told to clean off the desk, pick up cleaning and the like. Women in these jobs are often seen as surrogate wives, mothers and servants—even to other women.

Many times, when a secretary makes creative contributions she is not given her due. The work is changed slightly by the person in charge, who takes the credit. Most secretaries live in an area between being too assertive and being too passive. Often a secretary feels she has to think twice before stepping in and correcting the grammar, even when she knows her "superior" can't frame a good sentence.

Envy

When after three months I announced to my co-workers that I was quitting, I was met with kind goodbyes. In some I caught a glimpse of perhaps a gentle envy, not filled with vindictiveness at all, but tinged with some remorse. "I'm just a little jealous that someone is getting out of prison," admitted one woman. "I wish I'd done that years ago," said another.

Their faces remain in my heart. They stand for all the people locked into jobs because they need the money, because they don't know where else to go, afraid there's no place else, because they don't have the confidence or feel they have the chance to do anything else.

I was lucky. I escaped before lethargy or repressed anger or extreme eagerness to please took over. Before I was drawn over the line, seduced by the daily rewards of talk over coffee, exchanged recipes, the photos of family members thumbtacked to the wall near the desk, the occasional lunches to mark birthdays and departures.

I am free now, but so many others are trapped in their carpeted, respectable prisons. The new-woman myth notwithstanding, the true tale of the woman on her own most often ends that way.

As I see it, the slave mentality is alive and well. It manicures its nails. It walks in little pumps on tiny cat feet. It's there every time a secretary says, "Yes, I'll do that. I don't mind" or finds ashtrays for the people who come to talk to someone else. The secretary has often forgotten her own dream. She is too busy helping others to realize theirs.

Questions for Discussion and Writing

1. Kenyon describes the unspoken pecking order women office workers find themselves in. If you have worked in an office, do you agree with Kenyon's perception? Is she exaggerating the problem? How could the inequities she writes of be changed?

2. Kenyon writes that today more women than ever before are working but that most of them are in clerical positions and very few in management. Why are so few women in managerial positions? What factors continue to make it more difficult for women than men to break into upper level positions?

3. "The slave mentality is alive and well," yet we will always need secretaries and clerical workers. Can you imagine ways that "the slave mentality" can be changed, or will women clerical workers always be viewed as second-class citizens?

MONARCHY AND ABUSE OF POWER

William Edenstein, **"Monarchy"**

Monarchy, "the rule of one," was the earliest form of government, finding its origin in humankind's primitive past and still existing in various forms today. William Edenstein outlines an extended definition of monarchy and traces how it has developed and why it has changed.

Key Concepts

Despotism, tyranny, and **autocracy** have all been defined in earlier readings; see pages 305 and 320.

Imperial expansion (page 343), like colonial expansion, involves a stronger nation taking power over a weaker one, exploiting it economically.

For a definition of **aristocracy,** see page 320.

The **bourgeoisie** (page 344), a Marxist term, is the middle class, or those above the working class.

Monarchy is a form of government in which one person is the sovereign.[1] The word derives from the Greek "monarchia," the rule of one. The Greeks, however, distinguished the legitimate one-man government of monarchy from the illegitimate one-man dictatorship of **despotism** or **tyranny.** In the latter system the ruler rules in his own interest rather than in that of the governed. In a monarchy in its pure (and original) form, the ruler combined in his person the supreme authority and power in legislation as well as in administration and adjudication.[2] In later stages of evolution, the monarch frequently still retained his position as the supreme law-giver, but handed over the judicial and administrative functions to specialized agencies, generally subordinate to him. Above all, the monarch was originally, and long remained, the commander in chief of his nation's armed forces.

In early history, as among primitive peoples today, the monarchical form of government was virtually the only one known and practiced. Generally, monarchy was hereditary. In Asia and Africa monarchy persisted in its **autocratic** form until, beginning in the 17th century, **imperial expansion** by European states (England, France, Holland) put an end to native monarchical autocracies. Native monarchies were often retained, however, as instruments of control over conquered populations. Where such European imperial influence has been only short-lived—as in Saudi Arabia—the despotic or autocratic form of monarchy has survived.

[1] Supreme ruler.   [2] Judicial rule.

In Antiquity

The Greeks discarded the monarchical system of government beginning in the 7th century B.C., although Sparta persisted in monarchical rule of an elective type. Monarchy did not fit the individualistic, rational, inquiring mentality of the Greeks, who may be said to have invented republican self-government in the Western World. Moreover, their main enemy in the 5th century B.C. was Persia, an empire under an absolute monarchy. Monarchy thus became in ancient Greece the symbol of external and internal servitude. Even after Philip and Alexander the Great had forced the Greek city-states into the Macedonian monarchy and empire, the institutions of self-government in the city-states were preserved by their Macedonian overlords.

The Jews opposed monarchy from very early times. According to the teachings of Judaism, God was sovereign, and no man could demand complete allegiance from his subjects. The Romans had their great period during their republican system of government. The establishment of monarchy in Rome coincided with the expansion of Rome from a relatively small city-state to a world empire. Although the Roman monarchy of the imperial type helped unite the empire, it symbolized the early decay of those civic qualities in Rome that were the foundations of its greatness.

In the Middle Ages

After the destruction of the Western Roman Empire in 476 A.D., monarchy continued in the Eastern Roman Empire centered in Constantinople. In the West, two types of monarchy gradually emerged. First, the bishop of Rome progressively established himself as the ruler of all Christendom, and he claimed monarchical prerogatives over all Christians in matters temporal as well as spiritual. Meanwhile, the German rulers sought to restore the Roman imperial monarchy under German leadership, claiming universal political allegiance throughout the Christian world. This Holy Roman Empire of the Teutonic[3] Nations was inaugurated[4] with the coronation of Charlemagne in 800 by the pope in Rome. Legally, it lasted until 1806, when Napoleon I destroyed it, but it had exercised little influence during the last few centuries of its existence.

In the Renaissance and Modern Times

The monarchy more than any other institution was instrumental in forging the modern nation-state. In general, the main force to be overcome was the **aristocracy,** which opposed increased royal power. But the new middle class, or **"bourgeoisie,"** which supplied much of the administrative personnel of the new nation-states, was willing to allow the monarch strong central authority so long as he could maintain law

---

[3] Northern European, particularly German.   [4] Formally begun.

and order, efficient communications, a stable currency, and protection against internal and external enemies.

England, in the 17th century, was the first modern country to abandon the concept of the absolute monarchical authority. The Civil War culminated in the execution of King Charles I in 1649, the establishment of a republic under Oliver Cromwell, and the ascendancy of the middle classes. The monarchy was restored in 1660, but the revolution of 1688 finally established the principle that political authority resides in Parliament. A century later, the French followed the English example and established a republic based on "liberty, equality, and fraternity." During the 19th century, monarchy was restored in France for short periods, but the concept of absolute monarchy deriving its authority from divine grace was dead.

Where liberalism was weak, the monarchical form of government lasted until World War I. In Russia the monarchy was destroyed in 1917, and the emperors of Germany and Austria abdicated in 1918. Today, monarchy exists in Western nations where it has allied itself with democracy and liberalism, as in Britain, Belgium, the Netherlands, Denmark, Norway, and Sweden. In liberal societies the monarchy served as a symbol of national unity and continuity.

Questions for Discussion and Writing

1. Summarize the definition of monarchy.
2. Describe the various degrees of monarchical rule, from a monarch who is just a figurehead to one who exercises absolute power.
3. What pivotal role did monarchies play in the establishment of modern nation-states? Why did monarchs ally themselves with the bourgeoisie against the aristocracy?
4. What caused the demise of monarchies?
5. Several countries today, such as Great Britain, still retain figurehead monarchs, and other countries, France and Spain included, have witnessed small movements to restore legitimate monarchs. Why would people want to restore a monarchy? What would they stand to gain either from a figurehead or a fully functioning monarch?

Suetonius, *"Gaius (Caligula)"*

In the first century B.C., the Roman republic, a representative form of government, came to an end. Julius Caesar led Rome on its way to an empire. He was succeeded by a series of Caesars: Augustus, Tiberius, Claudius, Nero, and Gaius, among others. The Roman Empire stretched from England and Spain to Jerusalem and parts of Africa. But the empire was hard to maintain, at home and abroad, and the Roman emperors often succumbed to the temptation that absolute power placed before them. Rome fell in A.D. 476. Suetonius (c. 70–c. 160 AD) recounts Roman corruption in this excerpt from The Twelve Caesars *(c. 120 AD).*

So much for the Emperor; the rest of this history must deal with the Monster.

He adopted a variety of titles: such as "Pious," "Son of the Camp," "Father of the Army," "Best and Greatest of Caesars." But when once, at the dinner table, some foreign kings who had come to pay homage were arguing which of them was the most nobly descended, Gaius interrupted their discussion by declaiming Homer's line:

Nay, let there be one master, and one king!

And he nearly assumed a royal diadem[1] then and there, turning the semblance of a principate[2] into an autocracy. However, after his court-iers reminded him that he already outranked any prince or king, he insisted on being treated as a god—sending for the most revered or artistically famous statues of the Greek deities (including that of Jupiter at Olympia), and having their heads replaced by his own.

Next, Gaius extended the Palace as far as the Forum; converted the shrine of Castor and Pollux into its vestibule;[3] and would often stand beside these Divine Brethren to be worshipped by all visitants, some of whom addressed him as "Jupiter Latiaris." He established a shrine to himself as God, with priests, the costliest possible victims, and a life-sized golden image, which was dressed every day in clothes identical with those that he happened to be wearing. All the richest citizens tried to gain priesthoods here, either by influence or bribery. Flamingoes, peacocks, black grouse, guinea-hens, and pheasants were offered as sacri-fices, each on a particular day of the month. When the moon shone full and bright he always invited the Moon-goddess to sexual intercourse in his bed; and during the day would indulge in whispered conversations with Capitoline Jupiter (a statue), pressing his ear to the god's mouth, and sometimes raising his voice in anger. Once he was overheard threat-ening the god: "If you do not raise me up to Heaven I will cast you down to Hell." Finally he announced that Jupiter had persuaded him to share his home; and therefore connected the Palace with the Capitol by throw-ing a bridge across the Temple of the God Augustus; after which he began building a new house inside the precincts of the Capitol itself, in order to live even nearer.

Because of Agrippa's humble origin Gaius loathed being described as his grandson, and would fly into a rage if anyone mentioned him, in speech or song, as an ancestor of the Caesars. He nursed a fantasy that his mother had been born of an incestuous union between Augustus and his daughter Julia; and not content with thus discredtiing Augustus' name, cancelled the annual commemorations of Agrippa's victories at Actium and off Sicily, declaring that they had proved the disastrous ruin of the Roman people. He called his great-grandmother Livia a "Ulysses in pet-

---

[1] Crown.   [3] Entrance hall.
[2] Territory ruled by a prince.

ticoats," and in a letter to the Senate dared describe her as of low birth—
"her maternal grandfather Aufidius Lurco having been a mere local
senator at Fundi"—although the public records showed Lurco to have
held high office at Rome. When his grandmother Antonia asked him to
grant her a private audience he insisted on taking Macro, the Guards
Commander, as his escort. Unkind treatment of this sort hurried her to
the grave though, according to some, he accelerated the process with
poison and, when she died, showed so little respect that he sat in his
dining-room and watched the funeral pyre burn. One day he sent a
colonel to kill young Tiberius Gemellus without warning, on the pretext
that Tiberius had insulted him by taking an antidote against poison—his
breath smelled of it. Then he forced his father-in-law, Marcus Silanus, to
cut his own throat with a razor, the charge being that he had not
followed the imperial ship when it put to sea in a storm, but had stayed
on shore to seize power at Rome if anything happened to himself. The
truth was that Silanus, a notoriously bad sailor, could not face the voyage;
and Tiberius's breath smelled of medicine taken for a persistent cough
which was getting worse. Gaius preserved his uncle Claudius merely as a
butt for practical jokes.

Nor was he any more respectful or considerate in his dealings with
the Senate, but made some of the highest officials run for miles beside his
chariot, dressed in their togas; or wait in short linen tunics at the head or
foot of his dining couch. Often he would send for men whom he had
secretly killed, as though they were still alive, and remark off-handedly a
few days later that they must have committed suicide. When two Consuls
forgot to announce his birthday, he dismissed them and left the country
for three days without officers of state. One of his quaestors[4] was charged
with conspiracy; Gaius had his clothes stripped off and spread on the
ground, to give the soldiers who flogged him a firmer foothold.

He behaved just as arrogantly and violently towards the other
orders of society. A crowd bursting into the Circus about midnight to
secure free seats angered him so much that he had them driven away
with clubs; more than a score of knights, as many married women, and
numerous others were crushed to death in the ensuing panic. Gaius liked
to stir up trouble in the Theatre by scattering gift vouchers before the
seats were occupied, thus tempting commoners to invade the rows
reserved for knights. During gladiatorial shows he would have the can-
opies[5] removed at the hottest time of the day and forbid anyone to leave;
or take away the usual equipment, and pit feeble old fighters against
decrepit wild animals; or stage comic duels between respectable house-
holders who happened to be physically disabled in some way or other.
More than once he closed down the granaries[6] and let the people go
hungry.

[4] Public officials.
[5] Roof-like Covering.

[6] Grain warehouse.

Gaius made parents attend their sons' executions, and when one father excused himself on the ground of ill-health, provided a litter for him. Having invited another father to dinner just after the son's execution, he overflowed with good-fellowship in an attempt to make him laugh and joke. He watched the manager of his gladiatorial and wild-beast shows being flogged with chains for several days running, and had him killed only when the smell of suppurating[7] brains became insupportable.[8] A writer of Atellan farces was burned alive in the amphitheatre, because of a line which had an amusing double-entendre.[9] One knight, on the point of being thrown to the wild beasts, shouted that he was innocent; Gaius brought him back, removed his tongue, and then ordered the sentence to be carried out.

Gaius' savage crimes were made worse by his brutal language. He claimed that no personal trait made him feel prouder than his "inflexibility"—by which he must have meant "brazen impudence." As though mere deafness to his grandmother Antonia's good advice were not enough, he told her: 'Bear in mind that I can treat anyone exactly as I please!' Suspecting that young Tiberius Gemellus had taken drugs as prophylactics[10] to the poison he intended to administer, he scoffed: "Can there really be an antidote against Caesar?" And, on banishing his sisters, he remarked: "I have swords as well as islands." One ex-praetor, taking a cure at Anticyra, made frequent requests for an extension of his sick-leave; Gaius had him put to death, suggesting that if hellebore[11] had been of so little benefit over so long a period, he must need to be bled. When signing the execution list he used to say: "I am clearing my accounts." And one day, after sentencing a number of Gauls and Greeks to die in the same batch, he boasted of having "subdued Gallo-Graecia."

The method of execution he preferred was to inflict numerous small wounds; and his familiar order: "Make him feel that he is dying!" soon became proverbial. Once, when the wrong man had been killed, owing to a confusion of names, he announced that the victim had equally deserved death; and often quoted Accius' line:

Let them hate me, so long as they fear me.

Questions for Discussion and Writing

1. Suetonius recounts Caligula's offenses in graphic detail. What might his purpose(s) be in depicting the horrors of Caligula's rule so vividly?

2. Was Caligula sincere in his belief in his own divinity, or did he have some political purpose for his bizarre behavior?

3. Despite the severity and cruelty of Caligula's rule, four years passed before he was assassinated. Why did an entire nation endure his excesses? What political strategies might he have used to stay in power?

---

[7] Giving off pus.
[8] Unbearable.
[9] Double-meaning statement.

[10] Things that prevent or protect against.
[11] Medicinal plant.

4. Compare Caligula to more contemporary dictators. What strategies are still used today? How successful are they?

5. In what sense is fear a more powerful means of control than love?

Machiavelli, from **The Prince** ──────────────────────

Machiavelli's The Prince *(1513) has enjoyed both renown and infamy, depending on its audience. The author offered his work to the leaders of Renaissance states as a kind of guidebook to power through manipulation, deception, and force. The term "Machiavellian" has come to mean a cunning, devious approach or attitude. Like the contemporary Castiglione's courtier, the ideal of grace, the Prince embodies the ideal of power. The prince depicted here became a model of pragmatic and ruthless leadership. Some twentieth-century leaders who displayed a Machiavellian edge were Stalin, Hitler, and Mussolini. Machiavelli himself lived from 1469 to 1527.*

Every prince should prefer to be considered merciful rather than cruel, yet he should be careful not to mismanage this clemency[1] of his. People thought Cesare Borgia[2] was cruel, but that cruelty of his reorganized the Romagna,[3] united it, and established it in peace and loyalty. Anyone who views the matter realistically will see that this prince was much more merciful than the people of Florence, who, to avoid the reputation of cruelty, allowed Pistoia to be destroyed. Thus no prince should mind being called cruel for what he does to keep his subjects united and loyal; he may make examples of a very few, but he will be more merciful in reality than those who, in their tenderheartedness, allow disorders to occur, with their attendant[4] murders and lootings. Such turbulence brings harm to an entire community, while the executions ordered by a prince affect only one individual at a time. A new prince, above all others, cannot possibly avoid a name for cruelty, since new states are always in danger. And Virgil, speaking through the mouth of Dido, says:

My cruel fate and doubts attending an unsettled state force me to guard my coast from foreign foes.

Yet a prince should be slow to believe rumors and to commit himself to action on the basis of them. He should not be afraid of his own thoughts; he ought to proceed cautiously, moderating his conduct with

---

[1] Mercy.
[2] Italian Cardinal, political and military leader.
[3] Italian lands.
[4] Accompanying.

prudence[5] and humanity, allowing neither overconfidence to make him careless, nor overtimidity to make him intolerable.

Here the question arises: is it better to be loved than feared, or vice versa? I don't doubt that every prince would like to be both; but since it is hard to accommodate these qualities, if you have to make a choice, to be feared is much safer than to be loved. For it is a good general rule about men, that they are ungrateful, fickle,[6] liars, and deceivers, fearful of danger and greedy for gain. While you serve their welfare, they are all yours, offering their blood, their belongings, their lives, and their children's lives, as we noted above—so long as the danger is remote. But when the danger is close at hand, they turn against you. Then, any prince who has relied on their words and has made no other preparations will come to grief; because friendships that are bought at a price, and not with greatness and nobility of soul, may be paid for but they are not acquired, and they cannot be used in time of need. People are less concerned with offending a man who makes himself loved than one who makes himself feared: the reason is that love is a link of obligation which men, because they are rotten, will break any time they think doing so serves their advantage; but fear involves dread of punishment, from which they can never escape.

Still, a prince should make himself feared in such a way that, even if he gets no love, he gets no hate either; because it is perfectly possible to be feared and not hated, and this will be the result if only the prince will keep his hands off the property of his subjects or citizens, and off their women. When he does have to shed blood, he should be sure to have a strong justification and manifest cause; but above all, he should not confiscate people's property, because men are quicker to forget the death of a father than the loss of a patrimony. Besides, pretexts for confiscation are always plentiful; it never fails that a prince who starts living by plunder can find reasons to rob someone else. Excuses for proceeding against someone's life are much rarer and more quickly exhausted.

Returning to the question of being feared or loved, I conclude that since men love at their own inclination but can be made to fear at the inclination of the prince, a shrewd prince will lay his foundations on what is under his own control, not on what is controlled by others. He should simply take pains not to be hated, as I said.

The Way Princes Should Keep Their Word

How praiseworthy it is for a prince to keep his word and live with integrity rather than by craftiness, everyone understands; yet we see from recent experience that those princes have accomplished most who paid little heed to keeping their promises, but who knew how craftily to manipulate the minds of men. In the end, they won out over those who tried to act honestly.

---

[5] Careful judgment.   [6] Unstable, undecided.

You should consider then, that there are two ways of fighting, one with laws and the other with force. The first is properly a human method, the second belongs to beasts. But as the first method does not always suffice, you sometimes have to turn to the second. Thus a prince must know how to make good use of both the beast and the man.

Thus a prudent prince cannot and should not keep his word when to do so would go against his interest, or when the reasons that made him pledge it no longer apply. Doubtless if all men were good, this rule would be bad; but since they are a sad lot, and keep no faith with you, you in your turn are under no obligation to keep it with them.

Besides, a prince will never lack for legitimate excuses to explain away his breaches[7] of faith. Modern history will furnish innumerable examples of this behavior, showing how many treaties and promises have been made null and void by the faithlessness of princes, and how the man succeeded best who knew best how to play the fox. But it is a necessary part of this nature that you must conceal it carefully; you must be a great liar and hypocrite. Men are so simple of mind, and so much dominated by their immediate needs, that a deceitful man will always find plenty who are ready to be deceived.

In actual fact, a prince may not have all the admirable qualities we listed, but it is very necessary that he should seem to have them. Indeed, I will venture to say that when you have them and exercise them all the time, they are harmful to you; when you just seem to have them, they are useful. It is good to appear merciful, truthful, humane, sincere, and religious; it is good to be so in reality. But you must keep your mind so disposed that, in case of need, you can turn to the exact contrary. This has to be understood: a prince, and especially a new prince, cannot possibly exercise all those virtues for which men are called "good." To preserve the state, he often has to do things against his word, against charity, against humanity, against religion. Thus he has to have a mind ready to shift as the winds of fortune and the varying circumstances of life may dictate. And as I said above, he should not depart from the good if he can hold to it, but he should be ready to enter on evil if he has to.

Hence a prince should take great care never to drop a word that does not seem imbued with the five good qualities noted above; to anyone who sees or hears him, he should appear all compassion, all honor, all humanity, all integrity, all religion. Nothing is more necessary than to seem to have this last virtue. Men in general judge more by the sense of sight than by the sense of touch, because everyone can see but only a few can test by feeling. Everyone sees what you seem to be, few know what you really are; and those few do not dare take a stand against the general opinion, supported by the majesty of the government. In the actions of all men, and especially of princes who are not subject to a court of appeal, we must always look to the end. Let a prince, therefore, win victories and uphold his state; his methods will always be considered

[7] Failures.

worthy, and everyone will praise them, because the masses are always impressed by the superficial appearance of things, and by the outcome of an enterprise. And the world consists of nothing but the masses; the few have no influence when the many feel secure. A certain prince of our own time, whom it's just as well not to name, preaches nothing but peace and mutual trust, yet he is the determined enemy of both; and if on several different occasions he had observed either, he would have lost both his reputation and his throne.

Questions for Discussion and Writing

1. Machiavelli advises the Prince that it is better for him to be feared than loved. What is the logic of his argument? What is the argument against his position?

2. Machiavelli also advises the Prince to lie and teaches that "those princes have accomplished most who paid little heed to keeping their promises." How does he rationalize this doctrine?

3. How does Machiavelli describe the common person? To what extent would he agree with Plato's opinion of the masses as "the herd"?

4. Ultimate victory and preservation of "the state" are the ends for whose achievement Machiavelli advises almost any means of action. How important is preservation of the state? Should other principles be valued over government stability?

5. Machiavelli's work depicts the kind of world that "the Renaissance Prince" encountered every day. Review Machiavelli's advice and opinions. What can you infer about the political life of the time? How would you describe it?

6. What is the argument against the ends justifying the means? Have you been in situations in which you faced this dilemma? How did you respond?

7. Machiavelli's Prince is usually considered ruthless. To what extent is he also evil and cruel? How would you compare his political position to that of Caligula or Robespierre?

8. Is it possible for a powerful politician not to be somewhat Machiavellian in our modern political world? Why or why not?

THE COSTS OF COMMUNISM

Lewis L. Lorwin, **"Communism"**

Communism and Marxism are terms we encounter daily in newspapers, on radio and television. Yet apart from often having strong reactions to these ideologies, many people know very little about what they mean or how they were theoretically meant to function. Lewis Lorwin writes a brief introduction to communist doctrine, defining key important terms and making the distinction between socialism and communism.

Key Concepts

Capitalism (page 353) is an economic system characterized by private industry instead of state-controlled production.

The Marxist theory of **materialism** (page 353) states that all social and political institutions have an economic basis.

A **dialectical process** (page 353) involves a thesis and antithesis evolving into a synthesis: one thing clashes with its opposite and some new thing derives from the clash.

For a definition of **imperialism** and **colonialism,** see page 366.

In a **proletarian dictatorship** (page 354) the working class holds political control.

Collective ways of living (page 354) are cooperative efforts for the common good, or people working on a communal level, sharing both the work and the profits.

Communism is the term used broadly to designate a theory or system of social organization based on the holding of all property in common. Specifically and currently, it refers to the doctrines underlying the revolutionary movement that aims to abolish **capitalism** and ultimately to establish a society in which all goods will be socially planned and controlled, and in which distribution will be in accordance with the maxim "from each according to his capacity, to each according to his needs." It is to be distinguished from socialism, which means, by constitutional and democratic methods, to nationalize gradually only the essential means of production and to organize distribution on the basis of a just reward to each person for the amount and quality of his or her work.

Marx and Engels

The theoretical foundations of modern communism were laid by the Germans Karl Marx and Friedrich Engels in *The Communist Manifesto* (1848). Marx and Engels took over and modified the then current concepts of **materialism,** the Hegelian view of historic evolution as a **dialectical process** moving from thesis through antithesis to synthesis, the labor theory of value of David Ricardo, the critique of capitalism of the "utopian" French socialists, and the tactics of Blanqui. The synthesis of Marx and Engels consisted in formulating these and the dynamics of "world revolution." After Lenin's death, Joseph Stalin added to Communist doctrine his special ideas that socialism could be built in one country, particularly Russia, and that the Soviet Union was the base of the "world revolution."

According to these Communist elaborations, the present stage of world history is that of "finance capitalism" or **"imperialism,"** marked by the growth of monopoly and the control of industry by finance. It is the epoch[1] of the decay or "general crisis" of capitalism on the one hand, and of the "world revolution" on the other. The "general crisis" of capitalism, say the Communists, began with World War I. It is to be a prolonged process, during which there may be brief periods of world economic stabilization and development, but every such period will be followed by a new crisis and decline, bringing the final collapse of capitalism nearer. The "general crisis" of capitalism cannot be overcome, argue the Communists, because "finance capitalism" aggravates the disparity between the growing productive forces of society and the restrictive methods of distribution, between the capacity to produce and the ability of the people to purchase the products of industry. The Communists view these disparities as the cause of industrial and social conflicts within each country, and as the cause of increasing struggles between nations for the control of raw materials and markets. International animosities are further accentuated, they maintain, by political antagonisms between the great powers and the **colonial** and under-developed countries.

World War II, according to their theory, sharpened these antagonisms in such a way as to divide the world into two opposing camps—the "capitalist-imperialist" states led by the United States on one side, and the "socialist" countries led by the USSR on the other side. Between these two camps struggle is inevitable, though for temporary periods the peaceful coexistence of the two systems and an easing of international tensions are possible.

As a result of the "general crisis" of capitalism, the "world revolution," which, the Communists maintain, began with the Russian Revolution of 1917, is "maturing." This "world revolution" is conceived by the Communists as a whole epoch of class struggles, national wars, revolutions, and **proletarian dictatorships** in different countries, some of which may fail temporarily while others are successful. For an indefinite period, therefore, the Communists expect the world to present a spectacle of conflicting socioeconomic systems existing side by side.

Though their ultimate aim in each country is the establishment of a Communist society, the achievement of this aim, according to their theory, must be preceded by a transition period, during which industry will be nationalized, a planned economy organized, and the people accustomed to **collective ways of living.** The Communists call this period the "building of socialism" as the "first phase of communism." During the transition period the government will be organized as a "proletarian dictatorship," that is, as the class rule of the workers under the control of the Communist party which claims to be the "vanguard of the proletariat." Such a government will use all the powers of the state to crush resistance to its program. Thus, though the Communists claim that

[1] Period of time.

in some countries the revolution may initially be carried through by peaceful means, the fulfillment of the program involves the employment of violent and dictatorial methods.

Communism versus Socialism

Though both derive from Marx, socialism and communism parted ways in 1917-1919 and are now farther apart than ever. To the extent that they still hold to Marxian ideas, the democratic socialists have revised them to fit modern conditions of democratic freedom and social progress. The democratic socialists consider Leninism a Russian distortion of Marx and denounce Communist methods as antidemocratic and immoral. Nor do they regard the Soviet Union as a socialist country simply because it has nationalized its industries and introduced economic planning.

Questions for Discussion and Writing

1. What is the major difference between socialism and communism?

2. Which communist countries still aggressively pursue the revolutionary goal of abolishing capitalism? Why have many communist countries backed off from this position?

3. Define the concept of class struggle.

4. Review the key concept definition of dialectical process. How did Marx and Engels modify this model of historical evolution into an economic and political theory centered around the class struggle?

5. How is communism generally depicted on American television and movies? Cite specific examples.

6. Imagine how life in a capitalist state is depicted in a communist country. What stereotypes would the communist media make use of and why?

7. How do the Soviet and Chinese models of communism differ? Consider events such as the massacre in Tiananmen Square, the opening of the Berlin Wall, and other major changes in Eastern Europe. What economic, social, and cultural characteristics might account for differences between the two systems?

Alexander Weissberg from **The Accused** _____

Communism is an ideal of communal or popular rule. Josef Stalin's prolonged rule, from 1924 to 1953, illustrates how, despite this ideal, absolute power can corrupt. As a communist leader, Stalin instituted a reign of terror far surpassing Robespierre's. Under his rule, Russia came to epitomize the modern totalitarian state. In this excerpt, Alexander Weissberg, who spent three years in prison camps on trumped up charges, documents the history of Stalinist terror, a period that saw over eight million people arrested and many millions of people killed.

Key Concepts

For definitions of **totalitarianism, dictatorship,** and **tyranny,** see page 305.

In a **socialist revolution** (page 356), the people seize power from a centralized government and replace it with communal rule.

From the middle of 1936 to the end of 1938 the **totalitarian** state took on its final form in the Soviet Union. In this period approximately eight million people were arrested in town and country by the secret police, the G.P.U. The arrested men were charged with high treason, espionage, sabotage, preparation for armed insurrection[1] and the planning of attempts on the lives of Soviet leaders. After periods of examination which rarely exceeded three months, all these men, with very few exceptions, pleaded guilty, and where they were actually brought before the courts they confirmed their confessions in public. They were all sentenced to long terms of forced labor in the concentration camps of the Far North or of the Central Asiatic desert districts.

They were all innocent.

The victims were accidental. In those days the G.P.U. operated in such a fashion that there was no probability that the arrested would really be enemies of the Soviet power rather than harmless citizens. But still further, the general atmosphere of fear created by Stalin's slogan "Vigilance!," the spy scare and the encouragement of denunciation crippled the activity of those whose official task it was to track down the real enemies of the state.

They were doubly innocent. Not one of them was guilty of spying; not one of them had betrayed his country to the Germans or to the Japanese; not one of them had planned or carried out any act of sabotage.

But perhaps they were guilty in the sense of Soviet public policy at the time while not being actually guilty of the crimes with which they were charged? Perhaps they really were conspirators, not against the Soviet power as such, but against the Party leaders and the Party regime? Perhaps they had attempted by underground methods to overthrow Stalin's **dictatorship** in the Party? Perhaps the dictator's secret police had nipped their conspiracy in the bud and then denounced them as counterrevolutionaries and agents of a foreign power in order to deprive them of that general sympathy on which the enemies of **tyranny** can reckon at all times and in all countries?

Nothing of the sort. The arrested men were not enemies of the **socialist revolution** but its most ardent supporters. And the overwhelming majority of them were not even opponents of the dictator. Very few of them had actually been in opposition, and even these had long since capitulated and abandoned all illegal activity. The overwhelming majority had neither belonged to the opposition nor sympathized with it. Many of them were actually enthusiastic Stalinists who had

---

[1] Rebellion, uprising.

vigorously opposed the opposition. In short, the general political attitude of the arrested men was not one whit[2] different from that of the millions who had been lucky enough to escape.

The arrests were made indiscriminately. In the depths of their hearts the victims certainly opposed the dictator, but even this carefully repressed feeling was shared with the great majority of the population, and they never allowed it expression because they knew what an ill-considered word could mean to them and their families. If this carefully repressed feeling was the criterion for the arrests, then the G.P.U. arrested not eight million too many, but 152 million too few. After the happenings of 1932 and 1933 the feelings of the people certainly turned against the dictator. The peasants had not forgiven him the hunger years and the death by starvation of millions of their fellows. The workers and intellectuals in the towns had not forgiven him for stifling all liberty. But all these feelings were repressed. The hunger years came to an end. The economic system gradually recovered. And the Russian people began to hope that they would regain their lost freedom. Men began to forget the bitter years and to take pleasure in the progress of their country. This process of emotional recuperation was interrupted in August, 1936. A new era opened up in the development of the Soviet Union, the era of the Great Purge.

But liquidation of the politically conscious sections of Soviet society was only the preliminary to happenings which were so fantastically senseless that it is difficult to describe them—and still more difficult to persuade Western minds to believe them. Hundreds of thousands of old revolutionaries and old members of the Bolshevik[3] Party had been arrested. The very foundations of Soviet life had been shaken. But ordinary people still believed it was exclusively a conflict within the ranks of the ruling party. Then in the second half of 1937 the character of the action changed. The scale of the arrests increased enormously and extended to those who had never been members of any political party. Day and night G.P.U. vans raced through the streets of town and village, taking their victims from their homes, factories, universities, laboratories, workshops, barracks and Government offices. All walks of life were involved, and workmen, peasants, officials and professional men, artists and officers found themselves together in the cells. All branches of the economic system were affected. Officials of heavy industry, agriculture, education and the armed forces were among the arrested. There were fifty republics and autonomous districts in the Soviet Union with their separate governments, and about five hundred People's Commissars. Very few of these Commissars[4] survived the storm. Not a single one of all the big Soviet undertakings retained its director or its leading engineers. New men took their places, but within a few weeks they too were arrested.

[2] Little bit.
[3] Communist.

[4] Administrators.

The arrest of Marshal Tukhachevsky and eight leading generals opened the prison gates to the officers corps. The commanders of all Russian military districts, the strategic units of the whole system, changed their commands for prison cells. Their successors joined them a few weeks later before they had even had time to settle down in their new commands. Within the space of a few months some military districts changed their commanders half a dozen times, until before long there were not enough generals left and colonels took over, only to be relieved in their turn by majors. In the end many regiments were commanded by lieutenants.

The purge in the higher reaches of the Party and the labor unions was complete. At the head of the Communist Party is its Central Committee, which then consisted of seventy-one members and sixty-one deputies. These men had proved their revolutionary loyalty on a score of occasions. They had been picked out of hundreds of thousands of their fellow Party members. Every day of their lives had been carefully examined by the control organs of the Party and by the G.P.U. And yet more than three-quarters of them were arrested as spies. The Politburo[5] of the Party, which consisted of ten members and five deputies, is an even narrower elite. It is the personal staff of the dictator, the actual government of the country. And yet at least five of these men fell victim to the G.P.U.

Soviet cultural life was temporarily paralyzed and it never fully recovered. The control organs of the Party closely examined every new literary and scientific publication for "Trotskyist[6] contraband." An unhappy formulation was enough to seal the fate of its author. Many leading Soviet writers joined the masses in the concentration camps. Many of those who were spared stopped writing altogether for fear of suffering the same fate. Still others sought safety in writing only of the past and avoiding even the slightest reference to current affairs. Those who were totally unprincipled "fulfilled their social task," i.e., they wrote whatever the ruling group required of them. They turned their coats again and again, condemned today what they had held sacred yesterday, only to damn tomorrow what they praised today. The result was a deplorable decline in literary standards, and such books as were published were no longer products of imagination and talent but belletristic[7] comments on the decisions of the latest Party Congress. Ordinary people stopped reading them.

Scientific work suffered greatly from the G.P.U. excesses. The Terror paralyzed every creative endeavor. During the construction period the Soviet Government had spared neither money nor energy to build up a great network of scientific institutions. The scientist was the favored

---

[5] Executive committee of the Communist party.

[6] Followers of Trotsky, who opposed Stalin.

[7] Artistic but lacking informative content.

child of Soviet society. But when the Great Purge came he was not exempt. Many leading scientists were arrested and their colleagues were so intimidated that they stopped their work on the urgent problems of the day and turned to mere routine work in which they could not go wrong.

The victims of the purge came from all the peoples of the Union, but the national minorities were singled out for special attention. In all big towns there were small minorities whose main stock lived elsewhere, perhaps even outside the frontiers. The Germans had their independent republic on the Volga, the Armenians theirs in Southern Caucasia, the Uzbeks theirs in Central Asia. The origins of the groups of Letts, Lithuanians, Finns, Greeks, Bulgarians, Poles, Persians, and Chinese lay outside the Soviet Union. Groups of these peoples had lived for hundreds of years scattered over Russian territory without ever becoming fully assimilated. When they lived together in agricultural colonies, like the Germans in the Southern Ukraine, they obstinately retained their old national customs and their way of life. Lenin's nationality policy not only gave the oppressed nationalities political independence in their homogeneous colonies, but it also gave cultural autonomy to the smaller groups scattered over the territory of the bigger nationalities. It gave them their own schools, their own clubs and their own national theatres in which they could hear pieces performed in their own tongue, and it ensured them equality before the law. In the first years of the revolution none other than Stalin was People's Commissar for Nationalities, and under Lenin's guidance he implemented this just and far-sighted policy which ended the everlasting nationality squabbles in Russia and won the oppressed peoples for the revolution. And now all these minorities were liquidated by Stalin's own order. The men were all arrested, the women were banished from European Russia to Asiatic Russia and the children were often carried off to be brought up as Russian orphans in the children's homes of the G.P.U.

A small colony of about six hundred Armenians lived in Kharkov. One day in the autumn of 1937 over three hundred of them were arrested. Within six weeks the rest followed. Most of them were illiterate or semiliterate shoeshine boys, cobblers[8] or petty blackmarketeers. For a long time they were unable to understand what had brought them into prison. The Letts and the Germans had preceded them, and the Greeks and Bulgarians (who were among the most skillful gardeners in the country) followed them. After that came Poles and Lithuanians, Finns and Estonians, Assyrians and Persians, Uzbeks and Chinese, and many other ethnic groups Europe has never heard of. It almost seemed as though the G.P.U. were determined to ensure the racial purity of Russia's towns by administrative action. All these people had to be spies, the G.P.U. insisted. Germans, Poles and Letts had to have spied for Hitler; Chinese, Koreans and Mongolians for Japan; while Armenians, Assyrians and Persians had to

---

[8] Shoemakers.

have spied for the British Intelligence Service. The G.P.U. was a stickler[9] for order. The fact that the G.P.U. insisted that the Chinese should have spied for Japan, the archenemy of their own country, was a national injustice about which my Chinese cellmates—they were poor laundrymen—complained bitterly. On the other hand, in the examiner's office the Armenians entered the service of the British without much protest.

The final organization to go through the mincing machine was the G.P.U. itself. The examiners came into their own cells to keep their former victims company. Prisoners would often find themselves in the same cell with the examiner who had been in charge of their cases. And then all the old questions would be asked again. But the G.P.U. men had no idea what they had done or why they had done it. They had no more idea of the significance of the happenings than their victims. It was only years later, when the whole thing was over, that the more intelligent prisoners gradually pieced together a general picture of the happenings and sought by analyzing innumerable incidents, which taken on their own seemed insignificant, to discover the motives of the dictator in launching the Great Purge.

I was the companion of these people for three years in the prisons of the G.P.U. in Kharkov, Kiev and Moscow. During that time I was held in a dozen different cells, and innumerable batches of prisoners came and went before my eyes. I remained. I was a careful observer of the unique process going on around me and I made a note of the facts with the intention of one day giving them to the outside world. I talked to hundreds of prisoners, classified them in the general framework of the events and sought an explanation. At no time did I ever lose hope that one day I should be free again. With calm certainty I waited for the change which I knew must come.

We all waited for that change. We all knew that things could not go on in the same way much longer. At some time or other the disastrous process would have to be curbed unless the country was to go down to ruin. Someone would have to put a stop to the G.P.U. madness. At some time or other the dictator would have to recognize the full extent of the damage which was being done by the purge he had ordered. For two terrible years we waited, and the whole country waited with us. Then the change came.

On December 8, 1938, the organizer of Stalin's Great Purge, Nikolai Ivanovitch Yezhov, People's Commissar for Home Affairs and head of the G.P.U., was removed from his post. A few months later he disappeared from the Central Committee and then he was arrested. We were never able to discover whether he was shot or not. At the same time a unique trial took place in the Moldavian Republic, in the southwest corner of the vast Soviet Union. The leader of the local G.P.U. and four of his examiners

---

[9] Stubbornly insistent.

were charged before a military court with having arrested innocent people and forced them to make false confessions under torture. The accused pleaded guilty. But they did not defend themselves by saying that they had only carried out orders; instead, they confessed that they had acted under the instructions of a counterrevolutionary organization. They were found guilty, sentenced to death and shot. These men had done no more than every G.P.U. man had been doing with impunity[10] for two years from Arkhangelsk to Odessa and from Vladivostok to the Polish frontier. The indictment and execution of these minor G.P.U. officials was Stalin's signal for change. The Great Purge was over.

Questions for Discussion and Writing

1. Describe the "Great Purge." What motivated it? How was it implemented?

2. What were some of the direct effects of the purge? How did it affect the intellectual climate?

3. The Soviet Union includes many national minorities: Poles, Bulgarians, Persians, and so on. What motivations might Stalin have had for singling out these national minorities for special attention and vengeance?

4. Review Machiavelli's advice to his Prince. Which part of Machiavelli's instruction do Stalin's actions most reflect?

5. To what extent were the Stalinist purges similar to the Reign of Terror in France? Consider the ideological motivations as well as the events themselves.

6. What other communist countries suffered a reign of terror similar to Stalin's purges? Have noncommunist countries apart from France experienced the same terror?

7. Discuss changes in Soviet communism since *glasnost* and *perestroika*.

8. Could a purge or anything like the Reign of Terror ever take place in the United States, or do we have a system of political checks and balances strong enough to protect us from such arbitrary political action? Discuss the internment of Japanese-Americans during World War II, the McCarthy investigations, and Hollywood blacklists of suspected communists. To what degree could you compare these actions to those of Stalin?

Dianne Feeley, "The Family"

Although both Marxism and democracy profess a belief in equality, women under both systems suffer oppression. The author of the following article takes a radical position and criticizes the American Communist party for its acceptance of the family as the basic social unit, a revisionist[1] Marxist doctrine. To attain the first step toward a pure socialist state, Feeley supports the abolition of the family unit.

---

[10] Without punishment.

[1] Compromising or modifying revolutionary theory.

Key Concepts

The term **class society** refers to any nonsocialist society in which economic
distinctions between groups exist, such as middle class versus working
class.

For a definition of **capitalism,** see page 353.

For a definition of **sibling rivalry,** see Chapter 2, page 92.

In a **patriarchal family system** (page 363) power is held by the father or
eldest male relative.

Marxists maintain that the family is basically characterized by its
function as an economic institution. As an economic unit, each individual
family is responsible for providing for its own members—from the care
of the young to the welfare of the old. This is a tremendous economic
responsibility; for example, to raise a child adequately from infancy
through college in the United States requires anywhere from $75,000 to
$150,000 according to current estimates. Add in the hours of unpaid
labor that parents, usually women, perform in the home for tasks that
could better be performed socially—such as laundering clothes—and
one can begin to understand the financial commitment exacted from
each family.

In vetoing a national child-care bill, Nixon was quoted by the
December 10, 1971 *New York Times* as expressing distaste for the
"family weakening implications of the system it envisions. . . ." Of
course, as society provides more of its resources outside the structure of
the family, the family as an economic unit will weaken. But although this
course would be beneficial to society, it runs counter to the ideas of
class society and its cornerstone, private property. And that is why
those who rule this country have fought so hard against such steps as free
education, social security, comprehensive medical care, welfare benefits,
and now, against child-care centers. In fact, the ruling class tries to take
back wherever possible the few concessions already won from it.

Capitalism rules through its various institutions, which mirror and
reinforce the values of the dominant class. Such institutions—whether
the various agencies of the state, the church, or the family—function to
repress the individual, to tell people that they must accept their lot
in life, to spread the myth that things can't be changed. The family's
reactionary ideological function complements its economic one. Nixon
recognized this when in his speech vetoing child-care centers he
announced:

. . . good public policy requires that we enhance rather than diminish both
parental authority and parental involvement with children—particularly in those
decisive early years when social attitudes and a conscience are formed and
religious and moral principles are first inculcated.

The family transmits a reactionary ideology through its hierarchical
structure, training individuals to be submissive to "authority." Despite

the window dressing about the "partnership of marriage," the man is the "head of the house," while the woman and children are economic dependents. The man's economic role gives him a position of authority within the household while the role of the woman turns her into a domestic slave. Although fully 43 percent of all married women are also wage earners, their jobs are considered supplementary to what is considered their primary responsibilities, the maintenance of the household and the care of the children. Since the family is only able to carry out its socially assigned responsibilities by using the woman's unpaid labor in the home, her servitude is justified by cultural assumptions about a woman's "nature."

The family structure itself does not produce revolutionary fighters. Its authoritarian ideology is designed to teach passivity, not rebellion. Given the economic and political function of the family, one must conclude that the revolutionaries' first steps toward rebellion are most often taken against strong opposition of their families. Wilhelm Reich, author of *The Sexual Revolution* and *The Mass Psychology of Fascism,* noted:

It is not by accident that the attitude of adolescents toward the existing social order, pro or contra, corresponds to their attitude, pro or contra, toward the family. Similarly, it is not by accident that conservative and reactionary youths, as a rule, are strongly attached to their families, while revolutionary youths have a negative attitude toward the family and detach themselves from it.

Youth, after all, are under the control of their parents, without the protection of citizenship. Currently, an estimated half-million teenagers run away from home every year in rebellion against the oppressive and authoritarian atmosphere. Youth detention centers are filled with teenagers whose only "crime" has been their "unruliness" or their attempt to leave home. The despair, alienation, and resentment that young people feel is a logical reaction to the pressures of operating within a social unit whose binding tie is economic. The competition, **sibling rivalry,** and smoldering resentment within the family are at least as frequent as the appearance of love and harmony.

Parents are also the victims of the family system. They—and especially the mother—must take full responsibility for their children, with little free time of their own. They suffer psychologically when they are not able to fully provide for the needs of their children.

As a result of these economic and psychological pressures, people are forced to take out their frustrations on those who live closest to them, their family. Each year statistics reveal several hundred thousand cases of battered children. In reporting on the first two months of 1971, the New York Medical Examiner noted that the largest number of victims in the city's murders were wives killed by husbands. Next came husbands killed by wives. These two groups were followed by parents, children, aunts, uncles, cousins, and in-laws killing each other. Such information tends to confirm the contention that the **patriarchal family system**

serves to alienate family members from each other, rather than to promote concern for each other. Many feminists have concluded that the
oppression women suffer through the institution of the family is not
simply a wart on the nose of an otherwise healthy organism. This oppression is the very essence of the family institution. As they examine their
own childhoods, they can see how the young girl is programmed to
accept her role within the family. From the time she is wrapped in a pink
blanket and given a name that defines her sex, she is reared differently
from young boys.

The culture chooses to regard boys and girls as two separate
species, and the family is given the primary responsibility for beginning
the tracking system. Studies by Robert J. Stoller, Jerome Kagan and John
Money indicate that by the time the child is eighteen months old, the
family has successfully taught gender identification.[1] The family sends
out gender based signals in the way it handles the child, or in the kind of
language that it uses. As the child grows older, the masculine-feminine
models within the home, in books, and on TV, are so easily absorbed that
one need only look at the typical five-year old at play in the doll corner
for proof that the basic role differentiation has been learned.

The family, as the primary unit of society, has constricted the young
girl's mind and emotions as effectively as the pre-revolutionary Chinese
family bound the feet of its infant girls. Why, one must ask, have so many
women submitted to this grotesque distortion of themselves? Precisely
because woman's role has been limited to that of wife and mother. One
can't escape what is one's destiny. But further, girls are fed fairy tales and
cinderella myths. It can happen to you, too, these stories proclaim. For
those who see the reality a little more clearly, the woman is presented as
selfless and all-giving.

How many individual women can dare to refuse what society tells
them it is their nature to be? Only with the development of the women's
liberation movement have women come to see that the frustration they
feel is shared by others as well.

Unequal pay for women, the lack of child-care centers, the burden
of housework, and male supremacy—all derive from the family system as
an institution of class society. The only way to lay the basis for the
disappearance of the family as an economic institution is by eliminating
these conditions—through allowing women to be fully integrated into
social production, abolishing unequal pay, establishing free, twenty-four-
hour child-care centers for all, setting up low-cost, high quality laundry
services, take-out food services and dining facilities, and creating a mech-
anized public housecleaning service. These facilities are the socialist
alternative to the family system.

Capitalist society has made tremendous technological advances.
For the first time, society has developed the forces necessary to produce

[1] Knowing what male or female behavior
society expects.

the food, clothing, housing, and care people need. Why should these be the responsibility of the biological parents, and most particularly, the woman? The backward, insular[2] home is not able to provide the varied resources of the total society. Today the family unit is more and more at odds with the patterns of social interaction at work and at school. Narrow family loyalty, like loyalty to one's country, is constricting. An anachronism[3] that forces its members to limp along as best they can, the family unit condemns women to the most isolated world of household slavery.

But in a technologically advanced society, the possibilities for good medical care, a decent and stimulating environment, a broad education, and the chance to be more than a workhorse are within reach. As a consequence, socialists call for taking over the burdens that have been traditionally "women's work" by socializing them. High quality child-care centers, staffed by people who enjoy being with children, would be a welcome replacement for the haphazard and almost non-existent care of today. Free communal dining areas serving attractive, nutritious food or prepared take-home meals would insure a better standard of health, and a well-paid housekeeping service, utilizing scientific equipment, will help end the servitude of women. All of these services, controlled by those who use them, will free women from economic dependency on men and free children from their oppressed status within the home.

While the Communist Party in the United States justifies and glorifies the oppressive institution of the family, the rise of the women's liberation movement has begun a critical examination of one of society's most sacred institutions. Women will learn the truth about the Russian Revolution—in its initial gains, in its setbacks, and in the bureaucracy's betrayal of the revolution. More and more women are discovering the scathing Marxist critique of the family. They see the shallowness, selfishness, and authoritarian attitudes that the family system imposes on its members. Women are beginning to rebel against their oppressive roles. Women, including women in the USSR, can see that there are alternatives to the savagery of the individual household. There is a massive, and international feminist movement on the rise, demanding control by women over their lives.

It is absurd to speak of "magically" abolishing the family. The family institution must be replaced by something better. It can disappear only when society as a whole takes over the functions of the family in providing for people's needs.

Questions for Discussion and Writing

1. Are there governments or political systems today that advocate abolishing the family?

2. How does the communal family model operate?

---

[2] Isolated.

[3] Something outdated; throwback to another time.

3. Explain Feeley's statement that the family creates a "reactionary ideology" through its hierarchical structure. What does she mean by a "reactionary structure"? What examples does she provide?

4. Feeley points out problems with the family structure, many of which arguably seem valid: competition, sibling rivalry, perpetuation of patriarchal values, sexist gender roles, and so on. How valid are her criticisms? In what ways are these problems being addressed without abolishing the family?

5. Feeley writes about "taking over the burdens that have been traditionally 'women's work' by socializing them." How might this work in the United States with, for example, child care?

6. How does Feeley's rhetoric reflect her political position?

7. Imagine a socialist state without a family system as Feeley advocates. What would daily life be like? What new kinds of problems might develop?

8. Summarize the arguments, pro and con, for abolishing the family.

THE IMPERIALIST HERITAGE

Robin W. Winks, "Imperialism"

Much of the history of the world, even before that of "imperial" Rome and its extended colonies, has been the history of various forms of imperialism. Examples can be seen in the conquest of the Philippines, the Caribbean Islands, the American Southwest, Central and much of South America by Spain; the conquest of much of Africa by France, England, Belgium, and Portugal; the colonization of India by England; and the colonization of Indonesia by the Dutch. This reading briefly defines imperialism and questions the ultimate unfairness of a more powerful nation imposing its rule on another.

Key Concepts

Expansionism (page 366) is a political and economic policy of one nation's increasing control over another through a growing physical domination.

Imperialism is difficult to define or explain. This is so because, like the terms "republican" and "conservative," the word may be used in both praise and denunciation of the practice or policy for which it is the merest shorthand label. Further, "imperialism" often is taken as a synonym for "colonialism," with which it has a close relationship but from which it nonetheless should be distinguished.

Imperialism often is applied to the outward thrust of European society—the carrying of political, economic, and moral practices into non-European areas—which began in the 15th century. Most commonly, it refers to European **expansionism** in the period following the American Revolution, when Britain and France, in particular, shifted their interest from the New World and from colonies of white settlement to Asia and, later, to Africa, to colonies already populated by yellow, brown, or black men. Less often, imperialism is applied to ancient and medieval empires—to the growth of Rome, of China, of Islam, of the Mongols, or of the Incas. Preferably, the term should be used to describe the expansion of all technologically advanced peoples at the expense of the technologically backward, so that it embraces, for example, modern Japanese or even Indonesian expansion.

However applied, imperialism must involve at least three factors: the expansion of an advanced society at the expense of a society thought to be backward; the development of economic and political expertise in an area with an indigenous[1] population, without the intent of substantial colonial settlement; and the application of the imperial nation's force to areas well removed geographically from its base—with all the inherent problems of strategy and international diplomacy.

It is undeniable that all forms of imperialism, while often bringing stability, sanitation, education, and improved communications to an area, have also forced one people to advance at a pace set by another people. All imperialism, therefore, including that pointing toward the ultimate independence of the colony, implied that only the superior power could name the stages through which the inferior had to pass and would judge the degree and speed of that passing. As Kenya's one-time economics minister Tom Mboya remarked, "Efficiency is the last refuge of the imperialist." One might always find a test that another might not pass.

The most pervasive legacy of imperialism was the assumption that someone else had, by nature, the right to judge the progress of another people. For this reason, while many scholars might well judge the physical benefits of imperialism to have been high for both power and colony alike, many also would judge the psychological effects to have been harmful to both. Anti-imperialism usually turns on this point. Although the age of "imperialism" has passed, the word imperialism remains a battle cry because its effects have yet to be measured fully.

Questions for Discussion and Writing

1. Review the three factors Winks uses to define imperialism. What examples of imperialism do you see in today's world? How closely would the founding of America, based in part on the "winning of the West" and the defeat of the Native American peoples, fit Winks' definition?

2. What is cultural imperialism and what are its effects?

3. What is the myth of science and progress? How could it be considered "the last refuge of the imperialist"? How is it used as a rationale for imperialism?

4. Winks says that imperialism has a close relationship with colonialism, but the two are different. Explain the differences between colonialism and imperialism.

5. Explain the supposed advantages that imperialist expansion offers the colonized country and the advantages it offers the imperialist nation.

[1] Native.

W.E.B. Dubois, *"The White Masters of the World"* _____

W.E.B. Dubois was a famous black writer, educator, and pioneer of the civil rights movement. In 1909, he cofounded the National Negro Committee, which in 1910 became the National Association for the Advancement of Colored People. Later in life, he promoted worldwide black liberation and pan-Africanism. In 1961, he moved to Ghana. In this reading Dubois argues that Western society achieved power and wealth only through slavery and colonialism, which has led to a form of decadence and the collapse of Europe as a cultural and economic power.

Key Concepts

The **science of Darwin** refers to his theory of evolution and the doctrine of Social Darwinism; see Chapter 3.

Realistic literature (page 370) depicts common people in daily situations, using great detail to make scenes seem true to life.

What are the real causes back of the collapse of Europe in the twentieth century?

One of the chief causes which thus distorted the development of Europe was the African slave trade, and we have tried to rewrite its history and meaning and to make it occupy a much less important place in the world's history than it deserves.

The result of the African slave trade and slavery on the European mind and culture was to degrade the position of labor and the respect for humanity as such. Not, God knows, that the ancient world honored labor. With exceptions here and there, it despised, enslaved, and crucified human toil. But there were counter currents, and with the Renaissance in Europe—that new light with which Asia and Africa illuminated the Dark Ages of Europe—came new hope for mankind. A new religion of personal sacrifice had been building on five hundred years of the self-effacement[1] of Buddha before the birth of Christ, and the equalitarianism of Mohammed which followed six hundred years after Christ's birth. A new world, seeking birth in Europe, was also being discovered beyond the sunset.

With this new world came fatally the African slave trade and Negro slavery in the Americas. There were new cruelties, new hatreds of human beings, and new degradations of human labor. The temptation to degrade human labor was made vaster and deeper by the incredible accumulation of wealth based on slave labor, by the boundless growth of greed, and by world-wide organization for new agricultural crops, new techniques in industry and world-wide trade.

Just as Europe lurched forward to a new realization of beauty, a new freedom of thought and religious belief, a new demand by laborers

---

[1] Being withdrawn or self-denying.

to choose their work and enjoy its fruit, uncurbed greed rose to seize and monopolize the uncounted treasure of the fruits of labor. Labor was degraded, humanity was despised, the theory of "race" arose. There came a new doctrine of universal labor: mankind were of two sorts—the superior and the inferior; the inferior toiled for the superior; and the superior were the real men, the inferior half men or less. Among the white lords of creation there were "lower classes" resembling the inferior darker folk. Where possible they were to be raised to equality with the master class. But no equality was possible or desirable for "darkies." In line with this conviction, the Christian Church, Catholic and Protestant, at first damned the heathen blacks with the "curse of Canaan,"[2] then held out hope of freedom through "conversion," and finally acquiesced[3] in a permanent status of human slavery.

Despite the fact that the nineteenth century saw an upsurge in the power of the laboring classes and a fight toward economic equality and political democracy, this movement and battle was made fiercer and less successful and lagged far behind the accumulation of wealth, because in popular opinion labor was fundamentally degrading and the just burden of inferior peoples. Luxury and plenty for the few and poverty for the many was looked upon as inevitable in the course of nature. In addition to this, it went without saying that the white people of Europe had a right to live upon the labor and property of the colored peoples of the world.

In order to establish the righteousness of this point of view, science and religion, government and industry, were wheeled into line. The word "Negro" was used for the first time in the world's history to tie color to race and blackness to slavery and degradation. The white race was pictured as "pure" and superior; the black race as dirty, stupid, and inevitably inferior; the yellow race as sharing, in deception and cowardice, much of this color inferiority; while mixture of races was considered the prime cause of degradation and failure in civilization. Everything great, everything fine, everything really successful in human culture, was white.

In order to prove this, even black people in India and Africa were labeled as "white" if they showed any trace of progress; and, on the other hand, any progress by colored people was attributed to some intermixture, ancient or modern, of white blood or some influence of white civilization.

This logical contradiction influenced and misled science. The same person declared the mulattoes[4] were inferior and warned against miscegenation,[5] and yet attributed the pre-eminence of a Dumas, a Frederick Douglass, a Booker Washington, to their white blood.

A system at first conscious and then unconscious of lying about history and distorting it to the disadvantage of the Negroids became so widespread that the history of Africa ceased to be taught, the color of

---

[2] Suffering racial bias.
[3] Quietly accepted or went along with.

[4] Persons of Caucasian and black ancestry.
[5] Mixing of races.

Memnon[6] was forgotten, and every effort was made in archeology, history, and biography, in biology, psychology, and sociology, to prove the all but universal assumption that the color line had a scientific basis.

Without the winking of an eye, printing, gunpowder, the smelting[7] of iron, the beginnings of social organization, not to mention political life and democracy, were attributed exclusively to the white race and to Nordic Europe. Religion sighed with relief when it could base its denial of the ethics of Christ and the brotherhood of men upon the **science of Darwin,** Gobineau, and Reisner.

Together with the idea of a Superior Race there grew up in Europe and America an astonishing ideal of wealth and luxury: the man of "independent" income who did not have to "work for a living," who could indulge his whims and fantasies, who was free from all compulsion of either ethics or hunger, became the hero of novels, of drama and of fairy tale. This wealth was built, in Africa especially, upon diamonds and gold, copper and tin, ivory and mahogany, palm oil and cocoa, seeds extracted and grown, beaten out of the blood-stained bodies of the natives, transported to Europe, processed by wage slaves who were not receiving, and as Ricardo assured them they could never receive, enough to become educated and healthy human beings, and then distributed among prostitutes and gamblers as well as among well-bred followers of art, literature, and drama.

Cities were built, ugly and horrible, with regions for the culture of crime, disease, and suffering, but characterized in popular myth and blindness by wide and beautiful avenues where the rich and fortunate lived, laughed, and drank tea. National heroes were created by lopping off[8] their sins and canonizing[9] their virtues, so that Gladstone had no connection with slavery, Chinese Gordon did not get drunk, William Pitt was a great patriot and not an international thief. Education was so arranged that the young learned not necessarily the truth, but that aspect and interpretation of the truth which the rulers of the world wished then to know and follow.

In other words, we had progress by poverty in the face of accumulating wealth, and that poverty was not simply the poverty of the slaves of Africa and the peons of Asia, but the poverty of the mass of workers in England, France, Germany and the United States. Art, in building, painting, and literature, became cynical and decadent. Literature became **realistic** and therefore pessimistic. Religion became organized in social clubs where well-bred people met in luxurious churches and gave alms to the poor. On Sunday they listened to sermons—"Blessed are the meek"; "Do unto others even as you would that others do unto you"; "If thine enemy smite[10] thee, turn the other cheek"; "It is more blessed to give than to receive"—listened and acted as though they

---

[6] Famous Ethiopian king in Greek mythology.

[7] Melting and combining.

[8] Cutting off.

[9] Making saintly.

[10] Strike, hit.

had read, as in very truth they ought to have read—"Might is right"; "Do others before they do you"; "Kill your enemies or be killed"; "Make profits by any methods and at any cost so long as you can escape the lenient law." This is a fair picture of the decadence of that Europe which led human civilization during the nineteenth century and looked unmoved on the writhing[11] of Asia and of Africa.

It would be unfair to paint the total modern picture of Europe as decadent. There have been souls that revolted and voices that cried aloud. Men arraigned[12] poverty, ignorance, and disease as unnecessary. The public school and the ballot fought for uplift and freedom. Suffrage[13] for women and laborers and freedom for the Negro were extended. But this forward-looking vision had but partial and limited success. Race tyranny, aristocratic pretense, monopolized wealth, still continued to prevail and triumphed widely. The Church fled uptown to escape the poor and black. Jesus laughed—and wept.

The dawn of the twentieth century found white Europe master of the world and the white peoples almost universally recognized as the rulers for whose benefit the rest of the world existed. Never before in the history of civilization had self-worship of a people's accomplishment attained the heights that the worship of white Europe by Europeans reached.

Questions for Discussion and Writing

1. Dubois writes that "the real cause [behind] the collapse of Europe in the twentieth century was the African slave trade." Explain Dubois' argument.

2. In describing the egalitarian, humanizing influence of religions, Dubois praises Buddhism and Islam but condemns Christianity as supporting slavery, at least ideologically. Explain and evaluate his position.

3. How was Social Darwinism used to support the notion of white racial superiority?

4. Western society, according to Dubois, was built on "race, tyranny, aristocratic pretense, monopolized wealth," leading to decadence. How does Dubois argue that Western society is decadent?

5. What does Dubois' rhetoric reveal about his political orientation? Consider terms such as laboring classes, degradation of human labor, and wage slaves. What other phrases or arguments suggest his political position?

6. What effect does Dubois achieve through his imagery and organization?

7. How do you think Dubois would respond to the political theory of communism?

8. Dubois depicts European history very differently from how it is usually presented in most junior high school, high school, or even college books. To what extent does Dubois' historical perspective match what you have been taught? Do you accept his interpretation of history? Why or why not?

[11] Contorting in pain.
[12] Accused.

[13] Right to vote.

George Orwell, *"Marrakech"*

George Orwell (1903–1950) is best known for his novels Animal
Farm *and* 1984, *both satires of totalitarian communism. As an independent free thinker, Orwell also sharply criticized imperialism and life
under British colonial rule, as he does in this essay.*

As the corpse went past the flies left the restaurant table in a cloud
and rushed after it, but they came back a few minutes later.

The little crowd of mourners—all men and boys, no women—
threaded their way across the market-place between the piles of pome-
granates and the taxis and the camels, wailing a short chant over and over
again. What really appeals to the flies is that the corpses here are never
put into coffins, they are merely wrapped in a piece of rag and carried on
a rough wooden bier[1] on the shoulders of four friends. When the friends
get to the burying-ground they hack an oblong hole a foot or two deep,
dump the body in it and fling over it a little of the dried-up, lumpy earth,
which is like broken brick. No gravestone, no name, no identifying mark
of any kind. The burying-ground is merely a huge waste of hummocky[2]
earth, like a derelict[3] building-lot. After a month or two no one can even
be certain where his own relatives are buried.

When you walk through a town like this—two hundred thousand
inhabitants, of whom at least twenty thousand own literally nothing
except the rags they stand up in—when you see how people live, and
still more how easily they die, it is always difficult to believe that you are
walking among human beings. All colonial empires are in reality founded
upon that fact. The people have brown faces—besides, there are so many
of them! Are they really the same flesh as yourself? Do they even have
names? Or are they merely a kind of undifferentiated brown stuff, about
as individual as bees or coral insects? They rise out of the earth, they
sweat and starve for a few years, and then they sink back into the
nameless mounds of the graveyard and nobody notices that they are
gone. And even the graves themselves soon fade back into the soil.
Sometimes, out for a walk, as you break your way through the prickly
pear, you notice that it is rather bumpy underfoot, and only a certain
regularity in the bumps tells you that you are walking over skeletons.

I was feeding one of the gazelles in the public gardens.

Gazelles are almost the only animals that look good to eat when
they are still alive, in fact, one can hardly look at their hindquarters
without thinking of mint sauce. The gazelle I was feeding seemed to
know that this thought was in my mind, for though it took the piece of
bread I was holding out it obviously did not like me. It nibbled rapidly at
the bread, then lowered its head and tried to butt me, then took another

---

[1] Portable frame for carrying a coffin.   [3] Abandoned.
[2] Like a low, rounded hill.

nibble and then butted again. Probably its idea was that if it could drive me away the bread would somehow remain hanging in mid-air.

An Arab navvy[4] working on the path nearby lowered his heavy hoe and sidled towards us. He looked from the gazelle to the bread and from the bread to the gazelle, with a sort of quiet amazement, as though he had never seen anything quite like this before. Finally, he said shyly in French:

"I could eat some of that bread."

I tore off a piece and he stowed it gratefully in some secret place under his rags. This man is an employee of the Municipality.

When you go through the Jewish quarters you gather some idea of what the medieval ghettoes were probably like. Under their Moorish rulers the Jews were only allowed to own land in certain restricted areas, and after centuries of this kind of treatment they have ceased to bother about overcrowding. Many of the streets are a good deal less than six feet wide, the houses are completely windowless, and sore-eyed children cluster everywhere in unbelievable numbers, like clouds of flies. Down the centre of the street there is generally running a little river of urine.

In the bazaar huge families of Jews, all dressed in the long black robe and little black skull-cap, are working in fly-infested booths that look like caves. A carpenter sits cross-legged at a prehistoric lathe, turning chairlegs at lightning speed. He works the lathe with a bow in his right hand and guides the chisel with his left foot, and thanks to a lifetime of sitting in this position, his left leg is warped out of shape. At his side his grandson, age six, is already starting simpler parts of the job.

I was just passing the coppersmiths' booths when somebody noticed that I was lighting a cigarette. Instantly, from the dark holes all round, there was a frenzied rush of Jews, many of them old grandfathers with flowing grey beards, all clamouring for a cigarette. Even a blind man somewhere at the back of one of the booths heard a rumour of cigarettes and came crawling out, groping in the air with his hand. In about a minute I had used up the whole packet. None of these people, I suppose, works less than twelve hours a day, and every one of them looks on a cigarette as more or less an impossible luxury.

As the Jews live in self-contained communities they follow the same trades as the Arabs, except for agriculture. Fruit-sellers, potters, silversmiths, blacksmiths, butchers, leather-workers, tailors, water-carriers, beggars, porters—whichever way you look you see nothing but Jews. As a matter of fact there are thirteen thousand of them, all living in the space of a few acres. A good job Hitler isn't here. Perhaps he is on his way, however. You hear the usual dark rumours about the Jews, not only from the Arabs but from the poorer Europeans.

"Yes, mon vieux,[5] they took my job away from me and gave it to a Jew. The Jews! They're the real rulers of this country, you know. They've got all the money. They control the banks, finance—everything."

---

[4] Laborer.   [5] Old fellow.

"But," I said, "isn't it a fact that the average Jew is a labourer working for about a penny an hour?"

"Ah, that's only for show! They're all moneylenders really. They're cunning, the Jews."

In just the same way, a couple of hundred years ago, poor old women used to be burned for witchcraft when they could not even work enough magic to get themselves a square meal.

All people who work with their hands are partly invisible, and the more important the work they do, the less visible they are. Still, a white skin is always fairly conspicuous. In northern Europe, when you see a labourer ploughing a field, you probably give him a second glance. In a hot country, anywhere south of Gibraltar or east of Suez, the chances are that you don't even see him. I have noticed this again and again. In a tropical landscape one's eye takes in everything except the human beings. It takes in the dried-up soil, the prickly pear, the palm-tree and the distant mountain, but it always misses the peasant hoeing at his patch. He is the same colour as the earth, and a great deal less interesting to look at.

It is only because of this that the starved countries of Asia and Africa are accepted as tourist resorts. No one would think of running cheap trips to the Distressed areas. But where the human beings have brown skins their poverty is simply not noticed. What does Morocco mean to a Frenchman? An orange-grove or a job in government service. Or to an Englishman? Camels, castles, palm-trees, Foreign Legionnaires, brass trays and bandits. One could probably live here for years without noticing that for nine-tenths of the people the reality of life is an endless, back-breaking struggle to wring a little food out of an eroded soil.

Most of Morocco is so desolate that no wild animal bigger than a hare can live on it. Huge areas which were once covered with forest have turned into treeless waste where the soil is exactly like broken-up brick. Nevertheless a good deal of it is cultivated, with frightful labour. Everything is done by hand. Long lines of women, bent double like inverted capital Ls, work their way slowly across the fields, tearing up the prickly weeds with their hands, and the peasant gathering lucerne for fodder pulls it up stalk by stalk instead of reaping it, thus saving an inch or two on each stalk. The plough is a wretched wooden thing, so frail that one can easily carry it on one's shoulder, and fitted underneath with a rough iron spike which stirs the soil to a depth of about four inches. This is as much as the strength of the animals is equal to. It is usual to plow with a cow and a donkey yoked together. Two donkeys would not be quite strong enough, but on the other hand two cows would cost a little more to feed. The peasants possess no harrows,[6] they merely plough the soil several times over in different directions, finally leaving it in rough furrows, after which the whole field has to be shaped with hoes into small oblong patches, to conserve water. Along the edges of the fields

[6] Large frame with discs used for plowing.

channels are hacked out to a depth of thirty or forty feet to get at the tiny trickles which run through the subsoil.

Every afternoon a file of very old women passes down the road outside my house, each carrying a load of firewood. All of them are mummified with age and the sun, and all of them are tiny. It seems to be generally the case in primitive communities that the women, when they get beyond a certain age, shrink to the size of children. One day a poor old creature who could not have been more than four feet tall crept past me under a vast load of wood. I stopped her and put a five-sou piece (a little more than a farthing[7]) into her hand. She answered with a shrill wail, almost a scream, which was partly gratitude but mainly surprise. I suppose that from her point of view, by taking any notice of her, I seemed almost to be violating a law of nature. She accepted her status as an old woman, that is to say as a beast of burden. When a family is travelling it is quite usual to see a father and a grown-up son riding ahead on donkeys and an old woman following on foot, carrying the baggage.

But what is strange about these people is their invisibility. For several weeks, always at about the same time of day, the file of old women had hobbled past the house with their firewood, and though they had registered themselves on my eyeballs I cannot truly say that I had seen them. Firewood was passing—that was how I saw it. It was only that one day I happened to be walking behind them, and the curious up-and-down motion of a load of wood drew my attention to the human being underneath it. Then for the first time I noticed the poor old earth-coloured bodies, bodies reduced to bones and leathery skin, bent double under the crushing weight. Yet I suppose I had not been five minutes on Moroccan soil before I noticed the overloading of the donkeys and was infuriated by it. There is no question that the donkeys are damnably treated. The Moroccan donkey is hardly bigger than a St. Bernard dog, it carries a load which in the British army would be considered too much for a fifteen-hands[8] mule, and very often its pack-saddle is not taken off its back for weeks together. But what is peculiarly pitiful is that it is the most willing creature on earth, it follows its master like a dog and does not need either bridle or halter. After a dozen years of devoted work it suddenly drops dead, whereupon its master tips it into the ditch and the village dogs have torn its guts out before it is cold.

This kind of thing makes one's blood boil, whereas—on the whole—the plight of the human beings does not. I am not commenting, merely pointing to a fact. People with brown skins are next door to invisible. Anyone can be sorry for the donkey with its galled[9] back, but it is generally owing to some kind of accident if one even notices the old woman under her load of sticks.

As the storks flew northward the Negroes were marching south-ward—a long, dusty column, infantry, screw-gun batteries and then more

---

[7] British coin worth half a cent.
[8] Way of measuring a horse.

[9] Rubbed raw.

infantry, four or five thousand men in all, winding up the road with a clumping of boots and a clatter of iron wheels.

They were Senegalese, the blackest Negroes in Africa, so black that sometimes it is difficult to see whereabouts on their necks the hair begins. Their splendid bodies were hidden in reach-me-down[10] khaki uniforms, their feet squashed into boots that looked like blocks of wood, and every tin hat seemed to be a couple of sizes too small. It was very hot and the men had marched a long way. They slumped under the weight of their packs and the curiously sensitive black faces were glistening with sweat.

As they went past a tall, very young Negro turned and caught my eye. But the look he gave me was not in the least the kind of look you might expect. Not hostile, not contemptuous, not sullen, not even inquisitive. It was the shy, wide-eyed Negro look, which actually is a look of profound respect. I saw how it was. This wretched boy, who is a French citizen and has therefore been dragged from the forest to scrub floors and catch syphilis in garrison towns, actually has feelings of reverence before a white skin. He has been taught that the white race are his masters, and he still believes it.

But there is one thought which every white man (and in this connection it doesn't matter twopence if he calls himself a Socialist) thinks when he sees a black army marching past. "How much longer can we go on kidding these people? How long before they turn their guns in the other direction?"

It was curious, really. Every white man there has this thought stowed somewhere or other in his mind. I had it, so had the other onlookers, so had the officers on their sweating chargers and the white NCOs[11] marching in the ranks. It was a kind of secret which we all knew and were too clever to tell; only the Negroes didn't know it. And really it was almost like watching a flock of cattle to see the long column, a mile or two miles of armed men, flowing peacefully up the road, while the great white birds drifted over them in the opposite direction, glittering like scraps of paper.

Questions for Discussion and Writing

1. What does the opening description of the funeral and cemetery—the fact that "after a month no one can even be certain where his own relatives are buried"—reveal about colonial life in Marrakech? Why might Orwell have chosen to open his essay with this image?

2. What effect does Orwell's writing in the first person voice "I" have on the reader? Why might he have chosen this form of writing to communicate his opinions on colonialism?

3. How does Orwell make the point that the Europeans perceived the Moroccans to be somewhat less than human?

---

[10] Hand-me-down.   [11] Officers.

4. What is the purpose of Orwell's descriptions of the city worker begging for bread, the Jewish quarter, and the old Jews begging for cigarettes?

5. What is the implied message behind Orwell's portrayal of life in Marrakech? Consider what he chose *not* to describe and what he carefully chose to include.

6. Metaphorically, what could Orwell's description of the Senegalese soldiers represent? What does Orwell mean when he asks, "How long before they turn their guns in the other direction?"

7. Review all the situations and people Orwell includes in his essay. What effects did imperialism have in Morocco, on both the colonized and the colonizers?

8. Has the fear that colonial people would turn their guns on their masters materialized in Africa or other nations? Throughout history how successful have anti-imperialist revolutions been?

CONTEMPORARY TERROR

Baljit Singh, "An Overview of Terrorism" _____

Terrorism, both in the context of conventional warfare and as a violent form of political and social intervention, has probably plagued humankind since before recorded history. In fact, "resistance and violence . . . may well have begun with Creation and may not even end on judgement day," writes Baljit Singh. In the following essay, Singh analyzes the purposes, tactics, and effects of terrorism, particularly political terrorism, which has become a powerfully dangerous wild card on the contemporary political scene.

Sigmund Freud has argued that civilization, with its institutional restraints and the repression of human nature, guarantees discontent. His vision of the human condition suggests that society must be continually prepared to accept change and expand human freedoms or must face many forms of resistance as an unavoidable reaction for its intransigence.[1]

The agents of change, however, are often victimized by society which tends to label them as traitors and treats their ideas and actions as dangerous threats to civilization itself. The most dangerous element in a situation of change is not that a resister is victimized or killed for his ideas or acts but that it is often done without recognizing it or saying so and is hidden behind the mask of a "penal code." Resistance and vio-

---

[1] Refusal to compromise.

lence, therefore, may well have begun with Creation and may not end even on judgement day.

There is almost an infinite variety of violence of anti-social nature—homicide, acts of vandalism, arson, destructive rage, or other expressions of an essentially irrational urge to strike at someone or something. Political violence, on the other hand, occurs in acts designed to bring about social and political change both among and within nations.

Political violence may be grouped into two types: 1. conventional wars and intervention, that is, those actions that are related to achieving national objectives and that essentially fall within the Napoleonic mode, and 2. unconventional, an unimaginative category that encompasses all varieties of political warfare from subversion[2] to guerrilla warfare.

Political terrorism comprises only one type of violence activity subsumed[3] under the general heading of unconventional warfare. Furthermore, the scope of political terrorism has expanded radically through history. Perhaps the best known terrorists of yesteryear belonged to the Arab world's "Society of the Assassins." The Assassins were founded some 900 years ago by the religious teacher Hassan Ibn Sabah. Their Arabic name, Hashshasin, sprang from the terrorists' addiction to hashish. Because of their activities as killers, the word, assassination, came to mean political murder. The Assassins were a religious-political group whose power rested on the membership of fedawi (devoted ones) who killed at the command of their religious leader, believing that killing the unrighteous guaranteed their own salvation and assisted in overthrowing a corrupt order.

The Assassins remained a powerful force in the Arab world for 200 years and pitted their new weapon against their religious and political opponents, the Turkish military forces and Sunni Islam. Ultimately, they were destroyed by Mongol invaders, but two of their organizational practices—1. popular agitation or their attempts to spread their beliefs among the populace and 2. a strict code of secrecy among all members of the organization—have an exceptionally modern ring.

Political terrorism as an instrument of power came of age during the French Revolution of 1793-1794. Despite some indiscriminate killings during the early phases of the Revolution, a policy of revolutionary terror evolved clearly with the Jacobins. Robespierre, Saint-Just, and the Committee of Public Safety played a vital role in the organization and direction of what came to be known as the Reign of Terror. As Fromkin has remarked:

> Robespierre had coerced a nation of 27 million people into accepting his dictatorship. His followers sent many thousands either to jail or to their deaths; one scholar's estimate is 40,000 deaths and 3,000,000 arrests. Yet when retribution came and Robespierre and his group of supporters were executed, it turned out that in all there were only 22 of them.

---

[2] Undermining of a government.   [3] Included.

By no means is this the entire story of political terror during the French Revolution. The important point, however, is that a political group which should have been weak when judged objectively could wield such disproportionate amount of power. What made such a development possible can be explained only by analyzing the phenomena of terror.

Terror incorporates two facets: 1. a state of fear or anxiety within an individual or a group and 2. the tool that induces the state of fear. Thus, terror entails that threat or use of symbolic violent acts aimed at influencing political behavior. Despite its long history of use in many countries, political terror failed to score any significant successes after the French Revolution until 1921 when the British were forced to bow to the terrorist campaign in Ireland and granted that country independence under the terms of the Irish Treaty. The period between the Irish Treaty and the end of World War II saw little political terrorism, except as an adjunct to conventional warfare. The Germans, Russians, Yugoslavs, Japanese, French, British, and even Americans all engaged in some type of terrorist activity. The scope of it, however, was rather limited, and the objectives were well-defined.

Following World War II, political terrorism reemerged on the international scene. With notable exceptions in Cyprus and Algeria, it became one of the many tools used within the larger arena of nationalist movements for independence. From its minimal application in India to a substantial reliance upon it in Algeria, Cyprus, and Kenya, political terrorism encompassed a wide range of activities, including intimidation, abduction, sabotage, selective assassination, and indiscriminate killing.

During the 1960s, political terrorism appears to have entered into another phase. Pehaps the two most significant qualitative changes were: 1. its trans-national character and 2. its emergence as a self-sufficient strategy—that is, terrorists attempted to operate independently of the larger political arena. Several developments help explain this new direction.

The growth of political terrorism into a trans-national phenomena has been greatly facilitated through a revolution in communication— radio, satellite television, air travel, and tourism. Terrorist acts committed in the remotest parts of the world now receive instant coverage and their "propaganda by deed" is exploited to full advantage. The growth in international tourism has radically changed the composition of passengers aboard international airlines. Consequently, skyjackings emerged as tempting activities for contemporary political terrorists.

Terrorism's emergence as a self-sufficient tool to achieve political objectives is largely due to the vulnerability of our modern urban civilization. While Mao Tse Tung emphasized rural, peasant-based guerrilla warfare and thought in terms of an ultimate, armed, and open revolutionary conflict to attain victory, today's urban guerrillas view the modern city as the new battleground. Carlos Marighella in his Minimanual of the

Urban Guerrilla exhibits considerable insight into the delicate nature and the interrelationship of vital services in our modern cities. He also provides a detailed list of terror tactics and their most efficient usage, including political kidnapping, selective assassination, bombing, hijackings, and bank robbery.

The strategies and tactics employed by political terrorists are generally directed at three groups: the populace, the regime in power, and the terrorist organization itself. The overall objectives of these strategies and tactics are to: 1. gain popular support, 2. disrupt and destroy the military and psychological strength of the regime, and 3. achieve internal stability and growth.

If we accept the premise that political terror is primarily aimed at the psyche[4] rather than at "military hardware" per se,[5] a carefully selected assassination of an "important but unpopular" public official may boost terrorists' morale, create sympathy among the populace, and provoke the regime to adopt repressive measures that further alienate the populace.

These objectives are closely interrelated and are mutually reinforcing. Nascent[6] terrorist groups often attempt to accomplish multiple objectives through a single act. George Habash of the Popular Front for the Liberation of Palestine (P.F.L.P.) once remarked that "The main point is to select targets where success is 100% assured. . . . You should see how my people react to a successful operation! Spirits shoot sky-high." A successful operation therefore may also help achieve the long-term objective of gaining popular support.

Political terrorism essentially is propaganda by deed. Consequently, advertising the movement becomes an integral part of its tactics. The weak, who generally resort to terrorism as a weapon, have a great need for their cause to be widely noticed. Ramdane Abbane of the Algerian F.L.N. succinctly summarized this tactic when he said:

Is it better for our cause to kill ten of our enemies in a remote village where this will not cause comment, or to kill only one man in Algiers where the American press will get hold of the story the next day? . . . We must ensure that people learn about our struggle.

During the past few years the communication media has reported a wide variety of politically motivated terrorist acts designed both to gain publicity and to build organizational morale. The P.F.L.P.'s simultaneous skyjacking and subsequent destruction of four international airliners in September 1970, the Palestine Liberation Organization (P.L.O.) Commando's seizure of a Jewish high school at Maalot in May 1974 resulting in the death of two dozen children, and the death of some twenty innocent pedestrians in May 1974 when stolen cars packed with time bombs exploded in downtown Dublin, are but a few grim reminders of

[4] Mind.
[5] By itself.   [6] Just developing.

this tactic. However, to create a favorable image, such acts must be carefully targeted and efficiently executed; otherwise they may create an unfortunate first impression of the group and antagonize the populace. The so-called Symbionese Liberation Army's mindless abduction of Patricia Hearst followed by confused political rhetoric and material demands exemplifies the latter result.

Another important objective of political terrorism is the disorientation and psychological isolation of the individuals in the populace. The tactic of inducing an atmosphere of fear and general nervousness is designed to detach the individual from his social context "whereby he has only himself upon whom to rely and cannot draw strength from his customary social supports." To create a disrupted psychological behavior through inducing a state of fear and anxiety among the populace, terrorists engage in random, intense, and unpredictable violent acts. These tactics create an atmosphere of ever-present danger to the public's physical safety and tend to undermine its confidence in the ability of the regime to maintain stability and order. When a regime continually fails to maintain order, the populace is forced to accept whatever protection, cohesion, or guarantees may be extended by the terrorists. In their search for stability and safety, the populace submits to a new authority structure that can alleviate their anxieties, as they did in Algeria, Cuba, and Northern Ireland. In such a situation, however, the terrorists' authority to govern is highly tenuous, and they must continually engage in acts of terror to remain in control, thereby repeatedly testing their resourcefulness. Since excessive acts of physical violence to induce fear and psychological disorientation can be both costly and often are counterproductive, they generally occur with heavy doses of propaganda, the main purpose of which is to break the bonds that exist between the populace and the incumbent[7] regime. Fear, anxiety, and psychological disorientation among the populace greatly contribute to undermining a regime's authority and its ability for effective control.

The individual political terrorist, on the other hand, articulates himself through group participation. Group acts enhance his sense of political purpose and direction, his dignity and identity. Individual consciousness is welded into a group ideology that provides needed social and political supports.

Most political terrorists themselves lead a life of uncertainty and strain. Power struggles, factional fights, ideological debates, strategy disputes and discipline problems are common within these clandestine organizations. The need for obedience to commands and conformity in the organization often requires enforcement action, generally the actual physical liquidation of wavering members. The Irish Republican Army and Black September, for instance, have consistently eliminated dissident[8] members. A similar fate also awaits enemy agents, reformers, and collaborators. The objective of all these acts is to demonstrate, both

---

[7] Those in power.   [8] Those who disagree.

within and outside the group, the determination and the uncompromising stance of the leadership. In Algeria "executions of the traitors" by the F.L.N. far exceeded the number of French killed during the period of conflict.

The dominant forms of political terrorism today are but a reflection of the politics of our time. As the national independence movements were the natural products of colonialism, the contemporary political terrorists symbolize, often mistakenly, resistance against discrimination, exclusion, suppression, and abusive power and privilege all too manifest in social, economic, ethnic, cultural, and political spheres of society.

Questions for Discussion and Writing

1. Explain the two facets of Singh's definition of terrorism and give an example of each.

2. According to Singh, terrorism changed significantly in the 1960s. Explain the two most significant changes and the specific effects of advances in media, air travel, and increased tourism on terrorist activities.

3. Explain how a terrorist act can gain popular support as well as "achieve internal stability and growth" within the terrorist organization itself.

4. Terrorists sometimes engage in random violence against innocent civilians, risking the alienation of those sympathetic to their cause. Explain a terrorist rationale for random violence.

5. To what extent does Singh's definition fit what you have read about Caligula's rule, Robespierre's Reign of Terror, and the Stalinist purges?

Martin Oppenheimer, **"Defining Terrorism"** _____

Martin Oppenheimer, a professor of Sociology at Rutgers University and a political activist, is the author of The Urban Guerilla *and* White Collar Politics. *In this essay, he explores various definitions of terrorism. He points out that assassinations, sabotage, and hijackings are all recognized as terrorist acts, but he also includes police brutality, capital punishment, and the prison system. The article raises the issue of who defines terrorism, and it proposes that ruling political groups often adjust the definition of terrorism to maintain their political reality. Oppenheimer suggests that people confronting various degrees of institutionalized terror are justified in responding with terror—if indeed violence in response to terror should be viewed as terrorism.*

Key Concepts

Vigilantism (page 383) is unauthorized violence by a group supposedly organized to keep order and punish crime.

Institutional terror (page 383) is systematic violence employed by a part of the governing power structure against a specific population.

Terrorism is a label applied to certain criminal acts when the state doesn't like the criminal's politics. When the state, and those who support it, do like the politics, the label becomes more benign: freedom fighter or patriot. When politics are absent (or the state pretends that they are) the label becomes bandit, psychopath, or thug. Any act, violent or nonviolent, can be labelled criminal, and hence part of a terrorist conspiracy, when the state defines such behavior as dangerous.

Types of Terrorist Acts

Generally, we have come to think of terrorism as threats or acts of violence directed towards people in order to coerce them, or others (including governments), to change their policies. The terrorist seeks to prevent or stop some action. If necessary, this will be accomplished by the physical elimination of the actors, or by their forced withdrawal from a particular geographical area. Such terrorist acts include assassinations, kidnappings, sabotage, beatings, mutilations, cross-burnings, and other forms of harrassment. It also includes the broad category of **vigilantism**—when communities "take the law into their own hands" in the absence of official police, or when community values are in conflict with those of the law. Vigilante actions include night riders, mob lynchings, death squads, and pogroms.[1] Robberies committed to further political goals are labelled terrorism; other robberies, no matter how much they terrorize, are just robberies.

Terrorism is often one of a panoply[2] of tactics in a wider underground resistance and/or guerrilla national liberation movement. It is sometimes the first stage in the development of such broader movements. In such cases, the objective of terrorist acts may be more to raise political consciousness than to inflict injury or destruction. Some forms of terrorism may be ignored, condoned, encouraged, or even unofficially sponsored by the government or some part of it, to foster policies which it cannot officially acknowledge. Examples of this include the suppression of labor unions, keeping minority groups in "their place," and supporting exiles who carry out illegal actions in line with government policy.

Institutional Terrorism

Terrorism is always a response to **institutional terror.** It is an evasion to label some acts as terrorism, while ignoring the institutional terror which underlies this form of protest. This is true even though terrorist acts may be misdirected at scapegoats, who are sometimes provided by those responsible for the institutional terror.

The amount of terror inflicted by "terrorists," no matter how dreadful, is a thimbleful compared to official, legally-sanctioned terror.

[1] Systematic killing of Jews as in Czarist Russia.

[2] An array.

An example of state terror is the deliberate starvation of a population, as in Ireland during the potato famine. Other examples come all too readily to mind in this century; the brutalization of a population through poverty; child labor; slavery; the expulsion of a people from their lands; genocide based on religious, political, ethnic, and sexual identities; aerial bombardment; police brutality; official torture; the prison system in general and capital punishment in particular; and the systematic violence done by industry. To paraphrase Alfred McClung Lee from his recent book, *Terrorism in Northern Ireland,* more terrorists wear three-piece suits, ride in Rolls Royces, and sit in the seats of corporate power and government than lurk in dark alleys.

The Roots of Violence

The hijacking[s], like the car and truck bombings that have become an almost daily occurrence in Lebanon, . . . [are] best understood as an act of desperation by a people who have seen their homeland invaded and destroyed by forces infinitely more powerful than themselves. Faced with the overwhelming military power of Israel, which is sustained and encouraged by the world's most powerful nation, there is little the victims can do other than to strike back randomly through individual, frequently suicidal attacks. (In *These Times,* June 26-July 9, 1985).

Different kinds of disorder are defined in different ways by ruling groups. What rulers choose to do about any politically deviant behavior hinges on how they assess the danger, or the advantage, of such disorder. The survival of the established order requires the acceptance of the ruling class' definition of reality. The ruling class will enforce the definitions that are functional to it: black rioters or revolutionaries are defined as terrorists and shot, while more recently Ronald Reagan and New York City mayor Ed Koch had both refused to label other criminal acts as terrorism. These refusals have served as a quasi[3] official method of repressing certain subordinate and potentially dangerous populations: pro-choice women, the black "underclass," etc. The fact that these acts, like all vigilantism, have the support of a community of people makes them easier to ignore or downplay. . . .

Drawing Distinctions

At one level, as some pacifists argue, all terrorism is violent and therefore equally reprehensible. However, distinctions can, and should, be drawn. The concept of terrorism should exclude sabotage directed carefully and solely at property. The damaging of draft board files or missile components, while illegal, is nonviolent in that the consequent suffering, if any, is undertaken solely by the perpetrator. This is clearly not the case for the abortion clinic bombers, whose sabotage disregards the danger of death or injury to persons, even uninvolved bystanders. . . .

[3] Seemingly.

In crossing the threshold of violence, caution is in order. We are talking about times when the police appear blind in their right eyes, so to speak. Laws exist to protect us, but are not enforced. Nazi gangs terrorized German streets while the police looked the other way. Klansmen burned the Freedom Rider buses, as police and FBI watched. The houses of voter registration volunteers in '63 and '64 were bombed and shot at; calling the sheriff was futile. Peasants and farmers are legally evicted from lands farmed by their ancestors. When the law works to stop the Nazis, the Klan, and the landlords, and ceases to define their victims as "terrorists" for fighting back, then we will have law and order, and armed defense will no longer be utilized. Until then, some people will defend themselves with weapons of violence. Decency requires that we not lump them together with those who terrorize them. . . .

Community Values

Other forms of terrorism cannot be stopped, short of the kind of fundamental changes that eliminate the dissatisfactions which are its seedbed. This implies a serious reallocation of resources and vast changes in public ideology. Terrorist groups can survive for very long periods even in countries which overwhelmingly reject their goals. This is true even under conditions in which population movement is thoroughly monitored and civil liberties are far more restricted than in the U.S. West Germany is one such example, where there is widespread support for strict counterterror methods.

The U.S. is a relatively loosely-organized, poorly policed society with a long tradition of vigilantism. Today it is the most violent society in the industrialized world. Paradoxically, its citizens have, on paper, more protections from arbitrary police power than those of any other country in the world. It is clear, however, that these protections are hardly applied impartially. Whether it be street crime or "terrorism," the suppression of domestic disorder by the state requires the abrogation[4] of rights. As the clamor for order increases, the differences between the U.S. and other nations will decrease. The state will define street crime, as well as political disorder of which it does not approve, as "terrorism," and order, imposed by both the police and by vigilante groups, will tend to supplant law.

The alternative is to develop methods of community order which are both independent of the state, and nonviolent; that is, incorporating an ethic of problem-solving and reconciliation. Neighborhood anti-crime patrols may be a first step for some communities—a form of nonviolent vigilantism. On a wider scale, the task is formidable to say the least. After all, violence is as American as apple pie.

---

[4] Repealing.

Questions for Discussion and Writing

1. Review the examples Oppenheimer provides of institutional terrorism, including police brutality, the prison system, and capital punishment. How would Oppenheimer argue that these are acts of terrorism?

2. Oppenheimer quotes Alfred Lee as saying, "more terrorists ride in Rolls Royces, and sit in the seats of corporate power and government than lurk in dark alleys." Explain this statement. What specific examples could be used to defend it?

3. According to the author, why are bombers of abortion clinics and violent racists not called terrorists?

4. Compare both Singh and Oppenheimer's definitions of terrorism. What differences exist?

5. Review the examples of terrorist acts cited in both the Singh and Oppenheimer articles. Would there be conditions under which you could imagine yourself engaging in terrorist activities? Why or why not?

6. According to the author, the way in which ruling groups define different kinds of disorder really establishes the definition of terrorism: "The survival of the established order requires the acceptance of the ruling class' definition of reality." Is this an acceptable basis for defining terrorism? Why or why not?

Melanie McFadyean, "The Fingers on the Trigger" _____

Although Southern Ireland proclaimed its independence from Great Britain in 1916, Northern Ireland is still governed by Great Britain and is officially part of the United Kingdom. The battle lines have been drawn for hundreds of years. Most Catholics oppose British rule and support independence. Most Protestants support the British. Paramilitary groups from both sides continue fighting each other, and shootings and bombings occur frequently. Occasionally, IRA fighters attack targets in England, and the British Army increases its patrols and vigilance in retaliation. For many Northern Irish, the potential of violence has become a way of life. The following reading, written by journalist Melanie McFadyean, appeared as a newspaper article in The Guardian, *a major London newspaper, in 1988. McFadyean interviews two active members of what have often been called terrorist groups by their enemies and freedom fighters by their supporters: the Irish Republican Army and the Ulster Defense League.*

Key Concepts

IRA, the Irish Republican Army, is a secret organization, predominantly Catholic, working for Northern Ireland's independence from Great Britain through military means and unification with Southern Ireland (page 387).

UDA, the Ulster Defense Army, is a predominantly Protestant paramilitary organization based in Ulster, Northern Ireland, actively engaged in fighting the IRA and advocating a Northern Ireland separate from Southern Ireland (page 387).

The Troubles is a term for the conflict between Protestant and Catholic, British loyalist and Irish Republican (page 387).

ULSTER FREEDOM FIGHTER

"I didn't get actively involved until I was 16. I'm in the UFF, the military wing of the **UDA.** I am a freedom fighter, not a terrorist or a guerrilla. The **IRA** are terrorists and the problem with this country is the IRA. The UFF is a cell structure organisation. Like every organisation we have an intelligence section. Once we are given a known Republican we eliminate him or attempt to eliminate him. We would eliminate known Republican women as well. I have eliminated people on various occasions. It's a target that has to be eliminated. I never feel any feeling afterwards. I have eliminated six.

It's hard to sit back and watch Protestant people being killed. We know who to eliminate because of Intelligence. I'd rather not say where we get that from. You don't go out and shoot someone you haven't got a picture of. You have to know your target. I wouldn't stiff you (pointing at one person) if I meant to stiff you (pointing at another). I go into Republican areas quite often.

Our enemy are Sinn Fein, the IRA, IPLO, INLA. I would not attack the security forces, but they are not on our side. The security forces know it's the IRA doing the killings but very few are charged. There's nothing wrong with a shoot to kill policy. The RUC are British puppets. I believe the SAS would kill us if told to. There wouldn't be any qualms.

These **Troubles** would be sorted out if we had an independent Ulster. The ordinary decent working class Catholics have nothing to fear. As for the Unionist politicians, they have had twenty years to solve it. I wouldn't be prepared to live in a United Ireland either economically or in religious ways. If it happened the Northern Protestants would take up arms. I think of myself as an Ulster Protestant. I would say I was British. But I want an independent Ulster.

It's everybody's right to live—to a certain extent—except people who take up arms against the State. I think more innocent Protestants have been killed than Catholics.

I have never talked to Republicans. I don't see any future for them in this country, in Northern Ireland. I don't see any future for the Republican movement in Northern Ireland.

My earliest memories of the Troubles are lying in bed and listening to the riots in the Shankill and the Falls. I know a fellow who was shot, I didn't know him personally to talk to. It upset me.

The Troubles started when a lot of bigots, civil rights, upset the Protestants. It was the clergy and religious bigots on both sides. There were civil rights marches and things like that. I was too young to know what it was all about. The civil rights may have meant well but the majority of it was Catholic. A lot of it was started out by the Catholic Church, in my eyes. Then the Republican element came in. I feel the Republican cause gets put better.

Let me ask you—can you understand? I live here. I have a whole picture. We all live in the same conditions. You hear people screaming about the conditions of West Belfast—their houses are just as good as ours, or just as bad. There's no difference between Catholics of the Falls Road or Protestants in the Shankill. We don't live in large houses up the mountain. The IRA's arms come from Libya. The communists are paying for their arms. Arms are also coming from the USA, one of the greatest capitalistic countries in the world and yet the IRA are socialists.

There's no common ground. They go out and shoot people and blow them up. They are trying to force the IRA down our throats. They were fighting before Ireland has been in trouble, since the beginning of time."

IRA VOLUNTEER

I was about eight when it all began. I remember the British Army coming in and I remember being harrassed. I felt I wanted to do something. My parents tried to protect us but it was impossible. The area I'm from is not a ghetto, it's a "respectable" area but even there it was impossible.

A very close friend of mine was shot dead. Before that I saw arrests, I saw the British soldiers abusing children. I saw the way the British restricted our education and prevented us from learning about our culture and traditions. We are Irish and we have a culture and an identity and we're not allowed to fulfill that.

I am not married and I have no children. My family know of my involvement. I can't stay at home two nights in a row. You can't have a normal family relationship. Your social life is confined to Nationalist areas. I am a Catholic, I go to Mass on a regular basis.

All operations are discussed by volunteers involved. No volunteer is given an order that cannot be queried. Volunteers all have training. I've always queried reasons. I don't like to see any civilian hurt and would question any bombing, including ones if there were danger to British civilians.

Loyalists are definitely not our enemy. The IRA don't believe this is a sectarian war. The IRA will retain the right to execute known Loyalists, for example Lennie Murphy, the notorious Shankill butcher. The British Government are our enemy, and anyone they employ on a security basis, including building workers and contractors. Loyalists who are involved in death squads which are threatening our people would be legitimate targets for execution.

I would never have been involved in violence had it not been for the British presence. I don't feel our country should be governed by a foreign country. The means was the IRA and I volunteered.

I have been in prison, I did time and came out and rejoined. In jail we had an education process, reading about other people's struggles.

Do I think the IRA will succeed in getting the British government to withdraw from Northern Ireland? Look how Margaret Thatcher reacted after Brighton. The SAS executed a number of volunteers after that. After Ballygawley volunteers were assassinated. Despite Gibraltar there have been bombings—that proves we're not frightened. But we realise that military operations on their own can't succeed, there has to be dialogue with our political wing, Sing Fein.

Our main aim is to free our country and remove the British. Next year we will be into our third decade. This year and last year young volunteers were killed. The number joining is steady.

We're twenty years on and the risks are big. But if people could meet a member of the IRA they'd see we're human beings, we don't have a murderous mentality.

Questions for Discussion and Writing

1. Fighters from both the IRA and the UDA have been labeled terrorists. Sketch a rough profile of each man interviewed in the *Guardian* given what you have read. Consider social class, profession, and family life. Does reading this interview "humanize" them in any way or change the stereotype?

2. Why did the author choose to interview these men and then print their comments without any analysis of her own? What effect does this kind of interview have on the reader?

3. What psychological and social effects have these men experienced owing to their involvement in paramilitary fighting and assassination? How do each of these men "square their consciences" about the killing they have done? How has it changed them? Do they express any remorse? If not, why not? Do they show any friendship or compassion for each other's respective community?

4. What targets and victims do the fighters name? Does either of them justify the use of random violence?

5. The violence in Northern Ireland has often appeared on television and in newspapers. Imagine daily life in a Northern Ireland city with armed soldiers on the streets and armed paramilitary organizations gunning for each other. How does this situation affect children and people's daily lives?

6. Examine the language the two men use to describe their activities. The IRA man refers to himself as a "volunteer," and the UDA man as a "freedom fighter." What other political euphemisms do they use? What purposes do the specialized use of words like these serve?

7. Would you argue that these men are terrorists, freedom fighters, or volunteers in the Irish Republican Army? How would you decide on a basis for judgment?

BEYOND NATIONAL POLITICS

Anatolii Gromyko and Martin Hellerman, **Breakthrough: Emerging New Thinking, Soviet and Western Scholars Issue a Challenge to Build a World Beyond War** _____

This essay, coedited by a Russian and an American in 1988, is taken from Breakthrough: Emerging New Thinking, *a book written by Soviet and American intellectuals who met and discussed the daunting range of political problems the world faces and who explored alternative solutions to military intervention. Recent political events in Eastern Europe sound an optimistic note against the violence of Tiananmen Square and hint at the possibility of more global ways of perceiving political realities. The authors propose that we are entering a political paradigm shift and that nations must and will find new ways to solve world problems that transcend purely nationalist interests.*

Key Concepts

Nuclear imperative (page 390) is the obligation to respond to the possibility of nuclear war.

Coexistence (page 393) is the separate, peaceful existence of two or more nations of opposing ideologies.

Unilateral security (page 393) involves military action based on the interests of the initiating country.

Global thinking recognizes the interdependence of all nations and all peoples (page 391).

> *Global Thinking*
>
> *. . . we ought to recognize each other's humanity, as we move to solve today's complex problems dealing with political relations, economics, and social life.*
>
> *The most important message is that changes in human values, modes of thinking, and visions of the future are needed for us to live more sustainably and harmoniously—indeed to survive—in an interdependent world.*

The **nuclear imperative** is the setting for modern times. It drives us to take account, to take inventory. It calls us to examine our fundamental perceptions concerning our loyalties and allegiances. It summons us to lift our sights. It provokes us to ask what we have learned in history which will put us on a safer course, and what we are learning from science which will provide for our security more surely than has war, or the mentality of war.

To get us out of the present situation, new thinking will have to be more than a slogan. It will have to take into account these new nuclear dimensions of human life as surely as did Copernicus's discovery that the

Earth revolves around the sun. In the same way, new thinking will have to guide new conduct.

Global thinking begins with the beauty and the simplicity of the unity principle discovered by the cosmonauts and astronauts during their flights in space.

"What strikes me, is not only the beauty of the continents . . . but their closeness to one another . . . their essential unity." Yuri Gagarin

"From where you see it, the thing is a whole, and it is so beautiful." Russell Schweickart

There is one, unique, fruitful life-support system. All depend upon it. None can live without it. Men do not breathe differently in Omsk than in Omaha. If that is so, and surely it is so, then what damages the pure air for one part of the planet damages it for all. A nuclear reactor accident in one part of the world is an accident for us all. We are bound, beyond ideologies and religions, by an overwhelming number of common biological and physiological needs.

In the old perspective, before one could see with the help of television and astronauts all the way around the whole globe and back into one's own soul, blame for any predicament could always be placed on the invisible enemy over the sea, or across the mountains, in some strange land. From the new perspective, from the eye of the spaceship, there is no far-off place. There are no far-off people. All war is civil war. All humans are partners in a common endeavor. There is not some other place where people are responsible for ozone damage, or soil erosion, or injustice. In the new thinking, "everyone is responsible for everything." "The new thinking requires a radical change. . . . It means basic alterations in everything we think and do. It involves assuming a feeling of personal and historical responsibility for everything on the planet."

Such thinking produces a powerful change, and the promise of great improvement in the way we all treat each other.

To be "responsible," for example, means to avoid the conduct of lying. Stereotyping of another country, calling its people and leaders derogatory names, is deceitful and irresponsible. "They" are not vicious animals who live on the other side of the ocean, they are people. Of course we are culturally and politically different. But there are limits to our differences; and we are more alike than was apparent, or was the fact, before the age of international travel and global communications.

It is simply not truthful to blame life's disadvantages, history's inequities, failures of our economic systems, or failures of our foreign policies on any outside "enemy." It is simply not accurate to consider that all contradictions are conflicts among social groups and cultures can be explained by an evil which is found outside one's own society, but never inside. The view of the planet as a whole produces a more unified, comprehensive picture, a profoundly important fundamental premise:

We are all responsible. And there is a more profound opportunity. We all can help to solve any problem.

In the prenuclear world, before the global perspective, it would not have been so dangerous to be completely self-centered, or solely self-motivated. Today, that view transferred to nations has us on the brink of disaster. The view must shift to one which consistently responds to the question: What in the long run is best for everyone involved? And what are the means, consistent with that end, which I must choose?

Thinking globally requires discovery of the right relationship between the individual and the global community. Neither is insignificant. There has to be a healthy relationship between the community, the social order, the whole, and the individual.

We are all different in that each human is an original. But we are tied together, in that there is one global system in which the activities of each of us affect the lives of each other. We are separate in that each of us treasures different cultural and family values. Between these two realities, the whole and the individual, there is always tension. When the right relationship exists, the tension is worked out so that both the whole and the parts are healthy. When the relationship is wrong, war and violence are efforts to resolve that tension by imposing unity, one nation imposing its view upon another.

For centuries, war has been increasingly less effective as a means to reconcile the tension between unity and diversity. At least that has been true since the Augsburg Treaty in 1555, when a long series of battles to impose religious unity in Germany failed. The effort failed again during the Thirty Years War which ended in 1648. And the twentieth century has been replete with war's failure. Finally, in the nuclear age, war is utterly useless to resolve that tension. Large portions of the world have actually settled into a pattern of stable peace, a testament to the fact that war is accepted as unthinkable in those parts of the globe.

The mind-set[1] that, in a complicated world, one side can be eliminated is therefore totally obsolete. The new thinking must include, at a minimum, recognition of the reality that within global unity, diversity is a given. The threat of nuclear war now backs us up against the wall and demands that we live with that paradox, because to deny it will kill us. The long-term parallel continuation of capitalist and socialist systems is a given. There will be both global unity and diversity. We are one human species. But we are also all different. Not only will there be long-term differences between capitalists and socialists, there will be differnces between forms of socialism, and between forms of capitalism. It is the destiny of this generation to determine how such differences will evolve by nonviolent means.

Humans don't have to like each other, or even understand one another, to cooperate. Soldiers in the trenches in World War I—who were conditioned to hate each other, and ordered by their commanders

[1] Perspective, world view.

to fire at each other on sight—often stopped firing at dinner time. They just stopped. They let each other get up out of the trenches and go behind the lines and eat. Not just a few times, but regularly. When soldiers had been in one place in the lines opposite each other for a long time, they began to act differently toward each other. When they expected to be in those same trenches indefinitely into the future, it made sense for each side to ease up a little on the other, if the treatment was reciprocated. Both would live longer. Under those conditions, they evolved their own rules. They started to evolve civilization, while above and behind them commanders continued to push for noncooperation.

The soldiers discovered that cooperation evolves when the parties expect to be in a relationship—even if adversarial—for some time. They are nicer to each other when they expect to meet again—as the soldiers in World War I expected to meet again the very next morning. And they are nicer when they are dependent upon each other to survive. The parallel is clear. Nations which expect to do business again will learn to cooperate. Acceptance of long-term **coexistence** between capitalists and socialists is a precondition to cooperation, and an essential ingredient of global thinking.

Faced with the expectation of a long-term future together, it is simply common sense for all sides to keep the ends and means consistent. Repeated contacts will go better if that is so. Faced with a common future, it also pays to take care to preserve food and resources for future generations. The vision of global thinking is therefore of people who are dependable, interested in cooperation and right conduct, and caring. They are this way not because they are exhorted to be so, or bound by duty, ideology, or religion, but because it is human nature to find that way when the necessity demands. And—threatened by nuclear extinction—necessity now demands the highest level of exertion and consciousness.

There is a discipline imposed by the goal of coexistence. There are requirements. Humankind is at the crossroads. We must choose. Something must be decided for, something left behind.

If we choose mutual survival, **unilateral security** is a concept to be left behind. From Nicaragua to the Middle East, from Grenada to Afghanistan, the military powers have sometimes acted as if they could decide independently what should be the course of Third World development. But development cannot be controlled by capitalist, socialist, rich, or poor states alone.

In a totally mixed and interdependent world, where no nation is free to take unilateral action, security can only be multilateral, universal. "Security in the nuclear age means security for all." Which means that there can be no "just" war. Not of any kind, for any purpose. Not anymore. "The superpowers must take this into account as they presently engage in small wars such as those in the Persian Gulf, Afghanistan, Nicaragua, Iran-Iraq, and Africa," says resistance fighter of World War II Ales Adamovich.

It is the diversity of interests and systems which is the source of strength for the peoples and economies of the globe. The doctrines of exclusive interest, messianic doctrines that only one politico-economic system has the right to exist, are a thing of the past.

. . . it is impossible to export revolution. Revolutionary transformation cannot take place unless favorable conditions exist inside that society. Rejecting the aggressive messianic approach is consistent with this understanding. To go out with aggressive messianic fervor and try with force to impose revolution upon other societies against the will of the people won't work.

This then must be included in new thinking: Dogmatic arrogance and messianic fervor, whether capitalist or socialist, are no longer realistic. "Following the past is far from realism."

The overwhelming experience of this century is that war is obsolete. It failed to solve the distribution and equity problems that preceded World War I. It failed to achieve an empire for Hitler, or for the Japanese. War in this century has not quelled the cries of the cultures, the languages, the religions of the globe for expression through democracy and economic well-being. Nor is it working now in Central America, in Afghanistan, in the Middle East, in Africa, nor in Ireland. War is a blunt and brutal tool. War thinking is the opposite of new thinking.

"New thinking," concludes Professor Anatoly Gromyko, "stands for a process where we ought to recognize each other's humanity . . . . We live on the same planet Earth, our common home . . . . it is impossible to secure a unilateral[2] advantage for oneself to the detriment of the other side without ultimately impairing one's own interests." Gromyko quotes from Leo Tolstoy:

Misinterpreters of the truth usually say that reason can't be trusted because it speaks differently in different men . . . . But such a claim is quite the opposite of the truth. Reason never speaks differently. It always speaks alike in all men . . . . Whether God is said to have appeared in a pillar of fire, or Buddha to have ascended on sunrays, or Mohammed to have flown to the heavens, or Christ to have walked on water . . . rational men, always and everywhere answer in a similar manner: This isn't true. But, to the questions "Is it right to do unto others as you would they do unto you? Is it good to love and forgive them, do good to them?" The reason of all men throughout time has said: "Yes, it's right and worthwhile."

Humankind is on the move, emerging from a chain reaction of cause and effect that stretches back for billions of years. Now this species has the power to affect its own evolution by conscious choice.

The choice is not one which can be built upon fantasy or utopian hope about war. But the choice, if it is made, can have a solid foundation. It can be built upon a confidence in the capacity of the human to be responsible, the will of the human to do right when to do so is required

[2] For one side.

to survive, the experience of each human with every alternative to ending war, the love of the human for home, and the recognition—which is the hallmark of this century—that this whole planet is now home.

Questions for Discussion and Writing

1. The authors stress the need for "long-term coexistence between capitalists and socialists." Why must unilateral security be abandoned if long-term coexistence is to be achieved? To what extent is this feasible?

2. Explain how the nuclear imperative is the driving force behind the shift to global thinking. What other factors influence this paradigm shift? What effects are they having?

3. Take the ideological position of a hard-line communist and a hard-line capitalist. How would each of them argue against the authors' proposals?

4. What would be the argument against the following world view: "The history of humankind is a history of war. People have been fighting each other since long before written history. It is human nature and has never been different. It is not possible to 'affect [our] evolution by conscious choice.'"

5. What evidence indicates an international trend toward global thinking? Are we seeing more intercommunication and exchange between nations? How pervasive is the effect of television, radio, and other media?

Chapter Writing Topics

1. Under a democracy, all people are entitled to equal rights and full political representation. When people are deprived of these rights, what means can they justifiably use to regain them? Develop your argument in essay form, considering the following points.

   (a) Have Americans at any point in their history been deprived of their rights? Consider the civil rights struggle and the feminist and gay movements, among others.

   (b) How would Sidney Hook, James Farmer, or Malcolm X argue for or against the use of civil disobedience or the use of violence as a means of gaining equal rights in a democracy?

   (c) Is violence ever justified? Has it ever yielded positive results in a democracy? What methods have yielded the greatest results?

   (d) Are there still inequalities to be dealt with in the United States? Is legislation addressing the problems adequately? What methods of change or protest do you endorse?

2. Compare and contrast the oppression and discrimination faced by blacks with that which women from ancient Athens to present-day America have endured. Address the following issues.

   (a) How were both groups oppressed? What rights were they deprived of? Who were the oppressors? What were/are the psychological and economic effects on both groups? Refer to Farmer, Riencourt, Kenyon, and Feeley. You may also want to review the Rose article in Chapter 1.

(b) Analyze the psychological, economic, and political reasons for the oppression. Review Dubois' argument on colonialism and slavery, Orwell's conclusions on imperialism, and Carol Christ's critique of patriarchal values (in Chapter 2).

(c) What gains have blacks and women made? How did they achieve these gains? Refer to the Hunter College Women's Collective essay. What did they share in common as oppressed groups? How are they alike? How are they different? What does the future hold for each group politically, economically, and culturally?

3. The Gromyko/Hellerman reading describes a political and social paradigm shift designed to create new ways of perceiving the interdependence of nations and peoples. This is the "global political view," the view of the world as a "global village." Analyze the authors' argument. To what extent do you agree or disagree with their assessment of a changing world view?

(a) Review and summarize the authors' position. Explain the change to a global world view. What are the driving political, economic, and technological forces behind it?

(b) How feasible are the authors' forecasts of long-term coexistence between major powers? Consider how relations have changed between the Soviet Union and the United States in the past decade, as well as recent political events in Eastern Europe.

(c) Examine and then address the counterargument against Gromyko and Hellerman's position that it is not possible to change our evolution "by conscious choice" and that the history of humankind is a history of war. Refer to readings from this and previous chapters for evidence.

(d) Do we have cause to be optimistic? What other choices are available to us?

4. Historically, both communist and democratic states have practiced some form of imperialism. Explain the rationale for imperialist policies from a democratic and/or communist point of view.

(a) Review Winks' article and clarify your definition of imperialism.

(b) List examples of imperialism or actions that could be defined as quasi-imperialistic: the securing of North America from Native Americans; Spain's conquest of Central and South America; the recent U.S. incursion into Panama, both politically and militarily; the Soviet invasion of Afghanistan; the Soviets' political and economic control of Eastern Europe;the European powers' colonization of Africa; and so on.

(c) List and analyze the reasons for imperialism: protection of national borders; Manifest Destiny; keeping avenues of trade and national defense open; the need for raw materials; the desire to bring civilization and culture to a "primitive civilization"; religious duty; and so forth.

(d) Analyze the typical defense of the imperialist position. What benefit did it bring to the aggressor country? What other policy, if any, could the country have chosen?

5. Review the Singh and Oppenheimer readings on terrorism. Have there been or are there political situations today that justify the use of terrorist tactics? Develop an essay that examines this issue.

(a) Consider discussing the problem of defining the term *terrorism,* since Oppenheimer uses it to describe police brutality as well as such things as the PLO bombing of an airplane, child labor, and institutionalized poverty, as well as hostage-taking. A well-thought-out definition will be crucial for this essay.

(b) Present your definition. Discuss some specific examples that are or are not justified: Stalin's purges, Robespierre's Reign of Terror, Caligula's rule, and so on. The readings and your familiarity with history and current events should provide you with numerous examples, and/or you may want to propose your own hypothetical situation.

(c) Explore the terrorist's motives and the effect on the victims as compared to the ultimate outcome of the political situation. For example, weigh destruction of property as opposed to the taking of human life. Consider random violence against innocent civilians versus violence against military personnel. "The ends versus the means" may become part of the philosophical question.

6. Write an essay exploring the degree to which racial equality has been achieved in the United States. Did the civil rights movement achieve all its goals, or are we still witness to a significant amount of racism and discrimination?

(a) Provide some background and context to the question. What were conditions like for black Americans before the civil rights movement. Consider equal education, employment, voting rights, segregated facilities, access to media, and the like.

(b) What gains were achieved through the civil rights struggle? Which laws were changed? How is daily life different for blacks and other minorities today?

(c) Some black leaders still raise the question of overt racism and discrimination in our society, pointing to racially motivated killings, growing racist attitudes on campuses against blacks and other minorities, the continued presence of the Ku Klux Klan, and continued police brutality. How justified are these claims?

Philosophical
Perspectives
え

Introduction

Philosophy is the systematic, logical inquiry into the nature of the world and our consciousness of it. Philosophers seek to establish logical models of what reality is, how it works, and how we come to know it. Some of the fundamental scientific and spiritual issues that philosophers have devoted themselves to exploring over the centuries include how the human mind operates, what reality and consciousness mean, how logic and feeling provide or create information about the world, which ethical codes lead to the greatest happiness, and so on. The issues of philosophy, though often highly abstract, can have very practical effects on the kind of life an individual chooses to live. Perhaps it is for this reason that the major thinkers in the Western tradition, from mathematicians to historians, scientists to theologians, have been absorbed in attempts to formulate philosophical doctrines that help people make sense of their lives and guide them in their actions.

In the first reading in Chapter 6, "An Overview of Western Philosophy," D. P. Dirk sketches a broad historical and thematic view of the philosophical tradition and characterizes the major historical periods through the twentieth century. The history of philosophy in the West traditionally has its roots in ancient Greece. Plato and Aristotle are the most widely acknowledged sources of Western philosophical thought; their ideas still inform contemporary philosophical schools, though no single historical continuum exists. From the time of the Greeks, philosophy has been interrelated with art, politics, religion, and science. All fields of research and knowledge begin with certain philosophic assumptions about the nature of reality and the human mind.

The remaining readings in this chapter present specific philosophical doctrines from the ancient and modern worlds. Interspersed with these are

articles that discuss or illustrate choices, dilemmas, and problems encountered in contemporary life. Thus, as you read, you will have the opportunity
to examine contemporary situations from various philosophical perspectives,
assessing how completely and effectively they account for and offer solutions
to the complexities we face in daily life. As you work through the readings,
you may also find yourself calling into question your own philosophical assumptions. For most people, developing a philosophical perspective is a
continuing, ever evolving pursuit. Academic study of philosophy is one way
of testing out different perspectives, both to learn about the past and to help
define individually the issues and values that matter most in the present.

D. P. Dirk, *"An Overview of Western Philosophy"* _____

The philosophical schools of ancient Greece never ceased to be a
significant influence in Western thought and culture. Throughout the
history of Western philosophy one frequently finds that the great
thinkers placed themselves in the thought-world of ancient Greece,
making alliances with some figure or school and opposing others. At the
same time, the advent of new ideas provided continuously varying tex-
tures to the great philosophies, often moving them further away from
their ancient Greek roots. There have been many such new ideas over
the past two millennia, yet three stand out as most significant—religion,
humanism, and scientific naturalism. With the ancient Greek schools as a
base and these three ideas as themes of change, it is possible to sketch the
story of Western philosophy from the time of the ancient world's end.

Religion, in particular Christianity, was quite clearly the most
important catalyst for change in philosophical thought during the decline
of the Roman Empire and for quite a long time afterwards. During this
period the ancient Greek figure who enjoyed greatest prominence was
Plato. What has turned out to be an extremely influential revival of his
philosophy which we call Neoplatonism began in the third century A.D.
The most important figure in this movement was Plotinus (c. 203-296), a
native of Egypt who had moved to Rome. The Neoplatonists adopted
Platonic ideas like the exaltation of the rational aspect of humans and the
denigration of sensation and desire, while they embellished the doctrine
of the Forms and that of the Platonic theory of creation. These latter
doctrines were given a new shape in the theory of emanation. According
to Plotinus, everything has its ultimate origin in The One, or the First
Principle, which is simple, without parts, and which performs no actions.
Everything ultimately emanates as rays from the sun, from The One, but
it does so in successive stages. What emanates directly from The One is
Nous or Mind, which is identical to the Platonic Forms. Psyche or Soul
emanates from Nous, and everything else gradually emanates from
Psyche. As in Plato, the soul's highest office is to contemplate the Forms,
so for Plotinus, the role of the soul is to contemplate Nous. But there is a

higher purpose to the contemplation of Nous, or the Forms: mystical, ecstatic, communion with The One.

One of philosophy's most important features in these early times was Christianity's adaptation and transformation of Neoplatonism. For early Christian Platonists like St. Augustine (354-430), a native of North Africa, The One is roughly identified with God the Father, Nous with God the Son Jesus Christ, and Psyche with the Holy Spirit. Because Christ is consequently identifed with the Forms, Christ for Augustine becomes the proper object of contemplation, the Teacher who in turn allows one to achieve communion with God. Despite these changes, Christian Platonism retains many of the themes of the older Platonisms. Possibly the most significant theme that it retains is what might be called the unifying idea of Platonism: human beings are radically dependent on something that transcends us for the good in life. Plato held that goodness in human life is ultimately to be attained through controlling sensation and desire, and living the life of reason through intellectual contemplation of the Forms which transcend us, which are higher than us. The Forms should be authorities in our lives. Augustine believes the same, except that he thinks the transcendent authority on whom we are radically dependent is the trinity God of Christianity.

Christian Platonism was the dominant philosophy in the West until the thirteenth century. In the twelfth and thirteenth centuries, however, the renewed availability of Aristotle's works occasioned a profound change in Western thought. Aristotle's works had up to this time been studied especially by Islamic philosophers, but they had not, for the most part, been translated into Latin, the intellectual language of the West. Around the time that these works became available, the University of Paris developed into the most important center for theological and philosophical studies in Europe. The most famous thinker to work there was Thomas Aquinas (1225-1274), who remains the most important philosopher and theologian for the Roman Catholic faith.

The thinkers at Paris created a synthesis of Christianity, Aristotelianism, and the Augustinian/Neoplatonic tradition that had prevailed until then. Aristotelian thought encouraged humanistic change. Aristotle, and consequently his medieval followers, did not share Plato's idea of human radical dependence on the transcendent nor Plato's exaltation of the rational at the expense of the sensation and desires. As did Aristotle, Aquinas thought that we apprehend truth through our sensation and reason working together, that the apprehension of truth is not to be achieved just through the purely rational contemplation of transcendent Forms of God. Analogously, the nature of the good for humans is not to be found by means of rational contemplation alone, but through human desire modified by reason. Thus, in contrast with the various Platonisms, truth and the good are not to be acquired through denying part of human nature and focusing on the transcendent, but through the use of all of the human faculties—reason, desire, and sensation. It should be emphasized, however, that the thinking of Aquinas and of other medieval Aristotelians was to a significant extent still influenced by Neoplatonism. Possibly the most significant example is their retention of the idea of a mystical communion with God, in the beatific vision, at the close of life's spiritual journey.

From this time until the sixteenth century, the history of Western philosophy is mainly that of the development and entrenchment of medieval Aristotelianism. There are exceptions, however. For instance, Neoplatonism was quite popular in early Renaissance Italy and was an important influence on the art of that time and place. During the Renaissance, in the fifteenth century, Platonic currents made more significant gains. Within the Catholic Church there was a revival of Augustinian thought; this was an important catalyst of the Protestant Reformation. Both the Lutheran and the Calvinist branches of the Reformation leaned heavily on Augustinian ideas, such as radical human dependence on God for truth, the goodness and the idea of God as a transcendent authority (although these movements are much more complex than this characterization may indicate). Possibly a sign of the Platonic tendencies of Calvinists and Lutherans is their shunning of "sensual" adornment in their churches, their elimination of stained glass windows, paintings, and images from places of worship. In the Catholic Church itself, splits between Platonic and Aristotelian groups occurred, possibly the most famous of which was the division between the Jesuits, a religious order greatly influenced by Aquinas, and the Augustinian Jansenists in France.

The seventeenth and eighteenth centuries were a period in which European philosophy flourished. This period is called the period of modern philosophy, probably because this is what the early nineteenth-century philosopher Hegel called it. The Frenchman Rene Descartes (1596-1650) is usually thought of as the founder of modern philosophy. Descartes' thought, though influenced by the Aristotelian tradition, is more heavily Platonic, especially in that it exalts reason and denigrates sensation as faculties in the quest for truth. It is partly for this reason that Descartes is called a rationalist. One aspect of Descartes' philosophy that makes it revolutionary is its emphasis on science. Descartes not only lived during the scientific revolution, but also was one of its most important catalysts. In contrast to the Platonists, what Descartes focuses on as apprehensible by reason are the properties of bodies that are clearly geometrically describable, such as extension, shape, size, duration, and motion. These are the properties that figure into a mechanistic account of the physical universe. Nongeometrical properties, such as color, taste, and smell, are not apprehensible by reason and thus, following the Platonic tradition, are not real. The image for the physical universe which Descartes helped to bring to dominance in the seventeenth century was that of a clock, a complex machine, all of whose parts interact mechanically.

But there is more than mechanistic matter in Descartes' universe. Descartes is dualistic; he divides the universe into two kinds of substances—material and mental. Human beings have both a mind, a mental part, and a body, a material part. Thus, in an account of the entire universe there must appear two kinds of explanation—a mechanistic explanation for the material part, and a mentalistic explanation (an explanation that employs notions such as ideas, sensations, desire, reasons, and choices) for the mental part. John Locke (1632-1704), an English philosopher, basically accepted this dualistic framework. He differs from Descartes in an important way, however, in that he is less rationalistic than Descartes. Locke believes, like the Aristotelians, that sensory ideas are those from which one must proceed to acquire knowledge. This theory about knowledge is called empiricism and is often opposed to a rationalist theory of knowledge according to which reason can apprehend truth directly without having to rely on sensory ideas. Both Descartes and Locke were forerunners of the eighteenth century period called the Enlightenment. The seventeenth century scientific revolution culminated in the successes of Isaac Newton, who became the greatest intellectual hero of the eighteenth century. The Enlightenment was an age celebrating scientific and eventually moral reason as well. Old authorities like religion were no longer considered necessary. Religion, if maintained at all, was reinterpreted so as not to include the idea of radical dependence on a transcendent God. Infinite scientific and moral progress was thought to be possible, through human reason alone, liberated from any external tutelage.[1]

Many regard the Enlightenment thinker Immanuel Kant (1724-1804) as the most influential philosopher of the modern era. Kant tried to orchestrate an agreement between the various philosophical theories; for instance, he incorporated elements of both empiricism and rationalism into his system. At the same time he attempted to make room for science on the one side and, on the other, religion and humanistic morality, which according to many were being threatened by the idea that natural science explains everything. He did this by arguing that the realm of scientific explanation is only the realm of appearance and that behind the appearances, there is a realm of things in themselves about which science has nothing to say. We can't have any experience of things in themselves, but we can, we even must, have beliefs about this realm. In particular, we can hold the humanistic belief that we in ourselves are free and that God, even though he is not an object in the realm of science, exists as a thing-in-itself.

Kant had a tremendous influence on the thought of the nineteenth and twentieth centuries. To the one side, those who were interested in maintaining the integrity of religion and morality in the face of science often sought a Kantian solution to their problem. Conversely, those who were interested in a theory of science and knowledge also frequently looked to Kant's theory for guidance. Although Kant was an Enlightenment figure, he helped usher in a new period, Romanticism. The most

[1] Guidance.

important philosopher of the Romantic period was G.W.F. Hegel. His Romantic emphases included the importance of feeling and desire in acquiring knowledge of truth and the good, the cultural and historical factors that contribute to human nature, and the importance of seeing the history of thought and the history of the world as a single big picture with unifying themes.

It is important to note that Hegel's thought does not represent a complete break with the Enlightenment. For instance, two Enlightenment ideas that are central to Hegelian philosophy are the belief that everything can be rationally explained and the notion that the human race will progress as far as possible through reason.

Karl Marx (1818-1883) was a German Jewish philosopher who received his philosophical education when Hegelianism was dominant. His own thought is indebted to Hegel and yet is very different. Among the cultural and historical factors that mold human beings, Marx thinks the economic to be the most important. Marx believes that progress to a communist classless society, from his point of view a utopia, is inevitable. This progress will take place through internal conflicts and inconsistencies, in all of the economic systems that precede communism. Marx's thought remains influential in the world today, and a large scholarly community continues to interpret and reformulate his ideas.

It is often thought that existentialism had its origins in the nineteenth century, and the Danish philosopher, Soren Kierkegaard (1813-1855), is sometimes said to be the first existentialist philosopher. In his writings, two major existentialist themes can be found: an emphasis on the role of the individual in the determination of meaning in life, and an emphasis on free choice. Kierkegaard is unlike many twentieth-century existentialists in that he thinks that the best life to choose is a Christian life of commitment to God. The German philosopher Nietzsche (1844-1900) is also often considered to be a forerunner of existentialism. In contrast to Kierkegaard, he attacked the Christian religion and Christian religious morality, saying that they cultivated weak aspects of human character like humility, pity, and repression of desire. Christian morality is a slave morality, he said. What people should try to develop is a morality of the superman Ubermensch, emphasizing the strength and nobility of human character.

The twentieth century is a century of great philosophical and intellectual variation. There are many divisions and differences among schools and individual thinkers. Yet, one can identify powerful thematic currents, one of the most prominent being scientific naturalism, which states that everything there is can be explained by natural science, by physics in particular. The logical positivists of the Vienna Circle developed this idea in the first half of the century. According to them, all talk of the transcendent, for instance, all talk about religion, is meaningless; all meaningful language must be linked to sensory experience. Logical positivism lost much of its influence after the first half of the century, but in its place came possibly more rigorous scientific naturalisms. For the scientific naturalists, the most difficult aspect of the universe to accommodate is the mental. An early attempt to naturalize theory of mind was behaviorism; after that failed, the computer soon became the scientific naturalist's favorite model of the mind.

Existentialism and phenomenology represent an important humanist current of thought in the twentieth century. Martin Heidegger and Jean-Paul Sartre are possibly the two most famous philosophers of this tradition. Sartre believes that life in itself is meaningless, that there is no God, no eternal moral order to give it meaning. Meaning in life is achieved through individual free choice, through the choice of a project. The existentialists typically do think, however, that there are restrictions on the type of project that can make one's life meaningful. For Sartre the choice of project must not be in bad faith: one cannot be self-deceptive in one's choice. This allows Sartre to rule out projects that we would generally think of as evil from the realm of those that can give meaning to life.

Sartrian existentialism, like scientific naturalism, rejects the transcendentalism of Platonism and religion. Possibly the most unique aspect of twentieth-century thought is the fairly widespread acceptance of the loss of God and the loss of intellectual and moral standards that hold for everyone at all times. To be sure, not everyone in the present-day philosophical community rejects the transcendent in this way; there are still many religious thinkers and others who argue for theories that include transcendent intellectual and moral standards. The present age in philosophy is pluralistic;[2] to say that there is a single identifiable direction to modern thought would be a mistake.

Questions for Discussion and Writing

1. Which aspects of Platonic philosophy might have made it appealing to early Christian theologians? Consider the Platonic and Neoplatonic emphasis on rational thought, suspicion of the senses, and belief in an ultimate, unifying force.

2. Aristotelian philosophy teaches that we must use all our faculties—reason, desire, and sensation—to understand truth and goodness. How does this belief set Aristotelian thought apart from the Platonic and Neoplatonic philosophical schools?

3. Dirk suggests a connection between Descartes' philosophic views and his historical period—the age of the scientific revolution. Do you see a relationship between Cartesian philosophy and traditional scientific values? How might the theories of Descartes and Locke have helped shape the attitudes endorsed by Enlightenment thinkers?

4. In what sense is Kant's philosophy Romantic? Consider his desire to unite rational thought and empirical data (information gained through the senses). How is his philosophy a form of idealism, as in Plato?

[2]More than one.

5. Dirk points out that Marx drew on Hegelian philosophy to develop his own thought. How are the two schools of thought related?

6. In your opinion, can an existentialist also accept scientific naturalism as a valid philosophical stance?

7. In what way(s) is twentieth-century philosophy a radical departure from most preceding theories and beliefs?

8. Does the academic tradition of philosophy reflect actual views which you and your peers hold? Which of the specific philosophic schools discussed in Dirk's essay comes closest to the views you hold or consider acceptable? Do any seem unacceptable to you? Why?

9. Do the various schools of philosophic thought discussed in the essay bear resemblance to the moral values taught to you at home? Explore the possible heritage of your family beliefs or their similarities to and differences from the Western philosophical tradition.

10. Articulate your personal views on each of the following questions.
    (a) Which is the more reliable source of knowledge about the world— information gathered through the senses (empirical observation) or information created through a process of reasoning (rationalism)?
    (b) Are we limited to our own perceptions and consciousness, or can we transcend the limitations of the individual mind?
    (c) Do we need religious faith to live a good life, or is human reason a sufficient moral guide?

ANCIENT PHILOSOPHICAL ATTITUDES/CONTEMPORARY SITUATIONS

Francis Henry Sandbach, **"Stoicism"**

Stoicism remains a very common philosophical attitude, though today we take it to mean self-containment and forbearance, the calm acceptance of things that happen to and around us. The original Stoic attitude developed by the Greek philosopher Zeno (c. 340–265 B.C.) emphasized the relativity of virtue and the use of reason, as the article below details. Classical Latin authors kept the Stoic philosophy alive, mainly in literary works. Seneca (c. 4 B.C.–A.D. 65) is the most well known of the Roman Stoics. His philosophy served as a source of balance in the cruel and decadent Rome of Caligula's day, and may have helped Seneca himself to carry out his own execution at Caligula's command. As a systematic philosophy, Stoicism no longers exists, but traces of it mark Christian thought, and as a perspective on life it colors some modern philosophies.

Philosophy is the pursuit of the correct way of life, and the center of gravity of stoicism lies in ethics. To be virtuous is necessarily good, to be vicious is bad. Everything other than virtue or vice is neither good nor bad, for nothing else necessarily affects the moral nature of man for good or bad. The usual objects of desire, health, wealth, honors, a spouse, children, etc., are not necessary to a virtuous life and often in fact lead to vice. They are therefore morally indifferent. So far the stoics reproduce the attitude of the cynics, but they realized that to stop there would make of virtue and vice names without any positive meaning; virtue cannot merely be a refusal to consider anything good except virtue or bad except vice. Those things which are morally indifferent and cannot be called good or bad are for the most part not absolutely indifferent, but possess relative values; these values are not permanent, but some things, e.g., health or friends, usually have "worth" and are "preferred," while others, e.g., sickness or friendlessness, usually have "unworth" and are, to imitate the somewhat uncouth stoic terminology, "demoted." Exceptional circumstances may change the usual values: disease might be preferred to health if one might thereby escape conscription[1] to fight in an unjust war. Such things, in themselves morally indifferent, constitute the field of action in which virtue and vice can be displayed; virtue consists in making the right choices, in recognizing the true values and attempting to secure them.

Man shares with other animals impulses that cause him to choose among the morally indifferent things; these impulses are directed not, as

[1] The draft.

the Epicureans maintained, towards pleasure but towards self-preservation and preservation of the species. But man differs from animals in that
he is rational, and his reason should shape his impulses and his choices.
This means not only that he can take a long-term view of his own
interests and so on occasion reject what appears immediately advan-
tageous, but also that, knowing himself to be but a part of the universe, he
should realize that the apparent interests of the part must be subordinate
to the interests of the whole. Zeno defined the end at which man should
aim as "life in accordance with nature": by "nature" he meant not only
man's instincts which lead him to choose "the primarily natural," i.e., life,
health, etc., but also the whole nature of the universe, which is identical
with God. Every event in the whole universe is necessary, providential
and due to the divine will. Since man cannot wholly foresee the future,
he is bound sometimes to choose what his own nature suggests but what
fate will prevent his attaining. "So long as the future is uncertain," wrote
Chrysippus, "I shall cleave[2] to those things that best promise to give me
what is in accordance with nature; God himself has made me a creature
that chooses so. But if I knew that it was fated for me to fall ill today, I
should have an impulse to fall ill."

Actions chosen by man's reason are called "appropriate" actions;
they are actions which, though not necessarily right, can be reasonably
defended. Some actions, e.g., to be brave, are always appropriate; others,
e.g., to take care of one's health, are usually so; others, e.g., to give away
one's possessions, only exceptionally so. If a man were completely wise,
his choices would always be right and evinced[3] as such by the course of
events. His actions therefore would be not only "appropriate" but "correct" too. Externally they might not differ from the merely appropriate,
but in essence they would be distinct, as being the product of knowledge
and not of guesswork.

Wickedness is closely associated with the passions; these arise from
mistaken judgments by which we suppose that indifferent things are
good or bad; on these judgments follow unreasonable and uncontrolled
movements of the soul. There are four cardinal passions: desire, pleasure,
fear and sorrow. Desire arises when an object of choice is thought to be
intrinsically[4] good; the true stoic knows that he does right in usually
choosing, for example, the course of action that promises to secure him
his health, but his goodness does not depend on his actually being
healthy; therefore he is emotionally detached, he neither desires to be
well nor fears sickness, neither feels glad in health nor sorrows if he falls
ill. The passions are wrong from their inception[5] in the false judgment
and must therefore be, not moderated, but extirpated[6] along with the
falsehood. The wise man is not, however, without emotions; his correct

---

[2] Stick, keep.   [5] Beginning.
[3] Demonstrated clearly.   [6] Destroyed.
[4] By its real nature.

judgments (that virtue and vice are good and bad) lead to moderate movements of his soul; he feels joy in his own virtue, repugnance for ill-doing and a wish to help his fellow-men to be good.

Questions for Discussion and Writing

1. In the popular view, Stoic philosophy is often characterized as an attitude of self-control and passive endurance of life's events, whether painful or plea-surable. How closely does this view match the original formulation of Stoicism, as Sandbach describes it?

2. Consider how a classical Stoic might view the situations described below (or suggest other situations that pose similar ethical questions). Compare your responses to those of other class members to see if different interpretations of Stoic values are possible.
   (a) The loss of a loved one
   (b) Dropping out of school
   (c) Teenage pregnancy
   (d) Joining a religious cult

3. According to Stoic philosophy, "Wickedness is closely associated with the passions." In how many other philosophical schools of thought do we see this attitude expressed? Consider especially Platonism, Christianity, Romantic philosophy, and medieval views.

4. Stoicism was an influential school of thought during the time of Caligula, as depicted in an excerpt from Suetonius in Chapter 5. Can one say that the historical reality made people more disposed to accept Stoic values? Would you expect to see a resurgence of Stoic values in later periods of political terror and chaos? Consider the situations depicted in the excerpt from Tuchman's *A Distant Mirror,* Parry's "Robespierre's Bloody Virtue," and Farmer's "A Night of Terror in Plaquemine, Louisiana, 1963."

5. Sandbach explains that for a Stoic, many of the things traditionally considered good in themselves, such as health, wealth, and reputation, are morally indifferent. Does this belief make the philosophical school of Stoicism more in tune with or less relevant to contemporary attitudes?

Sharon Curtin, **"Letty the Bag Lady"** _____

The problem of the homeless today has gained much attention from the media, but little social change has occurred and the street population of the United States continues to increase. The homeless are a diverse group: their numbers include families displaced by unemployment, single parents with children, the mentally ill discharged from public hospitals, substance abusers, runaways, and other Americans for whom traditional patterns of living are impossible, unavailable, or undesirable. In the following essay, Sharon Curtin describes one homeless person whose situation illustrates some of the harsh realities that face the poor and dis-enfranchised today, women and the elderly in particular.

Letty the Bag Lady lived in a "Single Room Occupancy" hotel approved by the New York City welfare department and occupied by old losers, junkies, cockroaches and rats. Whenever she left her room—a tiny cubicle with a cot, a chair, a seven-year-old calendar and a window so filthy it blended with the unspeakable walls—she would pack all her valuables in two large shopping bags and carry them with her. If she didn't, everything would disappear when she left the hotel. Her "things" were also a burden. Everything she managed to possess was portable and had multiple uses (a shawl is more versatile than a sweater, and hats are no good at all, although she used to have lots of nice hats, she told me). Or was something she had to have, like the oversized leatherette covered Bible occupying a full quarter of one bag, in five-color-illustrated glory.

Letty was pretty crazy and she knew it. I think she even liked being old and frightening. "Scare babies in the womb, I do, this face of mine never was pretty, and time pulls and tugs it in all different directions like an old sweater sagging; and people stop and stare at me in the street. Stupid bastards, I say, someday you'll be old and ugly and hungry. And I'll be among the heavenly hosts, laughing my fool head off—at all of you with your wrinkle cremes and diet soda and wigs and paint. Dead before you live, I say, all of you are dead before you live. Ugly as sin but leastways I had a real life!"

So Letty and I agreed that she was pretty crazy, and she thought I was insane, should be locked up for morbid interests in old rotten bodies. Tested for queer ideas, and stopped from bothering people. She couldn't accept my simple-minded well-I-just-want-to-know explanation. And if I made things more complicated she'd shake her head and call me a mind-bending fool.

The first day I saw Letty I had left my apartment in search of a "bag lady." I had seen these women around the city frequently, had spoken to a few. (Including one episode early in my New York experience when I offered, Wyoming Girl Scout fashion, to carry an old woman's bags. Her response was direct, sudden, and a true learning experience. She whomped me with her umbrella.) Sitting around the parks—Tompkins Square, upper Broadway, Union Square—had taught me more about these city vagabonds. As a group, few were eligible for social security. They had always been flotsam and jetsam, floating from place to place and from job to job—waitress, short order cook, sales clerk, stock boy, maid, mechanic, porter—all those jobs held by faceless people. The "bag ladies" were a special breed. They looked and acted and dressed strangely in some of the most determinedly conformist areas of the city. They frequented Fourteenth Street downtown, and the fancy shopping districts uptown. They seemed to like crowds but remained alone. They held long conversations with themselves, with telephone poles, with unexpected cracks in the sidewalk. They hung around lunch counters and cafeterias, and could remain impervious to the rudeness of a determined waitress and sit for hours clutching a coffee cup full of cold memories.

Letty was my representative bag lady. I had picked her up on the corner of Fourteenth and Third Avenue. She had the most suspicious face I had encountered; her entire body, in fact, was pulled forward in one large question mark. She was carrying a double plain brown shopping bag and a larger white bag ordering you to vote for some obscure man for some obscure office and we began talking about whether or not she was an unpaid advertisement. This immediately caught her interest, because part of her code was that nobody could ever cheat her or take advantage of her. I asked her if she would have lunch with me, and let me treat, as a matter of fact. After some hesitation and a few sharp glances over the top of her glasses (this is at high noon in a big city. I don't know what she was afraid of; I guess I just looked weird to her), Letty the Bag Lady let me come into her life. We had lunch that day, the next, and later the next week.

Being a bag lady was a full-time job. Take the problem of the hotels. You can't stay too long in any one of those welfare hotels, Letty told me, because the junkies figure out your routine, and when you get your checks, and you'll be robbed, even killed. So you have to move a lot. And every time you move, you have to make three trips to the welfare office to get them to approve the new place, even if it's just another cockroach-filled, rat-infested hole in the wall. During the last five years, Letty tried to move every two or three months. "You can't ever fix a place up, you know, really clean it or put up curtains and maybe a picture or two because you can't stay, can't get attached. Seems to me I been moving in and out of the same hotel room for the last seven years. Shit-colored floors, shit-colored walls, and the john down the hall a mile, with no lock on the door. Never any time to just settle in, or make a friend. You can't trust anyone, they'll say they're your friend today and tomorrow be pounding you on the head and stealing your things. Like I didn't want to talk to you, you didn't look like a junkie or a pross, but I was afraid you thought I was some rich eccentric, I walk around in these rags because I want to, and the bags are full of money. I been mugged so many times by kids thinking I had money. I may be plenty eccentric, but I sure ain't rich. Maybe I could get a sign or a button like all the kids wear that says I am just as poor as I look, and I look this way because I'm poor. I used to love pretty clothes, I'd save all my money to buy a dress to wear just once. And now I'm lucky to have a change of clothes for the change in seasons."

Most of our conversations took place standing in line. New York State had just changed the regulations governing Medicaid cards and Letty had to get a new card. That took two hours in line, one hour sitting in a large dank-smelling room, and two minutes with a social worker who never once looked up. Another time, her case worker at the welfare office sent Letty to try and get food stamps, and after standing in line for three hours she found out she didn't qualify because she didn't have cooking facilities in her room. "This is my social life," she said. "I run around the city and stand in line. You stand in line to see one of them fancy movies with people making love right in front of everybody and calling it art; I stand in line for medicine, for food, for glasses, for the cards to get pills, for the pills; I stand in line to see people who never see who I am; at the hotel, sometimes I even have to stand in line to go to the john. When I die there'll probably be a line to get through the gate, and when I get up to the front of the line, somebody will push it closed and say, 'Sorry. Come back after lunch.' These agencies, I figure they have to make it as hard for you to get help as they can, so only really strong people or really stubborn people like me can survive. All the rest die. Standing in line."

Letty would talk and talk; sometimes, she didn't seem to know I was even there. She never remembered my name, and would give a little start of surprise whenever I said hers, as if it had been a long time since anyone had said "Letty." I don't think she thought of herself as a person, anymore; I think she had accepted the view that she was a welfare case, a Medicaid card, a nuisance in the bus depot in the winter time, a victim to any petty criminal, existing on about the same level as cockroaches.

Over and over again, she would ask me why I bothered to talk to her, and when I said that I just wanted to get to know a "bag lady" she would laugh and say, "Yeah. A bag lady. To you I'm a bag lady."

Letty didn't show for our next meeting. I walked the streets, seeing hundreds of old ladies like her, but no Letty. I didn't know where she lived, didn't even know her last name. There was no way to find her; I couldn't go to the police or any agency. She may have died in one of those weekly fires New York has in old hotels; she may have become so freaky she was locked up in Bellevue. Her body could have been in any one of the alleys on the lower East Side, or she could be buried in Potter's Field.

Questions for Discussion and Writing

1. Define the term *bag lady,* using Letty and her situation as an example.

2. "Letty the Bag Lady" was written in 1972. Is Letty typical of the street people seen in American cities and towns today?

3. Analyze how Letty's attitudes toward possessions and survival in the "big city" can be considered Stoic. Are newcomers to American street life, such as displaced families, likely to express views similar to Letty's? Why or why not?

4. Which parts of Letty's life-style could be endorsed by a Stoic, and which would be considered "inappropriate," as you interpret Stoic values?

5. In one view, the homeless are victims of our government's failure to provide for the poor; in another, they are seen as willful dropouts from the social order who refuse to seek jobs or other means of bettering their situation.

From a Stoic point of view, is the street person likely to be held responsible for his or her situation? Is the condition of living on the streets, as embodied in Letty's situation, a necessarily evil one, as a Stoic would define evil?

Joseph Epstein, *"The Virtues of Ambition"* _____

Writing in defense of a more honorable tradition of ambition than what he believes the term evokes today, the contemporary essayist Joseph Epstein sees ambition as a necessary ingredient of the full life. His appeal may find a sympathetic response among certain social groups of contemporary society, such as the young upwardly mobile professionals. He places aspirations for success in the context of a larger philosophic tradition, however, rather than in terms of social class.

Ambition is one of those Rorschach[1] words: define it and you instantly reveal a great deal about yourself. Even that most neutral of works, Webster's in its Seventh New Collegiate Edition, gives itself away, defining ambition first and foremost as "an ardent desire for rank, fame, or power." Ardent immediately assumes a heat incommensurate[2] with good sense and stability, and rank, fame, and power have come under fairly heavy attack for at least a century. One can, after all, be ambitious for the public good, for the alleviation of suffering, for the enlightenment of mankind, though there are some who say that these are precisely the ambitious people most to be distrusted.

Surely ambition is behind dreams of glory, of wealth, of love, of distinction, of accomplishment, of pleasure, of goodness. What life does with our dreams and expectations cannot, of course, be predicted. Some dreams, begun in selflessness, end in rancor; other dreams, begun in selfishness, end in large-heartedness. The unpredictability of the outcome of dreams is no reason to cease dreaming.

To be sure, ambition, the sheer thing unalloyed[3] by some larger purpose than merely clambering up, is never a pretty prospect to ponder. As drunks have done to alcohol, the single-minded have done to ambition—given it a bad name. Like a taste for alcohol, too, ambition does not always allow for easy satiation.[4] Some people cannot handle it; it has brought grief to others, and not merely the ambitious alone. Still, none of this seems sufficient cause for driving ambition under the counter.

What is the worst that can be said—that has been said—about ambition? Here is a (surely) partial list:

To begin with, it, ambition, is often antisocial, and indeed is now outmoded, belonging to an age when individualism was more valued and

---

[1] Psychological personality test.
[2] Not equal.
[3] Pure; unmixed.
[4] Fulfillment, satisfaction.

useful than it is today. The person strongly imbued[5] with ambition ignores the collectivity; socially detached, he is on his own and out for his own. Individuality and ambition are firmly linked. The ambitious individual, far from identifying himself and his fortunes with the group, wishes to rise above it. The ambitious man or woman sees the world as a battle; rivalrousness is his or her principal emotion: the world has limited prizes to offer, and he or she is determined to get his or hers. Ambition is, moreover, jesuitical;[6] it can argue those possessed by it into believing that what they want for themselves is good for everyone—that the satisfaction of their own desires is best for the commonweal.[7] The truly ambitious believe that it is a dog-eat-dog world, and they are distinguished by wanting to be the dogs that do the eating.

From here it is but a short hop to believe that those who have achieved the common goals of ambition—money, fame, power—have achieved them through corruption of a greater or lesser degree, mostly a greater. Thus all politicians in high places, thought to be ambitious, are understood to be, ipso facto,[8] without moral scruples. How could they have such scruples—a weighty burden in a high climb—and still have risen as they have?

If amibition is to be well regarded, the rewards of ambition—wealth, distinction, control over one's destiny—must be deemed worthy of the sacrifices made on ambition's behalf. If the tradition of ambition is to have vitality, it must be widely shared; and it especially must be esteemed by people who are themselves admired, the educated not least among them. The educated not least because, nowadays more than ever before, it is they who have usurped the platforms of public discussion and wield the power of the spoken and written word in newspapers, in magazines, on television. In an odd way, it is the educated who have claimed to have given up on ambition as an ideal. What is odd is that they have perhaps most benefited from ambition—if not always their own then that of their parents and grandparents. There is a heavy note of hypocrisy in this; a case of closing the barn door after the horses have escaped—with the educated themselves astride them.

Certainly people do not seem less interested in success and its accoutrements[9] now than formerly. Summer homes, European travel, BMWs—the locations, place names and name brands may change, but such items do not seem less in demand today than a decade or two years ago. What has happened is that people cannot own up to their dreams, as easily and openly as once they could, lest they be thought pushing, acquisitive, vulgar. Instead we are treated to fine pharisaical[10] spectacles, which now more than ever seem in ample supply: the revolutionary lawyer quartered in the $250,000 Manhattan condominium; the critic of

[5] Colored with.
[6] Imposing one's values.
[7] Everyone's well-being.

[8] By the facts themselves.
[9] Accompanying objects.
[10] Hypocritically self-righteous.

American materialism with a Southampton summer home; the publisher of radical books who takes his meals in three-star restaurants; the journalist advocating participatory democracy in all phases of life, whose own children are enrolled in private schools. For such people and many more perhaps not so egregious,[11] the proper formulation is, "Succeed at all costs but refrain from appearing ambitious."

The attacks on ambition are many and come from various angles; its public defenders are few and unimpressive, where they are not extremely unattractive. As a result, the support for ambition as a healthy impulse, a quality to be admired and inculcated in the young, is probably lower than it has ever been in the United States. This does not mean that ambition is at an end. That people no longer feel its stirrings and promptings, but only that, no longer openly honored, it is less often openly professed. Consequences follow from this, of course, some of which are that ambition is driven underground, or made sly, or perverse. It can also be forced into vulgarity, as witness the blatant pratings of its contemporary promoters. Such, then, is the way things stand: on the left angry critics, on the right obtuse supporters, and in the middle, as usual, the majority of earnest people trying to get on in life.

Many people are naturally distrustful of ambition, feeling that it represents something intractable[12] in human nature. Thus John Dean entitled his book about his involvement in the Watergate affair during the Nixon administration *Blind Ambition,* as if ambition were to blame for his ignoble actions, and not the constellation of qualities that make up his rather shabby character. Ambition, it must once be underscored, is morally a two-sided street. Place next to John Dean Andrew Carnegie, who, among other philanthropic acts, bought the library of Lord Acton, at a time when Acton was in financial distress, and assigned its custodianship to Acton, who never was told who his benefactor was. Need much more be said on the subject than that, important though ambition is, there are some things that one must not sacrifice to it?

But going at things the other way, sacrificing ambition so as to guard against its potential excesses, is to go at things wrongly. To discourage ambition is to discourage dreams of grandeur and greatness. All men and women are born, live, suffer, and die; what distinguishes us one from another is our dreams, whether they be dreams about worldly or unworldly things, and what we do to make them come about.

It may seem an exaggeration to say that ambition is the linchpin[13] of society, holding many of its disparate[14] elements together, but it is not an exaggeration by much. Remove ambition and the essential elements of society seem to fly apart. Ambition, as opposed to mere fantisizing about desires, implies work and discipline to achieve goals, personal and social, of a kind society cannot survive without. Ambition is intimately con-

---

[11] Very bad.
[12] Hard to control.
[13] Central part.
[14] Different.

nected with family, for men and women not only work partly for their families; husbands and wives are often ambitious for each other, but harbor some of their most ardent ambitions for their children. Yet to have a family nowadays—with birth control readily available, and inflation a good economic argument against having children—is merely an expression of ambition in itself. Finally, though ambition was once the domain chiefly of monarchs and aristocrats, it has, in more recent times increasingly become the domain of the middle classes. Ambition and futurity—a sense of building for tomorrow—are inextricable. Working, saving, planning—these, the daily aspects of ambition—have always been the distinguishing marks of a rising middle class. The attack against ambition is not incidentally an attack on the middle class and what it stands for. Like it or not, the middle class has done much of society's work in America; and it, the middle class, has from the beginning run on ambition.

It is not difficult to imagine a world shorn of ambition. It would probably be a kinder world: without demands, without abrasions, without disappointments. People would have time for reflection. Such work as they did would not be for themselves but for the collectivity. Competition would never enter in. Conflict would be eliminated, tension become a thing of the past. The stress of creation would be at an end. Art would no longer be troubling, but purely celebratory in its functions. The family would become superfluous as a social unit, with all its former power for bringing about neurosis drained away. Longevity would be increased, for fewer people would die of heart attack or stroke caused by tumultuous endeavor. Anxiety would be extinct. Time would stretch on and on, with ambition long departed from the human heart.

Oh, how unrelievedly boring life would be!

There is a strong view that holds that success is a myth, and ambition therefore a sham. Does this mean that success does not really exist? That achievement is at bottom empty? That the efforts of men and women are of no significance alongside the force of movements and events? Now not all success, obviously, is worth esteeming, or all ambition worth cultivating. Which are and which are not is something one soon enough learns on one's own. But even the most cynical secretly admit that success exists; that achievement counts for a great deal; and that the true myth is that the actions of men and women are useless. To believe otherwise is to take on a point of view that is likely to be deranging. It is, in its implications, to remove all motive for competence, interest in attainment, and regard for posterity.

We do not choose to be born. We do not choose our parents. We do not choose our historical epoch, the country of our birth or the immediate circumstances of our upbringing. We do not, most of us, choose to die; nor do we choose the time or conditions of our death. But within all this realm of choicelessness, we do choose how we shall live: courageously or in cowardice, honorably or dishonorably, with purpose or in drift. We decide what is important and what is trivial in life. We decide that what makes us significant is either what we do or what we refuse to do. But no matter how indifferent the universe may be to our choices and decisions, these choices and decisions are ours to make. We decide. We choose. And as we decide and choose, so are our lives formed. In the end, forming our own destiny is what ambition is about.

Questions for Discussion and Writing

1. Define Epstein's concept of ambition in your own words.

2. According to the classical Stoic, "Every event in the whole universe is necessary, providential and due to the divine will." Given this belief, can a Stoic be an ambitious person, using Epstein's definition of ambition?

3. By using the term *virtues* in his essay title, Epstein makes his topic an ethical issue. Can you construct an opposing view of ambition as not an ethical but a practical issue of survival? Consider ambition as a psychological or biological function, for example.

4. How does Epstein connect ambition with concern for the collective good? Do you accept and can you find support for his view that the two are related?

5. Describe your conception of how an ambitious student behaves, using Epstein's definition of ambition. Do you endorse this model of student behavior? Why or why not?

George K. Strodach, from **The Philosophy of Epicurus** _____

Like Stoicism, Epicureanism has also become obsolete as an actual philosophical school, but as an attitude it too has influenced post-classical philosophical thought. In common use, the term "Epicureanism" suggests an attitude of abandon and pleasure-seeking, and an "Epicurean" sometimes means a person of sophistication, sensuality, and refined taste. These modern connotations have very little to do with the ancient philosophy of the Greek Epicurus (342?–270 B.C.), who emphasized avoidance of pain, not indulgence in pleasure; balance, not excess. In the following passage, the author clarifies the original doctrine and distinguishes it from hedonism, the more accurate term for "pleasure-seeking."

The Epicurean theory of the good life—that is, the life that is simultaneously satisfying and moral—had two aspects, one negative and the other positive. Before one can enjoy the fruits of living, one must free oneself of certain crippling liabilities. These liabilities, specifically, are the fear of gods, the fear of death, and the fear of the torments of hell. Both Epicurus and Lucretius took great pains to neutralize these fears and to show that they were utterly goundless.

The positive aspect of Epicurus' ethical teaching is known as hedonism, from the Greek noun for "pleasure." His hedonism has two basic assumptions, both materialistic in character: (a) the moral good is the same as pleasure, either physical or mental, since the experienceable range of pleasure is very wide and extends to more than one level; and (b) that moral evil is the same as pain, whether physical or mental.

Moral acts involve deliberate "choices" of possible concrete pleasures and "aversions," i.e., the deliberate avoidance of prospective pain. An act is moral if in the long run, all things considered, it produces in the agent a surplus of pleasure over pain; otherwise it is immoral. This working principle is applicable in literally thousands of cases of individual "choice and aversion" and can readily be illustrated by examples from our life today:

1. A student decides to cheat in a college exam in order to pull up his grade. Is this act moral by Epicurus' standards? (We will forget, for the time being, all other possible standards.) Suppose the student "gets away with it" this time. His "pleasure" is increased, but at the same time he is a little worried that he may have aroused the instructor's suspicions. Pleasure and pain are more or less evenly balanced, and it is impossible to tell in this instance whether the act is moral or immoral. Encouraged by this previous success, the same student decides to make a habit of cheating. Several alternatives are now possible: (a) The student may finally be detected and thrown out of college, in which case pain outweighs pleasure and the act is immoral. (b) The student may be clever and consistently avoid detection but at the same time experience a nagging anxiety, in which case pain probably is greater than pleasure and the act immoral. Or (c) he may consistently avoid detection and feel no qualms or anxiety whatever (and there seems to be plenty of this kind of student in the colleges today). In this case Epicurus would be forced to admit that the act is completely moral, since only pleasure is produced by it! However, the habit of successful cheating in college may well be carried over later into cheating in marriage and dishonesty in business, where the consequences may turn out to be more painful than pleasurable. The long-term effects of our habits are always pertinent judgments of moral and immoral.

2. A convivial[1] drinker who loves martinis may consume ten or more at a party and stay on his feet. Is this act moral by Epicurus' standards? We have to take into account not only the short-term effects (our friend enjoys himself hugely for two hours) but all the consequences. If he suffers no ill effects during the night or the next morning, the act is wholly pleasurable and therefore wholly moral; otherwise it is probably immoral, depending on the intensity of his hangover. (It was this sort of example that gave Epicureanism a "black eye." Epicurus himself would have frowned on it, since he disapproved, on principle, of sensuality, raw pleasure, and overindulgence. Nevertheless it is characteristic of "epicures" in every age and is certainly pertinent to modern living.)

---

[1] Liking food, drink, and good company.

This basic description of hedonism still needs certain important qualifications in order to fit Epicurus' own meaning of the term, but for the time being it is obvious that: (1) The pleasure-pain principle is extremely flexible and can be used to uphold both conventional and unconventional moral values. (2) Hedonism proceeds to judge an act as moral or immoral not by the act itself, nor by any hard and fast rules of behavior, nor by the dictates[2] of reason, but by the experience it produces, specifically the feelings of pleasure and pain resulting from the act. For Epicurus believed that these feelings were the only true and natural foundation for an empirical ethics. "Every pleasure is a good by reason of its having a nature akin to our own, but not every pleasure is desirable. In like manner every state of pain is an evil, but not all pains are uniformly to be rejected. (3) The ethics of hedonism is relative and not absolute, and the morality of many acts is ambiguous, since the value of a given act does not depend on the a priori[3] character of the act itself but on its psychological consequences, which of course differ from person to person and from time to time.

a. Pleasure is neutral or negative in meaning. The doctrine that pleasure is the highest ethical good lends itself immediately to serious misunderstanding because of the unfortunate ambiguity of the key term "pleasure." The Epicureans have been purposely misrepresented as sensualists and "high livers" by their rivals and detractors, both ancient and modern; for "pleasure" has been a "dirty word" in the eyes of many moralists and laymen in all periods of history. Actually the strict Epicurean sectarian[4] was rather ascetic[5] and even puritanical, both in teaching and in practice, and this fact is borne in on anyone who reads the surviving texts sympathetically. Epicurus regarded "pleasure" as the logical opposite of "pain"; in other words, for him pleasure meant nonpain, or the relative absence of pain in mind and body, i.e., both physical comfort or well-being and peace of mind. The good life, then, is quite simply one that daily and yearly conduces[6] to these ends. It is emphatically not a life of sensual enjoyments, excitement, competition, social prestige, and monetary success—all of which we in this country tend to believe constitute the good life, or what we call the "American way of life."

The good life for the Epicurean involved disciplining of the appetities, curtailment of desires and needs to the absolute minimum necessary for healthy living, detachment from most of the goals and values that are most highly regarded, and withdrawal from active participation in the life of the community, in the company of a few select friends—in a word, plain living and high thinking.

It will be seen from this that the Epicurean ideal is hardly what we

---

[2] Orders or commands.
[3] Theoretical.
[4] Member of a group.

[5] Strictly disciplined.
[6] Leads.

mean by a life of pleasure or even a pleasant life. The conception of pleasure is wholly negative—the minimizing of all the pains of living, great and small, and of the three besetting fears, and the maximizing of inner peace, serenity, and well-being. The ideal, then, in its strict interpretation is practically Oriental—the achieving of a Buddha-like tranquillity—with the difference, of course, that the Epicurean asserted the full reality of the physical world and did not seek to be absorbed into a mystical nirvana.[7]

b. Hedonism emphasizes rational selection of pleasures and pains. Although every pleasure is a natural good in itself and every pain a natural evil, not every pleasure is desirable, nor is every pain to be avoided. At this point a kind of prudential[8] process of calculation enters in, to prescribe the necessary conditions for a mature hedonism. Reasoning overlays the naivete of nature with wisdom and tries to guide it aright. Thus if one knows beforehand that ten martinis will result in a hangover, it is the part of wisdom to take only five. By the same token if surgery is indicated, it should be undergone for the sake of future comfort and safety. And if the typical American wants to "succeed" today, he must be sensible and undergo the pains of four years of college education. His present discomforts will pay handsome dividends in the future.

For example, if confronted with a choice between a simple and a luxurious diet, between obscurity and fame, between a life of contemplation and a life in politics, the strict Epicurean would always choose the less obvious value—simple diet, obscurity, and contemplation. He would much prefer to be a Thoreau or a Frost than board chairman of U.S. Steel or President of the United States. And indeed to choose the simple life has a certain wisdom, though from the American point of view it looks like sheer inertia, defeatism, or stupidity. It means choosing the way that very probably presents the fewest pains and disappointments rather than the way that seems to promise the largest number of positive satisfactions but contains many hidden frustrations, not to mention ulcers. The defensive and negative attitude to life was wisdom distilled from an age of troubles, when it did not pay to be either optimistic or enterprising.

c. Hedonism is deficient as a social ethic. The self-protective and individualistic attitude of Epicurus' hedonism prevented it from turning outward toward society at large and developing into a mature social ethic. True, it did emphasize friendship and the practice of gentleness and loving kindness among its members, and in fact actual religious fervor, in spreading the gospel of atomism[9] as a counterirritant to the phobias generated by popular religion. But these are not the same as a comprehensive theory for the welfare of society as a whole, such as John Stuart Mill developed in Victorian England from a hedonistic base. The altruistic[10] spirit of Mill's "greatest good for the greatest number"

---

[7] Union with God.
[8] Careful.

[9] Individualism.
[10] Selfless concern for others.

(which, incidentally, included the British working classes) was far different from Epicurus' introverted escapism: "Withdraw form the world;
avoid the pains and dangers of involvement; seek your own security and
serenity."

From the egocentric question, What acts are likely to bring me pain
or pleasure? it seems not too huge a step to the altruistic questions, What
acts of mine are likely to bring pain or pleasure to others? Do I have a
duty to increase the happinesss of others as well as my own happiness?
Can I be happy myself if I ignore the unhappiness of others around me?
Am I ever to suppress and sacrifice my own pleasure for the good of
others, including at times the community? A modern hedonist, with his
social conscience enlarged by the impact of Mill and others, would be
bound to seek answers to these questions and then go on to apply a new
version of the pleasure-pain principle to pressing current problems such
as anti-Semitism, racial discrimination, world overpopulations, ther-
monuclear war, the growth of Communism, and others. The student
should let his mind play over the whole range of these social and political
problems, consider their vast implications for human happiness and
unhappiness, and then finally ask himself whether Epicurus' advice—
"Seek your own security and peace of mind"—is adequate for our own
age of troubles.

Questions for Discussion and Writing

1. Strodach uses examples from daily life to illustrate how Epicurean thought
   works. Generate in class discussion several examples of situations that
   involve ethical issues (such as exaggerating work experience on a resume,
   deciding not to tell a friend that the friend's boyfriend/girlfriend asked you
   out) and analyze their moral worth in Epicurean terms.

2. How might a purely hedonistic person behave in contemporary times?
   Would any of the interests and activities you imagine as part of a hedonistic
   life-style be judged morally worthy according to classical Epicurean values?

3. If you have or plan to have a family, would you find Epicurean teachings a
   satisfactory basis for the moral education of children? Explain the reasoning
   behind your response.

4. Using Strodach's summary of Epicureanism in paragraph 8, determine the
   degree of similarity to Epicurean thought in the ideas of the following figures.
   (a) Socrates (in Plato, *Symposium,* Chapter 1)
   (b) Martin Luther (in Grimm, "The Growth of Lutheranism," Chapter 2)
   (c) Emerson (in Atkinson, "Emerson," Chapter 2)
   (d) Freud (in Kagan and Havemann, "Psychoanalytic Theory," Chapter 3)
   (e) Robespierre (in Parry, "Robespierre's Bloody Virtue," Chapter 5)
   (f) Malcolm X ("The Ballot or the Bullet," Chapter 5)

Margaret Halsey, **"What's Wrong with 'Me, Me, Me'?"** _____

*In the following polemical essay (a strongly argued opinion piece),
Margaret Halsey condemns the uninhibited pursuit of selfish satisfaction*

*that she contends has pervaded—and helped corrupt—American society
since the 1960s. Adopting Freud's often negative view of human nature,
she rebuts the notion of a perfect inner self that the individual can and
should seek out and nurture. Written in the context of the affluent American consumer society, her essay addresses a more contemporary notion of
Epicureanism that what the classical philosopher Epicurus had in mind.*

Tom Wolfe has christened today's young adults the "me" generation, and the 1970's—obsessed with things like consciousness expansion
and self-awareness—have been described as the decade of the new
narcissism. The cult of "I," in fact, has taken hold with the strength and
impetus of a new religion. But the joker in the pack is that it is all based
on a false idea.

The false idea is that inside every human being, however un-
prepossessing, there is a glorious, talented and overwhelmingly attractive
personality. This personality—so runs the erroneous belief—will be
revealed in all its splendor if the individual just forgets about courtesy,
cooperativeness and consideration for others and proceeds to do exactly
what he or she feels like doing.

Nonsense.

Inside each of us is a mess of unruly primitive impulses, and these
can sometimes, under the strenuous self-discipline and dedication of art,
result in notable creativity. But there is no such thing as a pure,
crystalline and well-organized "native" personality, though a host of
trendy human-potential groups trade on the mistaken assumption that
there is. And backing up the human-potential industry is the advertising
profession, which also encourages the idea of an Inner Wonderfulness
that will be unveiled to a suddenly respectful world upon the purchase of
this or that commodity.

However, an individual does not exist in a vacuum. A human being
is not an isolated, independent thing-in-itself, but inevitably reflects the
existence of others. The young adults of the "me" generation would
never have lived to grow up if a great many parents, doctors, nurses,
farmers, factory workers, teachers, policemen, firemen and legions of
others had not ignored their human potential and made themselves do
jobs they did not perhaps feel like doing in order to support the health
and growth of children.

And yet, despite the indulgence of uninhibited expression, the
"self" in self-awareness seems to cause many new narcissists and members of the "me" generation a lot of trouble. This trouble emerges in talk
about "identity." We hear about the search for identity and a kind of
distress called an identity crisis.

"I don't know who I am." How many bartenders and psychiatrists
have stifled yawns on hearing that popular threnody[1] for the thousandth
time!

---

[1] Sad, grieving song.

But this sentence has no meaning unless spoken by an amnesia victim, because many of the people who say they do not know who they are actually do know. What such people really mean is that they are not satisfied with who they are. They feel themselves to be timid and color-less or to be in some way or other fault-ridden, but they have soaked up enough advertising and enough catch-penny ideas of self-improvement to believe in universal Inner Wonderfulnesss. So they turn their backs on their honest knowledge of themselves—which with patience and cour-age could start them on the road to genuine development—and embark on a quest for a will-o'-the-wisp called "identity."

But a search for identity is predestined to fail. Identity is not found, the way Pharaoh's daughter found Moses in the bulrushes. Identity is built. It is built every day and every minute throughout the day. The myriad[2] choices, small and large, that human beings make all the time determine identity. The fatal weakness of the currently fashionable ap-proach to personality is that the "self" of the self-awareness addicts, the self of Inner Wonderfulness, is static. Being perfect, it does not need to change. But genuine identity changes as one matures. If it does not, if the 40-year-old has an identity that was set in concrete at the age of 18, he or she is in trouble.

The idea of a universal Inner Wonderfulness that will be apparent to all beholders after a six-week course in self-expression is fantasy.

But how did this fantasy gain wide popular acceptance as a realiza-ble fact?

Every society tries to produce a prevalent psychological type that will best serve its ends, and that type is always prone to certain emotional malfunctions. In early capitalism, which was a producing society, the ideal type was acquisitive, fanatically devoted to hard work and fiercely repressive of sex. The emotional malfunctions to which this type was liable were hysteria and obsession. Later capitalism, today's capitalism, is a consuming society, and the psychological type it strives to create, in order to build up the largest possible markets, is shallow, easily swayed and characterized much more by self-infatuation than self-respect. The emotional malfunction of this type is narcissism.

It will be argued that the cult of "I" has done some individuals a lot of good. But at whose expense? What about the people to whom these "healthy" egoists are rude or even abusive? What about the people over whom they ride roughshod[3]? What about the people they manipulate and exploit? And—the most important question of all—how good a preparation for inevitable old age and death is a deliberately cultivated self-love? The psychologists say that the full-blown classic narcissists lose all dignity and go mad with fright as they approach their final dissolution. Ten or fifteen years from now—when the young adults of the "me" generation hit middle age—will be the time to ask whether "self-awareness" really does people any good.

---

[2] Many.

[3] Roughly, without respect.

A long time ago, in a book called *Civilization and Its Discontents,* Freud pointed out that there is an unresolvable conflict between the human being's selfish, primitive, infantile impulses and the restraint he or she must impose on those impulses if a stable society is to be maintained. The "self" is not a handsome god or goddess waiting coyly to be revealed. On the contrary, its complexity, confusion and mystery have proved so difficult that throughout the ages men and women have talked gratefully about losing themselves. They lose the self in contemplating a great work of art, or in nature, or in scientific research, or in writing poetry, or in fashioning things with their hands or in projects that will benefit others rather than themselves.

The current glorification of self-love will turn out in the end to be a no-win proposition, because in questions of personality or "identity," what counts is not who you are, but what you do. "By their fruits, ye shall know them." And by their fruits, they shall know themselves.

Questions for Discussion and Writing

1. What does Halsey mean by the term *the cult of 'I'?*
2. Halsey argues that the "real" person is a collection of selfish, primitive urges. How does that notion conflict with the "me" generation's definition of self, as Halsey reads it?
3. Does Halsey's view of human nature reflect the view of it promoted by Epicurean philosophy? In the Epicureans view, where does evil come from?
4. To what extent do you find evidence of the "me generation" in the media and entertainment fields? Consider examples from the music, film, television, and advertising industries: do they promote the kind of aesthetic that Halsey argues against?
5. Do the characteristics of the "me" generation described in Halsey's essay apply to the "yuppies" of the 1980s? If so, how? Do you think the 1990s will have its own version of the type, or can we expect a swing back to more community-oriented values and definitions?

Gwendolyn Brooks, **"The Pool Players"** _____

The prize-winning African-American poet Gwendolyn Brooks explores in her work the common experience of blacks, particularly urban blacks, in modern American society. "The Pool Players" captures the urban aesthetic, the street life charm that lures many young people with its flash and fast pace. It also suggests the price that living the aesthetic exacts.

"The Pool Players"

Seven at the Golden Shovel

We real cool. We
Left school We

Lurk late. We
Strike straight. We

Sing sin. We
Thin gin. We

Jazz June. We
Die soon.

Questions for Discussion and Writing

1. Describe your reactions to reading the poem. Which of its features catch the reader's attention—the imagery, the rhythm, the personality of the speakers, some other element(s)?

2. Does Brooks seek to make the reader feel the pleasure of the pool players' life-style, or is the reader meant to take a dim view of it?

3. Why did Brooks choose to use the collective voice "we" as the speaker in her poem?

4. Can the attitudes of the pool players be considered Epicurean? Why or why not?

Farrand Sayre, from **The Greek Cynics** ————————————————

In ancient times, Cynicism was not a systematic philosophy in the same way as Stoicism or Epicureanism. Because indifference and apathy characterize the Cynic's attitude, none of the classical Cynics chose to write down any formal theory. Accounts of the life of the famous Cynic philosopher Diogenes (412?-323 B.C.) do exist, however, and many stories that illustrate his views have been handed down over the ages. Following Sayre's essay is an example of one such tale of Diogenes' life, this one recounted by the ancient fabulist Aesop.

The object of Cynicism was happiness.

The Cynics sought happiness through freedom. The Cynic conception of freedom included freedom from desires, from fear, anger, grief and other emotions, from religious or moral control, from the authority of the city or state or public officials, from regard for public opinion and freedom also from the care of property, from confinement of any locality and from the care and support of wives and children.

As a result of the quest for freedom the Cynics were extreme individualists. The quest was personal and the Cynic had no loyalty to family, state, or race. He did not discriminate against any race or nationality because he did not favor any. "We should not give thanks to our parents—either because we were born, since creatures are generated by nature—nor on account of what we are for this results from a combination of elements. And there should be no gratitude for what comes by choice and purpose." "Whoever trusts us will remain single, those who do not trust us will rear children. And if the race of men should cease to exist, there would be as much cause for regret as there would be if the flies and wasps should pass away."

The Cynic virtues were the qualities through which freedom was attained. The description of Cynicism as "the pursuit of virtue" mistakes the means for the end and is misleading. The most important of these virtues was callousness, insensibility or apathy; it was associated with indifference. Julian is inconsistent in saying; "Apathy they (Cynics) regard as the end and aim," for apathy was only a means to an end. The Cynics regarded peace of mind as happiness or an essential element of it.

An important Cynic virtue was hardihood, ruggedness or endurance. It may be regarded as the physical form of apathy. It was said to have been attained or promoted by hardening exercises but with the later Cynics it came to mean the ability to endure the hardships incident to the Cynic form of life. The opposite of this virtue was softness, effeminacy or foppery, the vice most frequently and most severely denounced by the Cynics. Diogenes was said to have rolled in his earthenware jar over hot sand, to have walked barefooted over snow and to have embraced a bronze statue in freezing weather.

The Cynic principle of apathy naturally led to idleness, for if a Cynic engaged in any form of work he would thereby show a lack of apathy; and work under the control of an employer was inconsistent with the Cynic conception of freedom. Diogenes was quoted as saying; "Instead of useless toils men should choose such as nature recommends, whereby they might have lived happily." Chrysippus was credited with expressing many Cynic ideas and the following seems to be one of them: "What reason is there that he (the wise man) should provide a living? For if it be to support life, life itself is after all a thing indifferent. If it be for pleasure, pleasure too is a thing indifferent. While it be for virtue, virtue in itself is sufficient to constitute happiness. The modes of getting a livelihood are also ludicrous."

Poverty was an important Cynic virtue; it freed the Cynic from the care of property, from worry over losses and from confinement to any locality. It left him free to wander from city to city, from state to state and from country to country. It also partially explains the Cynic idleness, for he did not have the ordinary incentive to labor.

The Cynics did not express any sympathy for the poor for, in their opinion, the poor possessed the conditions of happiness, freedom and virtue. Neither were they friends, advocates and defenders of the poor, as they have sometimes been said to be. The possession of property was an encumbrance and a disadvantage. The Cynic's repudiation of possessions led them to ignore the property rights of other men and explains their thievery. One of the best known traditions of the Cynics was the following, which was attributed to Diogenes: "All things belong to the gods; the gods are friends of the wise and friends share all property in common; therefore all things are the property of the wise." The Cynics interpreted this to mean that they were free to take anything they wanted and could lay their hands on.

The Cynics held that laws were made by men no wiser than themselves and that customs and conventionalities differed in different countries and consequently had no validity. Their quest of freedom led them to disregard both; it also led them to disregard public opinion, reputation, honor and dishonor.

Disregard of honor and reputation was developed into open defiance of public opinion by shamelessness. "It was his (Diogenes) habit to do everything in public, the works of Demeter[1] and of Aphrodite[2] alike . . . Behaving indecently in public, he wished it were as easy to banish hunger by rubbing the belly." Epictetus says: "He ought not to wish to hide anything that he does, and if he does, he is gone, he has lost the character of a Cynic, of a man who lives under the open sky, of a free man." Julian said, "The cities of Greece were averse to the excessive plainness and simplicity of the Cynic freedom of manner." Lucian represents a Cynic as saying: "Away with modesty, good nature and forbearance. Wipe the blush from your cheek forever . . . Scruple not to perform the deeds of darkness in broad daylight. Select your love adventures with a view to public entertainment." Dio Chrysostom described Diogenes as terminating a discourse by squatting down and evacuating his bowels in the presence of his hearers. Epictetus said: "The present Cynics are dogs that wait at tables and in no respect imitate the Cynics of old, except perchance in breaking wind but in nothing else." This seems to have been a Cynic characteristic. Julian describes Diogenes as striking a youth with his staff for breaking wind in public and thus infringing on a Cynic prerogative. The Cynic displayed his hardihood, his apathy, his courage and his freedom by affronting and shocking public opinion.

The Cynics scoffed at the customs and conventionalities of others, but were rigid in observance of their own. The Cynic would not appear anywhere without his wallet, staff and cloak, which must invariably be worn, dirty and ragged and worn so as to leave the right shoulder bare. He never wore shoes and his hair and beard were long and unkempt.

Although the Cynics repudiated learning, they claimed to possess wisdom; for did they not know the road to happiness? "To the man who said to him (Diogenes), 'You don't know anything, although you are a philosopher,' he replied, 'Even if I am but a pretender to wisdom, that in itself is philosophy'." This seems to be an admission that the Cynic claim to possess wisdom was not based on learning. The Cynics asserted their wisdom by criticising and denouncing other men. Epictetus describes the ordinary conduct of a Cynic of his time as follows; "I will take a little bag and a staff and I will go about and begin to beg and to abuse those whom I meet; and if I see any man plucking the hair out of his body, I will rebuke him, or if he has dressed his hair or if he walks about in purple." "They (Cynics) are full of empty boasting and if one of them grows a long beard and elevates his eyebrows and throws his cloak over his shoulder, and goes barefooted, he claims straightway wisdom and courage and virtue, and gives himself great airs, though he may not know his letters, nor, as the saying goes, how to swim. They despise everyone, and call the

[1] Relieving oneself.   [2] Making love.

man of good family effeminate, the low born poor spirited, the handsome man a debauchee,[3] the ugly person simple minded, the rich covetous and the poor greedy." Lucian wrote: "As soon as I came to Elis, in going up by way of the gymnasium, I overheard a Cynic bawling out the usual street corner invocation to Virtue in a loud harsh voice and abusing every one without exception."

The Cynics claimed that, as wise men, they formed a class having special privileges; among these privileges was the right to collect contributions from every one, the right to be supported by the community and the right to express themselves fully to every one at all times. "Being asked what was the most beautiful thing in the world, he (Diogenes) replied, 'Freedom of Speech'."

The Cynic claim to wisdom raised a question as to how they attained it. Dio Chrysostom says that the wise man is "noble by nature" and "does not have to learn." Julian said that Cynicism, being a natural philosophy, "demands no special study whatever." Plutarch says: "The wise man, in a moment of time, changes from the lowest possible depravity to an unsurpassable state of virtue. . . . The man who was the very worst in the morning becomes the very best at evening. . . . He who was a worthless dolt when he fell asleep awakes wise." Plutarch ascribes this theory to the Stoics and he is opposing it, but he must have been referring to Cynics, for the Stoics did not class any one as wise, except Socrates and Antisthenes. For the Stoics, the wise man was an ideal. Wisdom was a goal which they might seek but could not attain.

The Cynics showed their apathy also in their attitude toward death and suicide. "Diogenes somewhere says that there is only one way to freedom and that is to die content." It is only in death that a man can attain complete apathy. "Diogenes, being asked who were the noblest men, said 'Those despising wealth, learning, pleasure and life; esteeming above them poverty, ignorance, hardship and death'." An empty, ideal and aimless life leads to nothing but boredom and misery; the Cynics may have shown some acknowledgment of this in their mention of suicide as "The open door." Teles says; "A man can readily find release, for just as he leaves an assembly, so he can take his departure from life—as Bion says 'to go out-doors' . . . Just as I depart from a banquet, so I will depart from life . . . I am not overly fond of life and I do not desire to prolong it, but as I am unable to find happiness, I will depart." Athenaeus quoted Antisthenes as saying, "Deliver your selves from life." Some of the stories of the death of Diogenes represented him as committing suicide.

The Cynics, in seeking freedom, rejected marriage and the rearing of children, repudiated obligations to parents and the state and avoided friendships. Lucian represents a Cynic as saying: "With wife and children and country you will not concern yourself. . . . You will live alone in the

---

[3] Someone perverted or morally corrupt.

midst of the city, holding communion with no one, admitting neither friend nor guest, for such would undermine your power." "They (Cynics) consider friends as insincere and faithless, consequently, they trust no one." Tertullian represents a Cynic as saying: "I have withdrawn from the populace. My only business is with myself . . . None is born for another, being destined to die for himself."

The Cynics were not Socratics; their teaching was opposed to that of Socrates in almost every respect. The distinction between right and wrong did not enter into Cynicism. It was the problem of the Cynic to seek happiness and freedom and the avoidance of what was wrong would restrict his freedom. The Stoics claimed succession from Socrates but we have no evidence that the Cynics did so.

The Cynics had no canon or authoritative writing, such as the Epicureans had in the writings of Epicurus. They were illiterates and wrote nothing. Julian said: "If the Cynics had composed treatises with any serious purposes . . .it would have been proper for my opponent to be guided by them . . . but nothing of that sort exists." Our knowledge of them is derived from observers who were not Cynics; but these were not all antagonistic. The Stoics regarded their origin as connected with that of the Cynics and were inclined to take a favorable view of them.

The Cynic traditions were oral and consisted for the most part of stories of Diogenes, a semi-mythical character; since little was known about him, he was a convenient vehicle on which the Cynics could locate stories expressing their ideas.

The Cynics attacked and ridiculed religion, philosophy, science, art, literature, love, friendship, good manners, loyalty to parents and the state, and even athletics—everything which tended to embellish and enrich human life, to give it significance and make it worth living. The callous amoralism expressed by the word "cynicism" reflects the impression made by them upon their contemporaries.

The Cynics did much to prepare the way for Christianity by destroying respect for existing religions, by ignoring distinctions of race and nationality and by instituting an order of wandering preachers claiming exceptional freedom of speech. Tertullian says that early Christian preachers adopted the Cynic cloak, and Augustine mentioned the club or staff as the only distinctive feature of the Cynics. Julian mentioned the similarity of methods of the Cynics and the Christians in their public discourses and their collections of contributions. Lucian describes cooperation between Cynics and Christians (Peregrinus). The early Christians worked side by side with Cynics for three hundred years and were to some extent influenced by them. We do not know of any early Christian arts, music, literature or sciences. Early Christian orders of priesthood accepted celibacy and poverty as virtues. The Dominicans explained their designation by saying that they were "Domini canes" (dogs of the Lord).

Aesop, "Diogenes on a Journey" _____

Diogenes, the Cynic, was traveling along a road when he came to a stream in flood and stood there wondering how to get across. A man who often carried people over saw his difficulty and came and took him across. Diogenes was grateful for this kindness and was just grumbling at the poverty which prevented his rewarding this benefactor when the man saw another traveler who couldn't get across and ran to do the same thing. Then Diogenes went to him and said, "Well, I won't waste any more gratitude on you since I see that you do this as a hobby and without any discrimination."

Men who do good services for the undeserving as well as for the worthy get no reputation for benefaction but are labeled as stupid.

Questions for Discussion and Writing

1. Make a list of the primary Cynic beliefs in order to formulate a definition of the term *Cynic.*

2. Why might the Stoics have been sympathetic to Cynicism—what basic principles do the two philosophical schools share?

3. In the final paragraph, Sayre states that Cynicism "did much to prepare the way for Christianity." How might Cynicism have laid a foundation for the emerging Christian religion? Consider the attitudes toward worldly goods and honor in particular.

4. How does the legendary incident that Aesop recounts illustrate Cynic beliefs as Sayre discusses them?

5. Do you believe the Cynic philosophy is likely to hold any appeal for people today? Give reasons for your response.

6. Consider possible similarities in the beliefs or behavior of Cynics and the following:
   (a) Hippies of the 1960s
   (b) Bag ladies/street people
   (c) Punk rockers

Eric Hoffer, "Long Live Shame!" _____

A generational split appears in Eric Hoffer's polemical essay: he writes to criticize the youth culture (the same one that Margaret Halsey objected to in "What's Wrong with 'Me, Me, Me,'?"), which he deems "flauntingly shameless." Hoffer cites historical traditions that promote what he considers to be a necessary, decent sense of shame, whose purpose is to instill and maintain a civilized way of life. Whether the high standards whose loss he mourns ever truly existed is a question worth pursuing.

The ancient Hebrews were alone in envisioning a troubled paradise. The Garden of Eden was not an abode of bliss but a place tense with suspicion and anxiety. For no sooner did God, in a moment of divine recklessness, create man in His own image than He was filled with misgivings. There was no telling what a creature thus made would do next. So God placed Adam and Eve in the Garden of Eden where he could watch them.

It is plain that Adam and Eve were ill at ease under constant observation, and in their isolation from other living things. They welcomed the snake's visit, confided in him, and listened to his advice. The expulsion from Eden was not the terrible fall it has been made out to be. It was actually a liberation from the stifling confines of a celestial zoo.

Now, what concerns me is the puzzling fact that when Adam and Eve followed the snake's advice, disobeyed God's commandment, and ate from "the tree of the knowledge of good and evil" they felt not guilty but ashamed—ashamed of their nakedness.

What connection could there be between the knowledge of good and evil and the impulse to cover the genitals with fig leaves?

It is conceivable that, to begin with, good and evil were not individual but social concepts. That was good which preserved the group, and evil that which threatened its survival. Now, there is one dangerous threat that no society can escape: namely, the recurrent threat of disruption by juveniles as a young generation passes from boyhood to manhood.

Since sexual drives are at the core of the destructive impulses characteristic of the juvenile phase, sex is seen as a threat, hence an evil. The primeval association of sex with shame is, like the taboos of incest and endogamy,[1] part of an apparatus devised to defend a society against rape by juveniles inside the tribe.

Through the millennia societies acted as if their safety depended upon the preservation of female chastity. Sex, of course, is not the sole threat to the group. Cowardice, weakness, bad manners are as dangerous, and they, too, are associated with shame.

Shame, far more than guilt, involves an awareness by the individual of being watched and judged by the group. It is to be expected, therefore, that the more compact the group, the more pronounced the sense of shame. The member of a compact group carries the group within him, and never feels alone.

Anthropologists distinguish between the "shame culture" of primitive groups and "guilt culture" of advanced societies. Actually, what comes here in question is not social primitiveness but social compactness.

It is true that the most perfect examples of social compactness are found in primitive societies. But a technically advanced country like Japan, in which the individual is totally integrated with the group, has as strong a sense of shame as any primitive tribe.

---

[1] Marriage within a social class or group.

By the same token one should expect the sense of shame to be blurred where socialization of the young becomes ineffectual, and social cohesion is weakened.

In this country at present the inability of adults to socialize their young has made it possible for juveniles to follow their bents, act on their impulses, and materialize their fantasies.

The result has been a youth culture flauntingly shameless. You see well-fed good-looking youngsters, obviously the sons and daughters of well-to-do parents, beg in the streets, pet in public, line up for pornographic movies, and vie with each other in taking advantage of every opening for skullduggery[2] offered by a social system based on trust.

The disconcerting thing is that loss of shame is not confined to juveniles. The adult majority is not ashamed of its cowardice, workers are not ashamed of negligence, manufactureres of marketing shoddy products, and the rich of dodging taxes. We have become a shameless society.

Our intellectual mentors strive to infect us with a sense of guilt— about Vietnam, the Negro, the poor, pollution—and frown on shame as reactionary and repressive. But whether or not a sense of guilt will make us a better people, the loss of shame threatens our survival as a civilized society. For most of the acts we are ashamed of are not punishable by law, and civilized living depends upon the observance of unenforceable rules.

One also has the feeling that shame is more uniquely human than guilt. There is more fear in guilt than in shame, and animals know fear. We blanch with guilt as we do with fear, but we blush with shame.

The fabulous Greeks made of shame a goddess—Aidos. She was the source of dignity, decency, and good manners. An offense committed against Aidos was avenged by the goddess Nemesis. Long live shame!

Questions for Discussion and Writing

1. What distinction does Hoffer make between shame and guilt, and why does he celebrate shame as a civilizing force? Provide examples to illustrate the distinction.

2. Connect Hoffer's view of contemporary adolescents with Cynic ideals. Would the Cynics admire the young people Hoffer condemns? Why or why not?

3. Is Hoffer's view a contemporary version of Puritan ideology (discussed in Wertenbaker's "The Rule of Conduct," Chapter 2)?

4. Of the three ancient philosophies you have encountered here—Epicureanism, Stoicism, and Cynicism—which best reflects contemporary notions of what is moral and immoral? Which (if any) of these philosophic attitudes should be revived as active moral codes for our time, and why?

---

[2] Deceitful acts.

Dick Gregory, *"Shame"*

Dick Gregory, a track star, comedian, and today a social and nutri-
tional activist, puts the abstract concept of shame into concrete, personal
form in this excerpt from his autobiography. He entitled his work Nigger
and opened it with the following dedication: "Dear Momma—Wherever
you are, if you ever hear the word 'nigger' again, remember they are
advertising my book." An impoverished and fatherless child, Gregory con-
fronted a society that sees both of these conditions as a sign of inferiority.
His concept of shame provides one response to Eric Hoffer's arguments in
"Long Live Shame!"

I never learned hate at home, or shame. I had had to go to school
for that. I was about seven years old when I got my first big lesson. I was
in love with a little girl named Helene Tucker, a light-complected little
girl with pigtails and nice manners. She was always clean and she was
smart in school. I think I went to school then mostly to look at her. I
brushed my hair and even got me a little old handkerchief. It was a lady's
handkerchief, but I didn't want Helene to see me wipe my nose on my
hand. The pipes were frozen again, there was no water in the house, but I
washed my socks and shirt every night. I'd get a pot, and go over to
Mister Ben's grocery store, and stick my pot down into his soda machine.
Scoop out some chopped ice. By evening the ice melted to water for
washing. I got sick a lot that winter because the fire would go out at night
before the clothes were dry. In the morning I'd put them on, wet or dry,
because they were the only clothes I had.

Everybody's got a Helene Tucker, a symbol of everything you want.
I loved her for her goodness, her cleanness, her popularity. She'd walk
down my street and my brothers and sisters would yell, "Here comes
Helene," and I'd rub my tennis sneakers on the back of my pants and wish
my hair wasn't so nappy and the white folks' shirt fit me better. I'd run
out on the street. If I knew my place and didn't come too close, she'd
wink at me and say hello. That was a good feeling. Sometimes I'd follow
her all the way home, and shovel the snow off her walk and try to make
friends with her Momma and her aunts. I'd drop money on her stoop late
at night on my way back from shining shoes in the taverns. And she had a
Daddy, and he had a good job. He was a paper hanger.

I guess I would have gotten over Helene by summer-time, but
something happened in that classroom that made her face hang in front
of me for the next twenty-two years. When I played the drums in high
school it was for Helene and when I broke track records in college it was
for Helene and when I started standing behind microphones and heard
applause I wished Helene could hear it, too. It wasn't until I was twenty-
nine years old and married and making money that I finally got her out of
my system. Helene was sitting in that classroom when I learned to be
ashamed of myself.

It was on a Thursday. I was sitting in the back of the room, in a seat with a chalk circle drawn around it. The idiot's seat, the troublemaker's seat.

The teacher thought I was stupid. Couldn't spell, couldn't read, couldn't do arithmetic. Just stupid. Teachers were never interested in finding out that you couldn't concentrate because you were so hungry, because you hadn't had any breakfast. All you could think about was noontime, would it ever come? Maybe you could sneak into the cloakroom and steal a bite of some kid's lunch out of a coat pocket. A bite of something. Paste. You can't really make a meal of paste, or put it on bread for a sandwich, but sometimes I'd scoop a few spoonfuls out of the paste jar in the back of the room. Pregnant people get strange tastes. I was pregnant with poverty. Pregnant with dirt and pregnant with smells that made people turn away, pregnant with cold and pregnant with shoes that were never bought for me, pregnant with five other people in my bed and no Daddy in the next room, and pregnant with hunger. Paste doesn't taste too bad when you're hungry.

The teacher thought I was a troublemaker. All she saw from the front of the room was a little black boy who squirmed in his idiot's seat and made noises and poked the kids around him. I guess she couldn't see a kid who made noises because he wanted someone to know he was there.

It was on a Thursday, the day before the Negro payday. The eagle always flew on Friday. The teacher was asking each student how much his father would give to the Community Chest. On Friday night, each kid would get the money from his father, and on Monday he would bring it to the school. I decided I was going to buy me a Daddy right then. I had money in my pocket from shining shoes and selling papers, and whatever Helene Tucker pledged for her Daddy I was going to top it. And I'd hand the money right in. I wasn't going to wait until Monday to buy me a Daddy.

I was shaking, scared to death. The teacher opened her book and started calling out names alphabetically.

"Helene Tucker?"

"My Daddy said he'd give two dollars and fifty cents."

"That's very nice, Helene. Very, very nice indeed."

That made me feel pretty good. It wouldn't take too much to top that. I had almost three dollars in dimes and quarters in my pocket. I stuck my hand in my pocket and held onto the money, waiting for her to call my name. But the teacher closed her book after she called everybody else in the class.

I stood up and raised my hand.

"What is it now?"

"You forgot me."

She turned toward the blackboard. "I don't have time to be playing with you, Richard."

"My Daddy said he'd . . ."

"Sit down, Richard, you're disturbing the class."

"My Daddy said he'd give . . . fifteen dollars."

She turned around and looked mad. "We are collecting this money for you and your kind, Richard Gregory. If your Daddy can give fifteen dollars you have no business being on relief."

"I got it right now, I got it right now, my Daddy gave it to me to turn in today, my Daddy said . . ."

"And furthermore," she said, looking right at me, her nostrils getting big and her lips getting thin and her eyes opening wide, "we know you don't have a Daddy."

Helene Tucker turned around, her eyes full of tears. She felt sorry for me. Then I couldn't see her too well because I was crying, too.

"Sit down, Richard."

And I always thought the teacher kind of liked me. She always picked me to wash the blackboard on Friday, after school. That was a big thrill, it made me feel important. If I didn't wash it, come Monday the school might not function right.

"Where are you going, Richard?"

I walked out of school that day, and for a long time I didn't go back very often. There was shame there.

Now there was shame everywhere. It seemed like the whole world had been inside that classroom, everyone had heard what the teacher had said, everyone had turned around and felt sorry for me. There was shame in going to the Worthy Boys Annual Christmas Dinner for you and your kind, because everybody knew what a worthy boy was. Why couldn't they just call it the Boys Annual Dinner, why'd they have to give it a name? There was shame in wearing the brown and orange and white plaid mackinaw the welfare gave to 3,000 boys. Why'd it have to be the same for everybody so when you walked down the street the people could see you were on relief? It was a nice warm mackinaw and it had a hood, and my Momma beat me and called me a little rat when she found out I stuffed it in the bottom of a pail full of garbage way over on Cottage Street. There was shame in running over to Mister Ben's at the end of the day and asking for his rotten peaches, there was shame in asking Mrs. Simmons for a spoonful of sugar, there was shame in running out to meet the relief truck. I hated that truck, full of food for you and your kind. I ran into the house and hid when it came. And then I started to sneak through alleys, to take the long way home so the people going into White's Eat Shop wouldn't see me. Yeah, the whole world heard the teacher that day, we all know you don't have a Daddy.

It lasted for a while, this kind of numbness. I spent a lot of time feeling sorry for myself. And then one day I met this wino in a restaurant. I'd been out hustling all day, shining shoes, selling newspapers, and I had googobs of money in my pocket. Bought me a bowl of chili for fifteen cents, and a cheeseburger for fifteen cents, and a Pepsi for five cents, and a piece of chocolate cake for ten cents. That was a good meal. I was eating when this old wino came in. I love winos because they never hurt anyone but themselves.

The old wino sat down at the counter and ordered twenty-six cents worth of food. He ate it like he really enjoyed it. When the owner, Mister Williams, asked him to pay the check, the old wino didn't lie or go through his pocket like he suddenly found a hole.

He just said: "Don't have no money."

The owner yelled: "Why in hell you come in here and eat my food if you don't have no money? That food cost me money."

Mister Williams jumped over the counter and knocked the wino off his stool and beat him over the head with a pop bottle. Then he stepped back and watched the wino bleed. Then he kicked him. And he kicked him again.

I looked at the wino with blood all over his face and I went over. "Leave him alone, Mister Williams. I'll pay the twenty-six cents."

The wino got up, slowly, pulling himself up to the stool, then up to the counter, holding on for a minute until his legs stopped shaking so bad. He looked at me with pure hate. "Keep your twenty-six cents. You don't have to pay, not now. I just finished paying for it."

He started to walk out, and as he passed me, he reached down and touched my shoulder. "Thanks, sonny, but it's too late now. Why didn't you pay it before?"

I was pretty sick about that. I waited too long to help another man.

I remember a white lady who came to our door once around Thanksgiving time. She wore a woolly, green bonnet around her head, and she smiled a lot.

"Is your mother home, little boy?"

"No, she ain't."

"May I come in?"

"What do you want, ma'am?"

She didn't stop smiling once, but she sighed a little when she bent down and lifted up a big yellow basket. The kind I saw around church that were called Baskets for the Needy.

"This is for you."

"What's in there?"

"All sorts of good things," she said, smiling. "There's candy and potatoes and cake and cranberry sauce and"—she made a funny little face at me by wrinkling up her nose—"and a great big fat turkey for Thanksgiving dinner."

"Is it cooked?"

"A big fat juicy turkey, all plucked clean for you . . . "

"Is it cooked?"

"No, it's not . . . "

"We ain't got nothing in the house to cook it with, lady."

I slammed the door in her face. Wouldn't that be a bitch, to have a turkey like that in the house with no way to cook it? No gas, no electricity, no coal. Just a big fat juicy raw turkey.

I remember Mister Ben, the grocery-store man, a round little white man with funny little tufts of white hair on his head and sad-looking eyes. His face was kind of gray-colored, and the skin was loose and shook when he talked.

"Momma want a loaf of bread, Mister Ben, fresh bread."

"Right away, Richard," he'd say and get the bread he bought three days old from the bakeries downtown. It was the only kind he had for his credit-book customers. He dropped it on the counter. Clunk.

I'd hand him the credit book, that green tablet with the picture of the snuff can on it, to write down how much we owed him. He'd lick the top of that stubby pencil he kept behind his ear. Six cents.

"How you like school, Richard?"

"I like school fine, Mister Ben."

"Good boy, you study, get smart."

I'd run home to Momma and tell her that the bread wasn't fresh bread, it was stale bread. She'd flash the big smile.

"Oh, that Mister Ben, he knew I was fixin to make toast."

The peaches were rotten and the bread wasn't fresh and sometimes the butter was green, but when it came down to the nitty-gritty you could always go to Mister Ben. Before a Jewish holiday he'd take all the food that was going to spoil while the store was shut and bring it over to our house. Before Christmas he'd send over some meat even though he knew it was going on the tablet and he might never see his money. When the push came to the shove and every hungry belly in the house was beginning to eat on itself, Momma could go to Mister Ben and always get enough for some kind of dinner.

But I can remember three days in a row I went into Mister Ben's and asked him to give me a penny Mr. Goodbar from the window.

Three days in a row he said: "Out, out, or I'll tell your Momma you been begging."

One night I threw a brick through his window and took it.

The next day I went into Mister Ben's to get some bread for Momma and his skin was shaking and I heard him tell a lady, "I can't understand why should anybody break my window for a penny piece of candy, a lousy piece of candy, all they got to do is ask, that's all, and I give."

Questions for Discussion and Writing

1. Gregory writes that Helene was a "symbol of everything you want." What does young Gregory want?

2. Why does Gregory's teacher come to the conclusion that he is "stupid"? How does his background lead her to make this judgment?

3. What emotional connotations does the term "you and your kind" come to have for Gregory? How is he branded by the term, the relief truck, and the plaid jacket?

4. Consider how Gregory's depiction of shame relates to Hoffer's defense of it. Is shame for the young Gregory a way of learning "dignity, decency, and good manners," as Hoffer argues in its favor?

5. Are the sources of Gregory's shame the same values that the Cynics criticized? Examine what it is that Gregory is ashamed of, and evaluate the moral worth of the values he seems to hold.

6. Relate the anecdote of Gregory and the wino to Gregory's earlier experience of shame. What are the sources of Gregory's shame in this incident? Do they show a change in his values or his sense of self?

7. Does the final incident with the grocer justify any Cynic values that Gregory may have adopted?

MODERN ATTITUDES TOWARD MODERN EVILS

Charles L. Glicksberg, **"Nihilism"** _____

Nihilism is a philosophical stance that denies the existence of absolute power, being, or value. As a philosophical attitude it has probably existed as long as religious belief has, for once the notion of faith exists, the notion of doubt inevitably arises. Nihilism extends doubt to its logical extreme: it calls for the recognition that life may be without meaning or purpose. Contemporary gang culture, in its apparent dismissal of the value of human life or a purpose in it beyond momentary pleasure, might be viewed as one expression of a nihilistic attitude.

What is generally meant by nihilism? Nihilism is difficult to define because it takes so many different forms, but it is a real enough experience. It is a spiritual crisis through which all thinking people pass at some time in their lives; and very few come through this ordeal unscathed. There is the passive nihilism of the Buddhist variety: life is an empty dream, action is futile, and striving for happiness, fulfillment, or perfection betrays the fact that one is still the slave of illusion. The second type, the nihilism of negativity, is derived from the special brand of nihilism that sprang up in Europe, especially in Russia, in the nineteenth century; it was a nihilism that, despite its professed rejection of all belief, rested its faith in the scientific method.

Then there is a species of nihilism that is active, Dionysian:[1] Nietzsche speaks of ecstatic nihilism. Nietzsche's nihilism is metaphysical rather than ideological. His attitude toward science is therefore not

---

[1] Pleasure-seeking.

worshipful; science is no more than a body of fictions, a set of conventions; it did not presuppose that it was based on truth. Nietzsche's nihilism was all-inclusive. He perceived no meaning in the world, no ultimate purpose, no sustaining principle of order. Man is saddled with the task of imposing order on a senseless universe. There is also the type of nihilism that is carried to the logical extreme of suicide. Finally, there is the nihilism that promotes and justifies an unconscionable[2] struggle for power. Life on earth is completely amoral in character; categorical imperatives[3] are human constructs; no law exists to prevent the rule of the strong—a doctrine that motivated the Nazi reign of terror.

Webster's New International Dictionary defines nihilism as "a viewpoint that all traditional values and beliefs are unfounded and that all existence is consequently senseless and useless: a denial of intrinsic meaning and value in life." Another definition that this dictionary gives is that nihilism is "a doctrine that denies or is taken as denying any objective or real ground of truth. In a more specific context this includes the philosophy of moral nihilism, which denies the objective ground of morality."

But if the truth that man pursues so eagerly is only a solipsist[4] illusion, then he finds himself trapped in a vicious circle of contradictions. Why speak? Why recommend one illusion as vastly superior to another? If truth is a myth, then all distinctions are abolished, and one might as well follow the erratic guidance of instinct and feeling instead of the promptings of reason.

The cult of nihilism tends swiftly to grow into a cult of violence and terror on the political scene, "expressing a total contempt for life . . . In an active or latent state, nihilism is at work throughout our civilization." Important, however, as is the social and historical background, it does not appear that nihilism is the special creation of the twentieth century, this age of crisis and catastrophe. The historical crisis of our time colors and accentuates the dominant motif of doom that crops up, but the nihilist strain has made itself felt in other cultures during the past, though in a less virulent[5] manner. Before the advent of the horrors of the holocaust, there were poets, dramatists, and philosophers, who faced the nihilist dilemma. From Sophocles and Lucretius to Schopenhauer, Nietzsche, Dostoevski, Kierkegaard, and Tolstoy, there is scarcely an important creative figure who has not at some time been stricken with the fever of nihilism. It is always there to be faced—and overcome.

I am assuming that the spiritual conflict that culminates in nihilism, far from being the mark of an unhinged mind or craven temperament or the characteristic but short-lived product of a time of trouble, is an archetypal[6] experience. The individual either passes through the dark night of the soul and beholds finally the glimmer of the light beyond,

---

[2] Inexcusable.
[3] Necessary actions.
[4] Egotistical.

[5] Angry.
[6] Original, basic.

however ambiguously it shines forth, or he never emerges from the darkness that hems him in. Though the nihilist has presumably abandoned the quest for ultimate meaning, he never actually ceases to question or cry out or seek a solution to the mystery of being. The dialectic of nihilism is charged with unresolvable elements of complexity. It is not the formal expression of a philosophical position nor is it a logically elaborated system of thought. If it embodies a world vision that is in the end forced to say No to life, it utters this categorical negation with different accents of conviction.

The rage of the nihilist against the ineradicable[7] absurdity of existence is an inverted expression of his love of life. Since his life goes on— he rejects, as does Camus, the expedient of suicide—he stops at some point in his career to ask himself: "How am I to live? What is to be done?"

It is apparent that the nihilist and the humanist share a common body of assumptions. Both believe that man is alone, both reject faith in the supernatural. But whereas the secular humanist then proceeds to declare that man is the measure, the sole source and touchstone of value, the nihilist repudiates all such man-made values as illusions, mere as-if fictions designed to hide from human eyes the emptiness and futility of existence. The nihilist will not conceal from himself the desolating "truth" of human dereliction. He will proclaim far and wide his discovery that the idea of progress, like the romantic faith in the perfectibility of man, is a spurious[8] myth. He harbors no revolutionary hopes; he does not look forward to the future for the redemption of mankind.

It is at this point of no return that the nihilist reverses his field, as it were, and takes up a position that, in defiance of the canons of logic, brings him to a closer understanding of the intense spiritual battle the religious Existentialist must wage before he can affirm his faith in God. Faced with the ultimate issue of death—his death—as annihilation, the nihilist wants to know how best to live the time of his life. But what is "good," what is "best"? Intellectually he is convinced that he has purged his mind of all religious traces, though his longing for God, as was true in the case of Nietzsche, never leaves him. But longing that never goes beyond that stage is not the same thing as the actuality of faith. The nihilist distrusts the coinages of the mind, the stratagems of the duplicitous[9] self, the abstractions that it creates and then hypostatizes[10] as sacred realities.

This encounter with nothingness forms the crux of nihilist literature, just as the experience of the dark night of the soul lies at the heart of Christian mysticism. Most people are sleepwalkers who take it for granted that life has a meaning beyond the mere living of it. It is this instinctive faith that the nihilist begins by questioning and then finally decides to reject. As soon as he does so, he finds himself trapped in a

---

[7] Unable to be destroyed.   [9] Deceptive.
[8] False.   [10] Makes an idea into something concrete.

spiritual cul-de-sac. He is unable either to affirm or to deny. He can neither act nor refrain from acting. How shall he act on his negative beliefs?

This life-negating dementia[11] constitutes a theme that has been pondered by poets, philosophers, mystics, and saints for over two thousand years. It is the archetypal concern of the tragic vision, the central, though not sole, preoccupation of religion. When human consciousness first arose, man must have formulated the question of questions: Who am I in relation to the cosmos? What am I doing here on earth? What purpose am I supposed to serve?

Nietzsche announced that God was dead and wrestled with the problem of what was to take the place of God. He sought to grasp the truth bearing on the human condition, without regard for the harmful consequences it might have for mankind. The relentless search for the truth at all costs is sustained by a moral principle, but it led Nietzsche to the ultimate of disillusionment. If truth is a myth, then the pursuit of truth must cease, for it leads nowhere. Nothing is to be believed, not even the empirically warranted conclusions of science. The upshot in Nietzsche's case is a nihilism that cannot be borne because it cannot be lived. As Karl Jaspers points out: "Even if his thinking appears as a self-destructive process in which no truth can last, even if the end is always nothingness, Nietzsche's own will is diametrically opposed to this nihilism. In empty space he wants to grasp the positive." He endeavors to formulate a vital faith, a transcendent affirmation that can inspire human life to nobler effort. Hence he glorifies strength, the elan vital,[12] the will to power, the ideal of eternal recurrence. This is a far cry, however, from any religious gospel that the general run of mankind can embrace. But the passion of striving, the stubborn hankering after the ideal, is abundantly present in his work; he is not satisfied with the finite, the merely human; he must break out of the nihilistic impasse.

Questions for Discussion and Writing

1. Glicksberg's essay opens with a listing of different versions of nihilism. Work with class members to come up with an example of each type, perhaps using well-known characters from fiction, movies, or other sources of popular culture. How do you rank each type in terms of philosophic worth?

2. In describing nihilism as a stage in an individual's psychological development, Glicksberg says that one "either passes through the dark night of the soul and beholds finally the glimmer of the light beyond . . . or he never emerges from the darkness that hems him in." Examine the images he uses and explain how they help illustrate the nihilistic state of mind.

3. Glicksberg claims that nihilism may play a role in the incidence of terrorism. Do you see parallels between nihilistic philosophy and terrorism as Baljit Singh analyzes it (in "An Overview of Terrorism," Chapter 5)?

[11] Mindlessness.

[12] Life force.

4. According to Darwin's theory of evolution, survival of the species is the force that directs life. Does the doctrine of nihilism contradict Darwin's biological view of life's purpose?

5. Using Dirk's "Overview of Western Philosophy," explain how nihilism, while it has ancient roots, seems a particularly modern philosophical viewpoint.

6. Construct a reading of Gwendolyn Brooks's "The Pool Players" that depicts the poem's speakers as Nihilists. Do any elements of the poem contradict such a reading?

7. Is atheism a necessarily nihilistic stance? Review Madalyn Murray O'Hair's essay (Chapter 2) and consider your own religious beliefs to address the issue.

8. Is the relativist stance that Stephen Toulmin explains in "Modern and Postmodern Science" (Chapter 3) a nihilistic view, as Glicksberg describes Nietzsche's version of nihilism?

Joan Didion, **"Death in El Salvador"**

Joan Didion (b. 1934) is a prominent contemporary American writer. She is famous as a stylist, a writer whose lean style embodies her sense of the emptiness, alienation, and almost moral bleakness of modern-day life. Note the physical descriptions that she includes in her essay, and consider how they reveal the feeling she associates with El Salvador's current state of political crisis.

The three-year-old El Salvador International Airport is glassy and white and splendidly isolated, conceived during the waning of the Molina "National Transformation" as convenient less to the capital (San Salvador is forty miles away, until recently a drive of several hours) than to a central hallucination of the Molina and Romero regimes, the projected beach resorts, the Hyatt, the Pacific Paradise, tennis, golf, water-skiing, condos, Costa del Sol, the visionary intervention of a tourist industry in yet another republic where the leading natural cause of death is gastrointestinal infection. In the general absence of tourists these hotels have since been abandoned, ghost resorts on the empty Pacific beaches, and to land at this airport built to service them is to plunge directly into a state in which no ground is solid, no depth of field reliable, no perception so definite that it might not dissolve into its reverse.

The only logic is that of acquiescence.[1] Immigration is negotiated in a thicket of automatic weapons, but by whose authority the weapons are brandished (Army or National Guard or National Police or Customs Police or Treasury Police or one of a continuing proliferation of other shadowy and overlapping forces) is a blurred point. Eye contact is avoided. Documents are scrutinized upside down. Once clear of the airport, on the new highway that slices through green hills rendered

[1] Passive acceptance.

phosphorescent by the cloud cover of the tropical rainy season, one sees mainly underfed cattle and mongrel dogs and armored vehicles, vans and trucks and Cherokee Chiefs fitted with reinforced steel and bulletproof Plexiglas an inch thick. Such vehicles are a fixed feature of local life, and are popularly associated with disappearance and death. There was a Cherokee Chief seen following the Dutch television crew killed in Chalatenango province in March of 1982. There was the red Toyota three-quarter-ton pickup sighted near the van driven by the four American Catholic workers on the night they were killed in 1980. There were, in the late spring and summer of 1982, the three Toyota panel trucks, one yellow, one blue, and one green, none bearing plates, reported present at each of the mass detentions (a "detention" is another fixed feature of local life, and often precedes a "disappearance") in the Amatepec district of San Salvador. These are the details—the models and colors of armored vehicles, the makes and calibers of weapons, the particular methods of dismemberment and decapitation used in particular instances—on which the visitor to Salvador learns immediately to concentrate, to the exclusion of past or future concerns, as in a prolonged amnesiac fugue.[2]

Terror is the given of the place. Black-and-white police cars cruise in pairs, each with the barrel of a rifle extruding from an open window. Roadblocks materialize at random, soldiers fanning out from trucks and taking positions, fingers always on triggers, safeties clicking on and off. Aim is taken as if to pass the time. Every morning El Diario de Hoy and La Prensa Grafica carry cautionary stories. "Una madre y sus dos hijos fueron asesinados con arma cortante (corvo) por ocho sujetos desconocidos el lunes en la noche": A mother and her two sons hacked to death in their beds by eight desconocidos, unknown men. The same morning's paper: the unidentified body of a young man, strangled, found on the shoulder of the road. Same morning, different story: the unidentified bodies of three young men, found on another road, their faces partially destroyed by bayonets, one face carved to represent a cross.

It is largely from these reports in the newspapers that the United States embassy compiles its body counts, which are transmitted to Washington in a weekly dispatch referred to by embassy people as "the grimgram." These counts are presented in a kind of tortured code that fails to obscure what is taken for granted in El Salvador, that government forces do most of the killing. In a Janaury 15, 1982 memo to Washington, for example, the embassy issued a "guarded" breakdown on its count of 6,909 "reported" political murders between September 16, 1980 and September 15, 1981. Of these 6,909, according to the memo, 922 were "believed committed by security forces," 952 "believed committed by leftist terrorists," 136 "believed committed by the rightist terrorists," and 4,889 "committed by unknown assailants," the famous desconocidos favored by those San Salvador newspapers still publishing. (The figures

---

[2] Musical work with a repeatedly developed theme.

actually add up not to 6,909 but to 6,899, leaving ten in a kind of official limbo.) The memo continued:

The uncertainty involved here can be seen in the fact that responsibility cannot be fixed in the majority of cases. We note, however, that it is generally believed in El Salvador that a large number of the unexplained killings are carried out by the security forces, officially or unofficially. The Embassy is aware of dramatic claims that have been made by one interest group or another in which the security forces figure as the primary agents of murder here. El Salvador's tangled web of attack and vengeance, traditional criminal violence and political mayhem make this an impossible charge to sustain. In saying this, however, we make no attempt to lighten the responsibility for the deaths of many hundreds, and perhaps thousands, which can be attributed to the security forces . . .

The body count kept by what is generally referred to in San Salvador as "the Human Rights Commission" is higher than the embassy's and documented periodically by a photographer who goes out looking for bodies. These bodies he photographs are often broken into unnatural positions, and the faces to which the bodies are attached (when they are attached) are equally unnatural, sometimes unrecognizable as human faces, obliterated by acid or beaten to a mash of misplaced ears and teeth or slashed ear to ear and invaded by insects. "Encontrado en Antiguo Cuscatlan el dia 25 de Marzo 1982: camison de dormir celeste," the typed caption reads on one photograph: found in Antiguo Cuscatlan March 25 1982 wearing a sky-blue nightshirt. The captions are laconic.[3] Found in Soyapango May 21 1982. Found in Meficanos June 11 1982. Found at El Playon May 30 1982, white shirt, purple pants, black shoes. . . .

All forensic[4] photographs induce in the viewer a certain protective numbness, but dissociation is more difficult here. In the first place these are not, technically, "forensic" photographs, since the evidence they document will never be presented in a court of law. In the second place the disfigurement is too routine. The locations are too near, the dates too recent. There is the presence of the relatives of the disappeared: the women who sit every day in this cramped office on the grounds of the archdiocese, waiting to look at the spiral-bound photo albums in which the photographs are kept. These albums have plastic covers bearing softfocus color photographs of young Americans in dating situations (strolling through autumn foliage on one album, recumbent in a field of daisies on another), and the women, looking for the bodies of their husbands and brothers and sisters and children, pass them from hand to hand without comment or expression.

Questions for Discussion and Writing

1. Is the kind of civil chaos depicted in Didion's essay likely to lead to increased nihilism on the part of those involved in the conflict, as well as in those observing it—reporters, photographers, and foreign government officials?

---

[3] Using few words.   [4] Used for legal proceedings.

2. What might Didion's purpose be in repeatedly detailing the mutilation of bodies? What effect does it have on the reader, and, by extension, on the people who actually view such scenes on a daily basis?

3. Does the final image of the silent, expressionless women searching for relatives among the pictures of the dead suggest a nihilistic attitude on their part?

4. Which response to the civil strife depicted in Didion's essay—joining a faction fighting for a particular form of Salvadoran government or adopting a classical Epicurean attitude of detachment and withdrawal from the political situation—seems the better course? Explain the reasons for your judgment.

Viktor E. Frankl, "Arrival at Auschwitz"

A survivor of the Nazi death camps, Frankl re-creates the stages of his immersion in what is considered one of the greatest atrocities of modern history. The process takes him through denial to the pragmatic stance that "a man can get used to anything." But the price for adapting, he finds, is a symbolic death of the former life.

Fifteen hundred persons had been traveling by train for several days and nights; there were eighty people in each coach. All had to lie on top of their luggage, the few remnants of their personal possessions. The carriages were so full that only the top parts of the windows were free to let in the gray of dawn. Everyone expected the train to head for some munitions factory, in which we would be employed as forced labor. We did not know whether we were still in Silesia or already in Poland. The engine's whistle had an uncanny sound, like a cry for help sent out in commiseration for the unhappy load which it was destined to lead into perdition.[1] Then the train shunted, obviously nearing a main station. Suddenly a cry broke from the ranks of the anxious passengers. "There is a sign, Auschwitz!" Everyone's heart missed a beat at that moment. Auschwitz—the very name stood for all that was horrible: gas chambers, crematoriums, massacres. Slowly, almost hesitatingly, the train moved on as if it wanted to spare its passengers the dreadful realization as long as possible: Auschwitz!

With the progressive dawn, the outlines of an immense camp became visible: long stretches of several rows of barbed wire fences; watch towers; search lights; and long columns of ragged human figures, gray in the grayness of dawn, trekking along the straight desolate roads, to what destination we did not know. There were isolated shouts and whistles of command. We did not know their meaning. My imagination led me to see gallows with people dangling on them. I was horrified, but this was just as well, because step by step we had to become accustomed to a terrible and immense horror.

[1] Hell.

Evenutally we moved into the station. The initial silence was interrupted by shouted commands. We were to hear those rough, shrill tones from then on, over and over again in all the camps. Their sound was almost like the last cry of a victim, and yet there was a difference. It had a rasping hoarseness, as if it came from the throat of a man who had to keep shouting like that, a man who was being murdered again and again. The carriage doors were flung open and a small detachment of prisoners stormed inside. They wore striped uniforms, their heads were shaved, but they looked well fed. They spoke in every possible European tongue, and all with a certain amount of humor, which sounded grotesque under the circumstances. Like a drowning man clutching a straw, my inborn optimism (which has often controlled my feelings even in the most desperate situations) clung to this thought: These prisoners look quite well, they seem to be in good spirits and even laugh. Who knows? I might manage to share their favorable position.

In psychiatry there is a certain condition known as "delusion of reprieve." The condemned man, immediately before his execution, gets the illusion that he might be reprieved at the very last moment. We, too, clung to shreds of hope and believed to the last moment that it would not be so bad. Just the sight of the red cheeks and round faces of those prisoners was a great encouragement. Little did we know then that they formed a specially chosen elite, who for years had been the receiving squad for new transports as they rolled into the station day after day. They took charge of the new arrivals and their luggage, including scarce items and smuggled jewelry. Auschwitz must have been a strange spot in this Europe of the last years of the war. There must have been unique treasures of gold and silver, platinum and diamonds, not only in the huge storehouses but also in the hands of the SS.

Fifteen hundred captives were cooped up in a shed built to accommodate probably two hundred at the most. We were cold and hungry and there was not enough room for everyone to squat on the bare ground, let alone to lie down. One five-ounce piece of bread was our only food in four days. Yet I heard the senior prisoners in charge of the shed bargain with one member of the receiving party about a tie-pin made of platinum and diamonds. Most of the profits would eventually be traded for liquor—schnapps. I do not remember any more just how many thousands of marks were needed to purchase the quantity of schnapps required for a "gay evening," but I do know that those long-term prisoners needed schnapps. Under such conditions, who could blame them for trying to dope themselves? There was another group of prisoners who got liquor supplied in almost unlimited quantities by the SS: these were the men who were employed in the gas chambers and crematoriums, and who knew very well that one day they would be relieved by a new shift of men, and that they would have to leave their enforced role of executioner and become victims themselves.

Nearly everyone in our transport lived under the illusion that he would be reprieved, that everything would yet be well. We did not realize the meaning behind the scene that was to follow presently. We were told to leave our luggage in the train and to fall into two lines— women on one side, men on the other—in order to file past a senior SS officer. Surprisingly enough, I had the courage to hide my haversack[2] under my coat. My line filed past the officer, man by man. I realized that it would be dangerous if the office spotted my bag. He would at least knock me down; I knew that from previous experience. Instinctively, I straightened on approaching the officer, so that he would not notice my heavy load. Then I was face to face with him. He was a tall man who looked slim and fit in his spotless uniform. What a contrast to us, who were untidy and grimy after our long journey! He had assumed an attitude of careless ease, supporting his right elbow with his left hand. His right hand was lifted, and with the forefinger of that hand he pointed very leisurely to the right or to the left. None of us had the slightest idea of the sinister meaning behind that little movement of a man's finger, pointing now to the right and now to the left, but far more frequently to the left.

It was my turn. Somebody whispered to me that to be sent to the right side would mean work, the way to the left being for the sick and those incapable of work, who would be sent to a special camp. I just waited for things to take their course, the first of many such times to come. My haversack weighed me down a bit to the left, but I made an effort to walk upright. The SS man looked me over, appeared to hesitate, then put both his hands on my shoulders. I tried very hard to look smart, and he turned my shoulders very slowly until I faced right, and I moved over to that side.

The significance of the finger game was explained to us in the evening. It was the first selection, the first verdict made on our existence or non-existence. For the great majority of our transport, about 90 per cent, it meant death. Their sentence was carried out within the next few hours. Those who were sent to the left were marched from the station straight to the crematorium. This building, as I was told by someone who worked there, had the word "bath" written over its doors in several European languages. On entering, each prisoner was handed a piece of soap, and then—but mercifully I do not need to describe the events which followed. Many accounts have been written about this horror.

We who were saved, the minority of our transport, found out the truth in the evening. I inquired from prisoners who had been there for some time where my colleague and friend P — — — had been sent.

"Was he sent to the left side?"

"Yes," I replied.

"Then you can see him there," I was told.

"Where?" A hand pointed to the chimney a few hundred yards off, which was sending a column of flame up into the gray sky of Poland. It dissolved into a sinister cloud of smoke.

[2] Pack.

"That's where your friend is, floating up to Heaven," was the answer. But I still did not understand until the truth was explained to me in plain words.

But I am telling things out of their turn. From a psychological point of view, we had a long, long way in front of us from the break of that dawn at the station until our first night's rest at the camp.

Escorted by SS guards with loaded guns, we were made to run from the station, past electrically charged barbed wire, through the camp, to the cleansing station; for those of us who had passed the first selection, this was a real bath. Again our illusion of reprieve found confirmation. The SS men seemed almost charming. Soon we found out their reason. They were nice to us as long as they saw watches on our wrists and could persuade us in well-meaning tones to hand them over. Would we not have handed over all our possessions anyway, and why should not that relatively nice person have the watch? Maybe one day he would do one a good turn.

We waited in a shed which seemed to be the anteroom to the disinfecting chamber. SS men appeared and spread out blankets into which we had to throw all our possessions, all our watches and jewelry. There were still naive prisoners among us who asked, to the amusement of the more seasoned ones who were there as helpers if they could not keep a wedding ring, a medal or a good-luck piece. No one could yet grasp the fact that everything would be taken away.

I tried to take one of the old prisoners into my confidence. Approaching him furtively, I pointed to the roll of paper in the inner pocket of my coat and said, "Look, this is the manuscript of a scientific book. I know what you will say; that I should be grateful to escape with my life, that that should be all I can expect of fate. But I cannot help myself. I must keep this manuscript at all costs; it contains my life's work. Do you understand that?"

Yes, he was beginning to understand. A grin spread slowly over his face, first piteous, then more amused, mocking, insulting, until he bellowed one word at me in answer to my question, a word that was ever present in the vocabulary of the camp inmates: "Shit!" At that moment I saw the plain truth and did what marked the culminating point of the first phase of my psychological reaction: I struck out my whole former life.

Suddenly there was a stir among my fellow travelers, who had been standing about with pale, frightened faces, helplessly debating. Again we heard the hoarsely shouted commands. We were driven with blows into the immediate anteroom of the bath. There we assembled around an SS man who waited until we had all arrived. Then he said, "I will give you two minutes, and I shall time you by my watch. In these two minutes you will get fully undressed and drop everything on the floor where you are standing. You will take nothing with you except your shoes, your belt or suspenders, and possibly a truss.[3] I am starting to count—now!"

[3] Support worn for a hernia.

With unthinkable haste, people tore off their clothes. As the time grew shorter, they became increasingly nervous and pulled clumsily at their underwear, belts and shoelaces. Then we heard the first sounds of whipping; leather straps beating down on naked bodies.

Next we were herded into another room to be shaved: not only our heads were shorn, but not a hair was left on our entire bodies. Then on to the showers, where we lined up again. We hardly recognized each other; but with great relief some people noted that real water dripped from the sprays.

While we were waiting for the shower, our nakedness was brought home to us: we really had nothing now except our bare bodies—even minus hair; all we possessed, literally, was our naked existence. What else remained for us as a material link with our former lives? For me there were my glasses and my belt; the latter I had to exchange later on for a piece of bread. There was an extra bit of excitement in store for the owners of trusses. In the evening the senior prisoner in charge of our hut welcomed us with a speech in which he gave us his word of honor that he would hang, personally, "from that beam"—he pointed to it—any person who had sewn money or precious stones into his truss. Proudly he explained that as a senior inhabitant the camp laws entitled him to do so.

Where our shoes were concerned, matters were not so simple. Although we were supposed to keep them, those who had fairly decent pairs had to give them up after all and were given in exchange shoes that did not fit. In for real trouble were those prisoners who had followed the apparently well-meant advice (given in the anteroom) of the senior prisoners and had shortened their jackboots by cutting the tops off, then smearing soap on the cut edges to hide the sabotage. The SS men seemed to have waited for just that. All suspected of this crime had to go into a small adjoining room. After a time we again heard the lashings of the strap, and the screams of tortured men. This time it lasted for quite a while.

Thus the illusions some of us still held were destroyed one by one, and then, quite unexpectedly, most of us were overcome by a grim sense of humor. We knew that we had nothing to lose except our so ridiculously naked lives. When the showers started to run, we all tried very hard to make fun, both about ourselves and about each other. After all, real water did flow from the sprays!

Apart from that strange kind of humor, another sensation seized us: curiosity. I have experienced this kind of curiosity before, as a fundamental reaction toward certain strange circumstances. When my life was once endangered by a climbing accident, I felt only one sensation at the critical moment: curiosity, curiosity as to whether I should come out of it alive or with a fractured skull or some other injuries.

Cold curiosity predominated even in Auschwitz, somehow detaching the mind from its surroundings, which came to be regarded with a kind of objectivity. At that time one cultivated this state of mind as a means of protection. We were anxious to know what would happen next; and what would be the consequence, for example, of our standing in the open air, in the chill of late autumn, stark naked, and still wet from the showers. In the next few days our curiosity evolved into surprise; surprise that we did not catch cold.

There were many similar surprises in store for new arrivals. The medical men among us learned first of all: "Textbooks tell lies!" Somewhere it is said that man cannot exist without sleep for more than a stated number of hours. Quite wrong! I had been convinced that there were certain things I just could not do: I could not sleep without this or I could not live with that or the other. The first night in Auschwitz we slept in beds which were constructed in tiers. On each tier (measuring about six-and-a-half to eight feet) slept nine men, directly on the boards. Two blankets were shared by each nine men. We could, of course, lie only on our sides, crowded and huddled against each other, which had some advantages because of the bitter cold. Though it was forbidden to take shoes up to the bunks, some people did use them secretly as pillows in spite of the fact that they were caked with mud. Otherwise one's head had to rest on the crook of an almost dislocated arm. And yet sleep came and brought oblivion and relief from pain for a few hours.

I would like to mention a few similar surprises on how much we could endure: we were unable to clean our teeth, and yet, in spite of that and a severe vitamin deficiency, we had healthier gums than ever before. We had to wear the same shirts for half a year, until they had lost all appearance of being shirts. For days we were unable to wash, even partially, because of frozen water pipes, and yet the sores and abrasions on hands which were dirty from work in the soil did not suppurate[4] (that is, unless there was frostbite). Or for instance, a light sleeper, who used to be disturbed by the slightest noise in the next room, now found himself lying pressed against a comrade who snored loudly a few inches from his ear and yet slept quite soundly through the noise.

If someone now asked of us the truth of Dostoevski's statement that flatly defines man as a being who can get used to anything, we would reply, "Yes, a man can get used to anything, but do not ask us how." But our psychological investigations have not taken us that far yet; neither had we prisoners reached that point. We were still in the first phase of our psychological reactions.

Questions for Discussion and Writing

1. Frankl paraphrases the Russian author Dostoevski's belief that "man [is] a being who can get used to anything." What are the stages of adjustment which Frankl and his fellows undergo? Is there a point at which they become totally divorced from their former lives?

2. Is there evidence in Frankl's retrospective account of his arrival at Auschwitz that he retained his "inborn optimism"?

---

[4] Give off pus.

3. Explain the psychiatric concept of "delusion of reprieve." What psychological function(s) might it serve?

4. Consider the situation of people like Frankl who survived the concentration camps. How might the horror of the experience have affected their sense of human nature and of their own identity?

5. Is the experience of such total disruption of normal life and the destruction of all familiar codes and expectations, as happened to the victims of the Holocaust, likely to push one to an extreme philosophical stance—pure nihilism, for one example, or absolute religious faith, for another?

Jean Paul Sartre, **"Existentialism"**

Jean Paul Sartre's reputation is fixed as one of the twentieth century's most influential philosophers. His existential theories had their greatest popularity in post-World War II Europe, especially in Sartre's native France. Often, new philosophies come into being during times of political turmoil, uncertainty, and change, when wars or other catastrophic events challenge the old order. Postwar Europe had suffered through two global conflicts, the coming of the atomic age, the partition of Germany and Eastern Europe, and the failure of many economies and governments. Existentialism teaches that such a disordered reality reflects life's universal absurdity, and places all responsibility for value and meaning on the individual, who must act in order to define his or her image of humanity.

Man is nothing else but what he makes of himself. Such is the first principle of existentialism. It is also what is called subjectivity. But what do we mean by this, if not that man has a greater dignity than a stone or table? For we mean that man first exists, that is, that man first of all is the being who hurls himself toward a future and who is conscious of imagining himself as being in the future. Man is at the start a plan which is aware of itself, rather than a patch of moss, a piece of garbage, or a cauliflower; nothing exists prior to this plan; there is nothing in heaven; man will be what he will have planned to be. Not what he will want to be. Because by the word "will" we generally mean a conscious decision, which is subsequent to what we have already made of ourselves. I may want to belong to a political party, write a book, get married; but all that is only a manifestation of an earlier, more spontaneous choice that is called "will." But if existence really does precede essence, man is responsible for what he is. Thus, existentialism's first move is to make every man aware of what he is and to make the full responsibility of his existence rest on him. And when we say that a man is responsible for himself, we do not only mean that he is responsible for his own individuality, but that he is responsible for all men.

The word "subjectivism" has two meanings. Subjectivism means, on the one hand, that an individual chooses and makes himself; and, on the other, that it is impossible for man to transcend human subjectivity. The second of these is the essential meaning of existentialism. When we say that man chooses his own self, we mean that every one of us does likewise; but we also mean by that that in making this choice he also chooses all men. In fact, in creating the man that we want to be, there is not a single one of our acts which does not at the same time create an image of man as we think he ought to be. To choose to be this or that is to affirm at the same time the value of what we choose, because we can never choose evil. We always choose the good, and nothing can be good for us without being good for all.

If, on the other hand, existence precedes essence, and if we grant that we exist and fashion our image at one and the same time, the image is valid for everybody and for our whole age. Thus, our responsibility is much greater than we might have supposed, because it involves all mankind. If I am a workingman and choose to join a Christian trade union rather than be a Communist, and if by being a member, I want to show that the best thing for a man is resignation, that the kingdom of man is not of this world, I am not only involving my own case—I want to be resigned for everyone. As a result, my action has involved all humanity. To take a more individual matter, if I want to marry, to have children, even if this marriage depends solely on my own circumstances or passion or wish, I am involving all humanity in monogamy and not merely myself. Therefore, I am responsible for myself and for everyone else. I am creating a certain image of man of my own choosing. In choosing myself, I choose man.

The existentialist thinks it very distressing that God does not exist, because all possibility of finding values in a heaven of ideas disappears along with Him; there can no longer be an a priori Good, since there is no infinite and perfect consciousness to think it. Nowhere is it written that the good exists, that we must be honest, that we must not lie; because the fact is we are on a plane where there are only men. Dostoievsky said, "If God didn't exist, everything would be possible." That is the very starting point of existentialism. Indeed, everything is permissible if God does not exist, and as a result man is forlorn,[1] because neither within him nor without does he find anything to cling to. He can't start making excuses for himself.

If existence really does precede essence, there is no explaining things away by reference to a fixed and given human nature. In other words, there is no determinism, man is free, man is freedom. On the other hand, if God does not exist, we find no values or commands to turn to which legitimize our conduct. So, in the bright realm of values, we have no excuse behind us, nor justification before us. We are alone, with no excuses.

That is the idea I shall try to convey when I say that man is condemned to be free. Condemned, because he did not create himself,

---

[1] Hopeless, alone.

yet, in other respects is free; because, once thrown into the world, he is responsible for everything he does.

To give you an example which will enable you to understand forlornness better, I shall cite the case of one of my students who came to see me under the following circumstances: his father was on bad terms with his mother, and, moreover, was inclined to be a collaborationist;[2] his older brother had been killed in the German offensive of 1940, and the young man, with somewhat immature but generous feelings, wanted to avenge him. His mother lived alone with him, very much upset by the half-treason of her husband and the death of her older son; the boy was her only consolation.

The boy was faced with the choice of leaving for England joining the Free French forces—that is, leaving his mother behind—or remaining with his mother and helping her to carry on. He was fully aware that the woman lived only for him and that his going off—and perhaps his death—would plunge her into despair. He was also aware that every act that he did for his mother's sake was a sure thing, in the sense that it was helping her to carry on, whereas every effort he made toward going off and fighting was an uncertain move which might run aground and prove completely useless; for example, on his way to England he might, while passing through Spain, be detained indefinitely in a Spanish camp; he might reach England or Algiers and be stuck in an office at a desk job. As a result, he was faced with two very different kinds of action: one, concrete, immediate, but concerning only one individual; the other concerned an incomparably vaster group, a national collectivity, but for that very reason was dubious, and might be interrupted en route. And, at the same time, he was wavering between two kinds of ethics. On the one hand, an ethics of sympathy, of personal devotion; on the other, a broader ethics, but one whose efficacy[3] was more dubious. He had to choose between the two.

Who could help him choose? Christian doctrine? No. Christian doctrine says, "Be charitable, love your neighbor, take the more rugged path, etc., etc." But which is the more rugged path? Whom should he love as a brother? The fighting man or his mother? Which does the greater good, the vague act of fighting in a group, or the concrete one of helping a particular human being to go on living? Who can decide a priori? Nobody. No book of ethics can tell him. The Kantian ethics says, "Never treat any person as a means, but as an end." Very well, if I stay with my mother, I'll treat her as an end and not as a means; but by virtue of this very fact, I'm running the risk of treating the people around me who are fighting, as means; and conversely, if I go to join those who are fighting, I'll be treating them as an end, and, by doing that, I run the risk of treating my mother as a means.

If values are vague, and if they are always too broad for the concrete and specific case that we are considering, the only thing left for us is to

---

[2] Person who works with enemy invaders.   [3] Effectiveness.

trust our instincts. That's what this young man tried to do; and when I saw him, he said, "In the end, feeling is what counts. I ought to choose whichever pushes me in one direction. If I feel that I love my mother enough to sacrifice everything else for her—my desire for vengeance, for action, for adventure—then I'll stay with her. If, on the contrary, I feel that my love for my mother isn't enough, I'll leave."

But how is the value of a feeling determined? What gives his feeling for his mother value? Precisely the fact that he remained with her. I may say that I like so-and-so well enough to sacrifice a certain amount of money for him, but I may say so only if I've done it. I may say "I love my mother well enough to remain with her" if I have remained with her. The only way to determine the value of this affection is, precisely, to perform and act which confirms and defines it. But, since I require this affection to justify my act, I find myself caught in a vicious circle.

Given that men are free and that tomorrow they will freely decide what man will be, I cannot be sure that, after my death, fellow-fighters will carry on my work to bring it to its maximum perfection. Tomorrow, after my death, some men may decide to set up Fascism,[4] and the others may be cowardly and muddled enough to let them do it. Fascism will then be the human reality, so much the worse for us.

Actually, things will be as man will have decided they are to be. Does that mean that I should abandon myself to quietism? No. First, I should involve myself; then, act on the old saw, "Nothing ventured, nothing gained." Nor does it mean that I shouldn't belong to a party, but rather that I shall have no illusions and shall do what I can. For example, suppose I ask myself, "Will socialization, as such, ever come about?" I know nothing about it. All I know is that I'm going to do everything in my power to bring it about. Beyond that, I can't count on anything. Quietism is the attitude of people who say, "Let others do what I can't do." The doctrine I am presenting is the very opposite of quietism, since it declares, "There is no reality except in action." Moreover, it goes further, since it adds, "Man is nothing else than his plan; he exists only to the extent that he fulfills himself; he is therefore nothing else than the ensemble of his acts, nothing else than his life."

Now, for the existentialist there is really no love other than one which manifests itself in a person's being in love. There is no genius other than one which is expressed in works of art; the genius of Proust is the sum of Proust's works; the genius of Racine is his series of tragedies. Outside of that, there is nothing. Why say that Racine could have written another tragedy, when he didn't write it? A man is involved in life, leaves his impress on it, and outside of that there is nothing. To be sure, this may seem a harsh thought to someone whose life hasn't been a success. But, on the other hand, it prompts people to understand that reality alone is what counts, that dreams, expectations, and hopes warrant no more than to define a man as a disappointed dream, as miscarried hopes, as vain

[4] A form of totalitarianism.

expectations. In other words, to define him negatively and not positively. However, when we say, "You are nothing else than your life," that does not imply that the artist will be judged solely on the basis of his works of art; a thousand other things will contribute toward summing him up. What we mean is that a man is nothing else than a series of undertakings, that he is the sum, the organization, the ensemble of the relationships which make up these undertakings.

When all is said and done, what we are accused of, at bottom, is not our pessimism, but an optimistic toughness. If people throw up to us our works of fiction in which we write about people who are soft, weak, cowardly, and sometimes even downright bad, it's not because these people are soft, weak, cowardly, or bad; because if we were to say, as Zola did, that they are that way because of heredity, the workings of environment, society, because of biological or psychological determinism, people would be reassured. They would say, "Well, that's what we're like, no one can do anything about it." But when the existentialist writes about a coward, he says that this coward is responsible for his cowardice. He's not like that because he has a cowardly heart or lung or brain; he's not like that on account of his physiological make-up; but he's like that because he has made himself a coward by his acts. There's no such thing as a cowardly constitution; there are nervous constitutions; there is poor blood, as the common people say, or strong constitutions. But the man whose blood is poor is not a coward on that account, for what makes cowardice is the act of renouncing or yielding. A constitution is not an act; the coward is defined on the basis of the acts he performs. People feel, in a vague sort of way, that this coward we're talking about is guilty of being a coward, and the thought frightens them. What people would like is that a coward or a hero be born that way.

Existentialism is nothing else than an attempt to draw all the consequences of a coherent atheistic position. It isn't trying to plunge man into despair at all. But if one calls every attitude of unbelief despair, like the Christians, then the word is not being used in its original sense. Existentialism isn't so atheistic that it wears itself out showing that God doesn't exist. Rather, it declares that even if God did exist, that would change nothing. There you've got our point of view. Not that we believe that God exists, but we think that the problem of His existence is not the issue. In this sense existentialism is optimistic, a doctrine of action, and it is plain dishonesty for Christians to make no distinction between their own despair and ours and then to call us despairing.

Questions for Discussion and Writing

1. One quality that makes us human, Sartre says, is our capability of "imagining [ourselves] as being in the future." What are some of the implications of this uniquely human ability, and why might it have philosophical significance?

2. Sartre states that a human being is "a plan which is aware of itself, rather than a patch of moss, a piece of garbage, or a cauliflower." How does that

logically lead to Sartre's belief that we are all responsible for our own lives and worth?

3. In your own words, explain Sartre's basic tenet that "existence precedes essence."

4. By being responsible for our own selves, how do we become responsible for all human beings? Review paragraphs 2–3 of Sartre's essay to work out his reasoning.

5. Why should rejection of belief in God make humans "forlorn" and "responsible"? Review paragraphs 4–6 to clarify Sartre's logical chain of thought.

6. Why is action the prime existentialist value? Apply the principle to examples in your own experience—attending college, committing yourself to a friend or lover, making some ethical decision, or some other choice or decision you have made.

Jack Henry Abbott, *"State-Raised Convict"* _____

Sent to reform school as a preadolescent and imprisoned in a state penitentiary at eighteen, Jack Henry Abbott was raised in—and, he argues, by—a system so repressive and cruel that its products may be forever incapacitated as citizens and individuals. Adjustment to prison, which the officials use as one criterion in parole hearings, is a logical and moral contradiction for Abbott, for it represents participation in injustice and corruption. Abbott's life since the 1981 publication of his book, symbolically entitled In the Belly of the Beast, *from which this essay is taken, provides evidence for his thesis. Within weeks of his release on parole, Abbott murdered a New York waiter in a misunderstanding about the use of a restaurant's restroom. As Abbott explained his actions later, his experience as a prisoner taught him that all encounters carry with them the threat of violence, and one must be ready to "defend" oneself, even to the point of murder.*

. . . My mind keeps turning toward one of the main aspects of prison that separates ordinary prisoners who, at some point in their lives, serve a few years and get out never to return—or if they do, it is for another short period and never again—and the convict who is "state-raised," i.e., the prisoner who grows up from boyhood to manhood in penal institutions.

I have referred to it as a form of instability (mental, emotional, etc.). There is no doubt (let us say there is *little* doubt) that this instability is *caused* by a lifetime of incarceration. Long stretches of, say, from ages ten to seventeen or eighteen, and then from seventeen or eighteen to ages thirty and forty.

You hear a lot about "arrested adolescence" nowadays, and I believe this concept touches the nub of the instability of prisoners like myself.

Every society gives its men and women the prerogatives of men and women, of *adults*. Men are given their dues. After a certain age you are regarded as a man by society. You are referred to as "sir"; no one interferes in your affairs, slaps your hands or ignores you. Society is solicitous in general and serves you. You are shown respect. Gradually your judgment is tempered because gradually you see that it has real effects; it impinges on the society, the world. Your experience mellows your emotions because you are free to move about anywhere, work and play at anything. You can pursue any object of love, pleasure, danger, profit, etc. You are taught by the very terms of your social existence, by the objects that come and go from your intentions, the natures of your own emotions—and you learn about yourself, your tastes, your strengths and weaknesses. You, in other words, mature emotionally.

It is not so for the state-raised convict. As a boy in reform school, he is punished for being a little boy. In prison, he is punished for trying to be a man in the sense described above. He is treated as an adolescent in prison. Just as an adolescent is denied the keys to the family car for *any* disobedience, *any* mischief, I am subjected to the hole[1] for *any* disobedience, *any* mischief. I will go to the hole for murder as well as for stealing a packet of sugar. I will get out of the hole in either case, and the length of time I serve for either offense is no different. My object is *solely* to avoid leaving evidence that will leave me open to prosecution out there in the world beyond these walls where a semblance of democracy is practiced.

Prison regimes have prisoners making extreme decisions regarding moderate questions, decisions that only fit the logical choice of either-or. No contradiction is allowed openly. You are not allowed to change. You are only allowed to submit; "agreement" does not exist (it implies equality). You are the rebellious adolescent who must obey and submit to the judgment of "grownups"—*"tyrants"* they are called when we speak of men.

A prisoner who is not state-raised tolerates the situation because of his social maturity prior to incarceration. He knows things are different outside prison. But the state-raised convict has no conception of any difference. He lacks experience and, hence, maturity. His judgment is untempered, rash; his emotions are impulsive, raw, unmellowed.

There are emotions—a whole spectrum of them—that I know of only through words, through reading and my immature imagination. I can *imagine* I feel those emotions (know, therefore, what they are), but *I do not*. At age thirty-seven I am barely a precocious child. My passions are those of a boy.

This thing I related above about emotions is the hidden, dark side of state-raised convicts. The foul underbelly everyone hides from everyone else. There is someting else. It is the other half—which concerns *judg-*

---

[1] Solitary confinement.

ment, reason (moral, ethical, cultural). It is the mantle of pride, integrity, honor. It is the high esteem we naturally have for violence, force. It is what makes us *effective,* men whose jꞌ ꞏgment impinges on others, on the world: Dangerous killers who act alone and *without* emotion, who act with calculation and principles, to avenge themselves, establish and defend their principles with acts of murder that usually evade prosecution by law; this is the state-raised convicts' conception of manhood, in the highest sense.

The model we emulate is a fanatically defiant and alienated individiual who cannot imagine what forgiveness is, or mercy or tolerance, because he has no *experience* of such values. His emotions do not know what such values are, but he *imagines* them as so many "weaknesses" precisely because the unprincipled offender appears to escape punishment through such "weaknesses" on the part of society.

But if you behave like a man (a man such as yourself) you are doomed; you are feared and hated. You are "crazy" by the standards of the authorities—by their prejudices against prison-behavior.

Can you imagine how I feel—to be treated as a little boy and not as a man? And when I was a little boy, I was treated as a man—and can you imagine what that does to a boy? (I keep waiting for the years to give me a sense of humor, but so far that has evaded me completely.)

So. A guard frowns at me and says: "Why are you not at work?" Or: "Tuck in your shirttail!" Do this and do that. The way a little boy is spoken to. This is something I have had to deal with not for a year or two—nor even ten years—but for, so far, eighteen years. And when I explode, then I have burnt myself by behaving like a contrite and unruly little boy. So I have, in order to avoid that deeper humiliation, developed a method of reversing the whole situation—and I become the man chastising the little boy. (Poor kid!) It has cost me dearly, and not just in terms of years in prison or in the hole.

I cannot adjust to daily life in prison. For almost twenty years this has been true. I have never gone a month in prison without incurring disciplinary action for violating "rules." Not in all these years.

Does this mean I must die in prison? Does this mean I cannot "adjust" to society outside prison?

The government answers yes—but I *remember* society, and it is not like prison. I feel that if I ever did *adjust to prison,* I could by that fact alone never adjust to society. I would be back in prison within months.

Now, I care about myself and I cannot let it happen that I cannot adjust to freedom. Even if it means spending my life in prison—because to me prison is nothing but mutiny and revolt.

. . . A round peg will not fit into a square slot. I don't think they'll ever let me out of prison so long as my release depends on my "good adjustment to prison."

In the beginning the walls of my cell were made of boiler-plate steel, and I would kick them all day every day, hollering, screaming—for no apparent reason. I was so choked with rage in those days (about sixteen or seventeen years ago), I could hardly talk, even when I was calm: I *stuttered* badly. I used to throw my tray as casually as you would toss a balled-up scrap of paper in a trash can—but would do it with a tray full of food at the face of a guard.

That is what I mean by a response to the prison experience by a man who does not belong there.

Hell, if I never went to prison, who knows what "evil" I would have committed. I'm not at all saying that because I don't *belong* in prison that I should not have been sent there. Theoretically, *no one* should *belong* in prison! I was sent there for punishment—and I happen to have gotten it. I do not think it is like that with most men who are sent to prison. Everyone hurts in prison, but not like that.

I *still* cannot talk to a guard, not unless I have his ass in a corner and am giving *him* the orders. I still stutter sometimes when I have to address a guard—address him without breaking rules. I can cuss one out very eloquently or insult him, but that's when I've broken a rule or don't care if I do break one. It is strange to contemplate: people with a stuttering defect in society can usually *sing* without stuttering; well, I can cuss without stuttering . . .

It's impossible. I'm the kind of fool who, facing Caesar and his starving lions, need only retract a statement to walk away scot-free but instead cannot suppress saying "fuck you" to Caesar—knowing full well the consequences. What is more, I *refuse to be martyred;* I don't accept the consequences, and whine all the way to my death. A death, it *seems,* that I *chose.*

If I *could* please Caesar, I would, I gladly would.

It's a fucked-up world, but it's all I got.

I have never accepted that I did this to myself. I have never been successfully indoctrinated with that belief. That is the only reason I have been in prison this long.

Indoctrination begins the moment someone is arrested. It becomes more thorough every step of the way, from the moment of arrest to incarceration. In prison, it finds its most profound expression.

Every minute for years you are forced to believe that your suffering is a result of your "ill behavior," that it is self-inflicted. You are indoctrinated to blindly accept *anything* done to you. But if a guard knocks me to the floor, only by indoctrination can I be brought to believe I did it to myself. If I am thrown in the prison hole for having violated a prison rule—for having, for example, shown insolence to a pig—I can only believe I brought this upon myself through *indoctrination.*

. . . I might have become indoctrinated were it not for the evil and ignorant quality of the men who are employed in prisons.

A prisoner is taught that what is required of him is to *never* resist, *never* contradict. A prisoner is taught to *plead* with the pigs and accept guilt for things he never did.

I have had guards I have never seen before report me for making threats and arguing with them. I have been taken before disciplinary committees of guards for things I have never done, things they all knew I never did. And I have been ordered to the hole for things they *knew* I never did.

My prison record has in it more violence reported by guards than that of any of the 25,000 federal prisoners behind bars today, and I am not guilty of nine-tenths of the charges. Yet there is nothing at all I can do about it.

If I were beaten to death tomorrow, my record would go before the coroner's jury—before anyone who had the power to investigate—and my "past record of violence" would vindicate my murderers. In fact, the prison regime can commit any atrocity against me, and my "record" will acquit them.

The government shows that record to judges if I get into court on a civil suit against the prison or on a petition for writ of habeas corpus.[2] It is designed to prejudice the judge—a man who relishes any opportunity to prejudice himself against prisoners.

Responsibility? I am not responsible for what the government—its system of justice, its prison—has done to me. I did not do this to myself.

This is not easy to say; it is not a *point of view* to hold. Why? Because it has cost me, so far, almost two decades of imprisonment. This I hold is the *greater* responsibility: I did not do this to myself.

I do not share in the sins of this guilty country; we are not "all in this together"! Who in America today would *dare* take the responsibility for himself and others that I and countless other prisoners like me have taken?

. . . I know you aren't mean enough to think I'm trying to shift the responsibility for my own "corrupt self." Indeed I am not. I have only tried to indicate the opposite: that I demand responsibility for myself. And in so doing, I have come to understand the reasons for it all. I myself can handle it quite well.

I do not have the confidence of a sleepwalker, and so my wish to better myself is in a spiritual sense a very conscious wish.

The Existentialists say they take all responsibility for their lives and the world upon their shoulders. Who can fault that? The world is amazed at how "cruel" it is! (This is very funny to think about!) And then, when the "chips are down" (Sartre's favorite expression), Sartre, who has never gambled but is enamored of the terminology of a kind of daring that doesn't involve getting his ass skinned, "martyrs" himself. It is the same kind of responsibility anyone takes upon himself by submitting to your

[2] Court-ordered personal appearance.

bad opinion of him by hanging his head and agreeing with all the accusations—and then, when he has done that, forlornly tells you he is sorry it rained last night, sorry the price of tea went up, etc., etc. He won't defend himself, because he is *truly* at fault and is too pathetic to be punished.

To say you are *not* responsible for the life of someone you killed in self-defense, not responsible for the circumstances that brought you to prison (and kept you there for two decades)—to say all that in the face of your accusers, accusers who also justify their mistreatment of you by those accusations, is to be really responsible for your words and deeds. Because every time you reject the accusations, you are held responsible *further* for things you are not responsible for.

. . . I've only lately discovered that at age thirty I began to exercise the ability to *think*. I'm more restless now than I was at age ten—and *nothing* could stop me then.

It is funny that some of us must not only get our bearings but must also know all the details of the world before we venture out into it. Only now do I feel I know enough to live, but it is not funny that what I have learned may demand that I throw my life away from me.

Questions for Discussion and Writing

1. Working with other class members and using Sartre's essay, identify the existential issues that Abbott raises in this excerpt. Consider the issues of responsibility and action in particular.

2. Abbott argues that state-raised convicts are different from people who have grown up in free society. Would Sartre accept his argument that society is responsible for the mental and emotional instability of these convicts? Explain the role of maturity and adult rights in Abbott's argument, and work out your reasoning for other class members.

3. Review Abbott's passage on the "hidden, dark side of state-raised convicts" (paragraph 9). Is he voicing an existentialist view in this passage? If so, in what way?

4. Would Sartre agree with Abbott that by adjusting to life in prison he would be unable ever to adjust to society? Why or why not?

5. Abbott writes, "I am not responsible for what the government—its system of justice, its prison—has done to me. I did not do this to myself." Would an existentialist accept his statement? Do you find any validity in it?

Richard Rodriguez, from **Hunger of Memory** _____

A social and literary critic, Richard Rodriguez has published essays on diverse topics, but his views on bilingual education and the experiences of Mexican-Americans have gained the greatest attention. The son of Mexican immigrants, Rodriguez learned as a child that to compete in Anglo society, he would have to adopt the language of the mainstream. But with the language came a sense of alienation from his home culture, an

*alienation exacerbated by his increasingly close association with and ul-
timate membership in the English-speaking community.*

> . . . I grew up victim to a disabling confusion. As I grew fluent in
English, I no longer could speak Spanish with confidence. I continued to
understand spoken Spanish. And in high school, I learned how to read
and write Spanish. But for many years I could not pronounce it. A
powerful guilt blocked my spoken words; an essential glue was missing
whenever I'd try to connect words to form sentences. I would be unable
to break a barrier of sound, to speak freely. I would speak, or try to speak,
Spanish, and I would manage to utter halting, hiccuping sounds that
betrayed my unease.
>
> When relatives and Spanish-speaking friends of my parents came to
the house, my brother and sisters seemed reticent to use Spanish, but at
least they managed to say a few necessary words before being excused. I
never managed so gracefully. I was cursed with guilt. Each time I'd hear
myself addressed in Spanish, I would be unable to respond with any
success. I'd know the words I wanted to say, but I couldn't manage to say
them. I would try to speak, but everything I said seemed to me horribly
anglicized. My mouth would not form the words right. My jaw would
tremble. After a phrase or two, I'd cough up a warm, silvery sound. And
stop.
>
> It surprised my listeners to hear me. They'd lower their heads,
better to grasp what I was trying to say. They would repeat their questions in gentle, affectionate voices. But by then I would answer in
English. No, no, they would say, we want you to speak to us in Spanish.
('. . . *en espanol.*') But I couldn't do it. *Pocho* then they called me.
Sometimes playfully, teasingly, using the tender diminutive—*mi pochito.*
Sometimes not so playfully, mockingly, *Pocho.* (A Spanish dictionary
defines that word as an adjective meaning 'colorless' or 'bland.' But I
heard it as a noun, naming the Mexican-American who, in becoming an
American, forgets his native society.) *'¡Pocho!'* the lady in the Mexican
food store muttered, shaking her head. I looked up to the counter where
red and green peppers were strung like Christmas tree lights and saw the
frowning face of the stranger. My mother laughed somewhere behind
me. (She said that her children didn't want to practice 'our Spanish' after
they started going to school.) My mother's smiling voice made me
suspect that the lady who faced me was not really angry at me. But,
searching her face, I couldn't find the hint of a smile.
>
> Embarrassed, my parents would regularly need to explain their
children's inability to speak flowing Spanish during those years. My
mother met the wrath of her brother, her only brother, when he came up
from Mexico one summer with his family. He saw his nieces and
nephews for the very first time. After listening to me, he looked away and
said what a disgrace it was that I couldn't speak Spanish, *'su proprio
idioma.'* He made that remark to my mother; I noticed, however, that he
stared at my father.

I clearly remember one other visitor from those years. A long-time friend of my father from San Francisco would come to stay with us for several days in late August. He took great interest in me after he realized that I couldn't answer his questions in Spanish. He would grab me as I started to leave the kitchen. He would ask me something. Usually he wouldn't bother to wait for my mumbled response. Knowingly, he'd murmur: '*¿Ay Pocho, Pocho, adónde vas?*' And he would press his thumbs into the upper part of my arms, making me squirm with currents of pain. Dumbly, I'd stand there, waiting for his wife to notice us, for her to call him off with a benign smile. I'd giggle, hoping to deflate the tension between us, pretending that I hadn't seen the glittering scorn in his glance.

I remember that man now, but seek no revenge in this telling. I recount such incidents only because they suggest the fierce power Spanish had for many people I met at home; the way Spanish was associated with closeness. Most of those people who called me a *pocho* could have spoken English to me. But they would not. They seemed to think that Spanish was the only language we could use, that Spanish alone permitted our close association. (Such persons are vulnerable always to the ghetto merchant and the politician who have learned the value of speaking their clients' family language to gain immediate trust.) For my part, I felt that I had somehow committed a sin of betrayal by learning English. But betrayal against whom? Not against visitors to the house exactly. No, I felt that I had betrayed my immediate family. I *knew* that my parents had encouraged me to learn English. I *knew* that I had turned to English only with angry reluctance. But once I spoke English with ease, I came to *feel* guilty. (This guilt defied logic.) I felt that I had shattered the intimate bond that had once held the family close. This original sin against my family told whenever anyone addressed me in Spanish and I responded, confounded.

But even during those years of guilt, I was coming to sense certain consoling truths abut language and intimacy. I remember playing with a friend in the backyard one day, when my grandmother appeared at the window. Her face was stern with suspicion when she saw the boy (the *gringo*) I was with. In Spanish she called out to me, sounding the whistle of her ancient breath. My companion looked up and watched her intently as she lowered the window and moved, still visible, behind the light curtain, watching us both. He wanted to know what she had said. I started to tell him, to say—to translate her Spanish words into English. The problem was, however, that though I knew how to translate exactly *what* she had told me, I realized that any translation would distort the deepest meaning of her message: It had been directed only to me. This message of intimacy could never be translated because it was not *in* the words she had used but passed *through* them. So any translation would have seemed wrong; her words would have been stripped of an essential meaning. Finally, I decided not to tell my friend anything. I told him that I didn't hear all she had said.

This insight unfolded in time. Making more and more friends out-side my house, I began to distinguish intimate voices speaking through *English.* I'd listen at times to a close friend's confidential tone or se-cretive whisper. Even more remarkable were those instances when, for no special reason apparently, I'd become conscious of the fact that my companion was speaking only to me. I'd marvel just hearing his voice. It was a stunning event: to be able to break through his words, to be able to hear this voice of the other, to realize that it was directed only to me. After such moments of intimacy outside the house, I began to trust hearing intimacy conveyed through my family's English. Voices at home at last punctured sad confusion. I'd hear myself addressed as an intimate at home once again. Such moments were never as raucous with sound as past times had been when we had had 'private' Spanish to use. (Our English-sounding house was never to be as noisy as our Spanish-speaking house had been.) Intimate moments were usually soft moments of sound. My mother was in the dining room while I did my homework nearby. And she looked over at me. Smiled. Said something—her words said nothing very important. But her voice sounded to tell me (*We are together*) I was her son.

(Richard!)

Intimacy thus continued at home; intimacy was not stilled by English. It is true that I would never forget the great change of my life, the diminished occasions of intimacy. But there would also be times when I sensed the deepest truth about language and intimacy: *Intimacy is not created by a particular language; it is created by intimates.* The great change in my life was not linguistic but social. If, after becoming a successful student, I no longer heard intimate voices as often as I had earlier, it was not because I spoke English rather than Spanish. It was because I used public language for most of the day. I moved easily at last, a citizen in a crowded city of words . . . .

Questions for Discussion and Writing

1. Both Jack Henry Abbott and Richard Rodriguez reveal that they were unable to speak clearly or that they began stuttering in certain situations—Abbott when he had to speak with a prison guard, and Rodriguez when he had to speak Spanish. How are their speaking problems a symptom of ethical struggles in each case?

2. Why does the term *pocho,* which translates as "colorless" or "bland," have negative connotations when it is applied to someone in Rodriguez's situation?

3. Why does Rodriguez's inability to speak fluent Spanish make others of his ethnic group openly critical of him? How does his language use relate to his sense of identity?

4. Is the belief of some of Rodriguez's acquaintances that "Spanish alone permitted . . . close association" an existentialist notion?

5. Rodriguez describes the guilt and sense of betrayal he experiences for learning English. In existential terms, how has his decision altered his identity?

6. Explain the young Richard's reluctance to translate the words of his Spanish-speaking friend for his Anglo playmate.

7. "Intimacy is not created by a particular language; it is created by intimates." Do you agree? Explain your response and provide evidence drawn from personal experience.

Chapter Writing Topics

1. The ability to examine an issue from multiple perspectives is a valuable problem-solving skill. The philosophical perspectives represented in this chapter can be used in this way to analyze a contemporary social, political, or personal issue. Select two or three philosophical perspectives and consider your chosen issue from these different angles. You could write on the abortion debate from an existentialist or Epicurean point of view, for example, or select an issue raised in the chapter readings. Topics that might be especially interesting and challenging can be drawn from Curtin's article on the homeless, Halsey's polemic against self-centeredness, Frankl's description of his Holocaust experience, Abbott's view of the effects of imprisonment, and Rodriguez's examination of cultural assimilation. The following issues can help you organize your exploration of the topic.

   (a) Identify the problem that you are attempting to analyze and perhaps offer a solution to it.

   (b) Summarize the first philosophical perspective that you will apply to it.

   (c) Adopt the perspective and apply it to explain the problem's sources, major elements, and possible solutions to it.

   (d) Consider the problem from a second philosophical perspective (summarize it for your reader first).

   (e) What new understanding of the issue has come out of the multiple-perspective analysis?

2. Examine the philosophical assumptions implicit in a religious code, scientific theory, or political doctrine detailed in earlier chapters (or one you know from other readings). Address any of the following questions which you consider relevant to the topic.

   (a) What view of human nature underlies the code, theory, or doctrine? Are people by nature good or evil? Selfish or altruistic?

   (b) Do people have free will or is human behavior programmed in some inescapable way?

   (c) Does a higher being or sphere exist?

(d) How definite is the knowledge we acquire? Can we ultimately find eternal, absolute truth?

(e) Can all people be held to the same rules of conduct? Are we created equal?

(f) What role should emotion play in determining values? Should reason prevail over feeling or desire?

(g) Which is more important, the individual or the community?

3. Discuss the issue of cultural difference and the philosophic problems it presents for the individual. Consider the experiences of Dick Gregory, Richard Rodriguez, Maxine Hong Kingston (in the excerpt from *The Woman Warrior,* Chapter 4), or other authors who discuss the effects of marginalization. How are questions of personal identity, social life, political activism, and educational choice affected by cultural difference from the mainstream? Synthesize the ideas discussed by the various writers listed by addressing the following questions; consider the authors' views from their probable personal, political, social, and educational perspectives.

(a) How might being "different" increase the pressure a person feels to formulate a specific philosophy in life?

(b) Do these writers act as spokespersons for their cultural group? Do they define the group's cultural identity, in existentialist terms?

(c) Which, if any, of these authors is likely to accept assimilation (the process by which members of an ethnic group move away from their home culture's traditions and adopt mainstream social customs and values) as the solution to marginal social status?

(d) What philosophic attitude toward prejudice would these writers be likely to adopt?

4. One of the major objections to rock music over the decades has been the apparently nihilistic stance that many of the groups promote through their lyrics, life-styles, and stage performances. Select a group whose work you know and analyze the music and image it promotes. To what extent does the group represent a nihilistic attitude? Does it actually promote some other value system? If so, identify the philosophical message that you believe more accurately characterizes the group's work. The following issues can be used to create an outline for your discussion.

(a) Explain why rock music has often come under attack for being nihilistic.

(b) Analyze why some groups may fall under that heading despite the positive message of their work: what in their image suggests a nihilistic stance? Focus on the group you plan to analyze in the essay.

(c) Identify the actual philosophical view(s) promoted by the group's work.

(d) Support your argument with quotations from song lyrics, examples of the group's social contributions, and other evidence that illustrates the group's values.

5. Illustrate the values of a particular philosophical view that appeals to you by telling the story of a person who lives life according to this philosophy. Clarify for the reader what the major beliefs and values are, and illustrate them by describing situations in which these values are put to the test. Come to some conclusion about the effectiveness and worth of the philosophical view by assessing the life this person has led. The person you describe may be real, fictional, or a composite of several sources. Consider the following ways of developing the discussion.

    (a) Compare or contrast the person's values to other philosophical views you have read about in this chapter.

    (b) Show how the person's views guide the decision he or she makes in common situations: academic matters (study habits, moral issues such as cheating), social life (attitudes toward friendship and love, views on the sources of pleasure and happiness), other major areas of experience.

    (c) Write the essay in the first person (the "I" voice) to give a real voice to the person whose life story is being told.

6. Choose a philosopher, religious figure, or social commentator whose ideas you have studied in the preceding readings and identify how this figure would perceive the contemporary world. Which issues, problems, and/or social practices would seem of greatest concern to him or her? Why? What would this person consider the most positive part of contemporary life? What overall impression would this figure probably have of the world we live in?

    (a) Use a figure from any of the preceding chapters. Consider the ancient Greeks, the medieval theologians, religious reformists, early and contemporary scientists, literary artists and critics, political theorists and activists, and philosophers.

    (b) Clarify for the reader what the philosophical values of this figure are.

    (c) Use these values to explain logically which contemporary issues would be of greatest interest to the figure and to determine the figure's general view of modern life.

CREDITS

Jack Henry Abbott, "State-Raised Convict." From *In the Belly of the Beast* by Jack Henry Abbott. Copyright © 1981 by Jack Henry Abbott. Reprinted by permission of Random House Inc.

Aesop, "Diogenes on a Journey." Reprinted from *Aesop Without Morals*, trans. by Lloyd Daly (A. S. Barnes & Company, 1961). By permission of the publisher.

Aristotle, from *Poetics*. Translated by S. H. Butcher, Macmillan Publishing Company, 1932.

Brooks Atkinson, "Emerson." From *The Selected Writings of Ralph Waldo Emerson*, edited by Brooks Atkinson. Copyright © 1940 by Random House, Inc. Reprinted by permission of Random House.

David Attenborough, from *The Living Planet* by David Attenborough. Copyright © 1984 by David Attenborough Productions, Ltd.

St. Augustine, *The Confessions of St. Augustine*, trans. by Rex Warner, New American Library, copyright © 1963. Reprinted by permission of Penguin USA.

Ian G. Barbour, *Issues in Science and Religion*. Copyright © 1966, pp. 40-43. Reprinted by permission of Prentice-Hall, Inc., Englewood Cliffs, N.J.

Bede, from *Life of Cuthbert* by Bede in *Lives of the Saints*, trans. by J. F. Webb (Penguin Classics, 1965). Copyright © 1965 by J. F. Webb.

Ruth Bleier, reprinted from *Feminist Approaches to Science*, Ruth Bleier, ed., Pergamon Press, 1988. Reprinted by permission of the publisher.

Gwendolyn Brooks, "The Pool Players." Published in *Blacks*. Copyright © 1987, and issued by The David Company, Chicago, Ill. Reprinted by permission.

sion of W. W. Norton & Company, Inc. Copyright © 1977 by W. W. Norton & Company, Inc.

Malcolm X, "The Ballot or the Bullet." From *Malcolm X Speaks: Selected Speeches and Statements*, Merit Publishers, 1965.

Sir Thomas Malory, from *Le Morte D'Arthur*. Reprinted with permission of Macmillan Publishing Company from "Sir Lancelot du Lac" in *Le Morte D'Arthur* by Sir Thomas Malory, R. M. Lumiansky, ed. Copyright © 1982 by R. M. Lumiansky.

Michel de Montaigne, "Of Not Communicating One's Glory." Reprinted from *The Complete Works of Montaigne*, trans. by Donald M. Frame with the permission of the publishers, Stanford University Press. Copyright © 1943, 1948, 1957, 1958 by Donald M. Frame.

Carolyn J. Mooney, "Sweeping Curricular Changes . . . at Stanford." Copyright © 1988, *The Chronicle of Higher Education*, Vol. 35, No. 16. Reprinted with permission.

Adalaide Morris, reprinted from "Dick, Jane, and American Literature: Fighting with Canons," by Adalaide Morris, *College English*, September 1985. Copyright © 1985 by the National Council of Teachers of English. Reprinted with permission.

"Oedipus." Reprinted from *Classic Myth and Legend*, trans. by A. Hope-Moncrieff, the Gresham Publishing Company, Ltd.

Madalyn Murray O'Hair, "Arguments for God, Historical and Contemporary, with Refutation." From "What On Earth Is an Atheist" by Madalyn Murray O'Hair. Copyright © 1972. Reprinted by permission of American Atheist Press.

Martin Oppenheimer, "Defining Terrorism." Reprinted from *The Nonviolent Activist: Magazine of the War Resisters League*.

George Orwell, "Marrakech." From *Such, Such Were the Joys* by George Orwell. Copyright © 1953 by Sonia Brownell Orwell and renewed 1981 by Mrs. George K. Perutz, Mrs. Miriam Gross, Dr. Michael Dickson, Executors of the Estate of Sonia Brownell Orwell. Reprinted by permission of Harcourt Brace Jovanovich, Inc.

Albert Parry, "Robespierre's Bloody Virtue," from *Terrorism: From Robespierre to Arafat*, by Albert Parry. Copyright © 1976 by Albert Parry. Reprinted by permission of Vanguard Press, a division of Random House, Inc.

Plato, from "The Apology of Socrates" and "Phaedo." Reprinted from Plato, *The Last Days of Socrates*, trans. by Hugh Tredennick (Penguin Classics, revised edition, 1969), copyright © Hugh Tredennick, 1954, 1959, 1969.

Plato, *The Symposium*, trans. by Walter Hamilton (Penguin Classics, 1951), copyright © Walter Hamilton, 1951.

Amaury de Riencourt, "Women in Athens." From *Sex and Power in History* by Amaury de Riencourt. Copyright © 1975 by Amaury de Riencourt. New York: Dell Publishing Company.

Richard Rodriguez, from *Hunger of Memory* by Richard Rodriguez. Copyright © 1983 by Richard Rodriguez. Reprinted by permission of David R. Godine, Publisher.

Mike Rose, "Crossing Boundaries." Reprinted with permission of The Free Press, a Division of Macmillan, Inc., from *Lives on the Boundary: The Struggles and Achievements of America's Underprepared* by Mike Rose. Copyright © 1989 by Mike Rose.

Rousseau, from *The Confessions of Jean-Jacques Rousseau*, trans. by J. M. Cohen (Penguin Classics, 1954), copyright © by J. M. Cohen, 1954.

Bertrand Russell, "The Copernican Revolution." From *Religion and Science* by Bertrand Russell. Copyright © 1935. Reprinted by permission of Oxford University Press.

Bertrand Russell, "Evolution." From *Religion and Science* by Bertrand Russell. Copyright © 1935. Reprinted by permission of Oxford University Press.

Francis Henry Sandback, "Stoicism." From *Chamber's Encyclopedia* (1964 ed.).

Jean Paul Sartre, "Existentialism." Copyright © 1947, renewed 1974. Reprinted by permission of Philosophical Library, Inc.

Farrand Sayre, *The Greek Cynics*. Copyright © 1948 by Farrand Sayre. Reprinted by permission of J. H. Furst Publishing Company.

Sidney Shalett, "First Atomic Bomb Dropped on Japan; Missile Is Equal to 20,000 Tons of TNT; Truman Warns Foe of a 'Rain of Ruin'," by Sidney Shalett in *The New York Times*, August 7, 1945. Copyright © 1945/74 by The New York Times Company. Reprinted by permission.

George Simpson, "Early Social Darwinism." Copyright © 1959 by the Antioch Review, Inc. First appeared in *The Antioch Review*, Vol. 19, No. 7 (Spring 1959). Reprinted by permission of the Editors.

Baljit Singh, "An Overview of Terrorism" in *Terrorism: Interdisciplinary Perspectives* by Baljit Singh. Yonah Alexander and Seymour Maxwell Singer, eds. Copyright © 1977 by the John Jay Press, John Jay College of Criminal Justice.

Sophocles, *Oedipus Rex*. The *Oedipus Rex* of Sophocles, copyright © 1949 by Harcourt Brace Jovanovich, Inc., and renewed 1977 by Cornelia Fitts and Robert Fitzgerald, reprinted by permission of the publisher. (CAUTION: All rights, including professional, amateur, motion picture, recitation, lecturing, public reading, radio broadcasting, and television are strictly reserved. Inquiries on all rights should be addressed to Harcourt Brace Jovanovich, Inc., Copyright and Permission Department, Orlando, Fla. 32887.)

George K. Strodach, from *The Philosophy of Epicurus* by George K. Strodach. Copyright © 1963 by Northwestern University Press. Reprinted by permission of Northwestern University Press.

Instructor's Guide to Accompany

THE COURSE OF IDEAS

Jeanne Gunner

UCLA

Ed Frankel

UCLA

CONTENTS

CHAPTER 1: THE ANCIENT GREEK TRADITION

<u>Religious and Artistic Narratives: Myth and Epic</u>

<u>Systematic Thought in Philosophy, Science, and Politics</u>

<u>Rethinking the Tradition</u>

CHAPTER 2: RELIGION: CHANGING BELIEFS AND ATTITUDES

<u>The Ancient World</u>

<u>The Middle Ages</u>

<u>Reform Movements</u>

CHAPTER 3:   REVOLUTIONS AND REACTIONS IN SCIENCE

The Historical Context: Medieval, Renaissance, Modern

Some Social Consequences of Scientific Progress

Rethinking Scientific Objectivity

CHAPTER FOUR: THE LITERARY TRADITION

Classical Texts

Medieval Tales and Renaissance Prose

CHAPTER 1: THE ANCIENT GREEK TRADITION

Religious and Artistic Narratives: Myth and Epic

Edith Hamilton, "Introduction to Classical Mythology"

1. Hamilton argues that the early Greek mythmakers were the first humanists. She offers her essay as context for reading the myths: one should approach them as products of a highly developed culture, not the religious or magical formulas of a primitive people. She wants to give the reader a framework for interpretation, and in this sense the piece is truly introductory: it attempts to sweep away traditional misconceptions and misreadings, posit a broad methodological approach, and offer readings of sample myths to illustrate it.
2. The rituals of truly primitive civilizations are unrelated to the sophisticated myths of the Greeks; the myths were developed by an advanced culture and put to human ends--entertainment and explanation of natural phenomena, or, in Hamilton's words, they served as "early literature as well as early science." The concerns dealt with in science fiction seem very human and are in this sense related to Hamilton's view on the nature of myths; the function of fantasy is similar to the entertainment value that Hamilton sees in them. Thus it seems likely that she would accept the parallel.
3. The thunderbolt of Zeus is a representation of the natural phenomena of thunder and lightning; the Dipper can never reach the sea because an angry goddess has cursed it. Other kinds of myth tell entertaining stories, as in the myth of the sculptor Pygmalion, whose statue of a beautiful young woman, Galatea, comes to life (retold in Shaw's Pygmalion and the play and film My Fair Lady, which can be taken as evidence of the myth's literary appeal). In their religious value, myths represent a moral system of right and wrong, as when Zeus punishes mortals for lying or breaking oaths.
4. According to Hamilton, the creatures of Greek mythology are, for the most part, attractive, and they have little direct influence on human life. They contrast to myths and legends featuring inhuman beings or powerful forces on human life, as in legends of dragons, goblins, and so on, and belief systems incorporating astrology or other occult arts. The rational basis of Greek civilization, Hamilton suggests, makes such elements irrelevant to the Greek culture, and so they generally are absent from the myths.

1

5. Rather than representing an absolute and unchanging code of moral conduct, the gods and goddesses of Greek myth reflect changing cultural values within the developing Greek culture. Thus the myths tend to reflect perceptions of the human condition, situations people face, desires they have, and so on, rather than specific moral precepts (in contrast to biblical parables, for example). That the figure of Zeus changes so radically is itself an argument against perceiving the myths as primarily religious in nature.

6. Voodoo, parapsychological phenomena such as ESP or telekinesis, and simple superstitions reflect a belief that invisible forces operate on the visible world, as do scientific theories and physical laws--gravity, for example. But scientific theories are based on phenomena that, while not apparent to the human eye, still physically exist and can be mathematically described. Where traditional scientists are likely to stand on this issue is open to debate. Traditional religions seem to depend on faithful acceptance of an invisible realm.

7. If we perceive the resources of the earth to exist only for human consumption--a belief common in religious teachings and in historical and political practices--we might expect this anthropocentric notion to lead to major environmental problems. The pollution of the earth's waters, depletion of the ozone layer, extinction of various species and so on can be traced back to the belief that the animal, plant, and mineral kingdoms are inferior in importance to human interests and thus can be fairly exploited for human gain. A disruption in the balance of nature is a logical outcome of privileging human needs and wants over animal rights, natural settings, and natural resources.

8. We ascribe human feelings and motives to pets quite commonly --love, envy, anger, jealousy, etc. We name prized possessions, from cars to stuffed animals, endowing the objects with our own sense of individuality and uniqueness. We may see natural phenomena in the same way: gloomy weather, angry rainstorms, relentless winds, playful breezes. The inverse of anthropomorphism can also be observed in the reduction of humans to objects, as may happen in instances of racism and sexism.

9. These figures reflect traditional American beliefs in rugged individualism and toughness (Wayne), tempered sometimes by a soft heart behind the gruff exterior; in rising from rags to riches and becoming "the king" (Presley), and having the fabulous riches that accompany such a station; of men having gorgeous, sexy, adoring women available, especially of the "dumb blond" type, though preferably good-natured and vulnerable (Monroe). The old west myths reflect the American sense of manifest destiny, the right and mission to expand our democratic empire, evident today, one could argue, in policies in central and South America as well as in other geographic areas.

10. [Personal response]

2

"Echo and Narcissus"

1. Myths have didactic content--they serve to explain and to
teach. In this sense, they can be said to possess a "thesis," a
main point, though the point is conveyed indirectly through
characters and dialogue. The storyteller and essayist use some
similar techniques (such as using convincing language and vivid
imagery), but they write with different audiences in mind. One
seeks to entertain and suggest; the other to lay out in analytic
form. In essay form, the story of "Echo and Narcissus" might
become an argument about the need to move beyond the limited world
of the self, on the one hand, but also to maintain the boundaries
of the self. Echo oversteps these boundaries on several occasions,
the ultimate one being her slavish devotion to Narcissus, which
leads to her tragic fate. The topic can elicit many different
readings of the myth's "thesis," which in turn can be used to
examine the idea of reader response.
2. The natural phenomenon of echoes is clearly one source of the
myth--how they came into existence, and why the phenomenon is
especially apparent in caves. The narcissus flower grows on the
edge of lakes; thus we see Narcissus lingering by the water.
Echo's punishment--to repeat the words spoken by others--and her
withdrawal to a cave explain the phenomenon and common locale of
echoes.
3. A narcissist might be described as someone who seeks always to
be the center of attention, who uses "I" more than any other
pronoun, who perceives events and conversations from a selfish
perspective. In ordinary usage, "narcissistic" and "egotistic"
have come to name very similar behavior patterns. The narcissist
might be said to have an overgrown sense of confidence and self-
esteem, unlike an egotist, who may be overcompensating for what is
actually a poor sense of self. The effects of either type of
behavior are likely to include hurt caused to others who care for
the person, as Echo is hurt and rejected; self-destruction brought
on by the self-absorption, literally so in Narcissus's case, but
seen also in the form of dependency on parental figures, immature
social skills, lack of responsibility, and so on.
4. Echo is in love, and we tend to view such figures
sympathetically. She is rejected by the object of her love
because of a personal failing--her inability to converse; many of
us may empathize on that level. The pain she feels at her
unrequited love and her hopeless devotion mirror common adolescent
reactions. On the other hand, she is a pest, and she seems as
narcissistic as Narcissus in her refusal to accept his rejection
and leave him alone. Narcissus comes across very badly to most
readers: he seems selfish, conceited, stupid, and so on. He is
desperately in love, though, and pines as fervently as Echo for
this cold, cruel object of love who flees from him, and thus he,
too, seems pitiful and pitiable.

3

5. [Personal response]

"Oedipus"

1. The ancient audience knew the events of the Oedipus myth in
full detail, yet they found the dramatic tension of Oedipus's own
discovery to be the main source of interest. The retelling of the
king's tragic fall was not seen as simple repetition but as a
strongly emotional process--what in the play <u>Oedipus Rex</u> would
become the basis of Aristotle's theory of catharsis, that tragedy
evokes pity and fear and cleanses the audience of these negative
emotions. Experiencing the feelings of Oedipus as he goes through
the steps of his well known fate was itself the source of
pleasure, and thus knowing the oracle's prediction (theoretically)
heightens the effect.
2. When Oedipus is abandoned as an infant on the slopes of a
mountainside, his feet are bound together in order to prevent his
crawling to safety. His ankles were pierced as part of the
process; his wound leads to the "swollen foot" name.
3. Oedipus seems a man of strong principles. He immediately
leaves Corinth when he learns of the oracle in order to avoid
harming his (supposed) parents. His royal blood and early
upbringing make him stand up to harsh treatment--treatment such as
Laius deals out. The encounter with the sphinx shows two of his
essential traits: his courage, and his extraordinary intelligence.
When he vows to find the king's murderer, he also reveals his
strong sense of law and justice; this sense may be what leads him
to prescribe his own punishment of self-blinding, in addition to
exile.
4. As a formerly great hero stripped of all the things that made
him great, he is punished in every waking moment by the knowledge
of how low he has fallen. He remains in life to serve as a symbol
of heinous sins, a walking representation of what can happen to
even the most lofty of men. Only he can bear the shame, which
offers the slight consolation that his nature is still a noble and
extraordinary one.
5. The myth can be interpreted in countless ways on this score.
Oedipus himself symbolizes the values of knowledge, courage, moral
strength; he also embodies a warning against unwavering pride,
violence, and impiety. The notion of facing up to one's fate might
also be read in the myth. The need for law and justice to prevail
over all people is a strong assertion as well.
6. Certainly the modern examples listed are treated as tragedies,
which points to the evolution of the term's meaning over the
centuries. We tend to see most unhappy events as tragic; why this
is the case is itself a good topic for discussion. Theoretically,
an event is tragic if it involves a person's fall from very high
status to a lowly position. The near-impeachment of former
President Richard Nixon is one possible example. A tragic hero

need not be morally impeccable but rather someone who possesses a
great trait that becomes the cause of his or her downfall. In this
sense, the assassination of Martin Luther King, Jr., can be called
tragic, for it was his message of peace and justice that brought
about the racist rage of his assassin.
7.   In Mafia legend, a code of honor demands that disloyalty be
dealt with swiftly and finally; the individual does not so much
atone as pay for his or her betrayal. Also, the victim is assumed
to have willfully committed the transgression, unlike Oedipus, who
was fated to commit his crimes. One could make an interesting
argument about the issue in the context of gangs: are gang members
fated by their environment to enter the life of the streets? Are
they less accountable for their "sins" as a result? Are incidents
such as drive-by shootings a form of personal retribution, or are
they terrorist acts designed to intimidate? In general, the modern
versions of the ancient principle seem to have moved away from
socially recognized justice into the realm of vendetta and power-
seeking.

Homer, from The Odyssey

1.   Odysseus devises a complex plan to save his men and himself
from the cannibalistic Cyclops. He is overmatched in size and
strength, on hostile ground, and without resources for direct
fighting. His use of the Cyclops' own sheep to pull off the
escape demonstrates his cleverness and cunning.
2.   Polyphemus is a shepherd, a rural type, which for the Greeks
suggested an unsophisticated, ignorant, uncivilized sort of
person. He is also portrayed as a sloppy drunk, further
strengthening the picture of his barbarous nature. His violence
and cruelty are inhuman, reflected in his physical form--he is
distorted, in body and values. Odysseus charges him with abusing
his guests, a great sin against Zeus, which makes him an evil
figure in classical Greek eyes.
3.   In defense of Odysseus, we can say that Polyphemus is
carefully depicted as less than human, perhaps to make the
violence of Odysseus seem less cruel. The Cyclops has sinned
against Zeus, and Odysseus is, in a sense, supplying a fit
punishment for his crime. Odysseus rejoices over his own
achievement as much as the Cyclops's fall. On the other hand, the
damage done to Polyphemus is grievous and horrible, even though he
is portrayed as a buffoon in his ravings.
4.   Odysseus is the cunning hero, and part of Greek culture
emphasized the right and worth of the hero proclaiming his
achievements. Odysseus has earned the right to gloat, though he
is walking a very fine line between the hero's prerogative and
ruinous pride. But as a hero, he takes the opportunity to
broadcast his name, adding to the fame of it, which is part of the
heroic warrior ethic.

5. In many ways, Polyphemus seems similar to the villains of
contemporary action thrillers and horror films. He is monstrous,
strong, cruel; he has no sympathy, shows no mercy, and seem bent
on total destruction of his prey. Certainly the graphic details
are highlighted in the action: we see the monster drool body parts
and we get a detailed description of the stake-in-the-eye routine.
Odysseus also has contemporary parallels in the hero who is not
above violence himself (or herself). He is seemingly immune to
death, highly confident, resourceful--all qualities seen in many
modern heroes.

Werner Jaeger, from _Paideia_

1. Refined from its early meaning of skill as a warrior, "arete"
is made up of personal superiority to others, in terms of moral
character and excellence in action. "Glory" might be the simplest
equivalent term.
2. Jaeger seems clearly biased in favor of the ideals of the
Greek heroes. He makes an authorial aside critical of modern
educators who no longer promote the chivalric notion of arete; he
cites the ancient Greeks as having "high educational ideals" that
attempted "to express the whole of human potentialities."
3. Odysseus tells Cyclops that Zeus forbids mistreatment of
guests, but his host proceeds to imprison and even eat some of
Odysseus' band of men. Odysseus must act on the principle of
nemesis to correct this imbalance in the system of justice; he
seems justified in wounding and taunting the creature. As a great
hero, Odysseus must show his superior mind and bravery, and it is
his duty to uphold the gods' system of justice and order.
4. [Personal response]
5. Jaeger's theoretical treatment of the ancient Greek heroic
values emphasizes the natural superiority of certain groups of
men, what he terms "high race." Such heroes have the right and
responsibility to act in aggressive ways to demonstrate their
power; they have the right to dominate--the right to rule over the
weak. Power and privilege are naturally joined, in this doctrine.
The heroes of antiquity have been traditionally viewed as models
worthy of imitation. Because much of Western culture sees itself
as the product of Greek culture, citing the ancients as precedents
for or originators of a doctrine tends to give it authority and
respectability.
6. On the one hand, the educational critique embedded in Jaeger's
essay suggests that he believes in a return to the ancient ideals.
His glorification of the Homeric heroes idealizes them as cultural
models worthy of imitation. On the other, one can say that he is
merely attempting to recreate the ancient attitude, to bring to
life the early Greeks' moral sense.
7. [Personal response]
8. Because the Homeric hero "estimated his own worth exclusively

6

by the standards of the society to which he belonged" and the opinions others held of him, the actions of Odysseus can be understood as his efforts to claim the recognition he deserves. He alone saved his men through his cunning. He asserts his right to be known publicly as the man who outwitted the giant, and so he proclaims his name and place of origin.
9. [Personal response]

Systematic Thought in Philosophy, Science, and Politics

Thomas H. Greer, "The Founders of Western Philosophy"

1. [Personal response]
2. The advantage to the Socratic method is that it forces students to articulate their answers carefully and to continually examine any potential weaknesses in their arguments. They learn to think for themselves and discover truth for themselves. One disadvantage to this method is that it sometimes frustrates students as it forces them to develop and use their own ideas and beliefs, rather than being handed a philosophical "system" in a formal instructional way by a teacher.
3. [Personal response]
4. The growth of the modern sciences of nature coopted much of the domain of traditional philosophy. Modern philosophers like Rorty, Derrida, Habermas, Gadamer, Ricoeur, etc., have turned to examining language, or doing various kinds of social inquiry. They remain isolated in academia, incomprehensible to the average person. Other philosophers continue teaching in universities, training students to think critically and adding voices of wisdom to fields like law and medical ethics, etc.
5. Plato opposed democracy because he believed that the common person did not have the political skills and wisdom to make political decisions and command the ship of state. Viewing the state as an organic whole, he believed that the foot should not be called upon to do the work of the head. In other words, those suited and trained to govern should do so. He might have argued that if you want to sail a ship, you hire a captain who has the expertise, rather than electing one of the crew, or running the ship by a direct democracy, an unwieldy way to make quick decisions. On the other hand, it may be true that one goes to a cobbler (the expert) to have a pair of shoes (the government) made, but only the person who wears the shoes (the people) knows if they fit properly.
6. Socrates and his student Plato believed in absolute truth, a truth that was hidden from people by their

7

"erroneous sense perceptions," but nevertheless lay buried
in the human mind. Plato saw the imperfections of perceived
reality concealing a "perfect, absolute, and eternal order."
The physical world, Plato proposed, may be only "an illusion
of our senses," but beyond it, behind the illusion, lay the
"real world of spirit," the eternal world of perfect ideas
and forms created by God. The Sophists refused to accept the
notion of absolute truth, believing instead that truth was
relative for each person. They cited Heraclitus's
observation that the world is changing every moment, as are
people's ideas and perceptions, and that there is no way to
identify absolute truth.
7. Christian theorists adapted Plato's teachings because
they too developed an ideology that saw the world of the
senses as illusory, transitory and impermanent. They
believed in the eternal world of spirit, "the other world of
divine order and perfection," and so Plato's world of
absolute ideas and forms, waiting in the philosophical
wings, was made to order for modification into Christian
theology.
8. [Personal response]
9. [Class exercise]

Plato, from Symposium

1. [Personal response]
2. [Personal response]
3. The steps Socrates proposes to reach the experience of
absolute truth and beauty:
- Appreciation in the realm of physical beauty: love of one
particular beautiful person.
- Generalized appreciation in the physical realm:
recognition of all physical beauty beyond the individual
level.
- Entrance to the spiritual realm: recognition of beauty of
soul beyond physical beauty (first transcendent step).
- Understanding of the abstract realm or world of ideas:
beauty in activities and institutions beyond the individual
spirit (second transcendent step).
-Advancement in the abstract realm: appreciation of science
or abstract knowledge (the stage before absolute ideality).
- Perception of the absolute: the ideal beauty, essential,
pure and complete (total transcendence of the
physical/sensible world).
4. If people begin a quest for spiritual truth on the level
of physical love and passion, they begin with real world
phenomena that are part of their everyday lives, rather than

abstract concepts like truth and beauty that can be difficult to talk about without referring to concrete examples. Starting in the real world of the senses is a logical first step in moving to the abstract and intangible.
5. [Personal response]
6. [Personal response]

Marshall Clagett, "Greek Science: Origins and Methods"

1. The shift in technology, from the Bronze Age to the Iron Age, facilitated the inexpensive production of better tools and weapons, allowing the Greeks to trade more competitively with their near eastern neighbors. The Ionian city/state Miletus, on the coast of Asia Minor, had continual contact with the more sophisticated cultures of the Near East as well as direct interaction with Mesopotamia and Egypt, which were both areas of higher learning and culture, and this contact and interchange provided an impetus for the development of Greek natural philosophy and science. Some scholars even postulate that the evolution of Greek mythology might have had an effect on the birth of Greek philosophy and science. Lastly, the adoption of the alphabet, some time after 1000 B.C., led to the broader development and spread of learning and education in Greece, where previously only the scribes and priests could read and write.
2. Other advanced civilizations, like the Egyptians, made impressive advances, particularly in fields like geometry. They developed "sets of empirical rules" to solve specific problems, but they never really developed a "generalized" science," as opposed to just empirical rules.
3. Induction involves examining and analyzing various examples or facts and formulating probable general conclusions from them. Deduction starts with a general law or hypothesis against which it tests ideas or examples.
4. [Personal response]
5. Greek science "falls short" of modern science "in the maturity and univerality of its use of mathematical-experimental techniques." In other words, althought the Greeks practiced experimental techniques in rudimentary forms in optics, statics, applied mechanics, astronomy, zoology and physiology, the Greeks did not consider these techniques as their primary tools in all areas of scientific investigation. When Rome rose to power, the development of Greek science leveled off, due in part to the rise of Christianity and the subsequent shift of

potential scientific thinkers from science into the ranks of
Christianity and theology. In addition, the late Hellenistic
period witnessed a generalized spread of "non-critical
spiritual forces" throughout the Mediterranean that deterred
progressive scientific thought.
6. [Personal response]

Hippocrates, "The Sacred Disease"

1. Rather than viewing illness as caused by God, Hippocrates
believed illness to have natural causes. Hippocrates accused
other healers who viewed disease as divine in origin to be
magicians, charlatans and quacks, treating illness with
purifications, incantations and not allowing the sick to
bathe or eat certain foods. Hippocrates' approach
illustrates the development of the rational method in that
it was "secular and non-mythological." It did not attribute
all phenomena to the direct intervention of the Gods. It
also reflected a generalized theory as to the cause of
disease and relied on observation as well as inductive and
deductive thought.
2. the "quacks, magicians, and charlatans" could claim
success for their own methods and cures if their patients
recovered. If their patients failed to recover, they could
protect their reputations by blaming the divine will and
intervention of the Gods.
3. Hippocrates might be implying that eating goat can be
unhealthy or "unsuitable for sick folk." He uses this
example to stress the incompetence of healers who make use
of superstitions and purifications rather than understanding
the natural causes of disease.
4. The symptoms of epilepsy include heightening of the
olefactory, auditory, and visual senses, often accompanied
by hallucinations before the actual seizure. The seizure
itself involves body rigidity and spasms and occasionally
temporary loss of consciousness.
5. Hippocrates did believe that illness was caused by
"things that come to and go from the body," indicating the
rudimentary beginnings of a generalized theory of germs and
contagion. However, he also incorrectly believed that "cold,
sun, and the changing restlessness of the winds" caused
disease. Hippocrates believed that each disease had its own
cause and thus its own cure, although he incorrectly
attributed the cause of disease to the changing of the
seasons.

Moses Finley, "Politics"

1.   Finley defines government as a system of making and
administering rules, providing community services (from
establishing armies to maintaining roads, for example), and
establishing courts. Politics, on the other hand, he defines as
public discussion of and decision-making about the system itself.
In Greek-style politics, members of the public have authority over
the system they agree to be ruled by, typically through voting
rights. Families, classrooms, and workplaces may or may not,
therefore, involve politics, according to how much democratic
control over policy the participants in each situation have.
2.   The term "Athenians" (or "Spartans") emphasizes that the
political entity is composed of individual citizens, not an
abstract governmental system. Finley emphasizes the distinction
because it goes to the heart of his essay--the distinction of
politics from basic government.
3.   Matters of state in the ancient Greek world were perceived as
strictly mortal matters; the gods and religious laws were
concerned with different aspects of experience. In European
history, church and state law often came into conflict: the pope's
power posed a threat to the authority of absolute monarchs. Thus
the division arose between church and state, with state ultimately
gaining the upper hand. Religious persecution occurred frequently
as the result of this political struggle. The traditional American
separation of church and state grew out of the first settlers'
determination to preserve religious freedom.
4.   Because political conflict involves the airing of different
views and discussion between those in opposition, it preserves
political life; it involves community members in discussions,
disputes, possibly even civil wars, but such events lead
ultimately to consensus, re-establishment of community, and a
reaffirmation of rules, according to Finley. Our consitutional
rights include the right to express our views openly, regardless
of state policy, and in this way we can say the same tolerance of
conflict exists in America today.
5.   In direct democracies, citizens vote on actual issues, rather
than voting for representatives, who then have the power to speak
and act in the name of the people. Thus in democratic societies
such as the U.S., our power to influence policy is at several
removes. In a direct democracy, each of us would be able to vote
on actual legislation and other civic issues. In practice, the
size of our eligible voting population would create enormous
difficulties for a direct system; the benefits are open to
question.

6. Since the Athenian citizens had direct control of their
government through their voting privileges, they had very great
power as a block within the state. To increase their small
numbers through liberal citizenship laws might have diluted their
power, as groups with interests beyond their own gained
influential voices and votes. Thus women, immigrants, or slaves
could help restructure the laws and policy of the state. The
male, land-owning citizens were jealous of their citizenship
power.
7. Finley argues that politics requires that citizens have the
right to vote, which means having the power to discuss state
matters in open arenas and to determine binding laws. This right
was withheld in the ancient tyrannies, though other rights were
granted--the right to own land, etc. Because democracy depends on
the right to vote, either directly or through representatives,
tyranny violates its central precept. Modern democracies are
posited on the voting principle, and other forms of government are
perceived as repressive. The notion of an all-powerful ruler who
can extend or abridge civil rights violates the modern revival of
the classical notion of individual voice in politics.
8. [Personal response]

Plato, from "The Apology of Socrates" and "Phaedo"

1. Socrates does, one can argue, present his own best interest--
staying alive--as being in the best interest of Athens. He argues
that the judges will be committing a serious sin in executing him
and that he is trying to save them from acting in a way that
of reverse psychology on his judges in order to save himself.
2. Given the honor bestowed upon Socrates by all his friends, who
themselves are renowned figures in Athenian society, Socrates does
seem to have the standing that makes for arete. He is superior in
his calm, his demeanor, his concern for honoring the gods. That he
does not die in battle reflects the changing notion of arete, as
Jaeger points out: as Greek culture developed, arete became less
and less a warrior ethic and more a code of personal glory in the
public perception.
3. Using Finley's description of political decisions, we may find
it hard to fault Socrates' judges--they act as a whole, the direct
voice of the people's will. Thus their decision must represent the
prevailing sentiment that Socrates was guilty and deserved the
ultimate punishment of death.
4. The material world of the senses is, according to Plato, but a
pale and inferior reflection of the ideal world and thus a place to
seek deliverance from, not something to be cherished for itself.
Socrates displays his sincere belief in this doctrine. Because no
one can say that this world is to be preferred to the next, he has
no rational basis for clinging to life or regretting its loss.

5. The vagaries of the judicial system are much greater today:
Socrates would be judged by a panel of peers, not by the
collective society. No higher authority existed than the Athenian
judges; today, the appeal process moves from level of jurisdiction
to a higher one, culminating in the Supreme Court. The execution
itself would be more formal, more impersonal, and, many would
claim, more violent. Because we do not attempt to legislate
morality today, at least directly, a basis for criminal charges
against Socrates would not exist. It seems more than likely that
Socrates would be seen not as a threat but as a type of celebrity
today.

Rethinking the Tradition

Carolyn J. Mooney, "[Stanford's] `Western Culture'
  Program"

1. [Personal response]
2. [Class exercise]
3. The Stanford debate centered around criticism by
minorities that the very focus of a Western Culture course
did not recognize the heritage and achievements of women and
minorities. It didn't "try to understand the diversity of
experience of different people," argued one student. The
other side argued that students would lose touch with their
Western heritage and traditions if the classics weren't
studied. As a compromise, Stanford's faculty Senate voted to
change the one year Western culture requirement to a new
requirement entitled "Cultures, Ideas, and values," which
would place "substantial attention" on "issues of race,
gender, and class," and include works of women and
minorities. The change in curriculum was a compromise in
the sense that students still study European based ideas but
also read works from at least one non-European culture. The
term "Western" is being removed and the program will be
called Culture, Ideas, and Values.
4. [Class exercise]
5. Teaching traditional western classics alongside of
contemporary minority books or even classical traditional
third world texts can enrich student appreciation of both
canons by identifying the universal qualities of the human
experience, while at the same time allowing students to
appreciate the different ways cultures have succesfully
dealt with the dilemmas of the human condition. Comparing
St. Augustine's spiritual experiences and development with
the life history of a Navajo man, for example, could open up
several areas of exploration: How does each culture view

sexuality, pleasure, and guilt? To what degree are the
spiritual experiences of each man similar or different? What
characteristics of each culture account for the different
religious and philosophical systems of each culture?
6. [Personal response]
7. [Personal response]
8. By not trying to understand the diversity of different
people, the dominant western culture keeps minorities
marginalized. In doing so, all of society suffers.
Demographically, America is changing dramatically; globally
third world countries are fast becoming powers in their own
right. By endorsing cultural diversity, and drawing
minorities in from the margins, American society will
benefit. We will "understand what made our society what it
is today," as one student remarked. More tangibly, as
minorities find their place educationally, economically, and
socially, America will only prosper more.

Mike Rose, "Crossing Boundaries"

1. Rose describes a canonical orientation in education as
measuring academic achievement by how much knowledge people
gain of an "historically validated body of knowledge." This
body of knowledge is a canon: books and ideas listed and
agreed upon by the academic authorities that be. This canon
can only be learned by returning to a "traditional literary
and historical curriculum" made up of the Western classics.
2. Defenders of the traditional canon argue that
disenfranchised students need access to the "language,
conventions and allusions" of the canon because it is the
language, the discourse of power, and people need to become
fluent in this discourse if they are to increase the
strength of their political and social position. The same
canon enhances democracy because it provides a common body
of ideas, experiences and ideals, a common "spiritual, civic
and cognitive heritage" that all young people can and should
have equal access to. It would provide a "stable and common
core" in an increasing instable and confusing world.
3. Marginalization as a political concept implies denying
minorities political and social power through a devaluing of
their culture, by withholding equal respect for their
language and ethnic heritage. Minorities are thus excluded,
pushed toward the outside of society, toward the margins of
the political and social arena.
4. [Personal response]

14

5. Rose believes that the canonical curriculum undercuts its supposed democratic intent by marginalizing and excluding much of our country's literature from our immigrants, working classes, Native Americans, Latinos, etc.. The only way to make the canon a true "democratizing force" would be to actually address and study the linguistic and cultural exclusion minorities still encounter.
6. Education becomes a "transmission" of information in the sense that students are encouraged to learn facts, dates, names, the "what" rather than the "how." The connections between the students' own lives and cultural histories are minimized for the sake of learning more information, information that will supposedly transform into wisdom if students just spend enough time reading the books. Truth, according to the canonist, "resides in the printed books."
7. Rose implies that the nontraditional students must overcome the boundaries of the canon oriented classroom and educational system that marginalizes them, devalues their cultures and subtly excludes them from acquiring access to the educational, political, and social power.

CHAPTER 2: RELIGION: CHANGING BELIEFS AND ATTITUDES

The Ancient World

"The Golden Calf"

1. Jehovah is angered at the Israelites for creating the Golden Calf because they have lost faith in Jehovah and indulged in idolatry. The story teaches the Jews that they must have faith in their God and not turn to other deities in times of difficulty, thus maintaining the continuity of the religion.
2. [Class exercise]
3. Moses pleads with Jehovah not to destroy his people by pointing out that the Lord has just rescued them from slavery in Egypt "with such great power and so strong a hand," that other people will view Jehovah as an evil God for saving the Israelites from the pharaoh, only to "exterminate them from the face of the earth." He also reminds Jehovah of his pledge that the Israelites would prosper as a people and would come to live in the promised land. As atonement for the sins of the Israelites, Moses asks Jehovah to "strike [him] out of the book [the Lord] has written," perhaps suggesting that Jehovah kill Moses, or completely remove his name from history and the Old Testament.
4. [Personal response]

15

"Jonah and the Whale"

1. Initially, the story raises the issue of obedience to
God. Jehovah commands Jonah to go to Ninevah and preach to
the people who have "in their wickedness, come up before
[him]." Instead of obeying Jehovah, Jonah runs away. The
sailors throw Jonah overboard but the Lord protects Jonah by
having him swallowed by the whale, punishing him, but at the
same time protecting him, which demonstrates the punishing
hand and power of God. The value of atonement, repentance,
prayer and faith is highlighted when Jonah praises God and
prays to him for mercy and is delivered from the belly of
the whale. The value of obeying God is again shown when the
people of Ninevah "turn away from evil" as Jehovah commands
and God forgives them and "withholds his blazing wrath."
2. From the belly of the whale, Jonah says a prayer of
thanksgiving, thanking Jehovah for saving him from the
"heart of the sea." He praises God and vows to obey God's
commandments. He declares that worshipers of "vain idols"
will not receive God's mercy. Jonah has learned to obey God
and trust in his mercy.
3. In Jonah's story, as in "The Golden Calf," Jehovah is
stern, punishing, but always capable of mercy. In "The
Golden Calf," Jehovah quickly becomes angry and threatens to
destroy the Israelites for turning to idolatry, relenting
only after Moses pleads with him. Nevertheless, many
Israelites who choose not to follow Jehovah are killed. In
Jonah's tale, Jehovah again appears harsh, threatening to
destroy the people of Ninevah for their evil, but forgives
them, when he sees they have "turned from their evil ways."
4. The stories reveal a people who developed strict
religious and social codes that were reflected in the image
of their god and the messages implied in the Bible stories.
The Israelites often found themselves struggling to survive
in a harsh, unforgiving environment, often at war with
neighboring tribes and peoples. Beset with adversity, a
people might develop a religion that could account for the
adversity it faced.
5. [Personal response]

Psalms Twenty Three and Twenty Four

1. In the first Psalm, God is praised for leading his people
to prosperity: "green pastures... still waters...," ... "a
cup [that] runneth over...." He is praised as a protector
against danger and adversity, and for providing guidance to

16

right action. In the Twenty Fourth Psalm, he is praised for
his might as creator and his strength and glory leading his
people to victory in battle. Those who want God's blessing
must be pure of heart and mind and neither vain nor profane.
2. [Personal response]
3. These Psalms still depict Jehovah as "the king of Glory,"
"strong and mighty in battle," much like the stern Jehovah
in the two preceding stories. However, God also appears more
gentle and beneficent in the Psalms as a "restorer of soul,"
a shepherd, and a provider of abundance.
4. [Personal response]

"The Prodigal Son"

1. The story teaches several religious and moral lessons:
- The younger son learns that squandering one's wealth on
loose living is harmful and morally wrong.
- Repentance for one's sins and mistakes is always the
correct action.
- Forgiving the sins of others is a virtue.
- The older son learns not to be jealous of others, when his
father welcomes the prodigal son home.
2. [Personal response]
3. If one interprets the father as God the father, then the
prodigal son could be the wayward or unsaved soul that has
strayed from God and the Christian life. The allegory then
teaches that God forgives all of those who repent and "come
home" to God, the union of the individual soul and the
divine.
4. Jesus usually taught to poor, uneducated working people,
most of whom could neither read nor write. Parables, fables,
and stories have long been ways of teaching and preserving
moral and religious lessons for common, often illiterate
peoples.
5. [Class exercise]

The Middle Ages

St. Augustine, Confessions

1. St. Augustine believes that complete abandonment to
physical love, lust and carnal pleasure is incompatible with
love of God and that we cannot enjoy both. He implies that
if one should find pleasure in physical love it should at
least be done with the purpose of "begetting children, as
your Lord prescribes," within marriage. Ultimately St.

17

Augustine asserts that it is better for a man "not to touch a woman at all" if he is not married. He implies that even a married man can not think about pleasing God as he usually "thinketh of the things of the world" and how he may please his wife.

2. St. Augustine continually refers to physical love and desire through negative terms and images: "...carnal corruptions of the soul ... I was on fire to take my fill of Hell... shady loves... muddy craving of the flesh... swimming mists of lust...whirlpools of vice... precipice of desire... illicit pleasure... madness of lust... sizzle and frying of unholy loves...."

3. Augustine believes that physical love and desire consummated in producing children in marriage is preferred to physical love outside of marriage but ultimately it is better "to become a eunuch for the kingdom of heaven's sake."

4. The bitterness could be interpreted as a continual, chronic dissatisfaction with physical love and lust. This dissatisfaction finally drives St. Augustine to give up physical love and seek love of God. Thus he thanks God for afflicting him with the bitterness.

5. [Personal response]

Bede, from Life of Cuthbert

1. [Personal response]

2. The Sheriff's wife could be suffering from convulsions. She is screaming "frightfully," grinding her teeth and "flinging her arms and legs about." She could also be experiencing some form of severe mental disturbance. Cuthbert diagnoses the wife's illness as demon possession. Because Cuthbert is filled with the holy spirit of God, the evil demon leaves the wife's body and flees at Cuthbert's approach. In chapter 1, Hippocrates describes people strickened with the "divine illness" as "delirious...groaning and shrieking" for no apparent reason... "darting up and rushing out of doors...," sometimes rational, other times highly disturbed, symptoms quite similar to those of the sheriff's wife.

3. Bede implies that living a good Christian life will provide protection against "the deceits and frauds of the devil." Although God sometimes allows innocent people to be "blighted by the devil in mind and body," the Holy Spirit heals and wins out in the end.

4. Cuthbert's saintly qualities include the power to banish evil spirits, heal the sick, foresee the future, and provide

blessings.
5. [Personal response]

Barbara Tuchman, from A Distant Mirror

1. The image of a distant mirror could suggest that by
carefully analyzing the writings, history, art, teachings,
etc., of the medieval church as artifacts, they will reveal
to us, reflect like a mirror, that which we cannot directly
see to analyze: details of daily life during the "distant"
times of the Middle Ages.
2. The "winds of discontent" that Tuchman writes of refer to
the growing dissatisfaction and outright anti-clericism
people expressed toward the Catholic church's corruption,
abuse of power, accumulation of wealth and monopolization of
knowledge. People like William of Occam represented a
growing hunger for intellectual freedom, and the poverty
movements pressed the church for a return to original church
doctrine and renunciation of the material world. A wind of
"worldly discontent" appeared in challenges to the church's
political power as well.
3. The Fraticelli, a Franciscan order, condemned the church
for accumulating vast wealth. The Fraticelli argued that
Christ had lived without possessions, and that the church
should return to an "imitation of Christ."
4. A doctrine like "no salvation outside the church"
benefits the church itself by investing it with extreme
power since people's souls could only be saved by
affiliation with and subordination to the church. Although
"few were saved" and most were damned, the doctrine at least
offered believers the hope of a better existence after the
trials and tribulations of worldly life, giving some
potential protection against the very real dangers of
eternal damnation and Hell.
5. The medieval church was "comforter, protector and
physician" and church representatives ministered to the hurt
and soothed the distressed. The saints even performed
miracles. Oedipus also saw his role as protector of the city
and his people and even performed his own quasi-miracle by
saving Thebes from the Sphinx.
6. [Class exercise]
7. The church viewed Occam's nominalism as a dangerous sign
of incipient secular intellectual freedom. Since the church
had almost complete control over education and learning, any
direct learning and knowledge of the world that could be
gotten outside of the church would erode the church's
power.

19

8. [Class exercise]

Harvey Cox, "No More Holy Wars"

1. Both Christianity and Islam share a common source of
religious revelation: The ten commandments and the teachings
of the biblical prophets. Both faiths recognize the Virgin
Mary and Jesus of Nazareth and both honor an apostle for the
early development of their respective religions, Paul for
Christianity and Muhammad for Islam, both of whom
"translated a particularist vision into a universal faith."
Cox points out that Muhammad was "considerably influenced by
Christianity and may almost have become an Abyssinian
Christian. Both Islam and Christianity share the practices
of faith, fasting, alms, prayer and pilgrimage. The major
ideological difference between the two faiths is Islam's
refusal to recognize the divinity of Jesus.
2. Sibling rivalry refers to competition and hostility
between brothers and sisters. Christianity and Islam can be
viewed as ideological siblings, born of the Old Testament
faith and fighting over who will be the best loved of "the
parents" and who will achieve dominance.
3. St. Augustine might condone the fasting, faith, and
dedication to prayer in the Moslem faith and would probably
respect the fervor and devotion often associated with Islam.
Any of the Islamic religious practices that minimized
pleasure, sexual or otherwise, would probably receive St.
Augustine's approval.
4. The dichotomy between religion and civil polity that Cox
refers to can be translated as the separation of church and
state, a separation Moslem fundamentalists do not recognize
as part of their faith. Theocracy, government rule by
religious leaders, is pro forma in orthodox Islam and is
similar to th powerful political control the Catholic church
wielded in the Middle Ages.
5. Cox recognizes that the "rival truth claims" between
Islam and Christianty need to be faced and difficult
questions such as the following need to be addressed: Why
have two religions that share so much in common fought so
much historically? Why are Americans "less sympathetic to
Islam than any other religion?" Both sides have to recognize
their mutual similarities and scrutinize the prejudices they
maintain toward each other.
6. [Personal response]
7. According to Cox, Westerners often stereotype Moslems as
"lecherous, argumentative, irrational, cruel, conniving and
excitable, while enforcing oppressive legal codes or being

overly sentimental."
8. [Class exercise]

Excerpt from The Koran

1. God is depicted in both texts as powerful, wise,
omnipotent and omniscient. The Koran excerpt also recognizes
God as "creating heaven and earth in six days" and ruling
earth from his heavenly throne similar to the biblical God.
2. The language of the Koran resembles Old Testament text in
sentence structure as well as imagery. Note the similarities
in the use of antithesis in these Koranic verses:
     grants life and brings death...
     he is the first and last...
     the outward and innermost...
     comes down from the sky... soars up into it...
     wraps night up in daytime and daytime in night...
3. Although many parts of this excerpt do not exactly
resemble the Old Testament word for word, the language,
images, and messages, correspond closely to Biblical
scripture.

Dante, from Inferno, Canto XXVIII

1. Although intended as a criticism of his contemporaries as
well as a political tract, the detailed realism and care
taken to describe exact punishments that fit particular
crimes, as well as the terrifying quality of the depiction
of hell supports Tuchman's view that the medieval vision of
hell was literal.
2. In medieval society, the church constituted the primary
social as well as religious institution and thus was
invested with immense social and religious power.
Schismatics, people like the Fraticelli, whom Tuchman
mentions in her writing, criticized the church, whipped up
"winds of discontent" and called for reforms in church
policy and practice. The church, always vigilant in
protecting its power, as well as truly believing that it was
spiritually mandated by Jesus Christ to be the only true
"mother church," naturally feared the dissent, the "scandal
and schisms" that the schismatics preached.
3. Muhammad is depicted split open from chin to anus, as is
his "apostle," Ali. Both punishments correspond to the

21

schismatic nature of Islam, which threatened the religious
hegemony of the church.
4. St.Augustine would probably approve of Dante's depiction
of hell as he writes of hell and sin in a very literal way.
St. Augustine describes physical love as "taking his fill of
hell," and his writing implies that he believed God was
punishing him and responding to his sins in a very direct
way, indicating his belief in the very real nature of God,
heaven and hell. The metaphors he uses to describe physical
love also support the notion that he envisioned damnation in
hell quite literally as punishment for sin.
5. [Class exercise]

Reform Movements

Harold J. Grimm, "The Growth of Lutheranism"

1. The "winds of discontent" that Barbara Tuchman writes of
led to the emergence and survival of the Reformation. Like
the Fraticelli that Tuchman mentions, Martin Luther
attempted to recreate a religion like the primitive
Christian church, replacing the "hierarchy of the medieval
church with the democracy of the New Testament." This
"reformation" responded to the growing criticism of church
corruption, misuse of power, and growing alienation of the
common people from the church itself.
2. The Reformation could not have happened during the Middle
Ages because of the powerful central social, political and
religious function the church maintained during this time
and the general lack of secular intellectual and political
freedom. The Reformation in Germany and the rest of Europe
corresponded with the emergence of political states which
eventually challenged the authority of the church. The
sixteenth century also witnessed the growth of secular
enlightenment learning and an ambitious middle class,
factors which supported Reformation ideology.
3. Luther believed that the Bible was "primarily a lively
dynamic force" and that all people should have access to the
Gospel, not in Latin which they could not understand or read
for themselves, but in the vernacular, their own language.
He wanted to make the liturgy and service intelligible and
more meaningful for its participants, which also increased
the participation of the congregation in the daily function
of the church.
4. Although the Catholic Church viewed Luther as a religious
radical and revolutionary, Grimm points out that his
theology demonstrated "innate coservatism." The "overzealous
activities" of some of his followers deeply troubled Luther
and he was careful not to encourage either social or
religious revolt, telling followers to "carry on reforms

[only] through duly constituted political authorities. He had no interest in radical social reform, declining to support the peasant revolts of the time. His "entire concern centered in a religious problem and excluded political, economic and social considerations."

5. Luther hoped that a return to the conditions of the early Christian church would involve the congregation more in the daily administrative concerns of the church, to replace the "hierarchy" of the medieval church with the "spiritual democracy of the New Testament church." In real terms, this meant that the congregation could decide doctrinal matters, choose ministers and teachers and decide how to collect and administer church monies.

6. Luther drew a clear distinction between the functions and domains of church and state. The state, the secular realm, was ordained by God to establish and maintain social order, an order citizens were called upon to obey. The church's domain was the spiritual realm, religion and ethics.

Thomas J. Wertenbaker, "The Rules of Conduct"

1. The Puritan religion was a form of Calvinism, a Protestant religion like Lutheranism that stressed innate human sinfulness and the uncertainty of salvation. Puritans saw worldly life as continually afflicted by the "dangers and temptations" of Satan. They developed strict rules of personal behavior and viewed any small daily pleasure, from enjoying a poem to smoking a pipe, as a possible opportunity for Satan to tempt them from their spiritual duty. They advocated a life filled with seriousness, constant readings of the Bible and prayer. Puritans established strict moral codes in their communities that often infringed on personal freedoms.

2. The Puritans viewed even small daily diversions such as enjoying a walk or cardplaying as a distraction from the strict self-searching and rigid code of conduct that they adhered to. Even the slightest diversions could be temptations of Satan meant to lure the less than vigilant Puritan from the ultimate goal of salvation.

3. Lutheranism distinguished the spiritual and secular realms much more clearly than Puritanism and did not infringe on personal liberty or view daily pleasures as severely as Puritanism. The Puritans put much more emphasis on the importance of vigilant daily behavior to counter the temptations of Satan than did Lutherans. Although Luther did recognize Satan as constantly conniving to destroy people's souls, he believed that God "would combat the forces of evil without man's efforts" and only "the preaching of the Gospel would provide victory."

23

4. Ascetics practice strict self-discipline, generally eschewing the pleasures of worldly life in an attempt to find union with God and achieve salvation.
5. [Personal response]

Ian G. Barbour, "God as Divine Clockmaker"

1. The image of God changed radically during the Enlightenment because the emerging modern scientific methods and major scientific discoveries were able to account for phenomena in the universe that before were attributed to God's divine creation and continual control. Some Enlightenment scientists hypothesized God's role in the universe as "first cause," that is, he set the universe in motion in a well planned and harmonious way. After this initial creation, the universe would "follow fixed laws, with material causes acting from their own necessity." God therefore, did not have an everpresent hand in the daily working of the world or in the fate of humankind.
2. The analogy of god as divine clockmaker describes a God who intentionally created a "skillful artifact," the way a clockmaker fashions a clock, and then steps back and allows the world to run according to rational scientific laws the way a clock, "once started runs its own independent course."
3. The notion of God as "retired architect" reinforces the image of an almost inactive God, completely removed from the running of the natural world and the affairs of men. It suggests the benevolent and rational God of Deism who created the world but provided no divine guidance, leaving people responsible for their own actions.
4. The analogy of God as "cosmic plumber" suggests a God who occasionally steps in to repair breakdowns in his system. These "leaks" in the system represent the area of scientific ignorance, phenomena in the universe that Enlightenment scientists couldn't account for or fit into their vision of the perfect mechanistic universe.
5. [Personal response]
6. [Personal response]
7. [Personal response]

Voltaire, "Of Universal Tolerance"

1. Voltaire's essay satirizes the intolerance and hypocrisy of people in general and Christianity in particular. Note the satire in his depiction of people as ants, absorbed in their self-importance, believing only their "ant-hill is

dear to God...and that only they will prosper and "others will be eternally unlucky"; his sharp parody of the "Fervent Dominican Inquisitor who tortures people to save their souls;"his mocking of the church that claims to know God's will and presumes to "decide before him the eternal fate of all men"; his satirical tone in describing the 40 million Europeans, doomed to hell, according to the Catholic church; the irony with which he questions whether a French ambassador would be able to do business with a circumcised non-Christian who in effect is damned to Hell; his final query as to whether the wise men of the centuries, Plato to Confucius, would be damned to Hell as pagans, while other historical villains may go to heaven, having taken the last rites of Catholicism.

2. A major figure of the Enlightenment, Voltaire uses reason, humor and satire to argue here for religious and intellectual tolerance and the right to pursue and express one's beliefs. Voltaire first proposes that people should have tolerance for each other and that Christians should even see non-Christians as brothers, pointing out the umlikely possibility that God would select one small group of people on this "speck" of a planet as the chosen people, blessed with the one true religion. He continues to argue for accepting people's natural differences by adducing the different dialects of a language people speak, questioning how one dialect could be the "infallible guide" and correct one that everyone should speak. He criticizes people's hypocrisy and and conceit for thinking they can "anticipate the Creator's decrees" and legislate religion for others, and points out the irrationality of believing that so many people on earth who believe in God but are non-Christians would be damned by the creator. He goes on to question how christians can justify acting so "un-Christian-like," and finally argues that we be judged by our deeds not our religious beliefs. He names important non-Christian historical figures who contributed to the positive growth of civilization and other avowed Christians who caused so much suffering and grief.

3. [Personal response]

4. Voltaire cannot accept the concept of "no salvation outside the church" because he reasons that people, as "insignificant little specks of time," can not possibly hope to " know all the ways of God and the full extent of his mercy." People should not be so self-esteeming in their infallibilty as to assume to know which religions will provide salvation and which will not.

5. [Personal response]

6. [Personal response]

7. [Personal response]

25

Brooks Atkinson, "Emerson"

1. Emerson reflected some of the Romanticist's reaction to
the mechanism, decorum, and the prescriptive precepts of the
seventeenth and eighteenth centuries. The expansive,
intuitive quality of Emerson's Transcendentalism
interrogates the Enlightenment's application of reason to
religion, politics, morality, and social life, and that
period's confidence in science and industrialization as
being completely beneficial to humankind's development and
well-being.
2. Transcendentalism is not a religious system but more a
form of idealism, a view of the world that finds reality in
ideas or spirit rather than just in material things. Early
American Transcendentalists found authority in their
intuition rather than in reason and physical experience.
They were pantheists who perceived the physical presence of
God in nature and saw themselves as part of God/nature. They
found God's "sweet natural goodness" manifested in all
aspects of reality, from the natural world to politics, art,
literature, and science.
3. Reviewers criticized Emerson's book Nature as
"pantheistic rapture" because it "charmingly" expressed
Emerson's perceptions of his mystical union with God and
Nature. They might have found it "without much significance"
because Emerson's philosophy was not based on rational
thought and logic. Many critics refused to accept Emerson's
spiritual excursions into the world of intuition or found
his ideas merely "wishful thinking." Others found his
identification of people with God bordering on heresy.
4. Nineteen sixties counterculture ideology might have
identified with Emerson's spirituality, his criticism of
materialism, his emphasis on intuition over reason, and his
pantheism.
5.Elements of Romanticism still influence our emphasis on
the freedom of the individual; the skepticism still
expressed toward the oppressive nature of organized society
and religion; our "romantic" conceptions of how art is
produced and our mythologies of how artists behave. A close
examination of Rock and Roll, and other popular musics, for
example, might reveal many traces of Romantic thought.

Madalyn Murray O'Hair, "Arguments for God, Historical and
Contemporary with Refutation"

1. O'Hair begin her argument by proposing that the burden of
proving God's existence is on the religious community and
theologians. Their continued attempts to prove his existence
verify that his existence is only a theory. If there really
were a God, they would not have to do any of this. "He could
just appear, just once, or give incontrovertible proof
...that would end the argument for all time." O'Hair
identifies eight major arguments for the existence of God:
    (1) Direct sensory experience of God
    (2) Faith
    (3) Accepting God on the word of some greater authority,
    i.e., church, holy book, etc.
    Three rational arguments:
    (4) The cosmological argument: originated by Thomas
    Aquinas, it proposes that everything, including the
    universe itself requires a "first cause" to account for
    its existence.
    (5) The teleological argument: Also known as the natural
    law argument, it proposes that since we can find so much
    order and planning in the world around us, i.e., the
    seasons, the stars, plants, etc., we must assume a
    planning intelligence had a hand in its creation.
    (6) The ontological argument: An argument of definition.
    "God's existence is defined by nature," which
    theologians go on to define. That is, if we can define
    perfection then it must exist.
    (7) Kant's moral argument: "...goodness, truth, and love
    flow from God and therefore he exists."
    (8) The pragmatic argument: Religion and belief in God
    "works" in the sense that it has served to advance
    humankind throughout history.
2. O'Hair develops her refutations in the following ways:
    (1) A sensory argument for God, personally talking to
    him, feeling his touch, seeing him would be considered a
    hallucination in today's modern world and theologians
    have long since abandoned this argument.
    (2) The "faith" argument is weak because it requires
    blindly accepting someone else's sensory experience of
    God or his/her intuition that there is a God.
    (3) Acknowledging God's existence on the acceptance of
    the authority of a book or religious institution is weak
    because whoever is in power rules and thus establishes
    the religious institution of the time. Which authority
    do you accept? Which holy book do you accept? The Koran,
    The Bible, The Vedas? There are many conflicting
    authorities and institutions.
    (4) The cosmological argument cannot account for the
    uncaused first cause. If something must have created the
    universe, then who created God?

(5) The teleological argument relies on the wondrous perfection of the universe and God's master plan, but fails to explain the pain, suffering, and apparent indifference which a benevolent God has inflicted on humankind.
(6) The ontological argument's weakness is that it is impossible to prove the existence of God just because we can define him. We can imagine and define all kinds of things, but that hardly proves their real existence.
(7) Kant's moral argument for God leaves unaccounted the problems of evil injustice and hate in the world.
(8) The pragmatic argument is vulnerable to the criticism that religion has not "worked" all that well and faith in God has not "advanced" humankind all that much.
3. [Personal response]
4. [Personal response]
5. [Personal response]
6. [Personal response]

Carol Christ, "Why Women Need the Goddess"

1. According to Anthropologist Clifford Geertz, religious symbols "define the deepest values of a society and the persons in it." Geertz conceives of mood as a "psychological attitude" such as respect or trust and motivation as the social and political action or direction that mood engenders. Religious symbols have psychological and political effects because they "create the inner conditions (deep seated attitudes and feelings) that allow people to accept social and political arrangements that correspond to the symbol system."
2. Patriarchal religions reinforce the political and social authority of males in society. Without necessarily being specific, Patriarchal religious symbol systems reinforce the notion that female power is never "fully legitimate or wholly beneficent." Even the creation myth depicts Eve as the evil temptress, hardly an uplifting symbol for women to relate to. Only man can see himself as created in God's image in a patriarchal Judeo-Christian religion. A women "can never have... her full sexual identity affirmed as being in the image and likeness of God." Western religion creates the "mood" in women of trust in the redeeming male power and "distrust of female power in herself... as inferior and dangerous."
3. Contemplating ancient and modern images of the Goddess can empower women both psychologically and politically. Psychologically it replaces the patriarchal devaluation of female power as "inferior and dangerous." As a new "mood," it engenders new "motivations" that can aid women in

28

relying on their own power both within their families and in society.

4. Christ says that women deal with the question of whether the Goddess exists "out there" or within women in three ways: First, through prayer and ritual, women can find the Goddess "out there" as a "divine personification." Second, the Goddess can symbolize life, death, and the regenerative energy in both nature and culture. Third, The Goddess legitimizes and affirms female power generally, as seen emerging in the feminist movement.

5. In orthodox Western religions, God is not conceived of as "the natural energy in [our bodies] and the world." However, Emerson's pantheistic belief in Nature as manifesting the physical presence of God could easily accommodate such a statement.

6. The author argues that the potent, archetypal female symbols of Eve and Mary both reinforce the view that female initiative and will are Evil. Eve, by "asserting her will against the command of God" brought on the fall from grace. Passive women, like Mary, who acquiesce to the will of a patriarchal God, embody goodness.

7. Recognition of the Goddess symbolism can help women examine and reevaluate their social and cultural heritage as well as the relationships they establish among themselves. Within our traditional culture, women have few models for establishing bonds between themselves. The literary canon, almost entirely authored by men, almost always depicts women in their relationship to men and there are few examples that "celebrate" women's bonds to each other. Most of our cultural narratives, like the Bible, generally focus on the father or mother's relationship to the son, but rarely on the important bond between mother and daughter. In fact, as Simon de Beauvoir argues, "the mother-daughter relationship is distorted in a male defined culture in which women are viewed as inferior." Goddess Symbolism, as seen, for example, in the myth of Demeter and Persephone, can help women recognize the inportant heritage passed on from mother to daughter and "reject the patriarchal pattern where primary loyalties" of women must be exclusively to men.

8. [Personal response]

9. [Personal response]

CHAPTER 3:   REVOLUTIONS AND REACTIONS IN SCIENCE

The Historical Context: Medieval, Renaissance, Modern

Friedrich Heer, from The Medieval World

1. Heer acknowledges the value of medieval scientific inquiry (if
the term is valid in this context) in that it led to later
development in the natural sciences, but he points out its
subjective, isolated, irrational basis. The religious and
political imperatives and biases of the era prevented science, as
it was later to be practiced, from existing in a recognizable way.
2. The female imagery reflects a sense of fear and secrecy in the
common perception of women and their sexuality. The womb image
acknowledges the life-giving nature of the female, but it remains a
symbol of forbidden territory. One can argue that the image of
"invasion" reflects a perception of women's bodies as a private
possession, presumably the male's, and any attempt by a strange
male to "know" the female is "unlawful" and forbidden. Science
thus seems to represent a threatening attempt to gain power and
illicit goods.
3. A belief in a world of the spirit may have made the notion of
empirical method seem insufficient and suspect. Without
formulated physical laws, scientists of the time had few means of
explaining the world beyond the magical and spiritual. Belief in
the possibility of "divine enlightenment"--direct knowledge of and
through God--further rendered the notion of human perception as a
route to truth suspect.
4. If one can claim to understand the "truth" of human life, one
has the power to explain mysteries, tragedies, and the future,
which endows one with great influence and hence power over
society. With the faith of the people goes economic power as well
as political power. Control over society is thus at stake. Each
side may have shared the power-seeking motive, though the Church is
typically depicted as the active enemy in the conflict. Both sides
sought influence in education, the key to social influence.
5. [Personal response]
6. [Personal response]
7. Within the world of higher education, belief in the occult
remains without institutional support, and practitioners of
nontraditional sciences continue to be treated as "quacks," often
provoking vehement institutional criticism (the controversy over
laetrile, a nontraditional treatment of cancer, is one example).
Outside university and college life, occult sciences continue to
thrive and are an important part of folk culture, especially
within ethnic groups. The intrusion of this personal and folk
tradition into national political life in the form of the Reagans'
astrologer created a major controversy; perhaps Americans would
like to believe that a more objective, scientific means of

conducting national politics exists--though this belief in itself
may be a kind of superstition.
8.   Issues related to reproduction seem to elicit the most
emphatic public reactions--abortion methods, artificial
insemination techniques, fetal tissue research, etc.   Other
medical procedures that suggest human control over life also stir
emotions--cryogenics, euthanasia, etc.   These seem to reflect a
medieval fear of overstepping bounds.   Other controversies are
reactions to excesses of science and technology--mainly
environmental issues.   What continues to be true is that
scientific controversies are very closely related to political
controversies--the two realms remain interrelated.

Bertrand Russell, "The Copernican Revolution"

1.   Russell quotes directly from religious figures, highlighting
the vehemence and (now apparent) irrationality of their views.   He
suggests that hostility to the theory was motivated by fear of
losing power and that church leaders unfairly sought means of
"branding it as heretical."   Finally, Russell's depiction of
Galileo picks up close to religious imagery, depicting him as a
martyr for his belief--scientific belief.
2.   The final sentence suggests an unbroken line of development
from era to era, with Newton stepping in to carry on Galileo's
work.   He promotes his implied argument in the text that
scientific advances were extensions of works done previously,
traceable back to the Greeks.
3.   The theory posits the existence of human life on a mechanical,
almost accidental physical system.   If life were not divinely
created, no force exists to give it meaning and worth.   No purpose
attaches to it; it becomes, one can argue, a static repetition of
physical laws.
4.   [Personal response]
5.   Many environmentalists argue that we continue to place human
interests above whole-world interests, that we see ourselves as
the center of importance and abuse natural resources for our own
selfish ends.   The Judeo-Christian tradition teaches that humans
are the "masters" of all else, a belief that has been used to
justify the exploitation of animals, etc., for human gain.
6.   [Personal response]
7.   [Personal response]
8.   The modern bias continues to be against nontraditional
theories and practices and for modern science and medicine.
Certainly the major social institutions--school and government--
promote traditional scientific fields and practices.   The media
tends to not take a stance but rather to sensationalize the
controversies.

Christe McMenomy, "The Scientific Background to the Industrial Revolution"

1. McMenomy analyzes the truly revolutionary nature of the shift to industrial society--the effects on class and gender, on social roles and personal well being. She describes society as a system thrown into a kind of chaos by the changes, with the many positive effects counterbalanced by negative ones. Thus the attention of the essay shifts away from the scientific and technological and to the human and social, providing a fuller context for the topic and illuminating how such progress can bring with it enormous social upheaval.
2. McMenomy uses Galileo as a way of dating historical periods in the opening line of her essay, assigning him status equivalent to the near-heroic image Russell creates of him in his work. She continues to use him as a historical point of reference throughout the piece. By doing so, she reinforces his status in the Western scientific tradition.
3. Bacon's view of science is very close to our contemporary view: "a national program...a fact-gathering method...with the ultimate goal being the control of nature for the benefit of mankind." Bacon emphasizes the value of research and exploration, and he seeks to establish scientific inquiry as a social institution rather than a lone experimenter's isolated pursuit, as medieval science often envisioned scientific practice.
4. [Personal response]
5. [Personal response]
6. McMenomy suggests that as science became more institutionalized, the scientist gained in status through such bodies as the Royal Society of London and other nationally sponsored groups. Today, we continue to have these national and international societies of scientists, as well as international awards such as the Nobel prizes. Scientists continue to be perceived as experts whose work benefits society and individuals; their work continues to be perceived as difficult, mysterious, and beyond the grasp of the average person; scientific fields continue to dominate university research. All these factors add to the status of the field, in addition to the professional organizations' work to maintain the field's prestige.
7. Many developing countries find that cultural conflicts are the greatest price they pay for technological advancement. Traditional ways are disrupted by urban growth, changes in social roles, and the shift to capitalistic values. Few countries seem to have successfully managed the shift, and many political movements have arisen as backlashes to industrial growth--Marxist revolutions in particular, a reaction to exploitation of labor and disproportionate economic benefits, with an increasing gap between rich and poor. As McMenomy points out, though, health improvements are a major benefit of industrialization; for poor countries, the availability of modern medical knowledge and

32

facilities is particularly valuable, and so the pattern of
interrelated benefits and drawbacks continues.
8. [Personal response]

Bertrand Russell, "Evolution"

1. The tenor of the outrage is treated somewhat differently in
the two essays. Galileo's critics are made out to be a very
powerful, vindictive social force, controlling the individual's
liberty and willing to impose terrible consequences on those who
hold heretical views. The critics of evolutionary theory come
across as more individualized voices, often with a comic edge.
They appear as moralizers rather than agents of the legal system.
2. Russell's thesis includes not only the three major tenets of
evolution but the social reception given the theory--in
particular, the growing discomfort with and rejection of
darwinistic thought. Thus he uses quotations from both a church
authority and an educator, suggesting the heat and breadth of the
opposing views. Both quotes illustrate the moral, not scientific,
basis to the objections, the popular perception that darwinistic
thought was by necessity an atheistic proposition.
3. Both systems emphasize the role of competition--one,
competition in the marketplace, and the other biological
competition for survival. In common terms, only the strong
survive, in each system.
4. Technological evolution results from improvements determined
by effective application--speed, simplicity, variety, etc. Change
is thus use- and practice-oriented. Social evolution is usually
conceived in political terms: we have increasingly enlightened
views of a problem or issue. As people's perceptions change, as
the degree of communication on a topic grows, change occurs. Thus
our sense of social evolution seems very different from what we
mean by biological or technological evolution.
5. As with the Copernican revolution, the theories of Darwin
seemed to debase human origins. Perceptions of natural
superiority and natural right to power were challenged by both.
Monkeys may have been perceived as especially bestial and
uncomfortably close to human form. We can easily see ourselves as
a community of chattering, bickering monkeys, taken up in
apparently frivolous pursuits and acting in a manner
embarrassingly free of shame.
6. Both directly challenge religious doctrine. Thus both
directly undermine church authority. The individual then faces
the dilemma of what and whom to believe. Struggle for allegiance
ensues on the part of the scientific and religious communities.
Whether the struggle is for power or faith remains open to
individual interpretation.
7. Mythological explanations of natural phenomena emphasize the
process of transformation; Ovid's <u>Metamorphoses</u> is an excellent

example. The move to an evolutionary perspective might thus seem
a logical one. Since Greek method emphasized the rational and
observable, the deductive logic of evolutionary theory would very
likely have found a positive reception. Also, the religious
objections that plagued the modern theorists would not have
arisen, since the ancient Greeks saw no conflict between faith and
science.
8. [Personal response]

Charles Darwin, from <u>The Descent of Man</u>

1. Darwin acknowledges at the start of this chapter that his
views are "highly speculative, and some no doubt will prove
erroneous," which functions as a kind of admission of fallibility
and humility, softening the challenge to doctrinal teachings. He
then goes on to assert his views within a professional, scientific
context, and he points out that other scientists have concurred
with his findings--spreading around the responsibility, in a sense.
He summarizes his data and shows that the findings relentlessly
lead to the conclusion he has offered. The truth resides in the
scientific data, and Darwin is simply the formulator of the
results, not a proselytizing voice. He writes with rhetorical
sensitivity, suggesting that he understands the need to defend
himself and his views.
2. Generally, the scientific writings of earlier centuries
employed highly rhetorical styles--direct address of the readers,
establishment of the authors' ethos, reference to shared values,
etc. Contemporary scientific writing is much more likely to use
an "objective" tone and voice, to attempt to present findings as
impersonally and "scientifically" as possible. The form has
changed as well: most theories are advanced in article form and
include quantitative data, using a more rigid format than Darwin
does.
3. Darwin uses an ecological context for his theory, which is
different from the anthropocentric view, or "humans first."
Darwin's system thus dethrones the human from the center and makes
us part of a chain that is more horizontal than vertical,
indicating we are not on "top."
4. The notion of progress, satirized by the likes of Voltaire in
<u>Candide</u>, champions change as steps forward, onward, and upward.
Thus whatever policy a nation currently holds is seen as an
advance over its earlier policies. Implicit in Darwin's view is a
notion of increasing strength, power, rightness, etc.
5. That the Fuegians were in Darwin's perception barbaric is
clear: he says they were "absolutely naked," using the adjective
to underscore his own shock and disapproval; their "tangled," long
hair further strikes him as evidence of savagery. Their
difference from European standards of personal appearance is to
Darwin evidence of their inferiority, their "dirtiness." They

34

seem closer to wild animals than to human beings, to Darwin.
Their lack of government, their superstitiousness, their different
moral codes, their violence all seem to Darwin to be repugnant and
inferior traits. His values of personal cleanliness, embarrassment
of nakedness, religious and civil laws, etc., have been used as the
basis for his disapproval. Thus his judgment of the Fuegians is
based on their failure to meet the standards of his society, not on
objective assessment of the Fuegian system.
6. [Personal response]

Jerome Kagan and Ernest Havemann, "Psychoanalytic Theory"

1. The house image would not capture the vastness of the
"subterranean" self. The power of the id is better represented by
the immensity of the submerged part of the iceberg, with the
conscious mind and social personality being a very small portion
of the total individual. The house image would overprivilege the
conscious mind.
2. The ego is the conscious mind, in Freudian theory, and its
purpose is to mediate between the external world and the desires
of the id. An egotist thus may be someone who indulges the id, or
selfish desires, in Freudian terms, though in common usage we say
such a person has a "big" ego--perhaps contradicting the Freudian
equation of ego and self-control, the meaning of a "strong" ego.
An egotist does not seem to have a distorted notion of reality but
rather a strong desire to place self-satisfaction above self-
control. A "wounded" ego might be seen as an overdose of the
reality principle: our ego is hurt when we are forced to see our
own unimportance, which violates the id's desire for supremacy and
omnipotence.
3. The superego is a kind of mental watchdog. It monitors our
thoughts, feelings, and actions. In the Oedipal stage, the child
is adjusting to the reality principle and must find a way to
control the id's impulse to possess the main source of love--the
parent. This impulse involves risk to the child, and so the child
feels fear, ultimately resolving the problem by identifying with
the parent's power and love. The child adopts parental values to
complete this identification process. Thus the superego is
developed, and the child has within his or her mind a "parental"
force that monitors wishes and actions. We retain the child's
sense of wishes and actions as equivalent things, and so we can
feel guilt for purely imaginary "crimes." Without the superego, we
would be unable to empathize with others or act in what is
typically considered a "moral" way. An overly active superego can,
nonetheless, create real misery for the individual, by making him
or her "pay" for imagined misdeeds.
4. We traditionally see infants as "new," unspoiled human beings,
free of the conflicts and desires that plague us later in life.
Thus the notion of infantile sexuality deflates this ideal picture

of early life. The infant is also physically undeveloped; we traditionally tie sexual feelings to physical maturity.
5. Freud cites such things as artistic creation or intense study as substitutive satisfactions. Sports, too, might qualify. We can also seek escapes in the form of entertainment, which can offer vicarious release.
6. By our nature, we are sexual and aggressive beings, according to Freud. Our natural desire is to place our own needs above those of others, to take what others have, even to kill others, if the act leads to some benefit to us. We are from the first driven by desire; innocence is a completely alien state, from a Freudian perspective.
7. [Personal response]
8. Freud says that we are expert at resistance and denial. Because Freudian theory presents a very unflattering, sometimes very threatening image of ourselves, we may follow an unconscious hostility and reject the theory, often very vigorously. We deny finding any correspondence between our own feelings and the model Freud has set up. Our defense mechanisms always push us to preserve our pleasure and fight against the reality principle; confronting Freudian theory can demand a disciplined mind and strong ego.
9. Much of Freudian terminology has become common usage. Despite the denial process, we seem to have incorporated Freudian concepts in our view of ourselves and the world around us. We acknowledge that we go through developmental stages, mentally; that we have egos, consciences, wishes, guilt, etc.

Sigmund Freud, "The Embarrassment-Dream of Nakedness"

1. [Class exercise]
2. Freud suggests that the dream of nakedness is an anxiety dream, and finds it to be a frequent dream among his neurotic patients. We wish to return to the paradise of childhood, a time before the cares and repressions of later life.
3. Before expulsion from the Garden, life was without shame, without fear, sexuality, conflict, sin and punishment. A benevolent, protecting parent figure took care of all of one's needs. Freedom from all the harshnesses of adult life typifies childhood, but awareness of that freedom comes only with its loss.
4. The child wishes for the paradise of early life, a place where the child can be free and satisfied; these desires intrude on adult life, however, and make us feel shame and guilt.
5. [Personal response]

Some Social Consequences of Scientific Progress

George E. Simpson, "Early Social Darwinism"

1. The argument about the cycle of poverty cites social
environment as the cause of a family's impoverished situation.
Social Darwinism cites the family's genes as the source of their
trouble. Adopting the latter view involves endorsing the idea of
the natural inferiority of the poor; in a democratic society based
on a belief in equality, this view seems untenable.
2. War allows for competition on a grand scale, so that one race
of people can rise over and crush another, according to Social
Darwinist thought. The loss of the best and brightest youth has a
fleeting effect in the larger picture; the race endures and
prospers.
3. According to proponents of imperialism, the natural order was
served by the stronger race coming in and taking over control of
the lower orders. If a people could be conquered by an invading
force, their loss was proof of their inferiority. With such a
"scientific" defense, imperialists were able to "justify" the
exploitation of others and to cloak their motives.
4. Many contemporary social critics have voiced concern over such
practices as amniocentesis, which reveals the gender of the fetus;
in some Asian countries, the abortion rate of female fetuses has
risen as a result of the process. Fear that such techniques might
be used to racist ends have also been expressed. Because of the
expense and education involved, these medical interventions in
reproduction are usually available only to the middle and upper
classes.
5. [Personal response]

Adolf Hitler, "Man Must Kill"

1. In Hitler's imagery, the stronger country is the hammer, the
active, powerful force. It imposes its force on a "host" nation
--the anvil. The hammer nation crushes the anvil nation,
flattening it.
2. [Personal response]
3. [Personal response]
4. The theory may appeal to the ego of an individual or group,
for it provides a sense of superiority and entitlement. It
creates scapegoats for social ills as well (much as the Jews were
used in Nazi Germany). Today, "skinhead" groups are often
paramilitary, eager for armed conflict with other groups, and
typically racist. Obviously, those groups more often threatened
might be the ones to actively fight against such philosophies,
along with political groups such as pacifist organizations.

Sidney Shalett, "First Atomic Bomb Dropped on Japan"

1. Both countries are depicted as feverishly devoted to war, as

the instigators of the war, and as extremist nations desiring to
pursue war to the point of one side's annihilation. The nations
are treated collectively--no reference to individuals appears.
2. The term carries with it a notion of total destruction and
omnipotence. Those who use it become the masters of the universe;
the political implication is that the U.S. is the supreme world
power.
3. With the nuclear energy plants that have been built all over
the country, American awareness of nuclear dangers has grown.
Plant accidents, radiation threats to workers, and compromised
quality control have all led to increased suspicion and policing
of nuclear energy plants. The idea that nuclear energy is a
factor in advancing civilization is open to serious question,
though nuclear deterrence, one might argue, has in fact led to
major and positive changes in world politics.
4. [Class exercise/personal response]
5. The development of the atomic bomb does seem to have had a
major effect on how we see the modern world. Its development has
been used as an historical marker: we live in the atomic or
nuclear age. We are capable of destroying the entire planet;
this, too, seems to change our view of human life, emphasizing the
power we have to destroy it and how quickly and easily it could be
destroyed.

Japanese Broadcasting Company, from Unforgettable Fire

1. Very little information about the effects of the Hiroshima
bombing were available at the time Shalett wrote his article. The
JBC piece is based on survivors' eyewitness accounts. The very
personal nature of the suffering is detailed in this piece; we
learn of the people's routine morning and experience the chaos of
the blast itself. We hear about how the ordinary things of daily
life were affected, from mothers with their infants to birds caught
in the explosion. The JBC piece includes the actual words of the
victims, giving the experience a human voice and face. The Shalett
piece records the historical context and scientific achievement of
the event.
2. The sheer extent of the damage, the flattening of the expanse
of the city, was mind boggling. The horrible effects of the bomb,
both the immediate injuries and long-term suffering, also were
previously unknown war experiences.
3. The opening description of daily life heightens the reader's
tension: we know what is about to happen, but we cannot prevent it
or speak out to warn the soon-to-be victims. We first see an
ordered world and are then immersed in the holocaust of the flash.
4. Conventional thought has Washington, D.C., and the surrounding
area, the seat of government and military operations, as a prime
target. Population centers might also be hit--New York being a
likely spot for mass destruction. But our isolated military

locations could also be logical targets. Some people have
suggested that nuclear power plants would be appealing hit sites,
increasing the power of the enemy-dropped bombs.
5. [Personal response]

David Attenborough, from The Living Planet

1. The natural system provides for continuation without
exploitation and depletion. The store of natural resources is
self-replenishing, unlike commercial harvesting of resources,
which interrupts the balance and has repercussions beyond the
particular resource's exploitation.
2. Attenborough suggests an approach to technology and
industrialization that takes the ecosystem into account. He
argues for an educated, balanced approach to modern innovations;
we need to avoid interfering with our world's life processes. He
calls for awareness and monitoring more than rejection of modern
technological and industrial practices.
3. [Personal response]
4. Extinction continues to threaten many species of animals and
plants, although laws have been enacted to protect certain of
these species, bans on ivory to protect elephants being one prime
example, and species that formerly neared extinction have been
helped to replenish their numbers. Concern over acid rain, the
depletion of the ozone layer, the greenhouse effect, etc., remains
high; actual changes in current practices that cause these threats
are slow, however. It may be fair to say that awareness has
increased but real change lags far behind.
5. [Personal response]

Rethinking Scientific Objectivity

Stephen Jay Gould, "On Heroes and Fools in Science"

1. The scientists of the era held beliefs about the nature of
life and the world that made preformationist assumptions very
logical. First, they believed the world was finite, and so
encasement was possible; second, without knowledge of the cell,
the lower size limit on the elements of living tissue was unknown,
and again encasement seemed possible. The way we think affects the
theories we develop, according to Gould, and we need to keep that
in mind before we ridicule earlier scientific theories or assume
our own to be superior.
2. Having a group of scientific fools allows those who would be
heroes to cast themselves in a good, contrasting light--fools
become a backdrop for one's own glory, in other words. The
heroes/fools framework allows the myth of progress to continue.
3. Gould opens his essay with accessible personal discussion.

39

The reader can identify with him, and he acknowledges his own
naivete about science, which helps the reader to be more
comfortable about his or her own scientific ignorance. Gould's
essay debunks the image of the scientist as an unerring, logic-
driven, godlike figure. A popularizer is thus a humanizer, a kind
of translator of specialized knowledge from professional style to
more colloquial modes, such as the story telling technique Gould
employs.
4. If some unnameable mystical vitalism is responsible for the
designs of the nature, its processes are forever beyond the grasp
of scientific method, which depends on observation. Thus one can
never locate the mechanisms of nature through the sense; one can
make no scientific discoveries.
5. The coding process of DNA seems as contrived, Gould says, as
the notion of encasement, and yet we accept the theory because it
seems to account for what we observe happening in embryos. We use
the metaphor of coding today; our way of thinking may seem as
ludicrous and misguided to later scientific thinkers as
preformationist theory seems to us.
6. [Personal response]
7. [Personal response]
8. Gould emphasizes the creative thought that goes into
scientific work, and in this sense he treats science as an art,
rather than an objective, precise activity bound by logically
determined rules. His argument that scientific thought is
constrained by cultural views and values makes his view
postmodernist, one can argue.

Stephen Toulmin, "Modern and Postmodern Science"

1. The postmodern scientist is aware that the traditional belief
in objectivity, in the scientist as outside spectator, is faulty.
The scientist brings with him or her interests, purposes,
assumptions, etc., that alter the object of study. Acknowledging
these interests is an equivalent way of saying one has a
multiplicity of interpretive standpoints.
2. Both Gould and Toulmin analyze the metaphoric basis of
scientific thought--we see in scientific theories reflections of
ways of thinking, ways of perceiving, that are common to the
individual scientist's cultural milieu. Both seek to point out
the way scientific knowledge functions--that it does not produce
absolute truth, but is more a means of describing the world.
3. As soon as we decide to study or observe some phenomenon, we
alter it by our presence--our physical presence, as in
anthropology, or our technological presence, as in physics. Thus
"objective" observation is an impossibility.
4. [Personal response]
5. [Personal response]

Ruth Bleier, Introduction to <u>Feminist Approaches to Science</u>

1. Bleier argues that preformationist theory is a product of male
cultural assumptions, specifically that women serve as passive
incubators of fully formed, male produced embryos. She
acknowledges that her essay is an attempt to correct the gender
biases of traditional science; one can argue that she does write
from a gender bias, though her acknowledged purpose is to do so.
Gould's defense of the preformationists, while not incorporating a
specific analysis of the role of gender bias, does agree with
Bleier's in that both recognize the role of cultural assumptions
in scientific theorizing.
2. The notion of objectivity gives scientific theory an air of
unbiased factuality; if in fact scientific methods and values
serve male interests, this notion helps to screen that self-
serving impulse. Claims to absolute truth, too, prevent
challenges to male scientific dominance, and the authoritarian
stance further diminishes the likelihood of being challenged.
Deterministic thinking puts the blame on nature, in a sense, and
deflects attention from the agenda of male dominance.
3. [Class exercise]
4. [Class exercise/personal response]
5. The status of the scientist in our society remains high. With
status typically goes power. We see this expressed within the
scientific community in the form of grant monies, prizes and
awards, etc. Thus the amount of personal power available within
scientific fields is great. The popular perception of the
scientist, however, is the inverse of this power model: the
scientist is usually seen as a humanitarian devoted to the pursuit
of knowledge that will directly improve the quality of life.

CHAPTER 4:   THE LITERARY TRADITION

Classical Texts

Sophocles, <u>Oedipus Rex</u>

1. While we attach the term "tragic" to the death (or other
extreme event) of a person who is not a major public figure, we
still experience a keen sense of loss when the person is well
known for some public service (even if this service has been
offered in the entertainment field). Thus the assassinations of
President Kennedy and John Lennon have each been perceived as
tragic events. Stature seems not to be a primary determining
element in our perception of tragedy, as was the case in ancient
tragedy, but it is an enhancing one. We continue to see a sudden
reversal of fortune as a tragic event: we speak of Nixon's fall in
Watergate as a tragedy, a sport figure's accident as a tragedy,

even a bankruptcy as a tragedy. The theory of the personal flaw
may or may not figure in our sense of what is tragic--in Nixon's
case, it certainly did.
Oedipus was a great man; his fall is thus greater--more tragic
--than if a lesser person experienced some loss. He is brought
down, one can argue, by the quality that made him great: his
boldness in discovering the truth, from the response he offers to
the sphinx to his insistence on finding the killer of Laios. He
struggles against the fate decreed by the gods and nobly bears it
when it strikes. He accepts his fate as punishment for his great
sins. This notion of fate and punishment plays little or no part
in our notion of tragedy, which is usually seen as a random event
and is heightened when the victim is completely innocent.
2. If we see Oedipus' desire to know as his tragic flaw, then we
can say he is both elevated and struck down by that trait. We can
also see overbearing pride as his tragic trait: he challenges fate
by fleeing his home in order to avoid (he believes) killing his
father and marrying his mother. This pride leads him to scorn
Tiresias and pursue his campaign to find the murderer. Our
contemporary notion of tragedy sometimes operates on this premise
of tragic irony; we often see the destructive excesses of popular
figures' lifestyles as the product of their great success. More
often, we see the waste of potential, of a bright future, as the
tragic element in an accident or death of a young person. One can
be a victim and be considered tragic today; in ancient times, only
the fall of heroes was considered tragic, and all other events were
examples of pathos.
3. Oedipus is perceived as a father figure, a protector of the
people and city. His heroic stature is also emphasized: the
priest appeals to his glorious reputation to deliver the city from
the plague. Oedipus reveals in his speech a sympathetic nature, a
sense of great moral and personal responsibility. He also
demonstrates his desire and ability to act through his revelation
of the steps he has taken to learn the cause of the plague.
4. [Personal response]
5. Oedipus seems to be infuriated by Tiresias' refusal to obey
him. Tiresias reminds him that he is not the equal of the gods;
this may be the point at which Oedipus has transgressed the divine
codes and committed a hubristic act. He does not recognize his
guilt, however, and instead doubles his vehement abuse of the
prophet. At this point, we see his human frailty: he begins to see
threats and enemies about him, and unjustly accuses Tiresias and
Creon of seeking his power.
6. By remaining alive, Oedipus actively participates in his
punishment and offers himself as a symbol of the crimes he has
committed. His self-blinding represents the blindness of human
perception, which he is guilty of. Jocasta, not equal to her
husband/son in greatness, cannot bear the shame of her sin, and
she takes her own life.
7. For the most part, women and lower class members are absent

from the action of the play. When we see a lowly type, such as
the shepherd, he is a cringing, fearful, though kindly man. The
play focuses on aristocratic, priestly, or other powerful figures.
None of the characters is realistic. They are stereotypical in
that they speak, look, and behave according to classical notions
of style--more refined for the upper classes, and so on.
8. [Personal response]
9. Oedipus believes his will is strong enough to guide him
through life; his fate reveals that we cannot consciously control
our behavior. If we don't listen to the warnings given us by
authority figures, we risk total destruction of our happiness,
love, and even physical being, as the play's events depict.
Oedipus symbolizes the Freudian truth that we carry within us
natural sexual urges and aggression, urges so powerful that they
cannot be controlled except through submission to laws.
10. The play's structure reflects the symmetry of Aristotelian
structure, its action the logic of cause and effect typical of
classical Greek thinkers. The story reflects the mythological
impulse to explain the human mind via specific characters and
situations. The emphasis on law that must be observed by all
citizens, even so exalted a figure as Oedipus, reflects classical
political values.
11. Traditionally, the term "Christian tragedy" has been viewed as
a contradiction, because Christianity is based upon a belief in the
possibility of repentance and forgiveness. The crimes that Oedipus
commits are not the most heinous ones possible within the Christian
ethical system. Heresy or other betrayal of God is far more
serious. Oedipus' repentance for failing to heed the gods would,
in a Christian system, lead to his reclamation as a member of the
community. By committing suicide, Jocasta, however, would be
condemned: she would be guilty of denying the possibility of God's
forgiveness, thus usurping his power by taking her own life.

Aristotle, from Poetics

1. Aristotle believes that by nature we learn through imitation,
and that the desire to re-enact is a supremely human trait. We
thus feel a natural pleasure in imitating or watching imitations
of human actions. Watching a play, then, is something we enjoy,
even if the actions depicted are unhappy ones.
2. Pity and fear are the elements of tragedy because they are
aroused only in certain situations, such as when a loved one turns
on a loved one. This kind of action is horrible and makes us feel
intense sympathy for all involved. These are the most unbearable
feelings in real life; to have them evoked and expressed through
tragedy thus allows us to rid our psyches of them. Art purges us
of dangerous feelings.
3. Tragic stories, particularly love stories, continue to be
popular as TV and film fare. But action thrillers seem to have

overtaken such stories, suggesting, perhaps, that pity and fear
are not the prevailing dangerous emotions. In modern life, what
might make us need films such as the Indiana Jones series, the
slasher/horror "Nightmare on Elm Street" series? Perhaps they
relieve the boredom of mundane, inactive life, the pent up
hostility that comes from social dissatisfaction, crowding, a
reduction of intimacy.
4. An academic essay without a beginning (an introduction) would
throw the reader into the middle of the argument without
background context, familiarity with the authorial voice, or a
clear notion of the author's thesis. Sometimes a writer might
wish to create this effect for some special text-related purpose,
but if the writer simply launched into his or her argument without
awareness of the missing element, the audience would most likely be
confused and the essay perceived as inadequate.

A sitcom without the middle section (the complicating part of
the plot that creates some threat of disaster, embarrassment,
etc.) would be a repeat of the opening, where life gets put back
together. Typically, comedy complicates life and then resolves
the complication, often giving the players some greater (though
usually platitudinous) insight into themselves or their lives.
The audience would be bewildered first because no action took
place but second because no problem arose that needed solving, and
so the good feelings offered by comedic release would not
materialize.

A biography without a conclusion about the subject would
frustrate the reader's sense of closure and might be uncomfortably
close to the tensions we face in our own lives--questions about the
future, about past decisions, etc.
5. The play is a complex action in which a great hero begins at
the pinnacle of his society and then faces a reversal of fortune.
In the case of Oedipus, the reversal and recognition happen at the
same time: he discovers himself to be guilty and is destroyed by
the discovery.
6. [Class exercise]
7. [Personal response]

Sigmund Freud, "Oedipus Rex"

1. Freud cites his extensive experience observing neurotics, thus
grounding his theory in scientific practice. He uses the
persistence of the Oedipus legend into modern times as evidence of
the psychological conflict he is defining; his purpose may be to
shift attention to its existence in the real world and away from it
as a mere theory he is promoting. He acknowledges that people
react to the idea of sexual relations with parents with
"indignation and astonishment," which seems a kind of appeasement
of his audience.
2. A child may cry to be with the desired parent whenever he or

she departs, rejecting the caretaker parent. Children often
openly identify with a parent, putting on some object of his or her
clothing, saying they are "Mommy" or "Daddy," etc. They are often
very direct in expressing their feelings--"I hate you" is a not
unusual phrase in a child's vocabulary.
3.   Freud calls the play a tragedy of destiny, but conceived
psychologically, not simply dramatically. Freud rejects the
reading of the play as a conflict between the gods and human will.
For Freud, the tragedy lies in the "curse" placed on all of us
before birth: to direct our sexual energy toward the opposite-sex
parent and to wish for the death of the other.
4.   None of us can avoid the oedipal struggle, and in this sense
we are destined to strive against the same impulses and horrors
Oedipus faced. We have to come to grips with the mismatch of our
desires and our power; life's earliest lesson is about how we must
learn to give up our greatest desire.
5.   Oedipus has come to believe he is more knowledgeable and wise
than others, including the seer Tiresias. He has also challenged
the oracle by attempting to evade his destiny--he has left home
and his (presumed) parents, thus challenging the gods' power to
predict the events of his life.
6.   [Personal response]

Medieval Tales and Renaissance Prose

Sir Thomas Malory, from Le Morte D'Arthur

1. The language is formal, courtly, and stylized. Readers
might perceive the characters as idealized, larger than
life, and less than realistic.
2. Aristotle defines a well-constructed plot as having a
beginning, middle, and end. It "must neither begin nor end
at haphazard." Malory's book is episodic, a collection of
stories, rather than one uniform work with an ending that
provides resolution.
3. Lancelot's bravery and mastery of arms is seen in his
confrontation with the knights in the Chapel Perilous and
his defeat of Sir Phelot in which he uses a tree branch
instead of a sword. He evinces virtue, restraint and his
devotion to the courtly love of his lady Guinevere as he
refuses to kiss the sorceress Hellawes. He demonstrates his
willingness to serve the weak and needy when he goes to help
the wounded Sir Gylbert and his duty to help ladies in
distress when he assists the woman with the lost falcon and
the woman being chased by Sir Pedyvere. He shows mercy by
sending Sir Pedyvere to Queen Guinevere for judgement rather
than killing him.

4. Lancelot is protected from the spells of Hellawes by his religious faith and virtue. He replies that God forbids him to kiss Hellawes and then prays to Jesus to protect him from the enchantress's magic.
5. Sir Phelot coerces his wife to lure Lancelot into putting down his weapons and climbing the tree; he intends to kill Lancelot eventhough he is unarmed and defenseless.
6. Sir Phelot's murder of his wife is a "horrible and shameful deed" not so much for the murder itself but because as Queen Guinevere says, it is "a great rebuke" of Sir Lancelot. Sir Phelot breaks the chivalric code with Lancelot. First, he breaks his promise to obey Lancelot after Lancelot stops him from slaying his wife. Secondly, he shames Lancelot by killing a damosel who is under his knightly protection.
7. Sir Pedyvere's penance requires that he carry his slain wife's body to Rome and the Pope. He is not allowed to stay more than one night in any one place and if he lies down to sleep he must take the body with him. In this way he will be constantly reminded of his sin and shame.
8. [class exercise]

Cervantes, from Don Quixote

1. Cervantes satirizes chivalry's emphasis on bravery and honor as well as courtly love in these two episodes. Don Quixote's attack on the imaginary giants in the windmills mimics the romantic tales of knights battling dragons and monsters and his overall concern with doing brave deeds; "having adventures" in which he can test his honor and bravery is also chivalric. What we see of his relationship to "his Lady" Dulcinea reflects Cervantes' satirization of courtly love: Don Quixote dedicates his adventure to "his lady"; he refers to himself as "a captive knight" lost in love, who sighs and utters "countless amorous lamentations"; he treats the peasant girl he imagines as Dulcinea with the chivalric courtesy expected of a knight errant.
2. [Personal response]
3. Don Quixote is significantly more realistic than the idealized stories and characters in Le Morte D'Arthur : The language Cervantes' characters use is sensible and down to earth. The peasant girls and Sancho Panza swear and curse and even Don Quixote's language seems realistic. The characters are described realistically; the peasant girl is "...a country girl...not very handsome... round faced and flatnosed," with garlic on her breath. The characters' actions appear realistic. Events happen as they

46

do in the real world; Don Quixote and his horse take an undignified fall; Sancho Panza chooses the fillies from Don Quixote's mares at home rather than a share of the spoils from Don Quixote's dreams of the spoils of adventure. The setting is real - no magical chapel or any supernatural goings on in the story.

4. As a sidekick, Sancho Panza plays foil and opposite to much of what Don Quixote symbolizes. Sancho, short, potbellied and full of commonsense, is the voice of realism, without a grain of spirituality or idealism. He is the working class common man making his entrance on the literary stage. Together with Don Quixote they symbolize the opposite sides of the Spanish national character or even the spiritual and earthly inclinations of humankind itself.

5. Incongruity and exaggeration account for much of the humor in these episodes. Note Don Quixote imagining the windmills as giants and charging at them at full speed challenging them to combat; Don Quixote on his knees praising the homely peasant girl as "the perfection of all desire." The peasant girl leaping into the saddle like a man just as Don Quixote is about to lift her gallantly onto her mount. Don Quixote generally believing all of Sancho's suggestions about the peasant girls including mistaking their donkeys for royal steeds.

6. Lady Dulcinea is the peasant girl Don Quixote imagines to be his lady before he sallies forth on his adventures. She becomes the satirized version of the courtly ladies we find in Malory: Guinevere, the "fair damosel," Sir Melyot's sister, the "fair lady" who loses her hawk, ladies who inspire chivalry in noble knights and who for Cervantes become part of his grand satire of the exaggerated chivalric romances of his time.

Castiglione, from The Book of the Courtier

1. Castiglione recommends expertise in wrestling, vaulting, horseback riding, and swordsmanship. Intellectually, courtiers cultivated the ability to speak eloquently and to be witty since participating in courtly conversation played an essential part in a courtier's life. The courtier was expected to display his physical abilities, gestures, habits, and intellectual abilities with cool, sophisticated, understated grace.

2. [Personal response]

3. The aspiring courtier is advised to seek out experts to instruct him and to also imitate the masters as much as

possible, to "make every effort to ressemble and...
transform himself into his master." The danger inherent in
this advice is that the courtier may become too extreme in
his imitation and end up copying traits, gestures, and
habits that are not necessarily intentional attempts at
sophistication and grace although they may be exhibited by a
much admired person. Castiglione describes courtiers
imitating King Ferdinand "twisting one side of his mouth" in
a certain way, which in fact was a physical malady and not a
stylistic gesture.
4. [Personal response]
5. Sprezzatura is an intentional attitude of nonchalance, an
attempt to make one's gestures, habits, movements, speech
appear effortless. When a courtier practices sprezzatura, it
reveals a much desired sense of understated grace and evokes
a sense of wonder and awe, since the courtier is
acomplishing something difficult while making it seem easy.
Courtiers' status in Renaissance courtly circles often
depended on their ability to both be entertaining as well as
skilled in the various courtly arts, and to do so with grace
and sprezzatura defined the ideal courtier.
6. Castiglione proposes that any art is devalued and
deprived of its sense of grace if any effort is detected.
"Ungainly effort" and affectation are the aesthetic taboos
for Castiglione's courtier, for they reveal someone who has
not completely mastered his art.

Michel de Montaigne, "Of Not Communicating One's Glory"

1. In the first example, Catalus Luctatus, after attempting
to stop his troops from running away from the enemy, joined
his troops in retreat in order to give the impression they
were following their commander and thereby cover up their
dishonor while disregarding his own reputation. Antonio de
Leyva, knowing that Emperor Charles had already made up his
mind, intentionally gave his master poor advice, so that the
Emperor would appear wise in acting against his counsel. The
mother of the Spartan Brasidas refused the public praise for
her slain son's heroism, pointing out that many other
Spartans were braver than her son. During the battle of
Crecy, King Edward declined to go fight alongside his
besieged son because he didn't want to diminish his son's
glory or assume any of the credit for the victory.
Theopompus refused to accept credit for governing Sparta
well but rather gave credit to its citizens who "obey[ed]"
well. The Bishop of Beauvais, fighting at the battle of
Bouvines, defeated several of the enemy but turned them over
to other knights to be taken prisoner or killed, thus
avoiding the glory of personal victory in combat.

2. Montaigne proposes that of all the virtues, giving up concern for reputation and fame is perhaps the most difficult. It is easier to embrace poverty, to give up health and even life than it is for people to surrender their vanity. Even the philosophers who write books about it want their books to still bear their names. Montaigne implies that true humbleness and modesty may be one of the purest virtues a person can attain.
3. Castiglione defines an ersatz modesty and humbleness. His sprezzatura does involve a grace that comes from concealing artfulness so that what one does appears to be effortless and without forethought. He recommends "art which does not seem to be art." Nevertheless, the ideal courtier does not want his grace to go unnoticed, even if he gives that impression. Here is where he would differ from Montaigne who points out the virtue of having one's achievements truly not be recognized.
4. [Class exercise]
5. [Class exercise]
6. [Personal response]

Enlightenment Satire and Romantic Heroes

Voltaire, from Candide

1. Voltaire uses absurd statements presented in a factual manner as one further source of humor. Pangloss's explanation of why we have spectacles is one example. He also deliberately misrepresents situations in a euphemistic way, as in the description of the "lesson" Pangloss gives to the young maid. Ironic juxtaposition is another comic technique: at the end of Chapter 1, we see kicking, slapping, and eviction taking place in what is described as "confusion in the most beautiful and agreeable of all possible castles." Understatement is yet another technique, as when Candide is "thunderstruck" in the wake of his kidnaping and torture.
2. The hypocrisy that Voltaire comically reveals ties to the real worlds of academe, philosophy, religion, family matters, and other human endeavors typically depicted as sacred or high-minded. The willful denial of real experience in favor of theoretical explanation is a common Age of Reason critique of metaphysical mumbo-jumbo in favor of the rule of common sense. Many of the horrible events put to a ridiculous end in the tale reflect actual history: the plundering and raping of native populations, the Inquisition, etc.
3. Candide accepts much at face value, though by the end he learns not to trust anything beyond his own experience. He is open to new ideas but also has the sense to question their

veracity. He is honest in his dealings with others, loyal in his friendships, generous, not spiteful, not any of the other negative qualities depicted as pervasive human flaws.

4. Optimism, taken to the extreme, denies the presence of evil in humans and nature. It forces rational explanations onto what ought to be judged moral outrages. If all is for the best, then all is permissible; the abuses done in the name of progress are just one example of how optimism can be used to justify excesses of all kinds.

5. A reformulation of the final line might be "accept what you have and make the best of it," or "the individual is responsible for himself or herself."

6. [Personal response]

7. Voltaire seems uninterested in naming the source of evil; instead, getting on with a rational life is the only important matter for him. Certainly if we fail to take care of our own responsibilities, we are at fault for the evils that befall us. But attempting to explain the larger issue of cosmic evil is a waste of time, for Voltaire.

8. [Personal response]

9. Voltaire seems to believe that differences arise from social, not natural, situations. He depicts these social pretensions as the basis of cruelty, inequality, and other social ills. His tale seems to support the notion that human nature is the same from individual to individual.

10. Voltaire seems suspicious of any claims of exclusive knowledge, absolute standards, or other attempts to impose a single belief system. Thus he would very likely argue for a liberal approach in the curriculum and against canonical requirements. As one of the "encyclopedistes," he would be likely to favor broad study rather than overly narrow educational plans (Pangloss being one example of the dangers of such study).

Jean Jacques Rousseau, from _Confessions_

1. Rousseau writes of his uniqueness, his absolute individuality. Thus the "I" voice is prominent in his style and subjects. His "I" is the center of his being, developed through his sensual perceptions.

2. Rousseau claims that his work has no precedent, unlike the biographical mode popular for centuries. He also claims that he is painting a natural, complete portrait, not a selective retelling of biographical points designed to construct an artificial, untrue image. He writes from the heart, which is the source, he believes, of truth, and so he will detail the good and the (apparently) bad, though anything that is the product of the natural man cannot be immoral, he claims.

3. Romantic love is love at close-to-first sight; it is a natural sympathy that draws two hearts together and keeps them eternally

bound (evidenced in his father's death scene). Romantic love is ideal, not basely physical, not tied to concerns of social standing and economics. Romantic love is also likely to be tragic, for by our very nature we are mortal, yet ideal love is immortal.

4. From his sickliness at birth, an air of pain and misery surrounds Rousseau, as he depicts himself. His mother's death is his "fault," his tragic mark. For the rest of his days this aura of tragic loss and depth of painful feeling cloaks him.

5. Popular novels, especially in Rousseau's time, are typically concerned with affairs of the heart or some extraordinary adventure, oftentimes correlating to inward journeys of exploration and discovery. Novels allow for imaginative transcendence of the daily and mundane. They allow for immediate sensation, for emotional identification. Scientific or historical works keep one tied to the realm of the limited, known world (the Romantic argument goes), stimulating not the heart and imagination, but the rational, logical mind.

6. Equality is not a major value among most Romantic writers, primarily because many of them held Rousseau's view of the unique self. A belief in equality contradicts this possibility of absolute individuality. As for natural goodness, this is Rousseau's central philosophical tenet. Society and its false, materialistic values corrupt its members, who are born into a state of natural goodness.

7. [Personal response]

8. Rousseau's philosophy is a kind of withdrawal into the self, a turning inward, away from the external, social world. Beauty becomes a matter of personal perception and sensation rather than an artificially contrived object. Preoccupation with the self takes precedence over social exchange. With the rise of the middle class, a kind of flattening of culture takes place; Rousseau's philosophical beliefs allow for difference on the individual level.

Mary Shelley, from <u>Frankenstein</u>

1. Dante envisioned not only some of the most vivid and detailed scenes of horror in <u>Inferno</u> but some of the most realistic disfigurations of the human frame in all of literature. Shelley's allusion captures the very human aspect of the monster in addition to the unnatural perversion of the human face and physique. It also conveys the devilish, hellish nature of the creature in Victor's perception of it.

2. The physical features of the creature are usually depicted fairly accurately, the major distinction being that Shelley's creature was agile and physically adept, unlike the stiff-legged, ungainly monster depicted on film. It is Frankenstein who rushes out of the laboratory in a panic, not the creature, in the original version; typically, films depict the "monster" as escaping

in a mad, violent panic. The film versions seem to want to make the human figure the hero, whereas Shelley endows the creature with supreme intelligence and enormous emotional sensitivity.

3. Victor's extraordinary sensitivity to external stimuli, the intensity of his feelings, and the daring of his imagination to conceive of creating life itself are all hallmarks of the Romantic hero, particularly of the Romantic over-reacher. The confrontation of the extremes within the individual's nature is also typically Romantic, and we see this in Victor's horror at his own creation. One can classify him as a tragic hero as well in that he possesses some unique quality that ultimately brings about his downfall--his will to create life both elevates him and brings about the loss of all that makes him human.

4. The Freudian analyst might see a mixture of wish fulfillment and self-punishment at work in Victor's dream. First, he transforms his mother into his future bride, indicating his desire to possess her. But he immediately transforms that wish into its punishment: he "kills" his mother, the object of his desire, and so deprives himself of the satisfaction he wishes, substituting great pain in its place.

5. Victor produces the creature at the cost of "infinite pains and care," like the labor of childbirth. The beauty of the perfect, tiny limbs has its nightmare equivalent in the gigantic proportions of the creature; the embryonic look that newborns retain adds to the horror, as does the weird coloration of the skin. The creature seeks out its "mother," making demands upon him/her. The creature also represents a kind of death-in-life figure, which many critics have traced back to Mary Shelley's own terrible losses through miscarriage and the early deaths of several children.

6. Certainly Victor embodies many of the traditional qualities ascribed to scientists: he is seen as possessed with and by his work; he is searching for the key to life itself, to total mastery of nature; he is "marked" in some way, indicating his superior status. The role of imagination is pre-eminent in Victor's case, however, more a Romantic than traditional value. His intensity of feeling is unlike the usual view of scientific detachment. One might say that Victor represents a kind of corrective to the masculine image of the scientist that Bleier critiques.

7. Many contemporary scientific fields of research have evoked the fears we see evident in the Frankenstein myth. Fetal tissue research as well as the whole array of artificial means of insemination have created intense public concern over the justifiable realm of the scientist. Artificial intelligence and genetic engineering are two more areas of major concern. The fear that we may go too far persists, and Shelley's monster retains its folkloric power to act as a caution against human interference with the processes of nature. The environmental effects of past scientific and technological developments are also often described in Frankensteinian imagery.

Tradition in the Twentieth Century

T.S. Eliot, from "Tradition and the Individual Talent"

1.   Eliot cites the critical tendency to assume that we have a tradition and an agreement on the values it embodies. What this traditional sense is has not been defined, and so he steps in to provide a detailed definition. Because we tend to judge new works of art according to what is new in them, not with an awareness of how they relate to tradition, we are left celebrating newness for its own sake, and we are likely to miss what is truly individual and best in a work of art.
2.   Colloquial speech reflects the language of the day and daily life to a greater extent than does formal, stylistically self-conscious prose. It is therefore more limited to its time, more "new" in the negative sense, than the kind of formal prose Eliot prefers. How prose relates to the prose tradition is the key to criticizing it, and so the individual voice will write with an awareness of that tradition.
3.   Tradition is not a blind imitation of past forms, not simple repetition. It involves an awareness of the past, of history, and of how it relates to contemporary values--a sense of "the timeless as well as of the temporal and of the timeless and of the temporal together." Tradition is thus a continuum that is forever reforming as time passes.
4.   The critic looks for the conformity and individuality of a work of art to determine its worth, according to Eliot. Consciousness of the past is a first element to look for; how the new work of art helps us see this past through the values of the present might be called the individual portion of the work of art.
5.   Concrete examples might best help illustrate the difference between "individual" and "different." For a traditional critic such as Eliot, a modern staging of <u>Oedipus Rex</u>, for instance, might be an excellent, individual work of art if it helps us to see how the essence of the ancient play continues to relate to our lives today. It might be simply different if the idea were to do a musical version of the play, with the musical aspect being the sole concern. This would indeed be different, but it would not address the play in its truly artistic form, in the power of the story of Oedipus. It would lack the historical sense.
6.   The ideal order of art is a constant, absolute notion. With the introduction of a new work of art, the order remains, though it takes on a new form, for the new work of art changes how we see the whole. We cannot imagine the works of Homer, for example, without an awareness of later works of art, such as the dramas and poetry of Shakespeare or Tennyson. Each new work of art alters how we perceive the whole.
7.   The extinction of personality ensures that what is simply

different will not be an element of the work of art. Personality
is difference, not individuality. Thus the elements that keep an
artist tied to his or her time must be erased from the creative
process in order for the individual, the relationship of present
to past, to emerge.
8. [Personal response]
9. If a work loses its status as a classic, then that work was
initially misjudged; true works of art are, for Eliot, eternal in
value. A work of an earlier age may become part of the ideal order
for later generations; Eliot himself is often credited for reviving
interest in the metaphysical poets, for example.
10. [Personal response]

Adalaide Morris, from "Dick, Jane, and American Literature:
Fighting with Canons"

1. Morris seeks to move attention away from the canon itself and
to the struggle that it reveals, the efforts of various groups to
be heard and recognized. Thus she speaks of "canons" rather than
"the canon" at the end of her essay. She criticizes the
traditional notion as a concept used to promote and to justify the
special interests of a privileged group in society, one that
eclipses the achievements and interests of women, minorities, the
working class, etc. The role of academia is also criticized: the
canon serves as the stuff of teaching, the selected knowledge that
is packaged and treated as more valuable than other kinds of
knowledge.
2. Obviously, her first disagreement is with Eliot's restricted
references to male artists and critics, for she corrects his line
to read "his or her." But rather than a tradition defined by
individual works of art determined to be great by special-
interest critics, she places art in a social context. This social
context is the full tapestry of various cultures that make up
American society.
3. Morris cites struggle as our common heritage. We have not had
a unified, centered cultural tradition, but rather a tradition of
conflict and difference. We need to learn to value such
differences, Morris argues, for our true tradition resides in the
conversations among the various communities that make up American
society.
4. Particular world views are presented in classrooms as models
of what is right, best, superior to other views. The assumptions
implicit in canonical works tie success and goodness to particular
beliefs--to Christianity, capitalism, and male superiority, for
example. We are socialized into treating the assumptions implicit
in canonical works as self-evident truths or absolutes, not values
tied to a particular social context or class.
5. [Class exercise]
6. A student outside the mainstream is likely to come to see the

mainstream culture as the "right" one, and his or her own as
inferior, lesser in importance, different, and secondary. The
message is that the mainstream does not value the student's home
culture. Often, a conflict develops: to be successful is to
identify with the dominant culture and reject one's own, a student
may come to believe.
7. It is Pecola's "fault" that she is black and so different from
the norm that guarantees happiness. If she had blue eyes, she
feels, then the rest--stable home life, love, friendship, etc.--
would naturally follow, as it seems to for those who make up this
mainstream group. She violates the ideal in her very physical
existence, and so she is to blame for her very less than ideal
situation. Only those who meet the mainstream standards deserve
love and happiness, she comes to believe.
8. [Personal response]
9. [Personal response]

Maxine Hong Kingston, from The Woman Warrior

1. At first, the silence is personal preference: Kingston recalls
that she was caught up in an imaginative world of possibility,
where the play/words would momentarily begin. The later silence
seems cultural; Kingston notes that Chinese girls did not speak--it
was not a behavior they were encouraged to develop. Fear of how
their voices sounded in English may have added to the silence, with
their awareness of cultural differences that they could not
articulate adding further to their discomfort.
2. Her parents are unfamiliar with American educational practices
and so react with fear, indifference, or stoic acceptance. They do
not understand the teachers' words or values, and so they cannot
help their daughter to negotiate the cultural differences she
encounters, to alter her behavior to meet expectations, or to
explain to others her individual beliefs. She does not report
shame at her parents' difference; she is acutely aware of it,
however, and seems bewildered, at the very least.
3. Her black friends help her to feel more free and confident
through their example as daring talkers and, in contrast to the
Chinese students, less inhibited behavior. Most likely the black
children are equally outside the mainstream, however. Yet their
reaction to that exclusion differs markedly from Kingston and her
Chinese playmates, and thus offers a model for adaptation other
than silence.
4. Kingston perceives the English "I" as oversimplified, missing
something, yet unashamed of its plain look. The Chinese "I" more
closely represented her own sense of inner complexity. She cannot
identify with the English symbol; the difference reveals an
identity conflict, a sense of not being able to fit into the new
culture she now inhabits.
5. More secure within the familiar Chinese context, the students

55

feel a sense of freedom in Chinese school. They are part of a
unified group, chanting their lessons together. They know the
system of rules and how to obey them; they are familiar with the
expectations of the adults who are their teachers. The
surroundings are also familiar, adding further to their sense of
belonging and security.
6.   Both seemed to be aware of their parents' difference as a kind
of handicap they faced. Both traced much of their identity
conflicts to language differences. Rodriguez writes as an adult
examining his childhood experience; Kingston recreates the child's
perception, and thus we get less direct analysis of her situation
and feelings. Rodriguez is aware of his parents' desire for him to
fit in and succeed; Kingston seems more instilled with the idea of
her difference and the impossibility of being one of the "ghosts."
7.   Certainly in the area of how she is judged academically,
Kingston's experience reflects Rose's argument. Her cultural
difference from the mainstream, her discomfort with the langauge
and customs of the classroom, is taken as evidence of intellectual
inferiority. She believes she has less right to speak, less
knowledge to share, than her classmates.
8.   Gregory's experience seems to be based more on a sense of
personal shame, in light of his public humiliation. He is less
focused on his cultural difference and more on his class
difference--on his poverty and his missing father. He develops a
sense of personal worthlessness that Kingston does not seem to
suffer; her experience is more generalized, tied to being a
"Chinese girl."
9.   [Personal response]

CHAPTER 5:   POLITICAL THEORY AND PRACTICE

Democracy and Oppression

Sidney Hook, "Democracy"

1.   A direct democracy is one in which all citizens vote directly
on all legislation, as was done in ancient Athens or in New England
town meetings. In an indirect democracy, citizens elect
representatives who "represent" their interests and who vote on
their behalf. Proper delegation of authority is crucial for an
indirect democracy to succeed because delegation of authority must
be reversible, "controlled by those who delegated it."
2.   The obvious benefit of a direct democracy is that it gives all
citizens a direct political voice in all of their governmental
affairs. An indirect democracy provides citizens of a larger
country, like the U.S., an indirect political voice through elected
representatives. Logistically, a direct democracy in the U.S.
would be impossible, but U.S. citizens, through democratic

representation have given up the direct voice an indirect
democracy affords.
3. Technically, a republic is led by a head of government
whose position is not hereditary. Therefore a republic can
be undemocratic, like Nazi Germany or the Soviet Union, or
democratic, like the United States.

4. Freely given consent describes the permission citizens
give to their representatives to vote and govern on their
behalf. Freely given consent requires a political climate
free of coercion or threats against public opinion; a free
press and freedom of speech and assembly; no complete
control of media by the ruling party. Conditions for freely
given consent are critical to the modern implementation of
majority rule, because they guarantee that different groups
have access to affecting and changing public opinion.
5. [Personal response]
6. When Mencken referred to the "dictatorship of the
booboisie he was implying that the common people were
"boobs" too stupid and incompetent to make informed choices
and decisions, but nevertheless entrusted with the power of
the vote. Plato and George Santayana argue in the same vein:
most people are "either too stupid or too vicious... to be
entrusted with selfgovernment." They argue that only an
intellectual and spiritual elite can have the knowledge and
hence the potential to govern wisely. Plato himself pointed
out the weakness to this position: Who will watch the
watchers? How will the good will of the benevolent despot be
ensured? Plato uses the analogy that the cobbler (the
elite) knows best how to make the shoes, but it is the
wearer (the people) who knows whether the shoes (the
government) fit properly.

Amaury De Riencourt, "Women in Athens"

1. As Greek culture developed, the status and rights of
women were continually eroded. Women lost the right of
inheritance through the mother; Women had no independent
status in court - they could not incur debts, enter into
contracts or initiate legal action. Women did not even
inherit their husband's property upon his death. Women were
often criticized harshly in Greek drama and literature, and
they rarely functioned outside the domain of the household.
2. Riencourt proposed that the strongly patriarchal,
misogynist nature of classical Greece originated in the
early Greek male understanding (in fact misunderstanding) of
his role as sexual inseminator. The Early Greeks believed

"men alone were endowed with generative power," and they saw
women as being "merely empty vessels... incubators" to bear
and nurture babies. Women became only tools of reproduction,
"wives to bear... lawful offspring... and faithful guardians
for [men's] homes."
3. The Greeks men used concubines as sexual companions,
often kept within the household for "the daily health of our
[their] bodies." The Hetairai were cultured, educated
courtesans, social companions rather than just sexual
partners, often of some influence and social standing. The
Traditional wives bore children and cared for the home.
4. [Personal response]
5. Widespread Greek homosexuality was both a cause and a
result of Greek misogyny because Greek men held in little
esteem the two most prominant feminine attributes: maternal
procreativity and female sexuality. Greek men often only
pitied "...men who could fall in love with women with the
same passion" as with men, an attitude that facilitated
Platonic homosexual love, further devaluing women even as
sexual objects.
6. [Personal response]

Albert Parry, "Robespierre's Bloody Virtue"

1. [Personal response]
2. The reign of terror was justified by French
revolutionaries as a means of "purifying" the corrupt,
villainous French government. Robespierre believed that
terrorism was the only way to insure revolution and to
"defend all the good citizens... by dealing out death to
the enemies of the people. He even claimed that by executing
antirevolutionaries he was ..."doing his victims the valiant
favor of restoring virtue to them and to society."
3. Robespierre saw the role of the revolutionary regime as
the necessary precursor to a constitutional regime. It was
an out and out war by the people, "the legions of freedom,"
against their enemies. The revolution was the creator and
the protector of the republic.
4. [Personal response]
5. Robespierre viewed himself as a true disciple of Rousseau
who believed people to be "good by nature and corrupted by
civilization." The only way to purify people of their
"meanness and criminality," to restore them to their state
of natural goodness, was the death penalty and the
everpresent guillotine.
6. According to Parry, the violence and terror of the French
revolution did not purify the nation but rather perpetuated

more violence and fear. As a "phraseology" rather than an "ideology," Robespierre's terrorist rhetoric blindly led thousands of people into his revolutionary religion and often up the steps to the guillotine.

Hiram Wesley Evans, "The Klan's Fight for Americanism"

1. [Personal response]
2. [Personal response]
3. Some of Evans' assumptions and fallacies:
    - "Americanism can only be achieved if the pioneer stock is kept pure."
    - "...a man [is] a poor American unless he has a racial understanding of Americanism and an instinctive loyalty to it."
    - "...few aliens can understand the [American] spirit."
    - " The white race must be supreme, not only in America, but in the world."
    - "...each race must fight for its life, must conquer, accept slavery or die."
    - "...the future of progress and civilization depends on the continued supremacy of the white race."
    - "...Protestantism must be supreme... for America to go forward..."
    - ..."the destruction [of Protestantism]... is the purpose of all other peoples."
    - "politicians cater to alien racial and religious groups..."
    -..."the Klan's ambition is to get race and religion out of politics..."
    - "The Klan's chief interest is in education."
    - "Jews and Catholics are lavish with their caustic criticism of anything American."
    - "For the alien in general we have sympathy, opportunity, and justice."
    - "...there is little hope ... for the assimilation of eastern European Jews into American society."
    - "The most menacing and difficult problem facing America today is this of the permanently unassimilable alien."
3. [Personal response]
4. Because the Klan would like to keep America's "pioneer stock pure," it is concerned with the immigration of any aliens who are not white, Anglo-Saxon Protestants. The Klan is suspicious of Catholics because of their alleged first loyalty to the Vatican rather than the U.S., but all "unassimilable " aliens threaten the the Klan's notion of

Americanism, particularly (at least when this article was
written) Jews. The Klan has special contempt and fear of the
eastern Jews, the Askhenazim, who it views as a "mongrel"
people with little desire of assimilating into the American
mainstream.
5. [Personal response]

Malcolm X, "The Ballot or the Bullet"

1. [Personal response]
2. [Personal response]
3. The opening line, "The question tonight, as I understand
it is ..." identifies the text as addressed to an audience.
The "front-stage" dramatic, almost sermonic quality of a
speech appears often: "I'm not here to discuss my religion.
I'm not here to change.... I'm not here to argue...."
Malcom X is obviously speaking directly to an audience when
he uses the second person you in an informal voice: "a
problem that will make you catch hell... you're going to
catch hell... we're all in the same boat..." Even the use of
"you" and "we" typifies political speeches: If we don't do
something real soon, I think you'll have to agree that...."
4.Malcolm X alleges that the Democratic party, traditionally
the party that most Blacks have supported, has done very
little to advance the condition of Blacks apart from giving
a few Black leaders "big jobs" in Washington. According to
Malcolm X, "a vote for the Democrats is a vote for the
Dixiecrats," southern Democrats with little real sympathy
for the political rights of Black Americans.
5. [Personal response]

James Farmer, "A Night of Terror in Plaquemine, Louisiana,
1963"

1. Non-violence succeeded because it brought the issues of
segregation and racism before the collective conscience of
America in a reverent but tenacious manner. The strong
religious overtones of non-violent philosophy, and the
Christian-like suffering many civil rights workers endured,
when demonstrated to America through a sympathetic news
media, had a powerful, lasting effect. More practically,
non-violent civil disobedience by a minority against a
dominant power structure was probably more feasible than
direct confrontation.

2. Malcolm X might have said that the nineteen six ties were
the time for Black Americans to stop turning the other cheek
and meet violence with violence. Some Radical Black
activists saw non-violence, as practiced by the Congress of
Racial Equality, and Martin Luther King's Southern Christian
Leadership Conference, for example, as a strategy that
worked too slowly; that made alliances with the Democratic
party that historically had only thrown political crumbs to
the Black community and as a strategy that ultimately
demeaned Black people.
3. It could be argued that non-violent civil rights
strategies successfully impacted the American power
structure, leading to the Equal Rights Ammendment and the
breakdown of segregation and wholesale descrimination. A
radical position might also point out that immediately after
the racial "riots/rebellions" that rocked Black Ghettos all
over America in the nineteen sixties, large ammounts of
Federal dollars and aid, "Poverty Programs" and community
development programs began appearing in Black communities.
4. [Class exercise]
5. [Class exercise]

Hunter College Women's Studies Collective, from Women's
Realities, Women's Choices

1. Althought the authors point out both the achievements of
the feminist movement as well as the considerable problems
and opposition it faces, the view of the early 1980's seems
more optimistic than pessimistic, since women's issues
dominated the public scene. Women began gaining
representation in religious organizations and made modest
gains in corporate and government sectors. Women in the arts
and media began receiving more attention. More women
acquired professional training. Sexism was put "on the
defensive" as sexist language in textbooks was scrutinized
and revised and women's study programs expanded at
universities. In the family, men began taking more
responsibility in child-care and more women with pre-school
children began working.
2. The authors predict a political backlash to the feminist
movement. They cite Ronald Reagan's opposition to the Equal
Rights Amendment and access to abortions; the reduction of
social service programs and defeat in 1980 of politicians
who supported feminist issues; antiabortion groups increased
pressure on politicians; traditional attitudes still
strongly promoted in the public sector; and many young women
considering traditional female roles as life options.

3. [Class exercise]

4. The authors concede that feminism has almost always been articulated and defended by those women who have the education and social position to make themselves heard - usually middleclass women. They point out however, that revolutions are often spearheaded by educated middleclass people. By citing abortion rights, welfare reform, equal pay for women etc., They argue that the issues the feminist movement addresses are hardly irrelevent to poor minority women. The authors claim that the goals of "liberal" feminists and more "radical" socialist feminists "are coming more and more to coincide."

5. The liberation ethic views achievement of equality for women as impossible within the capitalist system which is structured for the benefit of the few at the expense of oppressing the many. The hierarchical corporate ethic must be replaced with institutions that represent and speak to the need of all people. In this philosophy, women achieving equality with men will not solve the problems. The system itself must be changed. On the other hand, the egalitarian ethic seeks "equality immediately [within] the present system and ...existing institu.tions" which will provide more political and social power to push for even more equality and change. This ethic does not propose a "radical transformation of the system."

6. The authors argue that women should concern themselves with women's issues before social and humanitarian ones because historically "revolutionary systems proposed by nonfeminist theorists have not eliminated sexual equality or gender role structure." They cite the American Civil Rights Movement, the French and Russian Revolutions, and the British and American labor movement as examples in which women's issues consistently were relegated to the back burner, never to really be addressed.

7. [Personal response]

8. The fact that the authors identify themselves as members of a collective immediately suggests a progressive, possibly socialist political perspective, in which group interests supersede those of the individual. The authors' rhetoric and diction support this: power structure, oppression, oppression of women, neoconservative, ...survival strategies of many of our sisters; sisterhood; reference to the women's movement as a revolution; setting women's issues "in the present capitalist system"; the fact that they want to replace the business civilization's hierarchical structure with an egalitarian one; idealizing a society in which power will not be used to dominate others; referring to women as an oppressed class.

Karen Kenyon, "A Pink Collar Worker's Blues"

1. [Personal response]
2. Our society is still arguably very patriarchal in many
ways and gender discrimination still plagues the workplace.
The "old boy system" that has permeated big business makes
it very difficult for women to move up the management
ladder. In addition, gender stereotypes still tend to
relegate women to making the office coffee and working the
typewriters.
3. [Personal response]

Monarchy and Abuse of Power

William Edenstein, "Monarchy"

1. Derived from the Greek word monarchia, the rule of one,
monarchy is a form of government "in which one person is the
sovereign" and power is passed on through heredity. In early
history, as well as among many primitive peoples today,
monarchy was and is the common form of government.
2. The Greeks made the distinction between legitimate
one-person government and illegitimate despotism or tyranny
in which the ruler governed in his own interests rather than
those of his subjects. In early monarchies, rulers had
complete legislative, judicial, and administrative powers.
Later, the monarch often retained power as supreme law giver
but delegated administrative and judicial functions.
Monarchs also usually retained control of the armed forces.
In modern times, figure head monarchies, such as those in
Britain, Belgium, Sweden and Denmark symbolize national
identity but have little or no real political power.
3. Monarchs helped forge many modern nation-states by
establishing alliance with the bourgeoisie. The new middle
class supplied much of the administrative expertise that
made up the social and economic infrastructure of the new
nation-states and also aided monarchs in overcoming the
aristocracy which often opposed expansion of royal power.
4. The continued growth of the middle class, the abuse of
power by absolute monarchs, and the emergence of democratic
political and social ideals like the French republican
notions of "liberty, equality, and fraternity" signaled the
eventual demise of monarchies.
5. [Personal response]

63

Suetonius, "Gaius (Caligula)

1. Suetonius was a historian and a biographer. As such, he might have felt compelled to honestly depict in graphic detail the horrors of Caligula's rule. Suetonius refers to Caligula as a monster so he might have chosen to be graphic to accentuate the danger of absolute power wielded absolutely.
2. Judging from Suetonius's account, and the fact that it is widely believed he went insane after becoming seriously ill, Caligula might well have believed in his own divinity. Suetonius's description of his behavior in the third paragraph strongly suggests this, although it could be argued that by promoting himself as a God he would tighten his grip on the reigns of power.
3. Undoubtedly, Caligula maintained his power through a reign of terror and fear. This fact was certainly not lost on Caligula, who regularly quoted from Accius: "Let them hate me, so long as they fear me."
4. [Class exercise]
5. [Class exercise]

Machiavelli, from The Prince

1. Machiavelli takes a dim view of any innate goodness in people finding them generally "fickle, liars, deceivers, fearful of danger and greedy for gain." He advises the Prince to instill loyalty in his subjects with fear rather than love because people, being inherently "rotten," will not always perform dutifully out of love. On the other hand, people will obey out of fear if they know inescapable punishment awaits them if they disobey.
2. Those princes who have achieved the most success have not been those who have been honest but rather those who have lied and have known how to "craftily manipulate the minds of men." Machiavelli argues that using "laws," that is, dealing honestly, may be the most "human method" but it does not always insure victory. He insists that if people were "good," honesty might be the best policy, but since people are a "sad lot" who are dishonest themselves, the Prince should not feel at all obliged to be honest with them. Machiavelli explains that historically, political treaties and promises have been broken continually, and the Prince who ultimately succeeds is the one who knows "how best to play the fox." He doesn't advise evil for evil's sake; in fact a prince should not "depart from good if he can hold to

64

it," but should be prepared to "enter on evil [only] if he has to."

3. Machiavelli might agree with Plato's opinion of the masses as "the herd," thoughtless, dumb, and undirected, and he might even take Plato's pessimistic view of human nature even further, judging from the way he describes people as "ungrateful, fickle, liars, deceivers, fearful of danger, greedy, rotten, and a sad lot."

4. [Personal response]

5. Machiavelli's advice seems predicated on a political arena rife with deceit, doublecrosses and treachery. In fact, Machiavelli's first hand knowledge of Italian political squabbles and intrigue came from his experience as an envoy for the Florentine Republic and probably had strong influence on his thought and writings.

6. [Personal response]

7. Machiavelli praises ruthlessness toward one's political enemies but he doesn't advocate senseless cruelty as Caligula practices it. He doesn't advise evil for evil's sake and is strictly pragmatic in his use of force. Nor does he tout a phraseology/ideology as Robespierre does to justify terror and killing as purification of the nation and body politic.

8. [Personal response]

The Costs of Communism

Lewis L. Lorwin, "Communism"

1. Socialism aims to establish a society, through constitutional and democratic means, in which only essential industries are nationalized and the change occurs gradually. Distribution of products and services is based on the quality and amount of people's work. Communism views social change as only possible through revolution. All industries are nationalized and "from each according to his capacity, to each according to his needs" reflects the theoretical distribution of products and services.

2.[Personal response]

3. Class struggle defines the Marxist conception of the relationship between the proletariat, the working classes and the middle and upper classes in a capitalist society. Marxist theory sees the proletariat in constant struggle with the upper classes of the capitalist system who wield the economic and cultural power.

4. Originally Hegel developed a theory of historic evolution as a "dialectical process, moving from thesis through

65

antithesis to synthesis." Marx and Engels applied dialectics to world economics and politics. Communists would call our present stage of history imperialism, the growth of monopoly and the control of industries by finance. Despite periods of occasional stabilization, capitalism is in crisis. Eventually this crisis, brought about by an unequal distribution of wealth, will cause conflict and upheaval within capitalist countries, hence the tension and opposition between thesis and antithesis. Only communist revolution can end the crisis, distribute wealth fairly, and provide the synthesis.

5. [Personal response]
6. [Personal response]
7. [Personal response]

Alexander Weissberg, from The Accused

1. The "Great Purge" describes the mass arrest of approximately eight million Russians between the middle of 1936 and the end of 1938 by Stalin's secret police. Ostensibly arrested for spying or betraying their country to the Japanese or the Germans, most of the victims were arrested on trumped up charges and sentenced to forced labor in concentration camps. Weissberg implies that the purge was motivated by Stalin's almost paranoid fear of opposition and his obsession with consolidating his totalitarian power. The secret police carried out sudden wholesale arrests, singling out national minorities - Finns, Persians, Poles, Bulgarians, etc., but arresting people from all walks of soviet life: intellectuals, communist party members, high ranking army officers, common workers, even members of the secret police itself. Prisoners were interrogated harshly, and sometimes tortured. Eventually, almost all of them pleaded guilty and confirmed their guilt in staged public confessions.

2. The Purge traumatized the political, cultural, economic and military infrastructures throughout Soviet society. Art and literature declined as intellectuals and artists carefully avoided any controversial issues. Many scientists were arrested and creative scientific work diminished as researchers investigated only "routine" problems that could not be criticized or questioned. The effectiveness of the armed forces was even compromised, as hundreds of high ranking officers were imprisoned.

3. The persecution of Soviet national minorities could be attributed to Stalin's paranoid fear that the ethnic minorities were spying for the axis powers: "The Germans Poles and Letts for Hitler; the Chinese, Koreans, and

Mongolians for Japan; the Armenians, Persians, and Assyrians for the British Intelligence Service." Weissberg also suggests that the Stalinists desired to "ensure the racial purity of Russian towns" by singling out the minorities for persecution; hence Russian racism could have been a factor as well.

4. Machiavelli advised lying and using fear in counseling his prince. Both of these political pragmatics are apparent in Stalin's purges.

5. The heavy handed violence, mass imprisonment, and torture of the Purge greatly resembles the tactics employed by Robespierre during the Reign of Terror. In addition, the same sense of "cleansing and purifying" French society and the body politic can be found in Stalin's reign of terror along with the use of fear and intimidation as political tools.

6. One could find similarities to Stalin's purges in the Cultural Revolution in the People's Republic of China and in the devastating rule of the Khmer Rouge in Cambodia. Aspects of political terrorism and abuse can be identified in the communist regimes of Eastern Europe, particularly Czechoslovakia, Romania, Hungary and Bulgaria.

7. [Class exercise]

8. [Class exercise]

Dianne Feeley, "The Family"

1. [Class exercise]

2. Feeley admits that "it is absurd to speak of 'magically' abolishing the family," but she does advocate a socialized society that takes over the functions of the family. She sketches out a few specific details: Child care centers would take over the responsibilities of raising children, a job that's not being done very well at present; Communal dining halls would feed children and would provide take home meals for working mothers; Well paid housekeeping services would take care of homes in which women leave to go to work, freeing free women from the oppression of economic dependency on men.

3. Feeley criticizes the manner in which families teach people to submit to patriarchal authority. Although a great many women work, their position in the household is still seen as "supplementary" to the man's and they often finds themselves doing the bulk of the domestic work because of "reactionary" assumptions about women's "nature."

4. [Class exercise]

5. [Class exercise]

6. Feeley opens her essay by grounding her argument in Marxist theory. She criticizes the traditional family, making rhetorical assumptions that Marxist revolution is the answer to Western society's problems. Rather than looking for solutions within the present economic and social system, Feeley advocates major revolutionary changes in societal function and structure. She unhesitatingly uses Marxist termininology throughout the essay:
"...counter to the ideas of class society and its cornerstone, private property."
"Capitalism rules through its various institutions, which mirror and reinforce the values of the dominant class."
"...the role of woman turns her into a domestic wage slave..."
" The family itself doesn't produce revolutionary fighters."
..."the socialist alternative to the family system."
7. [Personal response]
8. [Class exercise]

The Imperialist Heritage

Robin W. Winks, "Imperialism"

1. Winks identifies three elements in his definition of imperialism. (1) The expansion and domination of an "advanced" society over a more "backward" society. (2) The domination of a society that is geographically distanced from the imperialist country. (3) No real intention to initiate colonial settlement.
2. Cultural imperialism is the exportation of culture from a dominant often more technologically advanced country into another society. Often economic leverage drives cultural imperialism. America has been accused of cultural imperialism in Mexico, Central America, and the Philippines, as have the French in Africa and Japan in Korea.
3. The myth of science and progress implies that scientific advancements and the development of industry and technology constitute important characteristics of a society that is advancing and that change, as such, within a society is both good and desirable. This myth could become the "last refuge of the imperialist" as Kenya's one time economics minister observed, because it provides a rationale for the "more advanced" imperialist country to maintain control over a less developed country, as it guides the less advanced culture into the "wonders and advantages" of the modern

age.
4. Colonialism, like imperialism. implies the political and
economic domination by a technologically more advanced
country over a less advanced country. Colonialism also
involves the migration of the colonizer's people into the
colony, whereas imperialism does not necessarily include
migration.
5. Imperialism often brings political, economic, and social
stability, education, and improved transportation and
communications systems. In return, imperialist countries can
gain natural resources, a market for produced commodities
and political and geographic control of an area.

W.E.B. Dubois, "The White Masters of the World"

1. Dubois argues that slave trade "degraded human labor" and
reduced Europeans respect for humanity in general. This
degradation of human labor was increased by the potential
for making huge sums of money from slavery and the
concomitant greed that accompanied slavery. Slavery helped
to usher in theories of "race" and racism: beliefs that the
white race was superior to all others. All the while, labor
was viewed as demeaning, the domain of the inferior races
and classes. White people were seen as destined to live off
the labor of the darker races. History was distorted to
verify the inferiority of the colored races and science,
sociology and psychology began proving this inferiority.
National heroes were created whose sins and excesses were
ignored as long as they perpetuated European imperialism and
colonialism. Ultimately Europe was wallowing in its own
decadence, a decadence caused by the overaccumulation of
wealth and the degradation of human labor initiated, to a
great extent, through slavery.
2. Christianity, particularly Catholicism, played a pivotal
role in European colonization throughout the world and the
enslavement of Native American peoples in both North and
South America. Ideologically, Christianity supported the
racism that accompanied slavery, using the Bible to justify
that "heathen Blacks," for example, bore the "curse of
Canaan," thus verifying their inferiority. Dubois points out
the blatant hypocrisy of Christianity that taught the
virtues of blessedness and meekness in sermons on Sunday
only to condone greed and slavery when business began on
Monday.
3. Social Darwinism proposed that people developed in a
manner consistent with Darwin's theory of biological
evolution and that "survival of the fittest" justified the

white Europeans' accumulation of wealth and power and their attitude of superiority over other races.

4. Dubois argues that European society was decadent because (1) It devalued human labor. (2) It built a culture on wealth accumulated through slavery and imperialism. (3) It defined the superior man as one of "wealth and luxury" who did not have to work for a living. (4) European cities were plagued with "crime, disease, and suffering." (5) History was distorted to justify European imperialism and white superiority. (6) Art and literature became cynical. (7) Christianity was interpreted hypocritically.

5. Dubois' rhetoric marks his political orientation as socialist, possibly communist. His use of words and phrases like "wage slaves," " degradation of human labor," "accumulation of wealth," "laboring classes," "race tyranny," and "monopolized wealth" suggests his familiarity with Marxist theory. His critical argument against European imperialism and his description of European capitalist culture as decadent would identify him as a Marxist, although in this essay he does not specifically advocate revolution as the only solution to European imperialism.

6. Dubois argues that slavery and colonialism led to the decadence and economic and cultural collapse of Europe. Defining Europe as both decadent and socially "collapsed" is a radical position and Dubois uses strong, sometimes, shocking images and little talked about facts to achieve this. Consider the wealth of Africa ..."beaten out of the blood-stained bodies of the natives"... and then distributed..."among prostitutes and gamblers in Europe..."; his depiction of idealized British heroes like Gladstone, involved in the slave trade, Chinese Gordon as an alcoholic and William Pitt as an international thief; his allegation that European children didn't learn the truth in school but rather, "the truth which the rulers of the world wished them to know and follow."

7. [Personal response]
8. [Personal response]

George Orwell, "Marrakech"

1. The fact that people may not even know where their relatives are buried suggests that for the colonized peoples in Marrakech, their lives are of little consequence and they lack even the basic human dignity of a recognized grave for family members. Opening the essay with the description of the funeral higlights the survival level quality of life colonized peoples often endured.

2. The first person voice brings an immediacy to the narrative. Readers might feel that Orwell is talking to them directly, intimately describing what he is seeing, smelling, hearing. It makes the description powerful, personal and very real.

3. To make the point that Europeans perceived the Moroccans as less than human, Orwell stresses how the abject poverty they live in, and "how easily they die," make it "difficult to believe you are walking among human beings." He also includes Moroccan laborers among all third world workers who "work with their hands [and are] partly invisible." He describes much of Morocco as "so desolate that no wild animals bigger than a hare" can survive there; yet, "long lines of women" eke out a survival subsistence crop from the barren soil. The old woman's surprise when Orwell notices her and gives her some money seems to "violate a law of nature" and he suggests that she sees her role in society as almost a "beast of burden." Orwell even admits that he felt more initial sympathy for the Moroccan donkeys than he did for the "people with brown skins who [were] next to invisible."

4. These descriptions serve to highlight the extreme poverty that Moroccans regularly endured, a poverty that drove old Jewish grandfathers, many of whom labored twelve hours a day, to beg for a cigarette, more or less an "impossible luxury" for them.

5. By describing the extreme poverty and deprivation of everyday life in Marrakech Orwell is highlighting the disastrous effects of European Colonialism and his dissatisfaction with it. He doesn't include in his descriptions any of the improvements colonialism may have brought to Marrakech, nor does he choose to write about the wealthy Moroccons or the wealthy Europeans enjoying lives of comfort in Northern Africa.

6. The Senegalese soldiers who served their colonial masters could represent the then still unawakened power of the indigenous peoples of Africa who one day would indeed revolt and "turn their guns in the other direction," that is, on their oppressors.

7. Orwell implies that both the colonized and the colonizers suffered adversely because of imperialism. The colonizers lost a basic respect for human life and dignity. The impoverished Moroccans also lost much of their human dignity under the oppression of imperialism which did little to improve their daily lives.

8. Almost all of the African countries have managed to liberate themselves from European imperialism with the exception of South Africa.

Contemporary Terrorism

Baljit Singh, "An Overview of Terrorism"

1. Singh defines terrorism as having two elements: (1) The
condition of fear introduced into an individual or group.
(2) The actual instrument used to produce the fear.
2. Terrorism has become a "trans-national phenomenon."
Before the 1960's, it was usually contained within a
particularly country or territory. Advancements in mass
media - satellite television and radio - and significant
increases in air travel and tourism have provided terrorists
the opportunities to find vulnerable targets outside of the
countries in conflict. Skyjackings have become a common
terrorist activity. Terrorist acts any place in the world
now can receive instant media coverage so that "propaganda
by deed" is exploited to full advantage. In addition,
Terrorism has emerged as the predominant political tactic in
many conflicts, whereas previously it usually served an
ancillary function. Terrorists have come to appreciate and
take advantage of the vulnerability of modern urban society
where kidnappings, bombings, assassinations, and bank
robberies can be easily effected.
3. Terrorists' acts can help gain popular support if they
are highly publicized and the sympathetic populace can be
impressed with the success of the terrorists' tactics.
Terrorism also serves to "achieve internal stability and
growth" within the terrorist organizaticn itself by
selecting targets "where success is 100% assured," thus
sustaining the morale of the organization.
4. Acts of random violence produce fear and anxiety in the
general population. As a strategy, this undercuts people's
confidence in the regime in power to maintain order and
social stability, causes general disruption and prepares
people to accept a new authority and structure when the
terrorist cause finally succeeds.
5. [Class Exercise]

Martin Oppenheimer, "Terrorism Is Sometimes Justified"

1. Oppenheimer defines institutional terrorism as systematic
violence employed by part of the governing structure against
a specific population. Taking a radical position,
Oppenheimer might argue that police brutality, capital
punishment, and the prison system could easily fit this
definition if operating in a country where a portion of

72

the populace has been brutalized through poverty, where
civil rights have broken down, and where the legal system is
only a rubber stamp for a tyrannical government.
Additionally, Oppenheimer points out that it is the ruling
class that defines disorder and further "the survival of the
established order requires the acceptance of the ruling
classes' definition of reality." Since the ruling class will
"enforce the definitions... functional to it," even in the
U.S., Black rioters and revolutionaries are labeled as
terrorists and shot, for example, whereas from a different
political perspective and reality, they might be defined as
freedom fighters.
2. Oppenheimer's quote from Alfred Lee highlights the
pervasiveness of institutional, legally sanctioned terror
throughout history. As examples Oppenheimer cites England's
deliberate starving of the Irish during the "potato famine,"
child labor, slavery, legalized genocide and official
torture.
3. Oppenheimer argues that abortion clinic bombers and
violent racists are not labeled as terrorists because both
groups help "repress certain subordinate and potentially
dangerous populations." Again, the ruling class is
enforcing" definitions that are functional to it."
4. Singh and Oppenheimer would probably both agree to a
technical definition of terrorism: "A state of fear or
anxiety" induced in an individual or group by "threat or use
of symbolic violent acts aimed at influencing political
behavior." Oppenheimer, ostensibly the more radical of the
two, might insist on pushing the definition even further to
point out that the dominant state or institution arbitrarily
defines what is terrorism and what is not, and that
sometimes, "terrorism is a label apllied to certain criminal
acts, when the state doesn't like the criminal's politics."
5. [Personal response]
6. [Class exercise]

Melanie Mcfadyean, "The Fingers on the Trigger"

1. Both men seem to come from the lower middle class or
working class. The IRA fighter doesn't come from a ghetto
but "from a "respectable area." He attends mass regularly
and his family "knows of his involvement." He's unmarried
and his social life has been changed such that he doesn't
sleep in the same place twice in a row. Both men come from
communities that maintain strong family and cultural
traditions. The IRA man expresses a particular concern about
the British "restricting ... education" and "preventing [the

Catholic Irish] from learning about [their] traditions."
2. Printing the two men's comments directly, without any
analysis or editorializing heightens in a quiet, understated
way, the stark, deadly realities these men navigate. In a
sense, the article's style recreates the matter-of fact
tones both men use to describe the danger and death they
have chosen to make part of their lives.
3. Both men seem hardened and inured to the violence that
they are involved in. The UFF man stresses that his
"targets" must be eliminated and that afterwards he has no
feelings at all. He refers to killing as "stiff"[ing]. He
has never talked to Republican Irish and sees "no future for
them in Northern Ireland." The IRA fighter stresses how he
was eight when he was exposed to British harassment and
abuse. He too seems hardened to the situation but insists in
the end that IRA people are "human beings" as well. Both men
indicate little compassion for the other side and "square
their consciences" by defining their activities as military
actions which defend freedom or aid in the struggle for
liberation.
4. The UFF man admits to having killed six known Republicans
and identifies as his enemies any members of the political
or military wings of the Republican cause. He doesn't refer
directly to random violence against civilians but claims
that "more innocent Protestants have been killed than
Catholics." The IRA fighter claims that he "doesn't like to
see any civilian hurt" and that he would "question" an
action that put British civilians in danger, although not
explicitly denying he would take part in such an action. He
identifies legitimate targets as the British government,
Irish working directly for the British, and any loyalists
like the UFF man.
5. [Class exercise]
6. When referring to the troubles, both men use language
that defines their respective actions as both political and
military. The UDA "Freedom fighter" labels the IRA as
"terrorists and guerillas." The UDA has an "intelligence
section" and a "cell structure organization." Protestant
people are "killed" by the IRA," they [the IRA] shoot people
and blow them up" but known Republicans are "eliminated."
Republican protests are "riots" instigated in part by
"bigots." The IRA "volunteer" refers to Republicans being
"shot dead... executed" by the British Special Forces or
"assassinated by "death squads." British soldiers "abuse"
Catholic children and IRA activities are labeled
"operations" and "peoples' struggle."
7. [Personal response]

Beyond National Politics

Anatolii Gromyko and Martin Hellerman, from Breakthrough: Emerging New Thinking

1. Unilateral security implies the privleging of one country's security interests over another. Coexistence in an interdependent world requires that no country "take unilateral action... security must be multilateral." Because of the threat of nuclear warfare, no country now can insist on unilateral security when the last stage scenario of conflict might be nuclear retaliation.
2. The nuclear imperative is a driving force behind the shift to global thinking because the potential for destroying life as we know it on earth is beginning to provoke us to "examine our ... loyalties and allegiances" and begin finding ways to ensure our mutual security other than warfare. Other factors that are encouraging global thinking have been space exploration and technological advances in television and the mass media which allow us to actually see the far off places of the world and even our planet itself from space satellites. This provides us with "a view of the earth as a whole, a more unified comprehensive picture," which prompts us to appreciate how interconnected we are as peoples; how our mutual survival depends on sincere cooperation; and how we can still retain our unique differences, even as captalist and communist, and still see ourselves as "partners in a common endeavor."
3. [Class exercise]
4. [Class exercise]
5. [Class exercise]

CHAPTER 6: PHILOSOPHICAL STANCES

D.P. Dirk, "An Overview of Western Philosophy"

1. Plotinus's theory of The One is compatible with the Christian conception of an all-powerful God, the ultimate source of life. Suspicion of the senses leads to a belief in some transcendent being, some force beyond the human mind and body, and so Plato's teaching that human senses are insufficient as the basis of truth is also compatible with Christian theology. Reason in both is the basis for moral judgement and the choice of the good over evil.
2. Typically, Platonic and Neoplatonic schools of thought saw desire as a negative thing, as evidence of some lack.

Aristotelian thought accepted desire and sensation as part of human nature and claimed it for the good, since nothing that is human is alien to what is good. The goal for Aristotle is not to transcend but to balance. Reason must work with and guide the sense to arrive at the truth, but reason alone is insufficient.
3. Descartes emphasized a physically describable scientific system, the basis for the later scientific method of objectivity and observation. The belief that one can separate mind and matter also leads into the scientific principle of objectivity and rejection of the subjective. Locke extended this systematic method so that one could make logical inferences based on data acquired through the senses to arrive at truth empirically. The Enlightenment emphasized reason, order, rules--in other words, systematic thought in all areas of human endeavor; the ideas of Locke and Descartes helped to define this mechanistic, logical view.
4. Kant championed a broader philosophic base than pure rationalism, thus making way for the Romantic reliance on truth that is more than the product of reason. He revived the Platonic notion of a realm of pure existence beyond the material objects of reality. Thus sensual perception, so valued by Romantic poets, could be the path to higher truth.
5. Hegel recognized the importance of history and culture, of social truth. Marx built on this perception of society as a kind of organism that evolves and attempted to identify the laws that directed its movement. He believed in a rational explanation of social evils, a materialist base to all actions and values. Both Hegel and Marx believe society progresses through stages, though only Marx believed that the ultimate stage of civilization was a classless, socialist society.
6. The scientific naturalist attempts to find specific, physical laws that explain the mind. The existentialist ties meaning to action, and is in this sense a materialist, but that term does not suggest that external laws exist to explain and give value to life.
7. Contemporary philosophy rejects the universal beliefs of preceding systems of thought, for the most part. Subjectivity has been extended to new areas of experience, from the scientific to the moral. The multiple points of view prevail in current philosophy, thus making the twentieth century more diversified philosophically in comparison to earlier ages.
8. [Personal response]
9. [Personal response]
10. [Personal response]

Ancient Philosophical Attitudes/Contemporary Situations

Francis Henry Sandbach, "Stoicism"

1. The original doctrine of stoicism had a seed notion of
indifference in that whatever was neither related to good nor to
bad was not a matter of ethical concern. This attitude evolved
over the centuries to a more generalized belief that stoicism
meant indifference or passive endurance of all tribulations.
Moderation, more than passive acceptance, typifies the ancient
school of thought.
2. [Class exercise]
3. Passion has been viewed historically with suspicion and
disapproval. It is commonly seen as the path away from God and
goodness, the exaltation of the temporal and physical over the
eternal and spiritual. Passion for Plato was an irrational and
dangerous state, likely to lead one to error. For Aristotle,
passion was problematic when it overshadowed other parts of human
nature, including reason. Medieval thinkers saw passion as a kind
of sinful possession, an indulgence in the sensual world of
illusions. Romantic thinkers saw the senses as a way to truth, and
so were more likely to view passion in a positive light, especially
if it were seen as a kind of excess of emotion rather than purely
physical heat.
4. [Personal response]
5. [Personal response]

Sharon Curtin, "Letty the Bag Lady"

1. [Class exercise]
2. Increasingly, the homeless include in their numbers many
families, especially single mothers with young children. Many
street people are the product of recent changes in public housing
of the mentally ill--the process called "dumping." Major cities
have seen huge increases in the homeless population, but smaller
towns are also experiencing a growth in the number of people who
have no permanent place of residence.
3. The reduction of material objects in one's life is a kind of
contemporary stoicism embodied in Letty's and other street
people's attitudes toward owning only what one can carry. The
lack of pleasure is a stoic value, but desire, sorrow, and fear
seem to abound in the homeless life, thus making it less than the
ideal the stoic aims at.
4. The lack of material excess in Letty's life would probably be
seen as a virtue, according to stoic ethics. The basic will to
self-preservation that we see in Letty is clearly a stoic value.
Her friendless state would be an ill, as would be her periods of
going hungry, the dangerous situations she faces on the streets,
and her mental illness.
5. The moral state of homelessness would be a relative one in
terms of stoic ethics. If one had left behind an abusive,
unhealthy home, then homelessness would be relatively good. If
one lost one's home through illness, etc., then the change would

be for the worse and thus lead to a bad state. One could take the stoic belief in appropriate action as an argument for the proposition that the homeless have themselves to blame, at least in part, for their situation.

Joseph Epstein, "The Virtues of Ambition"

1. For Epstein, ambition is the drive to succeed at some task that is socially meaningful. It requires dedication, effort, and discipline. It is not a purely selfish desire to amass wealth or status.
2. While the point is arguable, a stoic is unlikely to be ambitious, using Epstein's definition. Epstein places the worth of ambition in a social context, rather than in the stoic context of individual good or ill. Given the stoic belief in fate, the stoic is unlikely to see ambition as a route to altering one's personal or social destiny.
3. [Class exercise]
4. Ambition often relates to the welfare of the family, Epstein argues, and so has a social basis in this context. Ambition implies a will to improve the future state of one's life, in personal and social terms, and so again ambition serves a more than individual end. Epstein ties ambition to a new kind of work ethic, in a sense, and sees it as a positive force in American society.
5. [Personal response]

George K. Strodach, "The Philosophy of Epicurus"

1. [Class exercise]
2. Hedonism, which represents only one side of Epicurean thought, has a materialistic base. A hedonist values pleasure over all else, with pain being the ultimate evil. Because excess often leads to pain (as in excessive drinking leading to a hangover, etc.), the classical hedonist would not lead a life of total abandon but would observe moderation insofar as it allowed for the avoidance of pain.
3. [Personal response]
4. [Class exercise]

Margaret Halsey, "What's Wrong with 'Me, Me, Me'?"

1. The cult of "I" or the self is a kind of narcissism. The self is seen as the primary value and basis for judgment of what is good and bad. It is a self-referential doctrine: all things are judged according to the impact they have on the individual's life.
2. The "I/me" ethic has as its premise that the true self is a

78

unique, talented, positive being. All flaws are due to external sources--to parents, to social ills, etc. Again, the narcissistic urge described by Freud seems to be the impelling notion in this philosophical stance. Like Freud, Halsey believes this is pure delusion. The real self is a collection of conflicts and selfish urges; the "me" philosophy attempts to justify the worst part of human nature.
3. Fear is the source of evil, according to Epicurus. If we fear the gods, death, or hell, we are incapable of enjoying our lives, and thus we lead bad lives. The "me" philosophy can be connected to this view in that it advocates throwing off the constraints of morality and social responsibility (its critics argue). If we do not need to feel shame or guilt--if we reject fear of the gods and hell--then we can lead happy, pleasurable, good lives. Fear of death can be turned into the hedonistic view of "eat, drink, and be merry, for tomorrow we may die."
4. [Class exercise]
5. [Personal response]

Gwendolyn Brooks, "The Pool Players" (poem)

1. [Personal response]
2. While personal reactions to the poem will differ, many readers feel the appeal of the pool players' fast, lean, self-serving lifestyle. Brooks does not argue against it directly; the outcome of it serves as its own warning and condemnation.
3. The "we" voice allows the reader to identify with the speakers. It also reduces the individuality of the members of the group, which adds to the negative impression of the aesthetic/ethic the players represent.
4. Much of the action described in the poem produces pleasure of one sort or another, and pleasure is the fundamental yardstick in Epicurean philosophy in its hedonist guise. In strict Epicurean terms, though, the attitude of the players does not reflect the value of the absence of pain. The outcome--death--contradicts the idea of security and non-pain that lies at the heart of the philosophical doctrine.

Farrand Sayre, from The Greek Cynics

1. The Cynics believed in freedom from desires, fears, anger, grief or other strong feelings, religious or moral laws, external authorities, concern for public opinion, ownership, and family responsibilities. Individual concern was the only important one; concern for others was an unnecessary burden. The Cynic must be able to endure physical hardship, to face life with a kind of apathy, in order to be free from the above concerns. The Cynic also rejects employment, which, as Epstein argues in "The Virtues

79

of Ambition," involves a belief in and hope for the future improvement of one's condition. The resulting poverty leads to further freedom from the trappings of society.
2. Both seek to mitigate suffering by reducing involvement in and concern for the usual social and personal values. Both seek freedom from the burden of social status, replacing an external code of values with an inner system of what is good or bad for the individual. Both reject wealth and the claims of family, for example. The stoic, however, does not reject the notion of planning to improve one's future state; it is a less extreme philosophical stance.
3. The Cynics denied the values of this life. While they did not replace this value system with a belief in a life to come, they did much to foster questioning of a materialistic code, to suggest the illusory nature of material riches and social status. Their de-emphasis of individual importance is a kind of early parallel to the Christian valuing of humility and self-denial.
4. Those who act out of kindness and for the good of others are acting in an irrational, stupid manner. They get nothing for their efforts; their deeds are hollow and cannot lead to benefit to themselves. If they act indiscriminately for the good of all, they are in fact benefitting the evil as well as good members of society, and so their action may itself be evil.
5. [Personal response]
6. [Class exercise]

Eric Hoffer, "Long Live Shame!"

1. Shame, according to Hoffer, "involves an awareness by the individual of being watched and judged by the group." Guilt, as we learn from Freud, can be entirely internal, the product of the individual's fantasies and own self-punishment system. Shame is the product of external discovery and disapproval. To feel shame, one must have respect for the social group one belongs to. To feel part of this group, one must be socialized into it. One then gains a sense of interdependence, respect, and cooperation. Thus the socialized individual is likely to act for the good of the group and to maintain his or her status within the group. Hoffer suggests this is the process of civilization. An angry child who wishes his punitive parent dead may later suffer guilt; the rest of society does not play a part in the child's internal conflict and is unaffected (in a direct sense) by it. If the child were to curse at others on the street and be publicly rebuked, he or she would feel shame, and most likely would not want to undergo the same uncomfortable social disapproval by repeating the behavior.
2. Insofar as adolescent behavior draws upon the desire to show off material goods, physical beauty, stylishness, etc., the cynics would reject it. Their emphasis was on indifference to such worldly objects and concerns. The desire to perform for the

eyes/approval of others is also foreign to the cynic value system. Idleness, self-centeredness, unconventional behavior, a kind of nihilistic disregard for death--these are cynic values, and one could argue that the adolescent behavior Hoffer deplores does to a degree represent these cynic "virtues."
3. While some surface comparisons could be made, overall Hoffer is not endorsing a Puritan code. He does suggest that we are responsible for "policing" the behavior of others, to the extent that public shame can be considered such a force. But the Puritans were ascetics, and they observed a single, absolute belief system. Hoffer argues for a general code of social behavior, not for a particular doctrine of belief.
4. [Personal response]

Dick Gregory, "Shame"

1. Helene symbolizes the middle-class dream, plus some personal ambitions of Gregory. First, she has a stable home life, complete with a father. She does not lack for clean clothes, food, and the material extras of life. She has standing in society and the respect that goes along with it. She is personally a good person, especially as the young Gregory defines "good"--she is attractive, clean, smart, nicely dressed. Her sense of belonging in society is what Gregory wants, along with all the things that allow that membership.
2. Because he often goes to school hungry, having had no breakfast and perhaps no supper the night before, Gregory finds it hard to concentrate on academic tasks. His attention is on the clock, on lunchtime and the possibility of sneaking some food. His home life does not include extra reading time or other activities that assist a child to adjust to school. In the teacher's eyes, Gregory may have appeared to have a behavior problem, to be a lazy student, neither bright nor motivated.
3. Gregory feels reduced and humiliated by the term. It makes him a member of a faceless underclass, people without hope, without a future, without moral worth. Society can see the badge of membership in the relief truck and plaid jacket; these are symbols of his dependence and failure, of society's largess and his own incapacity.
4. Shame in the vicious public form that Gregory encounters seems incapable of producing dignity; it humiliates and strips one of a sense of one's innate worth. It makes one feel that society itself lacks decency, for one is treated in a most obscene way. And the "good manners" it teaches is an insistence on self-degradation, on acknowledgment of inferiority. The shame that Gregory describes is of a different order than the public conscience Hoffer endorses.
5. To a large extent, the ancient Cynics would criticize Gregory's concerns as foolish. He suffers due to his desires for things that are in themselves (the Cynics believe) worthless:

public recognition and social status, material goods, etc. Gregory's concern for the opinion of others enslaves him to them, the Cynics might argue. His situation is in fact an opportunity for freedom from all the sources of misery in life. The Cynic view is a harsh one, particularly if we consider it as a "solution" to the young Gregory's situation.

6. Having himself been the victim of social cruelty, of having to pay for the means of subsistence with his pride and dignity, Gregory feels that he should have been more understanding of the man's situation and come to his aid. He feels shame not in the sense of his external self and the public judgment it brings upon him, but in an internal, self-judging way.

7. The Cynic code would certainly explain and perhaps endorse Gregory's actions. As for justifying Gregory's Cynic views, the incident does seem to lend evidence to the Cynic view that selfishness, stupidity, etc., prevail in human nature, and to honor it is a stupid response.

Modern Attitudes toward Modern Evils

Charles L. Glicksberg, "Nihilism"

1. [Class exercise]
2. The phrase "dark night of the soul" creates an image of spiritual death, a sense of aloneness and isolation, of impossibility of escape. We have no power over darkness and can only wander aimlessly in it. Thus the image suggests that life is a series of directionless, random, even chaotic fumblings. But like dawn, some light may come to us; we may grasp onto something that gives us a general sense of change, possibility, and hope. Nihilism thus is a stage of perception, as night is a stage in the cycle of time.

3. Singh argues that terrorists seek to create a sense of isolation and disorientation within the populace. Terrorist acts create a sense of life as potentially and randomly dangerous, a sense of instability, inability to depend on social structures or standards of morality. People experience a loss of faith in social order. These are all qualities of a nihilistic sense of the world.

4. Glicksberg identifies several strands of nihilistic thought. One strand leads logically to an acceptance of suicide as a rational choice in the face of life's lack of meaning; this strand would be directly contradictory to Darwinian thought, which sees the propagation of life as the premier drive within us. The nihilistic notion of life can also be seen as the pursuit of power, the rule of the strong. One could fit Darwinian thought to this aspect of nihilism and use Darwin's theory to promote the notion that the strongest survive at the cost of the weak.

5. Nihilism seems modern in that it rejects the possibility of a

meaningful belief system. Much of ancient thought assumed that
such a system or systems exist and that our labor lies in
detecting them and naming their elements. Glicksberg points out
the unifying notion of the tragic, which is pervasive in ancient
thought as well as modern: the fear that life has no meaning has
exists throughout western historical literature and philosophical
thought. With the rise of rationalism, faith lost its primary role
in philosophical thought. Nihilism thus seems a modern inversion
of faith--a new belief in nothing.
6. The pool players have rejected school, symbolizing their loss
of faith in the value of any organized social system. They do not
see education as a way to some meaningful end. Simple being and
random action--lurking late and striking straight--make up their
experience. They celebrate evil--sing sin; they dull the senses
with drink and sensual indulgence. They face their inevitable
death without a sense of regret, urgency, or any other emotion that
would suggest the value of life.
7. [Personal response]
8. The relativity that postmodern science recognizes is not a
refutation of the possibility of truth, as Nietzsche's philosophy
suggests. The inescapability of cultural filtering of perceptions
is more the message in Toulmin's article, rather than a questioning
of any system of values.

Joan Didion, "Death in El Salvador"

1. Didion depicts a kind of moral vacuum, which seems an ideal
breeding ground for nihilistic attitudes. Human life seems
lacking in any value; the social structure is in total disarray;
supposed sources of authority are in fact engaged in terrorist
attacks against the populace--according to Glicksberg's analysis,
the stage of nihilism that we are likely to undergo as individuals
could be brought on as a social mindset in the horrifying milieu
depicted by Didion.
2. Didion seems to suggest the initial horror and then
routineness of such sights. The only result of the grisly
discovery is in the total body count compiled weekly--no arrests,
no public outcry, no action of any cathartic kind takes place.
The reader also finds it hard to take in the enormity of the
carnage. Thus the reports blend together in a kind of nightmare
effect, and the individual crimes seem less and less real.
3. One can argue that the women's quiet and passive demeanor
bespeaks their nihilistic loss of protest against such outrages,
but perhaps more convincing is a reading that interprets their
continued searching for the faces of their relatives as a
persistence of the human spirit. Their quiet devotion to finding
their loved ones is a tribute to the individuals they seek, an
acknowledgment of their continuing importance, an expression of
hope and love.

4. [Personal response]

Viktor E. Frankl, "Arrival at Auschwitz"

1. Frankl and his fellow sufferers go through an initial stage of
denial, the "delusion of reprieve." Their actual adjustment,
however, begins with the recognition that the life they knew has
ended and a new kind of existence has begun, one characterized by
total deprivation, fear, and powerlessness. All physical and then
mental ties with one's former identity are erased. A kind of
detachment then takes over, what Frankl calls a "curiosity" about
one's fate. The self in a sense becomes exteriorized and observes
the situation. It is a protective psychological device, a means of
coping with the incomprehensibly horrible. One's actual physical
life changes: the preferences and neuroses of the former life seem
to die along with that personality, and the prisoners find that
they are able to endure physical suffering they would never have
believed possible. Beyond this point, Frankl suggests at the end
of his essay, new adaptations take place, new losses occur, and new
strengths develop.
2. The humor that he and some of the other prisoners find in their
situation suggests at least some sense of hope or optimism; life
does not become a paralyzing state of fear. He learns to readjust
his sights, in a sense, becoming optimistic not about retaining his
material possessions but about his own inner ability to survive the
experience.
3. When we face death, the will to live is likely to be at its
strongest point, making us capable of the most (apparently)
irrational delusions. That we are about to escape or be freed
even when the executioner is approaching is the most vivid example
of the psychological process of denial. Ambrose Bierce's "An
Occurrence at Owl Creek Bridge" is a famous story employing this
psychological device. Denial, in its own way a form of insanity,
perhaps saves us from the unbearable confrontation of our own
death.
4. [Personal response]
5. [Personal response]

Jean Paul Sartre, "Existentialism"

1. To be aware of the future means to be aware of one's power
(and responsibility) for planning that future. One thus has
control over one's "destiny," to a significant extent, in
philosophical terms. Unlike lower orders of animals, we do not
simply act and react; we can take actions in the present that we
predict will alter the course of later events. Thus we remove
ourselves from simple existence for the moment and take on
responsibility for our future--and so the future of humanity.

2. We are not biologically coded to behave in specific, predictable ways, as is a plant, for instance. We are not mere existence, though we share that basic state with the plant world. Unlike plants or other simple organic matter, we can become something beyond our physical selves, our simple existence. An organic mass simply follows the rules of physical life; we have power beyond this level, and so we are responsible for defining the meaning of this higher level of life.
3. We physically are, and that is existence. What we are, what our lives mean, is not predetermined for us; we are responsible for defining ourselves beyond our physical being. This is our essence: what we become through how we act.
4. Because the definition of "human" is not a predetermined, static one, our meaning must be enacted--we must take action to show who and what we are. Since the unit of existence is the individual, the individual's actions sum up the meaning of humanity. The individual's vision of the self is the vision of what humanity is like. Thus every action the human takes makes a statement about the nature of all humanity, and so we are responsible for ourselves and all others.
5. Rejection of religious faith requires an acknowledgment that no absolute system of values exists. There is no definite code to guide us to a "good" life; we can be whatever we choose to be. The individual is forlorn because he or she has no other to look to for answers, standards, approval--all the functions that a god figure fulfills. This freedom from an external system of absolutes makes us responsible for defining our own individual ethical system.
6. Actions define the individual's beliefs and make them real. We can make our values have an effect in life by living them-- that is what gives them meaning. Thus action is the key to essence and worth.

Jack Henry Abbott, "State-Raised Convict"

1. [Class exercise]
2. Sartre might see Abbott's situation as the ideal one for existential action. By not taking the responsibility to deny what the state imposes as his definition, Abbott allows the state to control him--and all humanity. The existentialist would take a stand that defines human life in a way different from the authoritarian, animalistic regime that dominates Abbott. The resistance forces of World War II are an example of existentialism in action against a fascist force.
3. This conception of manhood is existentialist in its belief that certain actions define essence. The choice to define human essence as violent, power-hungry, and dispassionate is one that others are likely to condemn, though to fight against it they would choose to lead lives based on actions of valor, justice, concern

for society, etc. The evil essence defined by the "manhood" ethic
of the criminal Abbott describes thus could lead to a more moral
notion of humanity, ultimately.
4. The existentialist sees no absolutes, no eternal choices.
Thus Abbott could change, could redefine himself despite
adaptation. But Abbott raises a good point: to adapt is to accept
the value system of prison and thus to become truly a criminal.
5. [Personal response]

Richard Rodriguez, from _Hunger of Memory_

1. For Abbott, responding to the guard is acknowledgment of the
guard's right to imprison him. He would be recognizing the guard
as a valid authority figure and himself as a true prisoner, in
existential terms. Thus to speak is to commit to a specific value
system, one that he does not wish to accept. For Rodriguez, a
kind of betrayal of his home culture takes place when he speaks
English. He also cannot identify with the sound of his own voice
when he speaks this foreign language; it alienates him from his
home and his self, and so involves a painful conflict.
2. A "pocho" has lost the characteristics of the culture. As a
pocho, Rodriguez is no longer a member of the Chicano culture; he
becomes an outsider. He is not the "real thing" any longer, and
yet he is not entirely assimilated into mainstream Anglo culture.
Thus he is a "pocho" in both camps.
3. Speaking Spanish is a sign of membership and closeness, of
understanding of what life is like for Chicanos within Anglo
culture. As a kind of sign of solidarity, the language develops
symbolic significance. Rodriguez, unable to speak fluently, thus
seems a kind of turncoat. Others expect him to represent the
culture; his loss of fluency is a kind of betrayal.
4. If we take speaking the language to be an active choice and
statement of value, then it may be considered existential. But
actions can take other form, and one can identify in ways beyond
sharing the language--other actions of solidarity are possible.
5. He has chosen to become a part of mainstream Anglo culture,
which alters his very nature. As he chooses to pursue mainstream
education, he redefines himself as a person who believes in the
value of that education, the kind of life one leads as a student,
etc. He can maintain his earlier identity, but it is altered by
the new values he has defined through his choices.
6. [Personal response]
7. [Personal response]